A TEXTBOOK IN ANALYTIC GROUP PSYCHOTHERAPY

Other books by S. R. Slavson

AN INTRODUCTION TO GROUP THERAPY
ANALYTIC GROUP PSYCHOTHERAPY
THE PRACTICE OF GROUP THERAPY
THE FIELDS OF GROUP PSYCHOTHERAPY
CHILD-CENTERED GROUP GUIDANCE OF PARENTS
CHILD PSYCHOTHERAPY
RECREATION AND THE TOTAL PERSONALITY
CREATIVE GROUP EDUCATION
CHARACTER EDUCATION IN A DEMOCRACY
RE-EDUCATING THE DELINQUENT
SCIENCE AND THE NEW EDUCATION

A TEXTBOOK IN ANALYTIC GROUP PSYCHOTHERAPY

S. R. Slavson

INTERNATIONAL UNIVERSITIES PRESS, INC.

NEW YORK   NEW YORK

Contents

PAGE

INTRODUCTION   1
SETTING VERSUS PROCESS. EMPHASIS ON SPECIFICITY. THE SMALL GROUP
CONCEPT. CULTURE AND ETHOS. THE REPETITION PHENOMENON. STYLE
AND CONSTRUCTION. THE IDEAL AND THE ATTAINABLE.

I THE GROUP IN NATURE, CULTURE, AND PSYCHOTHERAPY   7
THE GROUP IN INDIVIDUAL DEVELOPMENT: *Nurture, Training, and
Schooling; Discipline and Repression; Social Hunger; The Eight
Basic Groups; Misconceptions of "Togetherness"; Individualism ver-
sus Individuality.* GROUPS IN NATURE AND SOCIETY. GROUPISM. FREUD'S
GROUP PSYCHOLOGY AND PSYCHOTHERAPY. EGO BASIS OF GROUP
PSYCHOTHERAPY. GROUP-INDUCED ANXIETY. THE EFFECT OF GROUPS
ON EGO AND SUPEREGO FUNCTIONS. GROUP PSYCHOTHERAPY AND
TRANSFERENCE NEUROSES.

II DIFFERENTIALS OF THERAPY AND NONTHERAPY GROUPS   36
DEFINITION OF PSYCHOTHERAPY: *Conation versus Cognition in Psy-
chotherapy; The Tasks of Psychotherapy.* ESSENTIAL VERSUS NEU-
ROTIC ANXIETY. CONFLICTS AND SIMILARITIES IN THEORIES. GENERAL
DYNAMICS OF GROUPS: *Interaction; Interstimulation; Mutual In-
duction; Identification; Intensification; Assimilation; Integration;
Group Cohesion; Polarity; Nodal and Antinodal Behavior in
Groups.* SPECIFIC OPERATIONAL DIFFERENTIALS: *Group Dynamics and
Group Psychotherapy; Differentials in the Light of Therapeutic
Criteria; Differentials in Synergic Movement.* ANONYMITY. THE
GROUP "EGO" AND "SUPEREGO." THE THERAPY GROUP AS A "CLOSED
SYSTEM." DIFFERENTIALS IN GROUP GENESIS: *Free-Associative Groups;
Motivated Groups; Forced Groups; Deliberating Groups; Planning
Groups; Action Groups; Structured Groups.*

III THE RELATION OF PSYCHIATRY AND GROUP
PSYCHOTHERAPY   75
THE UNITARY BASIS OF PSYCHOTHERAPY: *Meeting Individual Needs;
Contributions of Group Psychotherapy to Psychiatry.* SOME HIS-
TORICAL BACKGROUND. RECEPTIVITY TO GROUP PSYCHOTHERAPY. LEVELS
OF TREATMENT. SOURCES OF VARIATION AND CONFUSION. SOME CHAR-
ACTERISTICS OF THERAPY GROUPS. SOME AREAS OF DISAGREEMENT:
Specificity; Organicity; Terminology; Suitability; Integration.

CONTENTS

IV DIFFERENTIAL AIMS AND DYNAMICS IN GROUP
   COUNSELING, GUIDANCE, PSYCHOTHERAPY, AND
   PSYCHONURSING   98
   "Depth" of Therapy. Determined Individual Needs. Counseling.
   Guidance. Psychotherapy. Case Illustrations. Dynamic Dif-
   ferentials. Para-Analytic Group Psychotherapy. Psychonurs-
   ing.

V BASIC DYNAMICS OF GROUP PSYCHOTHERAPY   130
   Transference: *Types of Transference; Constants and Variables in
   Transference Phenomena; Effects of Transference Dilution; Reality
   Saturation and Transference; Group Psychotherapy and the Libido
   "Conserve."* Catharsis: *Resistances to Catharsis; Overloading the
   Ego; Types of Catharsis; Catharsis Accelerators.* Patterns of
   Group-Induced Resistances: *Resistance Solvents.* Insight: *Con-
   ditions for Deriving Insight; Types of Insight.* Reality Testing:
   *The Emergence of the Sense of Reality; Therapy and Reality;
   Group Psychotherapy and Reality Testing; Psychotherapy and
   Mysticism.* Sublimation: *Sublimation in Psychotherapy.*

VI CRITERIA FOR SELECTION   178
   Four General Criteria: *Minimal Primary Relations; Sexual Dis-
   turbance; Ego Strength; Superego Development.* Types of Indica-
   tions: *Positive Indications for Analytic Groups; Negative Indica-
   tions for Analytic Groups.* Application of Group Variables to
   Specific Patients: *As Exclusive Treatment; As Primary Treatment;
   As Ancillary to Individual Treatment; As Parallel Therapy; As
   Antecedent Therapy; As Tapering-Off Therapy; As a Testing
   Period.* Reliability of Criteria.

VII SOME GUIDES FOR GROUPING   198
   Status of Knowledge on Grouping. Sex as a Criterion. Strength
   of the Ego and Its Defenses. Homogeneity: *Nuclear Problem; The
   Two "Universals"; Counterindications of Character Homogeneity;
   Symptom Homogeneity.* Clinical Considerations: *Clinical Cate-
   gories.* Reidentification and the Supportive Ego. Homosexu-
   ality and Homoerotism. Heterosexual versus Unisexual Group-
   ings. Married Couples and "Family" Groups. The Factor of
   Age. Social and Intellectual Factors. Caste versus Class.
   Monopolizers. Psychological Literacy.

VIII THE BIO-QUANTUM NATURE OF THE EGO AND ITS RELA-
   TION TO ANALYTIC GROUP PSYCHOTHERAPY   233
   The Trend Toward Ego Therapy. The Misuse of Ego Therapy.
   Nature and Structure of the Ego: *A Definition of "Ego"; Ego
   Manifestations in Lower Animals and Man; Educability of the Ego;
   The Self and Nonself Polarities; Conditioning of Ego Functions;
   Family Influences and Ego Formation; Organic Foundations of the
   Ego; The Quantum Aspect of the Ego.* Seven Sources of Patho-
   genesis: *Impaired Libido Development; Blockage of Autonomous
   Strivings; Faulty Identification Models; Neurotic Conflict, Guilt,
   and Fear; Defective Self-Image; Ambivalence; Organic and Con-
   stitutional Deficiencies.* The Distribution of Ego Energies. Dy-
   namics of Ego Therapy: *Specificity; The Process of Ego Therapy.*
   The Group as Ego Therapy.

CONTENTS

IX COMMUNICATION IN ANALYTIC GROUP PSYCHOTHERAPY   259
VERBAL AND NONVERBAL COMMUNICATION. INTRAPERSONAL AND INTER-
PERSONAL COMMUNICATION. THE NATURE OF COMMUNICATION IN A
THERAPY GROUP. SPECIFIC FEATURES OF THERAPEUTIC COMMUNICA-
TION: *Threat Areas; Specificity and Concreteness; Exposure of Resistances and Evasions; Atomism.* COMMUNICATION VECTORS: *The In-
trapersonal Vector; The Patient-to-Patient Vector; The Patient-
to-Group Vector; The Patient-to-Therapist Vector; The Group-
to-Individual Vector; The Therapist-to-Patient Vector; The Thera-
pist-to-Group Vector.* CONGRUENCE AND MISUNDERSTANDING. TYPES
AND SOURCES OF FEEDBACK: *Status of the Communicant; Relevance;
Piquancy; Emotional Activation; Threat Areas; Levels of Comprehension; Empathy; Heterogeneity.* EFFECTS OF GROUP COHESION.
TEMPERAMENTAL DIFFERENTIALS. COMMUNICATION AND CATHARSIS.
DEFENSE AGAINST THERAPY.

X THE ANALYTIC GROUP INTERVIEW: PHENOMENOLOGY   283
THE EARLY SESSIONS. TIMING AND PSYCHOLOGICAL LITERACY. THE
IMPORTANCE OF TIMING. INDIVIDUALIZATION. DISCHARGE OF HOS-
TILITY. ILLUSTRATIONS OF GROUP ANALYTIC INTERVIEWS: *A Group of
Married Women; A Group of Young Adult Women.*

XI THE ANALYTIC GROUP PSYCHOTHERAPY INTERVIEW:
DYNAMICS   330
REALITY FIGURES VERSUS INTERNALIZED IMAGES. INTELLECT VERSUS
AFFECT. COMMON GROUP TENSIONS. ENDOGENOUS VERSUS INDUCED
ANXIETY. ARTIFICES AND DEVICES: *Recent Developments; Rallies,
Topics, and Themes; Manifest versus Latent Themes.* SIGNALS AND
CUES. THE FACTOR OF COMMONALITY. TYPES OF THERAPY WITHIN
THE GROUP. THREAT AREAS AND INTOLERANCE FOCI. PSYCHOLOGICAL
ENCOUNTERS: *Interpersonal Encounters; Intrapersonal Encounters;
Intragroup Encounters.* INTRAPSYCHIC ENCOUNTER AND NUCLEAR
PROBLEMS. "PHASES" IN GROUP ANALYTIC INTERVIEWS. FACTORS AF-
FECTING "PHASES." THE "AUXILIARY THERAPIST" FALLACY. STEREO-
TYPY. SILENCES: *General Individual Silences; Selective Individual
Silences; General Group Silences; Selective Group Silences.* MONOPO-
LISM: *Phenomenology; Causation; Treatment Indications.* BASIC
CHARACTERISTICS OF ANALYTIC GROUP THERAPY INTERVIEWS: *Tran-
silience; Dispersal; Focusing.* THERAPIST-INDUCED RESISTANCES.

XII THE ANALYTIC GROUP PSYCHOTHERAPY INTERVIEW:
REGRESSION AND ACTING OUT   370
ATTITUDES TOWARD ACTING OUT. THE PHENOMENOLOGY OF ACTING
OUT. ACTING OUT AND REGRESSION: *Therapeutic Regression; Pathologic Regression; Parapathologic Regression; Induced Regression.*
TYPES OF ACTING OUT: *Therapeutic Acting Out; Pathologic Acting Out; Parapathologic Acting Out; Induced Acting Out; Counterphobic Acting Out; Normal Acting Out.* FUNCTIONS OF ACTING
OUT: *As a Release; As Abreaction; As Resistance; As a Reaction
to Fear; As Provocation; As a Bid for Status; As Emotional Hypochondriasis; As a Defense; As a Test; As Contagion; As a Neurotic*

vii

CONTENTS

Symptom; As Narcissism; As a Character Disorder. THE CATE-
GORIES OF ACTING OUT: *As Regression; As Fixation; As Ego As-
thenia; As Ontogenetic Recapitulation; As Phylogenetic Recapitulation.* THE ADVANTAGES AND DISADVANTAGES OF ACTING OUT.
CHILD VERSUS ADULT ACTING OUT. THE THERAPIST'S ROLES IN ACT-
ING OUT: *Timing and Readiness; Evasion of Acting Out; Stimula-
of Acting Out; "Alternate" and "Post" Sessions.*

XIII THE QUALIFICATIONS AND FUNCTIONS OF THE GROUP
    THERAPIST   401
    PERSONAL QUALIFICATIONS: *The Importance of Definition; As a
Suitable Model of Identification; Maturity; Intuition and Percep-
tiveness; Empathy versus Sympathy; Detachment versus Indifference; Motivation; Imagination; Narcissistic Preoccupations; Frustration Tolerance; Omnipotence of Ideas; Specific Assets of a
Group Psychotherapist.* EDUCATIONAL QUALIFICATIONS: *The Scope
of Training; The Content of Training; Boundaries for Nonmedical
Psychotherapists; Integrating Rival Schools; Basic Psychiatry; Child
Development Studies and Their Values; Family Relations; The
Social Sciences; The Methods of Training; The Curriculum; Train-
ing Seminars; In-Service and Field Training; Educational Seminars
versus Therapy.* FUNCTIONS: *Four Functions; Passivity and Crea-
tivity.* CHARISMA AS QUALITY AND FUNCTION: *As Quality; As Func-
tion.* MACHIAVELLISM VERSUS SPONTANEITY. THE FACILITATIVE ROLE
OF THE THERAPIST. AN ILLUSTRATION OF THE THERAPIST'S FUNCTIONS.
COUNTERTRANSFERENCE: *The Inevitability of Countertransference;
Positive Countertransference; Negative Countertransference; Aim
Attachment; Ambivalent Countertransference; Countertransference
Toward the Group as a Whole.* DIFFERENTIAL ERROR VALENCES:
CUMULATIVE VERSUS COMPENSATING ERRORS.

XIV SUPERVISION   457
    GENERAL CONSIDERATIONS. THE SUBJECTIVE ELEMENTS IN SUPERVISION.
THE FACTOR OF SEX. ATTITUDES AND VALUES. INTERRELATIONSHIP
ROLES. FIRST STEPS. LATER DEVELOPMENTS. ENCOURAGING SELF-SCRU-
TINY. EGO FUNCTIONING OF THE SUPERVISEE. AWARENESS OF THE
SUPERVISEE'S BASIC PERSONALITY. DEALING WITH IMPASSES. THE
VALUES OF AFFIRMATION. SETTING ANTICIPATORY ATTITUDES. MULTI-
CENTEREDNESS: *Group-Centeredness; Patient-Centeredness; Situation-
Centeredness; Technique-Centeredness; Theory-Centeredness; Idea-
Centeredness; Philosophy-Centeredness.* REPETITION. SENSITIZA-
TION.

XV ANALYTIC GROUP PSYCHOTHERAPY WITH SOME CHAR-
    ACTER DISORDERS: AGGRESSION, HOSTILITY, AND
    WITHDRAWAL   473
    ON THE NATURE OF AGGRESSION: *Atavistic Aggression; Phylogenetic
Aggression; Ontogenetic Aggression; Instrumental Aggression.* AG-
GRESSION VERSUS HOSTILITY. AGGRESSION AND CULTURE. SOURCES OF AG-
GRESSION: *Character Aggression; Neurotic Aggression; Psychotic
Aggression.* EFFECTS OF AGGRESSION ON GROUPS. THE NATURE AND
TREATMENT OF WITHDRAWAL: *Definition; Inhibition of Spontaneity;
Failure in Sibling Rivalry; Withdrawal as a Reaction to Guilt; Nar-
cissism and Withdrawal; Reaction to Stigmata; Defective Self-*

viii

CONTENTS

Image; Submission to Parents; Schizoid Withdrawal; Catatonic Defense; Withdrawal as Retaliation; Withdrawal as Psychoneurotic Symptom. THE TRANSMUTATIONS OF WITHDRAWAL INTO AGGRESSION. GENERAL VALUES OF GROUPS TO WITHDRAWN PATIENTS: *General Release; The Consistency Element; Supportive Ego.* GENERAL PRINCIPLES OF THERAPY.

XVI GROUP PSYCHOTHERAPY AND THE NATURE OF
    SCHIZOPHRENIA   507
SPECIFICITY IN TREATMENT. THE NATURE OF SCHIZOPHRENIA: *Quantitative and Qualitative Aspects; The Three Basic Characteristics; Real versus Induced Schizophrenia; Schizophrenia as a Defense; Borderline Schizophrenia.* CATEGORIES OF SCHIZOPHRENIA. SYMBOLIC REALIZATION. BASIC PRINCIPLES OF PSYCHOTHERAPY OF SCHIZOPHRENIA: *The Four Tasks of Treatment.* THE PRINCIPLE OF GRADED REALITY: *Confrontation versus Exploration; Phantoms, Hallucinations, Delusions; Self-Identity and Schizophrenia.* HOSPITAL COMMUNITY PSYCHOTHERAPY: *Values of a Hospital Community; Staff.* PROGRAM: *Application of the Group Process; Effects of Small Groups; Reality-Oriented Groups; The Project Method.* GROUP PSYCHOTHERAPY IN OUTPATIENT TREATMENT. PSYCHONURSING. DEFENSE AGAINST THERAPY.

REFERENCES   548

INDEX   551

Introduction

The present volume is an attempt to organize systematically the outcome of fifty years of experimentation and observation with various types of group in and out of clinical settings, thirty years of which were spent in the latter. The basic orientation is frankly derived from Freud's formulations as to the structure and function of the human psyche and its misconstruction and aberrations. Experience with different types of clinical problems, the immense variety of neurotic and character structures and deviations, and especially the fact that the treatment was carried on in a group setting, necessitated modifications, as well as expansion, of Freud's basic concepts. Nonetheless, these diversional necessities in no way detract or counter the profound laws formulated by Freud. It is safe to assume that, were he active in the psychosocial climate of the present era and the current cultural and clinical settings, and with groups, he himself would have modified his practices, though hardly his basic discoveries. For did he not say about his work: "I have dug the tunnel; others will have to let in the light"?

SETTING VERSUS PROCESS

In group and social psychotherapy, more than in other types of this endeavor, special attention must be directed to the *setting* in which actual treatment is to be carried on. The therapeutic process, i.e., the interpersonal interactions, the cathartic process, the functions of the therapist, derivation of insight and the numerous concomitant occurrences and outcomes such as correction and reweighting of psychic forces, dissolution of onerous defenses, and acquisition of objectivity and allotropy, is, in group psychotherapy.

conditioned by the setting in which it is carried on. This setting consists of several interrelated elements: (a) the choice of and grouping of suitable patients, (b) the personality and the professional qualifications of the therapist, and (c) the physical milieu. To each of these, and many other factors, extensive portions of this textbook are devoted.

Even a greater part of the material contained herein is given over to the innumerable minutiae of the dynamic stream, the codirectional and conflictual intra- and interpersonal and intragroup interactions that take place in an active therapeutic context and process after appropriate settings are provided. These forces are further related to the phenomena that are subsumed in the clinical categories of neuroses, psychoneuroses, character disorders, and schizophrenia from which patients who come for treatment suffer.

EMPHASIS ON SPECIFICITY

Experience with several thousand patients has impressed upon us the importance of an exhaustive understanding of each patient: his background, his early formative relations, his medical history, psychic structure and dynamics, his organic and psychic pathology and ego functioning in interpersonal relations. These etiologic, nosologic, and social histories are essential in establishing an operational diagnosis even when a clinical diagnosis may be unclear. It is because the direction of therapy is determined by this knowledge that it becomes the crux of the therapeutic effort, and we have, therefore, apportioned considerable space to these pivotal subjects.

The same approach has been employed toward the use of terminology in this newly developing field. Serious confusion results from blanket, unclearly defined or entirely undefined usage of terms and phrases that lend themselves to variegated meanings. This condition has given rise to serious misunderstandings in practice and impediments in communication. An effort is being made here toward establishing clearer meanings for the terms employed in formulating theory and clarifying practice. Because of the nature of the concepts with which one deals in psychotherapy, many of the definitions have to be of necessity instrumental.

THE SMALL GROUP CONCEPT

The various and essential characteristics of a therapy group are discussed at length in the body of this volume. However, because some confusion still persists as to its nature in one respect, we deem it necessary to establish here a basic frame of reference for the student. This element is that of the size of a psychotherapy group.

The number of patients in a true psychotherapy group cannot exceed eight, and a somewhat smaller number may be advisable. The principle of the small group was first introduced by the present writer in 1934. It was a serendipitous discovery. Originally the intention was to supply recreational and "socializing" experiences for socially maladjusted "little sisters" in a Big Sister department in a child guidance clinic. The core of these group activities was "creative expression" with arts and crafts materials and trips and outings characteristic of social group work and "progressive education." The reports of the impressive improvement in the girls by their Big Sisters who had contact with them led us to conclude that the "creative achievement" was the source of this change. We therefore adopted the term "therapeutics of creative activity" as a designation of our project.

However, at an exhibit of the productions of the girls of several groups, doubt arose as to whether results of such, not-too-high, craftsmanship and art creations could have such sanguine influences on them. We proceeded thoroughly to study and analyze one year's record of the weekly sessions of a group with a view toward trying to discover the factors that had led to the improvement. This effort consumed approximately a thousand hours. We were able to identify twenty-six interpersonal situations in the group that may have affected the participants favorably, and we came to the conclusion that *it was the group per se* that held the therapeutic potential. As a result, we suggested the term "group psychotherapy" as the appropriate designation for our work. This term was unknown to us and had not been used by any of the psychiatrists and others who had employed groups for various reasons. It was sixteen years later that it was pointed out to me that the term had appeared once in passing in a publication, without defining it or suggesting techniques for its employment.

At first, the study referred to above led us to the conclusion that

3

the dynamics operating were release, acceptance, "unconditional love," relatedness, and similar operational phenomena. It was some years later, after we had worked with analytic groups, that we recognized that the operational dynamics were the same as those of Freudian analytical psychotherapy, though modified.

CULTURE AND ETHOS

Since psychotherapy involves the total personality of the patient (though it must of necessity focus upon its pathognomic areas), it must take into consideration the psychic structure of the individual and his value system. Different cultural values and the forces that condition the psyche as they operate in the family and in the wider social milieu, forge specific intrapsychic operations and determine pathology. It is by this complex of forces that the character of psychotherapy needs to be planned and applied. In the Introduction to the Japanese edition of *Analytic Group Psychotherapy,* this problem is stated in part: ". . . one must be very much aware . . . when psychotherapeutic procedures are transplanted from one culture to another. It will be apparent . . . that the problems with which we have been dealing . . . were derived from early family relations and experiences with the important persons in the individual's life; namely, parents and siblings. Obviously these relations and their symbolic and reality meanings vary in different cultures and civilizations, because of differences in family structure and social value systems—the ethos. Adjustments and variations in techniques of therapy, and especially the differences in the latent meaning of words must be considered. These adjustments must be left to the scientific investigations and judgment of local practitioners who know the indigenous forces that determined the ontogeny of each society. Thus the value of this volume will be in a large measure conditioned by the intelligent and discriminative application of the principles herein suggested and formulated; for above theory and preference, is the patient. It is the welfare of the patient that must motivate the therapist at all times and not his personal predilections or inflexible adherence to a set of principles." It is not only in divergent races and cultures that adaptations in the practice of

4

therapy are necessary. There are also regional and subcultural characteristics in a society and in a nation that demand attention from the psychotherapist.

THE REPETITION PHENOMENON

The reader will find references to ideas, principles, and processes repeated in various connections relating to theory, psychodynamics, and to the conduct of group interviews. Ordinarily, repetitions are both onerous and annoying, but in organizing the type of textbook which this is intended to be, such reiteration was found unavoidable. When a complex but holistic subject such as psychotherapy is to be presented with some degree of completeness, it is inevitable that the same ideas and phenomena should apply to, and reappear in, more than one relation and context. To have avoided them would have rendered each segment under discussion, which was only part of a holistic construction, barren and unrelated to the whole. The result would have been trite, severe, and impoverished. Thus it was decided that a facile treatment would be preferable to rigid avoidance of tautology. However, every effort was made to limit iteration to a minimum by employing it only when it added to clarity and relatedness.

STYLE AND CONSTRUCTION

While the intent in planning this volume was to present group psychotherapy to the student in a simple and systematic form, thereby avoiding vagueness and partial, pseudo, or twilight understanding, the aim was to avoid the dry, cryptic, and skeletonized statements characteristic of the typical textbook. The elaborative plan adopted in the writing of this book is particularly necessary for group psychotherapy, since no teaching facilities of adequate extensive and intensive nature are as yet available. "Training" is still limited almost entirely to techniques and to general concepts relating to these techniques—mainly available in inservice and residency periods on a supervisory or "control" basis. In other academically established subjects, the instructors elaborate on the summarized content of textbooks. In group psychotherapy, opportunities for this type of teaching are still nonexistent. It was, therefore, deemed advisable to treat some of the topics extensively and rather fully. This plan, it is hoped, will engender in the student perspective and an appreciation of the vastness of the field.

THE IDEAL AND THE ATTAINABLE

It will be obvious to the student that the professional standards set forth in this volume are of necessity rather high and, perhaps, maximal. We must strive toward them, at the same time recognizing that modifications and compromises are inevitable in the setting of reality. Nonetheless, as in all areas of life, it is of utmost importance that we set our sights on ideals so that we may approach them to the extent to which circumstances favor that realization.

Some parts of the content of this volume have appeared, in abridged form, in various publications. Chief among these are the *International Journal of Group Psychotherapy, The Psychoanalytic Review, The American Journal of Orthopsychiatry,* and *Acta Psychotherapeutica.* I wish to express my appreciation to Dr. A. S. Kagan of International Universities Press for his many courtesies during the preparation and publication of this and other of my books published by them, and Mrs. Irene Azarian and Miss Joyce Shaw for their editorial help. I am very grateful to Miss Elinor Bowles for her painstaking secretarial work and to Dr. Haim Ginott for his critical reading of the original manuscript.

S. R. Slavson
Croton-on-Hudson, N.Y., July, 1963

I

The Group in Nature, Culture, and Psychotherapy

THE GROUP IN INDIVIDUAL DEVELOPMENT

As a social phenomenon, grouping is not an invention or discovery of man, but has its roots in nature. Groupings are essential for the biological survival of lower animals and, because of his frailty, they are particularly important for man. They are also essential to man's psychological and spiritual life. Man consciously uses groups for enhancement of personality and for social survival. Psychosocial cravings originate in the family, being derived, at first, from dependence on parents or surrogates and from sibling relations and rivalries. They are further developed through various types of cultural values and emphases. However, despite the many artifices for their promotion, groups must be recognized for what they are—an extension of biological life and an integral part of nature.

The manifestations of grouping are present among all forms of life on our planet. In man, their management and organization are of special concern for society, for only through group relationships can the individual gain the greatest profit and satisfaction. Before discussing this further, some basic patterns of interpersonal relations at the early stages of development need to be discussed, because it is upon these relations that a sound educational superstructure and later psychotherapy are founded.

7

Nurture, Training, and Schooling

In modern society, an infant's and child's growth require, from persons responsible for their survival and development, three distinct relations, which, in actual life, may occur simultaneously. When the needs and demands of children are inappropriately dealt with by adults, in terms of these relations, pathology results. The three functions are *nurture, training,* and *schooling*.[1]

Included under the category of nurture are all the services accorded to the infant by adults when he lives a parasitic life, completely dependent upon the mother (or nurse). At this stage he is very much an extension of her. His life is in many respects similar to that of his intra-uterine existence. During this period, all his needs and wants, communicated by crying, are usually instantaneously met. Although the infant, and to a progressively lesser extent the child, is entirely dependent on others for his survival, he cannot yet *perceive* himself in a related way and, as a result, he behaves in an imperious and autocratic manner. During the period of nurture he is not normally subject to discipline or routine, nor is he expected to submit or to conform. He cannot yet conceptualize beyond his self-centered physical world.

As the infant enters childhood, an increasing number of limitations are progressively imposed upon him, making inroads on his autism. The first step in this direction is in the area of feeding, when sucking is replaced by spoon-feeding and, later, when solid foods supplement and replace liquids. Biting and masticating demand effort on the child's part. This change in the feeding pattern, and particularly the sensations during teething, give the human personality a special stamp. At this time there is less indulgence on the part of the mother (or nurse) and more external limitations are set on action and motility.

In addition to these processes, the child begins to become aware of the separateness between himself and other individuals, which lays the foundations for object relations. The onset of this awareness, coupled with external demands and the child's maturational-

---

[1] The totality of all nurture, training, discipline, expression, and interaction make up "education." Schooling is only a small part of education.

ly strengthened ego, enable him to adapt to the increasing discipline imposed on him. Training, which was concentrated on feeding, is expanded to the areas of anal and urethral activity, a process the child finds even less to his liking. Whereas, in the substitution of the glass and spoon for the nipple, he was still on the receiving end, he now has to give up part of himself (his feces) at the bidding of another person. As a result, the child puts up a struggle against this incursion upon his pleasures and self-indulgence. The attitude and manner of adults, in dealing with this struggle, determine to a great extent the child's organization of personality and the quality of his future object relations, as well as being a frequent source of much pathology which a psychotherapist has to deal with later on.

In our culture, official education, or schooling (the third stage) starts around the ages of five or six, when, through a definite regimen, the child begins to acquire skills and learn facts and acceptable social behavior.

One of the common sources of psychological difficulties in children, as well as in adults, is that either nurture—the stage of dependence and protection—was extended beyond the normal maturational period into the training phase, or training was initiated too early, taking the place of nurture. Children for whom the nurture phase has been extended too long are the overprotected, infantilized, and pampered. Being dependent, helpless, and usually of limited effectuality, they present problems of maladjustment because of a weak ego structure. Because of external factors or due to their inherent nature, they may become unsocial through demanding, exploitive maneuvers and expect to be cared for and protected. On the other hand, children who have been overcontrolled, rigidly disciplined, and unreasonably frustrated, whose conduct has been criticized and directed, when they should have had the security of love, develop behavior disorders of an aggressive nature and may become hostile, destructive, disturbing, provocative, and retaliatory. Such children feel themselves rejected, and many of them may become defensively withdrawn and isolated.

"Discipline," when properly applied, strengthens the ego so that one can deal adequately with inherent aggressive, pleasure-seeking and narcissistic tendencies. It can prevent the child from becoming a victim of anarchic impulses and self-indulgence; it can serve to overcome false feelings of omnipotence and prevent development of deleterious object relations. Discipline by parents and teachers, and later by various groups and institutions in society is, therefore, essential. However, it must be employed so as to lead not only to self-discipline—inner strength that inhibits unrefined and untrammelled impulse, without emotionally destructive consequences—but also to prevent the emergence of onerous attitudes toward social interaction. When discipline is properly applied, it leads to self-discipline; it leads not to punishment and frustration, but to identification and internalization of societal values, represented by benign parents, nurses, and teachers who personify these values. The recognition of this interpersonal complex is essential to the psychotherapist for establishing and dealing with transference-countertransference dynamics.

The struggle between the child and the adult is inevitable. The child cannot give up his narcissism without it. And, as in the case of sibling relations, this struggle is beneficial, for through it the child's ego is strengthened, unless he is crushed in the process by an overbearing manner and overwhelming threat from adults. An excitable, tempestuous, or irascible parent can render the child's ego weak, unstable, and incapable of dealing with difficulties in later life. On the other hand, the easy-going, tolerant, and reasonable reactions of important adults pattern the child's ego after their own. Through their conduct, adults *demonstrate* ways of dealing with life, and, even more important, they bring about an equilibrium in the child's psychic forces and strengthen his ego. While it is commonly understood that the superego is derived from parents, other important adults in the child's life, and the cultural climate, it is less recognized that these are also responsible for ego development and functions. The absence of constructive parental attitudes and behavioral modes need to be taken into account by the therapist in his reconstructive work.

10

Discipline and Repression

The structural relation between discipline and repression is a very close one, a fact that psychotherapists must recognize and sometimes make clear to patients. Certain primitive drives must be appropriately repressed if the individual is to make an adequate adjustment in life; and when this has not been achieved in childhood and adolescence, psychotherapy must find ways to correct such developmental defects. Repression must be established, but this must be accomplished without doing violence to basic drives and their associated emotions or to the personality as a whole. It is one thing to make an individual "moral" and "responsible"; it is another to render him, in the process, either weak and oversubmissive, hostile, emotionally frigid or compulsively anxious. Repression and discipline, first inaugurated through parental controls, are only a beginning. An individual cannot rise to the fullness of his potentialities or achieve personality integration through repression and discipline alone.

Social Hunger

In the development of the individual in our culture, extrafamilial relationships are also important. No one is adequately adjusted, however favorable his family climate may have been, who has not experienced meaningful relations with individuals and groups outside the home. In orderly development, object cathexes are progressively extended from the persons in the family toward persons outside it. In the world beyond the family, free associations in play and work take on utmost importance. The child progressively enters on new paths which lead him from the limited circle of the home toward the larger world and new and expanding experiences. When left free and encouraged to fulfill his maturational readiness and socially conditioned requirements, he gradually represses urges and cravings toward members of his family, especially his parents, and redirects them toward persons outside the home.[2] At the same time, and because of the child's

[2] During puberty and adolescence this transition constitutes the change from incestuous to nonincestuous sexual objects.

progressive maturation, new needs arise, the most important of which is the need to be with, and to associate with, friends. This we designate as *social hunger*.

Some of these associations are casual playmates, nursery and kindergarten groups, classmates, and later social clubs, and occupational and political groups. In orderly development, the modifications in adaptation that ensue from individual and group associations are structured into the character of the individual. The ego, the group-conditioned superego, and the various defenses that had their beginnings in early family relations are, in these social relations, advanced in their growth, modified, and brought to a state of more or less final formation. Spontaneous and planned group associations play a determining role in this.

The slighting of the group as an instrument in psychosocial and psychosexual development in our individualistic and family-centered culture is a serious defect in the education of all and in the therapy of many. In recent years, however, it has been recognized that this oversight is at the root of the maladjustment of numerous individuals and is the cause of much social pathology. Enlightened educators and psychotherapists alike are increasingly aware that the individual cannot be understood apart from his family and social cultures; that the totality of the conditions of his life, past and present—his biosphere—needs to be considered. His past and current life, their influences, relations, and his adaptations to them, are part and parcel of his personality. In fact, the socioeconomic milieu also affects infants and children, through parents and nurses who are affected by the conditions of their lives and society. Just as a plant cannot avoid the effects of sun, weather, and climate, so man cannot avoid the conditions of his interpersonal and social environment. Each person lives less in his macroculture and more in the microculture of his immediate surroundings, the kernel of which is the group. The capacity for adaptation to group relations and group living is the foundation for both individual health and a constructive democratic life pattern. Group associations are, therefore, a prime requirement of a healthy personality and are indicative of a well-balanced psyche. However, both isolation from group association and vehement pur-

12

suit of it reflect inner tension and a need for escape mechanisms.

Whatever the *raison d'être*, an important fact in understanding and dealing with people, in total education and in therapy, is that the craving for relationships, acceptance, and association is a primary one. One of the universal complaints of the neurotic is that people do not like him, and one of his fears is that of group association, which, according to him, must result in rejection and pain. Though the psychoneurotic's disturbance is intrapsychic, that is, it is structured in his own psyche, it originates in intragroup (family) relations and manifests itself most often as social maladjustment. His most urgent need is to overcome this handicap. But social maladaptation is not confined to the neurotic alone. Others are similarly afflicted. Whether an individual's condition falls within the clinical category of neurosis, psychosis, behavior or character disorders, or psychopathic personality—all of them *intrapsychic* malformations—his *manifest* difficulties are in relation to other people. It is therefore understandable that an effort should be made to explore the possibilities of employing the group as a developmental and corrective tool.[3]

The Eight Basic Groups

In the process of orderly growth, in our culture, an individual comes under the influence of eight types of groups. Table 1 lists these groups, in order of importance. While all of them contribute to ego building and social adaptation in similar ways, each makes specific contributions to the shaping of personality. Although these groups are disparate, most of them are coextensive, the individual coming under the simultaneous influence of several of them at any given time.

In addition to other values, these groups supply opportunities for sublimation of the many socially unacceptable urges and cravings lodged in instinct and the unconscious, both through activities and through constructive identifications and relationships. The

---

[3] For example, the author's *Re-Educating the Delinquent* (1954) demonstrated how groups can be effectively employed in the social rehabilitation of fairly hardened "delinquents."

13

TABLE 1

*Major Contributions of Successive Groups
to Personality Development**

Order	Group	Major Contribution
1	family	acceptance, unconditioned love
2	nursery or play	social experimentation (socialization)
3	school	creative-dynamic expression
4	same-sex	identification (socialization), sexual reassurance
5	heterosexual	heterosexual adjustment
6	occupational	social adequacy, economic security
7	adult voluntary	social acceptance (socialization)
8	family	mating, parenthood, self-perpetuation

* For more detailed discussion of these groups, see Slavson, 1938, 1939.

transition from self-centered egotropic to expansive allotropic personality is aided by the settings these groups provide.

Of particular importance are group relations during adolescence. At this stage of the transition from childhood to adulthood, from dependence to independence, the support that adolescents give one another is essential (Slavson, 1958). This is observably manifested in the spontaneous groupings of young people during this period. To be of greatest value, groups should provide a milieu in which the individual is accepted and respected; where he can function constructively at his maximal level of development and capacity, without the anxieties aroused by fear of failure and by real or fancied inferiorities. In cases where, in the course of development, these opportunities were lacking, re-education and psychotherapy should supply them.

Misconceptions of "Togetherness"

Criticisms of the growing trend toward "togetherness" cannot but fall on deaf ears, for man's very survival depends on this "togetherness." The opposition to this inevitable and irreversible development may be justified if "togetherness" is understood to mean *submergence* of the individual rather than his *mergence* with the group and the human race. "Togetherness" (admittedly

14

a poor term) is undesirable only if it is taken to mean the sacrifice of individual uniqueness and particularity. However, this is a misinterpretation of the concept of "togetherness," perhaps stemming from a confounding of the terms "individuality" and "individualism."

Few enlightened people would defend rampant individualism as a suitable system for social and race survival in the highly technological and logistically complex world of today. Even in societies committed to the "sacredness of individual enterprise and initiative," considerable inroads into this doctrine had to be made. Individualism as a philosophy of life is inconsistent with the best interests of society and individuals. Out of sheer necessity, curbs and controls have evolved to reduce to some extent, at least, the contradictions that these two forces generate. Widespread individualism had its beginnings in the Industrial Revolution and the scientific and technological developments that followed in its wake. The slaves and serfs assumed new stature and new values as they became the producers of wealth for the owning classes, and, as these members of the new wage-earning mass—labor—became aware of their power, they initiated the ultimately successfull struggle for a place in the sun, which has been carried on for approximately the last hundred years.

Whether by strikes, sabotage, or open rebellion, the motive was to acquire for the many some of the advantages of what they produced. In some of the most industrially advanced nations, surprising progress has been made in this direction so that the demarcation between owner and worker is now less distinguishable. This change was brought about partly by the very nature of industrial, and especially commercial, development, but the organization of labor greatly contributed to it. In this process, the efficacy of "togetherness" on the part of the workers was amply demonstrated, as it has been in many other areas.

At the same time, "togetherness" also appeared in the ordinarily competitive industrial and commercial enterprises, which have grown by leaps and bounds in number and size. As the incomes of the masses of the population have soared, the increased consumption of goods has stimulated production and the growth of corporations. These corporations have attempted to aggrandize themselves by combining into trusts, and when this was legally thwarted, they began to merge and consolidate into large single corporations.

Thus, co-operation, fusing, and merging have become the ascendant pattern of social life in all basic community and national efforts and are gradually extending across national lines. As suggested, these phenomena are the manifestions of processes inherent in the socio-technological evolution of man. However, the development of appropriate value systems and *Weltanschauung* has lagged behind. The pace was not maintained in the individualistic orientation which permeated the thinking and striving of individuals and social, economic, and governmental institutions.

While the individual derived his greatest fulfillment from and through groups and social institutions, agencies and associations, his needs for happiness and "success" did not include those of his near and remote neighbors. Similarly, industrial and commercial concerns while combining, at the same time carried on keen competition. These are among the many contradictory, tension-producing phenomena that have generated so much stress, both in individuals and in societies.

The recent awareness of the changing social climate which is described, rather erroneously, as "togetherness" in personal relations, is an automatic expression of the need to establish social homeostasis. It is a self-generating and self-regulatory social mechanism that serves to reduce contradictions in human affairs, which, if controlled with purpose and intelligence, hold promise for a less stressful climate for human life.

Individualism versus Individuality

In giving direction to this inevitable and favorable trend toward "togetherness," it is essential to understand and maintain the differences between *individualism* and *individuality* and between *submerging* and *merging*. It would be both folly and misanthropy to carry the banner for the two antecedent ideas in these antithetic pairings. Individualism is antiprogressive; it seeks to reverse the social evolutionary process; it leads to intrapersonal and interpersonal tensions, and mutual exploitation, both emotionally and

16

materially. Similarly, submergence of the individual in the group cannot but lead to a static society and the spiritual degeneration of mankind. This submergence can be achieved only by tyranny, and its inevitable effect is a static, nonproductive community.

The essential difference between individualism and individuality is that in the latter the dignity and especial uniqueness of each individual are preserved and respected, while at the same time he is *socially motivated*. That is, the individual is inextricably intertwined in his social matrix and does not view his actions and their outcomes in terms of personal advantage only. This becomes a problem of conditioning, motivation and evolving a new system of values. In the long run, nothing can be good for an individual which is not, at the same time, also to the advantage of mankind as a whole. This conviction is extolled in all religions, as well as in fiction, poetry, and drama. It is now necessary to assimilate it into the process of daily living, which is what "togetherness" implies.

The concept of individuality, by its very nature, rules out *submergence* in the horde. Rather, it implies that the individual *merges* with the group, with society and with mankind, in a benevolent interest in the happiness of all, and, above all else, in a feeling of responsibility for the improvement and perpetuation of such a plan of life. It also means subordinating one's narcissistic, self-seeking urges to the welfare of others—consciously subordinating self-interest for the interests of the group as a pattern of everyday life. However, one can still retain uniqueness, despite renunciation of those aspects of life and conduct that infringe on the well-being of others.

"Togetherness" need not be grim, if the community discriminates intelligently between those areas of life in which it is beneficial and those in which it may prove harmful. The outcome of a socially motivated individuality would be a new type of attitude, which could be described as "communalism"[4] (as opposed to individualism).

---

[4] This term is different from "communism," which, in its current application, is a travesty on both the term and the original idea behind it. *Communalism* means a plan of social life and motivations for conduct that will take into account the needs and interests of others, near and remote, and the community as a whole.

17

One of the points pressed on parents, educators, and therapists, in recent decades, is the importance of being aware of individual differences in capabilities and needs. Although socioeconomic demands and technology are forcing individuality and unique talent more and more into the background, the mental hygienist, whatever his specific field may be, is well aware of the pathogenic potentials in the trend toward uniformity. Neither productivity nor good health lie in this direction, for, as the leveling social conditions are increased and integrative and controlling inner forces are decreased, which is now the trend, social and individual pathology must of necessity increase. It is this dichotomy in modern society that is responsible, in great part, for the present rise in individual and social imbalance. It is this same dichotomy that forces the community to adopt alleviating measures, as represented by counseling, guidance, and therapy.

GROUPS IN NATURE AND SOCIETY

A popular misconception is that "the group" and "grouping" are the result of man's conscious planning and are indicative of his "spirituality." Studies of the habits of all forms of life, even the unicellular, yield incontrovertible evidence that what zoologists call "innate co-operation" abounds in nature and gives rise to clusters, colonies, schools, flocks, herds, hives, etc. This co-operation is in the service of survival—obtaining food and shelter, procreation, and protection.

Some of the commonly observed natural groupings are herds of wild horses, sheep, and other mammals; bee hives and ant hills; schools of seals; schools of salmon during the spawning season; flocks of birds during hatching and migration; and "slumber parties" of insects (such as the "solitary wasps," where both males and females group together at night and the "solitary bees" where only males gather for their sleep). The Russian geographer, Peter Kropotkin, observed that horses, attacked by wolves in the lonely snowcovered wastes of Siberia, formed a circle with their hind legs outward and kicked at their attackers from whatever point they approached. During cold weather, many snakes form a huge ball, intricately intertwined, which is in constant motion, so that no one snake remains exposed to the cold for any length of time.

Worms, paramecia, and various other low and high forms of animal life, have displayed greater endurance and better survival capacity under stress and toxicity when in groups. Allee (1938, page 58), after presenting a large array of experiments and observations, states: ". . .under a variety of conditions groups of animals may be able to live when isolated individuals would be killed or severely injured by unaccustomed toxic, chemical elements, strange to their normal environment." Another experimenter (Shaw, 1932) found that some fish, when their tails are cut off, regenerate them faster when a number of them are present in the water than when they are isolated. Allee (1938, pages 97-98) observed the same phenomenon in young tadpoles and found "a device . . . in nature [if] one or a few fish in a group find plenty of food, apparently without willing to do so they regurgitate some food particles which are taken by others, a sort of *automatic sharing.*"[5]

A great many observations have been accumulated to support the thesis that survival of life, in all its forms, is achieved through groups and grouping, either as a permanent pattern, or under specific circumstances or stress. Man is no exception. In fact, in man, groups have assumed wider and deeper significance than in other forms of biological life. Biologists have long recognized that the more complex an organism's environment is, the greater are the variety and the strain of adaptive requirements upon that organism. Species whose optimum adaptive capacities have proved inadequate to meet environmental change have become extinct. In species other than man, this law applied to physical survival alone. In man it also assumes psychological significance. In Western societies, the threat to physical survival has greatly diminished. Man's capacities for producing, storing, preserving, and distributing the provisions for his physical needs, his laws governing violence against his person, and his medical and technical advances, have combined to make his daily life more se-

[5] Italics are mine.

cure. However, urban life and the patterns of industrial-commercial society have accentuated another area of struggle, that of survival as a member of a social setting or, as some sociologists refer to it, as "a social atom." The struggle has been transferred from the arena of biological survival to the problem of maintaining individual status—survival as a psychological and social entity.

This newly emerged problem is a source of intense strain, anxiety, and guilt, especially to those who, for a variety of reasons, fall outside the norm or average of the value system of a given society. As society becomes more compact, decreasing the physical distance between people and standardizing their ethics and conduct, insularity becomes less serviceable as a personal adjustment. The so-called "herd instinct," or mutualism, observed in all nature ("social hunger" in man) is intensified by proximity and necessitates interaction. As with any other rudimentary trend in organisms, exercise intensifies its strength. Thus, the need for group formations of various types has so progressed that now groups are part and parcel of social life and operate in a multitude of forms in all areas of society.

Man can achieve psychic development and fulfillment only through groups, with the foundations being laid in the earliest relations with another individual (the mother). However, as indicated, this primary relation has to be extended beyond the family if mental health and intellectual development are to be assured. In this process, groups are of pre-eminent importance. Growth of personality cannot be derived from interaction with individuals alone, for in all groups one has to *deal with, and interact with, relationships among people,* as well as individuals. Even in families, the social molecule of Western society, the father not only has to deal with his children and his wife as individuals, but also with their relationships to each other. Similarly, the mother has to be aware of the relationships between her husband and children, and so on. Successful functioning grows increasingly more difficult as the number of persons involved increases.

There is a specific set of groups with which each individual must interact and in which he has to find his place and occupy a specific role if he is to survive adequately in his society. This set is part of a much larger phalanx of groups (to be discussed later).

GROUPISM

Lester Ward, the great American sociologist and foremost exponent of integrative knowledge, suggested (Ward, 1911) that the stages of development in nature were chemism, bathmism, zoism, and psychism. In a seminar on group work (in 1939) I suggested that the next stage in the evolutionary development of man is *groupism,* and elaborated this concept in *Child Psychotherapy* (Slavson, 1952a).

Some neurologists believe that imperceptible evolutionary changes are occurring in man's nervous system. However, these changes are so slight that eons will elapse before any observable effects can be expected that could result in changes in man's feelings and behavior. On the other hand, observable transformations in the social scene are continually taking place and man can, to some degree, control and direct his social destiny. If man can find a way to adequately deal with his atavistic hostility and evolve better means to apprehend, direct, and control his own unconscious, he will be able to direct his society and his development toward the creation of a more satisfactory world. Man's critical problem at the moment is how to subordinate his disruptive and destructive drives (individually and collectively) to his knowledge and his latent rationality.

Man has learned to harness the forces bound up in the realm of chemism, and to understand, train, and utilize animals in the realm of zoism. And now, in his desperation and bewilderment, man is trying to understand and direct *himself,* through the sciences of psychology and sociology, seemingly with relatively little result or benefit. It seems that the study of man as an individual or in large masses is not enough. The next step will be the exploration and training of his nature as he operates in the dimensions of time, space, and, most important, in his relationships with other human beings. He shall be forced, in the near future, to peruse his nature and potentials in the group, for it is

21

through groups that man's greatness is achieved and it is in groups that he will find the instruments of social effectiveness and self-fulfillment.

The new *science of groupism,* now in the process of development, and its instrumental application to life are the only hope mankind has for escaping impending catastrophe. We cannot entirely agree with H. G. Wells's prediction that man's future history is a race between education and catastrophe. Education alone cannot meet the needs of mankind nor prevent the tragedy Wells so prophetically envisaged—not unless we include in education the effect upon man of his total environment, including economic conditions, and moral value systems. We need to find procedures that will place man in a different relationship to his fellow men. We need to find means for forging the unconscious in such a way that man's hostilities and aggressions toward others and himself might be, if not eliminated, at least diminished and sublimated. This can be achieved only through human relationships and through groups, with their power to sanction, prohibit, control, accept, and reject.

That the *era of groupism* is in the making is evident from the extensive literature and vast quantity of experimentation current in group dynamics and group management. During the last few decades, the group has been the central theme of numerous publications in various fields. Although the profession most directly concerned with the group is understandably sociology, educators, psychologists, and psychiatrists, among others, are increasingly turning their attention to this subject. One example of this expanding preoccupation with the group as a tool in social and professional functioning is reflected in a symposium (Symposium, 1954) in which an imposing variety of professional interests were represented (in all of which, group techniques have been employed). These included government, industry, education, communications, community mental health, and others. In another publication on the subject (Slavson, 1956), wider application of these techniques has been noted.

Use of group methods has been steadily increasing in the fields of education, interracial relations, management and labor, industrial and commercial activities, family counseling, parent guidance and education, student mental health, training for medicine and psychiatry, hospital management, delinquency prevention and correction, prison management, treatment of addicts, and other management, therapeutic, and prophylactic activities too numerous to list.

It is understandable and inevitable that psychiatry should have been caught up in this evolving era of *groupism*. Society has many of the characteristics of an individual organism and is subject to reflex and referred reactions to important developments and changes that occur anywhere in the body politic. No significant change can occur in any part of the social organism without affecting, to varying degrees, the nature and functions of other areas.

FREUD'S GROUP PSYCHOLOGY AND PSYCHOTHERAPY

Few will gainsay that Freud has influenced, to varying degrees, every area of modern culture and civilization. Some efforts and thought systems have been completely transformed by his insights, some have been modified as to direction and content, and still others have been enriched by the addition of new knowledge. Much confusion in many fields, has been cleared up as a result of the new understandings that he contributed or that have been evolved on the basis of what came from his pen.

Freud's original impetus for his work came from an applied approach to healing emotionally disturbed patients, but his observations led him to construct a new system of individual and social psychology unformulated before his day. He threw light on the constitution and the dynamic processes of man's psyche, which, up to that time, had been in the realm of speculation, conjecture, or just ignorance. His formulations of the unconscious and its operation made clear much that had been enigmatic, and his theories of the libido, infantile sexuality, and oedipal strivings clarified what had been a puzzle in human behavior for ages. The patterns of functions and relations of the id, ego, and superego and the relation of instinct and social mores are now much more fully understood, as a result of his penetrating thought and prodigious work.

The arts, education, family life, the social sciences and humanities, psychology, the status of woman and her relation to life and work, the relations of men and women, parents and children, races and nationalities, the styles of dress and designing, industrial designs and merchandising, and countless other efforts, patterns, relations, and institutions have all been affected by Freud's discoveries and formulations; for these have struck at the very essence and psychological sources of life itself. Seldom does one man arise in the course of human history to enunciate such basic truths. Countless "truths" have been propounded in the past millenia, dealing with specific areas or ideas. But only rarely has mankind been witness to the discovery of such widely pervasive basic findings as those of Copernicus, Galileo, Darwin, and Einstein. What these foremost scientists have done for man's understanding of his physical world, Freud has done for man's understanding of himself, a far more difficult task requiring great penetration and courage.

Whether or not one accepts Freud's formulations *in toto*, whether one differs from him in psychological theory or therapeutic practice, no thinking person can remain unaffected by exposure to the mass of observations, information, and theory that came from his writings. A great many derivative and modified theories and practices have evolved since Freud lived and worked in the field of psychoanalysis. These have many names and special features and vocabularies of their own, but all are derived from and based on Freud's numerous suggestions, remarks, hypotheses, discoveries, and formulations. Even those who claim different origin have been stimulated by his work.

Freud was well aware of the differences between individual and group psychology. In his *Group Psychology and the Analysis of the Ego* (1940, page 94) he speculates on the relation of individual psychology and group psychology. He says, "The primal father had prevented his sons from satisfying their directly sexual tendencies; he forced them into abstinence and consequently into the emotional ties with him and with one another which could arise

24

out of those of their tendencies that were inhibited in their sexual aim. *He forced them, so to speak, into group psychology.* His sexual jealousy and intolerance became in the last resort the causes of group psychology."[6]

Freud based his deductions on group psychology and group behavior on the fundamental and quite correct studies of Le Bon and McDougall, and, to a lesser extent, on those of Trotter. We find here a contradiction that led Freud to some confusion as to what constitutes a group. Although his psychological definition of a group (Freud, 1940, page 83) conforms with our present-day understanding, there is obvious confusion in his treatment of the subject. Le Bon's and McDougall's studies dealt with large groups or *masses* rather than small groups. The latter were more the concern of Trotter, though not entirely so. While thoroughly aware of the differences in the dynamics of small groups and crowds or masses, Freud, in his discussion, nonetheless treats those two groups as one type and applies observations of one to the other. This is not correct, for intensification and mutual induction are both quantitatively and qualitatively effected by numbers.

Freud's conclusion that the "group is similar to the primal horde" has to be questioned. It would be more correct if the word "mass" were to be substituted for "group." "The psychology of such a group," says Freud (1940, page 91), ". . . the dwindling of the conscious individual personality, the focusing of thoughts in a common direction, the predominance of the emotions and the unconscious mental life, the tendency to the immediate carrying out of intentions as they emerge—all this corresponds to a state of regression to a primitive mental activity, of just such a sort as we should be inclined to ascribe to the primal horde."

We know that masses of people, such as mobs (in lynchings, riots, and strikes) and nations (in times of strong disturbance, such as war and revolution) behave in the manner described; but it is not in the nature of small groups to regress to such excesses or display such extreme behavior. The ego functions of each participant remain *more* intact in small groups than in large active

---

[6] Italics are mine.

25

masses, and the superego of each member retains much of its discriminatory controls rather than investing them entirely in the group leader or suspending them completely.

The seeming error perhaps arises from two separate sources. Freud's era in pre-World-War-I Europe was one of individualism. Group life as we know it today in a democracy was not known to even the most enlightened, although an awareness of irrational behavior on the part of masses and nations was recognized from observable behavior and from the vast information accumulated by ethnologists and anthropologists about primitive society and by historians about the more recent past. One hesitates, however, to ascribe to an intellect like Freud's a lack of comprehension of the difference between a group and a crowd or a mass. In fact, in a number of passages, he refers in passing to the importance of numbers in the behavior of groups. Consequently, one is rather inclined to attribute the confusion to an error of the translator. In a footnote, the translator explains that he had used the term "group" to substitute for the German *Masse,* and Le Bon's *foule* (the latter having been translated as "crowd" in the title of his book). In my opinion, then, the error has to be laid to the translator's inexperience in the theory of groups. In the light of this error, the similarity that Freud draws between the group and the horde is more understandable.

Freud wrote his essay on group psychology in the second decade of the twentieth century, but he anticipated later theoreticians when he emphasized the importance of the leader (among many other factors) in group formation and group functioning. In our day, the definition of a group includes leadership as one of its essential elements, for it is the *centrality* of the leader or a representative symbol that secures group cohesion. Freud was the first to call attention to the leader as a common object of libidinal cathexis and to point out that this cathexis holds the group members together. On this point we read his cryptic sentence: "The group vanishes in dust, like a Bologna flask when its top is broken" (1940, page 49). This observation has many implications for further study and for a better understanding of the more conscious and more appropriate role that leaders of all types of groups (including members of governing bodies) must assume for maximum effectiveness.[7] His parallels between the group leader and the leader of the primal horde are particularly apt in this regard. However, further observation of the unconscious projections of group members onto the person of the leader also reveals similarity to their attitudes toward parental figures, especially the father. This fact is even more pronounced in small groups, though it is also evident in masses. I have elsewhere suggested that one of the sources of mental health in a democracy lies in the fact that periodically the voters can reject their father substitutes (Presidents, governors, and others in authority); that is, they vicariously kill them off.

In small groups, particularly, because they are closer replicas of the family, individuals are stimulated to re-enact family-conditioned attitudes and behavior. Patterns of submission to or attack upon the leader, as the case may be, and the relationships with fellow group members are determined by, and stem from, the earlier family climate. It has been shown that the group serves *in loco maternis*. The leader usually represents, symbolically, the father figure, while the group represents the complimentary figure of the mother. In this sense, the original family constellation is re-established in all groups (including those in group psychotherapy). A group member can, with greater equanimity, tolerate sternness on the part of the leader than he can chastisement, disapproval, or rejection by the group. Each member expects the group to accept him and approve of him and each is more likely to adjust his behavior to the demands of the group than to the authority of the leader.[8]

To understand this dynamic process in therapy groups, Freud's

[7] Because of inadequate understanding of his role, a director of a professional organization, with a large staff, sought this writer's advice. When, during the interview, it was suggested in passing that his position places him in the role of a father substitute, he burst into involuntary laughter. His failure in his job stemmed directly from his inability to assume a parental role (having even refused to have children of his own). Successful directorships of organizations require the assumption of the role of the good, though firm, father who loves his children.

[8] Among the transferences that appear in therapy groups, "transference toward the group" is one that has to be considered in understanding the therapeutic process and the reactions of patients.

27

elaboration of the concept of identification is essential. In recognition of the importance of identification as a corrective, I have suggested the term "identification transference" to emphasize its presence and importance in psychotherapy. In *Group Psychology and the Analysis of the Ego* (1940) Freud develops this idea and suggests three types of identification: "First . . . the original form of emotional tie with an object; secondly, . . . introjection of the object into the ego; and thirdly, . . . perception of a common quality shared with some other person . . ." (page 65). All of these aspects of identification are operative in group psychotherapy, as they are in other types of small groups, and all must be viewed as part of the ego ideal of the individual. The psychotic is predominantly subject to the second type, i.e., oral incorporation in fantasy, so that other persons, especially the therapist, become part and parcel of his ego. The main characteristic of the psychotic is that, for him, the model of identification also becomes the target of intense hostility and destruction, a replica of his attitudes toward his parents.

Many concepts and dynamics since described by various writers on group psychotherapy, are mentioned, in passing, in Freud's essay (1940). Freud makes several references to the "group mind" (page 49), giving McDougall credit for the term. The phenomenon of bipolarity in groups (also present in therapy groups) is recorded in the following terms (pages 44-45): "It is to be noticed that in these two artificial groups each individual is bound by libidinal ties on the one hand to the leader. . .and on the other hand to the members of the group. . . . If each individual is bound in two directions by such an intense emotional tie, we shall find no difficulty in attributing to that circumstance the alteration and limitation which have been observed in his personality [by virtue of his belonging to the group]." Elsewhere in this volume, I have added a third pole.

Freud makes the following significant statement, in the light of group psychotherapy: ". . . where a powerful impetus has been given to group formation neuroses may diminish and at all events temporarily disappear. Justifiable attempts have also been made to turn this antagonism between neuroses and group formation to therapeutic account" (Freud, 1940, page 124).

This statement is of value to psychotherapists in a rather negative way. The question that it suggests is does the fact that a patient participates in a group and makes an adjustment to it, constitute therapy? Further, can the fact that some behavioral changes occur and some symptoms disappear be relied on as evidence of permanent change in the patient to the degree that he can carry on, in the future, the business of living, without the neurotic interferences? Freud's statement implies answers to these questions. These answers are derived from the experience of today's proponents of analytic group psychotherapy.

Analytic group therapists found, as did others, that some patients in groups give up their symptoms rather rapidly, but they recognize that such symptom improvement can be a screen for resistance to treatment, which is facilitated by identification with other group members and the group as a whole. The nature of analytic group interviews is such that direct suggestions, guidance and intellectual understanding are unavoidable. Because of their fear, discomfort, and resistance, some patients readily adopt the *ideas* thus gained as controls for their lives and act as though a basic change had occurred in their personalities. Others are suggestible or have a need to please, and be accepted by, the therapist or the group and so appear similarly improved.

Analytic group psychotherapy holds that improvements can be accepted as basic and relatively permanent only when problems are worked through in transference and through the analysis of resistances. By "worked through" we mean here that the anxieties bound up in the different traumatic situations in the patient's past have been released and his feelings and current reactions have been made available to the examination and, therefore, the control of the ego.

This position is indirectly supported by Freud in the statement previously quoted, which has two important elements. One is a "powerful impetus . . . to group formation" in the individual, the other is that neuroses *temporarily* disappear or *are diminished.*

Such improvement is readily supported through our observed experience. The diminution of emotional disturbances in individuals during an economic depression, war, or immediately after deeply disturbing major catastrophes is one example. The emotional disturbances reappear when the emergencies pass. Freud's statement is also supported by the many mental healing cults that produce apparently desirable effects on their adherents, although these improvements are conditional on continued membership and dependent on the support of the cult's beliefs or ritual.

Inasmuch as the statement concerns analytic group psychotherapy, it can be categorically averred that there is no "powerful impetus" in analytic groups for "group formation," nor is the aim to "diminish" the neurosis or to have it "temporarily disappear." We, and others, have pointed out on many occasions that group mobility, as opposed to group fixity, is the foundation of analytic group therapy. The group goal and unitary purpose necessary for "group formation" are absent in therapy groups and the aim is not temporary alleviation of symptoms or decrease in the neuroses. Rather, the aim is intrapsychic reorganization of the functions and relations of the id, ego, and superego. This aim is not a *common* aim; rather, there is a *similar* aim in each individual, as an individual.

EGO BASIS OF GROUP PSYCHOTHERAPY

Group psychotherapy partially derived its impetus from recognition of the ego's place in development and in therapy; hence, basic work was first done with children. Freud's preoccupation with, and concentration on, the psychoneuroses of adults and the techniques that stemmed from his work, have obscured other elements of the human psyche that significantly bear on mental illness and its correction. The chief member of these neglected dynamics was the ego, which was pushed into the background of Freud's elaborate and profound theories of the libido and its aberrations. Work with certain emotionally disturbed and socially maladjusted children, and, later, with older persons, as well as with mental patients, has revealed the importance of the ego in certain types of psychic illness.

The first practical demonstration of this fact, in clinical practice, was through Activity Group Therapy with children and its effect upon children with habit and character disorders. While, historically, the initiation of this technique was not prompted by any *a priori* theoretical consideration of the ego (See Chapter VIII), the awareness of its therapeutic significance soon became evident. This is especially true for specific clinical categories, which, with other related facts and considerations, will be taken up in later chapters. At this juncture it need only be said that, were psychotherapy to rely only on the libido theories and other classical therapeutic dynamics of Freud, correct and profound though they are, group psychotherapy could not have developed. Certain types of neuroses in adults, which are in the special domain of Freudian psychoanalysis, are not accessible to group psychotherapy. The distortions of the libido are still (and will probably always be) within the special purview of Freud's techniques; but other types of illness, within the domain of ego function and character structure, are more accessible to other approaches, among them, group psychotherapy.

Alfred Adler was one of the earliest clinicians calling attention to the possibilities in groups for the establishment and maintenance of mental health. While we cannot accept Adler's assumptions of "organ inferiority" and power drive as *primary* in the motivation of man, it cannot be denied that they do occupy important places in the hegemony of drives and behavior. This is not the appropriate place to discuss this point fully, beyond saying that they, too, are derived from the basic assumptions of Freud as are many other schools that have sprung up in recent decades purporting to be anti-Freudian. (See Chapter III for further discussion of the history of group psychotherapy.)

GROUP-INDUCED ANXIETY

The effect of groups on the individual is not entirely on the credit side. Groups can also be the source of anxiety and discomfort, especially in their early stages. All groups at first evoke anxiety in all people. No person can be in a group without at first feeling anxious. This anxiety diminishes as one becomes accustomed to the group, but one is never entirely free of it. The degree of anxiety is diminished with acquaintance and length of membership in the group; however, with rare exceptions, the average person never feels as comfortable in a group as he does with one individual. An individual is seldom as threatening as a group.[9] This is caused by several factors, alone or in combination.

Biologically, members of the same group, whether human or nonhuman, are a threat to one another. Though groups are protection against danger and favor survival, they are also sources of considerable tension to the individuals constituting them. Observations of other animals show that while they tend, because of the "instinct" of gregariousness and the need for security, to seek the proximity of one another, periodically there arise sudden combats between individuals in the group. Rivalries over food or the acquisition of a mate always arise. Antipathies arise spontaneously, and frequently for unexplained reasons, among humans as well as lower animals. Reasons are sometimes apparent, e.g., striking differences, membership in a different subspecies, an organic defect, or an ailment. The atypical member of an animal group is frequently subject to cruel attacks that often result in death.

Among humans, these reactions are vastly more complex and the aggressive and combative engram in each member of every group is a common source of anxiety. In humans, the anxiety is intense, since each person is, on the one hand, overtly or covertly in rivalry with every other person for status, recognition, acceptance and power. On the other hand, each person feels guilty about it. Anticipated group rejection is another source of fear and anxiety to everyone; the fear of being slighted, criticized, attacked, or humiliated is always present.

In addition to biological sources, anxiety in human groups stems from early family relations. Attitudes and responses toward groups are replicas of family experience. A person who had to be aggressive in order to get attention and survive psychologically in his family, or who had to ingratiate himself and be

---

[9] Except in some neurotic reactions. A boy in treatment once said: "Three is company, two is a crowd," thus revealing his fear of individuals and his need for the protection of a third person.

submissive with his parents, will repeat these patterns in other groups. The derivative hostilities and aggressions that accompany such adjustments are implicit in all group relations. Groups, therefore, threaten each member, because he expects attack, rejection, rivalry, and aggression. He is also afraid that the group will delimit and constrict his freedom of action and be critical of his unguarded conduct, his opinions, and his personality as a whole.

Still another source of group-induced anxiety is uncertainty regarding the ego functioning of others. While one can be certain, to some extent, of the ego functioning and behavior of an individual, one never feels the same confidence as a member of a group, and with strangers. A number of people in interreaction are not as predictable as a single individual.

THE EFFECT OF GROUPS ON EGO AND SUPEREGO FUNCTIONS

An element of uncertainty regarding the ego functioning of group members is universally observable. Ego functioning of individuals is altered by a group. Behavior of a person whose reactions are well known frequently differs in groups. Many feelings and responses untouched in individual relations are set off by groups: anxiety and insecurity are intensified, aggression and hostility are increased, and fear and withdrawal may set in. Drives toward domination, submission, and status and acceptance are activated by groups, just as in families. Group members who are subjected to anxiety may react in an unexpected manner and in ways that threaten others. A pattern of mutually induced anxieties and fears is activated and the ego-controls of each member are reduced and invested in the group, through its leader who takes over these controls. Restraints which are ordinarily exercised by the individual internalized superego are diminished, since the group as an entity is invested with the sanctions and prohibitions relative to the behavior of each. These dynamics create innumerable tensions in all members, as well as in the leader, for he, too, is caught up in the vortex of these feelings: one member may submit, where in ordinary relations he tended to dominate; another controls his usual hilarity and is quiet and withdrawn;

another reacts to a feeling of discomfort by a show of humor and volubility; still another, who is usually gentle in individual contacts, becomes overbearing. Even more confusing to the observer is the fact that one person may react in different ways at different times to different situations or different persons in the group, as well as to a small change in the total situation. In addition, a unique "physiognomy" or "character" emerges in every group, as well as a specific "group culture," something that has to be dealt with in addition to the individuals composing the group and to which its members both contribute and adjust.

A group arouses conscious misgivings and, even more important, unconscious and repressed feeling tones already associated with groups (family). Each member perceives the group as a possible source of danger, i.e., he fears being hurt, rejected, or discovered for what he thinks he *really* is and about which he feels guilty. As a result of these fears, some take on a façade of social amenities, while others may attack or withdraw.

Fear of group association is engendered by the protective mantle against narcissistic injury to the individual. Exposure to the gaze of others is threatening. Though the need to be accepted (social hunger) is one of the strongest needs in man, groups can also destroy one's self-esteem. Self-isolation can thus become a means of self-protection.

Therapy groups try the ego strengths of each participant, the therapist included. Group induced anxiety puts a strain on everyone present at the therapeutic sessions. The capacity that a patient acquires to deal with this anxiety, through therapy, is a reflection of his growing ego strengths. This is, however, only a part of the group situation. The group is a tangible, ponderable reality that threatens and makes demands on the individual. This is true of therapy groups as well as of other types of groups. In all groups, one becomes aware of the ego functions of each member, his defenses and "threat (sensitive) areas," and one behaves selectively. In therapy groups, patients pass through a series of stages, and when treatment is successful, ego restraints gain ascendence over id impulses. Thus, accommodative, selective, and inhibitive capacities are enhanced through the freeing of the psychic forces that have been bound up or drained by pathognomonic intrapsychic processes. The group setting is most effective as a corrective of the ego, because of its reality property, the inevitable multiple identifications and transferences, the catalytic influence of the patients on each other, its service as a field for testing one's ego functioning, its opportunities for improving the self-image, and its mirroring of reactions and behavior, as well as other effects of a similar nature inherent in a group.

GROUP PSYCHOTHERAPY AND TRANSFERENCE NEUROSES

Whether a group is as powerful in the treatment of personality disturbances mainly involving the sexual libido (as in transference neuroses) is open to serious questioning.

From my observation and study of several thousand patients in groups, I am inclined to believe that groups have only a limited application in the latter area with adult (nonpsychotic) patients. The nature, depth, and intensity of the biologically primary and highly cathected property of the human organism (sex) and its psychic concatenations are not subject to rational or experiential correctives. These types of psychoneuroses involve intense sexuality and form an integral part of the patient's psyche; they are autonomous and are strongly defended by neurotic needs and repetition compulsions. Even when they are ego-alien, the ego is helpless in counteracting, controlling, or negating them and, as a result, it reacts with anxiety. The transference neuroses require transference psychotherapy and the transference has to be vested in one person, as a parent surrogate, and not diluted in multilateral transferences or directed toward a collective entity, a group. Also, transference neuroses cannot be worked through in a group because the essential regressive free association is continually interrupted by other patients as they are activated to respond and participate. Still another reason is that the emotional and disturbed reactions of other patients to deeply psychoneurotic revelations reproduce the setting in which the neurosis originated. In the treatment of a transference neurosis, the other participants must remain calm and impersonal (Spanjaard, 1959) which cannot be achieved in groups, since the other group patients are invariably prone to react.

II

Differentials of Therapy and Nontherapy Groups

Before describing the characteristics of psychotherapeutic groups, an outline of the nature and process of psychotherapy will be helpful.

DEFINITION OF PSYCHOTHERAPY

A professional organization asked its members to define psychotherapy: The several hundred answers revealed enormous variance and glaring contradictions. A majority considered even partial symptom improvement as adequate psychotherapy; behavioral changes were viewed as sufficient; elimination of symptoms without basic changes in the personality was viewed as "recovery"; moral and ethical principles entered into the definitions; and religious and other considerations were included in definitions of the process and its aim.

The absence of a definitive formulation has been, and still is, a source of much misunderstanding in the field. A major difficulty lies in the fact that a large number of diverse theories and practices stem from *a priori* assumptions rather than validated clinical experience and reliable results. Many theories are derived from such unlikely areas as biology, reflexology, behaviorism, philosophy, and even mysticism, transcendental theories and esoteric concepts, rather than from phenomenological observation

36

and tested experience. Some show little understanding of the laws of personality formation and malformation. Many stem from a naïve assumption of the "omnipotence of words," giving rise to practices that rely mainly on cognition and conceptualizations.

Sound psychotherapy is concerned with the conative and irrational in man, with the unconscious and the revelation of inadequately repressed memories and conflicts or, when clinically indicated (as in some character disorders), with direct experience and external pressures from planned corrective situations. True psychotherapy (as differentiated from guidance or counseling), especially in the transference neuroses, can be effective only through the process of emotional regression and the reliving of traumatic feelings and memories of the past. Ideas and concepts alone are ineffective where the pathogenesis is in libidinal overcathexis, defects in ego and superego formation, or the correcting of a low self-concept derived through one's life experiences and conditioned by the attitudes of important persons in childhood.

The life force, the *élan vital,* is normally balanced in its inward (centripetal) and outward (centrifugal) flow to serve the needs of individual and social survival. It consists of both sexual and nonsexual segments. Personality disturbances occur when the libido is excessively invested in either the individual himself or an object. Thus, in narcissism, autoerotism, hysterical conversion, hypochondria, etc., the libido is invested in the subject himself, and in patients with dependency needs, homosexuals, parasitism, etc., it is invested excessively in an object. The objects are then said to be overcathected.

The human personality is a combination of biologically inherited features and psychic potentialities, shaped by the influences of the physical, economic, and human environments, all of which impose definite courses of adaptation on the individual, through their demands, pressures, and dictates. Involved are the total educative influences that shape the course of the individual's development, his quality and life pattern (including his value system) and result in a specific *pyschic physiognomy* (personality), ego functioning, and character.

Persons in need of psychotherapy are those whose life experiences have rendered them incapable of adequately assimilating and integrating all these educative influences. Instead, they are fixed in, or regress to, a pattern of adjustment more suitable to an earlier phase of development than their present, real chronological or social ages. In some instances, reconditioning or re-education, guidance or counseling may be sufficient to correct ego functioning. However, persons whose rigidities, affect, and anxiety are deeply bound up in their behavior require a more thorough reconstructive therapy. They require correction of intrapsychic forces to render them amenable to, and capable of, integrating educative influences. In this light, *psychotherapy can be defined as the process by which a patient is rendered accessible to the total educative influences of his world.* This is achieved through correcting the nature, functions, and relations of the libido, ego, superego, and self-image. The dynamics by which this is achieved are transference, catharsis, ego strengthening, correcting the superego, reality testing, and the acquisition of suitable sublimations.

Conation versus Cognition in Psychotherapy

Psychotherapy deals primarily with the irrational or conative elements in the human psyche. The rational or cognitive elements are utilized as secondary reinforcements in the reconstructive processes. A distinction is made between insight and understanding; between conceptualization and feeling. Insight and understanding occupy relatively minor places in the correction of psychic disorders, although ideas and "understanding" are the warp and woof of education and perhaps counseling. In a thoroughgoing psychotherapy, the essence is *reliving in affect* early traumata and eliminating the anxiety, fear, and guilt bound up in them; ideas and understanding are ancillary to this. This is fully recognized in psychoanalysis, where not only the transference attitudes, but also the physical setting receive special attention. The couch, subdued light, furnishings, and arrangement of the consultation room are all designed to utilize the patient's libido in the interest of relaxation, regression, and catharsis.

Special settings are designed also for individual and group play therapy with children. In occupational, recreational, and group therapies with adults, the physical setting and the atmosphere are also carefully planned for best results. Attitudes of patients are determined by the setting in which their therapy takes place— whether hospital ward, out-patient clinic, private office, military or residential treatment institution. Therefore, serious consideration must be given to the setting and procedures in each instance.

The Tasks of Psychotherapy

One of the tasks of psychotherapy is to free or dislodge the libido from the overcathected foci, whether they be within the person or in an object, so that a balance between the relation of the self and the object may be established. This therapeutic aim we designate as *libido redistribution*. The process by which this occurs in therapy, and especially in group psychotherapy, is described in Chapter V.

Another source of emotional tension and social maladjustment, which psychotherapy seeks to correct, results from inadequate ego development. This requires, in some instances, the correction of constitutional deficits through chemotherapy. Where this is not the case, ego strengths are established by corrections in identifications and individuation, and the overcoming of blocks to autonomous trends. Therefore, the second task of psychotherapy is *ego strengthening* and establishing adequate ego defenses.

The superego in psychoneurotics is usually overstrict and is a source of conflict, guilt, and anxiety, although in some types of character disorders (psychopaths, for example) the superego is too lax, rendering the individual maladapted in social living and in interpersonal relations. Thus, the third aim of psychotherapy is to *correct the superego*, while the fourth is to *improve the self-image*.

The symptom picture presented by those needing psychotherapy includes difficulties in interpersonal relations; these always stem from intrapsychic tensions. Correction can be achieved by freeing the libido from its overcathected anchorages in the self or in other persons, that is, through the process of *cathexis displacement*.

Elimination or reduction of excessive overt and covert anxieties is the mission of psychotherapy. The sources of anxiety are many: it can proceed from internal and external conflicts, guilt, ambivalence, fear, feelings of inadequacy, and many similar problems. The term anxiety, as differentiated from fear, designates tensions set up by *inner* threats, e.g., the conflict between the id and the prohibitions of the superego, or threats to ego defenses. Fear, on the other hand, is a reaction to a realistic, *external* threat. Some of the usual results of anxiety (which psychotherapy has to correct) are defective reality testing, ambivalence, impulsivity, and conflicting object relations. Free discharge of hostility in the therapeutic encounter is essential for effective psychotherapy. The overriding feelings of anger and rage, whether deeply repressed or close to the surface, must be discharged and their sources examined and understood. The patient must also become reconciled to residual aggressions. Much of the anxiety and guilt in patients stems from unexpressed hostile urges and fantasies, which must be cleared up if intrapsychic balance is to be achieved. The therapeutic situation provides channels for free discharge of noxious feelings without generating guilt. This is assured only when both the therapist and the group accept and understand the patient.

ESSENTIAL VERSUS NEUROTIC ANXIETY

The impression is frequently conveyed that psychotherapy aims to free patients of *all* vestiges of anxiety or that it is possible to do so. This is misleading, since not only is it implausible, but it is also undesirable. All sentient life is endowed with anxiety, both because of engrammatic (internalized) fear of destruction by members of other species in the struggle for survival and because anxiety is an essential driving force in life. Disturbances in kinesthesis and homeostasis generate a type of *organic anxiety* that propels the organism to re-establish balance. Without this mechanism, life would not only be static, but would become extinct. The dynamism and creativity of living stem from the perpetual states of tension and anxiety generated by the alternation between imbalance and equilibrium.

If hunger and the sexual urge were not felt as anxiety, animal life on earth would not survive very long; and if man were incapable of *moral anxiety,* his achievements in the arts, ethics, and general culture would never have taken place. The characteristic that sets man off from all other forms of animal life is his capacity for moral anxiety, in addition to the organic anxiety universal among all animal species. Both forms of anxiety propelled man to build civilizations and cultures. The summation of these two forms of instinctual anxiety we shall designate as *essential anxiety*.

The most universal source of essential anxiety in man is guilt. Only man is capable of feeling guilty. Guilt originated in the social necessity engendered by his role as a social atom. The conditions of communal living require codes for conduct that check animalistic drives and acts. Superstition, gods, and hobgoblins have served to frighten man away from conduct opposed to the codes proclaimed by chiefs, medicine men, and shamans, who personified the group interests and who later were displaced by organized religions, priests, and laws. The codes of group life, personified by parental figures and the various substitutes for them, are gradually internalized through fear and identifications, in each new generation as "right" and "wrong" in the superego. Divergencies from these codes generate guilt and anxiety.

Neurotic anxiety is differentiated from essential anxiety. While felt and managed by the ego, neurotic anxiety stems from the superego, that segment of the human psyche which sits in judgment over acts, thoughts, and unconscious strivings. Under certain conditions, the pressures and demands of the superego may become overstrict and tyrannical, generating an uninterrupted stream of guilt and anxiety. Or, the superego may be so underdeveloped as to fail in adapting the individual to his social milieu.

Anxiety may also result from prolonged and, more or less, continuous threat to physical survival or to the individual's status as a psychological entity. Persistent imbalance in organic and psychological homeostasis during formative years, can produce hypersensitivity and overreaction. It can also build into the psyche an expectation of, and preference for, suffering and disaster, referred to as *traumatophelia*.

Psychotherapy addresses itself to neurotic anxieties mainly by

41

resolving, eliminating, or reducing them. It cannot deal with the basic, essential anxiety inherent in the nature of man, and as already indicated, it would not be desirable to do so.

Conflicts and Similarities in Theories

On the surface, the various "schools" of psychotherapy appear to emphasize a specific dynamic in pathology that is central to each, while setting forth a unique system of treatment. An unbiased view of the structure of human personality and the multitude of possibilities for its disturbance brings to light the serious error in this overspecialized position. To insist on any one treatment method for all types of maladies is to ignore the fact that personality disturbances result from innumerable causes, and that sound clinical understanding can only lead to the antithesis of a monistic approach. This is as true of group psychotherapy as it is of individual treatment.

This does not mean that psychotherapy is devoid of systematic theory or organized techniques. There are basic generic laws, governing the formation and malformation of personality, by which therapists should be guided. But the astronomic possible variations in the personality structure of individuals rules out any one technique as being suitable in every case. Even within the same clinical category, to be effective, treatment has to be modified to suit the needs of a specific patient and again modified with the same patient at different stages of the treament.

A therapist cannot hold rigidly to a set method or technique (or theory) in psychotherapy to the exclusion of all others without jeopardizing his effectiveness, for he inevitably limits the therapeutic possibilities as a result. Rigidity is even a greater deficit in group treatment than it is in individual psychotherapy. Variations in the personalities and pathologies of the different patients in each group require the therapist to adopt a variety of approaches and procedures to meet the needs not only of each patient as a specific psychologic entity, but also the needs of the same patient at different periods, as he presents specific problems in his progressive or regressive emotional development.

Adherence to a single technique applied inflexibly in a blanket fashion to all patients and groups regardless of their nature, structure, and locale cannot but limit or defeat therapeutic effectiveness.[1]

This does not mean that the therapist should, or indeed can, carry out his tasks without a *basic* orientation in psychology, psychopathology, and psychotherapy. Such a frame of reference is necessary as a source of emotional security and intellectual clarity. However, at the same time, he must recognize the infinite varieties of personality and problems and the vast number of possible combinations. He must be ready to abandon bias for the best means in each case. To be most effective, a therapist needs to have the flexibility essential to intelligent and discriminative eclecticism.

It is with considerable concern that one witnesses the appearance, in recent years, of a number of philosophical and abstract speculative theories as frames of reference for psychotherapy. Many of these are mystical and transcendental and their application to scientific endeavor and an instrumental effort, such as psychotherapy, is highly questionable. A small number of psychotherapists have thrown themselves into promoting these theories, with no validation or proven effectiveness. This scientific irresponsibility could put psychotherapy into disrepute and cause untold harm to patients.

Anyone who knows the structure of neuroses, for example, is aware of their autonomous nature, their persistence, and the compelling need of the neurotic to live by them (repetition compulsion). Experience also shows that neuroses are not therapeutically accessible to conceptualization, reason, or principles. Religion, suggestion, and mysticism may offer some guidance and temporary relief, but recovery or lasting improvement can be achieved only through the tortuous and painfully long procedures that constitute psychoanalysis and some of its derivative methods.

---

[1] I found it necessary to devise seven distinct techniques of group psychotherapy and guidance to meet the requirements of various types of patients by age and clinical indications. Even these are not employed rigidly. Rather, a variety of techniques and approaches are employed in five of the seven, while in the remaining two, best results can be obtained only by rigid adherence to the specified procedure.

It should be noted that despite different assumptions and "methods" in the different "schools," beneficial results, in varying degrees, are achieved by most. One wonders, therefore, whether a particular treatment method becomes effective because of the therapist's confidence in it; because of its suitability to his temperament and intellectual bias, or because he employs it with skill. These possibilities are all concerned with the person of the psychotherapist; but it is not altogether unlikely that the nature of the problems in *specific* patients and their personalities and transference needs are better met by one method than by another, and that the technique employed is fortuitously suitable for some patients and not for others. More often, however, a different understanding of what constitutes improvement plays a part in the evaluation of the particular effectiveness of a treatment method. There are, also, basic, common elements implicit in most of the so-called "schools," which are underplayed because the adherents of each school are more preoccupied with differences than with similarities. (For further discussion of these points, see Slavson, 1952.)

"Experience shows that despite theoretical unanimity among practitioners in any field of endeavor, including psychotherapy, each differs somewhat in the application of the theory. A practitioner cannot escape the imperatives of his own personality, and inevitably makes modifications as a result of his attitudes, temperament, and understanding. Thus, there is at present considerable variation in the application of such a well-defined practice as Freudian psychoanalysis, even though there is full theoretic consonance." (Slavson, 1952a, page 135.)

In sound psychotherapy, practice, theory and assumptions have to be selected and modified as demanded by the patient's needs. The blanket use of only one method of group or individual therapy, will result in harm to patients and frustration for the therapist. While there are underlying principles in group psychotherapy, experience shows that for some patients a certain type of group may yield the most effective results. For others, whose difficulties can be resolved only through individual treatment (or not at all), group treatment may be definitely unsuitable. Still others may require less intensive group exposure such as guidance or counseling. In the treatment of children, for example, not only is the type of problem an important consideration, but age and sex are also determining factors.[2] Similarly, the techniques of group treatment employed for adult psychoneurotic patients must be modified to meet the needs of psychotics and those with other types of character disorders.

GENERAL DYNAMICS OF GROUPS

Interaction

Persons in any type of active group participation set up specific dynamics that are more or less universal in nontherapeutic groups; some of these are also discernible in therapy groups. It is inevitable that, where there is action in a group, there should also be *interaction* among its members. Such interaction is greater among free-acting, self-directed, voluntary groups, and is largely determined by the type of leadership function involved. In groups where the leader is either authoritarian, directive or assertive, the interaction of members will be less, both in frequency and intensity, than in a group in which the leader remains in the background and assumes a democratic attitude. The interaction of a number of people without a leader may generate varying degrees of tension and, under specific conditions, may result in mob violence and group disruption, due to overstimulation.

In order to be constructive and productive, social, educational, and all other aim-directed groups must set limits to the freedom of interaction allowed their members. At certain periods, a common aim or agreement must emerge (group code) that holds the group to a tacitly accepted or codified purpose. If the tensions in a group prevent movement toward the group aim, means can usually be found to resolve those tensions. *Compromise* is the most common and essential mechanism in social, political, and aim-directed groups and is the outcome of another process that may be termed *neutralization*. When emotional drives are counteracted or the individual entertaining them is won over by placation or

[2] See Slavson, 1943, 1944, 1952, 1958.

some other ego-gratifying strategy, neutralization of his feeling occurs. Among the chief neutralizing agents in groups is the leader, who represents, in the unconscious of the members, a parental figure. When he assumes the role of the good parent, the members submit to his expectations. This neutralizing effect of the leader is exerted in therapy groups by the therapist, though it is accomplished differently and with a different intent.

Compromise is partial, not total, neutralization. "It comes about through . . . (a) finding a common ground for agreement . . . This permits at once self-determination (even though a partial one) for all concerned and meets group needs. The group leader's chief function is to act as a catalytic agent in this neutralization process." (Slavson, 1939, page 78.)

Interaction, and not compromise or neutralization, is at the very core of the group therapeutic interview, for it is through the various forms of impact of patients on each other that transferential feelings are made manifest and can be worked through. It is essential that interaction should not be stimulated or forced by the therapist, rather, it should arise from the interviews and the significance of the reactions of the various group members. Interaction among psychotic patients, however, needs to be guided and controlled.

Interstimulation

Another dynamic present in ordinary groups, is *interstimulation* (which is an outgrowth of interaction). That is, the phenomenon of mutual activation that occurs among persons engaged in a common objective and effort, through attitudes, conduct, specific acts, emotions, and ideas. In constructive efforts, interstimulation can produce most desirable results; but it can be devastating when exercised destructively, as in the case of mobs.

As in the case of interaction, interstimulation has to be a natural outcome of verbal and nonverbal communications from patients in the group and the emotional and intellectual stimulation they engender. At times, this dynamic may heighten emotions in a therapy group beyond a permissible level and the therapist's intervention, by deflection or exploration and interpretation, may be required. This procedure is the core of the "here and now" treatment method. Interstimulation, as well, has to be regulated with psychotic patients or they may get out of hand.

Mutual Induction

Of less obvious nature, but equally universal and similar in process and effect, is the dynamic of *mutual induction*. This is confined to the area of feeling and emotion, whereas interstimulation occurs largely in the realm of action and ideas. The term "induction" is borrowed from the electrical phenomenon, wherein a coil placed in the field of another coil becomes charged although the coils are not in direct contact. People induce attitudes and feelings in one another without verbal or other observable forms of communication. The inductive processes are enhanced through close association and intimacy, as in the case of close friendship, marriage, family groups, and in other groups (including therapy groups). The closer and more prolonged emotional and physical association is, the more responsive people become to the inductive effect of one another, and the more empathy is heightened.

Because of their emotional fragility and weak ego defenses, patients in groups are particularly susceptible to emotional induction, a process that bears watching in therapy groups. Induction has a direct effect on anxiety and hostility and may have deleterious results on the therapeutic climate of a group. Induction too, may at times require exploration and interpretation, but unlike other dynamics, it is intangible and involves greater emotional resonance and subtlety.

Identification

In all associations of people, positive and negative *identifications* occur, according to the emotional prototypes of each participant. Identifications take place as a result of similarities in constitution, background, and experience, that make people feel alike.[3] Being based on emotional resonance, identification is particularly impor-

[3] The dynamic of identification is employed here in its simplest form.

tant in therapy groups for it makes possible vicarious catharsis and spectator therapy. It is for this reason that patients assigned to the same group should, as far as possible, have common central or nuclear problems, even though their symptoms and clinical diagnoses may be dissimilar.

Identification operates differently in a nontherapeutic group. "The most cohesive groups that act in concert and with unified purpose are those in which there is mutual identification (commonly designated as sympathy or 'understanding') among their members. In a group where there is a great degree of such understanding there also exists the possibility for concerted action: here the positive elements are intensified. Mutual identification is at once the most potent and the most nearly universal socializing influence in society. The 'homogeneous' groups (common-interest groups, social coteries, economic classes, cultural groups, etc.) are groups in which there is mutual identification. Patriotic organizations and all types of sects originate in mutual identification among their members." (Slavson, 1939, page 79.)

Intensification

One of the undesirable by-products of interaction and interstimulation is the resultant *intensification* of feeling and acting out. Where a number of persons share a common emotion, especially that of hostility and aggression, their tonus is heightened through removal of ego and superego restraints due to group consent or approval, and the need to be at one with the group, which is an outcome of *social hunger*. An example of intensification of emotion, in a negative manifestation, is the behavior of mobs where id impulses are uncontrolled. In a similar fashion, constructive and benevolent emotions and acts can be intensified through group example, pressure, and demand. Here, the "group superego" reinforces that of the individuals who constitute the group.

Because of the nature and content of therapy groups and the susceptibility of patients to emotional contagion, the dynamic of intensification is likely to reach high levels and, unless skillfully dealt with by the therapist, may lead to disintegration of the group.

Assimilation

Assimilation is another tendency in nontherapeutic groups that aids in the socializing process and group cohesion. It is accomplished by lessening self-assertion. The infant and child accepts the parent as a controlling force and becomes a part of, and is assimilated into, the family group. The youth and the adult find substitutes for these early gratifications in groups. The disposition to become assimilated in a group is at least partially conditioned by a favorable early family life. Other elements that come into play are the native capacity for social development in the individual and his balance between masochism and sadism.

From a sociological point of view, assimilation is highly prized by society; through it the individual becomes fused with society and can be held in check and utilized to societal advantage. The aim of all groups is to maintain stability and security both at the cost of and for the benefit of, the individual. Thus, society is essentially conservative and nonprogressive. Progress is initiated by individuals pursuing a path of self-determination. Only individuals, not society, as such, can be creative. From the point of view of society, the creative person, the innovator, is a nonconformist. Dr. Abraham Myerson's aphorism aptly states this: "Mankind has always lived upon its geniuses and crucified them." But what about the "creative society," of which one hears so much? A creative society is one which provides for and encourages the work of its individual creative citizens: Only in that light can a society be creative.

Assimilation is antitherapeutic and should be avoided in analytic therapy groups.

Integration

Another dynamic operative in functioning groups is *integration*. Integration is here defined as the process by which an individual becomes an indivisible part of the group, by renouncing, to varying degrees, his individuality and self-determination. The integrative tendency in the organism (demonstrated by studies such as those of Sherrington and Cannon in physiology and the Marsdens and Wertheimer in psychology) is present in group living as well as in the organic realm. Complete absorption in a "total situation," or a group Gestalt divests the individual of his autonomy,[4] while at the same time it promotes the vigor of the group. The fine balance between these two opposing trends is one of the major concerns in a democratic society.

Excessive loyalty limits the field of one's experience and checks the social and cultural expansion of the individual. Under favorable circumstances, one's horizons constantly expand through new experiences, from which wider and deeper understandings emerge. While groups and associations are the means through which personality expansion is achieved, they also limit and restrict. For example, desirable as family loyalties are, when they are overintense, they limit growth. This is also true of other groups such as political factions and social, philosophical, and religious aggregations. Such group loyalties can be in opposition to personality and social development (Slavson, 1937, pages 21-22). Growth is achieved when the balance between individuation and group integration is maintained and when shifts from one group to others are made. A secure person can detach himself from a given group with comparative ease and re-establish himself in another group. The ability to withdraw from one group and to adjust to another is one indication of a healthy dependency and a strong and stable character. This is especially necessary in a complex and interdependent society, where daily living inevitably brings one in contact with many and varied individuals and groups. In the light of the preceding definition, a therapy group, to remain therapeutic, must prevent its members from becoming integrated into the group.

Group Cohesion

Group cohesion evolves from the amalgamation of individuals

---

[4] This fact should be kept in mind in relation to therapeutic groups, where group cohesion, assimilation and integration must be avoided. This topic will be discussed later.

around a common objective or interest entertained by all participants in a common effort. This commonness of purpose and centrality of aim cathexis erases or subordinates individual aims and interests. Group cohesion occurs when empathy and socio-cultural homogeneity predominate. The group is fused into a unitary whole, as with integration, but there is an important difference.

In integration, the operational focus is the individual, as he relates to other members of the group. The acceptance of him need not be universal. Different relationships and attitudes can exist. These can be more cordial or more friendly with some than with others. Integration can occur even when feelings are moderately antagonistic on the part of a subject toward some other members of the group or on their part toward him. It is only necessary that he "go along" with the group's major objective or interest and conform to its aims, code and mores.

This is not the case with cohesion, where *emotional* considerations predominate. A cohesive group is one that operates as a unit with negligible or little friction or sense of individual differences. A group working on a project can have a high degree of co-operation and still not be cohesive, if the mutual fidelity that may exist is not of a predominantly personal (emotional) nature, but is rather a result of the binding force that is the common aim, central interest, or affective focus. For a group to be cohesive, however, the basic common, underlying *feeling* must be one of unconditional mutual acceptance and affection.

To varying degrees, all functioning groups draw their mutuality and harmony from their conscious or unconscious feelings toward their leader. This trend is even more pronounced in the case of cohesive groups. Cohesion among members of a group may stem from widespread affection or widespread hostility toward the leader. In the first instance the group is productive and survives, while in the second it is destined for disruption. In a very subtle sense, cohesion arises from the unconscious recognition of the leader's wishes and submission to them by the group members. This submission in turn arises from the feeling of gratification derived by the members, as the leader recognizes and responds to the common overt and especially covert needs of his followers. Because of the emotional and psychological implications of this, cohesion in therapy groups is antitherapeutic.

Excessive *loyalty* toward a specific group in society, or *gestalt*, has still another effect. As a result of it, the individual tends to reject change. A well-knit group is nonprogressive; it is inhospitable to newcomers and to new ideas. It either rejects them altogether, or accepts them only after prolonged hesitation and opposition. Such an attitude on the part of the group is undesirable, for though it assures its survival, it is, at the same time, the root of conservatism. A prime objective of a healthy society is to eliminate the insecurity from which resistance to change stems. One of the evidences of improvement in therapy groups (both childrens' and adults'), for example, is the ability to accept new members into their midst. In activity group therapy, newcomers are used to test this, for here, the patients re-experience the feelings they once had toward siblings, especially at their birth. Readiness to accept new members is an index of emotional strength and inner security.

Because of the importance of individuation in psychotherapy of ambulatory patients, assimilation, integration, or cohesion should not be encouraged in therapy groups. While the aim of therapy is to render the individual able to cooperate, this facility must be achieved through "working through" fears, reservations, and submissiveness with some patients, or hostilities, aggressions, and domination with others. The ultimate objective is to free the individual of noxious inner states and thus make fusion with groups possible for him in a way that will enhance both his own and the group's development and satisfaction; but he should not be placed in a situation where this is demanded of him before he is psychologically prepared for it, as is the case with therapy groups.

Polarity

Another dynamic manifestation of groups is *polarity*. "Group polarity, . . . the center around which a group gathers, be it a person, idea, ideal or an issue, is always more or less definite. Nearly all groups are polarized around some such center . . . the most stable and most vital groups are those that have very sharp and emotion-arousing poles or centers . . ." (Slavson, 1937, page 89). In this regard, therapy groups are vastly different from the ordinary groups in a community. Polarity tends to produce rigidity and fixity, while therapy groups must be fluid and mobile. Interaction must be spontaneous and each patient's role must alter with his personality integration and emerging ego strengths. A rigidly determined place, status, or relation to fellow patients prevents personality change. As the individual changes, his functions and roles in the group also change. Where this does not occur, the corrective and re-educational process of therapy is prevented. To assure personality change, freedom and flexibility are essential in interpersonal relations as experiences in self and reality testing.[5] Since rigid polarity prevents essential flexibility in the roles and functions of group members, it generates *group fixity*.

In ordinary groups, there is fixed polarity; in therapy groups, variable and *multiple polarity* exists. At the start, the therapist may serve as the central pole because of his transferential importance to each patient as a cathected object and as an object of dependence. However, because he does not personify an idea or aim common to all, his hold on the patients is dissimilar to that of the leader of a movement, for example. The cathexis is felt by each member separately and in a different way than in the others. In some patients, the feelings are positive; in some, hostile; and in some others ambivalent or indifferent. As feelings in a therapy group gradually emerge, patients also become objects of different feelings in the others; thus there arises a multiplicity of poles. Yet a third pole of cathexis is the group-as-a-whole.

Nodal and Antinodal Behavior in Groups

In human interactions (as well as in the behavior of groups of animals) the phenomenon of *nodal* and *antinodal* behavior occurs in all gatherings of three or more. The larger the number and the

---

[5] This is one reason why it often becomes necessary to involve members of a patient's family in treatment. Their unbending attitudes and rigid insistence on the patient's past role in the family, and elsewhere, prevent his improvement.

FIGURE 1

Fixity and Mobility in Groups in
Relation to Polarity

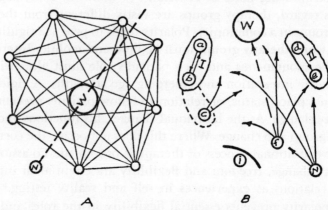

A illustrates schematically the compactness of a "fixed" group. Lines representing relationships emanate from each one of the members to every other. The therapist (*W*) is in the center. The newcomer (*N*), must cut through—adapt or force through —the maze. It may require considerable flexibility (partial de-egotization) or inner strength to make his way into the group through domination or adaptation.

B is a schematic representation of a "mobile" group. In configuration *I* there is a strong relation between the two individuals (bilateral) in the solid ellipse, (*c*) having a loose and partial relation with (*a*) and (*b*). He also moves about freely, as shown by the arrows, and relates himself to all or some co-members at different times (multilateral relation). *II* is a configuration of a bilateral relation permitting little or no invasion. *I* illustrates a *symbiotic* relation where (*a*) and (*b*) depend upon each other; *II* on the other hand, illustrates a *supportive* relation, where (*e*) is the support of (*d*); (*f*) is a "free-floating" individual who may or may not attach himself temporarily to different persons or configurations. He is shown here as having a strong attachment to the therapist, which for therapeutic reasons he must be helped to resolve (Fig. 2); (*i*) is an isolate who works by himself and has little or no contact with the other members of the group. (*N*), the newcomer, need not cut through "lines of relationships" to feel acceptance and comfort. There are many possibilities for him to establish relationships.

freer they are, the more intense are the acting out periods (nodal) and the more prolonged are the periods of silence and comparative inactivity (antinodal). Periods of the nodal aspect of group behavior are characterized by mounting animation and communication, rising noise, and a general atmosphere of interaction and conviviality. When the noise and chaos reach a high level of intensity, sudden quiet sets in. This alternation is usually observable in all free gatherings, such as parties, and other types of assem-

54

blies. Even mobs finally spend their energies and quiet down. In groups of children, especially, nodal and antinodal behavior appears in an almost regular pattern. (Although no time study has been made of the frequency and duration of the changes in this pattern, observation suggests that there may be a mathematical modality in this phenomenon.)

FIGURE 2

Schematic illustration of periodicity of nodal and antinodal phases in therapy groups at early sessions (A), later sessions (B), and when group becomes a "working group."

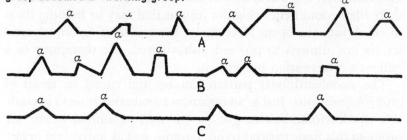

α represents the stages when antinodal phases set in.

The rise to the nodal level stems from interstimulation. However, as it progresses and becomes intensified, a state of tension is engendered in the participants due to the physical exertion and emotional drain. The overstimulating and chaotic state, into which the gathering falls, activates organic anxiety and produces a reaction in each participant. As a result, silence and inactivity (rest) set in.

The alternation between nodal and antinodal behavior also occurs in therapy groups. There are periods of considerable interaction, interstimulation, and intensification. There may be mutual induction and reinforcement of hostility and aggression toward a single target, usually one of the patients. In activity therapy groups, this process is allowed to run its course so that the ego and superego may become involved in the behavior. Personality growth and integration can then occur as the participants bring themselves under control on their own. However, in analytic groups of adult patients, this type of acting out of feelings is checked at the appropriate time by the therapist, who helps them recognize their behavior in the light of therapeutic "understanding." His action at once brings the nodal state of the group to a halt. As the patients investigate their immediate actions and prevailing feelings in the light of current or past emotional experiences and attitudes, the behavior is changed to that of an antinodal character.

Prolonged silence in a therapy group (extreme antinodal behavior) is rare. One of the patients, usually the most anxious and insecure, will break the silence. When this does not transpire automatically, the therapist will ask the group for the meaning of their silence and help bring the reasons that may be holding them in check into the open. Here again, the course of "group dynamics" is not allowed to proceed unhampered; the therapist's or a patient's intervention prevents it.

The nodal-antinodal pattern can be understood in terms of *group homeostasis.* Just as an organism automatically seeks to establish equilibrium, human groups (as well as animal herds) are prone to this basic natural trend. Groups, just as individual organisms in a state of tension, generate counterirritants to excessive activation and hypertension. These are manifested in the antinodal phase, a process analogous to exertion and recuperation, to tension and relaxation.

In psychotherapy, the point of transition from nodal to antinodal behavior needs to be considered from the point of view of personality integration and ego strengthening. Though autonomic factors are involved, it is through the controls emanating from each of the participants that the group passes to a state of constructive effort or quiet. This state is an indication of the emerging capacity of each member to master his impulses. At first it occurs in an unconscious way, but as therapy progresses, it can become a conscious effort, which is carried over into everyday life. Intrapsychic effects occur at the point where antinodality sets in. It is here that ego controls and personality integration occur. Nodal behavior among adults is naturally much less intense and less frequent than among children.

In observing a therapy group for any length of time, one notes that the alternation of these two modalities grows less and less frequent, as does their intensity.

SPECIFIC OPERATIONAL DIFFERENTIALS

Group Dynamics and Group Psychotherapy

Whether group dynamics, in the ordinary sense of the term, arise in therapy groups, specifically with nonpsychotic adults, is a pivotal question. If such dynamics are operative, much of what we understand the process in group psychotherapy to be, would have to be revised, and its practice—which is clinical therapy and not sociological theory—would have to be altered. Whether we deal with the group as a *unitary entity* or with the patients *as individuals* may well determine the course of the development of group psychotherapy, both as a science and as a therapeutic tool (Slavson, 1951, 1953). A common unsupported assumption is that patients improve merely because they seemingly adjust to a given group, have a "good influence" on it, or have "good relationships" with fellow members. This claim cannot be substantiated. In psychoneuroses, for example, improvement or recovery cannot be judged by behavior only, but rather by deeper personality changes which can accrue only from the patient's being freed from the anxieties bound up in the neurotic nucleus, from his acquisition of insight, and from his corrected self-image. Only when improved relationships and group adaptation are an outcome of these inner changes can they be considered as indications of a satisfactory therapy.

Many individuals with problems seek out groups and social movements as an escape or a source of relief and many *do* experience a degree of comfort, even showing improved behavior for a time. But these changes do not last, for one who finds relief by these means becomes dependent on them. Also, while neurotic tension may be temporarily abated, it will reappear as the stimulus wears off.

In order to clarify these concepts, it will be necessary to draw on other experiences and operational systems. First, let us define, on the basis of its inherencies, nature, and functions, what a "group" is (keeping in mind that not every collection of persons

57

is a *group*). Because of the differences in number, motivation, aims, and interpersonal relations, human gatherings are variously designated as masses, crowds, assemblies, audiences, congregations, mobs, groups, etc., all of which imply the existence of different relationships among their constituents.

A reasonably accurate definition can be formulated as follows: A group is a voluntary gathering of *three or more persons*, in a free, face-to-face relation *under leadership*, who have a *common goal* or aim and who interact with each other relative to the common goal, as a result of which, personality growth may occur. The salient features of this definition are: (a) a group consists of a small number of persons so that meaningful face-to-face relationships can take place; (b) it has leadership; (c) it has a purpose *common* to all (or to a majority) of the members; (d) the members are in a dynamic interaction with one another (interpenetration); and (e) the group can foster personality growth.

Using this definition, which is acceptable to professional group workers (as differentiated from group therapists), as a frame of reference, let us examine therapy and social groups.

Numerical Parity

A minimum of three persons are required to activate the dynamics that tie them into a *group*. This is because the emotional components of a group are threefold in their nature, requiring that number as a minimum. The first component is the emotional tie of the group members to the leader; the second component consists of the network of interactions of the group members to each other as individuals, and the third component arises from the relations of each member to the relations that may exist among other members. This latter dynamic is the one that fuses discrete individuals into the unitary entity which we conceptualize as a group. A common illustration is a family of three, where reactions operate between husband and wife and between each of them and their child; but were these the only threads of emotional ties present, the family would be a much simpler complex than it is. Each member constantly projects feelings to each of the other two individuals, and, in addition, also to the *relation* of the other two. It is from this characteristic that most interpersonal difficulties arise in groups. It must be noted that, in many instances, a third person may be present as a phantom in a cathected memory or image of the past.

FIGURE 3

Interrelationships of a Group of Three Persons

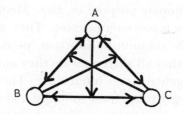

In therapy groups, the therapist cannot serve as the third person involved in the group-emotional network; therefore a minimum of three members is necessary, though three patients in a prolonged relation may set up a repetitive vicious circle of emotional cathexes. Dilution and redirection, through the incursion of additional members, is essential. A minimum of five members is, therefore, a requirement.

Leadership

A therapy group does not have a leader in the usual sense of the term. A leader can be defined as one who personifies the conscious and unconscious (especially the latter) needs, trends, and urges of the group constituents; and who initiates or sets the pace in achieving the *common aim* of all, or most of, the membership. An ordinary group can survive only if it accepts its leader. In therapy groups, neither the therapist nor any of the patients assume such a role. In a therapy group, the therapist is the recipient of libidinal, and other, transference feelings and is an object of dependency. He is, therefore, periodically the target of positive, negative, and ambivalent feelings. If he functions adequately in his therapeutic role, he does not usually serve as an initiator nor does he ordinarily set the pace for the group, though he may, at times, have to help some patients focus their discussion, garner the significance of their communications and feelings, and acquire insight.[6]

Commonality

Perhaps the most important difference between social, educational, and special interest groups, on the one hand, and therapy groups on the other, is to be found in the characteristic of *commonality*—common purpose or aim. Members of a therapy group do not have a *common* purpose. They are not gathered to discharge a specific community function, pioneer a cause, or advance an interest they all share; nor do they meet for the pleasure derived from congenial social intercourse. Their motive for coming together is to get relief from suffering and overcome deficiencies that prevent, or interfere with, enjoyment of life and human relationships. Each is driven to what is, most often, a resentful compresence, in quest of relief from unhappiness, tension, fear, and anxiety. The motives for attending therapy groups may be said to be the same in all or most of the participants, namely, to improve; but because each seeks *his own* salvation, it does not have the nature of a common motive in the sociological or educational sense. Each seeks to achieve his aim *as an individual,* for his own individual ends, and not for the benefit or advantage of the group as a unit nor for the sake of a common group goal. The patients do have the *same* purpose, but it is not a *common* purpose. It is this factor, more than any other, that prevents the emergence of the usual "group dynamics" and cohesion.

Synergy

The basic integrating force that assures the survival and achievement of ordinary groups is *synergy*. Synergy is the drive, purpose, aim and effort common to all the individuals constituting a group, or a mass. The cohesion in these groups lies in the personal homogeneity of their members or their interest or goal, whatever it may be, which is represented by a leader, or by a

---

[6] For a discussion of the four main functions of a group therapist—directional, stimulative, extensional, and interpretative—see Slavson, 1952. See also Chapter VIII in the present volume.

cathected idea or ideal. This element is absent in therapy groups. In fact, its presence prevents therapeutic gains for patients. Instead of the coherence essential to social and educational groups, therapeutic groups feed on interpersonal conflict and overt expression of hostility among their members, who are in positive, negative, and ambivalent transference relations with each other and are mutual objects of paratoxic projections and distortions. Essentially, in therapeutic groups, patients are held together by anxiety and not by pleasure-yielding participation. The need of each patient is to find relief from that anxiety, through talk, acting out, and insight. No other type of voluntary group could survive under similar conditions, with aggression so rampant and anxiety so pervasive. It must be noted, however, that the leader in ordinary groups and the therapist in therapy groups are both the center of the emotional cluster of the constituent members. In order for the group to survive, these feelings toward the leader must be positive in ordinary groups, while, in therapy groups, they alternate between the extreme poles of positive and negative feelings.

Dynamic Interaction

There is a distinct similarity between, and confluence of, the two types of groups in the presence of *dynamic interaction* among the group members. In the social-educational groups, however, dynamic interaction is largely in the realm of ideas or camaraderie, even though these are not altogether free from emotional undercurrents. In the psychotherapeutic groups, on the other hand, the interactions are almost exclusively in the realm of feeling and emotions. Even ideational differences and conflicts mask feelings, especially hostility and resentment; these are always present in each participant, for it is the presence of excessive feelings of this nature that makes them "patients."

Personality Growth

There is seeming similarity between therapy and nontherapy groups in their fostering of *personality growth*, which, however, proves illusory on closer examination. The aim and result of social-educational groups is to implant and activate social attitudes and values, to help acquire tools of social living, and to uncover interests and talents. In "special interest" groups, concerned, for example, with art, literature or dramatics, the aim and effect is to activate latent talent and interest and bring them to fruition through training or "self-expression." Under the stimulation of leaders and teachers, talents and powers are uncovered and expressed. Occasionally, this also occurs in therapy groups, as blockings and inhibitions are removed; but the expressed aim of therapy groups is rather personality repair, as a result of which talents may or may not become manifest. Analytic psychotherapy does not directly aim at discovering talent; rather, this can result from the released ego powers and enhanced self-esteem and self-confidence achieved through psychotherapy.

Differentials in the Light of Therapeutic Criteria

In order to test the applicability of group dynamics derived from the behavior of voluntary social, educational, and action groups to therapeutic groups, let us examine them now from a clinical viewpoint. The operational elements of group psychotherapy, as of all psychotherapy, are transference, catharsis, insight, reality testing, and sublimation. A comparison of these elements in the two types of groups, shows great dissonance.

Transference Differentials

The nature and manifestations of transference are quite different in nontherapy and therapy groups: in the former, it is almost always positive and largely nonsexual, while in the latter, it is libidinized and bipolar.

Differentials in Catharsis

No nontherapeutic group could survive long if its members were to reveal their unmoral and immoral acts, fantasies, preoccupations, and urges, past and present, as they do in psychotherapy. Nor would such groups hold together if their members attacked and abused one another as they do in therapy. No social-educational group could survive under the impact of free catharsis. The crosscurrents of hostility would easily deteriorate it and disintegrate it. Nor could a social or educational aim-directed group withstand the uncovering and interpretations of hidden motives and latent meanings, which are not always the noblest or purest in nature.

Insight

While interpretation (as differentiated from explanation), that leads to insight (as differentiated from understanding), alleviates anxiety in a therapy group, such interpretation would only intensify anxiety in a social-educational group. In everyday relations, interpretation and even explanation of basic, unconscious, and preconscious motives and meanings generates a high degree of anxiety and resentment because they are essentially attacks on normal and necessary ego defenses.

Reality Testing and Sublimation

Since reality testing and sublimation of primitive drives are carried on constantly at every point of the individual's life, they are present in all relations, group and individual, and since they are minor elements in the actual therapy group situation of adult, nonpsychotic patients, only cursory mention of them is necessary here.

A therapy group, however, is a *conditioned* reality, planned and structured by the therapist, with a therapeutic aim in mind and a concern with the group's suitability for the participants. This is part of the "closed system" of therapy groups. Such conditioning is not essential in social-educational or action groups, whose membership is self-chosen on the basis of some element of homogeneity.

Differentials in Synergic Movement

The dynamics here described are present, in varying degrees, in all groups and gatherings in which free interaction is the rule, but their applications and significance are vastly different in different types of groups. This difference is particularly marked in the case of therapy groups. Whereas, in all other groups, the dynamics are directed, largely by the leader, toward specific goals, interactions in therapy groups run their course so that their psychological sources and interpersonal roots can be explored and their significance to each person uncovered. The pivotal difference in the operation of psychotherapeutic and ordinary groups lies in the fact that *in the latter, group dynamics remain the operational instruments of the synergy of a group. In therapy groups, individual reactions are explored and interpreted in terms of intrapsychic determinants in each patient.*[7]

Even the most basic group dynamics are not permitted to run their full course, for it is the task of the therapist (often taken over by patients) to uncover the underlying and, most often, hostile feelings from which they flow. As a result, dynamics in therapy groups are automatically nipped in the bud, for, just as soon as responses are analyzed and related to individual emotional sources, they no longer operate for the group as such. It is this process in therapy groups that prevents the emergence and operation of the group dynamics manifested in nontherapeutic groups. Therapeutically directed exploration, uncovering, and insight, also prevent group synergy which demands accommodation of the participants to it. Thus, *the therapeutic process, by its very nature, is antagonistic to group formation and group dynamics.* Reinforcement of feelings and the intensification that periodically set in, should they be permitted to run their course, do result in specific dynamics. In analytic therapy groups, however, this is prevented by the intervention of the therapist and by his and other members' interpretations, thus dissipating the building up of group patterns and group effort. By their very nature, therapeutic groups favor interpersonal *interaction,* rather than group patterns.

In discussing the synergic or collaborative activity of a number of people, Freud says, ". . . experience has shown that in cases of collaboration libidinal ties are regularly formed between the fellow-workers which prolong and solidify the relation between them to a point beyond what is merely profitable. . . . The libido props

[7] An exception to this is when, at times, all the patients are involved. However, the intent is always to work through individual reactions.

itself upon the great vital needs, and chooses as its first objects the people who have a share in that process." (Freud, 1940, page 57.) In a therapy group collaboration is not a virtue. Most of the time it is entirely absent; at other times, it is present to a minimal degree and is fleeting in duration. Patients in groups do not "collaborate" for any length of time, in the sense employed in the preceding quotation. Patients *react* to each other and at times may help each other, but they are not engaged in a common (collaborative) project or process, and therefore, no strong ties among them are, or should be, established. The libido cathexes among patients in a therapy group emanates from transferential projections which have to be analyzed and dissipated. When emotional ties arise among patients and their negative transference feelings are eliminated too easily in treatment, the therapeutic effectiveness of the group is diminished and even vitiated as a result.[8]

ANONYMITY

In keeping with the principle of maintaining a transferential relation among patients in a group, during its therapeutic phase, it is best that patients do not have any relations with each other beyond the group sessions. Maintaining relations, other than those that arise in the course of therapy and during the group sessions, affects the quality of the catharsis and the content of the communications. Intimacy may give rise to warm friendships in some instances and sibling hostilities in others. In most cases, intimacy will deter frankness in reactions and criticism, as well as increase defensiveness against being exposed by the newly acquired "friends," so as to maintain an idealized façade, as is the case in all relations except therapy groups. Intimacies acquired in therapy groups, and carried on outside, interfere with the therapeutic role of each, toward self and toward others, which leads to confusion in roles. Outside contacts impose a relationship role vastly different in nature than that of a therapy group.

[8] It is conceivable that a therapy group, near its termination, may become a "cohesive," collaborating group as a result of prolonged treatment, but this rarely occurs and when it does the group needs to be terminated.

The objectivity with which patients must view others (and, later, themselves) vanishes, when either warm, antagonistic, or ambivalent attitudes arise, as they must, in such friendships. When these feelings manifest themselves as a result of group interactions, they become subjects for exploration, leading to symbolic meanings and reawakening memories and feelings. This "working through" is impossible and would be inappropriate in relationships carried on outside the group.

The importance of anonymity among patients frequently presents difficulties for some private practitioners and more often, to community clinics which draw their patients from residents in one neighborhood or small town, for, in addition to the other considerations, the members in these groups withhold essential information about themselves so as not to lose face with their neighbors. This diffidence is a serious impediment to the establishment of therapy groups, a diffidence which should be overcome through psychotherapy as patients' ego-ideal defenses are diminished and they become more secure and more accepting of themselves. However, because of self-protective needs, patients usually cannot engage in a group therapeutic experience to overcome their diffidence. In such conditions, individual psychotherapy may be instituted to work through defensive secretiveness before assigning patients to groups, or the patients may be submitted to parallel individual and group treatment. In dual treatment, patients can deal with the most sensitive areas of their lives in one, while in the other they can ventilate and discuss behavioral and relationship matters. These dual experiences usually aid each other and the therapeutic process as a whole.

Anonymity is an important consideration in selection of patients for a group, i.e., in grouping them (see Chapter VIII).

Often, one of the outcomes of extragroup contacts among patients of heterosexual groups is sexual acting out. Since the participants are in a filial relation to each other, this phenomenon can be understood as the vicarious culmination of incestuous strivings. In most instances, the lines of attraction are not as direct, however. Rather, the incestuous strivings are toward the therapist *in loco parentis* and are displaced on the less forbidding object, a fellow patient. The likelihood is that patients who are prone to this type of acting out would do so in any event (Wolf et al., 1954), but the fact that the principals in the escapades are fellow members of a group in treatment presents particularly difficult problems. For one thing, the dramatic significance of the events, as they are brought to the interviews, are usually so arresting to the other members that an unpermissible portion of time is consumed on this topic to the neglect of the problems of other patients. The interest in the sexual escapades of a pair of members can also be used as resistance, by the others, to going on with their own treatment.

THE GROUP "EGO" AND "SUPEREGO"

Although the term "group ego" is usually employed only euphemistically, there actually is a group ego, invested in and personified by the leader. One of the tacit demands imposed by cohesive groups on each of its members, is that he modify his ego functioning, for, if each should act on his own drives, plans, preferences, and judgments, no group as such could exist for any appreciable length of time. A condition of group membership is *partial de-egotizing* of the individual; that is, a part of his ego must be given up to the group and especially to the leader as its representative. In other words, to be a part of the group, the individual has to submit to the group. Groups come into being and survive only because of this and it is out of these so-called "discarded" portions of the individual egos that a "group ego" is constituted. This can be represented schematically.

A part of the ego (represented by the shaded portions of the circles) of each of the constituent members is given up to form the "group ego," an essential survival process commonly referred to as "socialization" or "assimilation." The more "individualistic" a person is, the less he can give up of his personal ego and the less he is capable of becoming part of his social milieu. In mobs, for example, much larger portions of the individual egos are given up, and each individual is guided less by his ego than he is in democratic deliberative groups. During periods of violent mob action, the egos of the active participants are entirely suspended, while, on the other hand, the initiator or social reformer possesses a minimal capacity for being assimilated.

All group action, whether deliberative or uncontrolled, is a result of the groups "ego" (GE, Fig. 4) functioning which is personified or represented by the cathected and idealized symbol, the leader.

FIGURE 4

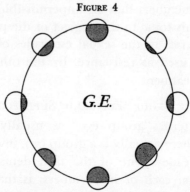

G.E.

What has been said of the ego is equally true of the superego. Superego judgments are weakened in each member by the group's *primary code*: its approval, sanctions, and prohibitions. The libido thus freed in each member is invested in the leader, who becomes the representative of the "group superego." When an individual's superego functioning is at great divergence from that of the group, he will either withdraw, or the group will reject him as a result of anxiety and guilt in himself and in the other group members.

By its very nature, psychotherapy utilizes ego and superego functioning in quite a different manner. Although psychotherapy is permissive and is based on freedom of action and expression, it does not divest the patient of *individual* responsibility. Rather, it encourages unimpeded exercise of the id, ego, and superego during the term of therapy, for only by manifesting them can they be exposed to correction. This is a characteristic of the *permissive culture* of therapy groups. The important tenet of psychotherapy is to give the patient freedom to act in accordance with the dictates of his superego and the strengths of his ego, while still remaining responsible for his own conduct, rather than having this responsibility relegated to a group or a leader. The power to exercise judgment must remain with the patient. It is through the expression of the patient's *real* ego and his *real* superego, and not their feigned character, that the patient discovers the *reality of himself* (self-confrontation), which has to be corrected and brought in alignment with outer reality. In effect, the individual in a therapeutic setting is on his own more thoroughly than he has ever been before, for it is only through this testing of himself against inner and outer reality that he can readjust his psychic forces. Even in activity group therapy of children, which is an extremely permissive method, the child is placed in a position where he must face the consequences of his acts. The more permissive an environment is, the more burdensome one's own task becomes, for freedom is the heaviest load an individual can be called on to carry.

In the differences in ego and superego functioning between ordinary groups and therapeutic groups, lies one of the major contrasts between the two groups. The dynamics that operate in one obviously cannot operate in the other.

THE THERAPY GROUP AS A "CLOSED SYSTEM"

From what we have said about the characteristics of therapy groups, it is evident that they operate on a "closed system." A "closed system" is a configuration of forces which feeds on itself and by its very nature does not permit, or does so minimally, the intrusion or impact of outside influences or forces. Its very existence depends on this inbreeding and exclusiveness. In the light of their definition and characteristics, nontherapeutic groups of various kinds operate on an "open system" plan. That is, they are, as groups, in contact with events outside the confines of their coterie and draw upon them for their activities and expansion, as well as being modified and influenced by them. Contrariwise, a therapy group, having a specific objective which can be obtained only by deeply intimate interactions, mutual induction, and mutual catalyses of its members, can reach its aim only when it remains undiverted and unaffected by the intrusion of outside pressures or influences. There are nontherapeutic groups, usually large in size and extension, that fall between these two extremes. Among these are some religious and semireligious cults and movements which are bound together and activated by a fanaticism and ardor that do not permit deviation, such as Jehovah's Witnesses, the Seventh Day Adventists, the Amish, and various religious cults, Nazi, and so-called Communist groups.

The "closed system" principle for true therapy groups is of major importance and is a cardinal consideration for their success. The nature of the transferences and mutual cathexes and catalysis in these groups is such that their effectiveness is intensified by the intimate freedom of the patients to express themselves and discharge their feelings of hostility and antagonism toward each other, as well as express their affinities and attractions. These transference feelings form one of the major grists for the therapeutic mill. The addition of a new member to an ongoing therapy group, for example, dilutes and interferes with the progressive deepening of feelings, due to "self-consciousness" and group-induced anxiety, present until the new member is accepted into the group.

Inevitable deceleration of the therapeutic process also occurs when patients introduce ideas, thoughts, and information that are not derived from a common group emotion and interaction and the patients' fantasies and preoccupations. Every therapist has had to face, at one time or another, the frustration of the group patients' conversations about occurrences in their personal lives, social events, or philosophical topics, that were not related or advantageous to the therapeutic intent. This has been experienced by both individual and group therapists and psychoanalysts, since diad therapy relations are also "closed systems."

The Yugoslav psychiatrist, Dr. S. Betlheim, analogizes the closed system of a therapy group to a kettle of boiling water, vividly illustrating the principle. If a kettle of water is to boil it must be a self-contained entity: if a stream of water is permitted to flow into it continuously while it is on the fire, it will never come to a boil. This example not only illustrates the principle of the closed system, but also gives a clear image of the dynamic process in psychotherapy. The patients, and the group as a whole, gain most out of the experience when they "boil," as it were. Therefore, anything that lowers their boiling point should be avoided.

Perhaps this analogy can be carried even further, especially as it relates to the adding of patients to groups at a high point of treatment, for adding even a small quantity of water to a kettle already in a state of violent boiling will abruptly stop the boiling until the temperature again rises. This phenomenon, too, is analogous to a therapy group; for the admittance of a new member stops or decelerates the therapeutic turmoil, which reappears only when the patient becomes a part of the group, that is, when he is raised to the "boiling point" or the therapeutic level of the other patients.

The breaking of the "closed system" rule bears more serious consequences in the case of adult therapy groups than it does with children and adolescents. Because of their greater tendency to defensiveness and entrenched self-awareness, adults are more vulnerable than are children to being exposed to the scrutiny of a "stranger." Their communications are more weighted with guilt and shame than are those of younger patients.

DIFFERENTIALS IN GROUP GENESIS

In the Western cultures, groups can be classified in accordance with their origins, which give them a special stamp, character, and function. Accordingly, groups can be classified as free-associative, motivated, forced, or structured. From the point of view of their function in a democratic culture, they can further be classified into deliberating, planning, or action groups.

Free-Associative Groups

Groups that spring up spontaneously in response to a common social or occupational interest are *free-associative*. Among these are transitory or permanent street groups or gangs of children, adolescent clubs, and various social associations and lodges of adults (such as the Masons). Special interest groups such as neighborhood improvement groups, philatelist clubs, and similar aggregates of adults with a common objective or interest, can be included. Among youth they may take the form of airplane modelling clubs, arts and crafts groups, hiking clubs, and the like.

Motivated Groups

Motivated groups are introduced by persons, or institutions, and draw in their members through various devices, prizes, or status and social recognition. Among these are various scout, religious, and political organizations, some of which offer distinction through uniforms, grades, medals, social approbation, certificates, prizes, etc.

Forced Groups

Forced groups are those in which membership is required and imposed. Families, school classes, the military services, and some occupational aggregates can be counted among these.

Deliberating Groups

A *deliberating group* is a gathering of people, with a single and common aim, who meet for the purpose of considering and clarifying the nature and purpose of that aim and the means and possibilities of achieving it, and to implement action through committees or other suitable means. A variety of opinions, differences and disagreements are not only permissible in such a gathering, but are essential both for the preservation of democracy and maximum effectivenes. In such a democratic procedure, the compromising and fusing of opposing and complementary ideas can produce most suitable results.

Planning Groups

A *planning group* is considerably smaller in number than a deliberating assembly and is also more cohesive, with the individuals constituting the group in greater consonance as to aims and procedures. Its function is to formulate plans and strategies to carry out decisions of the planning assemblage and, in order to do so, it is essential that this group be very much smaller and that differences and antagonisms must be at a minimum among its members. Frequently, the same group functions for both deliberating and planning, passing, in its development, from the former to the latter.

Differentials of Therapy and Nontherapy Groups

Action Groups

Action groups are usually chosen by planning groups, and serve as committees to put in operation the plans arrived at and approved by the other two groups. In order to be effective, this is always a very small group, consisting of persons who are in full accord with each other as to aims and means. Lacking this unanimity, no constructive action can be evolved or carried on.

Structured Groups

Structured groups are inaugurated with a defined aim in mind: not only must members meet specific requirements as individuals, but also certain interrelationships are anticipated. An example of a structured group is a committee set up for planning or action, in which the specialties and knowledge of each participant has to be taken into account, *along with* the prospects for their harmonious co-operation. Therapy groups are structured groups *par excellence,* for each patient included is thoroughly studied, his suitability for treatment determined, and the most advantageous grouping for him is judged in advance.

TABLE 1

The Dynamics of Nontherapy and Therapy Groups

Nontherapy	Therapy
Interaction	Interaction
Interstimulation	Interstimulation
Intensification	Intensification
Induction	Induction
Neutralization	Neutralization
Total	Partial
Compromise	Resolution of conflict
Identification	Identification
Assimilation	None
Integration	None or partial
Motivations	Motivations
Collective impulse	Recovery
Cohesion	None
Synergy	Individuation

73

TABLE 2

Expansive and Constrictive Influences of Nontherapy and Therapy Groups

Nontherapy Groups		Therapy Groups*	
Expansive	Constrictive	Expansive	Constrictive
Self-expression	Group induced anxiety	Status	Group cohesion
Creative effort	Interindividual threats	Acceptance	Homoerotism
Social intercourse	Antipathies	Freedom	
Suppression	Rivalries	Security	
Sublimation	Antagonisms	Restitution	
Identification	Restriction of behavior	Knowable character of group	
Allotropism	Ego functioning of others		
Transition to social participation	Reduction of ego controls		
Transition from family to ethos	Reduction of superego judgment		
Enhancement of self-esteem	Reinforcement of the id		
Development of responsibility	Defense against narcissistic injury		

* For further evaluation of therapy groups see Chapter IV.

TABLE 3

Types of Functional Groups

Free-Associative
Motivated
Forced
Deliberating
Planning
Action
Structured

III

The Relation of Psychiatry and Group Psychotherapy

THE UNITARY BASIS OF PSYCHOTHERAPY

Sound group psychotherapy, as a treatment method for emotional disturbances and social maladjustments, is derived from and based on concepts that are common to both it and individual psychotherapy. It draws its insights, methodology, and techniques from the special knowledge and skills of dynamic psychiatry. Group play therapy, for example, is a direct extension of individual play therapy, and analytic interview group psychotherapy is a derivative of individual psychoanalysis. Even activity group therapy, which at first glance may seem to differ from these, actually embraces all of their basic elements, though in a different guise. For instance, instead of verbal catharsis, *activity catharsis* is its forte. Both are psychodynamically similar and both serve the same therapeutic ends. In individual treatment and in analytic groups, interpretation is by means of spoken language. In activity groups, the therapist's expressed reactions, or his abstention from expression, both serve the same ends. The pattern of nonverbal reactions we have named *action interpretation,* and instead of *direct* insight, *derivative* insight is attained.

Top reality testing, an essential ingredient of all psychotherapies, is favored more by a group situation than a one-to-one relation. The emotional re-education incidental to all types of psychologic treatment also occurs in group therapy. But there it is probably more rooted in reality. Diagnosis, on which all psychotherapy must be based, is strictly adhered to by responsible and well-trained psychotherapists before the choice of appropriate treatment is made. An added consideration in group treatment is the assignment of patients to the proper groups for optimum results.

Group psychotherapy is neither a blanket substitute for individual treatment nor is it a universally applicable method. Only patients with specific difficulties can be helped by it; many cannot accept it or respond to it and others may be actually harmed if placed in a group. It is for these reasons, among others, that a thorough knowledge of the psychic structure, physical state, and psychodynamics of each patient must be determined before assignment to a group is made. This emphasis on the psychiatric base of group therapy does not mean, however, that only psychiatrists should practice it,[1] but it does mean that nonmedical therapists need psychiatric consultation and, when indicated, control or supervision. It is essential that the group therapist possess a thorough understanding of, and orientation in, dynamic psychiatry, so that he may function with professional competence and be able to utilize psychiatric supervision. Extensive experience leads to the conclusion that cases such as psychoses, and psychosomatic and hypochondriacal disorders should be treated or supervised by medically trained therapists.

Once knowledge of the dynamics of personality and psychopathology have been adequately acquired, and after extensive controlled experience, psychologists, psychiatric caseworkers, and specialists in group psychotherapy may be able to make competent decisions as to selection and placement of patients in groups. There are, however, appreciable numbers of patients who require medical assessment and psychological testing before treatment can be safely initiated. Such evaluations may also be necessary when the conduct of a patient already in a group manifests unusual or suspicious reactions.

[1] See Chapter XIII for a discussion of qualifications.

Meeting Individual Needs

In order that one may appropriately meet the needs of each member of a therapy group, the diagnosis of each patient must be established. Both assignment to groups and methods of treatment will be determined by it. For example, a patient with a behavior or character disorder may be restrained from acting out, while in the case of organicity, psychoneurosis, or neurotic character, the therapist will eschew restrictions or apply them only with the greatest caution. He may additionally involve the patient in individual treatment, and, in some instances, perhaps substitute it for the group, while in other cases he may suggest medical treatment. To discern the correct step requires knowledge of psychopathology and extensive clinical experience.

Sound group therapists utilize the scientific knowledge that psychiatry provides, in addition to the insights and perceptiveness of interpersonal and group reactions. Only then can the multiplicity of group situations be profitably utilized for each group member. At joint conferences between group therapists, caseworkers, psychologists, and psychiatrists much valuable general information is elicited and a more comprehensive knowledge of each patient is derived. Each specialty contributes from its own store of knowledge and the outcome is a better understanding of the treament procedure that will be of most value to each patient and group.

A major function of a modern hospital, clinic or agency is to train psychiatrists, psychologists, and caseworkers in group psychotherapy. This training must have general psychiatry and individual treatment as its base. This can be acquired through "in-service" training, practicum seminars, and conferences. Continuous seminars for workers in group therapy, in which both theory and practice are discussed, are particularly valuable. The content of these should be based on the literature of the field and, even more important, on records of group sessions and case material. Individual psychodynamics and the dynamics of interpersonal situations, the function of the group therapist, and the details of practice, form the basis of the conferences. The trainee must be made aware of the therapeutic needs of each group member and must understand the latent implications of manifest behavior and statements, penetrating the disguises under which pathology is concealed. He must also know how to deal with them. The task of the group therapist is further complicated by the interplay of the personalities of the group members and the effects they exert on each other that give rise to a variety of situations.

Group psychotherapists, especially those who work with analytic groups, need to have broad experience in individual psychotherapy and must possess a thorough understanding of emotional processes as they are activated through the multilateral stimuli in a group. They should possess information on a variety of subjects, which group discussions inevitably bring forward. Therapists who work with children must, in addition, have skills in arts and crafts.

The practice of group psychotherapy can be undertaken only by persons who, in addition to prolonged training and experience in dynamic individual psychotherapy, have specific personality traits, such as a high degree of intuition, insight, frustration tolerance, self-confidence in group situations, and objectivity.

Contributions of Group Psychotherapy to Psychiatry

It should be noted that psychiatry's contribution to group psychotherapy is not a one-way process. Group psychotherapy has, in turn, contributed to the development of psychiatry.

With the advent of the group in psychotherapy, psychiatry has acquired an instrument of treatment whose effectiveness is indisputable with *specific cases,* including character and behavior disorders in children and adult patients, certain types of acting out neurotics, and patients in mental hospitals. As a derivative of group psychotherapy, the "therapeutic community" in hospital treatment emerged as a real revolution in that field. In the United States the concept of the therapeutic community has, in turn, given birth to a rather erroneous concept and a dubious practice dubbed "the open door."[2]

[2] It is doubtful if just leaving doors unlocked is advisable or effective, without first preparing patient-residents for group responsibility which is the core of the "therapeutic community."

Historically, it was activity group therapy, introduced in 1934, that first demonstrated the place of the ego in psychotherapy and in which the earliest experiments in so-called "ego therapy" were pioneered. It was first applied with children, which served to focus attention on it, so that it was soon integrated into the treatment of adults and has since made inroads into neo-Freudian psychoanalytic practices. Group psychotherapy was instrumental in re-emphasizing the significance of interpersonal and relationship factors in both development of, and correction of personality. An awareness of social and milieu relationships had already existed among certain leaders in the fields of psychology and psychiatry, but it was the effective employment of the group in treatment that brought this awareness into more cogent view, as well as instrumentalizing it as a therapeutic aid in psychiatry.

SOME HISTORICAL BACKGROUND

In 1944, the present writer suggested to the Executive Committee of the American Group Psychotherapy Association that it consider the needs for training practitioners.[3] Members of the Committee felt that, while interest in group therapy had greatly increased and a number of agencies and clinics had adopted group treatment as a part of their facilities, not enough qualified persons were available to carry out these programs. The Association, therefore, undertook to sponsor a training institute for a small number of experienced psychiatrists, psychotherapists, and caseworkers. Representatives of the Association and of agencies in a number of cities met and formulated plans for such an institute.

The original intention was to have hospital and child guidance clinics release workers for two days a week to receive this type of training. Students were to be enlisted from New York and nearby cities. Agencies in Boston, Washington, and Philadelphia, and in Connecticut and New Jersey towns, agreed to send mem-

[3] The pages that follow were presented as a paper at the Fourth Annual Conference of the American Group Psychotherapy Association in New York City, January, 1947, and appeared in *Meneal Health*. XXXI:386-396, 1947.

bers of their staffs for training. It was planned to have the students remain in New York one or two nights a week, so as to spend approximately two days in training and study.

Because of war conditions at the time, this plan proved impracticable and was modified. A seminar in group therapy, one morning a week, was offered instead, and the student body was limited to members of agencies and clinics in Metropolitan New York and cities within commuting distance. Only psychiatrists and highly experienced caseworkers on a supervisory level were accepted.

The Association felt that the curtailed program might have the effect of setting a standard for training and decided to withdraw from the project. A committee consisting of directors of a number of child guidance clinics undertook to sponsor the institute, with the present writer as instructor. Seven agencies and clinics were involved.

In all but a few instances, tuition was paid by the agencies, and most of the caseworkers and psychiatrists were released from their duties to take the training. The institute had seventeen students, of whom three were psychiatrists, four group therapists, nine psychiatric caseworkers, and one a psychologist. Each session was of three-and-a-half hours duration, with a twenty-minute recess. Thirty sessions were held. The seminars consisted entirely of the reading, analysis, and interpretation of protocols of group sessions and of case discussions. Records of activity groups, play groups, and "interview" (analytic) groups with adolescents and parents of children under treatment were read and analyzed. Considerable theory in psychodynamics, psychopathology and general psychology grew out of the discussions, but emphasis was on techniques and procedures in the practice of group therapy itself.

One indication of the value of the institute is the fact that all but one of the students continued their studies for a second year through the actual practice of group therapy in their own agencies and clinics. The instructor supervised some of these projects in Connecticut, New Jersey, and New York City. Some of the participants continued in another seminar the following year, which included therapists from several European countries.

It may be of value to record some impressions of this first project in the training of group therapists.

One was impressed with the fact that only persons with a sound understanding of psychopathology and a record of experience in general psychotherapy could undertake the practice of analytic group therapy. No one without a thorough knowledge of, and prolonged experience in, general psychotherapy could be trained to do group therapy with any degree of adequacy, for dealing with groups is more complicated than dealing with individuals. In the treatment of an individual, the therapist may, according to his understanding of the patient's needs at a given time, encourage or discourage the patient's production; he can direct the interviews by means of a leading question or a remark; he can go passive and uncommunicative; or he can actively give interpretation. In therapy groups, these powers are greatly curtailed and at times abrogated. In a group, the therapist has to be alert to numerous situations and a network of interpersonal tensions not present in individual therapy. This is as true of analytic group therapy as it is of activity groups. It is for this reason, among many others, that only highly skilled and self-confident therapists can function well in a group treatment situation.

Another observation derived from that first training experience (and verified through subsequent experiences) is that group psychotherapy is not a specialty apart from the general practice of psychotherapy. A group therapist, whether medical or nonmedical, must have the knowledge that an individual therapist has; he must know and understand the backgrounds of the patients and their intrapsychic problems and treatment needs, as must the individual therapist. One cannot master group techniques apart from these general understandings, essential to all psychotherapy.

The following passage, from the paper mentioned at the start of this section, has historical interest:

"Because of the need for knowledge of general psychotherapy as a background for the practice of group therapy, the founding of a graduate training school for psychotherapy was undertaken some years later.[4] Not only because the lack of medically trained psychotherapists is a serious handicap, but on purely technical grounds, it has become increasingly evident that medical training as such is not essential for the practice of sound psychotherapy providing the therapist does not attempt to deal with psychotic and with organic patients. The lay therapist cannot be too cautious in this respect, however. He must be able to recognize patients who do not fall within his purview and be bound, both legally and in honor, not to undertake to give treatment beyond his competence. He should in all instances have a prospective patient examined by a general physician, a neurologist, and a psychiatrist. (To this list a psychologist should be added.)

"In order that much needed services in psychotherapy be supplied to some extent, at least, qualified persons, both medical and nonmedical, need be trained more widely than is done at the present time both in clinical and didactic settings in the science and art of individual and group psychotherapy as a step toward licensing both medical and nonmedical psychotherapists.

"To qualify practitioners in psychotherapy, the following tripartite curriculum of *four-year* (full-time) duration is suggested:

"I. Orientative studies in biology, zoology, genetics, embryology, anatomy, physiology, neurology, endocrinology, child development, general, abnormal and social psychology, sociology, and contemporary family problems.

"II. Professional courses, including depth psychology, basic psychiatry, diagnosis, individual psychotherapy, and group psychotherapy.

"III. Field work and practice in a clinical setting under competent training supervisors.

"It is suggested that this training be open to university or college graduates with degrees in psychology, to students with premedical training, and to graduate physicians, and should be, preferably, an integral part of a medical school.

---

[4] The Group Psychotherapy Institute, Inc., was licensed by the University of the State of New York and operated during 1950-1952, under the direction of the present writer.

"A degree of Master of Psychotherapy and Doctor of Psychotherapy should be granted to students who complete the required schedule of studies and pass the qualifying examination of a board set up for this purpose. Psychiatrists as well as lay candidates should be required to take the qualifying examinations . . . and the degrees of Master and Doctor in Psychotherapy should be bestowed upon them, in addition to their medical doctorates." (For further discussion on the training of group psychotherapists, see Chapter XIII.)

RECEPTIVITY TO GROUP PSYCHOTHERAPY

Group psychotherapy, unlike innovations in most other fields of human endeavor, has met a singular receptivity from all the related professions, including psychiatry. One of the more thorough and systematized schools of psychotherapy did not officially join in the otherwise prevalent acceptance of group psychotherapy, but it did not openly or militantly oppose it. However, this coolness, which is no longer universal among its members, is its characteristic reaction to all divergencies from its own rather rigid lines. Barring this one group, the readiness with which group psychotherapy has been welcomed augurs well for its future, at the same time placing more responsibility for the maintenance of high professional standards on the shoulders of its proponents.

In the history of human culture, significant new ideas that survived the natural resistance to change have had to pass through four stages: being ignored, encountering active opposition, meeting derision, and, finally, acceptance. Group psychotherapy was spared these birth pains, partially because of the fascination of the concept of "the group," its inherent truths, and its indisputable effectiveness with many patients. However, more extraneous and practical circumstances, coinciding with its infancy, aided in its acceptance. Specifically, during the Second World War, group psychotherapy became widespread as a means of treating psychogenic "battle fatigue," a debilitating emotional disturbance effecting military personnel. Another cause of the relatively small opposition to group psychotherapy, even in the decade preceding the war, was the lack of extravagant claims made by its proponents, who systematically pointed out its limitations.

However, since group psychotherapy is still a new technique, skepticism as to its methods and value, though rapidly diminishing, still exists. This is both understandable and desirable. In the interests of the patients, no new therapeutic technique should be accepted without the safeguards that skepticism, analysis, evaluation, testing, and validation provide. Many of the doubts concerning group therapy, on the part of some professionally trained persons, are the result of a lack of empirical knowledge about this method of treatment and are, rather, derived from the theoretical and constructional hypotheses. Much of the skepticism also stems from an even more important and more cogent assumption; namely, that *all* psychotherapy, to be effective, must deal with deep unconscious content in a one-to-one transference relation. Actually, this is not so. While experience supports the view that massive psychoneuroses, especially of the transference neuroses category, do require such intensive treatment, one finds, in the daily practice of psychotherapy, that a large number of patients do not require (although some could benefit from it) such profound and thoroughgoing psychoanalytic therapy.

When asked what she had gained from her (exclusively) group treatment, a very attractive and intelligent young woman, married to an older man, said: "One thing that is important to me that I got from this treatment is that I deal with my husband with less disturbance and strain. [Her husband was an impatient, quick-tempered, and quarrelsome man.] In the past, I'd fight with him, but the fights in the group and how we resolved them taught me that I can handle my husband without fights. I just say to him, 'You are mad now and unreasonable. I'll talk to you when you calm down.' And it works." Thus, although the group had not at that point resolved her oedipal fixation on an older man who resembled her father in his behavior, the family climate and the mates' general relations greatly improved and their child also benefitted from the improved home atmosphere—one less neurotic personality will be bequeathed to the next generation. Significantly, this patient was aware of the deeper oedipal meaning of her marriage, but she consciously accepted it as an adequate adjustment for herself.

A more seriously disturbed patient was the young woman whose mild agoraphobia was associated with the term "walking the streets." This, in turn, was derived from her fear of being approached by men and was a reaction of her susceptibility to them based on her incestuous feelings toward her now dead father. Following group psychotherapy, the patient was able to go out of the house, get a job, and function moderately well, without having resolved her unconscious conflict. It is true that she remained a sick woman and that the *neurotic residue* of her problem required a thoroughgoing psychoanalysis. However, the financial outlay was out of the question for this young woman and the less profoundly-affecting type of therapy had eliminated what Dr. J. H. W. van Ophuijsen referred to as "the representative in the conscious" of the unconscious conflict.

Levels of Treatment

Sound analytic group psychotherapy does not operate only on superficial levels. This is demonstrated by the patient who, in addition to many functional and adjustment problems, suffered from psychogenic eczema, a condition that created many problems for her both as a mother and housewife. Her relationship to her husband, as well as to people in general, was masochistic in nature. Having been intensely rejected by her mother and made to feel inferior to her siblings, she hugged the thought that her deceased father had really loved her. It was the one sustaining idea to which she clung. She maintained this and other defensive fantasies throughout her life. As a result of analytic group treatment (only) and skillful interpretation of the transference, this woman came to recognize, quite on her own, that her father did not really love her but "was sorry" for her. A number of repressed associative memories then came tumbling, one of which was the memory of her father fondling her naked sister, when the latter was twelve years old. She also became aware that she accomplished little because, in her "unconscious," she had always expected that her father would come and help her with her tasks; this despite the fact that he had been dead for many years. The alteration in this woman's life pattern and personality, following analytic group psychotherapy, were indeed impressive.

A young woman, who carried on extramarital relations with older men only, for small sums of money, after one and a half years of group treatment inadvertently said, "As a child when I wanted something I had to *warm it up* for my father." She meant she had to be sweet to him and cajole him, but when the phrase "warm it up for my father" was called to her attention, she blushed and freely associated it with her current behavior. She soon abandoned her delinquent practices.

These few illustrations demonstrate that group psychotherapy does not operate only on the ego and behavioral levels, but also involves the unconscious. Most thoughtful psychotherapists hold that groups do reach the preconscious and conscious but have serious reservations as to whether unconscious material can come through. In the practice of *true* analytic group psychotherapy, conducted with insight and competency, unconscious material *does* come through, as we shall illustrate in the course of this text.

This doubt, more than most others, shows the misconceptions that can arise from lack of actual experience with this method of treatment. Patients in groups *do* all the things that seem impossible to the uninitiated, except, of course, that not all the patients necessarily go through the same process. The needs of some are met by less intensive uncovering, while others improve their lives through strengthened or altered ego functioning.

In a group (as in individual) psychotherapy, the levels of treatment have to be adapted to *the needs* and *the possibilities* of each patient. Some patients require individual psychotherapy or psychoanalysis, while others, if properly chosen and placed, can do as well or better in groups. Groups offer opportunities for new identifications and, for that very reason, they also supply possibilities for improving the ego and the superego structure. The examination, analysis, and elaboration of behavior and attitudes by a number of peers, with honesty and good intent, cannot help but have a telling effect on the participants. The therapist must be able to recognize when the defenses and rigidities of a given patient make him impervious or inaccessible to group therapy. It is these patients, among others, who would require one-to-one treatment, if they are willing and able to submit to it. It is, therefore, a matter of carefully choosing each patient and matching him with the type of therapy that will best serve his needs.

Discussions and reactions in a group may exceed a particular patient's ego tolerance. This is one of the serious considerations that should and does preoccupy responsible group therapists. This subject is discussed extensively in other chapters. Suffice it to say here that techniques for "rescuing" patients are at hand in groups, through deflection, diversion, and sparring, and that care in selecting patients for groups is an assurance against untoward eventualities. Many responsible group therapists insist on projective tests, as aids to clinical diagnoses, for all patients before including them in groups.

There exists, in some, a fear that groups may be used for "re-education," rather than for a facing of the rigid and stubbornly self-perpetuating mechanisms of full-blown psychoneuroses. No responsible psychotherapist, who understands the nature and psychodynamics of such psychoneuroses and the various types of character disorders, will expect group therapy alone to deal with such problems. Accordingly, individual treatment is resorted to, alone or in combination with group therapy, or placement in a hospital may be recommended. The multiple gradations of depth and complexity in work with patients, such as education, support, counseling, guidance, psychonursing, psychotherapy, and psychoanalysis (which is a special form of psychotherapy), are discussed at length in Chapter IV.

There is a view of group psychotherapy that stems from the assumed "law" that *all* treatment is the resolution of conflicts between the id and the superego. However, one of the very important constituents of the psychic triad, the ego, has not been considered with a sufficient degree of adequacy in the past.

There are innumerable maladjusted and difficult persons whose ego functioning, in terms of intrapsychic controls and external behavior, can be vastly improved by less intensive procedures than psychoanalytic ones. These are the nonpsychotic adults who have

87

character disorders, schizoid personalities, and borderline schizophrenia, and the psychopaths who are not accessible to the well-established psychoanalytic technique indispensable for the psychoneuroses. There are also numerous adults, suffering from mild neuroses and neurotic traits, who can keep their neurotic patterns under control once their ego is strengthened. Groups are immensely effective in ego reorganization and reinforcement; in fact, they are more effective than individual therapy, largely because of the opportunities they offer for establishing healthy identifications.

Reidentification is one of the essential dynamics of psychotherapy; and in groups, dynamic affect-laden interaction or encounter among the members and with the therapist constitutes a very telling and tangible process of reidentification. There is also the element of identification with the "group as a whole." In fact, in group psychotherapy, corrective identifications are so important that we have suggested the terms "identification transference," "vicarious catharsis" and "spectator therapy" as their operational processes.

An important element in psychotherapy, frequently minimized or overlooked, is that of "reality testing." This is understandable with regard to one-to-one therapy, since there, the major preoccupation is with the relation between patient and therapist, that is, the transference-countertransference phenomena. Actually, the patient's dealing with and response to reality *outside* of the diad situation must be viewed as an integral part of individual therapy as well as a test of the patient's improvement. The group, on the other hand, with its network of interactions, demands, and restraints, is an indigenous tangible reality with which the ego of each member must deal. In fact, psychoanalysts who recognize the value of this refer patients to groups as a "tapering-off" device. Some analysts believe that every analysand should have a group experience before terminating treatment.

In general, one could say that any therapist who avers that group psychotherapy can reach the same levels of the unconscious as individual psychoanalysis suffers from *countertransference to his craft*, certainly from an overidentification with it. Each type of therapy, guidance, or counseling has to define the optimum limits of its possibilities and stay within those bounds.

Scientific method requires clear definition of the subject under study and comparison with a subject in an identical category. It would be more cogent and more profitable, for example, to *specifically* discuss the relative natures of group psychotherapy and psychoanalysis in the treatment of, say, an obsessional neurosis, rather than to draw parallels between them as *forms* of psychotherapy in its *generic* meaning. Psychotherapy will grow both as a science and a practice when specificity, rather than generalities, is integrated in it. It must deal with *each* patient, select the proper treatment for his special needs at each different stage, and recognize the possibilities and limitations of the different techniques.

SOURCES OF VARIATION AND CONFUSION

It is inevitable that an expanding theory and practice, such as group psychotherapy currently is, should acquire a multitude of peripheral, divergent, and fringe theories and techniques. This is true of any early pioneering period in human effort, before testing and validation have selected the wheat from the chaff. It is also true that variations, conflicts, and divergencies are more liable to proliferate where a theory and practice is outside the exact sciences, and psychotherapy is in this category. It is currently not possible to formulate with exactitude either a theoretical or instrumental blanket science of human personality and behavior in a group *generally,* though predictions may be possible with regard to a *specific* individual.

The plethora of schools and principles in the fields of psychology and psychotherapy arises from two sources: the complex nature of the dynamics of human personality and behavior and the predilections and preferences of the observers and students due to their own personality set and educational conditioning. The primary cause for this multiplicity of approaches in the field of group psychotherapy stems from the confusion and lack of a common ground in individual psychotherapy.

Group psychotherapy can never stand alone as a separate thera-

89

peutic tool. By its very nature, it must always base its methods, techniques, and understanding on individual psychotherapy. Fundamentally, the focus of treatment in a group is still the *individual* patient and the dynamics of the individual personality. Group psychotherapy is only a modification of individual psychotherapy and not a completely different method. An exception to this is activity group therapy for specially selected children in latency.

Some Characteristics of Therapy Groups

In analytic group psychotherapy, as in all analytically oriented psychotherapies, the aims are: redistribution of the libido where it is excessively cathexed either on oneself or on an object; strengthening of the ego so that it may deal with inner and outer demands and pressures and regulate the impingement (or lack of it) emanating from the superego; and correction of the self-image.

The *aim* of true group psychotherapy is the achieving of a relatively permanent intrapsychic change, rather than the alleviating of symptoms or behavior improvement only. The next consideration is the *process*. Neither "relationships," "understanding," or "re-enactment" (action) are adequate procedures for achieving "cures" or lasting changes in emotionally disturbed patients. Explanation is not interpretation, and understanding is not insight. Action as a form of therapy may be adequate for some highly selected, mild behavior and character disorders in children, if it is carried on in a specially designed environment and in a group (not individual) setting. The more disturbed, even among children, and all adult nonpsychotic patients cannot be therapeutically affected by abreaction, acting out, or re-enactment alone. In true psychotherapy, action and reflection go hand in hand, and the latter (reflection) can stand alone, but not the former (action). Nor is it enough for the ends of real psychotherapy with adult patients to foster relationships. There is no proof that a better adjustment to a therapy group, and more friendly and tolerant relations among its members, results in lasting inner changes in the individual patient that carry over to other areas of his life.

Improvement in behavior and attitude nearly always results from any type of friendly and constructive individual and group associations, but no one who really understands the structure and dynamics of character and of neuroses can confidently claim that they can be changed or dissolved by such superficial means as "relationships in a group."

Analytic group psychotherapy, with nonpsychotic adolescent and adult patients, relies on free associative verbal communication by each individual, interpretation of individual and group resistances, interpretation of the individual, multiple, and collective (group) transferences, and the attainment of insight by *each* of the participating group members *as individuals*. True psychotherapy can hardly be expected to occur if the sexual and nonsexual libido is not involved and primary and secondary hostilities and aggressions are not worked through.

Such "working through" cannot be achieved in guidance and counseling or in the so-called psychotherapies that rely on artifices for behavioral change. Working through can be achieved only through regressive infantile memories and feelings in a transference relation to a parent surrogate. This process is especially indispensable in the treatment of real psychoneuroses.

Action without reflection is insufficient. "Role taking," which is sometimes suggested as the sole therapeutic tool, cannot affect the personality structure so profoundly as to alter it. What is necessary to reconstructive psychotherapy is not re-enactment, but rather the reliving of past affect-laden traumatic events with all the accompanying distortions and fantasies. But this must occur in a setting devoid of the original threats and anxiety-inducing reactions and situations. In addition to freeing ego energies consumed in dealing with these unconscious pressures, the deeply affecting emotional experiences are here relived in the light of new and more mature attitudes, with the help of the therapist and fellow patients. Thus, the second requisite of true group psychotherapy with nonpsychotic patients is free verbal catharsis that leads to early memories of traumata with the associative anxieties (though it may also involve regressive acting out).

The third requirement for real group psychotherapy is *free and spontaneous* participation and response from *all* members of the group, as feelings, memories, and ideas are stirred up (catalyzed) by fellow patients. Any technique that does not permit this is invalid. The concatenation set up in the unconscious of individuals (and sometimes in the group as a whole) must be permitted free flow. It is through this freedom (which the neurotic was not permitted in his past history) that the noxious elements in the psyche are thrown off.

From this point of view, techniques such as psychodrama, didactic therapies, and role playing in a *structured* situation or pseudo-relations, do not conform with sound group psychotherapy or, for that matter, any kind of psychotherapy. It is the free flow of stored-up memories and feelings that lead the patient to the core of his problem, help him unburden himself of his psychic tensions and anxieties, and allow him to acquire insight into his mechanisms and reactions.

Devices and artifices often play into the resistances that patients inevitably present. These resistances are part and parcel of sound psychotherapy. However, where there is no free cathartic flow in the interviews, patients can be activated to communicate, but this communication is not therapeutically meaningful. Such devices as "forced," "contractual," "transactional," or "imposed communication" have no therapeutic validity (Slavson, 1953). Verbalization, in all psychotherapy, is effective when it releases associated and bound-up affect and anxiety stored in the unconscious, and occurs most tellingly by overcoming censors and resistances. Facilitated statements do not place the individual in a position to encounter himself and his unconscious and, therefore, do not constitute a true therapeutic experience.

The fourth requirement for effective group psychotherapy is correct selection and grouping of patients. Initially, diagnoses must be established for each patient and his suitability for one of many types of treatment determined.

A fifth requirement of a therapy group is that it meet the corrective needs of each patient according to his unique personality structure and clinical indications.

A sixth and important requirement of a true therapy group

is that it remain small (not exceeding eight persons), so that interpersonal reactions and interactions can take place. But in a group that is too small, say less than five, prolonged relations would tend to reinforce the patients' problems and play into each person's neuroses without interactions, neutralization, cathartic elaborations, and other corrective dynamics. Mutual induction occurs in inverse geometric ratio to the size of the group, since the neutralizing and diluting elements stem from the variations in personality and ego functioning between the group members.

The small group provides a narrower field for emotional operation and, therefore, greater concentration of affect. It prevents a loss of self-identity and pits individuals against each other more poignantly and more directly than is possible in larger groups. A small group is more likely to reactivate and reawaken the hostilities and discomforts experienced by the patient in his natural family. Since, aside from constitutional predispositions, psychic distortions predominantly stem from relations with members of one's own family, the duplication of these relations in a therapeutic setting and the process of working them through are the key to psychic reintegration. This can be achieved in a small group in a face-to-face relation, in intimate and affect-laden interpenetration.

We can therefore say, with justification, that *group psychotherapy had its beginnings with the introduction of the small group.* It is only in a small group that free-associative catharsis can occur, that valid interpretation can be given, and that telling insights are acquired.

It was the present writer who, in 1934, introduced the concept of a small group consisting of eight members. This number has since been universally accepted by therapists. Experimental studies of communication by group dynamists, conducted more than twenty years later, have shown that eight is the optimum number for the spread of significant emotional induction and deep interpenetration among people. In my opinion, eight is actually the *maximum* number for a truly psychoanalytically oriented therapy group; five to six patients would yield better results. The number eight, as a limit for the size of groups, was originally set for activity groups for children and was adhered to by us when analytic group psychotherapy (first known as "interview group therapy" to differentiate it from "activity group therapy") was added.

The "hunch," that led us to the use of small groups in therapy, was derived from our work, since 1911, with various types and sizes of groups, in and out of classrooms, in "group work," in leisure-time occupations, and in formal and informal education. Many years prior to the inauguration of therapy groups, we had recognized that interpenetration of personalities cannot occur in large groups, where interactions are, of necessity, diffuse and perfunctory.

SOME AREAS OF DISAGREEMENT

Specificity

The group psychotherapist needs to take into consideration the setting in which he is practicing, as well as the particular types of patients he is working with. Procedures are, to a certain degree conditioned by the setting in which they are carried out. Whether the therapy is being done in private practice, on a hospital ward, in a convalescent home, or in a restraining institution, will affect patient-therapist relationships, patient attitudes, and the ease with which communication is established. In a child guidance clinic, for example, the primary preoccupation of adults in treatment is centered around their children and their relationship with them. In a prison setting, on the other hand, the focus is complaints against the prison and its personnel, conflicts with society, lawbreaking, and the prisoners' "innocence." In the one instance, significant communication is much more easily established than in the other, and the patients are less distrustful and less fearful of the therapist. The treatment aims, as well, are different in the two settings.

The specific applications of group psychotherapy extend to patients with defined syndromes or ailments. Special groups are conducted for psychoneurotics, psychotics, delinquents, epileptics, the senile, patients suffering from psychosomatic symptoms, the tubercular, addicts, and patients with hypertension and cardiac maladies (See Slavson, 1956).

94

Organicity

Another characteristic, reflected in the literature and in current practice, is what may be called *organicity*. Group psychotherapy has evolved an organized body of characteristic knowledge, theory, nomenclature, and techniques. Though proceeding from, and rooted in, individual psychotherapy, it is distinct as to its methods. Seemingly, there is variety and conflict in the theoretical orientations of practioners, but in actuality, the contrasts are more in concepts than in clinical practice. Though one's thinking and approach inevitably reflect one's personality, preferences and bias, there is considerable congruence in the principles acceptable to large numbers of group psychotherapy practitioners (Slavson, 1962).

Even when practice becomes more uniform, explanations and assumptions will probably still be subject to controversy. (This is true of all human endeavor and cannot be viewed as a particular defect or handicap.) Of singular interest is the fact that in all fields, most practitioners who appear to disagree on theoretic foundations have been found to perform their tasks in substantially the same manner. The difference, in most instances, is in emphasis on *one* element as against others. A similar situation exists in group psychotherapy and will probably persist for some time. To wish for unanimity among practitioners is futile. The best one can expect is that there will be unity of effort in the study, testing, evaluation, and free exchange of experiences and ideas.

Terminology

The terminology of the field, as part of its organic growth, presents a somewhat confused picture.[5] It is to be expected that a new practice, involving special procedures and newly identified dynamics, will result in an extensive and unique terminology. The

[5] The Second and Third Editions of the *Psychiatric Dictionary* (Hinsie and Shatsky, Eds., Oxford University Press, 1953, and Hinsie and Campbell, Eds., 1961, respectively) include more than thirty terms on group psychotherapy supplied by the present author.

literature reveals, in addition, a tendency on the part of some to employ terms that are frequently no more than rhetorical expressions or colorful restatements of old and well-used concepts in psychiatry, psychology, and psychotherapy. Frequently, they are of linguistic or semantic coinage that does not represent new formulations and does not identify new phenomena. Fortunately, this is not a universal tendency. Only a few are given to this, but these few do create considerable confusion on occasion. Not only is there a semantic difficulty, but their terms convey the impression that group psychotherapy is different and apart from other mental therapies. Actually, the fundamental processes and dynamics that operate in group psychotherapy are, in every regard, the same as in all good psychotherapies, even though they are modified by the compresence of a number of persons.

Suitability

There is also considerable variance as to the suitability of group therapy for particular patients. Some tend to limit the practice to less disturbed patients and to those in definite clinical categories. Others place patients in groups indiscriminately. There is considerable variance, also, in the matter of grouping, which is influenced by age range, sexual homogeneity, the patients' clinical and diagnostic categories, the advisability of having families or couples in the same groups, and other elements of the group therapeutic setting. These are among the questions discussed in subsequent chapters.

Integration

Another factor to which attention must be given is the processes by which group treatment can be integrated into other types of psychotherapy. Group psychotherapy has been fully accepted by the Armed Forces in the immediate rehabilitation of patients in acute states of anxiety and minor maladjustments and is fully accepted and widely practiced in veterans hospitals and institutions for mental patients. It is also widespread in the private practice of psychiatry and psychotherapy, and in child guidance centers, youth consultation, and all other types of community clinics. An increasing number of medical schools are including group psychotherapy in their advanced curricula for postgraduate training of psychiatrists. There also exist an impressive number of techniques derivative from the parent body of group psychotherapy.

IV

Differential Aims and Dynamics in Group Counseling, Guidance, Psychotherapy, and Psychonursing

"Depth" of Therapy

"Depth" of therapy, as a concept, is a subject of intense controversy, a controversy that has also been a topic of varying and opposing views in individual psychotherapy and psychoanalysis for many years and is, therefore, not the concern of the group therapist alone, but of all who are engaged in mental treatment. Some who do not subscribe to the concept of "depth" in treatment, hold the position that treatment has to be evaluated in accordance with the needs of the patient—what may be superficial therapy for one is deep for another. To them, the concept of "depth" is not absolute; rather, it is relative and conditioned by the specific circumstances and specific patients.

Others view "deep" psychotherapy as an absolute value, which includes regression, recall of traumata and intense affect. To them "depth" connotes involvement of the sexual libido, deeply repressed memories, defensive ego mechanisms, and the freeing of the individual from the throes of inhibiting or conflicting states of mind; in short, the reorganization of the patient's psychic economy, so that the id, ego, and superego function more harmoniously to achieve more efficient and more satisfying sets of adaptive patterns and responses.

Most psychotherapists differentiate the depth in personality change achieved through classic psychoanalysis and that achieved by the less thoroughgoing psychotherapies. These psychotherapies aim at improvement in attitudes, adjustment, and function. Some affect "symptom improvement," only, without basic changes in the relation of intrapsychic forces and dynamics. Unfortunately, in the absence of accurate measuring devices for alterations in the psyche and changes in function and attitude, much of this must remain in the realm of speculation. However, the giving up of a symptom may be an indication that some improvement in the psyche has taken place, even if fleeting or transitory. The services of the symptom as a defense, as a channel for discharging tensions, or as a means for resolving inner conflicts, are no longer needed. There is, as yet, no quantitative validation of these, nor can we measure the "representative in the conscious" of the intrapsychic conflict (Slavson, 1952a).

Much of current practice in the field depends on finding answers to these questions. Group psychotherapists need not feel that finding these answers is their responsibility alone, however, for these are generic problems of psychotherapy and psychiatry. One cannot subscribe to assertions like, "Group psychotherapy is more psychoanalytical than psychoanalysis," regardless of the source. The same is true of the claim that "nothing that can be achieved by individual psychotherapy cannot also be achieved by group psychotherapy." Such extravagant claims must await confirmation. Until tools for validation are at hand, these comparisons are insidious.

The terms "guidance" and "counseling" are employed to describe treatment, both individual and group, where lesser results are sought than in psychotherapy and where only specific problems in the dimensions of time and space (as differentiated from intrapsychic problems) can be resolved. Clinical diagnoses are not employed, since the intention is to focus on a definite situational stress with which the individual may be unable to cope by himself. Sharp demarcations are necessary between the concepts of psychotherapy and those of other techniques, which deal with people in difficulty who need not, cannot, or are unready to, work toward a radical inner change. Much of the work characterized as group psychotherapy may actually be group guidance or group counseling, and a good part of the confusion and disagreement among group psychotherapists lies in this fact. This confusion will be cleared up only when agreement is reached as to what actually constitutes psychotherapy as differentiated from schooling, education, counseling, and guidance.

This lack of clarity is reflected in characterizing recreational activities, playing in a band, group reading, singing and hand clapping in unison, dancing, parties, lectures, movies, and didactic teaching, as group therapy. While these and similar occupations may be "therapeutic," in so far as they constitute a part of the living situation of patients in a hospital and occupy them constructively, they do not, however, constitute psychotherapy as such.

In recent years, psychotherapists, especially caseworkers, have taken cognizance of differential levels in therapy. The terms "casework therapy," "supportive therapy," "insight therapy," "intermediate therapy" (between supportive and insight in intensity), and "psychoanalysis," attest to this awareness of the differences in intensity and depth of treatment and the "layers" of the personality that can or should be involved in it.

These distinctions apply to group psychotherapy as well. There is definite need for a cogent differentiation of "levels" in the patient's psyche to which group psychotherapy can address itself and which it attempts to reach. We have, therefore, suggested the terms *group psychonursing, group counseling, group guidance,* and *group psychotherapy* to emphasize the differences.

In the movement from infancy to maturity, nurture, discipline, education, schooling, counseling, and guidance are the stages through which every individual in Western culture must pass at the hands of parents, teachers, religious figures, peers, and the community. In primitive societies, nurture and discipline were the only adaptation mechanisms employed. With the onset of civilization, schooling and education were added as essential for the individual to have in meeting the new and vastly more complex demands placed upon him. As the complexities of society have increased, counseling and guidance were added to help individuals, especially the young, to find their way. Educational, vocational, marriage, family, and personal counseling and guidance have, as a result, become indispensable in the complicated culture of the West, and, recently, also of the East. Those who, for a variety of reasons, did not or could not fully benefit from the early formative influences and find themselves in disharmony with themselves and, therefore, inevitably with their surroundings, become candidates for psychotherapy.

Determining Individual Needs

We are here concerned only with that area of counseling and guidance which is preceded by the term "personal." Educational, vocational, premarital, marital, and family counseling are not specifically within our purview.

Individuals who become aware of difficulties in interpersonal relations, who suffer somatic symptoms or emotional tensions and unhappiness may seek help and it is the responsibility of the therapist to determine the nature and intensity of the patient's needs. An examination of the patient's history and the various facts involved, will lead him to determine the appropriate course to pursue in each case. This course may be individual or group counseling, guidance, or psychotherapy, and in some cases, to be discussed presently, psychonursing.

Counseling and guidance deal specifically with ego functioning and to a lesser extent with the self-image. Psychotherapy is also concerned with these, but in addition seeks to unravel the intrapsychic malformations that give rise to these and seeks to affect basic corrections in the personality.

Counseling

In counseling, the counselor, who may or may not be a trained psychotherapist, leads the counselee either to arrive at or to accept from the counselor, a solution of the immediate difficulty for which help was sought. The counselor addresses himself to that difficulty, whatever it may be, and helps the counselee to resolve it, by indicating to him, and supporting him in, a line of action that would alleviate the dilemma. The content of the interviews, which are usually few in number, is focused on realities in the interpersonal or situational difficulty; the *explanations* are reality oriented; that is, only the actual events related to the felt problem and their meaning and effect are evaluated and discussed. Solutions are considered and selected according to the needs of the situation as seen by the participants, these solutions being within the counselee's existing capacities or talents.

The counselor is an *active agent,* although he should follow that precept of all good teaching which stresses that the best solution is the one which the learner arrives at through his own effort and, as far as possible, by himself. Thus, while he leads the counselee on and opens doors to him, as it were, his aim is, nonetheless, to consummate a suitable resolution of the counselee's problem. The counselor is equipped for this by his superior understanding of the forces involved: the personality structure and ego functioning of the counselee, to which the latter may be blind. The counselor's experience and awareness should indicate to him whether the counselee can carry out the plan. Above all, the fact that he is uninvolved and views all elements objectively places him in an advantageous position.

Counseling should be done on a one-to-one relation. As we view it here, group counseling is by far more difficult, if not impossible. Since, in counseling, there is always the *specific* aim of helping a specific individual seeking practical and immediate help, the interference of other members of the group with the direct pursuit of this aim may prove a serious stumbling block. The variety of reactions and opinions, inherent in the group, may take the discussion far afield, into areas and ideas not related to the *immediate* problem or situation for which a given individual is struggling to find a solution or a helpful line of action.

GUIDANCE

This is not the case in guidance. Here, unlike counseling, the attitudes, and sometimes even the feelings involved in the guidee's problems, are exposed for his own consideration, even though the underlying unconscious motivations and their sources remain untouched. A person requires guidance when the emotional significance of the problem is beyond simple ego functioning. In counseling cases, it is assumed that the ego is capable of dealing with the problem as a course of action is made clear. There is a minimum of blockage, due to anxiety or affect, in carrying it through. In guidance, on the other hand, the emotional charge such as guilt feelings, for example, is such that the ego cannot function adequately until the feelings involved are brought to awareness and are understood.

Support and clarification are two essential elements. Because of the accompanying affect, the patient is unable to act on the solutions which he himself may have come upon or which he was helped to arrive at. The support of the therapist, as a parent surrogate, and his permissiveness release the necessary ego strengths which are otherwise blocked by fear, anxiety, guilt, superego prohibitions, and other similar intrapsychic, as well as circumstantial, impediments.

One of the dynamics operative in this process is the *reduction of the ego load* through communication and objectification. The dilemma in which the patient finds himself is, at least in part, due to the strain to which the ego is subjected. This strain is a result of the unconscious urge to act and an equally unconscious (and sometimes conscious) fear or guilt as to the outcome of the act. This conflict not only engenders ambivalence, hesitancy, and vacillation, but consumes much of the ego energies that could otherwise be used for action. By exposing the elements involved in the conflict, a resolution can be expected which will clear the decks for decisive action. The ego energies bound up in conflict are released to carry out the intention.

Several factors are involved, of which clarification is the first. But, in most instances, such clarification cannot be achieved without elimination of the feelings of guilt, fear or anger that may be involved. Since, in guidance, these are not traced to their neurotic sources, improvement is accomplished by the therapist's support, that is, by his empathy, acceptance, and permissiveness.

He thus assumes a superego role. It is obviously impossible to delineate, with any degree of definiteness, a specific role that anyone, let alone a therapist, plays in life to the exclusion of all others. But it seems clear that in counseling, the counselor is predominantly an auxiliary or supportive ego to the ego of the counselee. In guidance, he serves in that capacity as well, but his additional role is one of counteracting superego prohibitions and so-called "pangs of conscience." This latter role predominates over his ego-supportive functions.

When the patient is brought into greater harmony with himself, and the conflictual syndrome is dissolved, other dynamic elements are set into operation (which we have already indicated). There are the clearing of the way for action and the development of the capacity to mobilize ego energies for that action.

From the nature of the process involved, it can be seen that guidance requires a considerably longer period of time than counseling and involves many more interviews (the exact number of which is determined by the needs and capacities of a given patient and the depth and intensity of the affect involved). In guidance, even though feelings are dealt with on a superficial level, establishing the necessary transference attitudes takes considerable time, which varies with each individual. Also, to prevent shock or hurt to the patient, it is often necessary to move slowly, until he is able to confront his own feelings and his own part in creating his difficulties. These, and other factors, delay or extend the process far beyond that of the more direct approach employed in counseling.

In most instances, groups accelerate the guidance process. Group guidance, especially when the problems of the participants are of a similar nature, is not only more economical but is actually more effective. Exploration of the elements involved in the dilemmas of the participants is greatly accelerated by their interactions and by the light thrown by the ensuing interchange. Of even greater help is the removal of guilt and the feeling of difference and uniqueness, which results from the patients' similarities. The discovery that one is not alone or peculiar in having problems and seeking help reduces stigma and guilt and preserves one's self-esteem. These steps are extremely valuable in freeing ego energies and strengthening the ability to carry out decisions. Universalization reduces inner constraint and corrects superego demands.

The experience of belonging to, and being accepted by, a group is far more gratifying to the patients or clients for whom guidance is indicated than would be acceptance by only one individual. Both the symbolic and biological significance of a group and the satisfaction of instinctive social hunger enhance the individual's confidence and security. They dispose him toward more socially approved reactions and relationships, in addition to the release and help that they supply. An accepting, harmonious group helps each participant to grow disposed toward feelings and behavior that, not infrequently, automatically resolve environmental conflicts and difficulties. This is in addition to the clarifying and supportive effect the group discussions may have.

As stated, a guidance group is more effective when its members are preoccupied with the same or similar problems. The practice of forming groups for marital or premarital problems, family problems, parents of children with problems, or special handicaps or illnesses, adolescents, delinquents, etc., is sound, from this point of view. This type of homogeneity crystallizes the group into a unit in which each member identifies with the others and all are able to help each other because of emotional empathy and mutual understanding. Such homogeneity also favors universalization, from which reduction of feelings of guilt and uniqueness results. Group "cohesiveness" of this nature, not desirable in psychotherapeutic groups, is essential in guidance groups.

Unlike counseling, guidance requires that the group leader be a professionally trained person with experience in psychotherapy. Guidance borders on psychotherapy, in so far as it deals with and aims at correcting feelings, the nature and sources of which have to be understood by the therapist, even though they may not be deeply involved in the process; that is, they are not worked through in their relation to unconscious and repressed memories, associated affects, and the bound-up anxiety. If the leader (therapist) is not qualified to work on this deeper level, much harm may result to some patients from his guidance work. The technique of guidance, and also its aim, is to hold anxiety within narrow boundaries, for once it reaches high intensity, its abatement can be achieved only by working it through, which involves psychotherapy and means the procedure has to be altered as a result (a development that may be undesirable either for clinical or practical reasons or both). In some instances, however, guidance may be a planned preliminary step as an easement to or a motivation for psychotherapy.

The leader-therapist, in both individual and group guidance, must at all times be aware of the "threat areas" of patients. He has to be equipped to recognize the onset of anxiety beyond permissible levels in each patient and, when he works with groups, in the group as a whole. This is essential, for the forced transition into psychotherapy that would result may prove deleterious to patients who had not been selected and grouped with that intent in mind. Criteria for the two practices are in very telling respects at variance with each other. Thus, the leader-therapist needs to be able to employ skills other than those in psychotherapy. Much of his efforts have to be bent toward *avoidance, instead of the unrestricted exploration* involved in uncovering and free catharsis. The latter are employed only to the extent that they bring feelings and behavior to awareness and give them their proper significance in the client's current life and relationships. They are not employed for reconstruction of his personality, however, though some changes are inevitable (as is the case with every significant experience in life).

When deeper recesses of the repressed painful memories in the unconscious are activated, the leader-therapist must deflect the flow of communication. However, such stratagems have to be employed in a manner that does not appear authoritarian, rejecting, or interfering. Many psychotherapists find it difficult to adapt their techniques to guidance. Almost imperceptibly, they "slip into" therapy, often with deleterious effects. They have to be constantly "pulled back" during supervision for long periods before their awareness is fixed and controls established. (For further discussion, see Slavson, 1958.)

PSYCHOTHERAPY

A distinct difference between guidance and psychotherapy is that communication, in the latter, is *free associative*. It is only occasionally centered around a current topic, while in counseling and guidance, current and specific topics are the pattern of the interviews or discussions. However, in psychotherapy as well, patients do talk for a period about *top realities*, but these periods are transient, part of a larger intent—intrapsychic change. Unlike the counselor and guidance worker, solving practical problems is not the ultimate concern of the psychotherapist.

Free association cannot but bring forth painful memories, highly charged feelings and anxiety. None of these are permitted to make their appearance in guidance, and cannot occur in counseling, by its very nature. The ego defenses are, of necessity, threatened in psychotherapy, which sets up resistances to communication (catharsis). The analysis of these resistances are an integral part of psychotherapy, as are the various transference reactions. Within broad limits, no precautions are taken against arousing anxiety. "Threat areas," that is, areas within which anxiety, guilt, hostility, and resistances are mobilized, are not respected. As these reactions make their appearance, the psychotherapist does not deflect them or retreat from them. Rather, since they reveal the real personality of the patient, he encourages their manifestations so that they can be used in the therapeutic process.

The aim in psychotherapy is not to resolve a single conflictual situation or an external relationship syndrome. *The aim is to change the personality structure more or less permanently,* so that it may function more adequately. As already pointed out, this involves correction of each of the intrapsychic triad—id, ego, and superego—and their balance and relations. The aim of counseling and guidance then, is to help the individual to deal with *specific* situations, while that of psychotherapy is to make him permanently capable of dealing with *any* situation. Ego weaknesses and dependency may in no way be affected by counseling; they are improved in relation to a specific problem in guidance and may even be carried over to other related functions purely as *secondary outcomes;* but in psychotherapy, these are *primary* aims and the psychotherapist directs his efforts toward achieving them.

This involves the development of insight in the patient, in addition to recognition and understanding, a process that necessitates reduction or elimination of ego defenses and emotional rigidities, as well as the less important fact of intellectual comprehension. Emotional and transference regression, an integral part of the therapeutic process, is either absent or is held within boundaries in counseling and guidance. In psychotherapy, traumatic memories, ensconced in the catacombs of the unconscious, and their associated disturbing feelings, are dislodged and examined in the light of their current significance and existing adult realities, which is avoided in the other two practices. Here, only reality-testing and minimal transference reactions are employed. The leader-therapist remains as passive as the counselee or guidee will allow him to, but, by the very nature of the intent, he is more active than he would be in psychotherapy. In the latter case, his activity is one of periodic assertion and withdrawal, the assertive role being assumed when interpretation or explanations are indicated, or when resistance blockage sets in which the patient cannot break through on his own.

The course of therapy is fraught with much ambivalence and resistance; it oscillates between positive and negative transference feelings, communication and silence, confidence and distrust, frankness, deceit, and avoidance. All these have to be worked through as products of conscious and unconscious needs and causes. The patients pass through mood swings between elation and depression, submission, hostility, and aggression, expansivenes and diffidence. These need to be observed and their meanings understood. All this takes a very long time, much longer than does guidance and even more so than counseling. Much of the time is consumed in evolving a positive transference, so that patients will grow secure enough to reveal themselves. This relation is strongly tinged with sexual libido. The therapist is invested with strong libidinal significance and may become the patient's sexual object or aim. While the degree of regression to the pre-oedipal and pregenital stages is at its height in true psychoanalysis, the patients' attitudes, in all real psychotherapy, are colored by these irrational, infantile strivings.

In groups, as in individual treatment, transferences and resistances are explored and interpreted and their libidinal components uncovered; they are traced to unconscious sources, determinants, and traumata (which is avoided in counseling and guidance).

CASE ILLUSTRATIONS

After the preceding theoretic discussion of counseling, guidance, and psychotherapy, it may prove helpful to illustrate their application to the actual situations one meets in clinical practice.

A woman was referred for treatment by her husband, because of her unending conflicts with her two sons, sixteen and twelve years old respectively. Her main complaint was that they did not keep their room in proper order. The constant haggling had, for years, engendered a climate of tension in the home, and the husband, being of an unassertive and passive disposition, felt disturbed but helpless. The older boy was exceptionally brilliant in his schoolwork and gave promise of becoming an outstanding scientist. His father also had a quasi-scientific occupation.

During the only interview held with this woman she elaborated and reiterated her annoyance with her boys. Her special preoccupation was with the "messy" condition of the boys' dresser drawers, the disorder in which they were kept, and the difficulty in finding things in them. She spoke feelingly about the subject. It seemed to have great meaning to her.

At one point during her recital, the therapist (counselor) asked: "How long have you been trying to teach your sons to be orderly with their dresser drawers?" "Oh, about seven or eight years with the older boy," was the answer. The therapist then smilingly asked: "Isn't it possible that since you did not succeed in teaching them for so long a time, you may have used a wrong method?" "What can one do then?" asked the woman. "I don't clearly know, not knowing all the facts. One way, of course, is for you to straighten up the drawers for them. Another is to let them keep their drawers in whatever shape suits them." This seemed quite unacceptable to her, though she did not respond verbally.

We were aware that this woman did not intend to return for further interviews and that her complaints would not be worked through, and we waited for an opportunity to say something that would be of significance to her. Toward the end of the hour she said: "I can't understand it! My father who lives with us is such an immaculate and orderly person, why can't they be like him?" The therapist in a calm voice responded: "Well, then he has some other faults. No one is without faults." The woman seemed somewhat startled and for a brief moment remained silent, and then as though speaking to herself said quietly: "That's true; he never earned a living." With this the interview ended. The therapist did not give her the opportunity to go on with this topic or to decrease the impact of her discovery.

On meeting the therapist informally some months later, the husband said: "We have no more trouble in my home about the boys' orderliness. What did you do to my wife? She keeps on talking about you and what a bright man you are!"

The above example of a rather simple procedure illustrates the process of counseling. Obviously there were considerable unconscious determinants in this woman's attitudes and values; chief among these was her need to please her father. This remained untouched. She had the intelligence to understand the principle involved (that each person has some faults) and the ego strength to bring herself under control. It is our belief that the abrupt ending of the interview which prevented the diminishing of the impact of her own formulation about her father was a major determinant in her changed behavior.

Another illustration of counseling, that also took up only one session but was emotionally somewhat more complex, was that of the woman, referred by her family physician, planning for her eight-year-old daughter's schooling. She wanted her girl to attend a certain private school with a progressive education program, but hesitated to send her there. The woman was separated from her husband, a medical specialist, toward whom she entertained intense hostility and distrust.

Her communication of almost a full hour, was consumed in discussing her indecision about her daughter's school plans. We were puzzled throughout as to what was actually on her mind, since it was clear that she strongly favored the school in question as against any other. We guessed that the husband had something to do with her difficulty. A few questions revealed that, by court order, her husband was allowed to see the girl for a half day each week at his apartment and during parts of the summer holiday. It became evident that the mother was disturbed by the relation between the father and daughter. We then asked how the girl reacted to her visits. With considerable emotion, the mother said: "My daughter thinks he is a horrid man! And she is right." "By the way," we asked, "where does he live?" The woman seemed to be taken aback, reddened, and in a somewhat subdued voice said: "He lives right across the street from the school." "Are you afraid that your husband will see your daughter more often and will alienate her from you?" we asked rather directly. "Yes," was the answer, delivered almost in a whisper.

We then explained to this worried woman that a young child, especially a girl, has an intense need for its mother and the fact of current residence being with the mother, and not the father, strengthened the feeling to such a degree that no one could alienate the child from her. In addition, the girl's own statements concerning her father (which of course may have been a blind for the girl's strong affection for him—but this we did not touch upon) should give her no concern on that score. The woman meekly asked: "Do you really think so?" "Not only do I think so, but I would stake my professional reputation on it," was our unequivocal response. The woman visibly relaxed.

The referring family physician reported later that the girl was placed in the school in question without any unpleasant consequences and that the woman had been most pleased with the "guidance" she had received.

A more complicated situation was presented by Mrs. J. who,

though requiring psychotherapy to fully solve her problem, was able for practical reasons to receive only guidance.

Mrs. J. sought help for herself because she was concerned about her increasing need for alcohol, her marital incompatibility, and general restlessness. At the very first interview, she spoke of her problem with her husband who was indifferent to sexual intercourse because, she thought, of his excessive masturbation. She and her husband were of different religions and she insisted on adhering to her own, even though it was a verbal adherence rather than a ritualistic one. Mrs. J. continued coming for interviews on a weekly basis. She later revealed that she had had extramarital sexual relations and had a general tendency to flirt. She was "on the make," in her own words.

Mrs. J. was not a very attractive woman. Her dress and general personality tended to be slovenly. Despite her flirtatiousness, she obviously was not interested in making herself attractive or "playing up" her femininity. As the interviews progressed she spoke of her feelings about her father and mother. The former was a likable and kindly man whom she adored, but she did not go into her fantasies or wishes about him, nor was she encouraged to do so. She saw her mother as a hostile, domineering woman whom she disliked. Here, too, Mrs. J. was permitted to ventilate her feelings without arousing or exploring their deeper libidinal significance.

Gradually, Mrs. J. displayed some understanding of father's role in her relations to men. She began to feel greater warmth toward her husband and their sexual relations improved. She no longer emphasized the religious difference between them. She stopped drinking. Preceding these developments, she had begun to dress more carefully; she had improved her coiffure and presented a neater appearance generally. Altogether, there were forty-six interviews.

There was considerable unconscious material that actually should have been brought out in this case; however, due to a number of practical factors it was deemed inadvisable to launch into a full course of psychotherapy. Individual guidance was, therefore, pursued. We felt that group guidance would not be suitable for her. Mrs. J. came for help because of a specific problem—heavy drinking. If this were all, she could have been placed in a group; but her sexual maladjustment and delinquencies, home and religious conflicts, masculine identifications, and homosexual trends, if brought out in a group, would create more anxiety than a guidance group could tolerate. These problems can be treated in a therapy group after a course of individual psychotherapy. Individual guidance served only to pull her out of the confusion in which she had found herself at the time. How long she remained "in the clear" is not known.

The last case is that of a man who, at the age of forty-two, found himself unable to go to his office and was generally in such a state of anxiety and restlessness that his relations with his wife and children deteriorated to a degree that alarmed him. He had suffered from this state of anxiety for more than a year. At first he was able to "force" himself to go to the office a few times a week and a fast automobile drive would usually dissipate his tensions. In time, however, these remedies no longer had any effect on him. He was unable to go to his office altogether and his car jaunts only made him more tense.

When he called on the phone, an appointment was made for him for four o'clock in the afternoon. After he stated his problem, we asked him to tell us something about his current family and later about his parental home. As a young man, whose mother was dead, he had worked for his father, now also dead, in a small business. The father cooked most of the meals in a small apartment, which the patient, his father, and a brother occupied. They ate most of the meals together and also kept house. The mother had died when the patient was about sixteen years old and he spoke of her in glowing terms—her kindliness and "goodness," and her warmth and patience. He described how deeply he had mourned her death. The father never remarried. According to the patient, his own sexual adjustment was entirely adequate.

We let Mr. K. talk for an hour and a half, trying to get a clue to his reactions and behavior, but we could not identify the *nuclear problem.* Evidently he had left something out. We then told him to come in the next morning at 8:30 A.M. He was instructed not to engage himself in any business enterprises or other matters that would divert him, but to come to the office directly after breakfast.

The next morning we asked him if he had anything to add to what he had told us the evening before, and he told us that three of his friends, about his own age, had recently died in quick succession, and he described in detail how he had learned, from a woman acquaintance, of the death of one of them, during a visit to a hospital where one of his boyhood friends was confined.

I told him quite directly: "Your present severe anxiety was brought on by the deaths of your friends and this is somewhat connected with the death of your mother."

This statement seemed to open up the sluices of his locked-up memories which now came tumbling out in quick succession. One of the significant memories was that for some years after his mother's death, he had vomited whenever he ate *between* meals. He was able to hold the three regular meals, but could not retain even slight refreshments, such as ice cream, between meals.

Apparently the death of his contemporaries, who obviously had strong emotional meaning to him, had reawakened the anxiety hysteria dormant for a quarter of a century.

Mr. K. was advised to submit to a thoroughgoing psychoanalysis.

Perhaps a situation involving differential application of counseling, guidance, and psychotherapy, in a single complaint may further clarify the differences between them.

A man comes to us having consistent bad reactions to his employer, as a result of which he finds it difficult to adjust to his job and his fellow employees and is in a constant state of irritation, worry, and economic insecurity. Several (and sometimes only one) interviews may reveal that his antipathy toward his boss is displaced on fellow employees because of his *general state* of dissatisfaction and irritability and, what is more important in such a situation, they may reveal the source of his attitude toward his employer.

This may be (1) characterological incompatibility, ideological conflict, or difference in opinions as to the conduct of the job; (2) a result of the patient's generalized rebellion against authority as a continuation of his attitude toward significant figures in his childhood; or (3) reaction formation of unconscious passive homosexual and submissive wishes toward the employer. In most instances, counseling would be indicated in dealing with cases in the first category, group guidance may be sufficient for persons in the second, and psychotherapy is essential for the third.

DYNAMIC DIFFERENTIALS

If we consider work with groups from the point of view of therapeutic dynamics and aims, we find that the difference is both in degree and in kind.[1] The aims of a thoroughgoing psychotherapy are: libido redistribution, ego strengthening, correction of the superego, and improvement of the self-image. The dynamics by which these are achieved are: transference, catharsis, insight, reality testing, and the acquisition of sublimations.

In counseling, the libido is largely not involved; in guidance, it is only involved to a minimal extent; in psychotherapy, however, it is a major focal point. In counseling, the ego is strengthened only in relation to a specific situation, as a result of the support it receives from the counselor. In guidance, it may be strengthened, in addition, by the removal of the drain to which it had been subjected by conflictual emotions. Once the conflicts are eliminated, the load the ego had borne is reduced. In psychotherapy, the same results are obtained but to a much greater extent and on a much deeper level. Heightened self-esteem (self-image) always results from psychotherapy; it is also partially achieved through guidance and may be affected in counseling also, but to a limited or almost negligible degree.

Therapeutic dynamics are also variously involved. We have already indicated that transference is of a superficial nature; it is

[1] These and other therapeutic elements and dynamics are described more fully in the next chapter.

fleeting and of shallow intensity in counseling; it is considerably more intense and more prolonged in guidance and is of heightened strength, with concomitant fantasies and wishes toward the therapist, in psychotherapy. In counseling and guidance, transference feelings are uniformly positive, while in psychotherapy, they pass through positive and negative phases.

The relative content and depth of communication and catharsis in the three techniques have already been elaborated in considerable detail and will, therefore, not be repeated here (this also applies to insight). Concerning reality testing, it can be said that in counseling, the reality testing is confined to the specific problem under consideration. A person who is selected for counseling has the capacity for general reality testing (as contrasted with reality perception). If he is not adequately capable of it, counseling would not be the procedure of choice.

There is the probability that the capacity for reality testing in those patients who are selected for guidance may be of a low level, especially in the areas or relations in which they experience difficulties, and would require special attention. In psychotherapy, especially in group psychotherapy, the interpersonal impacts of the group-as-a-whole are tangible realities forcing awareness upon each participant and requiring of him new perceptions and new adjustments. Reality testing in groups, therefore, forms an important element in the therapeutic process.

Development of sublimations of instinctual urges is not an objective in counseling or in guidance. Persons selected for these types of help usually have acquired either adequate sublimations or repressions, as measured in terms of the average population. The fact that they have difficulties with some specific problem does not indicate real pathology. When the latter is present, the patient is placed in either individual or group psychotherapy, or in both, depending on the need.

Para-Analytic Group Psychotherapy

We employ the term *para-analytic group psychotherapy* to designate a type of therapy which, though having the same base and orientation as analytic therapy, is lesser in depth. While the problems of some patients may still stem from the unconscious, the process of their therapy cannot, for a variety of reasons, proceed along conventional analytic lines and is modified accordingly. Instead of employing free association and predominant therapist passivity, the prevailing subjects of the interviews may be top realities and their content drawn from the conscious and the preconscious, rather than regressive memories and feelings and recall from the unconscious as is the case in psychoanalytic therapy.

There are individual patients and categories of patients for whom a lesser depth of uncovering is indicated, but for whom counseling and guidance would be inadequate, because their superficial nature would not solve the patients' problems. There are also patients whose difficulties require intellectual clarity or change in attitude, which they cannot achieve without first dissolving some rigidities and resistances. However, despite this need, the patients' egos could not withstand the assailment and stress of a fully uncovering, analytic therapy, and a less stressful procedure has to be employed.

We shall describe at some length, later in this volume, the precautionary measures necessary in the treatment of latent and borderline schizophrenic patients, but at this juncture it can be said that though an analytically oriented therapy can be employed with some of them, it must be of a low degree of uncovering and exploration. When concepts of a depth nature are employed, great care must be exercised against causing disturbance or agitation in such patients.

Another category of patients for whom lesser depth therapy is indicated is adolescents. The state of maturity and life experiences of adolescents makes them unfit for introspective plumbing of the unconscious. The surface nature of their incestuous and libidinal urges and their transferential antagonism to adults (and, therefore, the therapist) militate against their entering into a relation and into their own psyche, as required by a true analytic therapy (Slavson, 1958). On the other hand, adolescents whose inner stress brings them to therapy, cannot be helped by counseling or guidance alone. Consequently, another approach is needed

—*para-analytic group psychotherapy,* the treatment of choice for most adolescents.

Para-analytic group psychotherapy is also most suitable for the aged (not the senile), whose descending libidinal quantum and ascending egotistic drives engender a radical reorganization of their psychic structure. In the treatment of patients in this category, limits to self-confrontation and the unraveling of unconscious strivings have to be tightly drawn, partly because of diminishing inner resources and partly because of the automatic and largely unconscious disengagement process that goes on in all elderly and aging persons.

The comparative dynamics of para-analytic psychotherapy are as follows: transference is of the same level of intensity as in analytic groups; catharsis is considerably less regressive than in the latter; the same levels of insight cannot be reached in para-analytic, as in analytic, therapy (though they are much higher than in guidance); and reality testing and sublimations are more or less of the same nature. The greatest difference, and the most telling one, is the activity of the therapist. In para-analytic group psychotherapy, the therapist is much more active in leading and also, at times, directing the interviews. He offers explanations and interpretations, suggests ideas, principles, philosophies and guides for conduct and living, and he may assume the role of a discussion leader at certain points. However, as in analytic psychotherapy, he follows the leads and cues from the group and is careful to relate comments and questions to the subjective meanings and unconscious strivings of the patients, although universalizing them more often than personalizing them.

In para-analytic group therapy, dreams are employed just as they are in analytic groups and unconscious material is allowed to come through and is utilized to advance interviews whenever indicated, or avoided when it is not to therapeutic advantage. Actually, para-analytic maneuvers and levels are employed in *all* types of individual and group psychotherapy, as they are needed, except that they are of transitory duration and short lived, while with patients requiring therapy of lesser intensity, para-analytic procedures form the major pattern of the treatment.

The general rules for the application of para-analytic psychotherapy are as follows: the therapist must not press for regression in his patients to deep levels of the unconscious; the interviews consist predominantly of top realities, dealing with current problems and preoccupations; only a minimal level of anxiety is permissible; rise of the anxiety level has to be prevented, allayed or diverted; introspective or uncovering therapy, if used at all, needs to follow the acquisition of "psychologic literacy" which involves conceptual understanding (as differentiated from emotional insight) ; free association is not demanded or expected; rather, associated thinking is prevalent, that is, horizontal association of ideas, thoughts, feelings and events (as differentiated from vertical, regressive free association); the therapist is much more active than in analytic psychotherapy; and by-and-large, the therapist addresses himself to behavioral patterns of the patients and their ego functioning and is less concerned with the libido and superego than he would be in analytic therapy.

The following condensed record of a session of a group of 16-year-old boys illustrates some of the above precepts. Six boys were present, all intellectually superior, well-informed, and sophisticated, but emotionally rather immature. All have been referred by the high school authorities, because of underachievement.

Thomas and Kim came on time; the others came in late. The therapist and the two boys began the session and Thomas initiated a discussion of the various types of "ham" radio equipment, of which he had a considerable variety. Thomas was very interested in the subject and held forth with an air of authority. The therapist asked a few questions and this warmed Thomas up to the subject. After a while, Kim changed the subject to school by asking Thomas what his best subject was. Thomas said that he was doing "all right in math and getting pretty good marks in other subjects." French was the most difficult subject for him, he said. Kim offered a solution to the problem by saying, "Why don't you think in French when you are doing math. That way you'll get practice in a difficult subject while you're doing a good subject." At this point the other four boys came in: Bernard, Richard, Abe, and Stanley. The four boys, who came together from the school they all attended, displayed a spirit of camaraderie. [Abe, who was referred because he was an isolate and had no friends, glowed with pleasure at having made friends now and was in a somewhat boisterous mood, which was rare for him as he usually appeared rather stolid.]

The boys had obviously been to a refreshment stand. Stanley was holding a package of French fried potatoes and Bernard was sipping malted milk from a paper cup. The gay mood continued as the boys took their seats. Bernard sat to the therapist's right and Stanley to his left. Richard and Abe took their usual seats. Stanley (an aggressive boy, bordering on delinquency) at once proceeded to tease Thomas about not having any French fried potatoes. Thomas did not respond to him.

When the gaiety died down somewhat, the therapist blocked further hilarity by turning to Thomas and saying, "We were talking about French, weren't we, Tom?" A brief silence ensued, but Thomas soon responded by declaring that it was just a pretty difficult subject for him. Kim repeated his suggestion about thinking in French when doing mathematics. Stanley poked fun at this suggestion. Richard, however, proceeded to talk about his dislike of his teachers, especially his French teacher, who was "very strict" and always insisted "on things being done a certain way." Abe expressed his dislike of his English teacher who, he said, was very British; in fact, came from England. If a boy did something the teacher didn't like, the boy had to write on a piece of paper, one hundred times, "I will not talk in class again." The therapist tried to pull together the boys' feelings toward teachers by saying, "I get the feeling that there's something all teachers do that you boys don't like." Stanley actively responded to this remark as though he expected it and became facetious. He mumbled something to Richard that brought forth laughter from the latter. The therapist asked Richard what Stanley had mumbled. He didn't answer, but his face reddened as if he had been caught at something prohibited. Bernard said, "You don't have to mumble here, Dick, you can talk right out."

Stanley began to talk about a teacher whom he called "mumbles." This teacher, he said, expected you to learn, but he walked around talking under his breath and nobody could understand what he said. Abe, Stanley, Richard, and Bernard actively described teachers they did not like. Bernard summed it up by saying, "When I'm in a class with a teacher who pushes me around, I can't think any more. I stop studying and learning in that class."

The therapist said, "You know, I get the feeling that sometimes you boys get a feeling about a teacher even before the teacher does anything." Stanley said, "I always do that. Somebody tells me so-and-so is no good and I walk into class waiting to have a fight, and the teacher hasn't done anything to warrant a fight." Richard agreed, saying that sometimes boys develop opinions about teachers not out of their own experience, but based on what they have been told by other boys. Bernard asked the therapist whether this was unusual. The therapist said, "Not particularly unusual, but I wonder if sometimes feelings about teachers don't come from experiences with someone else that a teacher might remind one of." Richard immediately said, "All teachers remind me of my mother. I always expect a teacher to give me a hard time the way my mother does." At this point, Stanley (who was in inordinate conflict with his mother) began to act up. He said something the therapist didn't hear and then said to Richard, "Your problems are your sister, you just aint getting enough." (Obviously a sexual reference.) Richard broke into forced and embarrassed laughter. (Richard's sister was adopted about eight months before he was born.)

Bernard tapped the therapist on the forearm and went on to tell him: "When I get into a class and I see a teacher that looks like my father, I know I am in for trouble." Therapist: "What do you mean?" Bernard: "I'm having problems with my father. He keeps telling me not to steal the car. I don't get that guy. You know what my father used to tell me? He always used to brag to me about how when he was a kid, about thirteen years, he used to burn out the clutch of his father's car. He and his father always used to fight because he was stealing his old man's

121

car. Now he tells me not to steal his car!" Stanley said, "Well that is how parents are, sometimes. They're always telling you what not to do because they did it themselves." The therapist voiced interest in this seeming contradiction, saying "You mean your parents tell you not to do things that they themselves did?" Richard joined the discussion and said, "That always happens. For instance my mother always tries to teach me nice manners and how to behave, and all I have to do is look at my mother and see how rough she is when she talks to people and I know there is something screwy here."

Kim became uncomfortable and said, "Don't pay attention to your parents. Parents are people. Just treat them like people. This shouldn't be any problem." Richard jumped in and told Kim to "shut up. I've heard this from you last time." Kim did not pursue the subject.

As Bernard was lighting a cigarette, he was reading the printing on the package and said, "According to this, I'm going to get a grade A cancer." Everybody, including the therapist, burst into laughter. At this, Stanley said, "Let's sit here and tell dirty jokes." This suggestion was met by giggling from the boys and Richard asked, "Okay, why don't you tell a dirty joke?" Stanley pulled back at this, looking embarrassed. Richard said, "Okay fellers, let's tell dirty jokes." [There was a teasing quality in his manner.] The therapist countered by asking, "By the way, do any of you have an idea why dirty jokes are so popular in our society?" Abe responded by telling a story about his being in Chicago and going to a night club where a comedian was telling jokes. The best ones were the "dirty ones. Everyone laughed the loudest at them." The therapist took advantage of this and explained that "dirty jokes" are popular because one of the subjects about which it is most difficult to talk is sex, so people get around "that little man who is a censor inside of them" by telling jokes. Richard said, "I get a funny feeling telling a dirty joke in your presence." Stanley facetiously suggested that the therapist leave the room so the boys could sit around and tell "dirty jokes." The therapist asked, "What makes it so hard for you to tell such jokes when I am in the room?" Stanley scratched his head and said, "It's

funny talking about this subject in front of a grown man."
Bernard leaned over and asked the therapist, "Can I ask you a
personal question?" Therapist: "Go ahead." Bernard: "Are you
married?" Therapist: "Yes." Bernard: "It's even harder telling
dirty jokes in front of a married man." Richard: "It's funny
talking sex in front of a grown person." The therapist: "Has it
never happened to you?" Richard: "No." Therapist: "Well, I am
glad you boys were able to tell me how you feel about it."

Suddenly, Bernard began to talk about his father and the fact
that his father was punishing him for having "stolen" his car.
(Bernard made it a practice to drive the family car illegally, as
the father consistently left the keys in the car overnight.) His
father prohibited his leaving the house for several nights. Bernard said his father was very upset and did not know what to do.
The therapist said, "What would you expect your father to do,
Bernard?" A sudden silence fell on the group, with Bernard
saying, "That is a good question. I think my father doesn't know
what to do with me anymore." Abe said, "Why do you take the
car?" Bernard replied, "Just for fun." "Just for fun?" the therapist asked. Bernard turned to the therapist and said, "That's not
the whole reason. I want to get even with my father. I am mad.
I am so mad I just want to hurt him." The therapist said, "Can
you tell your father how you feel?" Bernard responded, "Not in
the way I can tell you how I feel. My father doesn't listen to
me. I don't see any difference between my father and Hitler.
When I try to explain to my father how I feel, he takes his
fist and he pounds the table and says, 'Children don't talk back.'
So what am I supposed to do? I want to hurt, and I'm hurting
him by taking the car." (As a result of further discussions,
Bernard came to recognize the absurdity of his behavior and,
about ten weeks later, stopped "stealing" the car.)

Stanley spoke up, saying that his father was planning to punish
him by prohibiting his leaving the house the following week end.
He felt that it was an empty threat, because his father and mother were going away for the week end, and how could his parents
enforce the punishment since they would be away? Bernard asked
what had happened. Stanley said he had come home late one

123

night after a party. It was eleven o'clock. "How can you get home from a party at eleven o'clock when the fun just begins to happen around 10:30?" he asked. This brought forth a discussion, concerning parties, between Abe, Richard, Bernard, and Stanley, and about how unfair it was to be forced to come home at 10:30 or 11:00 when the fun just starts. Richard and Stanley were jokingly suggesting ways of "getting even with parents," such as not "showing up at all," etc. The therapist said, "It seems from what you are saying, boys, that a lot of your time is spent thinking about how to get even." Richard: "You're not kidding! I even dream about it. Like once I dreamt I saw my mother dead." Stanley: "A boy I know dreamt that he saw his mother on the ground and an elephant had its paw on her head." Bernard laughed at this and said, "I bet the mother said, 'Hey cut that out, you stupid elephant.'" All laughed uproariously.

When the laughter subsided, Stanley changed the subject by saying "a couple of the boys in school want to get into this group," and he asked the therapist if it would be all right to invite "guests." The therapist asked the boys what would be the purpose of having guests, and Stanley said, "A lot of boys at school have problems with their parents and they have nowhere to talk about it, and they know about this group and maybe they can talk about it here." "I have nothing to do with having boys come to the group, but if you wish, these boys can apply to the Center and get into a group," the therapist replied. Stanley said, "Well, maybe they ought to apply to the school psychologist first, because that is how most of the boys got to the Center." The therapist agreed that that might be a good idea.

Stanley then said, "Okay, boys, I'll tell you a dirty joke now." Richard said, "Oh, come on, Stanley, cut it out." Abe (the shy, inhibited boy), however, kept urging Stanley to tell the joke and Stanley very embarrassingly told a story about two nuns who were walking down the street. One said to the other, "My brassiere is awfully tight. My tits hurt." The other responded: "Oh, such a way to talk! That's a horrible way to talk!" The first nun: "So what should I say, my cup runneth over?" This brought laughter from the boys.

When the laughter had subsided, the therapist asked the boys, "Have any of you had a chance to talk about this subject with adults?" Richard said, "You mean sex? Yeh. You should hear the way me and my mother talk about it." He then said that he had a very good friend to whose home he went every so often. One day, for seemingly no reason at all, his mother told him not to go to this friend's house. Richard wanted to know the reason and his mother seemed to become infuriated and said to him, "I'm sick and tired of you and your friend masturbating one another." Abe then narrated how his father once tried to discuss sex with him, but gave him a "very scholarly lecture about animals." He summed it up by saying, "My father made sex sound like a pretty dry subject." Bernard told how his father always "lectured him on never using dirty words." Once Bernard went to his father's office and was sitting in the outer room while his father was on the phone. His father did not know that he was outside and he heard his father using "atrocious language on the phone." Bernard added, "I guess that is okay, but my using dirty words once in a while aggravates him."

Stanley again began to act up by teasing Richard about masturbation. He said with an air of bravado, "Beating the meat is good for you." Bernard said, "Yeah, I guess it is good for you," but it was quite obvious from the tone of the boys' voices that they had a great deal of anxiety about it. The therapist commented, rather casually, that most boys, in growing up, have a lot of questions about this subject and sometimes are not so sure of the answers. Richard became very serious and said, "Can you get hurt from, you know, masturbating?" Therapist: "What do you mean, Richard?" Richard: "My mother told me it would ruin my married life if I masturbate." Therapist: "Masturbation is a normal part of growing up the same way that eating is a normal part of living. But you know that overeating, or eating all the time isn't very good. The same applies to masturbation." (This subject was discussed in later sessions and the mental health aspect was considered.) Stanley asked, "Is it true that you can get syphilis from masturbating?" Therapist: "Syphilis from masturbating?" Bernard: "Yeh, venereal disease." Stanley explained that his father had once told him that if he masturbated he would get venereal disease, or syphilis. Therapist: "Stanley, masturbation does not lead to syphilis." Stanley: "That's what I thought. I always thought that syphilis comes from having intercourse, but my father made me feel that if I masturbate I'll go crazy in the head."

It was now some minutes past time and the session ended at this point. (Note: Two months later the therapist gave the boys information on sex, pregnancy, and birth, illustrated with charts in textbooks.)

PSYCHONURSING

Counseling and guidance can be viewed as forms of *psychonursing*. Since no fundamental cure is sought or attained, the client or patient may be expected to return whenever he is presented with a difficulty in the future. In practice, this form of "nursing" is frequently all one can achieve with many very disturbed and also psychotic patients, and with patients whose resistances, intellectual or psychological limitations, or constitutional deficiencies impose limits on therapeutic effort. One should not underestimate the value of this form of practice. In a striking number of cases it enhances the mental health of the community, through preventing or diminishing conflict and tension; it helps to establish harmony between the individual and his environment and in crucial interpersonal relations such as marital and family relations, in employment, and in general social adjustment. As we have attempted to show, this can be achieved in comparatively few interviews, or it may be a prolonged process, even longer than psychotherapy. In fact, many a course in individual or group treatment is actually guidance or psychonursing, according to our definitions.

In the treatment of borderline or latent schizophrenic patients, whose ego integration is at best tenuous, a prolonged period of counseling and guidance is essential. In the majority of cases, this is all that would be allowed, so as to prevent the ego fragmentation that could result from deep psychotherapy. However, in less serious cases, especially in those of pseudoschizophrenia, psychotherapy may be cautiously attempted after ego reinforcement and strengthening of the defensive structure are achieved through the less threatening procedures of counseling and guidance, i.e., psychonursing (which may be required for decades in a case of true schizophrenia).[2] Psychonursing is employed with senile patients, with persons with physical or mental deficiencies, the intellectually retarded, and with dying patients.

The findings of this chapter can be briefly summarized as follows: *Through counseling and guidance we help people; through psychotherapy we change them.*

<hr />

[2] For a fuller discussion of this topic see Chapter XVI.

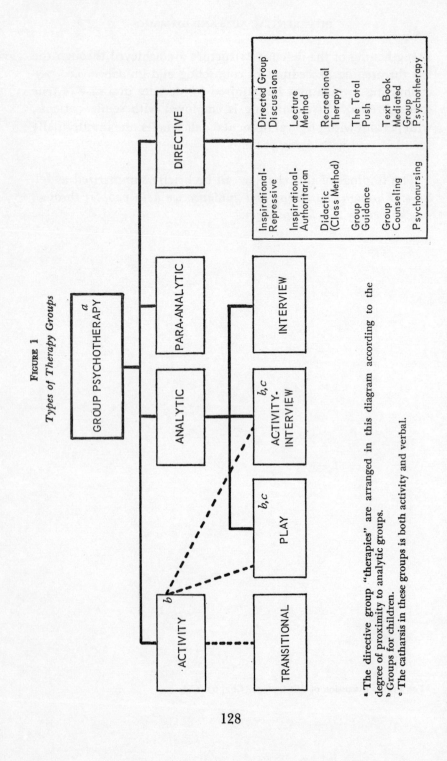

FIGURE 1
Types of Therapy Groups

GROUP PSYCHOTHERAPY [a]

ANALYTIC — PARA-ANALYTIC — DIRECTIVE

ACTIVITY [b] — PLAY [b,c] — ACTIVITY-INTERVIEW [b,c] — INTERVIEW

TRANSITIONAL

Inspirational-Repressive	Directed Group Discussions
Inspirational-Authoritarian	Lecture Method
Didactic (Class Method)	Recreational Therapy
Group Guidance	The Total Push
Group Counseling	Text Book Mediated Group Psychotherapy
Psychonursing	

[a] The directive group "therapies" are arranged in this diagram according to the degree of proximity to analytic groups.
[b] Groups for children.
[c] The catharsis in these groups is both activity and verbal.

128

TABLE 1

Aims and Dynamics in Counseling, Guidance, and Psychotherapy

Aims	Counseling	Guidance	Analytic Psychotherapy	Para-Analytic Psychotherapy
Libido redistribution	none	none	present	partial
Regulation of superego demands	none	slight	present	partial
Strengthening of ego	none	slight	present	present
Improvement of self-image	none	slight	present	present
Solution of immediate problem	present	present	transitory	present
Dynamics				
Transference	slight, positive	moderate, positive	intense, cyclical	intense
Catharsis	none	moderate, associative	regressive, free associative	associative and free association
Insight	none	slight	deep	moderate
Reality testing	present	present	present	present
Sublimation	none	possible	present	present

V

Basic Dynamics of
Group Psychotherapy

The general aim of all psychotherapies is identical: to improve or cure the patient. Whatever the theoretical formulations may be, this is achieved in all psychotherapies by involving the basic elements of personality: the libido, ego, and superego. However, the psychotherapy processes, though fundamentally similar, vary in respect to a number of factors, which we shall consider in this volume. In this chapter, we shall discuss the therapeutic dynamics in analytic group psychotherapy,[1] the influence of the compresence of a number of patients on them, and the consequent variety of interactions. It must be remembered that whatever modifications of dynamics are introduced, they are procedural only, for psychological repair can be affected only by the employment of specific reconstructive experiences, regardless of the way they may be employed by individual therapists.

The pathology and defective elements in personality need *specific* correctives, whatever the techniques adopted may be, and we have seen that these are in the areas of libido distribution, ego strengthening, adjusting the superego, and correcting the self-image, and are achieved through transference, catharsis, insight,

[1] Unless an additional designation is specified, for the sake of brevity the terms "group psychotherapy" or "group therapy" indicate "analytic group psychotherapy."

reality testing, and sublimations. Whatever operational differences may exist, true psychotherapy occurs only when these are involved.

TRANSFERENCE

Types of Transference

Transference in psychoanalysis is, in its purest form, unilateral; it is directed from the patient toward the analyst. In less intensive individual psychotherapies, transference is bilateral. That is, while the patient's transference is substantially the same in nature, though much less intense, the therapist, in turn, responds to him with empathy, interest, and encouragement. This response is made necessary largely by the face-to-face setting and the greater involvement of the ego than is the case in classical psychoanalysis. In group psychotherapy, the patient-therapist transferences are further modified by the presence of others. Here, early feelings and inadequately repressed memories, relating to siblings as well as parents, are activated. Thus, a patient who projects parental transference feelings on the therapist may, at the same time, also react to other members of the group, as siblings. These varied affects and attitudes set up a network of emotional tensions peculiar to therapy groups.

To differentiate these types of transferences, we use the terms *libidinal transference* (for feelings derived from and related to parents), *sibling transference* (for feelings emanating from relations with siblings), and *identification transference* (where the patient identifies with the therapist and other members of the group and desires to emulate and be like them—they serve as ego-ideals and models of identification). The element of identification is present in all transference attitudes, though this fact is not sufficiently recognized. A special phenomenon of psychotherapy groups is that they provide a number of identification models, instead of just one—the therapist—as is the case in individual treatment.

Identification is the outstanding single force in the genesis of personality and the humanizing of man. It is not possible to add much to Freud's studies in this area beyond emphasizing the importance of identification in shaping character and in ego formation (including the ego-ideal). The individual's psychic entity and self-identity are derived from these two functions. Confused identifications, not only in respect to sexual image and role, but as internalized models for feeling and conduct, disorient self-identity and relations to the world. Without internalized identification, the personality is fluid, lacking solidity and substance, a state characteristic of psychopathy and psychoses, and, to a lesser degree, of other pathologic problems.

In orderly development, the original identifications are established in childhood through parents, especially the mother. As the child grows older, identifications expand to include other adults and peers; still later, impersonal models, such as mythical and historical figures, are singled out for admiration. As the individual grows into maturity, these models may be amplified or replaced by groups, ideals, social movements, and religious sects. The variegation of identification objects gives the personality richness, as well as adaptability, and is conducive to mental health, provided that each object of identification is, or was, adequately rooted in the psyche. Transient identification after adolescence, when one flits from one object to another, reflect emotional instability, shallowness, and, in some instances, pathology.

One of the characteristics of Western man is that his identification models also include groups. Some of these are the religious sects, professional, and other groups that characterize an urban industrial society. As individual models do, these groups, too, influence character and ego organization in accordance with their significance (cathexis) in the psychic economy. In the Western culture, some group identifications are considered essential requirements for mental health. In fact, too implacable identifications derived from childhood without modifications, elaboration, and expansion, constitute a form of neurotic fixation and character rigidity. They are also characteristic of psychoses.

According to Freud, identification goes beyond a feeling of sameness or empathy alone. It manifests itself in three mechanisms: imitation, internalization, and oral incorporation. The nature of schizophrenic and psychotic identification, for example, includes cannibalistic oral incorporation of the object (See Chapter XVI). This urge manifests itself in psychotherapy by the patient's basic drive to hurt and destroy the therapist (by symbolically ingesting him). In psychotherapy with nonpsychotic patients, occasionally one also finds intensely orally fixated or regressed patients with similar, though less murderous, reactions. But by and large, transference identification is present, in less raw and less violent forms, in all patients, with imitation and internalization predominating.

Man, as all primates, is an imitative animal, and the structure of his family, social, and community living aids and encourages the native faculty to imitate. Community codes, both primitive and advanced, aid, abet, and at times force, the imitative propensities of the individual. When the model adopted for imitation assumes a cathected role in the libido of the individual human, he not only imitates, but internalizes, absorbs as it were, the personality of the model and makes him a part of himself. This constitutes part of what may be described as *nonbiological heredity,* which determines and shapes the feeling tone, behavioral patterns, and responses of the individual. Internalization, goes beyond imitation, however. In imitation, superficial mannerisms and ways of conduct are adopted from the model, which are displaced by others as the circumstances of life change. Not so with internalized identifications; they form the warp and woof of the texture of character and personality.

Thus, internalization of the pathology of a cathected parent can determine one's destiny and one of the main and most difficult tasks of psychotherapy is to place the patient in a relation wherein he can give up these *primary identifications* for a new and, hopefully, more wholesome internalization. This is the main, if not the sole, task in the treatment of induced or pseudoschizophrenia and a great many nonpsychotic conditions.

Destructive as pathogenic identifications are, the absence of adequate identifications may be even worse. Individuals with early histories of shifting from one foster home to another, of having rejecting and frustrating parents, of being institutionalized children, and others who had no healthy and permanent identification objects, are in many respects at even a greater disadvantage. Their personalities are as unstable as shifting sands. They give a picture of schizophrenia — though pseudoschizophrenia withal; they may acquire "inadequate personalities," or "psychopathic characters."

Persons who have not had a base in adequate early identifications may become subject to *transient identifications*. In some respects, this phenomenon is dynamically similar to "floating libido." In such patients, the identifications are of short duration and depend on an available model. As a result, they may adopt values, patterns of conduct, mannerisms, and speech idiosyncrasies which are temporary, being retained only until another, more attractive model appears. Then, the former values, manners, and behavior are abandoned and new ones adopted.

This phenomenon, in a mild form, is characteristic of normal adolescence and, to a lesser degree, of latency; but when it is excessive in adolescence or carried over into adulthood, it has to be viewed as a personality defect requiring therapeutic intervention. Transient identification is characteristic of borderline and latent schizophrenics, due to their weak ego organization and few strengths. There are also nonschizophrenic persons with inadequately developed ego resources who, in their lives and conduct resemble the schizophrenic. They fall in the category of *pseudoschizophrenia*. Such patients require individual therapy where they can establish a primary identification with an *individual*. Group identifications alone are not sufficient. Identification transference, both in its imitation and internalization aspects, however, is a matter of consideration in all psychotherapies and psychoanalysis.

Identification is of particular significance in group psychotherapy. The multiple transferences in groups, provide multiple models and objects of identification. Thus, each patient who becomes a cathected object because of the content of the unconscious of another, is either imitated or internalized. This points to the importance of, and the need for, criteria of grouping patients for favorable therapeutic outcomes. In one instance, for example, identification with a promiscuous woman in a group led another patient to act out in a similar manner, although up to that time she had been a virgin. Not infrequently, delinquent patients lead others to delinquent acts by becoming models of identification, in addition to their actively involving them in transgressions.

Constants and Variables in Transference Phenomena

Similarity in the nature of transference in individual and group psychotherapy is most recognizable in its *positive* and *negative* phases. In a group, just as in individual treatment, the *basic transference* toward the therapist must be positive, while the negative phases *transitory* (Slavson, 1952), otherwise patients would break off treatment. In group psychotherapy there is also the important element of *transference toward the group,* which must be positive. Favorable transference attitudes toward the therapist alone are not sufficient, for when the group attacks, threatens, or rejects a patient, he will be unable to participate in, or gain from, it. Patients whose basic difficulties stem from fear of, or antagonism to, groups cannot be included in group psychotherapy as a first step; they usually drop out early in treatment. Fear and antagonism stem from memories or engrams of the pain and discomfiture in one's early family. A family (group) climate imbued with tensions, fear-inducing interpersonal relations, rejection, neglect, and threats to personal autonomy, psychologic survival, status, and self-esteem, conditions the individual for defensive attack on, or avoidance of, groups. Such preconditioning is a counterindicant for placement in group psychotherapy. Group psychotherapy requires fairly consistent positive transference toward the group as a whole in addition to the various individual transferences.

When the ego of an individual is unable to deal with group induced anxiety and a state of negative transference toward the group results, the patient requires a preliminary course of individual treatment to overcome these initial fears and aggressions. A patient may be unable to participate in a group because of the presence of members whom he cannot countenance, as they evoke recall of painful experiences in his past with persons whom they may resemble in some way. The patient cannot function in their presence. The aroused fear or rage overstrains his ego controls and he may uncontrollably act out or quit the group.

One modification of the transference phenomena in groups is *transference dilution*. In individual therapy, the therapist is the only transference object; but because groups provide a number of objects, *target multiplicity* occurs. The multiple targets of hostility, in the persons of fellow patients, diminish the intensity of the transference on any one person, though the total *quantum of affect* may be multiplied many times. This quantum is particularly high in the negative transference phases, as a result of reinforcement, intensification, induction, and intragroup identifications.

While there is an alternation of positive and negative transferences toward the therapist, it is essential that the basic transference be positive. Negative transference, though essential and inevitable, should be short-lived and temporary. Pain, suffering, and discomfort bring a patient to treatment, but he continues with it because he has confidence in the therapist and faith in his genuine interest. The resurgence of negative and hostile feelings inevitably appears as a displacement of these toward parents and other family members. In fact, if improvement is to be effected, such feelings must be encouraged (though seldom activated) by the therapist so that they may be brought to the surface and worked through. Negative feelings must not, however, become dominant or the treatment will break off. *Temporary phases can be negative, but the basic transference must be positive.*

This rule holds for both group psychotherapy and individual treatment, although the situation is more complicated in groups, because the basic transference has to be positive not only toward the therapist, but also toward the group as a whole and negative feelings toward members in the group cannot be so intense as to be intolerable to the participants. It is also more complicated because of the possible induction and intensification of hostility in groups.

While there are important similarities, the differential nature of the transferences in individual and group psychotherapy must be carefully considered. Theoretically, in individual therapy, transference attitudes flow in one direction: from the patient to the therapist. Ideally, this condition can be achieved only in a couch psychoanalysis. In the less intensive face-to-face treatment of most psychotherapists, counterfeelings by the therapist do not escape the patient's notice and they must, of necessity, be positive if the patient is to continue in treatment. In groups, transference feelings are directed toward a number of persons at the same time. We use the terms *unilateral, bilateral,* and *multilateral* transferences to describe these varying phenomena. Ideally, unilateral transferences can be achieved only in psychoanalysis and in activity group therapy with children. Bilateral transference is present in all other forms of individual psychotherapy, and multilateral transference is present in groups in addition to a variety of bilateral transferences.

TABLE 1

Transference Phenomena in Group Psychotherapy

Positive	Transitory	Libidinal	Diluted*
Negative	Permanent	Sibling*	Intensified*
		Identification	Multilateral
		Group*	Bilateral

* Indicates phenomena exclusively present in group psychotherapy.
Others are present in all therapies and, in modified form, in groups.

Thus, in analytic group psychotherapy, with nonpsychotic adolescents and adults, significant modifications of the transference emerge as an inevitable result of the presence of more than one patient. Here, transference is modified, diluted, and divided; identifications can be established with fellow patients as well as with the therapist; there is a more favorable climate for acting out; and opportunities for reality testing are at hand. The catalytic effect of patients on each other, and that of the group as a whole, accelerates catharsis, as does universalization, support, group consent, and target multiplicity. There are, however, also factors that retard catharsis; among these are fear and shame, group-induced anxiety, group contagion, negative group transference phalanx, and others.[2]

[2] For further discussion of transference in therapy groups, see "countertransference," Chapter XIII.

Effects of Transference Dilution

In a group, the transference upon the therapist is less intense and less libidinally charged, diminishing the intensity of the therapy. The diminution of the transference prevents deep regression and the emergence of many fantasies which become available through more involving transference feelings as in individual psychoanalysis. This, together with other factors, renders groups unsuitable for treating massive psychoneuroses requiring a transference neurosis as part of the treatment. Generally, groups cannot affect as deep a psychotherapy as can individual treatment in these and similar cases.

Reality Saturation and Transference

Psychotherapy, to be effective, must draw on analysis of the fantasy projections and distortions with which the patient operates in life. The actualistic top realities are, at best, only first steps, though they may be periodically interspersed as they obtrude themselves in later communications. These actualities, however, are useful in the therapeutic process when the fantasies and distortions are brought out and made available to examination by the ego. This process can be conceived as rendering ego alien what has been ego syntonic.

In its reality-testing aspect, psychotherapy relieves the patient of his habitual need to perceive reality in a negative light, largely through improved ego functioning and a more suitable defensive system. His paratoxic distortions and fantasies, derived from unhappy past experiences, predispose him to negative responses. The repetition, in the therapeutic situation, of similar occurrences, events, and relations reactivates defensive fantasies and aggressions. The presence of these within the therapeutic setting also activates the neuronic engrams involved in the stimulus-response Gestalt, and, what is even more important, it justifies the patient's behavior in his own eyes. Were the therapist to treat the patient in a manner, or with an attitude, similar to that of the latter's parents, for example, the patient would feel entirely justified in his negativism and even violence, and therapy would bog down.

Sound psychotherapy relies on memories, affect, and fantasies and their interrelation, and aims to dissipate their painful aspect and reduce their hegemony in the psychic economy. This cannot be done by conceptual and philosophical formulations or mysticism, to which the autonomic nature of psychoneuroses does not respond. Consideration should be given to the deterrent effect of massive "realism" in the therapeutic setting and to the hegemony of fantasy in psychotherapy. A patient's reality sense is strengthened and diminution of affect occurs as fantasy recedes from the arena of his perceptions and becomes dissociated from a given situation or response. The presence of noxious elements in the therapy itself supports the patient's parataxic distortions and fantasy, giving them psychic reality. It is reality distilled from fantasy that constitutes the therapeutic grist.

By the very nature of groups, reality is more pervasive in them than in individual treatment. In groups, patients' interpersonal reactions and their setting arouse the timidities, discomforts, hostilities, and aggressions lodged in the unconscious and operative in the conscious as vestiges of the past. The characteristics and personalities of the various members arouse irrational feelings and responses in each other. These, and numerous other developments, interactions, and events in a group setting, favor regressive conduct; but the distortions and fantasy are less available here than in individual treatment and this is why group psychotherapy cannot be as deeply affecting as is individual therapy, where distortions and fantasy are provoked through the patient's own uninterrupted intrapsychic activity.

The presence of excessive reality factors in therapy, which we shall designate as *reality saturation,* should be prevented. This includes the therapist's attitudes and conduct as well as physical setting. Another source of reality saturation is a grouping of patients in which they might relive the stresses of their lives too realistically, with little or no opportunity for throwing the light of objectivity on them. This is the case, for example, when parents and children or husbands and wives are included in the same groups. In such groups, the resentments and hostilities are brought forth by the same irritants and stimulators as in real life and, when not controlled, are acted out with all their vehemence and rancor. To subject feelings to adequate analysis is both impossible and inadvisable under these circumstances. The corporeal presence of the pathogenic persons may not inhibit free discharge of feelings, but it would prevent the appearance of the fantasy and distortions with which psychotherapy in its essence must deal.

How does reality saturation affect transference toward the therapist and toward fellow members? It is recognized that, for best results, the therapist should remain as inactive as the situation permits, leaving it to the patients to work through their productions as far as they can, helping them only at points where resistances set in or when clarification becomes necessary. Such comparative passivity can be more easily maintained by the therapist when the patients' communications deal with memories, fantasies, and projections than when they deal with the actualistic content of their lives. It is difficult, if not impossible, for the therapist not to be drawn into the explosive emotional vortex of the group and into the clashes of persons who are not symbolically but *actually* in serious conflict in real life. Psychotherapy deals with *reliving* situations, not with *living* them.

This does not mean that psychotherapy is detached from life. It proceeds from and focuses on life, but only as it is perceived or felt by the patient and not with its actualities. The latter are the concern of guidance and counseling and not of psychotherapy. The unavoidable involvement resulting from reality situations in groups changes the therapist's role and, hence, also the transference. The therapist becomes not a symbol of a parental figure, but a real parental figure, and thereby justifies the patient's attitudes toward him and acts against him. Such an eventuality brings about collapse of the subtler effects of treatment or its termination.

Group Psychotherapy and the Libido "Conserve"

In every type of psychotherapy, a period is reached in which the patient, as part of the transference-countertransference process, displaces his preoccupation from himself to the person of the therapist. He grows interested in matters of a personal nature concerning the therapist and attempts to understand and to "figure out" his character, motivations, and intent. Such attempts may occur only once during the course of treatment or may recur as therapy progresses. This phenomenon may be viewed as a spontaneous reversal of roles, which the patient had experienced, or sought to affect, in relations to his parents; it can represent the patient's effort to get emotionally closer to his mentor; often, it is an act of hostility and a resistance maneuver. It is as though by better understanding of the therapist, the patient seeks to buttress his hidden or overt need to unseat the therapist from the lofty throne on which the patient believes he has placed him.

In individual treatment, this phase can be viewed as an emerging phase of negative transference and as a means of abetting resistance. The patient perceives that downgrading the therapist will free him from the need to submit and from continuing in the discomfiture of his place as patient. It is at these periods of the therapeutic nadir that the therapist's perceptiveness and skills are tried to their utmost. It requires a high level of inner freedom not to fall prey to countertransference feelings. The patient's hostility and his urge to free himself during these phases, are repetitions of his earlier reactions toward his parents; they constitute the essence of the transference neurosis. Even patients whose *nuclear* or core problems do not require the development of transference neuroses in the treatment setting are subject to these phases, which are a product of hostility and resistance.

This mechanism does not appear as inevitably in group psychotherapy as it does in individual psychotherapy. The phenomenon of target multiplicity not only dilutes the transference, but also distributes the libido among a number of objects, thus preventing intense hostility toward the therapist. Remaining comparatively more in the background, he does not become the exclusive focus of love and, therefore, also of hate. Also, these ambivalent and alternating feelings projected on fellow patients can seldom be as intense as they are toward the parental figure. As a result, the libido that is used as a resistance strategem becomes available for the reconstructive process of the patient himself. This mecha-

141

nism, *libido conserve,* is counterindicated in massive transference neuroses.

CATHARSIS

Catharsis is the process by which a patient communicates his problems and preoccupations. As the term implies, it is a way of purging oneself of noxious states of the psyche; it is the way through which disturbing feelings, memories, and ideas are dislodged or disgorged, as it were, from the preconscious and unconscious and brought to the surface. It involves splitting off, from the compact structure of the individual's psyche, hitherto integral feelings and thoughts, which, though creating tensions and stress, were still a part of the total psychic organization.

The effort to effect this cleavage is usually very great and very difficult. The difficulty arises from the stress that is caused by the threatened disturbance in the equilibrium of the psyche; the discomfort arising from revelations of superego-alien and, therefore guilt-inducing thoughts, actions, memories, and feelings; and the diminution of one's self-esteem. These and other impediments and restraints constitute *resistance,* the most universal and the most intransigent of all dynamics in psychotherapy. Communication is not, in itself, therapeutic, unless it is free-associative, involves emotional regression, is accompanied by concomitant affect, and releases bound up anxiety. Not all communication is therapeutically valid just because its content is personal or proscribed. The material must be emotionally significant and produced through a slow, regressive process in a transference relation, with attention given to the feelings that accompany the statements. Ego tensions may thus be relieved by "unloading" guilt-producing thoughts and memories and the result may be temporary improvement in function and adjustment. However, the aim of psychotherapy is to establish a more adequate psychic balance with a new emotional and intellectual orientation and not just make the patient comfortable.

Assigning value to "confessionals" shows a misconception of what psychotherapy is. Patients in groups do tend to diminish resistance and restraints in each other by reducing superego demands through universalization, mutual support, identification, and group approval. However, mere communication becomes of little value and can even be meaningless.

The literature reveals many devices and artifices employed by group therapists. The gamut runs from the authoritarian approach of A. A. Low to the didactic and inspirational method of Joseph K. Pratt and his followers, as well as to the application of Freudian psychoanalysis and some metaphysical and mystical teachings of more recent vintage.

Many of these methods were stimulated by World War II army practices for relieving acute states of emotional disturbances. Patients suffered acute and temporary disturbances for the most part, and therapeutic efforts were directed toward rehabilitating them as quickly as possible for further military service. Directed group discussions, abreaction, visual aids and inspirational methods have all undoubtedly helped many soldiers overcome transient emotional strain and have prevented serious mental disturbances, but there is no evidence that they permanently changed the patterning of psychologic structure, which is the objective of good psychotherapy.

These methods, though effective in the setting of a field army hospital with their limited aims, cannot but be misleading when transplanted into civilian psychiatry and psychotherapy, in which patients, for the most part, are not in acute states of disturbance. They have lived with their problems for long periods and have perhaps grappled with them throughout their lives. The difficulties do not arise from a specific threat or situation,[3] such as the battlefield, but are rather a result of psychic reserves inadequate to deal with the total life process. The need, therefore, is not to work through an acute immediate problem, as is the case in the armed forces and in civilian counseling and guidance, but rather to alter the psychic equipment of the patient. A different approach is necessary for this.

[3] Even so called "situational neuroses" stem from intrapsychic weakness which is revealed by a stressful social situation. The situation does not generate the neurosis, however, as is implied in this misleading term.

Resistances to Catharsis

It is really not too farfetched to say that no adult can be treated by psychological means; that only children are accessible to psychotherapy. This is to say that the adult has to become a child before he can be treated, and the way back from adulthood to childhood is *regression*. Through regression, the adult returns to his childhood, becomes emotionally dependent on the therapist, and relives the events of his past with their associated feelings. This involves submitting to the therapist as a child submits to his parents; it involves the child-parent relation and a returning in memory and feelings to earlier stages of development. This is understandably difficult, for regression constitutes a threat to one's self-esteem and is, therefore, strongly resisted.

The most important single dynamic in psychotherapy, and one that requires utmost skill on the part of the therapist, is inducing a flow of catharsis by overcoming the various *resistances* of the patient. The leverage by which resistances are overcome is the transference, and especially its positive phases. In fact, so difficult does resistance to communication (catharsis) become, in some adult patients, that a series of *catharsis inducers* have been developed. Among these are various chemical means for reducing cortical inhibitive controls, and hypnosis, in addition to psychotherapeutic maneuvers.

The ease with which a patient communicates has a direct relation to his ego strengths and the state of his defenses. By and large, a weak ego does not allow self-revealing communication. The weaker the ego the stronger are the defenses and resistances. While a normal quantum of ego defenses are essential to normal adaptation, overstrong defenses do not permit effective function and satisfactory social adaptation—they also mobilize resistances in psychotherapy. These defensive maneuvers serve to prevent anxiety in psychoneurotics and to a lesser degree, in other types of patients.

Overloading the Ego

As a corollary to these considerations, the therapist should prevent *overloading the ego* in patients with inflexible defenses and constitutional deficiencies. These precautions are especially urgent in latent and pseudoschizophrenics whose egos may be fragmented when anxiety becomes too massive. Even in nonpsychotic patients, such as hysterics, temporary psychotic-like withdrawal from reality may be induced by overloading the ego. One latent schizophrenic patient, for example, began to hallucinate during the couch psychoanalytic session. An ambulatory psychotic woman insisted on sitting up, instead of lying down, during her treatment by a male analyst. When later asked why, her answer was, "I was afraid of my analyst." In the first case, the revelations and regression in free association overwhelmed the patient's ego defenses, a problem he solved by withdrawing from reality; in the second case, the regressive incestuous and probably homicidal urges were too threatening, and sitting up was a defensive and precautionary reaction. Many nonpsychotic manic-depressive and cycloid patients, and those with anxiety states, have to be protected at times against too rapid and too deeply affecting productions. The therapist has to exercise judgment on the basis of his knowledge of the specific patient's ego strengths and defenses. (See also "Therapeutic, Parapathologic and Pathologic Regression.")

Types of Catharsis

Catharsis can be divided into two major categories: *verbal catharsis* (employed with nonpsychotic adults and adolescents) and *activity catharsis* (employed in the treatment of children and some types or stages of adult psychotic patients). Individual and group play therapy and activity-interview group therapy with children, and occupational and recreational therapies with adults in mental hospitals rely in part on activity catharsis. It is the sole means employed in activity group therapy with specially selected children and is suitable for treatment of adult psychotics and regressed, chronic schizophrenics. It is not recommended for adult nonpsychotic patients. Where activity therapy with children is followed by exploratory associations aiming at insight and understanding, the combination of the two types, characterized as *activity-verbal catharsis*, is employed with neurotic and emotionally laden patients in latency. This is analogous to "play therapy" in individual treatment.

Both verbal and activity catharsis can take the following forms: free association, associative thinking (or action), directed, induced, forced, and vicarious.

Free Association

Free association (which stems from psychoanalysis and is also an important operational tool in other derivative psychotherapies) refers to the process by which the patient, in his communication, follows, without impediment, the concatenated sequences of thoughts, memories, and feelings, as they arise through the activation of the unconscious and preconscious. Through this maze of seemingly illogical, unrelated, and confused ideas, past traumatic occurrences, which have resulted in disturbed feelings concerning the self, other persons, objects, and situations (that have caused emotional and behavioral disequilibrium) are recalled.

While the ultimate value of catharsis lies in regression, its immediate service to the patient is diminution of tension and anxiety. As repressed feelings and hostilities are discharged, tensions are diminished, although in some instances further anxiety may be generated as the ego defenses are threatened and the ego-ideal (self-image) suffers setbacks. What young children gain through therapeutic play and acting out in a planned therapeutic setting, adults and adolescents achieve through verbal communication. In individual and group play and activity therapy, for example, not only the acts, but also their sequences throw light on the child's problems and preoccupations. What seem to be discrete, impulsive, or explosive and seemingly unrelated acts, may have a genetic and sequential thread running through them, which follows the flow of the subject's unconscious associations of feelings and fantasies. For example, a child's helter-skelter running, shooting, and playing dead, and his attacking of playmates or objects, followed by sudden moodiness, reflect inner turmoil, fears, hostilities, aggressive intent, and resultant guilt. Such nonverbal communications by children are as meaningful as verbalizations. This is also the case with adults.

With adult patients, the free-associative character of activity and verbal catharsis occurs in individuals in groups and in groups as a whole. An act or a statement by one member may set off a chain of ideas and feelings in the others by the associative process, catalysis, mutual induction, identification, and empathy. However, in a group, patients do not indiscriminately and consistently take up cues; rather, they respond selectively. Selectivity is determined by similarity of problems, temporary mood, and other factors; but more often because the catharsis of one patient activates the unconscious of others or dissolves their censors. Frequently, reactions may, on the surface, seem unrelated to a stimulus, when actually they are very related, though the relation may be difficult to discern. This *chain reaction* may infect an entire group or only some of its members. When the entire group is involved in aggressive catharsis, it is in a phalanx of negative transference toward the therapist. Whenever there is unanimity in a group, there is hostility toward a common object.

Action and communication may become very intense, mobility inordinately increased, voices grow strident, and acting out mounts, creating a tense atmosphere. This tumultuous and chaotic state continues for a period and then, with equal suddenness, things may quiet down. In activity group therapy, the children return to their individual occupations and interests, their mood for constructive effort reborn. Periods of hilarity and hyperactivity reappear periodically, to be succeeded by periods of quiet. This alternation is common in activity, as well as in analytic, groups and disappears entirely toward the end of treatment, when the group behavior levels off, reflecting inner stability in its members. (This alternation of hyperactivity and quietude we have previously described as *nodal* and *antinodal* behavior.)

Free association has the following major characteristics: (a) it does not necessarily have a theme, nor does it follow a "logical" line of thought; it is not always organized but may consist of a series of memories and/or current ideas as they seem to relate to each other in the patient's unconscious or preconscious; (b) the productions move from the present to the past; (c) it includes dreams, and recalls memories and feelings that lead to traumatic experiences and events long vanished from consciousness; (d) its direction is *vertical,* starting with the present and leading to the past, a characteristic that contributes to the regressive process; (e) to be most effective, it must be accompanied by affect and anxiety bound up in the traumatic memory; and (f) it has manifest and latent content.

Catharsis and regression in adolescents and adults is predominantly verbal and may take a *horizontal* direction. That is, patients may re-enact and relive, in the group, feelings they have stored up or currently experience toward parents, siblings, husbands, wives, and other significant persons in their lives. This is particularly valuable to diffident patients with tendencies toward psychic masochism, for whom it is a form of reality testing that results in ego reinforcement as well as ventilation of feeling. The discussions in analytic group psychotherapy are not always friendly or placid. Patients grow tense, attack each other, disagree violently and project on fellow members and the therapist. These interpatient encounters, so essential in group treatment, are analogous to the cathartic physical activity of children.[4]

In psychotherapy, individual equilibrium has to be achieved through prolonged intra- and interpersonal struggle. The therapist must not assume the role of the repressive parent who demands control of hostile impulses or a placid group façade. Hostility is an essential part of therapy. A regimen that suppresses it is contratherapeutic.

Uninhibited expression of hostility toward the therapist and fellow patients is the major grist in the therapeutic mill; where there is no hostility there is no therapy. By his accepting attitude the therapist aids the discharge of feelings and demonstrates his own strength, thus becoming a suitable identification model. To their surprise, patients discover that open hostility does not devastate anyone.[5] In psychotherapy, as in no other situation, the patient feels

[4] This is one reason why the timid and withdrawn gain more rapidly than do others from all types of group therapy. They can cast off their timidity, first guardedly and then more boldly, as they discover safety in the group.
[5] For further discussion of this dynamic see Chapter X.

148

free to expose his real self. This is tantamount to living over pre-oedipal stages in growth, where restraints were few and pleasures ran their course. Because of this feeling of unbridled freedom, he can permit himself to throw off caution and suspend the inhibitions growing out of his superego. By revealing his real self to himself and to others, he can then accept himself. Self-acceptance dissolves the defenses that impede emotional maturity and thus clears the arena for a more realistic adjustment to life.

The therapist should always be vigilant, because overaggressiveness and acting-out in a group can become too disturbing. Every group has its limits to the intensity of hostility and aggression that it can bear, and the therapist must foresee the point of saturation and deal with it before the limit is reached.

Patterns of catharsis reactions in group psychotherapy, vary in some respects from those in individual treatment, though their similarities are equally impressive. Associative thinking and free association are present in both individual and group treatment. However, in groups, the former may continue for longer periods. Because of fear of the group's reactions and the uncertainty of one's status, a patient may withhold some facts and feelings for longer periods than he would in individual treatment. (There are, however, patients who are more productive in groups.) Events in the life of patients may be so deeply cathected or they may be so intensely ashamed of them, that they cannot bring themselves to reveal them before others. This is why some patients require parallel individual and group treatment. What a patient cannot relate in a group, he may be able to relate in the one-to-one sessions with the therapist. But the group, through the dynamic of catalysis, activates this productivity in the parallel individual interviews.

Associative Thinking

Associative thinking or action (See Slavson, 1952), refers to a patient's productions that relate primarily to his *current* life, experiences, and concerns. The contents of these involve the dimension of time and have temporal immediacy.

As such, they can be described as *top realities*, which are nearly always the starting point in all psychotherapies. All psychotherapy begins with associative thinking, for patients come for treatment because of pressures and discomfort in their immediate lives and adjustments. Unlike counseling and guidance, in psychotherapy top realities are only the starting point, for, as the upper layers are peeled off, memories, feelings, and thoughts about the past, rise up by the process of free association. Through associative thinking the patient divests himself of immediate pressures, worries, and anxieties and reduces the load on his ego. By sharing his concerns and receiving sympathetic understanding (support) and discovering that others are in similar plights (universalization), the psychic burden is diminished and feelings of guilt and inadequacy are lightened. The characteristics of associative thinking are: (a) it deals with current matters (top realities); (b) it moves in a horizontal or lateral direction (in contrast to the vertical direction of free association); and (c) regression is at a minimum.

In this process, traumatic memories are not uncovered, relived, or re-examined in a new light and the psychic organization of the individual is affected but little. Yet, it may bring relief and lead to a better intellectual understanding of a situation. In psychotherapy, associative thinking at times inevitably runs parallel with free association, even in its more advanced phases. However, contemporaneous problems must be viewed as steps or doors leading to past events.

In counseling and in guidance, associative thinking is the major, if not the sole, mode of communication; through it, the maze of current involvements are unraveled and the light of understanding thrown on them, enabling clients to deal with their problems more realistically and effectively. But associative thinking leaves untouched the matters locked in the unconscious which only free association can release.

Directed Catharsis

Directed catharsis refers to the procedure in which the therapist (or fellow patients) ask leading questions in an attempt to uncover specific facts or memories relevant or important at a given time. This practice becomes necessary at certain points, even where free association is the prevailing mode, and it is used in analytic groups as well as in individual treatment. In the so-called "authoritarian" and "inspirational" therapies, it is a major or exclusive technique.

Directed catharsis is also likely to appear in analytic groups with great frequency, due to the fact that patients spontaneously interrogate one another, ask for explanations, and offer suggestions. Both identification and curiosity are aroused in fellow participants by the communications of a patient. Group interviews frequently force a patient to carry a point beyond his intentions or to alter the direction he would have pursued without such "interference." In fact, at times it may become necessary for the therapist to "rescue" a patient from the interrogations of fellow group members when the exploration becomes too disturbing to him. Directed catharsis, while occasionally employed by all psychotherapists as a deliberate, though infrequent and transient, technique, is *unavoidable* in groups because of their interstimulation characteristic.[6]

Induced Catharsis

Induced catharsis in groups is an inevitable outcome of the catalytic effects of identification, empathy, and mutual transferences on the part of patients and frequently also of the therapist. Facial expression, mannerisms, body tensions, and other types of nonverbal expression, and especially affect-laden statements, arouse responses by the process of induction. This activates patients to communicate their feelings and memories which, in

[6] This is only one reason why patients cannot be considered "auxiliary therapists." They lack the trained perceptiveness and judgment needed to distinguish relevance, significance, and, especially, appropriateness in conducting an interview; nor do they understand the latent content of communications or the benefit or harm that their statements and questions may have on a given patient. Because of their emotional involvement in the ongoing process and their own unconscious needs and transference reactions, they could not exercise the same highly appropriate judgment and control as a trained therapist, even if they understood the significance of their questions and remarks. The fellow patients' "interferences" in the free associative communications of a true psychoneurotic is one more reason why a transference neurosis cannot be resolved in a group, since these "interferences" block the essential regressive process toward early traumata.

many instances, they may not have done on their own initiative.

Induced catharsis is inherent in therapy groups. One of the major dynamics of groups is *mutual induction* or what is sometimes referred to as "emotional contagion." Because of similarity of interests, preoccupations, and difficulties, it can be expected that an affect-laden statement by one patient would inevitably stimulate reactions and associations in others in the group. Usually, the less-conflicted members initiate a chain of inductive reactions which is taken up by the more conflicted and timid members. Sometimes, the most anxious, because of their intense anxiety, may bring forth topics or reflections that the more integrated and better controlled would not raise on their own. Induced catharsis is a major advantage of groups over other types of treatment for resistive, suspicious, and insecure patients. Where resistances and blockings are intense, groups can be used with great effectiveness. The inductive effect dissolves barriers to catharsis, though it can, at times, also generate impediments to its free flow. Psychotherapists frequently report patients who presented insurmountable difficulties in individual treatment, but did well in groups. Induced catharsis is one of the factors that makes such patients more accessible.

Forced Catharsis

Forced catharsis is a paradoxical term, as anything forced cannot be truly cathartic. It is included here for completeness and because it is employed in certain authoritarian settings. The term "forced catharsis" describes the process in which patients are required to give specific information as an act of submission to the authority of the therapist or as part of disciplinary requirements such as one encounters in punitive institutions or in an army.[7] In a sense, revelations made by patients under pharmocological influences and hypnosis can be included in this category.

Forced catharsis is not efficacious in analytic groups, and when patients attempt to press another group member to reveal himself

[7] This technique has also been referred to as "contractual group psychotherapy," one of the many artifices to facilitate the work of the therapist.

beyond his readiness, they should be diverted. Forced catharsis must never be employed by the therapist: it is basically unsuitable for analytically oriented psychotherapy, and its use points to a fundamental misconception of what constitutes psychotherapy.

Vicarious Catharsis

Vicarious catharsis is of major value to a certain type of patient in group psychotherapy. This self-confrontation and release emerges as a patient identifies with another when a communication or feeling fortuitously mirrors his own problem and feelings. Where a patient, either because of neurotic anxiety or character impediments, cannot formulate his feelings or bring them to awareness or communicate them, he is frequently benefited by identifying with the reflections of another, through which he gains insight. This type of covert catharsis is contingent on a high degree of similarity of problems and a capacity for identification which, in varying degrees, are always present among group members. Thus, a patient may participate vicariously in the catharsis of another when his problem is mirrored by the latter, but will remain little affected if the content does not touch off a response in him, or if the two patients are devoid of emotional resonance.

In addition to the mirroring quality of vicarious catharsis, it may also be conditioned by personality similarity as well as by the similarity of pathology or problem. On purely theoretic grounds one can say that the identification essential to this experience would hardly be possible in persons who are too divergent in their outlook or make-up. Where reactions are at great variance, empathy is difficult, if not impossible. However, in any group of patients, there exist, at all times, sources for vicarious catharsis, as all patients have in common resentments toward their parents, and many have had difficulties with siblings and problems of sexual adjustment. Even patients who are unable to verbalize their difficulties experience covert vicarious catharsis and the resulting *spectator therapy.*

TABLE 2

Types of Catharsis

Verbal	Free Association (vertical)
Activity	Associative Thinking (horizontal)
Activity-Verbal	Directed
	Induced
	Forced
	Vicarious

Catharsis Accelerators[8]

Target Multiplicity

Groups supply each patient with a number of targets for his repressed or overt love or hostility in the persons of his fellow patients. This phenomenon, *target multiplicity*, has the effect of weakening the libidinal transference on the therapist. It aids catharsis because it reduces the fear of piling up hostility on one person, especially the one *in loco parentis*. Hostility can be "spread around" or divided, as it were, which has disadvantages as well as advantages.

The single most important condition for successful therapy is the development of positive-negative transference attitudes toward the therapist which are worked through in the course of treatment. This is important because psychotherapy essentially consists of bringing to the surface and working through the hostilities and ambivalent feelings which are debilitating and destructive to the psychoneurotic and, to a lesser degree to patients with character disorders. Thus, any setting, process, or set of reactions that blocks or dilutes the fantasy-laden, distorted, and ambivalent feelings of love and hate, dependence and rejection, dilutes the intensity of the transference and, hence, also that of the therapy.

This situation is unavoidable in groups. The compresence of a number of patients causes the libidinal investment of each to be divided, rather than focused on one person (the therapist). As a result, fellow patients become, for each, a target for love

[8] See also Chapter XII.

and hate according to the patient's current needs and the images and phantoms locked in his unconscious. This is particularly disadvantageous when the hostility meant for the parental figure, the therapist, is displaced on a fellow group member. While a perceptive, vigilant, and experienced therapist will recognize this *libido displacement* maneuver and deal with it therapeutically, the potency of the affect will still have been reduced and dissipated in the process.

Target multiplicity also has advantages. Where a patient is too timid to reveal negative feelings or is masochistic, submissive, and placating, he can, through the catalytic effect and support of the group, first permit himself to be aggressive and behave in a hostile manner to sibling substitutes (group members) in transition to expressing such feelings toward the therapist.

Catalysis

As patients reveal themselves, they activate the other patients to do likewise, frequently in areas difficult or impossible to reach without such stimulation. In induced catharsis, for example, it is clear that patients activate other patients to bring forth their concerns and feelings, participate in the interviews, and reveal their hitherto repressed or withheld memories and ideas. The effect of patients on each other can be described as catalytic and the process termed *catalysis*. Catalysis is another important advantage of group psychotherapy. Many patients, uncommunicable and otherwise inaccessible, are helped to overcome their diffidence and fears by the catalytic effect of others and by the nonthreatening climate of the group. Catalysis is present in, and is a function of, induction.

Mutual Support

Another aid to catharsis, derived from groups, is *mutual support,* especially in the area of hostility toward the therapist as a parent substitute and in the constructive areas of ego functioning. Some patients can, with comparative freedom, express their aggressions, while others, because of fear or painful memories in analogous past situations, are unable to reveal negative and aggressive feelings. This has a deleterious effect on the therapeutic effort. In group psychotherapy, the awareness of solidarity among the patients gives each the security to express hostilities, without which no improvement can be expected.

Support can also be withdrawn from a patient, by other group members, when he becomes unreasonably aggressive or is consistently negative toward the therapist. One or more members of the group may defend the therapist, usually for one of the following reasons: dependence on the therapist, a need for ingratiation, or anxiety resulting from the attack upon a parental figure, a remnant from childhood. However, by and large, aggressive trends are supported in groups and are the reason for the greater incidence of acting out, as compared with individual psychotherapy.

The mutual acceptance and empathy in groups reinforce the ego-functioning of each member and raises self-esteem. As a result, patients can assume a more constructive role in their everyday life, in relation to others in their envoronment, and can deal with reality more appropriately and more effectively. Universalization and insight derived from group discussions reduce guilt and offer support to each participant. Identification plays as important a role in support as it does in the inductive process, as support is commensurate with mutual identification. However, because of individual dissimilarity in psychological syndromes, feelings toward parents, and other needs and attitudes, patients may not always approve or countenance direct aggression toward a therapist.

Mutual support also exerts less tangible influences that affect patients' attitudes. The feelings of *mutuality* and of belonging, so alien to a large majority of patients, ultimately make their appearance in the group and have very salutary effects on observable attitudes and overt behavior. As inner tensions and interindividual hostilities are worked through, a heartwarming closeness develops and feelings of being wanted gradually emerge. Above all, the individual himself feels that he is worthy of acceptance. As treatment progresses, this inner warmth gives rise to a hitherto unexperienced emotional hospitality and mellowness, which bridges the rift that formally existed between each patient and his fellow human beings. This phenomenon is sometimes referred to as "emotional re-education."

It is this emotional comfort and the manifest improvement in interpersonal relatedness that so frequently strongly impresses therapists, the patients themselves, and their relatives and associates. Such manifest outcomes, however, should not be mistaken for a "cure." They should be viewed by the therapist with reservation and objectivity. Similar changes may result merely from the pleasure and comfort of human relatedness (gregariousness), the satisfaction of affective and social hungers that are common to all, but intensified in patients. Such improvements cannot be considered basic or lasting. The fact that gratification brings on more relaxed, more tolerant and warmer feelings is no assurance that they have been internalized or structured into the psyche. They may be only temporary responses to a new-found, but transient security, gratification of dependence needs, or signs of temporarily increased self-esteem and self-worth. To be accepted and to be the object of affection is no small source of happiness, but to the clinician, such emotions may represent a compelling need for dependence and are signs of ego deficiency. A patient who entertains such feelings does not necessarily possess a psychologically healthy personality. Exaggerated independence and self-reliance, as well as overintense craving for relatedness and support, are correctly considered as signs of psychic deficiencies and a faulty self-identity.

Thus, observable improvement in attitudes and conduct in adult nonpsychotic patients should not be overvalued; one must be assured that internal, more or less lasting changes have occurred, changes that will free the patient of dependencies, fantasies and phantoms in his unconscious and of his self-alienative trends.

Identification

We have already seen how *identification* is involved in the transference, inductive, catalytic, cathartic, and supportive processes, which are commensurate with the degree of mutual identification that exists between the patients in a group. Mutual identification points to the problem of selection and grouping (particularly the

157

latter) so that an adequate degree of identification can be engendered and thus facilitate communication in the group.

Universalization

Another aid to catharsis in groups is the dynamic to which we have given the label *universalization*. This mechanism has received considerable attention from psychotherapists largely because patients in groups invariably become aware of it and verbalize it. An individual's awareness of intra- and interpersonal difficulties cannot but generate a feeling of stigma, difference from others, and inferiority. Such feelings stem from one's internalized ego ideal contrasted with one's defective self-image derived from the attitudes of parents, peers, the social milieu, and cultural values and mores. Feelings that one has failed to live up to expectations and values or achieve status, can be magnified by the reactions of the community. In group psychotherapy, self-alienative self-criticism and self-deprecation are greatly allayed through the discovery that others have the same or similar problems, and are victims of urges and impulses similar to one's own. This discovery mends deflated self-esteem (self-image) and reduces guilt feelings and resultant anxieties—all of which diminishes the load carried by the ego in its effort to maintain emotional equilibrium and aids psychic integration. A further result is that defensiveness and fear of self-revelation are reduced, thus making repressed and guarded memories accessible to therapy. As the overloaded ego is freed of this burden, its energy reserves are turned toward repair and expansion of the personality and become available for the controls required in interpersonal and social adjustments.

TABLE 3

Catharsis Accelerators In Group Psychotherapy

Target Multiplicity
Catalysis
Mutual Induction
Mutual Support
Identification
Universalization

PATTERNS OF GROUP-INDUCED RESISTANCES

Resistance is, dynamically, closely related to catharsis and its occurrence in group psychotherapy is common. Some resistances are found in both individual and group treatment, while others are indigenous to therapy groups. Groups supply opportunities for escape from participation that are not available in individual treatment. Resistances that appear in both individual and group treatment are absenteeism, lateness, displacement, deflection, planned communication, associative thinking, irrelevancy, distraction, abruptness, general or selective silence, passivity, and acting-out.

Absenteeism can be readily employed in a group. The guilt feelings of the resisting patient are not as deeply aroused as in individual therapy, because he knows that the group interviews will take place without him. He is not as fearful of the therapist as he would be if he were the only patient and thus would disappoint him by absence. There is comparative anonymity in the group, as well, which is not the case in individual therapy. Similarly, *lateness* is not as apparent in a group; a patient can come late without being as embarrassed as he would be if he were the only attendant, for it does not interfere with the progress of the group interview.

Displacement consists of redirecting or re-attaching feelings from one person to another or to an object, because of fear or discomfort at the idea of expressing the feelings directly at the original target. In therapy groups, displacement frequently occurs when patients redirect the hostilities and aggressions they feel for the therapist toward a fellow patient. By this process, a patient can relieve himself of tensions set up by his hostile feelings; the substitution of a less threatening target prevents the rise of anxiety and fear in himself. Since direct expression of such emotions to a (substitute) parent is one of the necessities in equilibrating the psyche, this phenomenon, as a form of resistance, may have to be dealt with interpretively.

Patients who grow uncomfortable when they become the center of attention of the group, or when the content of a discussion generates tension or embarrassment in them, may *deflect* the

159

group's preoccupation toward another focus. This mechanism is in many respects similar to that of "abruptness," to be described presently. It varies in that interest is not cut off as in abruptness, but rather is allowed to continue with the focus of attention changed. Thus, when a group attempts to explore the personality or conduct of a patient, he may deflect it into generalized or universal terms away from himself; or he may include another patient in the category with himself and gradually render the latter the central target.

Planned communication is resorted to by patients who are threatened by free-associative revelations and spontaneity, which they feel may expose some of their carefully guarded thoughts, feelings, and experiences. They therefore come to the group with a planned discussion, frequently dreams, thus blocking off the therapeutically essential regressive memories in their unconscious and preconscious. This façade is more difficult to maintain for any length of time in a group than it is in individual treatment.

Associative thinking is the term we suggested to describe the content of one of the most stubborn of resistances in group interviews. This term designates the communication process in which only current happenings are detailed, without early experiences and traumatogenic emotions or dreams being evoked. The content of associative thinking is top realities, which, as already pointed out, are valid as a starting point in psychotherapy, but not as a prolonged practice.

A common means of resisting self-revelation and escaping anxiety generated in group interviews, as well as asserting oneself, is to introduce a subject, thought, or joke that is *irrelevant* to the ongoing conversation or theme. This strategy serves not only as an escape device, but also as an act of hostility against the group and the therapist.

In a group, a patient can *distract* the communication of another when it causes him discomfort or anxiety. This is, in a sense, analogous to deflection, but instead of diverting the stream of catharsis, the patient in a group can use a number of means for distracting such as changing the subject, laughing, telling a story, joking, interrupting, or in some other way preventing the completion of anxiety-provoking statements.

Abruptness is a form of distraction that blocks the progress of a communication or discussion by peremptory termination or peremptory interruption of other patients.

Silence is the most commonly employed escape artifice in groups. Yet, as a common pattern of resistance, it is less endurable in groups than in individual treatment. Silence can be selective or general. *Selective silence* refers to a patient's withholding comments in a specific situation or about a specific subject that has particular meaning to him because of its emotional significance. Contrariwise, it can also signify that the topic does not set off any response in the patient because of its irrelevance to his life and experience. Recurrence of selective silence, as is the case with all diverting and inhibiting maneuvers, may serve as a key to a patient's nuclear problem and threat areas. *General silence* is employed when a patient is resistant or fearful and refrains from participating in any or all interviews. General silence of the *entire* group, however, may have particular significance. Such silence may stem from anger toward the therapist; may be a phalanx of resistance; may be a reaction to a deeply moving event or shock; or may be a reflective mood stimulated by a highly significant thought projected by a patient or the therapist, which the whole group mulls over.

Passivity results in comparative silence and nonparticipation in the group interviews and needs to be understood in terms of each particular patient. Passivity may be a form of resistance, as in cases of passive-aggressive personalities; it is also characteristic of schizoid characters and it can be part of the individual's native temperamental disposition. The therapist needs to ascertain the nature and source of passive conduct and deal with it accordingly.

The appearance *of stereotypy* in group interviews is a signal that further progress cannot be made or that the patients refuse to take further steps. The repetitive return to the same subject, theme, or topic blocks the therapeutic process and the therapist must understand this and take steps to eliminate it. Stereotypy may serve as a means for preventing anxiety in the patients; it may be a tool for annoying the therapist and, thus, be a vehicle for hostility; it may be a topic of particularly strong cathexis to one or more patients requiring resolution; or, more often, group stereotypy serves notice to the therapist that the topic or situation was not adequately clarified. The steps the therapist will have to take to overcome this form of resistance will depend upon its meaning and intent.[9]

Acting out is one of the twilight areas in psychotherapy. Just as it can have profound therapeutic value as a form of catharsis, so it can also be employed as a potent resistance mechanism and as a block to the therapeutic process. Acting out is most frequently resorted to, by adult patients, when their ego defenses are threatened by the communications or acts of fellow members. It can also serve as an escape from self-revelation and self-confrontation that might result in anxiety. Since improvement comes only from revealing painful material, acting out that serves the patient as an escape from painful situations must be viewed as a form of resistance and is deleterious to psychotherapy with adults. This is not true of children, for whom acting out is the most suitable form of catharsis and communication. Whether in individual play therapy, group play therapy, activity-interview, or activity-therapy groups, acting out is the normal pattern for children. When a child abstains from action he is in resistance. Thus, acting out is a form of resistance in the treatment of adults, but not in the treatment of children.[10]

TABLE 4

Patterns of Resistance In Group Psychotherapy

Absenteeism	Associative thinking	Selective silence
Lateness	Distraction	General silence
Displacement	Irrelevancy	Passivity
Deflection	Abruptness	Stereotypy
Planned communication		Acting out (by adults)

[9] For a fuller discussion of this topic, see Chapter XI.
[10] For a more detailed discussion of acting out see Chapter XII.

Resistance Solvents

Analytic groups facilitate the acquisition of insight because patients in such groups come to grips with resistances, ego defenses, and character rigidities much earlier and in more telling ways, due to the reactions of fellow group members, than do individual therapy patients. The group at once reacts to a patient's obvious unwillingness to accept a new point of view, to examine his feelings and values, and to yield to efforts at reaching or altering them. At points in interviews, patients may verbally attack one of their number who persists in remaining silent or proves too "stubborn" or unyielding. This concerted pressure and disapproval affects him more, and certainly much faster, than efforts at explanation by a therapist in individual treatment. Group consensus is always impressive, and one is likely to quickly yield to it.

Displacement of blame or aggression is readily dealt with by fellow members who seldom countenance what seems to them "unfairness." Similarly, deflection, distraction, irrelevancy, and abruptness are not always successful when patients in the group are genuinely interested in a topic and aim to work on it. Associative thinking is swept aside by exploration and questions directed by patients toward the resistive member. A patient is shaken out of his silence by groupmates who directly address a question to him or become critical if he persists in a state of withdrawal for long periods.

However, resistances in groups are also overcome in less direct ways. There are inherent solvents of resistances that are considerably more subtle in their operation and effect. Some of these have been included in the discussion on catharsis. All of the aids (accelerators) of catharsis automatically counteract resistances, for catharsis, in its very nature, occurs in opposition to resistance and through its dissolution. Identification, universalization, and mutual support have the effect of overcoming defensive resistances in individuals. Catalysis and induction have the same consequence. Associative thinking, for example, yields to exploration, universalization, catalysis, and induction, while silence is

163

overcome largely by catalysis and support. Thus every form of resistance is affected to varying degrees, in different patients, by one or more of the catharsis accelerators.

INSIGHT

Conditions for Deriving Insight

The degree of insight derived from psychotherapy is conditioned by the acquisition of emotional flexibility, reduction of the ego defenses, and intellectual comprehension and conceptualization. To attain insight into one's own mechanisms and motivations and to understand and be willing to face their causes in one's constitution and background, one must first be freed of infantile fixations and cravings and be able to give up one's narcissism to a considerable extent. This is achieved largely through decathecting libidinal, pleasure-yielding areas of the body (libido redistribution) and eliminating urges that have remained at levels no longer appropriate to the chronological age of the patient and unsuited to the demands of reality. The persistence of immature desires and infantile methods of gratifying them fosters interpersonal and social disharmony and inner tensions which, among other things prevent true intelligence and the emergence of insight.

When the ego is constrained to defend itself irrationally, because of a low anxiety threshold or a need to maintain tenuous self-esteem, or when ego boundaries are overextended, as in the case of children, the individual cannot respond receptively to the processes involved in acquiring insight. In fact, the major impediments to insight are impelling ego defenses and character rigidities. They serve as a breastwork against any idea, memory, or thought that assails or blemishes one's self-ideal or depreciates self-esteem. Defenses are perpetually vigilant against narcissistic injury and guard the ego and the self, against anything that may tend to inflict such injury, by cloaking, rationalizations, or, at times, through too-ready submission which serves to cushion the damage.

Insight cannot be achieved by intellectual comprehension and understanding as long as resistances are present. Dissolution of these is a precondition for insight which requires self-confrontation (intrapsychic encounter) in a transference relation and through the regressive catharsis made possible by such a transference. Insight in psychotherapy necessitates progressive interpretation by the therapist in accordance with the patient's emotional readiness.[11] In groups, some "interpretation" is supplied by fellow members, which however, is not infrequently inappropriate to a patient's current ego strengths or "psychological literacy."[12]

Types of Insight

Activity group psychotherapy with children revealed that insight could be achieved without verbalization. Despite their age, children in latency become aware of the changes in their own attitudes and values and they recognize that their frustration tolerance has increased. These changes are communicated through both verbal and nonverbal channels. Freedom from defensive needs, ego reinforcement through the group, improved self-images, and the resulting relaxed state make it possible for even young children to become aware of changed intrapsychic reactions. Such spontaneously derived awareness has also been observed in adult patients, both in individual and group treatment.

In activity group therapy, the therapist is a neutral figure and a permissive parent surrogate. Despite the fact that he keeps his verbalizations to a minimum, his movement through the room, his differential response in action to children's acts, statements, questions and demands, constitute a form of interpretation. This *action interpretation* leads to some forms of insight.

To differentiate the two types of insight—that which is derived

[11] Interpretation must be differentiated from explanation, which is quite different in nature and therapeutic relevance. See Slavson, 1952, pages 54-55.

[12] Herein lies still another reason for the inappropriateness of considering patients as so-called "co-therapists." Lacking the professional training and judgment, they all too frequently "run ahead" of their fellow patients in their *explanations*, thus preventing self-discovery and progressive unraveling of the associated circumstances and feelings essential to real psychotherapy. They frequently disturb fellow patients with their poor timing. In fact, this is one of the weaknesses of group treatment for certain types of neuroses, though it is helpful for patients with character disorders.

from verbal interpretation and which automatically emerges as a result of emotional growth—the terms *direct insight* and *derivative insight,* respectively, are suggested. It has also been observed that patients acquire *differential levels of insight.* The depth of insight is determined by the needs of a specific patient, the type of therapy employed, the circumstances under which it is acquired, and (though seldom recognized) the *capacity* of a specific individual to acquire insight.

Because of the state of transference and the variety of cathartic processes in groups, the levels of insight that a patient can attain are less deep than in psychoanalysis. However, some patients, through the aid of groups, reach deeper levels of insight (and improvement) than in individual treatment with therapists of comparable skill. None the less, the potential for plumbing the depths of the unconscious and the past (essential to the treatment of transference neuroses) and for unraveling profoundly disturbing and inadequately repressed feelings, are generally much greater in individual treatment than in group psychotherapy. If this is reversed in practice, it is to be attributed to the skill (or lack of it) of the therapist or to the nuclear or core problem of the particular patient, and not to the relative inherent potential of the two therapies.

The interstimulation of thoughts, ideas, and understanding in a group is more conducive to acquiring derivative insight. However, the level of direct insight may be expected to be at a lower level, as the libidinal transferences toward the therapist are less charged and interferences from other patients are frequent. There is an organic unity between transference, catharsis, resistance, and insight. As one is affected, the others are reflectively influenced.

In analytic groups with young children, even of preschool age, interpretation is given by the therapist, but it is carefully geared to the child's perceptive ability and comprehension. In activity group therapy, on the other hand, no explanations or interpretations are given. The insight is entirely derivative and, as already indicated, a considerable degree of such insight is acquired through the groups.

TABLE 5

Types of Insight In Group Psychotherapy
Direct
Derivative

REALITY TESTING

The Emergence of the Sense of Reality

A major capacity, that at once contributes to and is an index of, the maturity of personality, is reality testing. In his orderly development, the individual normally alters his perceptions and understanding of reality from a narcissistic, omnipotent view to a more veridical one. To the child, reality is an extension of himself and he fantasies unlimited power over it. As he grows older, his perception is modified by experience and interaction with persons, objects and events. External reality—actuality—may grow to represent danger or comparative security, depending on his experience with it, and on the role of mediating persons in the environment, such as parents, teachers, and other adults. During his life, by interacting with his animate and inanimate environment, the individual tests its real nature as well as his own relation to it. He may find it friendly or hostile, constructive or destructive, a threat or a comfort. As with all other attitudes, his evaluations of reality and his attitudes toward it are determined by early experiences with the significant persons in his life. It is their treatment of the infant and child that lays the basis of the *quality* of his attitudes, first toward them as representatives of external reality and later toward actuality itself.

The important process in this interaction, as it concerns maturity, is that perception of reality has to undergo continued revision through experiencing and testing. The response to experiences and their meaning to a given individual are conditioned by his receptivity to them and to his evolving powers, understandings, and comprehensions. However, in nearly all persons, infantile perceptions of reality persist in some areas and to some degree. All persons retain vestiges of their childhood attitudes that interfere with adjustment in the adult world. (Among these, for

167

example, are feelings of omnipotence, or a belief in magic and miracles.) Few people are able to deal realistically with actuality in *all* areas. Most people can accept reality and deal with it effectively in some areas, but tend to be less mature in others. Despite this dichotomy, the average person can function with comparative adequacy; that is, he is operationally effective in achieving physical, psychological, and social survival with a normal amount of effort and stress.

Therapy and Reality

Patients who come for psychotherapy are deficient in some of these respects: their relation to their environment is a source of excessive difficulty, either as overt conflict, or because of the intense inner strain required to deal with it. Patients are always in conflict with the outer world, with themselves, or with both. Because of this common characteristic of patients, some therapists put direct emphasis on interpersonal relations, excluding or minimizing the personality sources of the difficulties. Dynamically this approach puts the cart before the horse, for correction of interpersonal relations first requires correction of the intrapsychic states that cause the conflicts and stresses.

"Re-education" in relationships can be effective with those persons in whom the disturbances are of a surface nature. When reality distortion is an internalized mechanism and an integral part of the personality structure, as in psychoneuroses, such directness cannot be effective. No real therapy can be achieved by dealing with the symptom rather than with the underlying causes. A technique that addresses itself to, and utilizes only, reality (actuality) is not true psychotherapy. It may be effective in counseling or guidance, but not with those deeply disturbed and conflicted patients who need reweighting and reorganizing of their psychic forces, before they can become free of stress and slough off their fantasies about reality and its perils.

Reality testing—or better still, reality retesting—is an important element in psychotherapy, since its aim is to achieve constructive and adequate adjustment to, and in, reality. The values of therapeutic intrapsychic experiences lie in this fact. Inner experience makes it possible for one to re-evaluate conditions and reactions in a more receptive mood and diminish defensive projections of negative, hostile feelings. Because psychotherapy establishes inner harmony, it places the individual in a more hospitable, charitable and objective attitude toward people and events. As self-hatred and discontent are reduced, there is a corresponding reduction in hostile feelings toward others; as self-blame is diminished, excessive blame placed on the external world is correspondingly reduced, as is the need for hostile or defensive aggression. Thus, interpersonal relations and a sanguine attitude toward the world generally are results of reconstitution of the personality, rather than alteration of one's "philosophy" or ideas.

Reality testing is an automatic process. As the individual functions in the world, he registers his reactions and difficulties. His self-esteem or self-image is affected accordingly. If he is successful in dealing with reality, repair to the self-image results; but when he fails, he is aware of shortcomings and the need for correction. The patient thus comes to the treatment situation, where he can examine reality and his own reactions, with the aid of the psychotherapist and the group. Reality testing is a major and integral part of emotional maturity and is always present in the therapeutic process, whether it occurs in the treatment situation itself or in the operational world.

Group Psychotherapy and Reality Testing

The therapy group presents a tangible reality to patients; it makes certain demands which each member must meet if he is to remain a part of the group. Among the many pressures a patient has to deal with is the ego functioning of the other group members. As a result, he has to show or withhold his responses, employ restraint or compromise, attend to discussions and expose himself to scrutiny. Ultimately he has to learn to deal with his likes and dislikes, attractions and antagonisms, and to absorb attacks on himself and control his attacks on others.[13] Actually, these demands for adaptation are not limited to psychotherapy; they are imposed

[13] These demands for control make group therapy intolerable for some patients. They require individual treatment before they can participate in or gain from a group.

in day-to-day living and functioning in the world. They may not be as concentrated and intense as in a therapy group; nonetheless, the patient constantly meets them. Few in our culture can escape interpersonal encounters.

There is, however, an advantage to being exposed to them in the therapeutic setting, where the affect generated by them can be expressed and worked through—analyzed, interpreted, and understood. In a group, it is more difficult to disguise reactions. The immediacy of the events and the actualistic approach by group members and the patient himself render the reality factor more telling and therapeutically more effective. This is *reality testing in situ,* as differentiated from *reality testing ex situ,* which occurs outside the treatment setting.

Reality testing *in situ* has given rise to a group therapeutic technique described by its proponents as the "here and now" method, in which the sole therapeutic process consists of helping patients understand their inappropriate emotional reactions to each other and to the therapist, by analyzing the "group tensions" as they appear in the interviews. The repressed memories and unconscious conflicts that prompt behavior are not examined. The claim is made that the patient has to be viewed not in historic perspective, but in the context of his current life and behavior and that when he understands these, he improves. This approach omits what is essential in the treatment of neuroses: the deeper determinants cannot be eliminated by intellectual understanding alone; neuroses are autonomous; their basic sources have to be worked through in the light of memories and earlier relationships and the bound up anxieties and guilts must be released, for only then can the noxious psychic sources be eliminated.

The way the therapist deals with conflicts and tensions in the group serves as an example for the patients. His calm and self-confident manner are a living demonstration of ego strength and objectivity which patients can emulate, and with which they can identify. Ego functioning is, for the most part, conditioned by identification with, and emulation of, parents, especially the mother. Where parents are excitable, afraid, panicky, and anxious, the children grow up incapable of dealing adequately with pressures and tensions. The therapist's strength and calm, under the conditions of stress that frequently arise in therapy groups, serve as corrective models which patients first imitate and later incorporate in their personal lives. Group members, too, serve as models for each other. This is one of the "re-educational" aspects of group psychotherapy.

Reality testing and acting out in a group situation may be compatible with, or antagonistic to, the ongoing therapeutic flow of the group. When catharsis, reality testing, or acting out aid the progressive flow of therapy, we can characterize it as *group syntonic*. When it is antagonistic to, or disruptive of, the treatment it can be considered as *group alien*.

Psychotherapy and Mysticism

The tendency to base psychotherapy on religion, ideologies, mysticism, and metaphysical and transcendental concepts must be deplored. To be effective, the frame of reference of all therapy needs to be reality, both "inner" and "outer" reality (actuality). The associative affects and fantasies have to stem from reality and the patient's paratactic distortions of it need to enter his awareness largely through his own efforts, though aided by the therapist and fellow patients. The introduction of transcendental theories and techniques cannot but vitiate the development of sound therapy, frustrate the therapist, and mislead and harm patients.

Philosophies borrowed from Eastern religions and cults and from indigenous religious dogmas serve persons with fragile egos only as escapes from facing and dealing with reality. These religions themselves are, in fact, being abandoned by increasing numbers, where they had prevailed for many centuries, as the facts of scientific and technological reality spread. To import such beliefs to the West only reverses the present trend toward a more dynamic confrontation of life. There is no guarantee that science will ameliorate the suffering and confusions of man, but there is more hope that it can be achieved through science than through mysticism.

Whatever philosophical adventures man is prone to, clinical practice should not be misled into the byways that lead away from rationality. The frame of reference must always be the reality of the human personality and its relation to, and interaction with, the actuality of the world around it. It is inevitable that the quest for truth, which is also the concern of psychotherapy, should at times lead into speculative thought and the exploration of ideologies and ethics. To block them off completely would be as erroneous as to make them the backbone of psychotherapy. When they are relevant and illuminating, abstractions are useful, but one must always be aware that they are essentially not suitable for personality reconstruction and may serve as a form of resistance for both patient and therapist.

TABLE 6

Types of Reality Testing In Group Psychotherapy

In situ	Group Alien
Ex situ	Group Syntonic

SUBLIMATION

To acquire acceptable sublimations for instinctual urges that are incompatible with social norms is one of the major aims of education, in its larger meaning, and when it fails, psychotherapy becomes necessary. Sublimations cannot be supplied to adults through the experiences in outpatient therapeutic situations, either group or individual. In inpatient treatment, ancillary techniques and activities are employed for this purpose, including various forms of recreational and occupational therapies, dramatics, sports, games, art, arts and crafts, and trades and services in the institution. Choice is made for the patients by the staff or they are encouraged to take part in activities that serve to discharge or redirect primitive drives into socially approved channels.

It must be recognized, however, that too ready sublimations may impede the psychotherapeutic effort or erase its effects. Unlike ordinary life functions, in psychotherapy it is necessary to bring remnants of instinctual urges present in the psyche into the open, in the raw, and work them through. Occupations and divergencies may cut this process short and establish a façade that will not hold up under the stress of living. First, psychic pressures and tensions need to be released and the ego must acquire and assimilate new strengths, or the tenuous sublimations will soon break down under the strain of outer pressures or inner conflicts. The individual then returns to his former problem-creating mode of life. To be effective, sublimations need to be established in childhood; failing that, they have to be arrived at through a grad ual elimination of primary drives by skillfully conducted psychotherapy. Sublimations are most effective and permanent when the primitive urges are channelled into suitable skills and talents, that conform with one's native disposition and predilections.

Sublimation in Psychotherapy

The value of sublimation, as part of psychotherapy, is being recognized by an increasing number of psychotherapists who employ social workers and specialists in the arts to work with patients. Some direct patients to outside individual and group occupations. Sublimatory activities, as such, are seldom offered in the private practice of group psychotherapy with adults, but for some patients belonging to a group in itself has salutary effects. Being part of, and accepted by, a group is, in itself, beneficial. Mutuality and the predominantly warm and friendly feelings that gradually emerge, and later become the dominant atmosphere in a group, produce deep gratification in most patients, sublimating and redirecting their hostile and aggressive trends and changing their habitually negative responses.

The craving to belong is in great evidence among children, but the same craving also dominates adults. Isolation and loneliness give rise to depression and intra- and interpersonal disharmony; they render one vindictive, irritable, and hostile. Being alone means being unwanted, a feeling that plagues the psychoneurotic. To belong to an accepting group that is interested in one, counteracts introversion, self-deprecation, and hostile reactions, self- and social alienation. A therapy group, though its aim is correction and reconstruction, rather than socialization, does satisfy social hunger. Even when the group exerts pressure which, at times, may be disturbing, it still yields gratifications because of the interest the group displays in the patient. This reaction is similar to that of a child who feels unwanted when parents do not correct or discipline him. The absence of attention, even if it is negative and restrictive, may symbolize lack of interest.

Sublimations do not necessarily have to be a part of the therapeutic setting itself. In the course of psychotherapy, adults are more and more liberated from their alienative compulsions and erratic behavior, and as their personalities become more flexible, they react more hospitably to the outer world and are able to evolve socially acceptable sublimations of their primary narcissism and instinctual urges. The psychoneurotic, and patients with character disorders, are unable to establish sublimatory channels because of repetition compulsion, defensive patterns, and character rigidities, as the case may be. Psychotherapy, in diminishing or eliminating pathology, lays the basis for evolving suitable sublimations within one's life-sphere.

The preceding comments are not as applicable to children as they are to adults, for defenses and character rigidities typical of adults are not fully developed or well entrenched in children. Dependent on age and experience, sublimations are either nonexistent or still rudimentary. The child reacts by direct acts, substitution, or displacement. Because of his nascent character, a child has to be helped, in the therapeutic situation itself, to evolve sublimations consistent with environmental demands. Viewed from biological and emotional aspects, the chief task of education —home, school, and community—is to help the child repress some, and sublimate other, primitive urges. Where these societal instrumentalities have failed, psychotherapy becomes necessary.

TABLE 7

Types of Sublimation In Group Psychotherapy

In situ

Ex situ

174

TABLE 8

Characteristics and Dynamics in Analytic, Activity and Directive Therapy Groups

Analytic Groups	Activity Groups	Directive Groups
Insight	Ego Strengthening	Understanding
Libido Activation	Libido Binding	
Libido Therapy	Ego Therapy	Ego Strengthening
Hostility Discharge against Therapist	Hostility Discharge toward Substitutes	
High Levels of Anxiety	Low Levels of Anxiety	Anxiety Held in Abeyance
Therapist Object of Libidinal Cathexis	Therapist Source of Support	Therapist as Guide
Therapist Active-passive	Therapist Neutral	Therapist Active
Direct Insight	Derivative Insight	Understanding
Verbal Interpretation	Action Interpretation	Explanation
Low Degree Reality Testing *In Situ*	High Degree Reality Testing *In Situ*	Low Degree Reality Testing *In Situ*
Emotional Interaction Only	Emotional and Active Interaction	Minimal Interaction

TABLE 9

Differential Dynamics in Group Therapies

Type of Group	Transference	Catharsis	Insight	Reality Testing	Sublimation	Resistance
Activity (Children)	Sibling Identification Multilateral Unilateral Group	Activity Induced Vicarious	Derivative	*In Situ*	*In Situ*	Absenteeism Lateness Passivity
Play (Children)	Libidinal Sibling Identification Multilateral Group	Activity Verbal Activity-verbal Free Association Induced Vicarious	Direct Derivative	*In Situ*	*In Situ* *Ex Situ*	Irrelevancy* Silence Passivity
Activity-Interview (Children)	Libidinal Sibling Identification Multilateral Group	Associative Free Association Activity Verbal Activity-verbal Induced Vicarious	Direct Derivative	*In Situ*	*In Situ* *Ex Situ*	Irrelevancy Silence Lateness Absenteeism Passivity

* Absenteeism and lateness are omitted since parents bring children under school age for treatment.

TABLE 9 (cont.)

Type of Group	Transference	Catharsis	Insight	Reality Testing	Sublimation	Resistance
Analytic (Adults)	Libidinal Sibling Identification Multilateral Group	Associative Free Association Verbal Directed Induced Vicarious	Direct Derivative	Ex Situ In Situ	Ex Situ	Displacement Deflection Distraction Abruptness Planned Communication Associative Thinking Irrelevancy Silence Absenteeism Lateness Acting Out
Para-Analytic (Adolescents)	Libidinal Sibling Identification Multilateral Group	Associative Free Association Verbal Directed Induced Vicarious	Direct Derivative	Ex Situ In Situ		(as above)

VI

Criteria for Selection

Four General Criteria

Even though individualization is the key to selection of patients for analytic group psychotherapy, it is possible to state several general generic guiding principles.[1] These are: capacity for minimal primary relations; degree of sexual disturbances; minimal ego strengths; and minimal superego development.

Minimal Primary Relations

To be able to withstand the impact of the multiple relations and interactions in a group, an individual must have had some satisfying relations with one or more persons, especially during his childhood. The capacity for relatedness stems from these early emotional experiences. Lacking these, his anxiety and discomfort would militate against his functioning in the compresence of others or his gaining from the situation. Group treatment as an initial or sole method is, therefore, not advised for patients whose relations, especially with parents and siblings, were nonexistent or extremely destructive. Such individuals possess little capacity for object relations, and are unable, as a result, to give up their egocentricity. Since relationships in groups are multilateral, the de-

---

[1] These, and other criteria in this chapter, were derived from the screening and treatment of some 6,000 patients of varied age, sex, race, and nationality, in a variety of settings over a period of more than twenty-five years.

178

mands are greater than they are in a person-to-person therapeutic setting. Before assigning patients to group treatment it is, therefore, necessary to determine whether they can fit into a group without deleterious effects to themselves and the other members. Early interpersonal deprivations may be revealed during the very first exploratory interview. Treatment by parents, family antagonisms, and sexual difficulties are among the central problems of all who seek psychotherapy and are among the first subjects they bring to the interviews. Patients frequently reveal themselves as lonely, emotionally isolated, socially uncomfortable people with interpersonal difficulties with mates, offspring, co-workers, and in social situations. Child patients show a general incapacity to have satisfactory relationships at school, with other children, and at home. Often, a single interview with their mothers uncovers a history of destructive parent-child relationships. Obviously, neither adults nor children with an intense emotional void could adapt themselves to a group.

Sexual Disturbance

The second general psychological vector for determining a patient's suitability for group psychotherapy is the intensity of his sexual disturbance. A patient whose symptomatology stems directly from the oedipal conflict, or who has been exposed to sexual overstimulation and the seductiveness of a parent, needs to develop a transference neurosis during treatment and requires an individual transference relation as a part of his therapy. Because therapy groups address themselves predominantly to ego functioning, the needs of such patients cannot be fully met in groups. Deep libidinal distortions require cathexis displacement onto a person who will deal with the aberrant wishes therapeutically. Adults whose *vita sexualis* is deviant, or charged with anxiety and guilt, are best helped in a transference relation in individual treatment, where id urges are exposed and can be worked through and made accessible to the superego and to the ego in a regressive and insight-evoking process. In some instances, a patient may require a period of individual psychoanalysis or psychotherapy before assignment to a group (after which he may not require the

179

group at all). There are still others who, for a variety of reasons, are unable to enter into a one-to-one relation with a therapist, but who can accept group psychotherapy, either as the sole treatment or as a preparation for individual treatment.

Ego Strength

The third consideration is the ego strength of the prospective group member. Although groups may offer escapes and protection, they also tend to expose patients to stresses and make demands on them that some may be unable to meet. This is particularly true of therapeutic groups. Therefore, patients are acceptable only when their egos are strong enough to withstand the stress to which they will be subjected. Unlike individual treatment, where the therapist can control the interviews and select therapeutically indicated content, the therapist in a group can exercise this prerogative only with great difficulty. The subjects discussed, the course the interviews take, and the emotional activation are in the hands of the group, which may overload the ego of some of the participants. Induced anxieties, fears, and guilts may be more than some of the patients should be exposed to at a given stage. This is an especially important consideration when interviews are held at long intervals and patients are thus compelled to live under increased stress in the interim.

Superego Development

In addition to ego sufficiency, it is essential that patients in group psychotherapy have at least a minimal superego development. Individuals devoid of feelings of right and wrong and driven by anarchic impulses and id urges, cannot internalize social criteria solely through group participation. The superego is initially derived from identifications resulting in the incorporation of the images and standards set by parents or their surrogates. The basic superego cannot be derived from group mores, though they reinforce and modify the original parental superego. Conscienceless and id-determined acts on the part of one group member evoke anxiety and, therefore, resentment in the other members, with little benefit to anyone. The foundations for superego development are established from relations with individuals and correction of its malformation has to come from identification with an individual therapist.

On the other hand, an overstrict superego can be relaxed through the permissive group climate and the support given to the expression of impulsiveness and aggression. However, in the case of anxiety-ridden, obsessional-compulsive patients, this may have the effect of intensifying feelings of guilt and increasing the quantum of anxiety. The criterion of superego sufficiency eliminates, from groups, also certain types of regressive infantile characters and psychopathic personalities who are deficient in superego development, and some psychotics.

TYPES OF INDICATIONS

Criteria for the selection of patients for group psychotherapy fall within three general categories: positive, negative, and positive-negative.

Positive indications appear when a clinical study of a patient's treatment needs show that they can best be met by a group, this method being either the temporary or sole treatment of choice. When the clinical study reveals that a patient would be traumatized by a group experience or that his specific difficulty would not be reached through a multirelational experience, a complex of *negative indications* appears. Where individual treatment is indicated, but the patient is unable to respond to or gain from it due to blockage in the transference because of fear and distrust, or because of an uncontrollable need to resist and to dominate all authority figures, group psychotherapy is recommended as preparation for, or as a parallel with, individual psychotherapy. These are *positive-negative indications*.

Among the "indications" suggested by some writers for assigning patients to groups is that of "social neurosis." Presumably, the term designates a condition that arises from reactions of anxiety, fear, or panic in relation to people and groups. Clinically, it would be difficult to justify such a diagnosis. A social or group situation can precipitate neurotic reactions only where a neurosis already exists. It would be difficult to demonstrate that an individual will react pathologically to groups and to social situations without the presence of some internalized noxious state that affects his personality and, therefore, his reactions. Social reactions cannot be divorced from inner conditions. Responses to interpersonal and social situations are only symptoms. It would seem correct to assume that patients with this specific manifestation should, sometime during their treatment, have a group experience as a reality-testing device in a "tapering off" process. However, the assumption that panicky anxiety in social situations can be treated through group interpersonal reactions is not, without qualification, justified and, in many instances, may even prove deleterious.

Positive Indications for Analytic Groups

Defensive Projection

Among the patients showing positive indications for analytic group psychotherapy, are those with the defensive mechanism of projection. Such patients persistently blame others for their own inadequacies, failures, and liabilities. Projection, as a defense, is very difficult to deal with in individual therapy. The therapist, being a parent substitute, is part of patients' fantasies as well as a target for their projections and blame. Any reaction on the therapist's part is perceived as criticism by the patient. In a group, this mechanism is rather effectively dealt with by the other members. Because they do not represent authority, projection is more accessible to confrontation and interpretation by fellow patients. The group, by its reactions, activates the patient to associate freely and to recall the early traumatic situations that gave rise to his defensive pattern. The group's reactions are tangible, direct, firm, and instantaneous. The effectiveness of group treatment for the self-defensive projective pattern has been amply demonstrated by clinical experience.

Biologic Destiny

Many patients' central need is reinforcement of their biological destinies, toward which their attitudes have been distorted through inadequate or unfavorable conditioning or identifications during the formative imprinting years. They are confused in sexual identifications and are at odds with the role they have to play in life. The valuable reinforcing of socially defined roles for an individual is an observable characteristic of all groups, educational as well as therapeutic. Barring massive pathology or perversion, the group's support of the individual's own unconscious wish to conform with social mores is very effective. For example, men who dress carelessly and women who prefer masculine fashions soon change their mode of attire through group influences. Patients who habitually neglect their persons become clean, comely, and trim. This kind of self-improvement may be attributed to fear of being stigmatized and unaccepted by fellow group members, reduction of homoerotism, or corrected identifications. Whatever the reason, the group supports the native trend toward healthy identifications and, as a result, has favorable repercussions in the patients' relations with mates, offspring, other relatives, and associates.

Additional effects occur in men patients. Through identification, imitation, and ego reinforcement, universalization and an improved self-image, masculine traits that had been neurotically submerged, come to the fore, at first cautiously and experimentally and later with more assurance and security. The patients proceed to test reality against their newly emerging strengths and soon take a more appropriate place in the family, on the job, and in other relations.

Character Disorders

Many difficulties stem from character deficiencies and patterns of ego functioning, as well as from deep-rooted psychoneuroses and sexual abnormalities. In the latter case, group psychotherapy must be used with caution, as there is no evidence of effectiveness in such cases. There is, however, sufficient evidence of effectiveness in the treatment of character malformations stemming from past accommodations to external relations and conditions. Character disorders, generally, yield to the ministrations of therapy groups. The group milieu is a new type of (substitute) family requiring accommodations of an altogether different type than those made by the patient in the past. What had to be guarded and covered before, can now be exposed in the light of feeling and understanding; what one has been ashamed of, one can now reveal with impunity. This is significant because it can be done without compunction, fear of punishment, criticism, or rejection. The therapist (as a parental figure) is permissive, tolerant, and understanding; and so are, by and large, the fellow patients (the new siblings). At times, patients may take one member to task; they may criticize him and correct him, but for the most part, it is done with an honest intent to help, not to punish or debase.

When a situation gets too tight for a patient, the therapist gives it meaning and significance, thus reducing the burden on the patient's ego. Most often, however, it is one's friends, the other patients, who explain and interpret. They not only help uncover memories and feelings of early childhood, but they also demonstrate, and teach one, how to react to situations in a different way. Even more significantly, they *compel* one to react differently than in the past, thus altering the pattern of adaptations and responses.

All groups, whether therapeutic, guidance, educational, or communal, modify behavior, whether temporarily or permanently. Of these, only therapy groups can alter intrapsychic states and inner balance. Limited only by hereditary resources, character is a result of interaction with people, experiences, and the impingement of demands and pressures during formative (imprinting) years. New ways of adapting, aided by a new awareness and favorable conditions, can alter character. The aggressive person, for example, is made aware of his aggressiveness because others in the group refuse to tolerate it, but they do not react to his behavior by rejection or punishment; rather, they wish to help, even if they are disapproving and firm in the process.

The passive and the diffident are encouraged by the group to become more outgoing and more reactive. Since there is, in all organisms, a trend toward centrifugal movement and aggression, such patients gain more readily from groups than do aggressive patients. Movement is the basis of life and survival and it automatically grows and evolves, unless it is inhibited or distorted at early stages. Psychotherapy, especially group psychotherapy, encourages the natural centrifugal flow of the libido.

One of the forms of character malformation that responds to group treatment is acting out. Where the acting out is ego alien, a neurotic conflict is present. Such patients may or may not be accessible to group psychotherapy, depending on the nature and intensity of their pathology. Where acting out is ego syntonic, however, the patient will present character resistances to change that are very difficult to reach by ordinary insight therapy. Such patients put up very strong defenses against change; they battle, as it were, with the therapist. Since their difficulties are not alien to their ego, they are devoid of conflict and deny the existence of a problem. Even though such patients, at times, feel discomfort over others' reactions to them, they are symptom-free so the discomfort is not intense enough to prevent their justifying themselves through defensive blame against other persons and external circumstances. They always fall back on the defense of projection.

The picture is different when the acting out is part of a neurotic syndrome, as in the anxiety neuroses, or when anxiety is, in itself, the symptom, as in the case of a neurotic character. Here, the need to act out is a resolution of deep-rooted and long-standing anxiety, originating in preverbal and preconceptual stages. Such compulsive acting out disturbs the group and its reactions may prove traumatic to the offending patient.

To be affected by group psychotherapy, impulse must be accessible to the ego, even if it requires the help of the therapist and fellow patients. When impulses are inaccessible to, or threaten, the ego defenses, and anxiety results, intensive individual therapy is indicated, because in such cases the group's criticism and disapproval may be harmful. The struggles of such an individual to control himself only add to the quantum of his anxiety, increasing his ego load and intensifying the disturbance. The prognosis for adults with neurotic characters is poor in any type of psychotherapy, including psychoanalysis, since the beginnings of

185

the problems predate the verbal stage of development and are structured into the personality. When acting out, however, proceeds from an inadequately formed ego and infantile omnipotence, or when it serves as a mechanism of control, a source of secondary gains, or a method of testing reality, the reactions of a saturated reality (such as a group) to these patterns is of definite effectiveness.

Character Resistances

Patients with character resistances fare better in groups than in individual treatment. The analysis of character resistances, as differentiated from superego and id resistances (Spotnitz, 1952), is a difficult, if not insurmountable, problem for the psychoanalyst and the psychotherapist. These difficulties are, in many respects, analogous to the ego defenses we have already described. Interpretation of these resistances are seldom fruitful because they are ego syntonic. The patient's ego refuses to recognize or accept the interpretations. As part of the character structure, the ego itself is involved in the process and, therefore, cannot examine itself. However, a patient can be made aware of his behavior and attitudes through the reactions of fellow group members. When resistances are repeatedly assailed and interpreted by a group, their dissolution is more likely to occur than in one-to-one interviews. The patient's need to be accepted by the group, his social hunger, motivates him to modify his conduct and reactions. Character resistances are much more tenacious than neurotic resistance and present a challenge to group psychotherapy. An integral part of character resistance is the patient's need to challenge and defeat the therapist as authority, which can also occur in transference resistance.

Transference Resistances

This type of resistance can be treated adequately in psychoanalysis. In the less-intensive individual psychotherapies, in which patient and therapist are in a face-to-face position, transference resistances present greater difficulties. The interviews may assume the nature of haggling dialogues and may degenerate into contentiousness between patient and therapist. In groups, the status of the therapist is much less prominent and, therefore, arouses less challenge. Since transference reactions are divided and diluted in groups, the urge for infantile oedipal struggle with the therapist is diminished. Because of the multiplicity of targets for hostile feelings (target multiplicity), this particular type of resistance can be more easily dealt with by a group.

All patients present transference resistances to some degree; they all have hostile attitudes toward their parents and suffer from inadequately resolved oedipal struggles. However, the intensity of the remnants of hostility vary, and other less involved patients confront the offending, resisting, or challenging fellow member. Because they easily identify with him, patients can appropriately interpret his mechanisms. Here, again, universalization, identification, and mirror reactions (and sometimes sibling hostility) favor therapeutic ends. The meaning of the reactions to the therapist may become the topic of discussion for a time. Memories and current attitudes toward parents and siblings are brought out by free association and a connection is made between these and attitudes and feelings toward the therapist and group members.

Another dynamic in this group syndrome is the "protectiveness" of some patients toward the therapist when he is challenged or attacked by a fellow patient. Their childhood fears and anxieties are reawakened when a parental figure is openly attacked and, to allay these anxieties, some patients defend the therapist or turn on the aggressive member.

Sibling Antagonism

There are patients whose nuclear problem is rooted in sibling relationships, even though the difficulties ultimately stem from the conduct of parents. There are advantages to placing such patients in a therapy group, where they can act out their feelings toward substitute siblings, in a conditioned environment which offers appropriate emotional reactions, suitable insights, and objective understanding. The tangible reality of other persons in a group activates the patient's conscious and unconscious difficulties

187

in a more telling way than solely verbal reconstruction. The replica of earlier tensions induced by the (substitute) family setting provided by a group brings out the partially repressed feelings associated with the original family setting. These feelings are then dealt with and worked through by the members of the group. While this may set off considerable group tension, it is therapeutically very profitable when analyzed and interpreted by the group as a whole, with the planned help of the therapist. However, patients whose hostilities toward siblings are overwhelmingly intense may be unable to tolerate a group; some may even leave because their hostile feelings reach an intensity which they cannot tolerate.

Repressed urges and feelings toward parents and sibling antagonisms are the greatest activators of group tensions. They constitute a fertile field for analytic group psychotherapy, where accumulated resentments and hostilities are discharged and worked through. While the light of understanding and the healing effect of insight are necessary, the analysis of group tensions cannot be the sole therapeutic tool. Rather, the analysis of the multiple transference relations that exist in every group should be brought out according to the patients' emotional backgrounds.

Some patients, who were only children in their families, expect, and sometimes demand, the narcissistic gratifications they received from their parents. They expect to occupy the center of attention in situations where such a desire is unrealistic. The estate of only-childhood also produces definite character traits, in which narcissism and faulty object relations predominate. Children who have not had the need nor the opportunity to share, are frequently deficient in this regard. Groups demand sharing and relating on a more mature base. This may prove difficult, and even distressing, to individuals without antecedent conditioning. Even when other problems of only-child patients require individual psychotherapy for their resolution, group psychotherapy is also indicated for them, as a reality situation in sharing and relating.

Schizoid Personalities

On theoretical grounds, patients with schizoid personalities are suitable for group treatment. The activation they require can best be supplied by groups. Special consideration, however, must be given to the nature of their problems and their ego strengths. Not every patient with a schizoid personality structure should be exposed to a situation where profoundly disturbing emotions can be touched off at any time. Patients in this category are better placed in guidance groups, which discuss top realities, current events and day-to-day interests. The schizoid person tends to remain apart from the flux of life, and he responds to it selectively and impassively. Mulling over the practical events of daily living is helpful to the schizoid patient. The more he is activated to participation, the narrower grows the schism between his mental preoccupations and actuality.

Schizoid patients remain, for the most part, quiet and withdrawn in groups; they participate but little. They are, however, among the more observant, astute, and insightful members, for despite their seeming detachment, they actually register everything that goes on in the discussions as well as nonverbalized and latent implications. Their remarks, though infrequent and brief, are usually penetrating and reveal a high level of reflective thought. They well confirm the adage, "Still waters run deep."

As the true schizoid personality has a constitutional base, therapeutic expectations must, of necessity, be limited. The schizoid's capacity for reactivity is comparatively low and his resources small. Despite these limitations, group association is indicated for the schizoid. Since they are not initiators, they remain, for the most part, uncommunicative in an individual relationship. In a group they are activated to a much larger degree. It is this characteristic that makes them more promising candidates for groups.

Psychic Masochism

Psychic masochists can gain from group treatment, giving up masochistic submissiveness with surprising rapidity. Interpretation by fellow group members, their support and encouragement and the resultant ego reinforcement, all help psychic masochists to achieve new ways of relating. Patients, have reported, with satisfaction and elation, their successes with increasing self-assertiveness, and newly found firmness and independence. They were

189

able to recall childhood situations, the family climate, and individual relationships that brought on their special type of adaptation, and were quickly helped to recognize the ineffectiveness of their attitudes and behavior. The support of the group (as a mother substitute) helped them overcome fears and encouraged them to challenge the persons to whom they formally submitted.[2] No evidence is presently available regarding the effectiveness of group psychotherapy with sexual masochists. However, it is unlikely that groups can correct this condition.

Borderline Schizophrenics

Borderline schizophrenics and other types of psychoses (to be discussed under "negative indications") have to be placed in groups only with great care. The measure of ego sufficiency of such patients must be ascertained in advance of assignment.

Negative Indications for Analytic Groups

The negative indications for group psychotherapy are more clearly definable than are the positive. As already noted, patients who lack a minimal capacity for object relations, ego and superego sufficiency, and those with serious sexual disturbances, are unsuitable for groups until their basic difficulties have been corrected by individual treatment.

Active or disturbed psychotics are unsuitable for analytic group psychotherapy where the analysis of the unconscious and intrapsychic processes form the body of the interviews.[3] Patients who hallucinate or have delusions, and those who fragmentize ideas and reality should be excluded from therapy groups. Among unsuitable patients are the nonpsychotics with very intensive and diffuse anxiety, those with transference neuroses, full-blown anxiety neurotics, the intensely narcissistic, the obsessive-compulsive, depressives, cyclothymic personalities, the suicidal, perverts, active

[2] See the case of Mrs. S., pp. 299ff.

[3] Participation in social, recreational, arts and crafts, occupational, and didactic groups are recommended for them, instead.

homosexuals,[4] compulsive talkers, and patients who cannot refrain from monopolizing the stage. Depending on the nature and etiology of the narcissism, however, some patients in this last category can gain from intimate group interaction. Among the character disturbances unsuitable for group treatment are the neurotic characters whose anxiety originated in the preverbal period. Such anxiety is not accessible to the ego; criticism and disapproval by the group only increases rather than allays their already intense discomfort.

Hypochondriacal patients have to be excluded because of their compulsive need to speak repeatedly, and sometimes continually, about their symptoms without any constructive focus or direction. Their viewing of reality in terms of physical pain, and their repeated reference to their ailments, cause annoyance and discomfort to the others in the group, blocking the group process and preventing therapeutic effectiveness. In fact, the cause of hypochondriacal somatization is not accessible to the group method. Narcissism and libidinal investment in the physical symptoms are so great that if the patient can be reached at all, it must be through a libidinal transference relation in a regressive process, such as is provided by individual psychoanalysis. Hypochondriacal symptomatology is, in many patients, a defense against psychosis and treatment for them has to be planned with the utmost care. The reality sense of the hypochondriac is greatly distorted, since events and occurrences are colored by physical discomforts and the expectation of physical catastrophes. He is inaccessible to group treatment and is a difficult patient for any type of treatment.

True hysteria is another negative indication for exclusive group treatment of adults. Hysteria, being the result of the oedipal complex operating on the genital level and being rooted in guilt concerning past sex thoughts or activities, requires a psychoanalytical-type of individual libidinal transference psychotherapy. In addition, since the hysteric's attitudes toward people are transient

---

[4] Active homosexuals placed with nonhomosexuals generate excessive anxiety in the latter. Recently, work was carried on with groups of homosexuals only. The efficacy of these experiments is still to be established.

and unpredictable, vacillating between extremes of affection and hatred with no apparent reason, his participation in a group may cause much stress and anxiety to others. Still another factor to be considered is the hysteric's susceptibility to suggestion; the group may become a source of pathogenic infection to the hysteric.

The foregoing negative indications for all group psychotherapies, are of two types. One set is derived from the clinical problems of patients, the other from the influence patients may have on each other and on the group. Both factors have to be considered in screening. Some patients, who might be otherwise suitable for group treatment, must be rejected because of the ad-

TABLE 1

Positive and Negative Indications for Therapy Groups
Adults and Adolescents

Positive Indications	Negative Indications*
Clinical	*Clinical*
Some psychoneuroses	Anxiety neuroses
Character disorders	Neurotic character
Some borderline ambulatory	Compulsive-obsessional
schizophrenics	Psychopaths
Schizoid personalities	Cyclothymic personalities
Psychic masochists	Active psychotics**
	Paranoiacs
Characterological	Depressives
Defensive projection	Perverts
Character resistances	Active homosexuals***
Confused identifications	Hypochondriacs
Defective sibling relations	True hysterics
Only children	
Drive to defeat therapist	*Characterological*
	Inadequate primary relations
	Inadequate ego development
	Inadequate superego development
	Intense sexual disturbances
	Regressive infantile characters
	Extreme narcissism

* Many patients included in this category can be treated in groups provided they also receive parallel individual treatment. The selection of patients for such parallel treatment depends on the clinical judgment of the therapist.
** This category refers to the inclusion of psychotics in groups with nonpsychotics.
* * * This refers to including patients with nonhomosexuals.

verse effect they would have on other members of the group or on its total climate. Accepting or rejecting patients, and grouping them, requires vigilance, objectivity, and prolonged training and experience with the various types of therapy groups.

Additional elements are the attitude and values of the therapist, which come under the category of countertransference. Suitable selections can be made only by therapists who know the variety of treatment methods available; are unbiased and free of rigid ideas and prejudices; are not motivated by material interests; are not committed to a particular technique; and who have an unreserved interest in their patients, being loyal to them rather than to a specific "school" of therapy.

APPLICATION OF GROUP VARIABLES TO SPECIFIC PATIENTS

In addition to the specific variables inherent in different settings (such as private practice, hospitals, institutions, and outpatient clinics) for which adjustments have to be made in treatment techniques, clinical approaches and staff relationships, other variables in the applications of group psychotherapy need to be considered. A decision must be reached for each patient as to whether, at a given time, group treatment will serve best as exclusive or total treatment, or whether other approaches are indicated. These indications are delineated briefly in the following pages, but experienced and perceptive clinical judgment is the best tool for making these decisions. At best, only general suggestions can be made here.

As Exclusive Treatment

By and large, exclusive group treatment is recommended for certain types of character disorders and mild neurotic states and anxieties in which transference neuroses are not essential as part of the therapy. Patients who, for character or clinical considerations, have to avoid being deeply stirred up (for whom guidance groups may be more suitable) or those whose affective problems are on a preconscious level can gain from exclusive group treatment. Some withdrawn, uncommunicative patients who need the activation of a group and the comfort of universalization can be placed in groups where vicarious catharsis and spectator therapy would be preliminaries for active therapeutic participation.

As Primary Treatment

Group psychotherapy can be central with patients devoid of massive psychoneuroses, whose symptoms appear predominantly in social adaptations and who suffer from so-called "situational neuroses." It can also be primary with patients who fear individual involvement and are blocked in communication. Group treatment is specially important where problems and difficulties are centered in reality situations and interpersonal and group adaptations, but do not contain profound sexual pathology.

Group psychotherapy can be considered as primary with patients whose difficulties stem mainly from inappropriate identifications and other character disorders and behavioral patterns that require corrective experiences and the impact of mirror reactions from others in an intimate face-to-face situation. Individual treatment may be additionally necessary to work through some idiosyncratic neurotic elements and resistances, help the patient recognize and accept the reality of the noxious elements in his personality, and to enlist his cooperation in combating them.

As Ancillary to Individual Treatment

Patients whose problems include intrapsychic distortions, intense conflicts, and sexual difficulties and who, for a variety of reasons, find it difficult to communicate to an individual therapist, may be placed in groups as a preparation for individual treatment. Some patients have problems that fall into both personal and interpersonal categories. The first are the focus of individual treatment, while the second are worked through in the group. As this simultaneous therapy progresses, some patients become suitable candidates for individual treatment only, while others may be found good candidates for group psychotherapy alone.

As Parallel Therapy

In this category are patients whose needs can be equally met

194

by either individual or group treatment, but who, because of their character structure, "dovetail" the two, each supplementing and stimulating the other. Some extroverted patients, and some with special entrenched resistance patterns (such as character resistances and "character armor"), deal with superficialities only in individual interviews. The impact of more neurotic and conflicted individuals makes such patients more introspective and induces greater self-confrontation. Through the group, they are motivated to utilize individual treatment more constructively, thus facilitating and accelerating therapy. However, while groups are effective in reaching them, their nuclear problems require individual transference therapy.

Some patients present problems so particular to themselves that the other patients cannot participate for the long period required in working them through. When commonality of problems is lacking, individual parallel treatment may be necessary for specific members of a group.

As Antecedent Therapy

Membership in a group is an effective preparation for individual treatment for patients who have intense difficulties in developing a positive transference relation and establishing communication with a therapist. Through the communication and the example set by other members of the group, the patient's discomfort and fears are abated. The observation the patient makes of the therapist's conduct, personality, and attitudes renders him less fearful and less distrustful of the therapist and less uncomfortable and restrained, thus preparing him for one-to-one therapy. This transitional experience is indispensible for some patients. According to their individual needs, patients may continue in the group, be transferred to individual treatment, or receive parallel treatment.

As Tapering-Off Therapy

Some patients can consolidate their gains in individual therapy through a period of membership in an ongoing, advanced therapy

195

group. The experience in meaningful, multipersonal relations, the exposure to the revelations of others, and the ease with which this is done opens a new facet of human encounter. The universalization of values and problems and the comparatively diluted climate of the group serve as a transition from the concentrated atmosphere of individual psychoanalytic therapy to the objective world which the patient is to enter independently and on his own.

As a Testing Period

Membership in a group can serve as an ending to individual treatment; it provides the patient with an opportunity to test the strength of his newly gained abilities for multipersonal relations, his comfort or discomfort in them, and to gauge his powers in dealing with anxieties. The group is employed here as an expanded arena for reality testing.

TABLE 2

Variables in Application of Group Psychotherapy

As Exclusive Treatment
As Primary Treatment
As Ancillary to Individual Treatment
As Parallel Therapy
As Antecedent Therapy
As Tapering-Off Therapy
As Testing Period

RELIABILITY OF CRITERIA

Despite theoretically established and empirically tested rules for selection, one finds, in practice, that these are never ironclad. Patients who, by all indications, should fit into therapy groups do not respond as expected and patients for whom group therapy seems to be counterindicated do surprisingly well. This can be explained by an error in diagnosis; by the presence of *unknowable factors* in the patient; by the presence of other patients in the group who unpredictably aid or block the patient's progress; and by the fact that some patients show only *partial improvement* (that is, they improve in some respects but remain unaffected in others).

One of the sanguine aspects of group treatment is that it presents definite safeguards against psychologic injury to its members. Patients can, and do, withdraw from groups when they find them unsuitable or too disturbing. Patients' self-protective tendencies and natural avoidance of pain is a safeguard against traumatization. Patients can also escape from harm through many resistance possibilities such as silence, absenteeism, and other devices favored by the group situation. The only type of patient that may be injured by an unsuitable therapy group placement is the borderline schizophrenic. Because of intense dependence, these patients may continue to come to groups despite the disturbance and turmoil created in them. The group psychotherapist must be extremely vigilant as to the effect of the group on schizophrenic patients

VII

Some Guides for Grouping

STATUS OF KNOWLEDGE ON GROUPING

The question of the most effective grouping of patients in psychoanalytically oriented group therapy is still a moot one. Ultimately, it can be answered only through controlled experimentation and empiricism. The possibilities for grouping of patients are almost infinite and the only reliable criteria now available are derived from unvalidated experience and considerations of clinical, character, and pathological syndromes. These will have to suffice until controlled tests and validations are available.

One serious impediment to the exploration of this area is the fact that private practitioners, who do much of the work in this field, do not always have a sufficiently large clientele from which to choose patients suitably for groups. Therefore, they tend to assign them on blanket basis rather than on the basis of specific considerations, a fact that militates against experimentation and validation. A small number of psychotherapists consider all but the most seriously ill of their patients suitable for group treatment, and a few even go so far as to practice group psychotherapy exclusively. Under these circumstances, criteria for grouping will have to come from hospitals, outpatient clinics, and social service agencies, whose large patient loads allow for experimentation and controlled investigation.

A true psychotherapeutic group presupposes the planned selection and grouping of patients on the basis of clinical diagnoses and the anticipated effect they may have on one another. The assumptions that criteria for grouping are not necessary, that patients can be thrown together without consideration of mutual suitability, or that all patients are suitable for group treatment, are serious misconceptions.

A perusal of the literature reveals a miasma of points of view and great variations in practice, the soundness of which are not substantiated, either by theory or results. Such determining factors as age, sex, and clinical diagnoses are underplayed. Schizophrenics and manic-depressives are grouped with anxiety hysterics and other neuroses, and with psychopaths, convulsives, and other neurological conditions, as well as with various types of mentally and emotionally disturbed patients. While absolute appropriateness in grouping cannot be achieved, such divergence of syndromes and pathology must prove inimical to psychotherapy. Anxiety patients become even more anxious in the presence of psychotics and convulsive patients. An attack by the latter would magnify their trauma, while the schizophrenic's ego defenses would be overwhelmed under such conditions. Our task here is to formulate some of the thoughts on grouping and criteria that we have derived from experience and observation. ("Thoughts" is employed here rather than "principles," being more appropriate, due to the absence of tested knowledge in this area.)

Sex as a Criterion

Grouping patients on the basis of sex is one of the considerations on which differences of opinion obtain. Some therapists prefer unisexual groups, while others claim that the presence of both men and women is preferable, since the resulting interstimulation reveals attitudes toward the opposite sex, adds transference possibilities which enrich the therapeutic content, and provides an element of reality to the latent nascent attitudes toward persons of the opposite sex. Others believe that patients in mixed groups inhibit one another because of their need to appear in a certain light before persons of the opposite sex: the men attempt

199

to exhibit their potency and the women their charm,[1] which blocks free association. In mixed groups discussions of sex may be overstressed or they may be shunned, developments that are not likely to occur in unisexual groups. Further, in heterosexual groups, the reality element of intersexual attitudes becomes too prominent (see "Reality Saturation"). Another eventuality that is obviated by unisexual adult groups is the sexual attraction that patients sometimes develop for one another, including promiscuity.

Dr. Francis W. Graham (1960), in a discussion of the inadvisability of including married couples in therapy groups, following Freud's admonition for continence between therapist and patients, points out that through their participation in the group interviews, husbands and wives are in a mutual therapist-patient relation and, therefore, cannot indulge in coitus. Dr. Graham's statement would seem equally pertinent for patients not married to one another.

STRENGTH OF THE EGO AND ITS DEFENSES

The group experience must not be injurious to patients and patients must not prove injurious to others in the group. In the first instance, injury can be prevented by not assigning, to a group, patients whose ego strengths would be tried beyond the permissible point of endurance. While intrapsychic stress cannot, and need not, be avoided, the maximal quantum of ego energies and the available ego defenses cannot be safely overridden; they must be preserved from possible onslaught by the group to which a patient is assigned. As far as possible, the transferences that may emerge, as well as extreme negative feelings toward a particular fellow patient, have to be anticipated and prevented. On the other hand, because of his special character or trauma, a patient may disturb or agitate others to a degree that is inconsistent with therapeutic efficacy. While tensions are worked through, some patients,

---

[1] Dr. Walter Briehl, of California, once found it necessary to separate the men from the women in one of his groups. He discovered "startling" sexual regressive material, which none of his mixed groups had ever before produced. This observation was also independently made by a woman therapist in Florida. (Personal communications.) These observations confirm the position I have held on the subject since the initiation of group psychotherapy.

or the group as a whole, may be unable to endure the strain involved. Overlooking such factors in structuring a group will vitiate the therapeutic effort and lead to disruption of the group. Constructive and destructive forces are always present in all groups, including therapy groups, and the group's capacity to resist the destructive forces may not be overstepped without adverse or dire results.

It has been suggested that group therapy should be carried on with an awareness of its "lowest denominator"; that is, the weakest members of the group. This is humane and necessary in some instances, but at the same time, it may deprive other group members of adequate therapeutic advantages. Causing injury to a patient is undesirable; it also disturbs the group as a whole. (For example, when a latent schizophrenic sustains a psychotic break, a hysteric loses control, or a convulsive has an attack during a group session.) Including such patients in groups and adjusting the treatment to suit them deprives others of the therapy to which they are entitled.

One criterion for grouping, therefore, is that—although problems and personalities may be at great variance—the range of the patients' ego strengths and defenses should not be so wide as to cause injury to, or breakdown in, the group.

HOMOGENEITY

Much of the ambiguity in the application of the term "homogeneity" to grouping patients arises because the common element of the homogeneity is seldom specified. In utilizing the principles of homogeneity and heterogeneity, it is essential that the frame of reference be made clear. For example, dynamics and practice with children vary enormously from those employed with adults; they also vary with psychotic, as contrasted with nonpsychotic, patients. Where specificity is so essential, a blanket statement cannot but be misleading. In some fields of endeavor, the unqualified term "homogeneity" may be sufficient to convey its meaning, since there may be only one universal involved. This is not the case with psychotherapy. The character, behavioral, clinical, gender, age, social, intellectual, and other factors involved, need to

201

be known when the term homogeneity is employed. No blanket or generic statement is adequate.

Nuclear Problem

It has been observed that patients gain most from a group session when they rally around a common topic that has emotional significance to all, or the majority, of the group. The interchange is livelier, emotional interstimulation is higher, and the catalytic effect proceeds more easily and naturally. On occasions, when an emotion or an interest common to the group arises, they bring forth strong transference feelings which are expressed verbally or acted out and are finally worked through. There are other positive, as well as negative, gains from a common problem that engages the libido of all or most of the group members. The more often these periods occur, in which all the members are emotionally involved and are interacting with one another (rallies), the more significant is the group interview and the more vital the total experience for each member. The fewer the common concerns, interests, and emotions, the less significant is the therapeutic interchange.[2]

Homogeneity of the patients' basic pathology or syndrome favors discussion of common problems and more intense therapeutic interchange, and is, therefore, conducive to therapeutic progress and increased empathy, vicarious catharsis, and spectator therapy. Empathy is lessened where emotional diversity, in fundamental psychological problems, predominates. Though patients may differ widely in ego functioning, in their defenses and symptoms, the best results are obtained when their *nuclear problems* are the same. When these are at too great divergence, an emotional Babel is likely to emerge. Words and phrases will have different significances to the different patients and will lack the force to stir feelings. Thus, the catalytic influence of patients on each other would not be triggered, since catalysis occurs only where emotional resonance is present.

---

[2] This characteristic has given rise to the differentiation between therapy *in* a group, *through* a group, and *by* a group.

The larger the number of group members to whom this applies, the more efficient is the therapeutic effort. When a problem is common, communication engages patients, some passively, others actively. In the latter case, a "rally" ensues. Empathetic response or psychological resonance temporarily binds the group into a unit, fusing it, for all practical purposes, into one patient. The advantages are obvious when compared with a group where each patient is preoccupied only with his own problems and fantasies, completely different from, or having little in common with, the others. This situation makes the practice of individual therapy *in* the group necessary, rather than collective therapy *through* or *by* the group. If this is carried on too extensively, it makes the patients who remain outside the therapeutic orbit resentful and increases their resistance, leading to disruption of the group.

The Two "Universals"

Even when there is great variance in nuclear problems, two basic emotions are present in all patients. These are, discontent with parents and sexual problems. In this, there is universal homogeneity; and since both are predominant in the formation and malformation of personality, greater latitude in grouping is afforded beyond the overstrict clinical considerations.[3] Anyone with experience in psychotherapy and psychoanalysis, where free association is encouraged, cannot but be impressed with the universality of these two problems. Whether it is the psychoneurotic with his conflicts and guilts, the character disorder patient with distorted identification, or the psychopath with weak controls over his pleasure urges and lack of superego judgments—all eventually turn to the subject of sex. Each may do so for reasons of his own, but each will display an intense interest in problems in the sexual area.

Equally intense feelings are bound up in memories about parents and siblings and the treatment received from them. Wheth-

---

[3] When highly charged problems, not common to the group, are recognized in individual patients, individual treatment parallel to the group treatment is usually instituted.

203

er the memories are true, exaggerated, or distorted, they are so real and so deeply affecting to the patient as to require living through and working through in therapy. Parent and sibling relations are inherently replete with negatives from which no one escapes, and the charged emotions associated with them constitute a major and universal theme in psychotherapy.

On these two grounds, therefore, there is considerable homogeneity in nuclear problems among all patients.

Counterindications of Character Homogeneity

Depth of affect cannot be obtained where the homogeneity is in the areas of character and ego functioning; only reinforcement and intensification of symptoms and problems result from it. Differences in ego functioning, in the group members, are desirable for generating clashes (interstimulation) and mutual catalysis. However, the divergencies must not be so basic as to completely prevent confluence as problems are worked on. On the other hand, group harmony as a permanent state, at any stage other than the final one, has no therapeutic validity.

Nuclear problem homogeneity needs to be differentiated from symptom or character homogeneity. The latter may still be at variance between individuals who have the same nuclear or central problems or who were subjected to similar traumatogenic experiences. The infinite natural predispositions and external factors in personality conditioning appear in innumerable variations. These differences and contrasts cannot but reveal themselves in the course of group interviews, giving them vitality and poignancy. On the other hand, similarity in ego functioning and personality types encourages inactivity, in the absence of the interstimulation that variety encourages, and are therefore, deleterious to the life of an analytic therapy group and to its therapeutic value. Therefore, in grouping patients for nuclear problem homogeneity, heterogeneity of ego functioning and ego defenses should also be taken into account.

In groups, there is a need for a variety of patients: those who activate communication through their assertiveness; who have poorly controlled aggressions and would act out; who, by their temperament or objectivity, can inject an element of poise and rationality into the interviews; and who, because of diffidence and constraint, remain observers and passive participants for periods of time. We have described patients by their behavioral façade; but while their behavior appears different, they may all be reacting to conflicts and guilts emanating from a similar source (oedipal guilts or incestuous wishes and acts, feelings of inferiority and insecurity, exhibitionism, etc.). The behavior is different, but the pathology is similar. Yet, each, though reacting to an identical nucleus, has additional problems which are *peculiar to him* and different from all others. Thus, there is variety within sameness, giving depth and dynamism to the interchange (encounters) in the group interviews. The deadening effect of sameness in groups is also prevented by the many *peripheral* or *secondary problems* in the preconscious, conscious, and unconscious, that differ from individual to individual. In group interviews, there is easy transition from nuclear to peripheral problems due to the differential reactions and interpretations of each of the participants.

Symptom Homogeneity

Symptom similarity or identity is not an automatic reason for placing patients in the same group. As already indicated, psychotherapy addresses itself to the causes of, rather than the manifestations of, behavior. Identity of symptoms in patients does not necessarily mean that their neurotic or psychosomatic syndromes are identical. There are, however, patients with certain physical symptoms that seem to have the same nosological base and that have responded well to therapy groups structured around them. Among these are adults with asthma, allergies, headaches, tachycardia, psychogenic hypertension, neurotic alcoholism, drug addiction, and other psychosomatic or psychogenic medical problems. These patients are suitable for grouping together because their central difficulties may be the same, which would result in a group with symptom, as well as syndrome, homogeneity.

None the less, in structuring a group, a therapist cannot rely

205

entirely on symptomatic evidence. While these may seem to predominate the clinical picture, further investigation may reveal that they are secondary in importance and that the real difficulty, which would determine the direction of the treatment, lies elsewhere. For example, take a patient whose presented symptom is only a part of a more involved hypochondriacal syndrome; a patient where somatic complaint is a conversion symptom of a psychoneurosis or hysteria; or a patient whose physical symptom is a defense against a psychotic break. If suitable for groups, these patients must be assigned in accordance with nosological considerations, rather than on the basis of somatic complaints.

<h2>CLINICAL CONSIDERATIONS</h2>

To illustrate the importance of clinical considerations and the difficulties involved in arriving at sound grouping guides, let us look at the two extremes in nonpsychotic patients—psychopathy and psychoneurosis, which represent the extremes on the scale of divergence in personality dynamics (and serve as counterindications for grouping them together). One involves the absence of superego development and minimal anxiety; the other, a tyrannical superego and all-pervasive anxiety. The psychosocial frame of reference of patients in these clinical categories will always conflict. Their responses to stimuli and, above all, to the ethical and moral considerations of behavior which inevitably arise in group discussions, cannot but be at extreme variance. On theoretical grounds, it is difficult to imagine that patients at these two extremes can find a common base; experience supports this view. The psychoneurotic and the psychopath never agree on matters of psychological or social significance.

Another example of clinical categories incompatible in therapy are the psychoneurotic and the full-blown schizophrenic. The incompatibility is due to the differing ego structures and ego defenses. Though constantly threatened by anxiety, the ego of the neurotic is structurally intact, while the ego of the schizophrenic is structurally defective and continually or periodically overwhelmed by external threats and internal tensions. Similarly, the ego defenses in a psychoneurotic are excessively rigid, while, in the psychotic, they are weak, tenuous and easily given up, causing the ego to retreat from reality into a world of delusion. The completely divergent needs of these two types of patients make them extremely incompatible as group members. In the one, ego defenses require loosening up, while in the other they have to be buttressed. With psychoneurotics, the analysis of defenses is a necessary part of the treatment; with schizophrenics, such an approach may result in a psychotic break. With the neurotic, regression is an essential requisite of the therapeutic process; in the psychotic it constitutes a threat to his psychic integrity, resulting in ego fragmentation,[4] unless the patient is supported by the therapist in individual interviews.[5]

Patients in different clinical categories often, though not always, attach different meanings to the statements and revelations of fellow group members. For example, the schizophrenic's intense oral aggression, devastating hostility, and fear of homicidal urges, which he holds in tenuous check, cause him to respond in a way that both confuses and frightens the psychoneurotic. Similarly, the schizophrenic becomes frightened at the directness, overt aggressions, and expressions of hostility of other members of the group, especially when the aggressions are directed toward him.

This does not mean that all latent and borderline schizophrenics must be excluded from groups containing other types of patients. In fact, if the indicated treatment includes a group, it is preferable that they be placed with nonpsychotic patients. The climate in an exclusively psychotic group can prove harmful, since, in the treatment of psychotics, reality and sanity must be emphasized. If all the members of a group were schizophrenic, pathol-

---

[4] In this context, I have suggested the terms "therapeutic regression," "pathologic regression," and "parapathologic regression" (see Chapter XII.)

[5] Some borderline patients can do well in groups, depending on their ego strengths; especially when they receive ego reinforcement in individual treatment. Psychotic patients have inordinately strong defenses against ego assailment, which they exercise by not registering or becoming aware of the attack. This I have described as *defense against therapy*. However, it is preferable that they be treated in guidance or counseling groups in which current events and reactions are discussed that do not threaten their ego defenses. (See "An Atypical Case" in Slavson, S. R., 1958, Chapter X.)

ogy would be intensified. A climate of insanity is no cure for the insane and is a detriment to the sane.

Thus, the number and type of schizophrenic patients that can be included in an analytic therapy group is a problem in clinical judgment. The best current opinion is that no more than two of the eight patients can be borderline schizophrenics; and they must be in good contact. A larger number cannot be properly assimilated. However, more important than the number is the intensity of the pathology and the quality and strength of the ego organization and defenses of the patients. Where the schizophrenic's ego is strongly cathected, his hostilities not sufficiently under control, and his anxieties and fears too intense, treatment groups should be avoided. In such instances, prolonged individual treatment, with a therapist skilled in this specialty,[6] is required before the patient can be included in a frankly analytic group. Such patients may, however, gain much from groups of lesser intensity, such as *paratherapeutic* groups of the guidance or counseling type. When treatment results in adequate mobilization of ego strengths and defenses and when some of the hostility is drained off, patients *may* then be ready for an analytic group in conjunction with individual psychotherapy.

Clinical Categories

The following is a list of clinical categories for grouping and antigrouping patients (useful both in planning treatment for specific patients and in grouping them): habit disorders, pre-oedipal and oedipal behavior disorders,[7] character disorders, transference neuroses, character neuroses, neurotic character, psychogenic psychopathy, constitutional psychopathy, latent and borderline schizophrenia, pseudoschizophrenia, true schizophrenia, and psychoses. These categories are in some respects arbitrary, yet, viewed in a flexible manner, they serve as valuable guides for understanding patients and planning treatment for them. For example, psychopathy can be viewed as a character disorder, but one having specific

[6] Experience with many psychotherapists has convinced me that in the treatment of schizophrenics, specific characteristics in the therapist are of pivotal importance.
[7] Habit and behavior disorders are predominantly found in children.

characteristics and presenting almost insurmountable difficulties in treatment. The schizophrenias and psychoses could also be included in character disorders. When habit and behavior disorders appear in adults, they usually fall in the category of "general maladjustment" or character disorders.

"Character disorders" is a generic term, and before assignment to a group is made, serious consideration has to be given to its nature in a specific patient and his suitability for a specific group or for group treatment altogether. For such patients, grouping needs to be considered in terms of the type of disorder and ego functioning. We have already noted the incompatibility of the psychopath and the neurotic; but some neurotics would also find it difficult to bear up under the domination and aggression of persons in any category and may feel so frustrated and disturbed as to withdraw from group treatment. For instance, the "monopolizer," for whatever psychodynamic or pathologic reasons, is a serious impediment to the treatment of patients with low frustration tolerance (which is characteristic of the neurotic). Thus, the aggressive, exhibitionistic individual should be placed in a group only with caution. A safeguard against the deleterious effect of such patients is to place them in a group that has met for some time and can, therefore, cope with them.

This strategy is valuable with patients whose assertiveness, monopolization, and domination stem from character sources and primary narcissism, but not where they are manifestations of neurotic needs and extreme anxiety. In the latter case, the restraints imposed by the group serve to intensify anxiety, add narcissistic injury, and further damage the self-image. Many latent difficulties in the psychoneurotic can be exacerbated by group criticism and rejection as his low self-esteem is further confirmed by the group's treatment of him. Sometimes, these reactions can be worked through, but often the depth of the resulting depression is not amenable to it. Nor infrequently, immediately following a group session, a patient, who was thrown into a depression must be seen alone by the therapist to meliorate his feelings.

Patients with tendencies to depression or frequent mood swings, if at all suitable for analytic group treatment, need careful as-

209

signment to groups. The psychodynamics and nature of depressions are such that group psychotherapy is not ordinarily the treatment of choice, except as a supplement to individual therapy. For patients who tend to have deep depressions, groups are counterindicated, since the depressive states can too easily be heightened by the content of the interviews and the negative treatment the patient may receive at the hands of the other members. The patients in depression can have a depressive influence on some group members, and an irritating effect on others. Psychoneurotics are ready subjects for emotional infection, while character disorders usually react unempathically and with aggression, which tends to intensify the problem for the depressive patient, and for the group as a whole.

This does not mean that patients with depressive trends can never be included in groups. Rather, it is suggested that special care be taken with them before assignment is made; it is necessary to know the nature and causes of the depressions, their frequency, depth, and accessibility. Such patients can be placed in groups in which aggressive acting out is at a low level. A prolonged course of individual therapy, partly for diagnostic purposes, should precede group placement. When assignment is made, it should be to an ongoing group, in order to forego the anxiety and tensions of the early stages in a group's life. The ongoing group may have already worked through initial hostilities and confusions and, thus, will present the newcomer with lesser disturbances.

The therapeutic process is more effective when patients of diverse clinical entities are grouped together than when the patients are clinically homogeneous. Clinical homogeneity, reinforces individual reactions, hindering the progressive flow of communication and the resolution of problems; the patients tend to "go around in a vicious circle," resulting in repetition that often leads to an impasse. Clinical and character variety with nuclear problem homogeneity, activates diverse feelings and ideas, which promulgates interpersonal reactions and, therefore, interpatient transference feelings. For example, if the ego functioning of a neurotic and a character disorder patient, do not clash so seriously as to produce an unresolvable conflict, both can gain from the interchange. Each can encompass the other's point of view and feelings, thus widening the empathic field in both; each discovers new possibilities for dealing with internal and external stress.

It would seem, at first consideration, that a group consisting exclusively of neurotics would favor greater "depth" of treatment; but this is not the case (though it is possible to achieve it in a well-planned group, through the choice of patients who, though neurotics, differ widely in character structures and ego functioning, having the same effect as the presence of clinically different patients). Homogeneity in character disorders, however, could not be as advantageous as in the case of neurotics for assimilation of the neurotic element is necessary for patients with character disorders which is supplied by neurotic fellow group members. Such mutual induction and interpenetration between the two is one of the advantages of group treatment.

REIDENTIFICATION AND THE SUPPORTIVE EGO

As already indicated, identification is a major dynamic in group psychotherapy and, therefore, must be considered when grouping patients. It would be of little value for a patient with inadequate or undesirable identifications, to be exposed, in treatment, to models as defective as, or worse than, himself. The automatic, and largely unconscious, identifications with therapist and fellow patients that inevitably occur, need to be *corrective identifications*. Under specific circumstances, men and women with confused sexual identifications, for example, can re-establish more appropriate identifications through the close emotional relations in a group. The process of reidentification is aided by the working through of earlier neurotic identifications in the corporeal presence of new models.

Identification with the ego strengths and ego functioning of fellow group members can aid and accelerate improvement, depending on the susceptibility of the patient and the model he chooses—for he may make the choice in favor of his antithera-

211

peutic motives as reinforcement of his own pathology or as placation of his superego. In some cases, when this occurs and the relation cannot be worked through and dissolved, separation may be necessary.

It is no simple matter to be able to anticipate all these eventualities. It is seldom possible to predict the lines that mutual identifications will take in a therapy group and the therapist, who structures the group, must be on guard.

A study of the personalities of the patients makes it possible to predict, to some degree, the attachments that may ensue in the group and their effects. By and large, patients tend to remain comparatively emotionally self-contained. Where relationships do arise, they are not of the equalitarian type frequently found in ordinary life. Rather, in therapy groups, they carry special emotional significance to one or both persons involved; they usually reflect transference and homoerotic feelings, and they are often of a parasitic and anaclitic nature.

To describe both the nature and function of the significant relations that emerge in therapy groups, I have suggested the generic term, "supportive ego." Observation of numerous relations between patients in therapy groups shows that the supportive ego relation develops out of the needs of one or both of the partners involved. These needs may arise from dependency feelings, insecurity, a need for protection, homoerotic attachment, or parent or sibling transference feelings.

The choice of a supportive ego is made on the basis of personality identity or personality complementation. This subject has not yet been adequately studied in adults (patients or nonpatients).[8] In activity therapy groups with children, both phenomena appear. Some children choose as their special friends (buddies) those who are like themselves (identity): a withdrawn child will strike up a relationship with another withdrawn child; an aggressive child will be drawn to another of similar ego functioning.

[8] For example, the importance of "buddies" in the military services, especially in active combat, cannot be underestimated. They constitute an essential source of security and libidinal cathexis. The principle of "supportive ego" is clearly demonstrated here.

However, there are children who follow what seems to be a need to complement themselves: a withdrawn child is observed most frequently in the environs of, and in play with, a more aggressive groupmate. There is also a sequential succession in the choice of supportive egos. The weak child who utilized another weak child (on the basis of identity) gradually, as his own ego grows stronger, moves on to associate with more and more aggressive and outgoing youngsters. Similarly, as treatment progresses, a disturbing, hyperactive boy will begin friendship relations with fairly average acting youngsters.

Adolescents and adults probably choose supportive egos in response to homoerotic feelings, internalized images, and memory traces. Fellow group members whose personalities and ego functioning resemble persons who were sources of pleasure in the past are accepted, while others, who remind one of unpleasant feelings, are avoided. The same identification object and supportive ego can be either harmful or therapeutic, depending on the patient's stage in the therapy. This is one of the therapeutic situations with adolescents and adults that requires particular vigilance on the part of the therapist. A patient with an especially weak ego organization and fluid identifications may choose an ego support that will prove detrimental to his emotional and social welfare. In one instance, for example, an oral dependent young woman had chosen as her model of identification a promiscuous fellow patient, duplicating the other's life to the point of becoming sexually promiscuous, although she was initially a virgin. When her first object of identification left the group, she chose another member as a model of identification, again altering her life pattern. The propensity to choose pathognomonic ego supports is more of a risk in sexually mixed groups than in unisexual groups because, among other things, they encourage sexual acting out.

The choice of an ego support is considered therapeutic where the model neutralizes or corrects undesirable ego functioning and defenses and replaces faulty identifications with those of a healthier character. In some instances, identifications that appear pathogenic *per se* may be therapeutic if they facilitate verbal catharsis, acting out, and discharge of noxious memories and feelings. Con-

213

duct of a patient activated by a supportive ego may be desirable in one stage of treatment and not in another (for example, acting out in the early stages against acting out in the final stages).

The dynamic of supportive ego is a phenomenon of major importance in group psychotherapy. In children's groups, those who develop such "supportive" relationships (and there are always a succession of them according to emerging strengths and needs) make better recoveries than those who remain isolated or only enter into superficial, floating relations. There is no evidence for a similar conclusion with either adolescents or adults, nor is it assumed that this phenomenon is as universal or essential in their case. There are, however, patients who may not remain in a group or who may find it strenuous without such aids. Supportive ego relations are also significant because they give the therapist a diagnostic clue regarding the patient's current and past dependencies and other needs. Along with the analysis of negative transferences, the examination of various types of supportive relationships gives the therapist tangible material for understanding his patients and gives the patients an impetus to self-examination.

Grouping patients with a view to the possibilities of supportive relationships is an added advantage, but, because of its intricacies, error and misjudgment must be expected. The incidence of such errors can be reduced when a patient can be added to an ongoing group, where the therapist already knows the ego functioning of the patients and their emotional needs. He can then add patients who may serve as a supportive ego to some group members who may need them. Occasionally, we have even found it necessary to deliberately seek out patients for inclusion in an ongoing group, to serve as activators (instigators) or supportive egos to individual patients already in the group. At times, this strategy proved exceedingly valuable. Of course, the new recruits should be therapeutically on a level with the group, either through prior membership in another group or through individual treatment.

HOMOSEXUALITY AND HOMOEROTISM

We have previously listed homosexuals as being among those for whom group psychotherapy is counterindicated. This particularly applies to their inclusion in groups of nonhomosexuals. The culturally-conditioned aversion to homosexuality, the guilt attached to it, the social stigma, and the anxiety derived from the susceptibility to it in everyone, all combine to generate extreme tension in groups that include acting homosexuals. This is especially true of the psychoneurotic members. (Therapists' reports tell of incidents of homosexual panic on the part of some male members of therapy groups and of their dropping out when the subject was touched upon.)

Recently, there have been reports of work with groups consisting exclusively of homosexual men. So far, these communications have been scanty and inconclusive. There have also been a few claims made of "cures" affected in homosexual men who were treated in groups with nonhomosexual patients. These reports are unauthenticated and may be the result of excessive enthusiasm on the part of the therapists, transient improvement in the patients or misleading information supplied by them. Occasionally, individuals have made spontaneous changes from homo- to heterosexuality, without the benefit of any therapy. However, these were not cases of true homosexuality, some habits being acquired as a result of circumstantial necessity and others being reactions to feelings of sexual inadequacy, or fears of, and fantasies about, the female body—all of which can be overcome by favorable circumstances and experiences, as well as by therapy. It would be difficult, however, to offer convincing proof of a permanent cure for *real* homosexuality[9] by any psychotherapeutic technique yet evolved. Certainly, where constitutional factors are obviously present, they would defy purely psychological effort.

The complexity of the true homosexual syndrome renders it inaccessible to a technique with the limited possibilities for depth analysis of group psychotherapy, and employing it with such pa-

[9] In cases where the sexual organ of one is the fetish of his partner, for example.

215

tients carries definite risks. In fact, most real homosexuals would not seek psychotherapy; their emotional needs, libidinal satisfactions, and ideological justifications do not dispose them to desire change or seek help. A homosexual who seeks out psychotherapy is in conflict with himself, which is not consistent with true homosexuality. It indicates that his condition is not the result of constitutional factors nor is he a pervert; rather, it is part of a psychoneurotic syndrome. My own observations lead me to believe that the practice of perversions can exist along with a neurosis; in fact, in some instances it can be a part of the neurosis, and, in such cases, psychotherapy can be effective. Where this condition exists, psychotherapy conducted by a therapist skilled in this very complicated anomaly can affect improvement. Whether it can be done in groups remains to be established.

One fact is certain: the presence of a homosexual patient, whether active or latent, in a group of nonhomosexuals greatly intensifies anxiety in the latter. Reactive anxiety becomes apparent even before the homosexual reveals himself as such. It stems from unconscious sources; from the threat to the equally unconscious repressions and superego defenses of fellow group members. One becomes aware of an unaccustomed tension and restlessness in the group and less focused productions. The climate of the group reflects a sort of fear resembling the restlessness of a herd of animals who sense the proximity of a dangerous enemy. Interestingly enough, we have repeatedly observed these reactions even in groups of boys in latency, in activity therapy, and have confirmed our suspicions by removing the offending patients, which, in all instances, normalized the groups.

Homoerotism, on the other hand, is widespread in the general population and even more so among persons who seek psychological help. In therapy groups, one observes the manifestations of homoerotism with great frequency. While it occurs among men, it is much more frequent among women. This is understandable, since their first love object was a woman and the transition to a heterosexual object is never completely made. In the boy, both the pregenital and the genital love object (the mother) is heterosexual. These differential relationships are a strong determining fac-

216

tor in attaining full genital development. Even when this is achieved adequately, which seldom occurs in persons who become patients, the unconscious homoerotism remains and has to be dealt with.

Homoerotic stimuli are always present in therapy groups. They may remain covert, but are frequently overtly manifested in women, as interests in each other's clothes, appearance, weight, hairdos, breasts, legs, and so on. In men, these interests are revealed through references to sexual activity, potency, masturbation, and occasional "friendly" pushing or touching. Homoerotism generates greater anxiety in men than it does in women, for reasons already indicated and because it is less unconscious and more likely to seek direct physical acting out due to the more active nature of the male. Married men in unisexual groups occasionally ask, "Why don't we have women in this group?" The question frequently stems from the homoerotic anxiety that the group has activated in them. Married women, on the other hand, do not request that men be added to their groups. They seem satisfied with each other.

Homoerotism, as any human characteristic, varies in degree of intensity. It is this feature that needs to be considered in grouping patients. It may be present to a degree that would set up homosexual anxiety in a psychoneurotic or a latent schizophrenic. The borderline between homoerotism and homosexuality, in many patients, is often a very thin one. This fact needs to be considered in grouping.

One would expect that the homoerotic factor would be diluted in mixed groups, since more of heterosexual interests are engaged. However, in the group's early stages, some members may take refuge in homoerotic dependencies. This is resorted to largely because of fear of heterosexual relations and neurotic insecurity with members of the opposite sex, which are diminished or vanish in time. If homoerotic ties continue, careful examination of its determinants is essential before the therapist attempts to deal with them, if he deals with them at all. The neurotic components and transference implications of the phenomena have to be unerringly understood or one may stir up a hornets' nest, as it were, that would

217

be detrimental to the group as a whole, as well as to the individual patient.

HETEROSEXUAL VERSUS UNISEXUAL GROUPINGS

Whether patients should be separated according to sex is a matter of disagreement among group therapists. This is another area that still needs further tests and controlled experiments. One cannot be certain whether present grouping preferences in this area are a question of therapeutic conviction or expediencey. In private practice, mixed groups are used with greater frequency than in clinics, where unisexual groups predominate. It is possible that availability of patients plays a part in determining the practice.

Unconscious attitudes, on the part of therapists, should not be overlooked in this regard, as well. Attitudes toward masculinity and femininity always have neurotic elements in humans, slight as they may be, and psychotherapists are not entirely free of them (and other countertransference reactions). Preferences for heterosexual or unisexual groups by therapists need to be considered objectively. A female therapist may understandably feel some discomfort in conducting an all-male group, for example; a discomfort which she is less likely to feel with an all-female group, unless her homoerotic or homosexual trends are pronounced. Both feelings are diminished or diluted by a heterosexual group, which may determine her preference.

Because of inadequately resolved oedipal problems or sibling rivalry, a male therapist may resent the presence of other men, having the need to eliminate rivalry and to "possess" all the women in the group. Another male therapist, because of unsatisfactory relations with his mother and/or sisters, may find the concentration of femininity in an all-female group threatening. Still another may prefer a mixed group because of unconscious fears of his own homosexual tendencies in an all-male group.

There are undoubtedly valid justifications for, and objections to, both types of group. Heterogeneous groups present patients with a more "normative" situation, which activates feelings and urges in consonance with everyday life. It is, therefore, to be expected that both verbalization and acting out would more faithfully reveal the personalities of the participants and reflect their desires (not necessarily needs) and adaptive patterns. Attitudes stemming from oedipal sources and sexual maladjustments make themselves known with greater speed and more "realistically." Behavior and reactions are "discussed" and examined from a more varied point of view and patients become "aware" of themselves as they are seen by their mates, and others of the opposite sex. Each can react to, and act out toward, persons of the opposite sex, just as they do in "real life"; their reactions can then be brought to their "attention" and evaluated by the others.

This process can be called, for the lack of a better term, *therapy in reality;* that is, the patients operate in a *social situation* in which their ego functioning and behavior determining affect are revealed and reacted to just as they occur in everyday life. This is understandably an impressive process that pleases the therapist, because of the "lively discussions," their seemingly pertinent content, and the interactions it generates and perpetuates. The patients, too, feel attracted by this, since they deal on the conscious level with problems that seem important to them and of which they are made aware in daily living. The group discussions, therefore, appear to have "real meaning" to them.

The arguments for unisexual groups lie more at the root of what psychotherapy is. If conceived as a didactic process or intellectual clarification, then therapy in reality is suitable. There are therapists who do not differentiate between guidance and psychotherapy and consider intellectual discussion and perusal of "here and now" matters as properly constituting therapy. But the therapist who is aware of the complexity of the human psyche, its rigidity, and the inviolability and autonomy of its conditionings, stands almost in awe before the immense task of changing it. Such a therapist cannot be satisfied with "therapy in reality," although it may, at times, have its place in the total therapeutic effort.

One needs to consider the concatenations, symbolisms, fantasies, and distortions that are embedded in the psyche and the magnitude of the task of unraveling and dislodging them, not so much from the conscious as from the unconscious. This cannot be done by dealing only with overt manifestations and awareness. One needs to dig deeper than the surface, or even the subsurface, to achieve it.

Sexual difficulties, as all affect-laden problems buried (as they are) in the unconscious, are better treated on a fantasy, rather than on a reality, basis. Actuality is less favorable to the reaching of the fantasy and distortion components of a problem than is a setting in which free association and regression take place. The presence of stimuli in reality favors *re-enactment* of behavior and feelings which may be adequate for some character disorders, but the psychoneurotic requires reliving of memories and buried feelings. An illustration of this is the dynamics set up when a parent attempts to treat his own offspring in psychotherapy. The validity and results of this effort are condemned to failure from the outset, even though under special conditions and with great difficulty a therapist may be able at times to treat his own prepuberal child. The failure is due to the absence of the essential transference phenomena. The patient cannot establish such a relation because the *actual* traumatogenic person is present and not a *transfer object*. The reality of the parent-therapist makes it impossible to bring out paratoxic distortions, early fantasies, and oedipal feelings. An offspring can do this toward the parent only in a state of rage, with no opportunity for therapeutically working it out with the parent-therapist. All the latter can do is defend himself against the onslaughts of his offspring-patient, and that with very little success.

The advantages claimed for the "realistic" situation in a therapy group need to be viewed critically. They lie largely in the fact that the group supplies accelerators for communication. They are not as advantageous where repressed, deep-rooted, and anxiety laden feelings are concerned. From this point of view, the presence of both sexes in a therapy group may be inimical to patients' living through and working through highly charged sexual problems. The presence of persons of the opposite sex, and which constitutes the nucleus of the difficulty, favors *regressive acting out* rather than exploration of *regressive memories* and the uncovering of fantasies and distortions.[10]

As similarity in nuclear problems is a criterion for grouping, the compresence of men and women would be counterindicated. The problems of life, the process of character formation, and the genesis of neuroses in the two sexes are different in many respects and in some matters, even diametrically opposed. Therefore, the foci of problem syndromes must be different as well, and the psychological significance of much that is communicated alien or obscure to members of the other sex. While differences in reactions and opinions help stimulate reflection and self-examination, the basic psychological frames of reference must be sufficiently common, to have value. If these are in opposition, or too far at variance, they lose their therapeutic potential. An example could be a discussion of sexual preferences between a heterosexual woman and a lesbian. In their *discussion,* no common ground will emerge, nor will either change in respect to her biological role.

Not only are the nuclear syndromes different in men and women, but their socially-conditioned psychological and biological frames of reference are also at variance. This leads to considerable confusion as to the latent meanings in interviews and inspires a great deal of tangential discussion and nontherapeutic argumentation, which do not have *therapeutic* bearing, though they may be intellectually stimulating or have educational value. Such difficulties are partially obviated in unisexual groupings.

It is not uncommon for male and female members of a group to line up against each other. This antagonism is not always instigated by the topic under discussion. Sometimes it results from a mood of one of the more effective members; from the intensification of the natural antagonism between the sexes; from certain feelings touched off in a group discussion; or from the resentment of members who feel neglected by the opposite sex. Under some circumstances, this material can be employed with thera-

[10] This is one of the reasons why group psychotherapy, especially in the case of transference neuroses, cannot reach as deeply into the psyche as individual psychoanalysis can; it is, however, more effective with character disorders.

peutic effectiveness. More often however, the situation creates an impasse, especially when the therapist is not skilled in dealing with this very complex intragroup tension.

In conclusion, heterogeneous grouping can be employed with patients whose psychoneurotic problems are not massive, where therapy on less deep levels will be adequate (as in character or special adjustment problems). Where the problem is highly disturbing and deeply rooted (as in psychoneuroses), a heterogeneous group is not suitable. Heterosexual groups can also be valuable as a "tapering off" experience in reality testing, after the psychoneurotic syndromes have already been worked through in individual psychotherapy or unisexual groups.

MARRIED COUPLES AND "FAMILY" GROUPS

The risk in treating married couples and whole family groups is great indeed and its effectiveness and advisability are highly questionable. Reports on this practice are largely unsubstantiated. One needs to be even more skeptical where whole families are involved—parents, children of varying ages, in-laws, and sometimes even grandparents.[11] The therapeutic results of groups of couples remains doubtful. In some instances, the couples have become "more frank with each other," but no successful intrapsychic changes have yet been reported, as far as the present writer knows.

If the only results so far obtained through group psychotherapy are greater frankness and ease between marriage partners, without inner change, one may well ask how it differs from "marriage counseling," which concentrates on these very outcomes. A few psychiatrists have dealt with childless couples in groups and, according to one report, fertility was markedly augmented (Levine, in Slavson, 1956), but no claim was made that basic changes had occurred in the personalities of the participants. Rather, certain blocks or attitudes had been brought to consciousness in some, while others had been motivated to seek appropriate medical help, previously eschewed.

---

[11] Here, too, the misunderstanding arises from not differentiating between counseling and "talking through," and true psychotherapy by "working through."

To help married couples feel at greater ease, be "more frank with each other," and trust each other more is undoubtedly worthwhile and should be encouraged, but a line must be drawn between counseling and guidance, and psychotherapy. Establishing family harmony is a needed service to mental health, but it should be placed in its proper perspective.

A large part of the group interviews with families are consumed by discussion of home situations and interpersonal "relations." Deeply rooted personality problems, memories, dreams, fantasies, and secret-laden acts, are not revealed in their fullness. For example, neither men nor women would bring to the group their compelling urge for, or actual practice of, extramarital sexual relations; their fantasies or practices of offensive perversions; or their underlying contempt and hatred for, or sadistic urges toward, the partner, during intercourse. While such communications are not replete in group interviews of even assorted patients, the point is that verbal catharsis is even less free among couples, where communications must be selective if the marriage is not to break up. This alone militates against true psychotherapy for families.

The therapeutic intent of these groups envisages revelation of stored-up or repressed malevolent feelings against a person, in the presence of that person, whether mate, child or parent. The disadvantages of the "reality saturation" and "therapy in reality" in such groups, are pervasive, extremely complicated, and more serious. A mate *is,* in a real sense, a transference object, for he or she is the recipient of intense projected and affect-laden feelings against parents, usually of the opposite sex. As Freud pointed out, the mate is also the recipient of stored-up hostility, and the aggressions and sadism that accompany "every act of intimacy." To openly verbalize these pernicious feelings and intentions, in the presence of their object, would strain the marital and amatory relation beyond the endurance of even the most psychologically literate person. It is doubtful whether the most thoroughly psychoanalyzed individual could remain unaffected by a recital of such hostile feelings toward him and if his affections could endure after that. Much in marital attitudes, as in all close relations, *must* be left suppressed or in unawareness only and should never be openly communicated. One takes serious risks in attempting to deal with intimate traumatogenic interpersonal relations in group psychotherapy with married couples and families. In such groups, one can deal with objective matters such as living arrangements, defining of roles and duties, and ventilation of the conflicting emotions that inevitably accrue as a result of living together, as is done in marriage counseling.[12]

In so-called "family psychotherapy," the difficulties are even more manifold than in therapy with couples, as the number of possible reactions of a group of persons to a given situation, when it is charged with a common emotion, increases in a manner generally similar to the permutation formula, $s=n$ $(n-1)$ $(n-2)$ $(n-3)$ ... $(n-n + 1)$.[13] The enmities and hostilities between parents and children, though universal and manifold, are seldom as intense as those between incompatible marital partners. This is so partly because the libidinal (sexual) involvement is of a different quality and lesser intensity, because feelings are distributed and diluted among a larger number of people, and the narcissistic injuries are less poignant. The presence of neutralizers also contributes to this process. Family group reactions are more varied and more involved, but are usually of lower intensity.

With the consent of a patient in individual treatment, an occasional family consultative session may be indicated, especially when the patient is a child. Such group interviews are helpful in arriving at a diagnosis, measuring improvement, and facilitating communication and understanding between the members of the family. In my work in family guidance and with individual young children, it has been my policy to visit the home at least once, observing the family's conduct during an evening meal and when the child retires for the night. This gives me an opportunity to observe the overt behavior and latent feelings of each member of the family and their relations to one another, in two critical situations in a child's daily life—eating and retiring. The selection of

---

[12] See the extensive literature on marriage and family counseling. For applications in a clinical setting see Ackerman (1958), Einstein (1956), and Slavson (1958).

[13] n = number of persons involved.

the specific time of day also afforded me a glimpse of the father and his role in the family.[14]

As in group therapy with married couples, no positive indications for "family group psychotherapy" can be given. Only counterindications can be pointed out.

What seems to be a less hazardous procedure in group treatment of families is what we have termed *coordinated family group psychotherapy*. In this method, father, mother, and child are each treated in a different group with separate therapists or leaders; the father is placed with other men, the mother with other mothers of children in treatment, and the child is assigned to a group appropriate for his age and psychological needs. The central factor of this technique is that all three therapists involved are under the supervision of one person, who is, as a result, apprised of the character, progress, and productions of each of the family members in his respective group. The information from each of the therapists is passed on to the other two during regular supervision conferences so that they can be guided in conducting the interviews in their groups. Periodically, four-way conferences are held on each of the families, with the supervisor and the three therapists (or leaders) present and, on occasion, with other professional staff, such as psychologists and psychiatrists, participating.

Being aware of significant situations and developments in the interpersonal relations in the families, each therapist can subtly canalize the discussions so that he and the other group members may help the involved patient to ventilate feelings, clarify the emotional network in the specific family conflict or situation or, when so indicated, work through intrapsychic cathexes or confusions.

Coordinated family group therapy has, so far, been successfully tried with adolescents in treatment and their parents in child-centered guidance groups and all who have been involved look upon it favorably. All were impressed with the increased pertinence of the discussion content, the ease with which parents comprehended its significance, and the promptness in application of learnings to

---

[14] So that the parents do not become aware that *they* are being observed, one must learn to *see without looking*, an acquired special talent of an activity group therapist.

the situations in their families. However, here, too, the proper choice and grouping of patients is of paramount importance, for many parents' serious personality difficulties render them inaccessible to guidance and their treatment of their children can be altered only by a thoroughgoing psychotherapy. Some require psychoanalysis and some are completely inaccessible to any type of treatment.

Impressive phenomena are the distorted views parents have of their conduct toward their children and their inordinate defensiveness toward their fantasied attitudes. In the group interviews, parents recounted acts and attitudes which were completely controverted by their mates and often, also, by their offspring, in their respective groups. These developments were of particular value to us in our attempts to normalize the family climate by canalizing discussion of these paratoxic behavioral distortions without direct confrontation and combat among the family members together in a therapy group.

THE FACTOR OF AGE

In private practice, and even in clinics, the issue of age is often determined by expediency. The lack of sufficient patients within a narrow age range, who are also suited to each other by other criteria, usually makes it necessary to include individuals in a group whose ages are too widely divergent. This is not a serious handicap, but it can create complications and may, for a time, retard the flow of communication. Because of wide age differences, patients respond to situations from value systems similar to those of parents and offspring. This may not only prevent a common base for interchange, but may too realistically activate displacement reactions of a parent-child type. At times these reactions can be usefully employed in treatment; but arguments ensuing from differences in the frame of reference due to age and life experience favor intellectualization rather than therapy.

According to the principles of psychological homogeneity in grouping, wide age distribution is inimical to therapeutic processes and progress. Not only are the attitudes and values systems of different generations inevitably different, but so are the psycho-organic maturational levels, the contrasts in range and variety of experience, and the nature of reactions to human affairs—all favoring conflicting responses and diverse understandings. The absence of temporal and maturational proximity, in addition to the other inevitable personality divergencies, widens the schism in intellectual, ideational, and ideological reactions and prevents the emergence of a common ground. A too-wide age range places some patients in the category of parents to others and, consequently, the basic transference is likely to be as negative as are their feelings toward their real parents. If at all workable, the situation becomes one of therapy in reality.

Patients should be in groups with persons of the same generation. The maximum span in adult groups should be within a twenty-year range (Slavson, 1952, page 243) and would be more suitable if it were lowered to ten. The younger the median age of the patients, the narrower the span should be. Thus, patients in the middle twenties, for example, should not be grouped with patients above 32 or 35, while patients above 35 may be combined with patients as old as 50. Groups of children in puberty can have a range of two years, while in the preschool or kindergarten ages, the range cannot be more than six months.

Social and Intellectual Factors

In a true psychotherapy group, economic and social status should receive no consideration. All other factors being favorable for grouping, these elements can be entirely ignored. Any feelings that a patient may have on this score, pro or con, need to be considered as an integral part of his problem and should be treated as such. All things being equal, being aware of social and economic status, and assigning undue significance to it, may be symptoms of a defective self-image, manifestations of primary narcissism, feelings of inferiority, or signs of even more serious intrapsychic difficulties.

Advantages may even accrue in groups because of cultural dissimilarity. Persons of higher cultural levels may serve as valid objects of identification and imitation, and may, themselves, give up some of the culturally embedded inhibitions, aversions, likes, and dislikes that perpetuate some of their limitations and restrict their social mobility. Cultural differences that may, at first, prove disadvantageous to a group, are those that stem from racially and nationally determined value systems, religion, customs, and life patterns. These may affect communication and mutual understanding and retard the emergence of a common base. Too great a disparity in culturally-determined child-parent relations, family rituals, and social value systems may present the group and the therapist with some difficulties during the early stages of therapy, but these are not insurmountable. The therapist must be aware of the difficulties and be sure that he and the group members come to understand them and each other. Such understanding makes a common base, creates therapeutically desirable interactions, and enhances the range of empathy.

Group members should be as nearly equal as possible intellectually, and possess at least minimal endowments and educational backgrounds, for while the focus, in analytic therapy groups, is on feelings, the means of communication and interchange are language and concepts. Patients must, therefore, be intellectually able to understand the concepts of the other group members.

CASTE VERSUS CLASS

In group treatment of wives of the personnel in a military establishment, the wives of both officers and enlisted men were included in the same groups. The groups experienced what proved to be insurmountable difficulties in getting started and, as they continued meeting, all the officers' wives invariably dropped out, after which, those who remained proceeded on their therapeutic way with comparatively little difficulty.

The compresence of officers' wives and enlisted mens' wives inhibited the members of the group. They acted distant and remained uncommunicative. The deeply entrenched chasm in the status and relations of officers and enlisted men in the armed forces divides them into definite castes with all the values and attitudes that characterize this particular form of schism. In the caste system, each group preserves its own strongly cathected images which make intermixture and mobility impossible. Each, especially the group of higher rank, is constrained to retain its image in the eyes of the other, which of necessity requires that all negative and devaluating facts be withheld.

The officers' wives, therefore, could not possibly have brought themselves to reveal their personal problems, which would inevitably involve showing their officer-husbands in an unfavorable light and placing themselves on a level with the members of the lower caste. These considerations were not entirely personal, for downgrading their husbands would affect the morale of the station with unfavorable and unpleasant consequences.

In grouping patients, caste is also a consideration in parts of the world where race and social values are rigid and feelings run high among the various sections of the population. Where feelings are not very intense, as in most democratic societies, especially where neighborhoods and schooling are unsegregated, ordinary prejudices can be overcome in therapy groups and the resulting mutual acceptance has a benign effect on the personality growth of the patients. However, where rigid segregation is the rule of community life and is charged with strong feeling, the chasm may prove insurmountable to a therapy group.

This is not the case in democratic communities, where the varrious segments of the population live in relatively intimate physical proximity, and can share the various economic and cultural facilities without the barriers that exist in a caste-dominated society. A democratic society is basically mobile when movement from one "class" to another is not prohibited or impeded by rigidly entrenched laws, rules or tradition, and, as a result, values grow more flexible and attitudes more hospitable. These serve as a base for equalitarianism and mutual acceptance by the members of varying nationalities, races, religions, and social and economic status. Where ordinary prejudices do exist, there is also an ideological base for overcoming them.

229

MONOPOLIZERS

A major consideration in the conduct of group interviews, are those patients who overassert themselves and pre-empt a disproportionate amount of the group's time and attention to themselves. Because of their conduct, they are characterized as "monopolizers." Their behavior blocks the free flow of communication in the group and frustrates and irritates the other members.

Depending on the quality of the personality of the monopolizer, the soundness of his contributions, and his status in the group, he may be welcomed, endured, quietly resented, or openly attacked. On the other hand, the monopolizer may, on many occasions, discharge a welcome service to some patients by playing into their resistances and making it unnecessary for them to participate and reveal themselves. Thanks to the monopolizer, they can remain quiet, believing that the monopolizer speaks for them as well as for himself. When they do respond, they address themselves to him and his words, thus making it unnecessary to uncover their own feelings and problems. This is especially true when the monopolizer is intellectually bright, cognizant in psychological matters, and held in high regard by his groupmates.

The reaction to him is not as sanguine, however, if he is ignorant or boring. These attributes result in feelings of disregard for, and annoyance toward, him. He may then be treated with direct aggression by some patients, while others may ignore him or show their irritation. In some instances, the offending patient becomes a scapegoats and target for derision.

There are, therefore, serious risks involved in placing a compulsive talker in a therapy group, where freedom of expression and participation is an essential precondition for therapy. Unless the therapist is confident of his ability to control or divert such patients, they should be excluded from group treatment until the source of their compulsion is worked through in individual treatment. To decide on the suitability of a talkative and exhibitionistic patient for a group, it is necessary to ascertain his psychogenic problems and their susceptibility to therapeutic intervention. Monopolization may be characterological, neurotic, or pathological; it may result from anxiety, extreme dependence, primary or secondary narcissism, urethral fixation, hostility, an authoritarian personality, sadism, or psychosis.

PSYCHOLOGICAL LITERACY

The ineffectualness of conceptualization and didacticism in the treatment of psychoneuroses has been previously pointed out. When affect and sexual libido constitute the core (nucleus) of a patient's difficulties, ratiocination is ineffective, which does not hold where ego therapy is indicated. In cases of character and behavior disorders, and with patients of certain chronological ages, such as the adolescent and the senile, concepts leading to ego controls can be pivotal tools in re-educating them and reconditioning their life patterns.

While mirror reaction and confrontation are the starting point that sparks the process, they have to be followed up by understanding of causes and motives for reactions and behavior. Knowledge of psychological facts and dynamics buttresses experience where the ego and behavior are involved and where affect is at its minimum. This process is predominant in counseling and guidance, but can be employed also with neurotics after the deeper emotional and unconscious factors have been worked through; hence, the practice of providing a group experience as a testing and tapering off procedure.

Intelligence connotes, among other things, the recognition of determinism and causality in life and should be extended to include the relation of cause and effect in human behavior, especially one's own. A knowledge of the general principles of dynamic psychology and how it operates in everyday behavior needs to be integrated into the psyche, so that its selective and control systems might be rendered more effective.

One method of diminishing the resistance to accepting and utilizing such knowledge in psychotherapy is to present it as general principles rather than personalizing it with the patients, though this, too, is not entirely ruled out when the patients can accept and assimilate such knowledge. In confronting patients

231

with character disorders, relevant information assures effectiveness. Thus, when aggressive conduct is under consideration, the therapist can elucidate on the patient's background and the sources that determined his reactions. In the case of psychoneurotics, an explanation of the essential and neurotic origins of anxiety and infantile sources of guilt can help them develop controls. First, however, the patients' readiness to utilize these concepts must be carefully considered.

Groups favor generalized ideas and principles because the ideas are not necessarily addressed to one individual, but rather involve the group as a whole and thus prevent invasion of personal threat areas.

VIII

The Bio-Quantum Nature
of the Ego and Its Relation to
Analytic Group Psychotherapy

In this chapter we shall explore one of the major elements in group psychotherapy—the ego—and the improvement of its structure and function through individual and group psychotherapy.

THE TREND TOWARD EGO THERAPY

The recent trend toward emphasizing the function of the ego in development and in therapy connotes a growing awareness of its importance in life and psychopathology. An increasing number of practitioners have recognized that, in many cases, resolving libido problems is not sufficient and correction of libido cathexes cannot be achieved without involving, at some point, the patient's awareness and his *conscious* effort to control inner reactions and overt behavior, namely, involving his ego. In psychoanalysis, this trend gave rise to "active psychoanalysis," which changed the role of the analyst from an entirely passive "sounding board" to one in which he actively, though discriminately, intervenes to clarify ideas, make suggestions, and even to advise or prohibit behavior that may involve the patient in undesirable situations or lead to serious outcomes.

This activity of the therapist is interspersed with his still predominantly passive function. The fact that some "psychoanalysts" and other types of psychotherapists have gone overboard, as it were, on their "activity," is a result of misunderstanding or a preference for a less strenuous role than that of remaining inactive for hours on end. The "functional approach" and "will therapy," which had brief sway some thirty years ago, still continue to be used under various names and guises.

THE MISUSE OF EGO THERAPY

Much that has been done in ego therapy followed didactic and directive lines, ignoring the fact that psychotherapy is a rather slow and gradual process of change in the structure of the psyche and the relation of its forces. However, the excessive enthusiasm for a new idea is gradually giving ground to a more balanced view and more effective application, as *ego therapy* is being integrated into multiphasial and eclectic therapeutic efforts.

An appropriate place is being assigned to the ego in the function of the psyche in behavior and in psychopathology and its correction. Because of preoccupation with full-blown psychoneuroses, early psychoanalytic theory and practice tended to overlook or underplay the ego. Now it is recognized that in behavior disorders, character disorders, psychoses and psychopathy, the ego may be the major, though not the exclusive, focus of attention. This does not mean that the ego can be completely isolated for treatment to the total neglect of other segments of the personality, for, even if this were desirable, the structure of the human psyche would not lend itself to such a plan. One cannot affect any part of it without involving, to some degree all the other parts.

Better comprehension of the nature and etiology of the ego in human life and behavior has not only modified the course of therapy itself, but has also given rise to various paratherapeutic efforts akin to therapy, though different from it in important respects (as counseling, guidance, and other types of directive and didactic groups). As noted, in these practices the therapist, or counselor, addresses himself almost exclusively to ego functioning and giving support and direction.

NATURE AND STRUCTURE OF THE EGO

The study of the ego, which has become increasingly important for the psychotherapist, can be approached from one of two points of view: the philosophical or metapsychological, or the instrumental. In the latter, the operational force in the life of the animal world, not only in man, is considered. Obviously, to the practicing psychotherapist, this is more pertinent and more necessary and we will, therefore, examine the ego from this narrower view.

A Definition of "Ego"

For the purposes of psychotherapy, the ego is a *function* of the psychic dynamism (of animals and man) which mobilizes and integrates energy for action, directs it toward effective ends, basically aimed at the survival of the individual organism and its species, and selects and controls motility and effort. In man, the ego has added functions. Because he is a social and moral animal, the functions of his ego are enormously more complex. It holds in check id urges and pleasure drives that are inconsistent with superego and social demands and approval; it selects out advantageous from disadvantageous lines of action according to existing conditions; it represses hostile and aggressive impulses; it deals with the anxieties to which man has fallen heir (essential anxiety) and those that are engendered in the course of his development (neurotic anxiety); and it restrains and directs the numerous other impulses, drives, and appetites. In summary, the ego is the part of the psyche which selectively mobilizes energies for action or restraint and deals with inner pressures and outer demands in accordance with an internalized regulative principle and external laws and dictates.

". . .of the three interrelated psychic factors—id, ego, and superego—the ego is the most complex. . . Charged as it is with the responsibility of serving as the intermediary between the id and the superego—in itself a strenuous task—it has a number of other functions almost as difficult. One of these is holding in check the anarchic impulses of the id; another is to mediate between them and the demands, pressures, and mores of the outside world; still another is to integrate the total personality resources as they relate to one another and to the world. Thus, the major, though not sole, function of the ego is to deal with inner and outer realities and to integrate and harmonize them." (Slavson, 1952a, pages 17-18.)

To most therapists, the term "ego" connotes a complex of directive and regulative forces inherent only in man. This impression is to some extent supported by Freud, who considered the ego (as an attribute of man) as "part of the id which has been modified by the direct influence of the external world acting through the Pcpt-Cs: in a sense it is an extension of the surface-differentiation." (Freud, 1927, page 28.) Thus, Freud views the ego as derived from the id. He says further: "The ego is not sharply separated from the id; its lower portion merges into it." (Freud, 1927, page 29.)

Ego Manifestations in Lower Animals and Man

My own view of the ego is that it is an instinct separate and apart from the id. If one interferes with the locomotion of an earthworm or a caterpillar by blocking its path or physically turning it about, it will repeatedly return to its course. Only after numerous trials, apparently when fatigue sets in, will it alter its direction. Similarly, a turtle whose movement is blocked by a log too large for it to crawl over, will move along the length of the log to reach its end. It then crawls in a diagonal direction until it is on line with its original path on the other side of the log. Repeatedly turning a turtle away from its course does not deter it from its purpose. It always returns to its original direction (which is usually toward a source of water). The same directional persistence is also found in ants.

The storing of food by insects, such as ants and bees, and mammals, such as rabbits and beavers, and the "gigantic" enterprise of the latter in building dams for winter habitat are other examples of the presence of a directive and organizing instinct in lower animals.

The flocking of birds for common protection during the hatching season and fish swimming hundreds of miles to spawn in shallow waters must be viewed as internal propelling forces apart from the immediate id gratifications. The denial of the id and its pleasure principle is well illustrated by the feeding process in birds, who bring worms and feed them into the beaks of their helpless young in the nests.

These are only some of the innumerable adaptations that illustrate the presence of highly complex procedures by which the life force finds its expression to assure survival. These may appear to be only manifestations of the id or the pleasure drive, but a closer look at the effort involved, the associated self-denial and abandonment of id gratifications, shows that the id is subordinated or suspended, to attain specific ends. It would seem that the highly complex patterns of behavior in lower animals *are derived from an instinctive ego which is in the service of the id or life force (élan vital)*. We shall presently see that, in some respects, the relation between the ego and id in man does not conform with this basic law in nature.

We derive the assumption of a biological base for the sources (not necessarily for the pattern) of functioning of the ego both from observation of animal behavior, and from inductive consideration of the nature of life itself. It is inconceivable that life and the struggle for existence in plants and animals, indeed within the atom itself,[1] can be equipped only with an urge (as the id in man) without the instrument to utilize and direct that urge toward realization of its aims in the interest of survival. Thus the *élan vital,* as we understand it, consists of two parts, both of which are inherent and instinctual: the urge or drive, and the mechanisms of implementation of that drive. It must be noted in this connection that in some insects, and, as Metchnikoff (1903) has suggested, also in higher forms of life and even man,

---

[1] Witness the conflict between the "anti-matter" and the "pro-matter" forces in the nuclear structure or process of the atom, for example.

237

"disharmonies" are present in this regard. The urge for pleasure and survival is in some instances negated by the absence of appropriate controls. Examples of this are the moth who flies into the fire to its destruction and the human child's indiscriminate eating of substances which may injure or kill him. This lack of the instinctive discrimination that should serve the interests of life, is what Metchnikoff termed "disharmonies in nature."

In the example of the moth and the fire, the instinctive ego is too weak to carry out the law of natural survival because of the chemical constitution of the moth, which responds with intensity to glow and heat. This tendency, also found in man, may have given rise to Freud's theory of the "death instinct." In our view, such a tendency in man appears only when the life force has been frustrated by internal debility or external deprivation to such a degree that the ego's energies become exhausted and its defenses break down.

The fascinating, intricate, and complex designs by which survival of individuals and, above all, the species is achieved in nature indicates that instinct is at work in rudimentary ego (instrumentality) as well as in the primary life urge. I can, therefore, only partially agree with Freud's statement that "the character of the ego is a precipitate of abandoned object-cathexes and that it contains a record of past object choices." (Freud, 1927, page 30.) This observation, astute as it is, applies to the patterning and *shaping* of the ego functions and not to the *inherent* ego. To assume, as does Freud, that "the ego uses borrowed forces," namely those of the id, and that "it constantly carries into action the wishes of the id as if they were its own," presents a dilemma. The urge to live and to perpetuate life stems from the id. But the id is only the *urge;* the adaptation and utilization of the mechanisms to carry out this urge emanate, in our view, from another biological property of the animal psyche—the ego.

Educability of the Ego

The bio-quantum theory asserts that the ego has its own instinctive forces. While one is on thin ice when applying anthropomorphic analogies to nature, it is nonetheless possible to speculate, with some degree of certainty, that where a natural urge is present, means of carrying it out are also there. Without a *modus operandi* the urge would die away. This principle is dramatically illustrated in the overwhelming intensity of cathexis of the body's three orifices (mouth, anus, and sex organs) which are involved in maintaining the life of the individual and in perpetuating the species. In the human, more than in other species, the ego is infinitely more strained in dealing with these three basic urges. But it also exercises control and selection of behavior, though with less strain, in other areas. (This is possibly because the three basic survival urges are not as subject to sublimation as are other urges —hostility, for example.)

Social life would be impossible if the ego did nothing but carry "into action the wishes of the id." Actually, the ego is also in opposition to the id and holds it in control on many fronts. The "selective capacity" (Roback) is the function of the ego. If this capacity and the ego's restraining and controlling powers were not inherent, the educability of man would be very limited indeed. All education and socialization of the human personality relies on the potential of the ego to respond to external influences in shaping it and utilizing its forces.

The forces that pattern the ego functions are many. Most are mechanical-adaptive, but identification does operate here on a basis of cathexes, as Freud suggested. The psychotherapist very often has to deal with negatively cathected internalized objects; that is, the objects that are invested with hostility and rage. The correction of ego function here requires that the patient dissolve his hostile feelings toward significant persons in his life and the accompanying anxiety and guilt which deplete ego resources.   . .

The Self and Nonself Polarities

The ego can be understood as being a product of the interaction of the *self* and the *nonself* that begins in early infancy and continues through childhood and probably, to some extent, to adolescence. It can be assumed that the "unconscious" part of the ego consists of its instinctive elements plus the added internalized experiences with reality of early (preverbal, preconceptual) childhood, while the "conscious" part of the ego consists of the learnings acquired later in life through accommodation, understanding, and the imposed, conscious controls necessitated by the demands of the outer world. Thus, the ego is a synthesis of the biologic self and the environmental nonself. These are its two structural poles. When either is insufficient or does not adequately complement the other, functional ego deficiency results. In the absence of organic deficiency, both poles are accessible to psychotherapy. Among other things, psychotherapy can help to bring into closer quantitative parity the conscious and unconscious parts of the ego, thus reducing anxiety.

A group aids in the fusing and complementation of the self and nonself polarities. The phenomena of identification, empathy, universalization, mutual induction, mutual support and common effort bring the self and nonself (other persons) in contiguity and dynamic interaction, thus integrating them into a more wholesome and more socially advantageous ego functioning.

Conditioning of Ego Functions

The ego, unlike the id, can be influenced and patterned by both internal and external necessities of the organism as, for example, in the domestication and training of animals. This is dramatically illustrated by the now-famous demonstration in which a cat, a rat, and a dog all lap up milk simultaneously from the same dish. The fact that antagonism believed to stem from primary instincts can be affected and modified by "training" has led some scientists to deny the existence of instincts. Actually, it is quite possible that the *mode of expression* of the instinct is altered and not the instinct itself. When a cat discovers that its needs can best be satisfied in the company of its biologic "enemies"—the rat and the dog—it accepts this company. But the fear and the hostility may reappear when this association no longer meets the cat's bio-organic needs. Behavioristic psychology also erred on these grounds. It is not the basic id that is conditioned, but, rather, the instinctive ego that is modified by conditions which meet the organic needs of the animal.

This mechanistic principle and distinction has a pivotal bearing on the human psyche, especially on the cultural aspects of man, as an individual and as a social atom. My assumption is that both the id and the ego have an instinctual base; only the superego is derived *entirely* through internalization of parental, and later, group demands, approval, and prohibition.[2]

Family Influences and Ego Formation

Selective capacities and the power and need to inhibit and direct motility are first acquired in the family setting and through family relations. While it is accepted that the superego is derived from the social climate, it is less recognized that the capacity to mobilize inner forces toward a specific objective and to operate as needed in a given life situation are also derived from the primary experiences in the home. While the potential, qualitatively and quantitatively, resides within the personality, the functioning of the ego, in Western culture, is conditioned by the examples set by, and the pattern of ego functioning of, the adults in the child's environment. The mother is of particular importance in this respect. The child is exposed to her influence more than to anyone else's during the most impressionable and imprintable period of his life. Whether parents meet life's stresses, large or small, with self-control and equanimity, or whether they respond with anger or panic, sets the example for the child's later behavior in similar situations. Example and imitation are not the only factors that foster and condition the embryonic ego. Internalization through identification is of even greater importance and has a more telling effect on the final outcome. It is doubtless the internalized image, behavioral and otherwise, of the parents that is sometimes referred to as the "unconscious ego." Early identifications, occurring frequently in the preverbal and preconceptual stages, are *structurally* integrated into the ego (and character) of

---

[2] Elsewhere, I have suggested the existence of a "group superego" as differentiated from the parental superego.

the individual and thus become a part of the store of his unconscious.

Ego structure and functioning are also fashioned by other important experiences to which the child is exposed, such as relations with siblings (which are actually a reflection of the attitudes of parents toward each sibling and the parents' relation to one another).

The conduct of parents and the other significant persons in his life demonstrates, to the child, patterns of reaction and control and methods of dealing with inner and outer realities. Both indulgence and rigid discipline affect ego development negatively. Indulgence encourages narcissism, vitiates the capacity for object relations, and impedes the emergence of the self-regulative forces, while excessive discipline tends to augment either submissiveness and/or rebelliousness and to prevent the development of true autonomy and self-reliance. Through the process of identification and ego ideal formation, weak parents induce defective capacities for reality testing and ego functioning.

In the final formation of the ego and the patterning of its functions, firm impediments, restraints, prohibitions, and *appropriate* punishment play an important role. They produce in the child an awareness of the boundaries of his ego and of the need for self-limited discharge of impulses and pleasure drives. Out of these arise some of the ingredients from which the superego is later formed, as well as the operation of the self-inhibitive and directive properties of the ego. However, the most potent single force in conditioning the ego for adequate functioning is security in childhood. The harmonious integration of the psychic forces and organic processes occur maximally when anxiety and fear do not drain psychic energies and do not interfere with the orderly metabolic growth and integration of the organism. *While the ingredients of the ego are resident in the constitution, its strength is determined by the nourishment it receives.* The basic element of this nourishment is security in childhood. I have elsewhere suggested the term "emotional vitamins" for a number of the supportive and nourishing conditions necesary for a wholesome development of personality.

242

Organic Foundations of the Ego

Having considered some of the psychogenic sources of ego formation, we now return to another biological aspect of ego functioning: the involvement of specific organs. It is a common observation that the behavior and general character of animals, such as dogs and cats, is greatly affected by castration and spading. Similarly, we note the altered characters of eunuchs. Further confirmation comes from persons who suffer from various glandular deficiencies and imbalances. The difference in ego controls is dramatically manifested in cases of hypo- and hyperthyroidism and pituitary, adrenal, and gonad deficiencies. People present impressive variations in their responses, controls, and self-determination when healthy and when ill. Deficiencies and debilities greatly affect the degree of frustration tolerance, the threshold of irritability, the capacity for equanimity, judgment, and self-control, and the mobilization of energies.

Thus, the functioning of the body-mind in all animals, and especially man, is not affected solely by psyche, a view promulgated by some students of psychosomatics. Somatopsychological processes, as well, have to be taken into consideration, if many is to be understood and if the various medical and psychological healing arts are to be responsibly practiced. In addition to endocrine deficiencies, there are various types of organ inferiorities, mental deficiencies, autonomic imbalances, and other types of neurological and constitutional deficits that limit ego development in the individual.

The ego load of man is heavier by far than it is in lower animals. Because he is compellingly a gregarious animal (and a moral one), the pangs of conscience and the demands of the unconscious segment of it, the superego, are a considerable strain on the ego. Even greater strain is exerted by the need to control the three basic appetites on which biological life depends: hunger, evacuation, and sex. The aim of the first two is to secure the survival of the individual, and the aim of the third is perpetuation of the species. In order that animals fulfill these aims, the orifices through which they are gratified have been endowed with highly charged sensitivity and cathexes and are high in the hegemony of the body.[3] In animals, these functions are discharged in accordance with a plan determined by instinct. They have not been placed in the dilemma in which man finds himself; he must regulate these urges and himself in order to maintain internal homeostasis and his equilibrium in relation to his physical and social environments.

Man is the only animal in which pleasure is divorced from purpose. Animals exercise the three primary urges to the extent to which they serve survival: Selection and intake of food are controlled by organic suitability and satiation; and the periodicity of sex has the same ultimate aim. But man's appetites are perpetual and the excesses to which he is prey constitute a major problem in education and in therapy. An example is the great difficulty some have in controlling their oral appetite, as manifested in obesity, addictions, and perversions. The ego is sorely tried in its attempts to check these appetites, even when the addict desires to do so. Similarly, the sexual urge is a source of endless difficulties for man (whether civilized or primitive). Here, too, in its extremes, pathological states can result, such as nymphomania and satyrism. Similarly, the anal orifice can become a source of such intense pleasure to the human animal as to lead him to all types of fixations and perversions. In all of these, what is striking is the marked separation of function (pleasure) from purpose (reality), a separation not found in any other animal.[4]

Training in proper exercise of these functions and their control, which begins in early infancy and continues to maturity, consists of calling the ego, as opposed to the id, into operation. One cannot possibly be fully successful in this. The residues of infantile urges, especially when encouraged and abetted by commercial and other interests in society, forever remain to plague

[3] This condition is exaggerated in psychoneuroses (and psychoses) and forms one of the major concerns of psychotherapy—libido attachment and redistribution.

[4] This could be considered as one of the "disharmonies in nature." Teleologically considered, the cathexis of the three primary orifices is nature's "bribe" to insure the exercise of biological functions and perpetuate the species. I have also suggested that man's general endogenous and exogenous conflicts are derived from this basic duality —separation of pleasure from purpose. (See Slavson, 1952.)

the individual. Whether in the conscious or unconscious, ego energies are always strained to deal with this conflict.

The Quantum Aspect of the Ego

The inevitable corollary of the biological theory of the ego is its quantum aspect. Observation, as well as inductive thought, suggests that, by virtue of their constitutions, there must be differential ego energy reserves in different individuals. Even if a person has been exposed to the most ideal nurturing and educational conditions, his energy reserves would still be limited by his bio-organic constitution. An ideal educational experience, however, cannot be achieved because of the inherent nature of man *vis-à-vis* the inevitable impingement of society upon him. Thus, the maximum available ego energies (reserves) are a product of the two forces —inherent organic adequacy and the totality of educative influences and pressures. This *quantum* of available (ego) energy must, therefore, be different for each individual, a fact that must be remembered by all those who exert authority over their fellow humans, such as parents, teachers, supervisors, etc. More than thirty years ago, I suggested that activities beyond one's daily occupational demands can be carried on where "excess energy" is available. I was interested to find that, many years later, Dr. Karl Menninger had come to the same conclusion quite independently (his "theory of excess energy"). The bio-quantum theory of ego reserves also forms the basis for an *organismic ethics* or *natural morality*. We cannot expect the same qualitative behavior and the same quantitative contribution to society from everyone. If we are to prevent tyranny, demands on the individual should be consistent with his capacities. Blanket or uniform demands, without consideration of individual resources and capacities, are unjust.

SEVEN SOURCES OF PATHOGENESIS

The biological, and, especially, the quantum hypotheses of the ego, lead the psychotherapist quite naturally to an interest in ascertaining the pathogenesis of its malformation. Such knowledge is essential for him as a preliminary to remedial steps. Impediment to the individual's development of maximal ego resources can arise from seven distinct causes: impaired libido development; blockage of autonomous strivings; faulty identification models; neurotic conflicts, guilt and fear; a defective self-image; ambivalence; and organic and constitutional deficiencies.

Impaired Libido Development

The most rapid development of the ego takes place during latency, when the oedipal libido urges subside and the establishment of identifications is accelerated. This period is marked by centrifugal interests away from the family, as play activities with contemporaries take ascendancy. New relations and excursions into the wider world demand a host of adaptations and inner and outer controls to make one acceptable to the microculture of peers. While the growth of the ego has its origin when the child is forced to give up his infantile feelings of omnipotence and rabid egocentricity and to recognize objects as separate from himself during the pregenital period, the growth of controlling and regulative principles are accelerated during the latency period and are continued, at a decreasing rate, probably throughout life.

If the libido has sustained damaging experiences in earlier years, in the preoedipal and oedipal stages, latency cannot reach its full measure, because remnants of the preceding libidinal strivings will inevitably persist; the transformation of the infantile sexual libido into the nonsexual libido, which should occur in orderly development, does not take place to an adequate extent. Thus, the pleasure principle continues to dominate the personality instead of giving way sufficiently to the reality principle. Freud has formulated this relation in the following terse sentence: "The ego is not sharply separated from the id; its lower portion merges into it." (Freud, 1927, page 28.)

This is also our position, even though we hold that the ego is not a derivative of the id. In our opinion, "Libido organization has a direct relation to ego function. The impairment or inadequacy of one is reflected in the other, and improvement in either inevitably affects the other. The ego is called upon to hold the psychological frontiers intact, but a weak ego cannot hold libidinal and infantile cravings sufficiently in check. Patients who require psychotherapy usually have such ego development. In some, this is frankly reflected in their lives and behavior; others evolve defensive façades that make them appear strong and able to manage their psychic forces. Actually, these are frequently overconditioned reaction formations, defensive pseudo-strength, as it were." (Slavson, 1952a, pages 46-47.)

Blockage of Autonomous Strivings

The blockage of autonomous urges and spontaneity in the child, as a deterrent to ego development, is too obvious to require elucidation. Like any other faculty, the ego grows in strength through exercise of responsibility. Free interaction with reality and experiences of its tangibility and impact engender both judgment and inner controls. Unfortunately, home, school, and recreation seem to conspire against the individual in this respect.

Faulty Identification Models

As already indicated, the child's ego is damaged by domineering, fear-inspiring, or weak and otherwise inadequate parents. This damage is not sustained in the home alone. During latency and adolescence, the child's progressive and fluid identifications with objects in the world outside the home also damage his development, though rarely as seriously as the identifications, ego ideals, and imitations derived from relations and experiences in the family.

Neurotic Conflict, Guilt, and Fear

Since neurotic symptoms are a result of inner conflict and the struggle between the id and the superego, in which the ego is involved as an unsuccessful mediator, the ego's energies and reserves are strained in maintaining psychic equilibrium, even though it may always remain "equilibrium under tension." (Slavson, 1952a, pages 68-70.) Feelings of guilt and thoughts, fantasies, and impulses that evoke either fear or anxiety (whether conscious or unconscious) are dealt with by the ego and consume ego energies that would otherwise be available for more constructive use. The psychic energies thus invested deplete the ego, and, where this occurs beyond permissible limits for the particular individual, a so-called "nervous breakdown" occurs; in extreme instances, where ego reserves are constitutionally limited and defenses tenuous, the ego retreats from reality and a psychotic episode may occur.

Defective Self-Image

An unloved, rejected, habitually punished, criticized, and demeaned child comes to perceive himself as inadequate and unworthy, incapable of achievement and success. Throughout life, he remains either hesitant or unable to undertake enterprises of value or to conclude them successfully if undertaken. Such a defective self-image is usually coupled with other neurotic mechanisms that incapacitate the possessor; he is unable to mobilize latent powers in his constitution and psyche that would otherwise be available to him were he free of the impediments generated through his childhood experiences. Psychotherapy improves the self-image by making available much of the ego energy blocked off from action and function.

Among patients (and in the general population) there are individuals in whom the reaction formation to feelings of inferiority is one of great activity, grandiosity, and outstanding achievement. The drive for power and recognition is intended, though entirely unconsciously, to counteract feelings of inadequacy. Such cravings for power and achievement can also be a bid for the parental acceptance which the patient has yearned for all his life: if he shows himself worthy of their affection, they may still replenish, for him, the gnawing craving for infantile love. This drive, being unconscious, can persist long after the parents have died and the world, generally, has been substituted for them in the unconscious.

The other aspect of this manifestation is that it absorbs the physical and ego energies to a degree well beyond the borders of mental health and physical well-being. The overcathexis of one focus of life (power, achievement or recognition, for instance), impoverishes other aspects of the personality and creates many problems in interpersonal relations and social adjustment. Thus, what appears on the surface as strength, because of apparent external power and success, is actually the obverse side of weakness and a pathetic inner hunger. In this connection, one cannot fail to note the relationship between the libido and the ego.

Ambivalence

Doubt, hesitancy, indecision, and the unresolved conflicts between conscious or unconscious positive and negative feelings in object relations—ambivalence—constitutes another major strain on the ego and a drain on its energies. Aside from the libido fluctuations characteristic of this state, the ego is involved in it as an arbiter, as it were. Its duty is to find an appropriate path for decision and action. This can be done only at a great expenditure of the energies of the psyche. In fact, quantitatively, the strain on energies may be by far greater in arriving at a decision than in carrying it out. A large part of one's *emotional* energies is consumed in dealing with ambivalent feelings. When freed of these opposing forces, one's energies are released for action.

This situation is a major consideration both in education and psychotherapy. The psychotherapist needs to be aware that part of his patients' ego deficiencies are caused by this condition, and correction of it will enhance their mastery over themselves and over the external world. Adjustment, adaptation, and mastery are greatly facilitated if doubt and hesitancy are eliminated.

Organic and Constitutional Deficiencies

The significance of constitutional and organic conditions in ego structure and functions has already been discussed in some detail. Their importance needs to be emphasized in relation to psychotherapeutic planning. Before psychotherapy is undertaken, it is essential that an adequate investigation be made of possible somatic causes for the patient's complaints. While psychotherapy or guidance may be of help even where the illness proceeds from physical sources (since all illness has a concomitant emotional reaction), mental therapy in these instances must be recognized as having limited effectiveness. In practice, one encounters conditions in which psychotherapy is definitely counterindicated. Such knowledge has value to the therapist, for, being aware of the limits of success inherent in a situation, he is less likely to feel frustrated and defeated.

TABLE 1

Sources of (Ego) Pathogenesis

Impaired libido development
Blockage of autonomous strivings
Faulty identification models
Neurotic conflict, guilt, and fear
Defective self-image
Ambivalence
Organic and constitutional deficiencies

THE DISTRIBUTION OF EGO ENERGIES

In the preceding pages we described the *quantitative* aspects of the ego and ways in which its energies can be dissipated. Drainage of ego energy through pathogenic states diminishes its services to personality expansion, social effectiveness, and the numerous other growth-producing possibilities that civilization and culture offer. In children, some of the most common manifestations of this are school phobias, learning disabilities, short concentration spans, conflict with or avoidance of playmates, etc. Functional ego deficiencies are displayed by nearly all adults, to some degree and in some areas, and are reflected in their inability to mobilize ego energies which, under favorable conditions, would be available to them. Since maximum available energy has definite limits for each individual and, since the quantum of these energies is absorbed in dealing with pathogeny, less energy is available for controlling impulses and feelings, for constructive activities, and for personality growth. Conversely, the less ego energies absorbed in holding down hostility and aggression, dealing with anxiety, fear and guilt, and in defenses and resistances, the greater is the quantum available for other functions. This relation and distribution of ego energies can be expressed in the following equation:

$EE=Eg+Ea+Eh+Er+Ef+Ed$ ... in which EE represents the total ego energy potential of an individual; Eg, the ego energies consumed in dealing with guilt; Ea, with anxiety; Eh, with hostility; Er, with repression; Ef, the ego energies required for general functioning in outer reality; Ed, the ego energies used in personality development and expansion, and so forth. It is evident from the equation that as Eg, Ea, Eh, and Er are diminished, Ef and Ed are correspondingly increased.

Where failures in adequate ego functions occur, the ego defends itself against bringing this fact to awareness, preventing the resultant anxiety. For this, the psyche employs a number of defenses including avoidance mechanisms and, in some instances, suppressions. Anna Freud (1945) lists these defenses as denial, repression, reaction formation, escape into fantasy, projection, and introjection. Other mechanisms of psychic avoidance are obsolescence, withdrawal, submission, catatonic defense, escape into reality, etc. The effect of these defenses is to prevent uncovering of the chasm between the actual ego and ego ideal (idealized self-image). The difference between these is always considerable and constitutes a perpetual source of potential anxiety, because of failure to reach the idealized image of the self. The ego ideal is derived from the social and group values and mores—the "social image" (Trigant Burrow). The feelings resulting from the different levels of the two—the actual ego and ego ideal—are one of the major focal points of psychotherapy, especially "ego therapy." In fact, so-called "ego therapy" is the preferred treatment method for patients in whom this difference in levels causes central difficulties.

DYNAMICS OF EGO THERAPY

Specificity

Psychotherapy and group psychotherapy can specifically serve as a corrective for ego malformation and can liberate its energies.

However, it must be remembered that no part of the human psyche can be dealt with without involving or at least affecting its other elements, and the soma as well. Thus, correcting the ego will involve psychic areas outside of the ego; the total psycho-organ will be affected.

It may be helpful to restate here, as a frame of reference, the general aims of psychotherapy. We conceive these aims as redistribution of the libido, strengthening of the ego, correcting of the superego, improvement of the self-image, and the finding of suitable sublimations. These are related parts that form a unitary whole. None of these aims can be achieved in isolation from the others; change in one brings changes in the rest. However, it is frequently necessary to segmentalize the whole for purposes of communication and intelligibility.

No blanket statement can be made as to how the ego can best be affected. Specificity is of the essence. Ego correction has to be determined by the degree and, especially, by the nature of its involvement in the total pathology. For the sake of brevity, we can point to the sharp differences in ego etiology in such psychologic disturbances as character disorders, psychoneuroses, and psychoses. In character disorders, psychotherapy would address itself to the ego and its functioning more than it would in cases of transference neuroses where the sexual libido is the focus of attention. In most of the psychoses, the structure of the ego and its defenses would receive the entire attention of the therapist. These generalized rules have to be further broken down for specific types and degrees, in each clinical category, which would be treated differentially both quantitatively and qualitatively. But in a treatise such as this is, which deals with generic considerations, only general suggestions can be made. In practice these have to be modified and elaborated to meet the needs of individual patients.

The Process of Ego Therapy

Examination of the pathogenesis of ego formation provides the clues to therapy. Where the libido development has been impaired, as in psychoneuroses, for example, direct dealings with ego functions alone, as in guidance or counseling, would be ineffectual. It may even be counterindicated, since it would constitute an attack on ego defenses, the sole source of the neurotic's security, for they are essential for his psychic stability until he can establish a new orientation through therapy. Here the dissolution of the libido fixation and the overcoming of the guilt and anxiety relative to libidinal strivings is necessary as a first step. All improvement is contingent on the diminution or elimination of these and other neurotic conflicts.

Where ego therapy is indicated, it is necessary to undertand the blocks to autonomy and self-assertiveness, sustained by the patient during his formative years. The stored-up rage, which he may, or may not, have suppressed as a result of early frustrations, needs to be ventilated or acted out in an atmosphere of freedom and acceptance, devoid of the fears of punishment and rejection which characterized the patient's childhood. This restitutive experience, in free self-assertiveness, provided by psychotherapy, drains off the accumulated emotional pressures, since no punishment or retaliation is experienced and no guilts and anxieties are generated. Thus, the load that the ego was carrying is reduced, freeing its energies that much more for productive functions. At the same time, the acceptance of his vagaries gives the patient a new awareness of his worth; that is, his self-image is improved. The fact that he is allowed to reveal himself as he really is and still be accepted without reservation raises his self-esteem.

In the group, the complete freedom to express judgments, opinions, anger, rage, hostility, and other prohibited feelings, without fear of retaliation or loss of status, serves to unload the weight borne by the ego, thereby increasing the quantum of energies available for personality growth and expansion and for dealing more adequately with the impact of inner and outer demands. The fact that this discharge of noxious affect occurs in the presence of others, who understand, empathize, sympathize, and accept such revelations, adds to one's feelings of self-worth. As a direct result of the repetition of these favorable experiences, the self-image is improved.

The self-image is also improved by the discovery that self-abasing, guilt-evoking, and anxiety-generating impulses, thoughts, fantasies, and acts are the property of others as well. One is not unique in this respect. The awareness of the universality of noxious elements similar to, and sometimes even worse than, one's own, diminishes guilt feelings and improves the self-image, thus freeing further ego energies for more constructive effort.

One cannot overestimate the significance of freedom in psychotherapy—freedom for self-expression and self-assertion. This freedom may take infantile and regressive forms, but therapy requires that the patient feel free even to regress, so that he can later retrace his steps upward toward sound emotional maturity under the guidance of the therapist and the group. Freedom gives him status and a feeling of worth. Self-worth comes when the therapist as a parent surrogate accepts him as he is, unconditionally, without reservation or question. But in cases where the center of treatment, i.e., the nuclear problem, is the ego rather than the libido, such extreme permissiveness should be employed only at the early stages of treatment. Unlike psychoneuroses, in ego-centered psychotherapy, the therapist plays an increasingly more active role. He may call attention to the patient's mannerisms and behavior, explain (as opposed to interpret) the effect of that behavior, and even suggest specific ways of dealing with the patient's own reactions and external circumstances. These strategies, if properly timed with regard to positive transference feelings, ego strengths, and defenses, serve as ego reinforcements. When the newly emerging strengths are tested against realistic life situations and the patient finds himself not wanting, the ego is permanently enhanced. However, where the object of the therapeutic effort is the neurotic nucleus, it is treated as a transference neurosis, letting ego repair take place automatically as described above and as the neurosis is dissolved. In such instances, ego retraining, if necessary, can be left for the end of treatment when the defenses are no longer of critical significance to the patient. Many psychoanalysts employ groups for this purpose, as an arena for reality testing and to check on ego strengths and the operation of defenses.

As already stated, the identification aspect of the transference situation was overshadowed by libidinal factors and did not receive the recognition that it deserves. Actually, an introspective examination of a patient's feelings toward his therapist reveals the latter to be a significant object of identification and ego ideal, since the choice of an object of identification is usually made on the basis of libidinal reactions. The therapist can correct the defective (ego) identifications that the patient made in earlier years. The patient unconsciously (sometimes quite consciously) models himself after the therapist in his manner of response, conduct, objectivity, dignity, imperturbability, and emotional control; that is, in his ego functions. When the central problem is ego functioning, such a model for emotional economy and efficient conduct can be of pivotal importance.

In all patients who come for treatment or guidance, the ego is *overloaded*. The overloading may be caused by the demands on its reserves from neurotic and other noxious properties of the psyche. As these are corrected and balanced, the wasteful use of ego energies is correspondingly diminished and these are made available for more constructive channels. Thus, after successful psychotherapy, patients not only live in better harmony within themselves, but also find new avenues for wholesome and socially useful activities and creative expression. Relations to people and to the outer world, generally, assume a new and more satisfying form and content; and, as conflicts and hostilities are diminished, energies become available for more humanizing feelings and for the sublimating and redirecting of primitive urges.

The ego can also be overloaded when an individual undertakes tasks and responsibilities beyond his (quantitative) ego strengths or allows himself to become enmeshed in situations which are alien or antagonistic to his (qualitative) temperament and ego organization. Perhaps the dubious term "situational neurosis" applies to circumstances where the ego is drained and irritability or other symptoms appear when one is compelled to remain in an unsuitable situation.

THE GROUP AS EGO THERAPY

The therapeutic process itself is no different in analytic groups than in individual treatment. In both methods, it occurs through transference, catharsis, insight, reality testing, and sublimation. Due to the presence of more than one patient, elaborations as well as modifications of these take place in a group. However, identification, transference, and reality testing are most involved in ego functioning and ego repair.

The accommodations that each patient in a group has to make, in order to be accepted, forces considerable modifications in ego functioning. The group situation is a severe testing ground for appropriate and inappropriate behavior, ideas, and feelings. Fellow group members curb or direct a patient's behavior and force him to *examine* his feelings and attitudes more readily, and in many instances, more effectively, than an individual therapist can do without damaging the transference relation. A patient can accept confrontation, suggestions, and criticism from fellow patients with greater equanimity than he could from a therapist, who represents authority and parent figures. A patient reacts with greater hostility to the therapist, who is *in loco parentis,* than he does to sibling substitutes in the persons of other patients.

In a group, the demands and pressures are tangible and realistic. Artificiality is reduced to a minimum and fantasy is subordinated to and tested against events. Each individual is compelled to navigate and make adjustments if he is to remain a member of the group. Due to their intrapsychic states, their hostilities, the threat to ego defenses, the weakness of ego controls, and similar conditions, patients may create considerable distress for themselves in a group. It is in these and similar situations and in dealing with group tensions that the skill of the therapist is tried. When he brings to the surface prevailing antagonistic feelings and helps the group members to face and analyze them, he not only aids in dissolution of libidinal distortion, but he re-educates their egos.

As each participant in the analytic discussion is led to *understand* his reactions to the behavior of another group member, he becomes more aware of the pattern and quality of his ego functioning and the unconscious displacement and transference mechanisms he employs. When patients reach this high point in group interviews, the therapist's and patients' interpretations become relevant and significant.

Groups help in this process immeasurably by the catalytic effect they exert on their members. The permissive climate of the group (reflecting the permissive attitude of the therapist) encourages each to reveal his ego functioning. As it is mirrored, and reacted to, by other group members, awareness is forced on each participant, leading to conscious examination and contemplation and ultimately to correction.

The self-justifying defenses (rationalizations) that patients inevitably employ in the beginning are not left unchallenged by fellow group members. Where a therapist would rightly hesitate to attack these defenses, fellow patients are not as restrained. Thus, an individual who lives by deviant mechanisms of escape from reality and distortion and who evades self-confrontation, is forced to face the devices that in the past caused him difficulties. This is particularly essential for patients with various types of character disorders. However, when such defensive strategies are charged with intense affect, they do not respond to ego-centered therapy. Therapy then has to be directed toward resolution of the inner neurotic constellation rather than toward ego functioning and behavior.

Defenses serve an essential purpose to psychoneurotics, and when these are threatened prematurely, dire results may ensue. In cases where constitutional, organic, or massive psychoneurotic bases for ego deficiencies exist, the boundaries of ego strengths have to be watched with great care. Within these limits, however, the mirror reactions of the other patients and their direct attacks on the defensive machinations of the ego (which alienated the patient from himself and outer reality) are among the major advantages of group treatment. In a similar fashion, character armor can be pierced and character resistances reached more easily by group interaction than by any other known method, provided that resistive mechanisms do not compel the patient to leave the group before it has had a chance to affect him.

Where the defects in ego functioning stem from models of identification, they can be changed, to a considerable extent, through corrective identifications in a group therapeutic situation. We have noted the importance of the identification factor in individual treatment. It is even more important in group therapy, where a variety of models are present in the persons of the other members as well as the therapist.

In general, groups provide avenues for more mature identification, since an adult's field of operation reaches beyond individual models. His horizons are wider and his interests have social direction. Therapy groups can have this meaning to patients. In fact, the capacity to develop loyalties to individuals and groups is one indication of improvement. But these feelings must be the gradual outcome of a corrected psyche. To be of therapeutic value, patients should not be *encouraged* to become atoms in the social molecule, the group; nor should there be a premium placed on "feelings of belonging."

As already indicated, "cohesiveness" in groups is antitherapeutic. But the dependencies and fears of some patients do lead them to use the group as support and as a substitute for their original families. When this occurs, the task of the therapist is to help the patient work through such dependency needs with the group as a frame of reference. To some degree, all members of all groups identify with, and depend on, the group, since social hunger, the need to belong and be accepted, is both biologically primary and psychologically imperative.

IX

Communication in Analytic Group Psychotherapy

The vastness of the phenomena of communication, in nature and man, precludes a complete treatise on the subject here. The discussion, therefore, will be confined to communication as observed in, and related to, interviews in analytic group psychotherapy, with nonpsychotic patients. Even this restricted area cannot be dealt with fully in a brief treatise. Therefore, only the essential factors that appear with comparative consistancy in the interviews will come under our purview.

VERBAL AND NONVERBAL COMMUNICATION

Communication in psychotherapy takes both verbal and nonverbal forms. In one, word symbols are employed; in the other, facial and ocular expressions, body tensions, movements, and stances, etc., manifest ideas and emotions, as they are activated. These reflect inner processes or states in the body-mind and are moderately specific to different emotional and physiological conditions. Emotions such as anger, fear, love, pity, indifference, worry, pleasure, joy and discomfort are recognizable by facial and bodily responses; illness, cold, heat, and hunger are also reflected in them. Particular communication also occurs through the tone of voice, the quality of speech, and numerous similar elements, which are part of verbal communication. The therapist has to ob-

259

serve and understand these various manifestations or he will not grasp the significance and meaning of the patients' intent.

There are more or less patent modes of communicating feelings and meaning, common to all human beings or to members of a particular culture. For example, raising of the eyebrows usually signifies disdain (though in one person I have known, it was a sign of fear in interpersonal relations); short or constrained breath may indicate anger or fear; sadness and depression are sometimes revealed by the eyes and mouth; and blushing or pallor have a number of different meanings in different individuals. Still, one needs to be aware of the particularized and idiosyncratic patterns of emotional expression in different individuals. Thus, in attempting to understand nonverbal communication, it is necessary to know the individual's personality and not just social stereotypes.

Since catharsis aids both in revealing the unconscious and in ego reorganization, in adult patients, verbal communication, rather than physical acting out, is the more appropriate medium. It is verbal catharsis and insight that establish a channel between the unconscious and the ego. They are in the service of "working through," which, in psychotherapy, is the process of making the unconscious available to the ego for evaluation and control. Nonverbal communication does not serve this end. Although valuable as an *indicator* of feelings, it still constitutes retreat rather than the self-confrontation essential for personality reconstruction. Feelings and fears remain untouched by nonverbal communication and they are stored up rather than released. If another patient does not rise to the nonverbal communication, the therapist has to take the cue and help the patient to verbalize his feelings, unless the patient is not ready for it or other counterindications are involved.

There are times when nonverbal communications may be even more significant to the therapist than are verbal formulations, for the latter can frequently be disguises or half-truths and may not reflect feelings as truly as the former. One of the outcomes of good psychotherapy is the acquisition of the inner freedom to use and respond to language honestly. At first, patients use language defensively to conceal and distort "truth" from themselves and from others, including the therapist and the group. They function on the "as if" principle. This is a common mechanism in the early stages of treatment and the numerous physical manifestations of repressed feelings and unexpressed thoughts are then of great value to the therapist for diagnostic understanding of the patients' unconscious, as are also abreactions, acting out, and re-enactments. Some disapprove of "acting out" in analytic psychotherapy, but any prohibition is inconsistent with sound practice (unless, of course, a patient's act threatens his or others' safety and well-being). There is little benefit in prohibiting anything to a patient, except with some obsessive-compulsive patients when, at the appropriate time in the course of treatment, a habit pattern has to be broken. While acting out by adult nonpsychotic patients is a form of regression (or resistance), with no inherent therapeutic value *per se*, it should not be prohibited but rather viewed as a form of communication and treated as such (see Chapter XII). Acting out is useful when its latent meaning is perceived and its significance to the patient's ego functioning is understood by the therapist and utilized in the course of the therapeutic effort.

The ability to perceive the covert meaning and significance of communication, whether verbal or nonverbal, is a talent indispensable to a therapist. The decision to explore, uncover, interpret, prohibit, or remain passive will be made on the basis of his correct perception of the hidden and latent feelings of a patient as manifested by his particular system of communication. A therapist should seldom, if ever, respond to an obvious, "logical" statement or question, unless he is convinced that the overt formulation corresponds to the covert intent. The statement or question has to be "thrown back" for further elaboration, through which the associated latent content and motivations can be revealed.

INTRAPERSONAL AND INTERPERSONAL COMMUNICATION

Communication is sometimes erroneously assumed to convey to others thoughts, ideas, and feelings. This interpretation may be adequate for common usage, but to the psychotherapist, the term has a vastly wider meaning and greater significance. To him, communication also includes intrapersonal integrative processes, in the total apparatus, between the innumerable neurons, endocrines, muscles, and cortical and thalamic activities that form the body-mind. This activity is referred to as *cybernetics* and is best illustrated by the integrative kinesthetic and homeostatic activity in an organism. As far as language is concerned, persons may be considered handicapped when their facilities for interpersonal communications are limited. However, a compulsive need to talk is also a symptom requiring attention. Loquacity is an unmistakable sign of excessive anxiety, of oral dependence or urethral fixation, among other things. Similarly, facial immobility or hypermobility, ocular placidity, body rigidity, or hyperactivity also communicate an individual's state of being. What is termed "emotional flatness," as reflected in the face, is usually a symptom of pathology.

Deviations in interpersonal communication are not primary phenomena; they may stem from defective intrapersonal communication. On the purely psychological level, this means that inhibitions and defenses are mobilized and ever vigilant against narcissistic injury through self-confrontation and that the unconscious is not available to the purview of the ego. However, neurological and endocrine defects and malfunctions, or even nutritional deficiencies, may be the primary causes for the observable functional peculiarities. Physiological and biochemical aspects of the personalties of patients should be part of the nosological investigations before treatment plans are formulated and the limits of possible improvement defined. Just as symptoms can be of psychosomatic origin, they can also be somato-psychological phenomena, that is, have their origin in the soma. Thus, interferences with both inter- and intrapersonal communication can be endogenous, originating in temperamental or organic sources, or internalized psychological blockage; that is, both the stimuli and the receptors can be within the personality itself, or the interferences can stem from externally originating stimuli which set up internal reactions.

An illustration of the latter would be a conversation in which, let us say, embezzlement is mentioned in the presence of a person who had committed such a crime and is either aware of it or has suppressed the memory of it. The mention of the subject causes him discomfort, against which he defends himself by failing to hear or comprehend what was said; or he may suddenly blush, begin to stutter, or lose the trend of the conversation. Thus, in addition to physical reactions, the block in inner communication interferes with interpersonal communication.

In this area, the objective of psychotherapy is to diminish the defenses, mobilized against narcissistic injury and structured in the psyche, that support neurotic defenses and character rigidities, and which prevent adequate self-confrontation. The resolution of this psychic state results from, and further facilitates communication between, the unconscious and the ego, thus placing the latter in control of the former. The channel of communication thus achieved is perhaps the most salutary outcome of psychological treatment, for it becomes a permanent facility in dealing more suitably with the self and with life's situations. Thus the task of psychotherapy is to facilitate intrapersonal communication and bring perception more in line with reality, as the ego is strengthened and the self-image is improved (self-acceptance). The result of improved *intrapersonal* communication is improved *interpersonal* relations and more salutary general adaptive mechanisms.

Interpersonal communication involves a communicant and a percipient. We prefer the term "percipient" to "recipient" because, due to defensive blockage and distortions, different individuals perceive (and react to) a communication differently. Cultural frames of reference, emotional states, and defensive systems, as well as organic determinants, assign to both verbal and nonverbal communications different meanings. The process is, therefore, one of perception and the person who so responds is the percipient.

Occasionally the idea is suggested that the sole or major process of group pychotherapy is interpersonal communication and that emphasis has to be on the group's "interactions." This view overlooks the nature of such communication and the conditions that inhibit, distort, and facilitate it. Since the difficulties in this form of relating stem from intrapersonal blockage (such as fear and the many forms of defensiveness), disturbances in interpersonal communication (using the term in its widest sense) are only symptoms of the inner disturbances to which psychotherapy has to address itself. What is necessary in such instances, rather than forcing communication is to correct those personality difficulties that interfere with it, and the patient can be free within himself. This inner freedom will allow him to integrate experience and feeling on a level involving the total personality—the instincts (id), the libido (pleasure), and the ego (understanding and control). As already indicated, this involves the reweighting and reconditioning of the patterns of functioning of these psychic ingredients, so that outer events and the inner responses are appropriate to the circumstances and situation confronting one. It is this freedom in inner relationships (intrapsychic communication) that leads to freedom in interpersonal communication and relatedness.

Hence, interpersonal communication, though being an *aim* in psychotherapy, can be achieved through intrapersonal communication. It is also true that intrapersonal communication can be achieved only in a therapeutic experience, whether individual or group, in which interpersonal communication is the central mechanism. Thus, interpersonal communication is both the aim and the process, but to be therapeutically valid, it has to flow from improved intrapersonal communication. It is essential that the psychotherapist keeps this differentiation clear in his own mind, as he participates in and guides the treatment process, and does not expect or force communication beyond the patients' readiness.

The Nature of Communication in a Therapy Group

In psychotherapy groups, the communicant is sometimes the entire group, as when it mobilizes hostility or uses one patient as a scapegoat, or an individual patient may communicate to the group; but, most often, communication is directed mainly to the therapist and peripherally to the group or to a specific fellow patient. Although it may appear that a patient is speaking to the group, his actual intent is to reach the therapist, since, being *in loco parentis,* the therapist can approve or disapprove, clarify or explain. This is inherent in the transference situation.[1]

Therapeutic communication in analytic psychotherapy *must be verbal.* Nonverbal communication does not serve the purposes of psychotherapy beyond its value in diagnostic formulations and as a source of infection or stimulation to the group. As an inhibitor of acts or verbalization, nonverbal communication borders, in a negative sense, on acting out. Inhibited or withheld feelings agitate both body and mind. Gross observation, as well as microphysiological studies, confirm the relation of organic concomitants to inhibition and ambivalent reactions. One of the basic requirements of true and competently conducted psychotherapy is that patients feel, and are, free to talk of all and any "embarrassing" subjects and reveal themselves without hesitancy or reservation.

Specific Features of Therapeutic Communication

Communication in analytic group therapy has four specific features: invasion and exposure of "threat areas"; specificity and concreteness; exposure of resistances and evasions; and atomism.

Threat Areas

The characteristic that forms the nucleus of a psychotherapeutic interview, as differentiated from ordinary conversation, is its involvement with "threat areas."[2] Everyone has areas in his psyche which, because of special circumstances, are most vulnerable. These may be a result of inferiority feelings, conditioned meaning to an individual, narcissistic injury, feelings of rejection and failure, cultural prohibitions, or numerous other constitutional and relational circumstances about which one is particularly sensitive. These constitute one's threat areas. For successful social and professional intercourse, one must evade the threat areas of others

---

[1] For a report of the striking difference in behavior, of a group of adolescent girls, in the presence and absence of the therapist, see Slavson, 1952, page 104. The completely different attitudes of adult patients, in the absence of the therapist (as in so-called "alternate meetings") is equally striking, though of a different nature.

[2] I am indebted to Mrs. Rose Switzer, for suggesting the term "threat areas" to me. Universal threat areas are one's religion, ethnic origin, sex, personal appearance, stigma, lack of achievement, and similar "personal" matters.

in ordinary conversation. In psychotherapy, on the other hand, dealing with the threat areas, of self and groupmates, is the ultimate aim of therapeutic communication.

An overabundance and wide range of threat areas tends to alienate a person from himself and limits his contact with and comprehension of outer reality. The defensiveness, on which threat areas feed, and the boundaries they set up, are inimical to acquisition of the inner freedom essential for interpersonal communication and, therefore, for satisfying social adjustment. For example, it is difficult to establish communication with persons who blush easily. The outskirts of their threat areas extend so far that even ordinary conversation becomes difficult. The threat areas of a schizoid character, are so extensive and intensive that they preclude ordinary contact with reality and people. The threat areas of small children (fear) and of adolescents ("self-consciousness") are common examples of this phenomenon. When these persist into adulthood they become more significant; in psychoneurotics they are of a particularly intense nature.

Psychotherapy aids in the diminution and narrowing of the threat areas. The patient eventually reaches a stage where he can feel more comfortable when subjects that were formally painful or embarrassing are touched on. In a large part, this is the essence of self-confrontation, which is a basic ingredient of inner freedom, self-acceptance, and successful intrapersonal and interpersonal communication. In a therapy group, incursion into threat areas occurs with greater frequency and impact than in one-to-one treatment. In the latter, self-confrontation is reached by gradual, almost imperceptible, growth of inner security, through a positive transference relation and the therapist's modulation in the conduct of the interviews. In groups, this graduation of impact cannot be maintained because of the assertivenes, aggressiveness, or sadism of group members toward each other, a situation that may sorely try the sensitivities and ego defenses of some patients. In extremes, the therapist may find it necessary to protect or "rescue" a patient from such onslaughts, which is particularly necessary with latent or borderline schizophrenics whose ego defenses are tenuous. But, despite the risks and strain involved, psychotherapy must deal with, and lead to diminution of, the strongly defended threat areas that tend to create anxiety and embarrassment and isolate the individual from his fellow men.

Threats can originate within the person (inner threats) or in the environment (outer threats). It is understandable that the latter are more likely to be recognized and consciously reacted to by patients. Defenses against recognition of inner threats (censors) are resisted with great tenacity. Ego defenses are quickly mobilized against inner threats, because of the incursions they make into the realms of the superego, ego ideals, and self-esteem, and guilt is aroused. The sources of outer threat can be used as targets for defensive projection (blame); the sources of inner threats cannot be so used. Paratoxic distortions and other defensive maneuvers of denial are used against them (outer threats, too, can be treated in the same ways) thus preventing the self from being invaded by guilt and anxiety. These strategies are ceaselessly in operation in the defensive phalanx of the ego and superego and require the perceptive attention of the therapist.

As mentioned, the group itself constitutes a threat, by the mechanism of group-induced anxiety: the fear of self-revelation, of being exposed by others, from the conscious and unconscious aggressive, and other guilt-provoking, urges, and of being victimized. It is important to create a secure, permissive, and nonjudgmental atmosphere in a therapy group, so that interpersonal and intragroup communication is facilitated. This climate primarily emanates from the personality, conduct, and values of the therapist.

As treatment progresses, threat areas are diminished in quantum, narrowed in extent, and defended with lessening intensity and affect. One of the most reliable indications of improvement in patients is the decrease in their defensiveness. As improvement in psychic equilibrium (especially in the self-image) emerges, areas that were vigorously denied or defended in the past are now accepted, allowed to be exposed, and faced with greater equanimity and with a constructive effort at self-correction. The individual is reaching toward a greater harmony with himself and grows less self-alienated. The increased inner harmony is the result of the inner psychic harmony and is partly attained through

267

the feeling of security given by persons (groupmates) who are nonjudgmental and nonpunitive and from the unformulated, but significant, "group code," which allows one to speak one's mind.

Specificity and Concreteness

In communication in therapy groups, the *level of abstraction* must be kept as low as posible. Here, the chief aim is to help the patient evolve to a level where he can face, and accept, inner and outer reality. The neurotic, one with a character disorder, and, especially, the psychopath and the psychotic, live by the "as if" principle. Although the fantasy content and its direction vary in these different states, patients (and everyone, for that matter) rely on the "as if" self-deluding devices as a form of ego and superego defenses and escape. This dependence on the miraculous is aided and abetted by various institutions of human culture. Actuality has always been a burden and a threat to man, and many symbolisms and devices have arisen as a defense against it.

Communication in therapy groups needs to be directed so that escapes into the realm of "as if" and abstraction and generalizations are prevented. Topics need to be drawn predominantly from actual experiences and from reactions to them by the patients, so that defenses, threat areas, and escape mechanisms can come to light. Abstractions and rationalizations, when employed as avoidance of self-confrontation and anxiety, are dealt with like any other type of resistance. To a great extent, the employment of theory and abstraction depends on the therapist. His consistent adherence to explicit matters and direct and simple (rather than involved) formulations, explanations, and interpretations set the pattern for the patients, and this manner of approach becomes a part of the group "code." This is not to imply that generalities, cognate philosophical principles, or cryptic, but enlightening, aphorisms are completely eschewed; these are, however, most effective when employed to culminate or illuminate a discussion of specifics. Such devices should be used sparingly and must be within the comprehension of the group members.

Exposure of Resistances and Evasions

A third element that differentiates communication in therapy groups from ordinary conversaion is the frank attacks made on efforts at self-deception (denial, distortion, rationalizations, and projections), which inevitably flows from the comparative disregard for threat areas. Unless he wishes to terminate a conversation or make an enemy, the communicant in ordinary conversation will avoid attacking the defenses or "sensitive areas" of the percipient. In group psychotherapy, attacking defenses is not only acceptable, but is an essential dynamic of the process and is encouraged. The therapist may wish to avoid doing this himself, due to his symbolic significance to his patients, but he permits and even encourages it in them. There are usually some members of the group who do not require much encouragement; their psychological needs, or early conditioning, impels them to act as inquisitors and explorers, frequently much to the discomfort of their victims,[3] and thereby they hew the interviews to a reality base.

Atomism

The fourth characteristic of group therapeutic communication is its *atomistic* quality. As indicated, generalizations and abstractions are kept down to a minimum. The discussions deal with the minutiae of living, experience, feelings, and situations. It is these minutiae and their elemental features that need to be recognized; and their effects on the communicant need to be explored and uncovered. This is not usual in ordinary conversations, and patients have to be conditioned to it by the therapist. He does this by exploratory questioning, until it becomes fixed in the patients' attitudes and, thus, a part of the (unformulated) group code.

In this connection, one needs to differentiate between full

---

[3] This is also one of the many objections to so-called "alternate meetings" (where the group meets in the absence of the therapist). Also, as already indicated, this is a reason why patients cannot act as therapists, "auxiliary" or otherwise. Only the trained therapist can respond to patients on the basis of an understanding of their therapeutic needs.

knowledge and twilight or threshold understanding. In the first, the individual comprehends the content and context of a set of facts or phenomena, while in the other, merely a hazy recognition or only partial awareness of these exist. Comprehension and knowledge can be clear and full, or only of a twilight nature. The rational and comprehension aspects, as differentiated from the irrational unconscious and the perceptual (i.e., the cognative versus the conative), has its place in psychotherapy, though one must be careful not to overexploit it. To a patient, the clearer his understanding is—against the background of emotional freedom and flexibility—the more thorough his improvement will be.

The elementaristic or atomistic feature of the group interview is important because it leads the participants to recognize those elements of interaction and reaction that arouse infantile emotions; it reveals the latent content in greater detail than a general statement; and it leads regressively to the core or nucleus of the patient's problem.

COMMUNICATION VECTORS

As we analyze the direction of the group's communications, we can identify seven directional vectors: intrapersonal, patient-to-patient, patient-to-group, patient-to-therapist, group-to-patient, therapist-to-patient, and therapist-to-group.

The Intrapersonal Vector

We have already discussed the nature of intrapersonal communication in terms of organic kinesthesis and homeostasis, organic integration, and availability of the unconscious to examination of and control by the ego.

The Patient-to-Patient Vector

This is stimulated by transference feelings, catalysis, spectator therapy, empathy, identification, and the total outcome of a sound analytically oriented psychotherapy and psychoanalysis. In the course of a group interview, empathy or emotional resonance or hostility and antagonism may bring into close interaction two patients, forcing the others at times into the role of spectators, some

270

of whom may implicitly or overtly react, while others remain passive and unaffected. The interaction between the two participating patients may be verbal or nonverbal. In the first instance, a prolonged dialogue may ensue. In the second, feelings—positive or negative, as the case may be—are communicated through the many channels already described. The quantum and quality of the patient-to-patient communication is conditioned by the libidinal investment the two have in one another, that is, the quality and intensity of the transference relation or homoerotic attraction (i.e., cathexis).

The Patient-to-Group Vector

Here, the patient addresses his communication to the group as a whole, without singling out any individual, though, as already stated, the therapist is always foremost in the mind of the communicant. This is usually the predominant pattern in the early life of the group. It may also occur at the outset of an interview, when a patient brings a personal problem for the consideration of the group or when he narrates an event from his past or one that took place in the interim between group sessions. Out of such a communication may spring a lively and free interchange between all the group members. Unlike communications addressed to the therapist or another member of the group, stimulus is supplied to the group as a whole and the group, as a whole, participates in the ensuing discussion or any part of it.

The Patient-to-Therapist Vector

Into this category, fall the communications directed toward the therapist, as an individual, and not toward other members of the group, though the response may come from the latter rather than from the therapist, usually a more desirable eventuality than the therapist's personal involvement.

The Group-to-Individual Vector

The group communicates to an individual patient when he stimulates an emotion or reaction that spreads through the group or a

271

considerable number of its members. This may result from universalization of a problem or statement, sympathy or empathy, disagreement, or an aggressive or hostile group phalanx engendered by his statements and ideas. Scapegoating, aversions, prejudices, and similar feelings that mobilize, in therapy (and other) groups, widespread or unanimous negative reactions, involve this vector; as do the more sanguine reactions such as attractiveness, forcefulness of personality, intellectual superiority, graciousness, and other positive qualities that find favor in the eyes of the group members.

The group may communicate their common positive or negative feelings to the target individual in the form of attitudes (nonverbal communication), but most often this is done verbally.

The Therapist-to-Patient Vector

Therapist-to-patient communication may occur on the basis of therapeutic indications or as countertransference reactions (See Chapter XIII). The therapist communicates his objective, analytical reactions; on rare occasions he may explain, elucidate, interpret, approve, agree, disagree, inquire, explore, elaborate, direct, and, in some rare instances, instruct or suggest to an individual patient in the group. The therapist's communication can also be nonverbal, such as a shrug of the shoulders, a nod of the head, or a smile, employed so as to "lead on" the patient, to evade committing himself, to prevent his becoming involved, or to support or encourage the patient.

The Therapist-to-Group Vector

Situations arise during group interviews in which the entire group, or a substantial part of it, is involved in a common emotion or reaction, presenting a unified phalanx toward one of its members or toward the therapist. Such a phalanx is also generated during a "rally" when a common or widespread interest engages the members, when the group is unavoidably involved in a project (which occurs very infrequently and should be discouraged), or when a universal feeling is under consideration. A group phalanx most often proceeds from a common negative transference toward the therapist. In all these, and similar developments involving the group, the therapist communicates to the entire group, since it acts and reacts as a unit, or nearly so.

Unlike patients' communications, the therapist's remarks, even when addressed to a single member, are registered by, and affect, the group as a whole. Because of his prestige status and the expectation the patients entertain for help and clarification from him, attention is centered on him and special importance is attached to both his utterances and nonverbal responses. Thus, whatever the therapist says or does becomes, *ipso facto* a communication to the group. In activity group therapy, for example, a child is never punished, even though it may be therapeutically indicated, because of the effect it would have on the other members of the group, who would perceive the therapist as a punitive parent and react to him accordingly. His treatment of one child is communicated to all the others, with resultant suspicion and distrust of him or open antagonism. There is, of course, greater latitude in analytic groups, since exploration and interpretation can cushion the negative effect of the therapist's conduct so that it is accepted in the light of its significance and intent. This cannot be done in activity groups, where interpretation and verbal communication of any emotional significance are completely avoided by the therapist.

CONGRUENCE AND MISUNDERSTANDING

One problem encountered in all communication is the differences in the meaning and significance that word symbols have for different persons. In a planfully structured group of patients, this hiatus would be minimized (though not eliminated) through nuclear problem homogeneity, similarity in other areas, and empathy and identification. The chasm is further narrowed as the group becomes a working group and evolves more or less uniform meanings.

The experiences of patients and the resulting feelings they acquired have many common elements which favor concordance in at least the most important concepts that appear in a therapy group, thus supplying a common frame of reference for word symbols. However, no consistency can be expected in this highly complex area. Rather, it can be assumed, guardedly, that conceptual resonance exists in therapy groups because of similarity in emotional and experiential bases of the participants.

Nonetheless, word symbolism may cause semantic misunderstandings in therapy interviews, as in other kinds of communication, and the therapist must be perfectly clear as to the meaning and intent of the words and phrases employed by the patients and by himself. This is one of his major responsibilities and skills. It does not mean therapy interviews need be turned into language analysis sessions or lessons in semantics, overshadowing the exposure of feelings. The intent is simply to call attention to the importance of clarity, so that the patients may participate on common ground and gain from the experience.

Because communication in psychotherapy is invariably charged with affect and contains latent content, which patients are disposed to conceal, the therapist has to attend to the feelings implicit in the productions as indices of the nature and intensity of their difficulties as well as the form of the communications.

TYPES AND SOURCES OF FEEDBACK

All communication is sustained by "feedback," and the greater the quantum and stimuli from that source, the more meaningful

TABLE 1

Phenomena in Communication in Therapy Groups

Specific Features	Vectors	Feedbacks
Threat areas	Intrapersonal Interpersonal	Status of Communicant
Specificity and concreteness	Patient-to-Patient Patient-to-Group	Relevance Piquancy
Exposure of resistances and evasions	Patient-to-therapist Group-to-Individual	Emotional activation Threat areas
Atomism	Therapist-to-Patient Therapist-to-Group	Levels of comprehension Empathy Homogeneity

and lively is the communication process. This is one of the reasons why a group conversation is likely to be better sustained and more vivacious than a one-to-one interchange. In therapy group interviews, the amount of feedback is determined by several factors, of which the therapist must be aware. These factors are: status of the communicant, relevance, piquancy, emotional activation, threat areas, levels of comprehension, empathy, and heterogeneity.

Status of the Communicant

Response to a communication (feedback) is determined to a large extent by the prestige status of a patient in his group. Patients at the top of the status ladder are likely to activate more feedback than the "indifferent" members. They serve as *instigators* and are more effective than are patients in the median category or the *social neuters*. All things being equal, patients who, by virtue of special characteristics (the charismatic characteristics and the intuitional or perceptive capacities rank high among these), are viewed with special regard by the group. They are more likely to activate response. A scapegoat has the same effect, though the response to him is of quite a different nature.

Relevance

A statement, from whatever source, relevant to the preoccupation of the group at the moment, receives more response than one which is not relevant. The libido being involved and focused on a subject of emotional significance or intellectual challenge, will keep the interchange going because of the interest and reactions of the individuals involved. An exception to this is when a member's statement diverts the group at a point of discomfort and thereby supplies an avenue of escape or of resistance to the group.

Piquancy

Piquancy will always attract attention and set off responses in a group. Elements of unusualness, pungency, and paradoxy provoke a deluge of feedback. This is not always to therapeutic advantage and is employed by patients as a form of resistance (de-

275

flection). It also serves as a form of exhibitionism and as a means of attracting attention and thus becoming the center of attention. When piquancy is employed for these ends, it requires working through with the aid of the therapist, if it is not dealt with by the group.

Emotional Activation

Feedback is at its highest in all interpersonal communication when intense feeling is aroused in the participants. This is true also of therapy groups. A communication may reinforce feelings, set off guilt, activate defenses or evoke intellectual disagreement. When these and similar reactions are stirred, one can expect a high degree of feedback.

Threat Areas

To the above list can be added the invasion of threat areas. Reactions to threat vary in different individuals and in the same individual at different times. It may induce a lively antagonistic response, a defensive disquisition, an angry act, or a withdrawal from the common arena. In the latter instance, there is a withdrawal of feedback, while the other types of responses may also terminate the verbal intercourse, since they threaten the communicant. However, in the more advanced stages of group treatment, invasion of threat areas may actually stimulate communication, as reactions and feelings are uncovered and explored. This occurs after ego defenses have been examined and ego strengths acquired by the participants. When this state of greater inner freedom and capacity for self-confrontation is reached, patients feed back even when their threat areas are exposed.

Levels of Comprehension

Feedback can be supplied by persons only when they comprehend the content of the stimulus. A communication which does not touch off an inner response in the percipient, because of its incomprehensibility to him, falls flat. For this reason, minimal intellectual and educational parity among analytic group therapy pa-

276

tients is a requisite, so that feedback is maintained and significance derived from communications. Of course, the lesser percipient may ask questions and seek further elucidation. This type of response, however, is a tenuous form of feedback, for the resulting interchange may reach so low a level that the communicant may lose interest or the dialogue become didactic. True feedback has to either maintain the intellectual and emotional level of the communication or raise it. Lack or drop in the level of the feedback tends to terminate communication.

Empathy

When a statement sets off an empathic response in another, the intellectual or emotional resonance (or both) brings the two persons into what may be termed an *empathic unit*. Such similitude begets a free flow between stimulus and feedback, aiding communication. However, a too thorough basis of agreement, too easily arrvied at, may have the opposite effect. It may choke off communication. Thus, even where there is empathy, sufficient difference must be present in the form of nuances, supportive ideas, causal foundations, or ego functioning. When these varying conditions exist — basic empathy and variance in thought and ego functioning—maximum feedback can be envisaged. This is one more justification for our criteria for grouping patients in analytic group therapy: homogeneity in nuclear problems and heterogeneous characters (and symptoms when possible).

Heterogeneity

Heterogeneity stimulates feedback, but the contrasting elements cannot be so far apart, or of such intense emotional significance, as to prevent a common base for continued communication.

EFFECTS OF GROUP COHESION

Group cohesiveness is attained at the cost of relegating part of the ego and superego functions and submission to the therapist, thus vitiating the therapeutic *living through* necessary for intra-

277

psychic change. The inhibitive effect of group cohesion can also be demonstrated by dynamics of communication.

To be therapeutic, communication has to be exercised against the opposing forces of resistance and must be accompanied by anxiety. The therapeutic value of communication (catharsis) does not lie in the fact that it occurs, but in the conditions under which it takes place; namely, whether it liberates bound-up anxiety and makes the repressed or traumatic subject, event, or situation accessible to the ego by breaking through resistances and dissolving censors.

When group cohesion is permitted to arise in a therapeutic group, and easy and close relationships emerge, the anxiety factor is disadvantageously eliminated or reduced. What should be a therapeutic interview (communication), turns into a social conversation, even when it is of a personal, episodal nature. In a completely friendly atmosphere of comfort and security in relationships, threat areas are carefully avoided or lose their sting *as far as the particular group is concerned.* Under these conditions, communication ceases to have therapeutic validity and the therapeutic effort is vitiated. One may be impressed with the content of a communication in a group, its frankness, self-confrontative quality and apparent "insight," only to find that the patient who presented this impressive façade within the confines of the group, does not carry over these attitudes outside it. This is obviously due to the fact that his intrapsychic difficulties were not worked through, but, rather, his ego has, consciously or unconsciously, accommodated itself to the particular group situation, where he now feels comfortable.

Harmony and unanimity, desirable in ordinary groups, are marks of resistance and hostility in a therapy group. In the therapeutic situation unanimity can be viewed, dynamically, as representing or reflecting a resistance or hostility phalanx. Unanimity tends to diminish communication and deteriorate it into "small talk." This occasionally occurs in therapeutic group interviews, but it should be of short duration only, and of infrequent occurrence. If it persists for too long, or becomes a pattern, the therapist's intervention is imperative. He has to deal with it as a form of resistance. In unskilled hands, the entire character of the group and the course of treatment may deteriorate through it. Usually, however, some patient will bring the group back because of his own pressing problems, which impel him to refocus the conversation.

TEMPERAMENTAL DIFFERENTIALS

When the phenomenon of communication is related to individuals rather than to the group, note must be taken of their native idiosyncrasies. Communicativeness is an instinctual disposition inherent to all animal life. Whether this is accomplished by sounds, odor, color, or light, it is universal in nature, although its intensity and manner of expression vary in each species and in individuals of the same species. The quantum and quality of communicative capacities and needs differ, also, in the different members of a therapy group. Most of these differences are psychologically determined; but as already indicated, constitutional dispositions and temperament, too, may be involved.

A person with a schizoid character cannot be as productive in social intercourse as the average individual or one with a neurotic or psychopathic character. Between the two modalities—schizoid withdrawal and massive loquacity and acting out—lie the varying degrees of communicativeness. In her studies of children from birth to puberty, Dr. Margaret Fries has found inherent differences in motility, at birth, which continued through childhood. As a result of her observation of a rather large number, she classified newborn babies as passive, active, and active-active, in accordance with the degree of their primary motility. She has also observed other behavior characteristics that seem primary and constitutional.

Thus, a paucity of communication in a particular member of a therapy group, cannot be considered prima-facie evidence of it having psychological significance, for individual dispositions have to be taken into account as well. Nor is the assumption justified that an uncommunicative patient remains unaffected. Communicativeness is not a function of improvement and silent patients

279

gain as much (and sometimes more) from group psychotherapy as the loquacious. The silent patients achieve this through vicarious catharsis and identification therapy and their own cognition. In one of our groups, the only quiet adolescent boy, on leaving the session after about three months, lagged behind the others to say to the therapist, "I hope you don't think that just because a guy doesn't talk, he doesn't know what goes on. He does, and understands everything that goes on and it helps him." He became considerably more verbal after this breakthrough. As a corollary, it is important to note that groups are usually the treatment of choice for nonverbal patients and those with low communication potentials, provided they are otherwise suitable. They are usually nonproductive in individual treatment, but are stimulated by group discussions to participate, as well as deriving benefit from being spectators.

COMMUNICATION AND CATHARSIS

It is evident from various parts of the foregoing discussion that there are special conditions which inhibit or favor communication. We have designated these, in regard to catharsis, as *resistors* and *accelerators*. However, communication, while embracing catharsis (as it is understood in psychotherapy), extends further. Catharsis is that part of the therapeutic communication constellation which relates to a specific intrapersonal difficulty and leads to its resolution through intrapsychic reorganization. It is charged with anxiety, has a regressive quality, and its function is to evoke affect and memories. The term communication, however, designates the total intra- and interpersonal means of informing, exchanging, signaling, contacting, and activating. Stimuli and mechanisms that have a salutary or inimical effect on the one, also influence the other. Thus, universalization, support, group consent, and target multiplicity, that aid catharsis, also aid communication. Ego defenses, fear of narcissistic injury, superego resistances, ego ideal, fear, shame, discomfort, and many other feelings, attitudes, value systems, and social taboos, that serve as resistors to catharsis, tend also to impede or block communication generally.

280

Communication, itself, can be employed to resist catharsis. This is observable in patients who, though maintaining a flow of conversation, reveal little or nothing that is of therapeutic significance. Reasons for such evasiveness, as well as the means for dealing with them as one type of resistance, are well known to the experienced psychotherapist. Such defeatist efforts on the part of patients, may be motivated not by resistance, but may serve as a most important defensive maneuver which we characterize as *defense against therapy*.

Defense Against Therapy

Communication, in group psychotherapy, can be withheld, in the service of maintaining health, as a *defense against therapy*, which may, in fact, be the case with many so-called "stubborn" or "inaccessible" patients. If the therapy applied is unsuitable to the patient's needs and the threat to his mental health is great enough, he may defend himself either by resisting or by terminating treatment. Thus, differentiation must be made between resistance and *defense against therapy*. This mechanism serves patients well as a protection against excessive anxiety or ego fragmentation, where the ego defenses are weak or tenuous (as in cases of latent or borderline schizophrenia or hysteria).

A therapist, no matter how experienced and perceptive, may overload some deeply hidden weaknesses in the psyche of a patient, inadvertently expose him to excessive strain, or employ a technique that is inappropriate for him. A case in point is the teenage girl who could not proceed with her psychoanalysis, but who might have been able to accept and benefit from ego-supportive psychotherapy. Another illustration is the couple, each in classical psychoanalysis, in which the husband began to hallucinate and the wife insisted on sitting up because she was "afraid" of her analyst. In each of these instances, the patients reacted not by resistance to treatment (in fact, the couple continued treatment, the husband returning to it immediately after our consultation), but by defending themselves against an inappropriate approach, one that would have proven disastrous had they submitted to the analysts' efforts.

A similar defensive maneuver was resorted to by the group patient who went silent when asked by the therapist if he had ever wanted to kill his mother. Had he permitted himself to be drawn into this line of investigation of his unconscious, he may have escaped from his delusional state into hallucination, or may even have committed homicide.

An even more transparent case of "defense against therapy," was the borderline schizophrenic woman, presenting many bizarre features and extreme anxiety and hostility, who was treated for two years in individual analytically oriented psychotherapy by skillful therapists. She was described as a most "resistive" patient who showed no improvement. She was then placed in a guidance group, in which all discussions were confined to reality oriented content and where she received considerable ego support from the group and the therapist. Her progress was so marked that her husband, an obsessional-compulsive cleric, voluntarily applied for treatment for himself. The patient herself was aware of her relief and when she met her former therapist, she said, "This (the group) is what I always needed. I couldn't talk to you about myself." The therapist stated that the patient had changed to such a degree that she, at first, had not recognized the woman. (See Slavson, 1958, Chapter X.)

Thus, the therapist should not consider all the patients' blocks to treatment as resistance. There may be profound reactions contained in seeming "resistances," which serve the ends of maintaining health and the wholeness of the personality. This particularly applies to schizophrenics whose instinctive perceptiveness is very keen indeed.

In this connection, a word of warning is necessary regarding the use of psychodrama and role playing with active and potential schizophrenics. Because the "conductor" and "auxiliary ego" are active participants in the treatment, they are particularly susceptible to overplaying their hand and forcing the patient into a defensive psychotic break, often during the dramatic scene. This also applies to analytic group psychotherapy, where such a patient may become the victim of pressure or attack from fellow patients.

X

The Analytic Group Interview: Phenomenology

THE EARLY SESSIONS

Group psychotherapy, as all sound psychotherapy, passes through a number of stages. At first, the group discussions are centered on problems and experiences in the patients' immediate lives and relationships, such as financial difficulties, children, the children's teachers, neighbors, landlords and apartments, employers, and similar matters that involve only minimal self-revelation and *top realities*.

In this period, the patients are cautious about revealing themselves. They observe each other's character, manners, responses, and the danger of being criticized, attacked or humiliated. There is an air of wariness and discomfort, which the therapist, according to the needs of the group, may seek to allay or may allow to run its course. In general, it is best to let the patients be exposed to this initial anxiety. However, if the patients find it difficult to get past this stage, the therapist may reflect the fact, by stating that they probably feel uncomfortable, which is natural when strangers come together, and that this discomfort will wear off as they come to know one another.

The therapist opens the first session by stating that those present have come to the group because they were uncomfortable and un-

283

happy and felt a need for treatment which would free them of their difficulties. The purpose of the group is to give them this help through talking through, together, whatever may disturb them. He then lays down two rules: everyone can say whatever he wishes, whenever it comes to his mind, even if it does not seem to relate to the ongoing conversation, and everything that transpires in the group should be considered confidential and not be repeated or talked about outside the interviews. These direct and forthright statements give an orientation to the proceedings, lay down the essentials of the group code, and engender a salutary feeling about the therapist, due to his frankness.

The choice of approach and the content of the opening statements are determined by a variety of factors: the therapist's judgment as to the intensity of the prevalent group anxiety or the anxiety of some particular patients; his own feelings of security in the situation; and his therapeutic objectives. If the aim is one of guidance or counseling, for example, he may prefer a less rigorous approach. If the aim is inner change, he may adopt more strenuous procedures. One consideration in favor of reducing initial group anxiety, at the outset, is to prevent the less emotionally sturdy patients from being frightened away from the group. This can be accomplished by offering the more disturbed patients a number of individual treatment sessions, preparatory to group placement (and whenever indicated later in treatment).

As the interviews proceed, the discomfort progressively lessens and communications flow with greater freedom. The patients become progressively less suspicious, less self-conscious, and less wary of each other. As the patterns of ego functioning of each participant are made manifest, the natural hiatus between the participants is bridged by relationships, both positive and negative. These are manifested as pairings, interpatient supportive or antagonistic reactions, consistent agreement or disagreement, empathic and sympathetic responses, and various other patterns of interrelationships.

As the sessions proceed, the appearance of sibling transference phenomena and a free discharge of feelings, signal the group's movement into therapy. After a period of free, unimpeded interchanges, when a member of the group does not do so, the therapist may explore the meaning of the communications and the accompanying feelings. However, this should not be done too early in the life of the group or it may shut off the cathartic flow, not only in the patients involved, but in all the others as well, because they will feel intimidated and uncomfortable. It is most essential to put the group at ease and render the members secure to reveal those components of their psyche which they have held out of view of themselves and of others.

TIMING AND PSYCHOLOGICAL LITERACY

The timing of the therapist's intervention is of supreme importance. Interpretation offered too early arouses resistance, both because of activation of ego defenses and because of the patients' *psychological illiteracy*. In the early stages, the patients, who have not been exposed to psychotherapy before, are unable to attach significance to their behavior or to the therapist's remarks. Forcing "insight" on emotionally and intellectually unready patients increases resistance, breeds distrust, and portrays the therapist as an unempathic person. "Interpretations" and explanations have to be delayed until patients attain awareness of, and ability to attach meaning to behavior. This can be achieved through their own efforts and, if necessary, the help the therapist may give should be of a *general* nature rather than specific to the patients involved.

After the foundations for such comprehension are laid, the therapist can expect the group to voluntarily and spontaneously seek out meanings for themselves and to help one another in this effort. When this understanding does not appear of itself, the therapist intervenes, through appropriate exploratory questions, explanations, and interpretations, much as is the case in individual psychotherapy. *Psychological literacy* and meaning are lent to the therapeutic experience by the therapist's encouragement and timely, though not too frequent, interpolations that help the patients find the meaning of feelings. This also gives meaning to the treatment process and motivates the patients to make the effort necessary for psychotherapy. Obviously, patients who have had preliminary treatment or are concurrently in individual treatment may not require this re-emphasis.

While encouragement can be given at the first session, it is more appropriate and more effective when given at later sessions. When a patient resists speaking of his distress, confusions, and conflicts, a statement like, "The best way to find a solution for it is to talk about it—say whatever comes to your mind and we'll see," emphasizes the significance of verbal catharsis. The following incident illustrates how this is learned by patients:

At an analytic group session of 15- to 16-year-old "delinquent" boys, one of the members was questioned by another as to why he had set a fire, an act for which he had been severely punished. This punishment had necessitated his being absent from the preceding session, which fact brought on the discussion. The boy described his feelings that culminated in the act as follows:

"I was mad at Mr. X for the way he treated me and I just couldn't take it. So as punishment he made me pick up the papers on the lawn. I was so mad that I was boiling inside. I thought I'd explode. If only I had some one to talk about my feelings I knew I'd feel better, but there was no one to talk to. I am not sure I altogether knew what I was doing, but I took out a match and set fire first to one piece of paper then to another 'til I had quite a fire."

"Yeh," said another boy, "if you talk about your feelings you don't have to do things."

The Importance of Timing

Both psychological literacy and the therapeutic process are enhanced when the therapist "picks up" significant statements made by one or more patients at appropriate times and gives them interpretation and insight, either in their general meaning or by their relevance to the *nuclear problem* of the specific patient. The therapist should withhold his intervention long enough to allow other patients the opportunity to examine their fellow patient's statement, and explore feelings and the meaning of the production. Failing this, the therapist may focus on the topic, or statement, that, in his understanding of the individual patient and the group as a whole, would lead to the uncovering of significant material. However, the therapist should not insist on pressing the patient, or his own line of thought, if he meets with resistance. Very often, a patient's withdrawal from a discussion means that he is emotionally unready and that his ego defenses are threatened. It is best to wait until further progress has been made in dissolving his defenses. Forcing the issue is inappropriate in therapeutic interviews; the patient's readiness is the guide to follow. If given a chance, other patients will usually pick up an idea and follow it through or turn it to another, equally valuable channel.

As far as possible, the interviews should be in the hands of the patients, with the therapist playing a minimal, but nonetheless important, role. In the first place, patients accept statements, explanations, interpretations, and advice from one another with more equanimity and less resistance than they do from a therapist. A statement from the therapist implies, at least in the fantasy of the patients, authority on his part and submission on theirs. Such feelings, distorted as they may be, are real to them and cannot but engender resentment and resistance. The same statement, criticism, or suggestion, if made by a fellow patient, is more acceptable since it comes from an equal and does not imply authority. These differential reactions can be employed in the transference interpretations at appropriate stages in the treatment.

Just as each patient observes the therapist and fellow patients, so the therapist must perceive not only the significance of verbal and nonverbal individual responses, but also the less tangible feeling tones of the group as a whole. His behavior, function, and statements have to fit the climate of the group and the readiness and receptivity of the individuals in it. Fine and sensitive judgment is essential in registering effects on individuals and the group as a whole.

INDIVIDUALIZATION

Because of the nature of the interviews it is inevitable that feelings toward important persons, in the early life of each patient, will be aroused in the group, and acted out, verbalized, displaced, and projected on fellow patients, especially those who in

287

some vague way resemble the earlier prototypes, either physically, in manner, or in accomplishments. Such patients serve as objects of affection, hostility, identification or dependence, rivalry, and jealousy. As in families and other groups, specific feelings may be mobilized toward various persons. These feelings may be positive, negative, or ambivalent; they may be transient or permanent. These are not *group reactions;* they are *individual reactions,* whose form, direction, and intensity are shaped by the history of each participant. The pattern of acting out or withholding, the manner of behavior, and the content and manner of verbalizations stem from the ontogenetic experiences of the individual. Each expresses his transference feelings in his own peculiar way. The fact that there may, at some time, be a common feeling in which all or most of the members share, does not necessarily make it a group feeling or a group reaction. The intensity of feeling, its deeper personal significance, and the impulse to act on it are vastly different. In fact, what appears to be a common feeling or attitude in a therapy group is actually not, for on exploring these reactions, one finds some individuals who are affected deeply, others who are only slightly affected and still others who remain indifferent. This is inevitable and understandable in the light of temperamental and superego differences, capacities for identification, past conditionings, and differences in the transference and projection mechanisms. Emotional contagion resulting in a "common" feeling is inevitable, but still the responses are individual. In fact, the outstanding feature of these reactions is that they are specific to, and characteristic of, each individual member.

Though free verbal and nonverbal interaction among patients is essential in group psychotherapy, a degree of caution is necessary. Aspects of a discussion, at a given time, may produce over-intense stress in one or more members or may be unsuitable for the whole group. The therapist can then use a *diversionary* tactic or call attention to the presence of disturbed feelings, which should be openly discussed. Such discussions are of the utmost value, because they open up channels of intrapersonal communication. Whether it is shame (ego ideal), disgust (sexual or anal inhibitions), anxiety (superego), fear (of authority or exposure), or discomfort (due to unusualness) that causes the emotional disturbance in individuals, clearing a path through these self-alienating blocks is an effective road toward mental health. However, here, too, keen clinical judgment has to be exercised as to the ego strengths, superego permissiveness, and psychological literacy of the patients before this "breakthrough" is attempted.

DISCHARGE OF HOSTILITY

The most important facet of psychotherapy is the discharge of hostility. Persons who seek psychological treatment are overwhelmed by hostility, usually to significant persons in their childhood. The fear and guilt associated with this hostility prevent the average patient from expressing it. Those who do express it are plagued by guilt and anxiety as a consequence. Mental health is conditioned by reducing hostility to a socially acceptable level, by being able to discharge it without guilt, by sublimating it in approved forms, and by coming to terms with it. The treatment process, therefore, requires that hostility be freely revealed and accepted by the group or by what can be tentatively designated as the *group superego*.

The emergence of this permissive group superego, which gives the individual the freedom required for free-flowing catharsis, is conditioned by three factors: the structure of the group, based on proper selection and grouping of patients; the stage in the treatment interviews; and, perhaps the most important, the therapist's own unconscious attitudes toward hostility.

The presence of too many rigid, compulsive, and obsessive patients retards the emergence of a permissive climate in a group. Their intolerance, their censorious shock and reactions, arouse guilt in their fellow patients who could otherwise discharge their hostilities in words and acts. Such inhibitive reactions block the flow of catharsis, generate guilt and anxiety, and further intensify the already strong hostility in the other patients, which in turn gives rise to more anxiety. Thus a vicious cycle is set in operation—only one of many developments that emphasize the initial importance of selection and grouping.

Expression of hostility is usually withheld in a new group until

289

patients feel a minimal security. Anger and impatience precede open hostile aggression, which first appears in the less controlled and the less conflicted. The majority delay their outbursts until they feel more comfortable in the setting.

A member of an all-female group, in talking about her children, said: "Sometimes I get so angry at my children that I want to kill them. I have to go out of the house. I am afraid I may do something to them." Another member responded to this by saying: "I, too, sometimes feel like killing my children."[1] It is interesting that none of the other group members reacted with shock or surprise at such frank admissions of infanticidal impulses; but such frankness cannot be expected in the early stages of a group's existence. It can appear only when patients feel a degree of security with one another and have worked through basic defenses. In a group of "delinquent" boys, one of their number said, in the fifth session, that "if he ran up against his mother [a feeble-minded woman who had abandoned her children] he would strangle her." This revelation came this early in treatment only because the boys, living together at an institution, already knew each other intimately and were, therefore, less constrained by the usual inhibitions.

However, the most potent deterrent to free expression of negative feelings is the therapist himself and his feelings toward his own hostility. A therapist posessed of a large measure of hostility may, unintentionally, activate it in his patients, on the one hand, or inhibit it in his patients as a reaction formation, on the other, in both cases creating a climate unsuitable for therapy. Even a therapist who has a "normal" quantum of hostility, but who feels uncomfortable with it, can unintentionally inhibit his patients. They sense his inner conflicts. It is, therefore, important that a therapist have freedom in relation to his own hostile feelings. Only a person who recognizes and accepts hostile feelings in himself can accept them with equanimity in others.

The flow of aggression is facilitated by increased security

---

[1] This is a good illustration of catalysis. From our knowledge of the second patient, we would not expect her to be able to verbalize such feelings without the encouragement of the first.

among the patients. This security is conditioned by the composition of the group, extended acquaintance, the various catalytic influences, and the accelerators of catharsis, all of which diminish superego censors and ego defenses. As hostile feelings are brought to the surface, their meaning recognized in terms of infantile and fixated attitudes, and the nature of their projective distortions examined, a fuller and more meaningful stage in treatment is reached.

The therapist must be cautious not to accelerate the process artificially. He must sensitively follow the psychic unfoldment of the patients as they divest themselves of their past, layer by layer. Significance is drawn from relevance, and relevance comes from readiness. The most effective therapeutic occurrences take place when patients are psychologically ready for them. The therapist must wait for the appropriate time. Then, his intervention, by leading questions, well-timed statements, and suitable explanations and interpretations, will advance the group's psychological literacy, stimulate self-examination, and activate catharsis. But his role should not become a dominant one. *His participation is one of periodic assertion and withdrawal.* He asserts himself by injecting a statement or question and withdraws as soon as the patients take up the discussion.

ILLUSTRATIONS OF GROUP ANALYTIC INTERVIEWS

The various theoretical and descriptive points we have made are illustrated in the following records of group analytic interviews.

A Group of Married Women

The group from which the first example is drawn consisted of six women in their thirties. The therapist in this group was a man. Many sessions had been spent discussing top realities: children, schools, home, neighborhoods, apartments, etc. Gradually, they began to emotionally interact with one another and share some common problems, still maintaining, however, their individual preoccupations. Gradually, much conflict and direct attack upon each other emerged. Finally, they began to reveal their disturbances, the causes of which were tied up with their developmental backgrounds and memories of painful experiences and relations. The particular session from which the following summary is abstracted, demonstrates some of the dynamics we have been discussing.

Present were four women, Mrs. B., Mrs. C., Mrs. G., and Mrs. S. Mrs. G., as she did twice before in earlier sessions, was defending Dr. L., who was currently on trial for killing his wife, and vehemently pressed her belief that the evidence against him was not conclusive. (Dr. L. was later convicted of the crime.) She seemed to be trying to make the point that some people, who committed murder in a moment of extreme passion or anger, may ordinarily be good people and should, therefore, receive special treatment. Mrs. C., who opposed this view, seemed much more perceptive and logical than Mrs. G. and, as a result, Mrs. G. backed down. Mrs. C. quickly commented that Mrs. G. gives up too easily, to which the latter responded that "it wasn't that important." During this interlude, Mrs. S. sat quietly. For a brief period the group seemed to be in a resistant mood and a short pause ensued, during which Mrs. B. arrived. Mrs. G. laughingly said to her, "Come and join the deadheads." This was followed by desultory conversation, during which Mrs. G. asked Mrs. S. if she had found an apartment as yet and suggested that she might have Mrs. C.'s apartment. (Mrs. C. had announced at the previous session that she would soon be moving to another part of the city.) Mrs. C. answered for Mrs. S., saying that Mrs. S. would not want her apartment because it is too close to Mrs. S.'s mother-in-law. Mrs. S. commented briefly that she and her mother-in-law "get along well —at a distance."

Another silence ensued. The therapist asked the group why they were so quiet today. Mrs. G., after a moment, said, in an aggressive and complaining tone, that she finds "the whole thing boring." She listens to talk about apartments, about other people's mothers-in-law and other such topics, implying that these had nothing to do with her. She felt that "nothing was happening." In a belligerently complaining tone, she reiterated this theme several times, and added that she "wanted help but did not get any. Nothing was happening" and she was "bored." She further implied that she had found nothing in common with what the other women were talking about, and added that she "had always gotten along well with her family." (This, despite an intensely disturbed family situation with problem children.)

Mrs. C. questioned Mrs. G., pointing out to her that the latter had never actually discussed herself, although she had participated in the discussions of other members of the group.[2] Mrs. G. maintained that she was quite willing to do this but again reiterated that she had not gotten any help and qualified this by stating that she had gotten help from individual treatment last year. During this discussion between the two women, Mrs. C. stated that she comes to the group because she finds it "quite interesting."

At this point, the therapist told the group that something must be wrong with him and his handling of the group, since Mrs. G. found it boring and of no help, Mrs. C. came only because she found it quite interesting, and Mrs. B. did not seem to care to participate.[3] Mrs. B. smiled at this. Mrs. C. responded quickly and with obvious sincerity. She stated that she did not see why the therapist should take the blame upon himself. She felt he was doing well; she found his questions and comments very helpful and some of his statements in reference to herself had helped her to understand her situation. The therapist repeated that, Mrs. C.'s statement notwithstanding, if the group was not going well, the fault must basically be his. Mrs. C. again disputed this. Mrs. G. also defended the therapist by saying that she did not see how it was his fault and then added that perhaps her "not being able to be helped in this situation" was due to her own temperament, but, at the same time, she repeated her statement that she was not "getting anything out of it," because she did not see what the problems she had heard the other women describe had "in com-

[2] Much later, after almost three and one-half years in group treatment, this woman finally stated to the therapist that she had never before "felt with the needs" of her fellow group members and she was only then beginning to do so.

[3] By this strategy, the therapist sought to bring the patients' hostility toward him out into the open.

mon" with her own. She then again reiterated that she had been helped in individual treatment.

Here, the therapist deliberately told Mrs. G. that her individual therapist had felt that a group would be more helpful to her because she had spent so much time telling him that she was not being helped by him and that nothing was being accomplished. Mrs. G. giggled self-consciously at this, but seemed to accept it quite readily, stating that this was possibly true. She now recalled that he actually did tell her this. The therapist then addressed himself to Mrs. G.'s complaint that she had nothing in common with the others in the group. He said that actually there was quite a common bond among them: all were having difficulties with their sons and though the individual problems may vary, there were common threads in the development of each of the women present from girlhood, to womanhood, and motherhood. Mrs. G. retreated at this, stating that perhaps "as usual" she was trying, as her husband often pointed out to her, "to get things done too quickly."

After the therapist's deliberate comment on her spectator role, Mrs. B. said she had always gotten along well with her father. She implied, by this, that she saw this as the only criterion by which to measure herself as a personality in terms of her relationship to her son (whom she dominated and effeminated). In response to this, the therapist commented that according to what all the members of the group had said, in the various group sessions, there seemed to be a close resemblance between their relationships with their sons and their fathers, but this should not be taken to mean that the daughter-father relationship is the only one of importance in a girl's life. In many ways, the relationship to one's mother was even more crucial since, in becoming a woman, the girl patterns herself after her mother, and depending on the personality of the mother, emotional difficulties could stem from that. Mrs. B., in a thoughtful manner, nodded confirmation to this. All the women grew thoughtful and remained silent, as though digesting the idea.[4]

[4] This is an illustration of helping patients become "psychologically literate."

The therapist then addressed himself to a remark made by Mrs. C., in the preceding session, when she had said in a discussion with Mrs. G., that men were not necessary at all as there was artificial insemination. He asked Mrs. C. if she does not get any satisfaction from sexual relations. Mrs. G. hastily interpolated the remark that last week she had wanted to tell Mrs. C. that "It's much more fun the natural way." Mrs. C. hesitated, seemed to have momentarily lost her self-assurance, and then, speaking cautiously, indicated that she had made the remark in a somewhat humorous vein as a response to something Mrs. G. had said. She continued to embellish her statement, but did not respond to the question directly. She tried to redirect the focus on Mrs. G. The therapist said that it seemed that Mrs. C. was finding it difficult to answer this question. Mrs. C. denied it, but then in a rather vague and indirect way, choosing her words very carefully, began by saying, "I'm not saying that sex is the most important phase of my marriage; in fact it is one of the least important." She then went on, with continued caution, to say that she participates in sexual relations with her husband in order to satisfy him, but that she derived "no real enjoyment from them" for herself.

Mrs. G. said that she does not claim that sex is the most important thing in her life, but that it is "pretty important," and then, with more conviction, added that she thinks it is "very important." A woman does not know what she is missing until she has really experienced "fulfillment in the sexual act," and added that she knew there were many women who have not had this satisfaction, despite having been married for years. In the first year or so of her marriage, she had little pleasure from sex, but then she had gone to a doctor to be fitted for a "diaphragm" and the doctor had asked her if she had ever had an orgasm. Somewhat humorously, Mrs. G. said that she did not even know what the doctor was talking about and asked him what he meant and the doctor had told her that if she "had had it," she would know what it is. Following this, she had been able to achieve orgasms with her husband and frankly and enthusiastically stated that she now enjoys her conjugal relations "tremendously." She then recalled a time when her husband had been away from

295

home for some weeks and how much she had "missed him." At one point, Mrs. C. again reiterated that sex was not "too important" in her life.

The therapist noted that on various levels there were rather strong differences emerging among the members in their attitudes toward sex, having children, and toward children themselves. He wondered what accounted for these differences.

As usual, Mrs. C. was the first to respond. She said that some of them had been raised in puritanical backgrounds, where sex was considered "dirty," and the word could not even be mentioned. Mrs. B. nodded affirmatively at this.

Mrs. G., as well, corroborated this. In her family this was something "you couldn't talk about." Until she was about fifteen years old, she did not know where babies came from and added that her family never was an affectionate one. Her parents did not even kiss each other or the children, except maybe when they left on a long trip. She recalled that she thought that kissing itself was bad and that, at fifteen, she was afraid that she might become pregnant when she once kissed a boy. In her own family now, they are "always kissing" each other.

Mrs. C. (who seemed resentful at Mrs. G.'s acknowledgment of sexual satisfaction), asked in a somewhat sarcastic, baiting manner, "Don't your children get in the way sometimes with all that kissing between you and your husband?" Mrs. G., with ease, explained that she was not referring to the "love-making" between her and her husband which they "save for the time when the children have gone to bed." What she meant was the kissing that occurs when her husband leaves for work and kisses her and the children. She added that she is always cautioning her husband to stop when he fondles her "in a sexual way" in front of the children.

Mrs. C. then began rather subtly to attempt to create the impression that Mrs. G. was oversexed. Mrs. G. defensively stated "Don't get me wrong; I'm not saying that I want it every night. In fact, my husband still thinks that I'm cold." Mrs. G. then talked of her background and her mother, describing the latter as a "cold person" who had probably never satisfied Mrs. G.'s father sexually. She indicated that now her mother is a widow and has an offer of marriage but has turned it down, saying that she does not want to have to get into bed with a man.

Mrs. C. and Mrs. B., who seemed to want to attack Mrs. G. (because of her acknowledgment of sexual satisfaction), then joined in asking her why she was trying to dominate her widowed mother and force her into marriage. In an abrupt, hostile manner, Mrs. B. asked: "Do you love your mother?" Mrs. G. did not seem fazed by this question and replied "of course I love my mother." When her mother comes to her house, she has an impulse to embrace and kiss her, but always restrains herself because she is unsure of what her mother's reaction would be.

Mrs. S., who seemed unusually quiet during this discussion, now said that there was something about her daughter, Lois, she had questioned. Lois, at five years of age, was interested in boys. However, Mrs. S. did not actually appear to be too involved in this question, as she spoke in an almost mechanical way. She recalled that there was a stage when Lois had expressed a desire to be a boy and had always worn dungarees (as did her older brother). (This repeats Mrs. S.'s own background. As a girl she was in keen competition with an only, and preferred, brother and probably indulged in sex play with him.)

The time was almost over, at this point, with only two or three minutes left. Mrs. C. got up and said that the "meeting was over. I guess we're finished," and began to leave. The therapist asked the group what they thought was the reason for Mrs. C.'s taking it on herself to close the session. Mrs. G. quickly commented that she had noticed that Mrs. C. had done this and that she herself always waited for the therapist to end the session. Mrs. C. defensively said, "Well, I have to get home in time to pick up my son from school." After she finished saying this, the therapist looked at his watch, and closed the session.

Interpretation

The women begin by being resistive. They discuss a current sensational trial and their apartments, instead of their personal problems, then silence ensues. Silences have a variety of meanings, but in this instance it represents resistance. The therapist "asserts" himself by asking why the silence. In this he exposes the resistance and conveys his disapproval of it. Resistance is then verbalized by Mrs. G. in her complaint that she finds the group useless. When the resistance in the group continues, the therapist makes a clean breast of it by taking blame on himself. This is a "tricky" strategy. In a sense it is for him a "status denial." He exposes himself as an inadequate person (which could boomerang against him) and the women become guilty. Because of his statement, they see in him the ideal, accepting parental figure. Instead of admonishing them (the children), he blames himself. This serves to overcome their resistance (antagonism to him) and they plunge into a defense of him.

Having been accepted by the group, he can now employ a flank attack against Mrs. G., who defends herself under the screen of individual treatment. He exposes her, as having used the same complaint in individual treatment, and forces her to "retreat."

The therapist's assertiveness brings Mrs. G.'s husband to her mind and Mrs. B.'s father to hers. They now see the therapist as a potent male figure to whom they have to defer, which helps some of these women, with their confused sexual identifications, to accept their role as women. He advances their "psychological literacy" by pointing out that their mothers, too, played a part in their personality formation.

One of the functions of a therapist, in a therapeutic interview, is to "recall" to his patients, ideas and statements of the past to "tie in" with the current productions. This he does in this interview by recalling to Mrs. C. her reference to artificial insemination. Now resistances are down and the women plunge headlong into the theme of the interview. The therapist can now withdraw and leave the field to the patients with the interplay of exhibitionism (Mrs. G.), jealousy (Mrs. C. and Mrs. B.), and Mrs. G.'s basic homoerotism ("My husband still thinks I am cold" and her desire to embrace her unloving, frigid mother).

The discussion of sex activates Mrs. S.'s guilt about it (her sex play with her brother) and she projects it on her daughter. This same theme had been brought forth by Mrs. S. during a number

of past group interviews. By calling attention to Mrs. C.'s terminating the session the therapist calls attention to her basic masculine drives, a point which is left for discussion at a future session. The assertive role the therapist assumed in this interview
was justified because three of the most active women have character disorders, two of them with masculine identifications and
protest. In certain types of character disorders, confrontation such
as here exercised by the therapist is indicated. Another value of
this experience, to the women, is that they were led by the therapist's strategy to submit to him and accept him as an adequate
male, which they had been unable to do in relations with other
males, including their sons. Mrs. S., who was a highly neurotic
woman with possible "induced borderline schizophrenia," could
not participate in this group "rally," partly because of her emotional fragility and partly because the "theme" was not relevant
to her problem. Dealing with her required an entirely different
approach. Both these facts are demonstrated in the following record of later interviews with the same group of women.

The center of interest here is Mrs. S., a 38-year-old psychoneurotic woman whose background has been very traumatic and is described, in part, in the interviews, so that it will not be recounted
here. Her general adaptation was strongly masochistic with underlying intense hostility. She was submissive and ingratiating,
fearful of taking a stand, especially toward her mother who
treated her brutally, and toward her husband. The husband
treated Mrs. S. with disdain and perpetually teased her, with the
intent of debasing his wife and giving vent to his sadistic feelings
toward her. Mrs. S. suffered for years with psychogenic eczema
on her hands, which seriously interfered with her functions as a
housewife, requiring her to wear rubber gloves as she did her
housework. One of the serious problems in her life, as she saw
it, was that she could not locate an adequate dwelling for her
family of four. Mrs. S. had two children, a boy and a girl, and
the whole family lived in a two-room apartment. She claimed that
though she tried for years to move from her present quarters,

where the family had lived for some fourteen years, she could not find any other apartment.

The cramped living conditions, the problems that her children presented, and the suffering she sustained as a child through the treatment she had received from her mother and brother, constituted the sole content of her productions at the group for forty sessions. She related her difficulties and problems in a pitiful manner and a whining voice, obviously seeking to evoke sympathy from the therapist and her fellow group members. In the group, she continually acted out her psychic masochism by attempting to provoke aggression, as well as pity, and she exploited her realistic deprivations and confusions in a form that can be characterized as *emotional hypochondriasis*.

Because of his awareness of Mrs. S.'s emotional (and possibly also ego) fragility, the therapist had not interfered with her functioning in the group, awaiting an appropriate opportunity to break through the pattern of her repetitive communications. This opportunity presented itself at the forty-first session. In this session, the other women took Mrs. S. to task for what she had been saying and attacked her violently. Sensing the disturbance that this caused in Mrs. S., the therapist came to her rescue, explaining what Mrs. S. meant by what she was saying and universalizing it so as to reduce the guilt in her. In a sense, he protected her against the group's attack. Mrs. S. responded to this maneuver by the therapist with a look of extreme gratitude and a smile of great pleasure (she had never smiled before in the group). Her facial expression conveyed the feeling that, for the first time in her life, she had finally found a friend.

Now that the therapist was assured of her positive feelings toward him and her trust that he was her "friend," he felt that he could become active with her rather than allowing her to continue in her stereotyped complaints. In the next session, when another woman in the group was talking, Mrs. S. interrupted her (which was her customary way, one by which she provoked aggression against herself and rivaled with her sibling substitutes in the group, as well as discharged her overwhelming disguised hostility) and changed the subject of that woman's narrative. The therapist turned to Mrs. S. and said, "Mrs. S., why did you change the subject just now?" Mrs. S. responded to this by an intense emotional shock as though she had been slapped. She became depressed and remained silent for the rest of the session.

The following meeting day of the group, a week later, was a holiday and the group, therefore, did not meet for two weeks. When the group reassembled for its forty-second session, the following events transpired.[5]

Mrs. S. was the first to enter the room at this session, just before Mrs. W. arrived. She said that she felt the therapist had helped her at the last session and recalled that he had called to her attention her pattern of changing the subject of the group's discussions. This had given her a clue to something. Last time when she had changed the subject another woman had brought up the Easter holiday, which reminded her of her father who had died during Easter many years before. She guessed that what was happening in the past few weeks was that, as a result of her thinking about what had occured in the previous group session, she had had to give up illusions about her father. She said that he was "nice" to her, but now she realized that in many ways he only "pitied" her, and she referred to a popular expression he frequently used in which he would tell her mother that one should feel sorry for her, Mrs. S., because of her eczema and because of her ungainliness and unusual height.

Mrs. S., in an intense and thoughtful manner, continued, "he was just good to me, and kind, and maybe there was some sex involved there, too." She then recalled that as an adolescent, she put on very tight brassieres, perhaps to show him that she "had something" and that she was "womanly." Yet her father wanted all his children to be boys. She reiterated, however, that despite this, he seemed good to her when compared with the treatment she received from her mother and brother, and that he was the only person she had had to lean on. Her mother gave her no

[5] The remarks by Mrs. S. are here highlighted and the remarks by the other women subordinated to them and omitted. By and large, however, comparatively little was said by the others, who deferred to Mrs. S.'s need to follow through on her feelings.

301

support and her brother kept throwing "salt into my wounds," especially in adolescence, when she felt that she was so big, and so different looking from everybody else. She also recalled that her father's standards were always extremely high and that he had to have the best in everything, including children. By this she implied that he must have been quite disappointed in her.

She recalled that once, while walking with her parents, she thought of how other families looked when they walked down the street and she took her father's arm. Her mother gave her "such a look" as if she had done "something dirty and degrading."

Mrs. W. eagerly entered the discussion at this point, to ask with strong feeling "why did they (the parents) always avoid anything physical; why were they afraid to mention sex to us?"

Mrs. S. then recalled her mother's embarrassed reaction to her first menses and guessed that her parents were "just ignorant." She recalled that at about the age of 12, she had received a terrible beating from her father just on the basis of her mother's complaint, without investigating the facts, and indicated that for a time after, she had had quite negative feelings toward her father.

Mrs. S. continued that she guessed that she was very unhappy as a child, since she was unwanted by her mother from the moment of birth and that, although her father "loved" her, he always "pitied" her. She wondered if perhaps she had a need to change the subject in the group because she was afraid she would come out with her feelings about her father. It had been always easy for her to talk about her mother because she was always completely against her mother, but she realized it would be much more difficult to talk about her father. She indicated awareness that if she were to realize that her father had not always loved her "in the right way," she would then have the feeling that she "had nothing at all" as a child; perhaps she wanted to hold on to the idea that her father was a perfect parent. She now realized that she could not find a suitable apartment for her family because "somehow I felt my father will come and help me."

She realized that she had recently been quite resentful toward Martin (her 12-year-old son) simply because he was a boy and a male and that this was tied up with the fact that at times he looked facially like her father. This indicated to her that she must have had considerable resentment against the latter.

Mrs. S. then spoke about her mother, first stating that she currently sees a change in her (widowed) mother's attitude toward her. Her mother now seems to perceive that Mrs. S. is "stronger in some way."[6] She said that she was now able to hate her mother openly for the cruelty she "had suffered at her hands," but she could also recognize that her mother "had paid plenty for all her cruelty," having been left a widow with five young children. She felt that she now saw her mother with a blend of contempt and pity.

She recalled a recent dream. In the dream she had just bought a house with a lot of rooms in it and her grandmother came and asked to live with her, but Mrs. S. could not make up her mind as to whether to let her do so or not. She thought she could figure out the dream rather easily. Her grandmother really represented her mother and Mrs. S. was, at present, not sure whether to accept her or not. She then guessed that she herself was like her father in that, like him, she pitied her mother. She then added "he was very wrong and very stupid also."

Mrs. S. continued. "I guess I always looked for pity and sympathy because that's all I ever got and that's all I knew how to get." She then recalled that at the age of 16, when her father died, she somehow did not react with the feelings she should have. She did not cry and in the coffin he did not look like her father. She wondered if this was because she "felt guilty or something." The therapist commented that sometimes we may want to deny an experience and block off the feeling connected with it so that we can pretend that it did not happen. Mrs. W. eagerly commented that this was exactly how she felt at her mother's death, and added that she was "so tremendously guilty," for she was pregnant at the time and felt as if she were "exchanging one life for another." . . . Mrs. S. described another incident, of punishment by her father, which she considered unjust.

[6] Obviously as a result of the (exclusive) group treatment she was receiving.

Mrs. S. then said that she now saw that perhaps she was "extending" some of these resentful feelings toward Martin (her son) as a male, and also toward her husband, adding that as she thinks about it, she is pretty sure she is doing this.

With what seemed to be genuine sincerity, Mrs. S. said that she wants to thank the therapist (then adding, politely, "the group also") for helping her "to see all this" and she implied that although two weeks ago, when the therapist pointed out some of her patterns, she may have been upset, she now saw that it was helpful to her.

The therapist said here that Mrs. S. seemed to have done a lot of serious thinking and seemed to have arrived at some quite sensitive self-understanding. The therapist then suggested, quite tentatively, that perhaps there was another possibility; perhaps, unaware to herself, Mrs. S. may have been attempting to please the therapist by telling him that what he did in the previous session was right. Mrs. S. in a serious and thoughtful manner stated she did not think that this was the case. . .

Mrs. S. stated that her husband needed a mother person and that was why he married her. Yet, he was at the same time resentful toward her for mothering him, because he is actually quite resentful of his own mother who had always preferred his older brother. Mrs. S. indicated that she is gradually helping her husband to see this. She herself, up to recently, did everything for him, just as his mother had done, but she no longer hangs up his clothes as she used to, for example. With determination in her tone, she commented, "Now they can crumble there on the floor."

Mrs. G. told Mrs. S.: "Now you have to let yourself be helpless and let him mother you." In a calm voice, Mrs. S. responded to this by saying that "this was not the way. I don't want to be helpless, just normal; he has his job and I have mine."

After this, Mrs. S. brought out some concern about Martin and his sister wrestling and her realization that there was "something sexual going on here." The other day she had heard her daughter asking Martin to kiss her and she also described how, recently, she got quite annoyed when Martin kept jumping up and down on the little girl. She finally told him that he could save his jumping up and down for when he is grown up and can do it on girls other than his sister.

Mrs. G. indicated that she had a similar problem with her two children. At least she insisted that they be dressed so that there would be "less the feel of each other." She felt, however, that Mrs. S. was wrong in what she said, because that was "too open and might put ideas in Martin's head."

There was some discussion about sexual instruction to children. Mrs. S. said that in the past, she had been unable to answer Martin's questions freely, but she now feels capable of doing it. . . .

Mrs. S. told how Martin had come into the house from playing ball and "he looked like such a real boy, I could have eaten him up." She expressed her extreme pleasure at his recently developed boyishness and masculinity and described a talk she had had with him in which he had told her, "You treat me differently now. You used to baby me." Mrs. S. recalled her past pattern, of which she had recently become aware, namely, that of treating her daughter like a boy, having wanted her to be aggressive and also dressing her up in dungarees . . . .

Mrs. S. pointed out that she had for a while been making Martin into a girl by treating him as "Ruthie" (her own first name) and not as "Martin." She no longer did this . . . .

This whole question and the possibility of mothers inhibiting natural boyish aggressiveness seemed to be of considerable significance to Mrs. B., who appeared to be both anxious about it and interested in it. In a tone of protest, she wondered if boys really had to fight and, at one point, stated, "I bet when Mr. X. (the therapist) was a boy he didn't fight." The therapist did not respond to this and she went on to imply generally that she did not think that boys needed to fight . . . .

Interpretation

Space will not permit a discussion of these productions in detail; nor is it necessary for the psychoanalytically oriented reader. It can, however, he pointed out that, through the positive transference toward the therapist and the group, this patient's ego was sufficiently strengthened to give up a number of its defenses, chief among those being the fantasy to which she had clung so tenaciously that her father loved her, and to face the fact that he had only pitied her. She was now freeing herself from the phantom of her dead father (who would help her find an apartment) and at the same time loosening herself from her mother, to whom she had been tied by hatred. But her emotional growth and maturity is made even more apparent when she begins to understand her mother's plight and forgive her ("I pity her").[7]

Because of her newly acquired strengths, she was now able (after forty-one sessions and through the instrumentality of the therapist) to recall events and bring forth from repression painful and humiliating memories and current events, that cleared her psyche for further strengthening and emotional maturity. In other words, true *catharsis* was taking place. (In a later session she recalled that her father once fondled her naked older 12-year-old sister. This she related with great feeling, since all her oedipal feelings were involved here, as well as sibling rivalry.)

Her *insight* is evident as regards her relations to her parents, but she now also recognized her displacement of resentment toward her father on her son and her husband, as males, as well as recognizing the fact that she denied her son's maleness by treating him as a girl, but now found pleasure in his masculine appearance. She also reached a point in insight where she could understand her own dreams and she recognized, quite on her own, the displacement mechanism. We know that Mrs. S. has never read anything on dream analysis; she was not a reader of psychological literature. She now recognized that her adaptive pattern was one of seeking pity because, in her words, "that is all I ever got and that's all I ever knew how to get." (In a later session, she spontaneously recognized the relation of her hostility to the eczema. She said, "When I feel like jumping out of my skin [angry] I get my rash.")

---

[7] One recalls, in this connection, Goethe's profound adage: "Everyone must understand his parents and forgive them." This is the only path to true emotional maturity and mental health and this can be attained only through regressive and insight therapy in transference.

At one point in the interview, Mrs. S. actually made an attack on Mrs. B. She could never have done this before treatment progressed to this point. She now also stood up against her mother, who had continued to tyrannize her even to this day, by prohibiting her mother (who lived nearby) to come to her house when she fed the children, because of her mother's criticism and interference. We learn from the interview that Mrs. S.'s mother now regarded her daughter with respect for her individuality ("I am stronger in some way"). Mrs. S. also prohibited her husband from humiliating her through his humor and insisted that he take a more appropriate and a more active part with their three children. (In fact she later threatened to leave him unless he altered his role in the family and his treatment of her.)

As Mrs. S. adopted a more realistic life pattern due to her intrapsychic changes and freely discharged anger and hostilities, her psychosomatic symptom completely disappeared. It had abated, to a great extent, even before the fortieth session, reappearing only during periods of stress. Later it was gone entirely. About five months after the discussion reported here, Mrs. S. found a five room apartment for her family. She was a little concerned about the increase in rent, but was confident the family could meet this financial strain, even if it meant that she would have to take a part-time job.

A brief statement may be in order, concerning the therapeutic maneuvers employed with this patient. The basic need for progress here was emotional security, so that she would be able to give up her fantasy about her father and relinquish the ego defenses that determined her need to cling to her belief in her father's love. This she could not do unless she received (substitute) love from someone else which, in addition to satisfying other needs, improved her feelings of self-worth. In the forty sessions preceding the one in which the therapist questiond her, this had been occurring. For the first time in her life, sibling-like persons and a parent surrogate accepted her and listened to her plaints and thoughts without ridicule or criticism. She had been accepted, so that even when the therapist asked her the crucial question, she did not feel rebuked or rejected, but was able to utilize it in the grist of her own therapy. However, she would probably not have been able to do so without the assurance of the therapist's (father's) unconditional "friendship" and interest in her, evidenced when he "rescued" her from the attack of her (substitute) siblings. This was the *critical event* in the treatment of this patient.[8] Thus, the therapist's watchful waiting for forty sessions bore fruit. It is this factor, more than any other, that led to Mrs. S.'s eventual improvement.

A Group of Young Adult Women

To illustrate progression in analytic group treatment interviews, we shall here examine three interviews, at different stages, culled at random from the recorded discussions of a group of young women in their early twenties, each of whom has had one child out of wedlock. Since most unmarried mothers have character disorders or reactive behavior disorders (See Slavson, 1956, "Unmarried Mothers"), the girls chosen for the group all suffered from rather serious psychoneurotic disturbances. They had all had complicated, and very pathogenic, home and interpersonal backgrounds. The group met weekly for ninety minutes. The therapist, in this group, was a woman.

The first brief abstract is from the third interview session.

On entering the room together, Mildred and Lizbeth exchanged some remarks about the book the latter was carrying. After seating themselves, Mildred, at the head of the table as usual,[9] inquired whether Judith was coming back to the group. She also inquired about another girl, whose name she did not remember, and pointed to the seat that Lizbeth occupied and where Beth had sat the previous session. Lizbeth also laughingly admitted that she did not remember Beth's name.

Mary wondered where they should start. The previous week

[8] For a definition and illustrations of this dynamic, see Slavson, 1943, pages 124, 217, 241, 266, 287.
[9] It is with a view toward preventing this kind of bid for status that we have recommended the use of round tables for group interviews with adults and adolescents.

she said they had "started and ended with sex." Lizbeth laughingly added that she remembered the discussion on "premarital intercourse." For some time the conversation centered around this subject, with Lizbeth reporting on her college studies in psychology, where the subject was discussed with varying opinions by different students. Mildred could not understand how there could be any opinion other than disapproval . . . Edna wondered how a man felt about a girl who "gave in" . . . Mildred discussed sex with her current boy friend, of a year's standing . . . She thought this was very important . . . Lizbeth agreed, but thought "other things in life are just as important." Mildred looked at her incredulously. "Such as what?" she asked. Lizbeth said "art" and Mildred asked "as a hobby or career?" Lizbeth replied, "Both, more or less." A silence ensued.

Mildred broke the silence by commenting thoughtfully, "the trouble is that I don't know the difference between love and infatuation." A protracted discussion followed, in which all the girls participated, on the difference between these two feelings, with Mildred giving illustrations from movies she had seen that dealt with "real" love.

Edna wondered whether there was a "reason" why one fell in love. Mildred looked at her and repeated "reason?" A silence fell over the group again. The therapist called attention to the silence, to which Mildred responded spiritedly by saying, "What we need is a teacher to talk to us and suggest topics, then we could talk about them." There was silence, she said, because the girls did not want "to reveal" themselves. They feel "gripped." Therapist: "gripped?" Mildred: "Yes, gripped in fear." The group would feel freer if someone "led the discussion." The therapist asked whether Mildred wanted to say something. At this, Mildred shot a look of disgust at the therapist. She then giggled briefly and turned to Lizbeth. "How do you feel about it?" Lizbeth, in a somewhat confused way responded: "I don't quite know where we are. I am lost."

Mildred said she had always wanted advice from people, and explained to the others how she used to ask older adults, and people her own age, for advice. She wondered whether Lizbeth had done that, but Lizbeth hadn't. She said she formed her own opinions and pretty much followed her own ideas. The therapist commented on this as being an interesting difference and wondered how they might account for it. Mary agreed that it was interesting and said that she related it back to childhood; at least that's how she felt about it and, looking directly at the therapist she said "I did not get this from books." She considered it a weakness, or at least she wondered whether it was. She thought that children get strength from the mutual love and respect of their parents. If they haven't been given this, if they haven't been trusted, they grow up to find they cannot rely on themselves. She pointed out again that she was not talking in generalities but felt that this has been her experience.

Lizbeth quietly asked whether Mary still felt that way. Mary said she did, but less so now. She learned that in asking people for advice, she got prejudices and opinions based on their own experiences and feelings. She could see that these were not the answer for her, because she is different from anyone else; different from all those who give her advice. She probably turned to people because she was not guided by her parents. She found that she tended to "make into parents" the adults of whom she asked advice. With eyes downcast, she explained that she had been separated from her family, had gone to live with her (two maiden) aunts, when she was a child, and "now I live alone." She felt more confident now and added, "I keep busy." She took lessons and attended classes and, of course, went to work. But every so often, these thoughts came back to her. Lizbeth said she thought it was a gradual process and one gradually grew more independent. Mary wondered why Lizbeth thought people did not have the strength of their own convictions; was it because they were immature? Lizbeth said she didn't think it was because of that. She didn't think that age (apparently confusing age with maturity) had anything to do with it. She said she knew self-reliant youngsters and she knew older people who were relatively "unselfconfident." . . .

During a period of a year and a half, the group went through a process of reorganization. Some of the original members dropped out for various reasons. One was not adequately motivated to continue, some moved away from the city; and Mildred married. Following one of our general principles of analytic group psychotherapy—that groups may remain "open" in the *early periods* of their existence—new members had been added as old members dropped out, until a *permanent* (closed) group had been established. Once this occurred and the patients progressed in working through some of their deeper problems, the group became a "closed" group (i.e., no new members were added).

Our second illustration of the progression in interviews is taken from the seventieth weekly session of this group.

This session, the group arrived almost simultaneously, except for Lillian, who was a little late. Frances had not seen the card announcing the birth of Mildred's baby and the therapist brought it along. There was a brief discussion about visiting Mildred by Frances, with little response from the others in the group.

Rose asked, "Where were we last week?" and Tessie recalled the discussion of mothers. Rose wondered how Tessie's "cold war" (with her mother) was coming. Tessie said it had abated somewhat; she and her mother were talking more to each other now, but since then there had been a new incident. On Wednesday night, Tessie was out, and her mother was "up in the dark," waiting for her, and stubbed her toes. Next day her mother went to the doctor and discovered that two of her toes were fractured. Tessie called both her and the doctor during the day, but went out with Chris that night. The mother obviously resented the fact that Tessie had not paid more attention to her. On the following evening, when Chris and she were at a relative's house five blocks away, and did not call for her mother, her mother was again very critical of Tessie and blamed her for the fracture. Rose moaned, and everybody else thought the mother's attitude was ridiculous. Frances suggested that Tessie's mother should turn on the lights after this, and Dorothy thought it would have been easy for her mother to take a cab five blocks home, without disrupting Tessie's date.

The therapist asked how Tessie felt about her mother's accusations. Tessie thought they were "slightly silly" (but there was evidently a feeling that it *was* her fault) and she said that maybe she should have given more attention to her mother, since the mother had been so solicitous of her when she, Tessie, was ill. Rose pointed out that the mother likes nothing better than taking care of Tessie since that ensures the "closeness" which the mother wants. Lillian came in at this point and Tessie recapitulated the discussion, for her benefit. Lillian, too, was amazed at the mother's blaming Tessie.

Tessie wondered what the others would have done in like circumstances. Frances said her father hurt his leg the day she left for the Middle West with her boyfriend. She hadn't thought of changing her plans nor had other members of the family, and her father would not have wanted them to. Her father stayed home with the grandmother and "made out fine." She did call home twice, while she was away, to ask about him and also let her folks know when she would return. She talked to her father on the phone; he was interested in her trip and how the car had held up. She had had a good time.

Rose returned to Tessie's problem and said that when her mother made accusations of neglect, Tessie still felt guilty. It was obvious that she had lots of doubts, and wondered whether there was anything for which her mother would not put the blame on Tessie. Dorothy, interrupting, said that she was reminded of Tessie's mother when she had had dinner with George and George's mother the preceding Monday night. (They all remembered the previous accounts of this garrulous, disturbed, sick woman.) Dorothy had been rather looking forward to the occasion, but was very distraught by the end of the evening because of his mother's behavior. The therapist asked her to describe her feelings. She felt "scattered" afterwards; "all in pieces." It took her several hours to regain some measure of composure. It is wearing to listen to such a woman (George's mother). She resents people who do not accept her opinions even if they do not share them. She "felt not listened to or respected." In fact, the lack of response meant rejection to her. This so affected

312

Dorothy, she said, that she wishes she could tell George, that she wants no more appointments with his mother. But she does not want to hurt him. His siblings refuse to see their mother because she is such "a nuisance and trouble maker." George is the youngest and the only one who has any relation with her.

The therapist asked why she felt that she had to protect him and wondered whether she felt that he could not refuse to see his mother as the other siblings had. Dorothy said she did not know why he would not. The therapist explored this. Dorothy grinned and agreed with what she thought the therapist had in mind, which was that it would make him feel too guilty. George was plagued by indecision in many respects and vacillated in his considerations of their plans for marriage, schooling, and a trip abroad. He was unable to discuss it fully with her, or anyone, but had felt better in the last six months since knowing Dorothy, and had said that he felt "somewhat closer to an answer" for himself. His indecision "gets to" her; "it reaches my own anxiety and indecision." She thought maybe that was why she pushed him into action, in order to counteract her own feelings, probably not so different from his own. Now he seemed to be less affected by his mother than she was. Frances commented that he was probably used to her.

The therapist wondered what Dorothy had expected of George's mother. She didn't know. She had always thought that he exaggerated in describing the way his mother was, but after she had met her, she found out that he had given "as full and awful a picture as there actually is." She told of the mother's gossiping and trying to talk Dorothy out of her warm feeling for George's aunt. Frances thought that this, too, must have felt like rejection, since Dorothy likes the aunt. Dorothy agreed. She said it had been a long time since she felt so "scattered." The therapist asked about her previous experiences with this feeling. She recalled that, in college, she couldn't concentrate and did not do as well as she might have. She felt pushed toward accomplishment by her mother.

The therapist casually wondered whether this coincided with her becoming pregnant. Dorothy recalled that it did, and remembered her feeling of relief at having a reason for leaving school.

313

Rose wondered why she had not just quit school. Lillian said, protectively, that that was hard to do when one was expected to finish. Rose wondered whether her mother had been "paying the way." Dorothy said no, but her mother had "tried to push." She guessed the mother was trying to take the father's role. She had not resented it in her father, but had listened and usually agreed with his "reasonableness." However, even when her mother was reasonable, Dorothy felt a strong urge to oppose her and to rebel.

She continued by saying that maybe she just did not get along so well with women. The therapist wondered if this referred to women who were mothers or who served in the place of a mother. Dorothy thought for a while, then said, "Maybe you have something there." She had looked forward to having a companionable relationship with George's mother and was disappointed when she realized it could not be. This was what she had wanted from her own mother, too—warmth and understanding. She should have known better than to expect it at this late date. The therapist asked if Dorothy felt pushed by George's mother, too. She said yes, and she resented it. The therapist remarked that it was natural that such feelings as she had about her mother would get "placed onto" her (the therapist) as well. Dorothy thought that was very true, although she had not thought of it in just those terms. She had never felt it with her individual therapist, except at the beginning. She knew her rebellion was her way of trying to "resist the push," and with her mother it was manifested as doing the opposite. She giggled as she said she guessed her resentment toward the therapist "came out" by her staying away from group sessions.

She could see it much more clearly with George's mother, and she knew she couldn't tolerate any kind of insistence which felt like extreme pushing. She recognized that it was easy to see this in someone else's mother. The feeling she had about someone else's mother was like the feeling she had toward her own mother, only heightened. "And easier to discuss," the therapist suggested. Dorothy responded by saying that that was definitely true. The others murmured assent.

Tessie had a question which she thought was "silly," but which she was going to ask anyway. She addressed it to Dorothy; "Do you love your mother?" Dorothy said, "Definitely, no." Maybe she had a "certain affection," but she did not consider it love. Somewhat defensively, she added that even the Bible says you don't have to love your parents, just "honor" them. Frances sarcastically interposed that "good girls love their mothers." All laughed. Lillian thought it was not only expected by themselves, but reinforced by society. The therapist wondered why Tessie had asked this question. Tessie said that recently she had had feelings of "actual dislike" for her mother, which she was not conscious of before. The therapist stated that it was natural in all relationships that there be ambivalent feelings. That was a concept Tessie had never thought of. The therapist remarked that this was clear in little children, who disguise their feelings much less. The therapist spoke, too, of the real but not final aspect of hurt, the wish for the mother to be *away*. Tessie could recall no negative feeling toward her mother as a child. She remembered being very mad at her, but accepted that "mother was always right." An attempt to get her to elaborate the feeling of being "mad" was not successful. She was then asked whether she had ever had any negative feeling toward the therapist. She grew very thoughtful and then said, "No." She knew she would always defer to the therapist. The similarity between her reaction to the therapist and to her mother was pointed out.

Lillian remembered hating her mother when she was little and telling her so, saying outright that she wished she was dead. Her mother had answered with the threat that Lillian would be placed in an orphanage if the mother were dead and her life then be nothing but hard work. The mother had thought that Lillian did not appreciate her life at home and she would some day recognize what a good life she had had. Lillian said that after this lecture, she went on hating her mother on occasion, but she never voiced it again. When asked about her reaction, she said she never was reasonable about it. If she had been, she would have thought of her loving aunts, who were always quite demonstrative, and whom she is sure would have taken her in, if there had been a death in the family. She guessed that she had felt powerless against

315

her mother's threat. The therapist said that that feeling was common to children and very frustrating. Lillian guessed it had led to the thought that maybe she could not get along without her mother.

Dorothy recognized this feeling in herself as well. The therapist wondered whether it did not make her feel guilty about expressing negative feelings. There was general agreement on this.

Tessie was thoughtfuly silent during this discussion. She now broke her silence and said that in the recent past, whenever she had arrived home and not found her mother there, the thought had immediately occurred to her that her mother may be dead. This had happened on very few occasions, however, because her mother usually always sat up waiting for her. Tessie thought there was probably some wish behind her "mental association," and yet she knew it was not the whole truth. The therapist supported this thought, without clarifying it.

Dorothy said she had had that feeling about George's mother and had actually "wished her dead," thinking that it "would solve everything." Yet, she recognized that if she could handle her own feelings about George's mother, it would not make any difference whether she lived or died. . . .

Interpretation

One striking feature of this interview is that these young women had become reconciled to their feelings of hostility (especcially toward their mothers) and the comparative absence of guilt, except in Tessie's case.[10] However, Tessie's former complete submission and servility to an extraordinarily demanding and frustrating (probably psychotic) mother was abated to the extent that she could make and keep appointments with a young man.

The girls' psychological literacy and awareness of cause and effect in the phenomena of behavior and feelings is apparent, as is the commonness or homogeneity of at least one of their problems (resentment toward their mothers). The absence of guilt in verbalizing it is a step toward overcoming and accepting their mothers for what they were, for, recalling again the words

[10] About a year later Tessie unsuccessfully tried to commit suicide.

316

of Goethe, the road to emotional maturity lies in understanding one's parents and forgiving them. Whether these young women can achieve that maturity, short of a thoroughgoing psychoanalysis, if then, remains to be seen, but the fact that they accepted their feelings had a salutory effect. They were able to free themselves of the mother phantoms to which they were tied by hostility and guilt, for all of the girls now had fiancés (except Tessie) and not long after, all (again except Tessie) were married.

We also witness in this interview, the therapist's greater participation and her security in leading her patients to clarify their thoughts and feelings, not merely ventilate them. This interview, as compared with the preceding one reported (the third), is characterized by greater emotivity, better focusing of the discussion, sustained interest, more penetrating insights, a higher degree of perceptiveness, diminished resistance, awareness of transference feelings, and enhanced motivation for therapy.

At the eighty-ninth session of this group, the center of the stage is occupied by Lillian, who is about to be married and, therefore, is filled with excitement. The group defers to her.

She starts by discussing her feelings at the prospect of separation (from the group). She said separation was "particularly difficult" for her, because of her feelings about her separation from her father (who, she felt, had "abandoned" her when he, an alcoholic, was divorced by her mother after prolonged tension, quarrels, and fights when Lillian was in her early teens). She had seen him since, but only very rarely.

She thought she had separated from others, to whom she was close, quite easily, like her mother and grandmother. She did not want to visit her grandmother to tell her the news of her coming marriage, for fear she could not handle the latter's inquisitiveness. She always felt she had to explain herself. She was sometimes still guilty over leaving her grandmother's house, and she realized that with both her mother and grandmother, absence did not mean emotional separation. She guessed that this was true of her father, too. She had been thinking of him in connection with the wedding. If it was to be a "big wedding," she would like to have him there. She thought she could trace him through an acquaintance.

About his "giving her away" (in marriage), she felt he had already done so; that is, "given her away (in leaving her), though not to anybody." She had never accepted her stepfather and had rejected his friendly overtures. She said she has always been disappointed that her father did not think enough of her to visit, though she could see the difficulties with her mother, who wanted the separation to be final. Lillian said, "I did not feel I belonged to anybody." She envied her fiancé in this regard, for he was sure that he wanted his father to be his best man.

She felt bad because, at the age of 15 when her father left home, she had not let him know that she loved him and had not supported him against her mother. She might even have gone with him if she had not been "cowardly," though she recognized that he had had no home for her. Most important, she had been afraid: she had needed a home and she could not oppose her mother. She now realized she would not have been homeless, and blamed herself for not realizing it then. The therapist wondered how she could have acted thus when she was feeling afraid and said that she was asking too much of herself to expect that, at 15, she could have felt what she only now was aware of. Lillian guessed she had been pretty fearful and insecure at that time, and the therapist generalized that fear does inhibit one.

Tessie agreed with this, and associated it with the previous week's session. She summarized, for Lillian, who had been absent, how Dorothy had expressed her disappointment in Tessie's not being free of her mother, even though she now lived apart from her. Tessie also had said that she had wished her mother would die, so that she could be rid of her feelings about her; yet she realized later that that was not a solution, since she would probably, in some way, feel responsible for her death. Lillian said she somehow knew that Tessie would feel that way, and commented that it was so much easier to see things in another person than in oneself. Tessie recognized and shared this feeling.

Tessie remarked that Lillian had seemed almost gleeful when speaking about the encounter her mother and Willis's parents would have. She said Lillian seemed almost to relish the opposition to her mother, because she expected her not to like Willis's parents. Lillian said that that was true. She knew her mother did not approve of the marriage, particularly because Lillian would be supporting her husband through his last year of college. Yet, she was also disappointed that her mother did not act more cheerfully about the forthcoming nuptials. Her fiancé's parents were "so different and are so pleased about the marriage." She described them as people who were not "fussy," who were generous and expressed their feelings, and who liked her. She knew her mother would disapprove of them, because they were different. She knew that no encounter, nor anything she could say, would change her mother's attitude. She believed her mother to be essentially unchangeable. She described her mother's life as "rigid, constricted, and narrow," and, yet, her mother did not see it for what it was. She thought her mother could never admit that there was any other way to live.

Lillian feared the problems of marriage, though; particularly *in regard to being like her mother.* The therapist commented that it was obvious that she was different from her mother, citing her coming "for help." She said that was true, but in other ways she was like her mother, mentioning her compulsive cleanliness. When she straightened and cleaned her apartment, Willis sometimes said to her, "For God's sake, Lillian, light!" He did not understand that she could not help herself. She did not like this aspect of herself and did not want to be like her mother. She tried staying away from cleaning, just to be different from her mother, and found that she could not tolerate it . . . .

The therapist encouraged Lillian to talk more about her fear of being like her mother. She said it did not come on her often, but when it did, it was "all-enveloping and very discouraging." She tried to fight it off, by acting as she thought her mother would not. When she felt like herself, she had more strength, was happier and surer, and looked forward to marriage; feeling good about it. The therapist led her on to describe this feeling further. Out of this, came the conviction that a part of her was exactly like her mother, "and this part would grow and grow. It was the inevitability of it that made it seem hopeless. There was no freedom to choose something else." In fact, she did not think that other adults were different. All adults became like their mothers. Being a grownup meant being disapproving, fussy, restrictive, and unhappy, and making others so. Lillian said she knew she might even control Willis and make him unhappy, just as her mother had done when she could not accept Lillian's father. Lillian feared that as she changed from a child to an adult, she *must* become like her mother. "Mother is the authority: the adult who represents all adults." This was the only way to be. The therapist asked whether this meant it was the way people *should* be, and Lillian said, "No, just that this is the way they are; the only way to be."

This "rang a bell" with Tessie and she said that though much of Lillian's problem did not seem the same as hers, regard for her mother as an authority symbol was similar; Lillian's feeling of inevitability was similar to Tessie's feeling that her mother was right, "just because she is Mother." . . .

Interpretation

In this session, Lillian revealed her deep-rooted oral dependence, with which she had struggled much of her life, and her "separation anxiety," or what may rather have been "mourning the loss" of every person who played any significant role in her life. Though she claimed that she separated easily from her mother and grandmother, she was afraid of the latter's rejection when she should disclose her marriage plans. She projected an act (rejection of her) on her grandmother, because she was afraid of being rejected (separated). We also have here a girl with an affect hunger of considerable intensity, which will probably be her lot until the end of her days.

The fact that she, out of her own free association, recognized that her feelings associated with separation stemmed from her feelings of having been abandoned by (separated from) her father, reduced the poignancy of the situation. Although Lillian had revealed and lived through her feelings on the subject in past interviews, the therapist could have re-emphasized this connection and the infantile memories associated with it. Though such rational and "logical" maneuvers do not constitute therapy, they do help the process where it is ongoing on the emotional level; reason is employed to buttress emerging emotional maturity.

Lillian's reactions and her continued ambivalence in relation to the significant persons in her life, as well as to the nature of her original problems, convinces us that only a thoroughgoing psychoanalysis can provide, for her, the treatment she requires. Even then, only limited results can be expected. However, the group therapy experience has helped her acquire an increased awareness of herself, her behavior, and her responses and has strengthened her ego so she can cope with the problems of life with somewhat more mature confidence and effect a marriage as the first step in that direction.

A comparison of the interviews with the two groups quoted supra, will throw light on some of the principles of grouping and communication discussed in the preceding chapters. The young women in the second group, as compared with the members of the first group, are obviously more involved and their interviews are more meaningful. This can be attributed to the fact, that in addition to sex homogeneity, they are contemporaries in age (age homogeneity) and their interests are, therefore, likely to be more analogous; they are also homogeneous as to the nuclear problem: hostility toward their mothers, to which they reacted by the same delinquent act (unmarried motherhood); they are intellectually on par and are clinically homogeneous, all being neurotic; and there is a high level of identification and empathy between them.

These requirements for high-level working groups are in less evidence in the group of the older women, and their interviews lack the vibrancy and intensity of the younger group interviews. They are less motivated and the group is composed of a variety of clinical categories—character disorders, confused sexual identification, psychoneurotics, and one borderline schizophrenic. These characteristics would not deter the group from working better if they were all homogeneous with regard to their nuclear problems, but such was not the case. The therapeutic prognosis for such a group is not entirely hopeless, but it requires more time and greater effort and skill on the part of the therapist, incomparably greater struggle by the patients.

Let us now summarize a later session (the 106th) and see what strides have been made by the young women of the second group.

The girls gathered in the waiting room and were discussing Tessie who had tried committing suicide. Lillian asked Dorothy whether she had heard from Tessie; she had not. When they settled in the meeting room they asked Frances how she was feeling. Frances had a sunburn, but was otherwise okay, she said. Dorothy wanted to report something. Saturday night, while sitting in a 42nd St. movie house with George, she had felt something on her shoulder and brushed it off. "You know what it was! Ugh!" She had been so disgusted that she "got right out of there," was almost ill and had had to be helped to the door by George (now her husband). Once home, she had washed her hands, thoroughly and soaped her mouth. She had felt creepy, dirty, awful. The thought of it still made her sick and she was still repulsed by any thought of "the male animal." ("It" referred to the penis of a middle-aged, drunken man.) . . .

Lillian wondered how Dorothy felt about George and his "maleness." Dorothy said that she put his "maleness out of her mind;" she "neuters" him, when she feels like "this." In her mind, she separated George from his penis and did not think of them together, did not think of his "having one." When she was feeling repelled by the penis, Dorothy could not stand to have George touch her. She had to have a "warning, to get prepared for lovemaking." It was only then that the penis gave her pleasure; but, if she was not ready for it, it was horrible.

Lillian said that she had to get herself ready, too. There had to be "a plan," something she knew about in advance, some warning before she and her husband went to bed. Otherwise, she had the fantasy that she was dry inside and the penis would scrape and cut her, leaving her insides raw and bleeding. After penetration occurs, when she knows this is not true, the fantasy would leave her. But she thought to herself: "I'll be glad when this is over," and had other thoughts, too. She remembered her mother and grandmother saying, "When a man wants you, there is nothing you can do." Dorothy related to this by saying she did not want to be "used." She felt that if she had intercourse when she did not want it, she was being "used, almost mechanically," as she had felt during intercourse before marriage.

Frances was silent and Dorothy noted this. Frances said quietly that she did not share their feelings. In fact, more often than not, she was the aggressor in sexual activity with Burt (her husband). Dorothy said that this had been true of her also, but only early in her marriage; in fact, she had complained to George about it (his not taking the initiative), so that sometimes now when she really did not want sex, George thought she was just teasing him. However, he had tried to be understanding and accepting of her moods.

Lillian wondered how Dorothy felt about George's penis in general. Dorothy said, again, that mostly she ignored it, *thinking of him as having none.* Lillian said she was very interested in Burt's (penis) and regarded it as a curiosity. For example, when he stepped from the shower, her eyes went to "it" immediately. She studied it, in different positions. After all, she had not seen many of them. The others laughed. Dorothy said she had not either; in fact, she couldn't tolerate looking at one before. Frances thought it was better that Dorothy could now at least pronounce the word and talk about it. Dorothy said she still shuddered a little when she used the word "penis" and admired the freedom with which Lillian seemed to talk about it.

Frances wondered whether Dorothy on Saturday night (when the incident in the theatre occurred) had thought of the "incident" (forced fellatio by an older boy, when she was 14 years old). Dorothy said not right away, but about five minutes later, she had recalled it. All she could think of at the time was how dirty she had felt, how sick, and how much she wanted to get out. The next day, Sunday, she had worked savagely around the house trying to get "it" out of her. ("It" in this instance referred to her tension, "a nearly frozen feeling in my muscles.") Lillian and Frances described minor incidents of being pawed in the subway and how, the next time it happened, they meant to call the police. Dorothy had thought of doing that, too, but did not want to get any more involved than was necessary. To a question from Frances, she replied that she had also thought that George might have called the police (at the movie theatre) or acted a little more involved than he had. She guessed that she resented his not being more active about it.

Yet, Dorothy feared that she had very small grounds for resentment. She complained of feeling very restless for some time. She found that her hands were completely restless and she had chewed on her nails and picked on her toenails. She had been trying to escape in reading. She wished she and George could go away together and not always be in "that damn one-room apartment." They went to two and three movies a week, more than she had ever gone before. She was much more aware of her feelings and described a decreasing ability to put them out of her mind. She wondered what she could do to feel less uncomfortable. She kept looking for answers. Her reading even included a book on psychoanalysis and "anything I can lay my hands on." She was very moody and experienced happiness only momentarily. Frances asked when these happy feelings came on her. Dorothy said usually right after intercourse, "but it lasts such a few minutes," she added sadly, and then she was back with her worries and uncertainties. She did not know what she wanted or why she was so moody. She said it was not just impatience about going to Paris (with George on his business). She guessed she had always been this way; only she was now much more conscious of it. The therapist commented on how much more uncomfortable it was for her now, because of her greater awareness.

Dorothy said the thought had come to her that she really held beliefs that were little different from those of her parents. All her behavior, particularly her sexual behavior, had been a big act and not a true mirror of the way she felt. (Dorothy had been inordinately promiscuous before therapy began.) She thought at heart she was really "a Puritan." She related how embarrassed she had been after a recent dream; she had lots of dreams lately. She narrated one in which she and "someone else" were underground and taking trains which always ended up in a shopping center, similar to the one underneath Rockefeller Center. She goes into a toilet and a man opens the door, and she is embarrassed because her soiled sanitary pad is there. Then a woman opens the door to the toilet. "It is all confused." Then Dorothy leaves the washroom naked, goes out in front of everybody with soap and water dripping from her legs. She has a towel, but it doesn't cover her.

She thought it was a weird dream. She had always been embarrassed about genitals, her own and other people's. They were something to "leave in the bathroom" and forget. Frances wondered whether Dorothy was embarrassed about her menstrual period, noting how Dorothy had tried to clean herself in the dream. Dorothy said she didn't think so. The therapist asked where she had held the towel and she said over her breasts. She said she had no idea what that was intended to mean. Maybe she had been reading "too much." She had read that the penis and breast are sometimes equated, since both protrude from the body. So far as she knew, she did not mind breasts, though. She always objected to men wearing tight bathing suits; felt it was disgusting and always averted her eyes. (At a previous session, she reported that she vomited whenever she came in contact with a penis other than via her genitals. It must be remembered that Dorothy was forced to commit fellatio on an older boy when she was 14 years old and then was blamed and rebuked by the boy for having done it.) But women in tight bathing suits did not bother her at all. She mentioned how she had always wanted closeness to her mother and how, as we are all aware, she had been trying to achieve that. She wondered whether maybe *the love of a woman was more important to her at that time.* And maybe, too, that was why she "neuters" George in her imagination, as if she were trying to make him "more like a woman."

Or maybe Dorothy wanted the penis for herself, Lillian suggested. Dorothy said she had thought about that, and had decided she "didn't want one and didn't need one." Frances thought that

Dorothy protested too much, like a girl pretending to pay no attention to the boy next door and then being overjoyed when he finally gets around to asking her for a date. Dorothy maintained that she had thought a lot about it and she certainly could not *feel* she wanted a penis. Frances asked about Dorothy's managing of George; how did that fit in? Dorothy admitted that she liked to run things, almost as if she were "wearing the pants in the family," but she also reminded the group that she had been dissatisfied when he did not take more initiative.

Frances wondered what Dorothy would do about her marriage if her problems were not solved before leaving for Paris. Dorothy said she would do all she could to hold the marriage together "at least until we get back." Certainly, she felt she would want to do that. She thought the fault was not in the marriage but in herself, her own confusions and moodiness which she was trying to understand and control. Frances said she had found that marital difficulties are not exclusively the fault of one or the other partner; Burt (her husband) had formulated this for her once, helping her see it. Frances said that in *this* pregnancy she would like to act like other young women having their "first baby" (Frances was now pregnant). She would like to make noises about every ache and pain and would like to see concern from her husband. She would love to be "babied" but realized that Burt would not do it. Also, she felt sheepish about asking for attention because, "I know what's going on inside me," and she had to laugh at herself when she attempted to exaggerate the situation. Dorothy wondered why Frances wanted this. Frances said she had always wanted to be "the star; on a pedestal." She would like to have verbal and demonstrated assurance that she is *"the* one," but Burt does not feel that it is necessary to show it all the time. She was very pleased the other day when he told his friends that he was going to be a father; then she did feel on a pedestal and thought how silly she had been for pressing him for reassurance, while, if she listened, it is there all the time.

Frances's sister-in-law was having a baby in January. Frances described with what pleasure she had received the news and how happy she was for her sister-in-law and her husband, because they had been "trying" for a long time. However, her second reaction seemed to be the truer one. She admitted she was not at all desirous of sharing the spotlight in the family with the mother of another grandchild. She wanted to be "unique, the only one. The hell with *her* baby" was her real feeling. Dorothy said she could appreciate that, and would probably feel the same way. Lillian said, rather wistfully, that it must be wonderful to be able to have a baby and share it—all the news about it—*openly*.

Frances said she had had a funny dream recently, about Jerry, her ex-boyfriend. They were walking along together near her old neighborhood, and Jerry was urging her to get a divorce from Burt and marry him. Then when they got to the same old street. Jerry did exactly what he used to do in real life, which was to ignore her and "cut up with the boys." She had told the dream to Burt, who laughed. Frances remembered being relieved, as she awakened, that she was not married to Jerry and did not have any plans to do so.

The time was up. Lillian said it had gone so fast; there was so much to talk about that she feels she'll be coming for "sixty years." Somehow, she felt she had just got started. Dorothy admitted to having that feeling, also. She assured Lillian that things would go faster now that Lillian was freer to talk. Lillian wondered whether we had noticed that Beatrice was not here. This surprised Lillian. It did not surprise Dorothy; in fact, she had expected that Beatrice would "wait a week" (because of the anxiety and guilt-laden subject matter of her revelations during the previous session).

Frances wondered who might be absent next time. All of them said they were going to come; they would not miss the group "for anything."

Interpretation

This interview shows clearly the psychological literacy of the girls and the ease with which they communicate intrapersonally and with each other. Their defenses and distortions are at a minimum. They are now able to view themselves, their impulses, and their psychological nakedness without fear or hesitancy. The ego of each, with the exception of Dorothy perhaps, is in control, where the id reigned before. Even in the case of Dorothy, her awareness is serving her in good stead. She knows that she needs to be prepared for intercourse and has a few minutes of real happiness afterward, which for her is a great event, because of her very tragic early life.

Without this awareness, she would have permitted herself to be "used" by her husband, as another girl put it, and her aversion, contempt, and hostility toward him would have mounted, possibly with disastrous results. Her awareness that she emasculates her husband in fantasy prevents her from showering *all* the blame on him for their sexual incompatibility and her recognizing her homosexual urges and tying them up with her mother, are the portals through which Dorothy will eventually solve her problem.

What is important here is that all the patients are *intimate with themselves.* They recognize and accept themselves, with all their perverse and not always admirable, urges and strivings. A communication channel has been established between their unconscious and ego. This gives them the strength to deal with reality, instead of being, as in the past, crushed by it and prey to the tyranny of their irrational impulsiveness, which they had acted out in its maximal form by becoming unmarried mothers.

Again, the high level of identification and empathy is seen in the accelerated communication, catharsis, uncovering, and clarification. We also see the value of interpatient stimulation and how directed catharsis takes place. Frances serves here *in loco psychotherapeutis,* as it were. By her leading questions she helps Dorothy explore deeply the unconscious sources of her feelings and reactions.

An informational by-product of the developments in this group, of value to psychotherapists, is the fact that marriage is no indication of cure or improvement. Reflecting our societal values, therapists sometimes offer as proof of their patient's recovery or improvement that the latter "got married." This is an erroneous criterion. Marriage does not solve any problem; rather, it creates more problems. The criterion should be whether the marriage is sustained and at what emotional cost to the partners involved.

Obviously, in Dorothy's case, it cannot be considered as an aid to emotional health; and to a lesser degree this is also true of some of the other young women though their complaints are not too different from nearly all women in modern times.

Note should also be taken, here, of the limitations of group psychotherapy. Much in Dorothy's personality cannot be reached by this method and the *neurotic residue* will require a more deeply affecting psychotherapy—psychoanalysis. In fact, before she left with her husband for Europe, Dorothy asked for, and was given, names of analysts whom she could consult in Paris.

Attention should also be directed to the fact that the sexual regression displayed by the girls could probably not have been reached in a sexually heterogeneous group, or in the presence of a male therapist.

XI

The Analytic Group Psychotherapy
Interview: Dynamics

REALITY FIGURES VERSUS INTERNALIZED IMAGES

Throughout the course of an interview, the therapist must always be aware that each of his patients is dealing with *internalized images,* or phantoms, of significant persons in his past, rather than with *reality figures.* Through therapy, these phantoms must be displaced by reality tested conceptions and values. Because these images are highly invested with affect and have long been lodged in the psyche, their elimination is an extremely arduous task. Indeed, it is doubtful whether they can *ever* be completely eliminated and, in some adults, even significantly weakened. Being strongly cathected, the attitudes toward these images are irrational; they are introjected into the very structure of the unconscious and irrevocably become an integral part of the psyche. It is, therefore, understandable, why psychoneurotic, let alone characterological, states cannot be altered by reason, exhortation, and explanation, or by any other form of "influence" or education. In most instances, it is possible to achieve modifications in the personality structure only be recalling, reliving, and re-experiencing the original emotions, in replica relations. By this means, the "edge" or intensity of internalized feelings can be dulled and the neurotic engrams can be weakened, but, in adults, hardly ever completely eliminated.

Psychotherapy, especially group psychotherapy, with adults, has to be content with eliminating that portion of the morbid internalized images that are, or can be, rendered ego alien.[1] It is for this reason, among others, that, even after a prolonged and expertly carried out psychoanalysis, there is persistence of remnants of the *basic* personality characteristics. However, along with this, there is unmistakable evidence of changed *quality of personality* and altered responses. The corrected or diminished ego defenses and object overcathexes that result from a sound therapeutic experience, competently conducted, *do alter quality.* But these changes, in adults, are in the peripheral, rather than the essential, character structure.

The imperviousness of these, and other psychic areas, stem from the fact that they are *ontogenetically archaic.* That is, they have their origin in the preverbal and preconceptual stages and have been experienced as organic (neuromuscular, vasomotor, and endocrinal), as well as psychological experiences. Responses in the formative stages of the organism establish neuronic as well as psychological engrams, or gestalt configurations, which are later reactivated by the same, or analogous, stimuli. These engrams involve either the total personality or, selectively, one or a number of areas. "Ego defenses," for example, can be shown to be a type of psycho-organic engram.

Experience confirms the theoretically sound expectation that psychotherapy with children is less difficult and less protracted and the outcomes are more basic and more lasting. This can be explained in terms of Freudian topology—id, ego, and superego—during their formative stages, as well as by the flexibility of the organism. The dependencies of the child, his ego formation and fluid identifications, his unformed superego and uncrystallized ego defenses—all of these and more render him pliable and subject to change through situations and relationships. This is borne out by the efficacy of good education with the ordinary child and by

---

[1] Rendering ego-syntonic traits, as in character disorders and psychopaths, into ego alien is sometimes erroneously described as turning nonneurotics into neurotics, thus making the patients accessible to psychotherapy. However, in cases where strongly repressed anxiety is present, it can be activated and neurotic states thus induced.

activity group therapy with children with certain problems. Because the neuronic engrams have not, as yet, crystallized, they can more easily be altered. In adults, they are rigid, especially where they are overcathected. The persistence of images and their cathexes form part of the resistance to therapy, for it is by this internalized "reality" that the patient has lived and it has become part of him. Giving it up would create a void with nothing for him to live by to take its place. The source of security on which he can draw during therapy is the positive transference on the therapist. Thus, the transition from internalized images to reality in relations is the positive transference toward the therapist, who has to mobilize all available means to help dislodge the noxious phantoms.

INTELLECT VERSUS AFFECT

Traditionally, catharsis consisted of verbal communication with its accompanying affect. More recently, other means have been devised to accomplish the same end. Among these, are the graphic and plastic arts, drama, and role playing. But it must be re-emphasized that the therapeutic effect is not encompassed in these expressional forms *per se*. They are only instruments of communication. Their value in therapy, especially with adults, lies in the interpretation and insight in which they should culminate under the direction of a skilled and perceptive therapist (and sometimes fellow patients).

While the intellect and understanding are not sufficient to effect therapy, they do play a part in changing affect-laden images and memories and the associated attitudes in the unconscious. Conceptualization cannot, of itself, bring this about, but it does aid the emergence of emotional clarity. An example is Lillian's connecting her current separation anxiety with the abandonment by her father. Another example is Mrs. S.'s intellectual formulation, relative to her father, after reliving in memory the emotional impact of her relation to him. It is erroneous to assume that once a patient makes a revealing disclosure, it has, *ipso facto,* a therapeutic effect. One has to differentiate between *logically appropriate* and *emotionally significant* statements.

In a group, patients intuitively perceive resistive rationalizations in a fellow member. Sometimes, they may explore a statement made by him until he is forced to recognize, or at least to attempt to recognize, its latent meaning. The group plays an even more significant role in aiding its members with their internalized images, as the members project them on each other, as well as on the therapist, in the reality (actuality) setting of the group. This mechanism is included in the dynamic of "target multiplicity" and serves to dissolve one of the most trenchant cores of neurotic reaction, the internalized images and distortions.

COMMON GROUP TENSIONS

The appearance of a "group phalanx," or "common group tension," may momentarily fuse the group into a single psychological entity in respect to a current emotion in which all the patients participate, keeping in mind, however, that despite the commonness of a feeling, its quality and intensity are different for each patient. When this occurs, the group can be treated as though it were a single person and the common feeling explored. The therapist may ask, "Why is everybody so silent?" or, "I see everybody seems upset; what is it that upset you?" or, "I see all of you are angry at me now. Shall we talk about it?" or, "What made you angry? What did it remind you of?"

Analytic group psychotherapists cannot accept "common group tensions" as an exclusive technique, if they are to help each patient to work through and live through his traumatic background in the light of new emotional content and understanding.

ENDOGENOUS VERSUS INDUCED ANXIETY

In conducting a group interview, it is necessary to distinguish *endogenous anxiety* from *induced anxiety*. Endogenous anxiety emanates from the conflicts within the patient's psyche or between him and his ordinary environment. These are the anxieties for which he seeks treatment. Induced anxiety is the additional state of tension, generated in a therapy group, which we have already described as "group induced anxiety." The therapist should be certain as to the type of anxiety a patient presents at a given moment. While group induced anxiety can be employed for therapeutic ends with benefit, it becomes undesirable if its intensity is excessive or prolonged. Though anxiety induction in therapy groups is unavoidable and is an integral part of group psychotherapy, it must not be allowed to become either the sole or the predominant climate. When a particularly disturbed and, at the same time, assertive patient consistently generates turmoil and tension for long periods, his suitability for the group should be re-examined.

A case in point is the obviously obsessional psychotic woman who was permitted to monopolize the group interviews and keep her fellow patients, all women, at a high pitch of anxiety for 135 sessions. At every session, she dwelt on her horrific impulses to torture and boil people alive and murder her children and her husband, talking continually at a rapid, compulsive rate, drowning out all the others. Her manner and the content of her talking understandably kept the group in a perpetually high pitch of anxiety, throwing the group into the silence of fear (Anthony, 1959). The effect of this woman on the group was that, instead of dealing with their own endogenous anxieties and problems, the participants were kept occupied with the problems of this one patient and kept at a high pitch of (induced) anxiety. Though it was reported that the woman in question did improve somewhat, the other members did not show any movement; and none could have been expected, since they had no opportunity to become involved in treatment, but were rather held captive by the monopolizer. In addition, the monopolizing patient buttressed natural resistance to treatment in the others by keeping them occupied with her recitals, rather than examining their own problems.

There were unquestionably common tensions set up in the group in this case. Certainly, her overwhelming hostility and murderous drives, so near the surface, could not but produce breath-stopping fear; but very little, if any, therapeutic progress can be made in a group with such a patient present. Instead of dealing with their own problems, all the patients were preoccupied with this one woman. Group psychotherapy can be effective only when each patient has an opportunity to deal principally with his own problems, as well as with the problems of his fellow patients. A common group tension is therapeutically valid when it stems from a *common* problem and does not exist simply because the members of the group become inductively anxious or react to exogenous or induced anxiety from one of its members. It is because of the therapeutic importance of individual, endogenous anxiety, that I have suggested the elimination of obsessional-compulsive and hysterical patients, whose psychodynamic mechanisms would impel them to obtrude themselves on the group. Such patients can be considered as *true foci of infection* in the group, blocking its progress and effectiveness.

Artifices and Devices

Recent Developments

In recent years, there have appeared, in the literature, numerous descriptions of a number of "devices" or "artifices" used in group therapy interviews, such as: "rallies;" "themes;" "alternate meetings;" "initial," "middle," and "terminal" phases; "transactional;" "mimetic;" "contractual;" and many others. In a sense, this is a reversal of the evolution of schooling. The old education was replete with "artifices," which the newer and more enlightened educators have renounced. Formerly, teachers were trained in facile methods of presenting subject matter and devices for making it easier for the child to grasp and memorize. The revolution in schooling, that began in the early years of this century, underplayed techniques and devices, focusing increased attention on the child as a person and his interests in, and motivations for, learning.

In group psychotherapy, we are witnessing a reversal of this process. In analytic group psychotherapy, as in psychoanalysis, spontaneity and free association predominated in the productions of patients. For reasons of various countertransference reactions and divergent theoretical assumptions, which culminated in "schools," some therapists have abandoned free association techniques and assumed a quasi-directive, teaching role. In a sense, this is a return to the "inspirational" and didactic techniques used with large groups early in the century, though perhaps less rigid and less authoritarian. Some practitioners employ these techniques even though they allegedly adhere to psychoanalytic psychology and its basic assumptions and findings.

Rallies, Topics, and Themes

The distinctive feature of therapy groups and, as we have pointed out, one of their major assets, is that patients stimulate each other's productions through the dynamic of catalysis—consent, support, universalization, suggestion, interstimulation, and induction—through nonverbal and verbal responses. Patients in groups periodically center around a specific subject or emotion which gives rise to "rallies" that may extend for varying periods during a group interview. The subject may be of extended or fleeting interest and when it is in the former category, it becomes the *theme* of the group interview. Rallies are part and parcel of therapy groups, for "Sooner or later," say Powdermaker and Frank (1953), "in every group we observed there appeared a phenomenon that we called *rallying around a topic;* because, instead of talking about the problem of a particular member, patients talked about a topic of interest to all." Actually, this is inevitable in the interchange in all groups, but it is more significant in analytic therapy groups. It is important that the therapist notes the role each participant assumes during rallies, his feeling tones, and general conduct, as well as the subject matter. The therapist must at all times maintain "free-floating attention."[2] Where the therapist is occupied with "rallies" and "themes" rather than with his patients' overt and covert reactions and anxieties, the process will suffer as a result.

"Rallies" and "themes" are sustained by a group when a topic strikes a common psychological resonance in patients; when group members empathically seek to help a fellow patient resolve a problem; when the members of a group have a common target for

[2] For a fuller discussion of this, see Chapter XIII.

hostility, either in a fellow patient, the therapist, or some other persons or symbol in their lives, that is, when a "group phalanx" appears; and when the group is in a state of common resistance. The therapist, therefore, has to be aware of the individual psychodynamics and the group tensions involved, each of which requires specific and suitable handling. Free-association and unrestricted expression of feelings and memories break into the sequentiality of a purely intellectual discussion, which is maintained only when the participants withold or restrain their free-floating feelings and fantasies. As a regular practice, this is not permissible in a therapy interview, since regressive catharsis should be activated by the participants through the catalytic effect they have on each other. Intellectual discussions may appear from time to time, for limited periods, especially when they represent, or are a product of, prolonged emotional working through of a specific problem. An orderly discussion can, therefore, be the culmination of emotional effort, with intellect called in to buttress the resolution of noxious feelings.

As the group interviews proceed, "themes" arise more and more frequently, for after a period of desultory and individual-centered productions, a degree of commonality emerges in the preoccupations or emotional interests of the patients. This commonality tends to rally them, at different times, around specific themes, with salutary effects.

The difference between a topic and a theme is illustrated in the group interviews cited in the preceding chapter. In fact, one may assume that the disparate free-associative and frequently unrelated interests (topics) by individuals in early sessions of groups, will inevitably diminish. In their stead, themes will appear, around which variegated and highly personalized reactions are expressed. At this stage, the group becomes a "working group" (which is sometimes misunderstood as being group cohesion).

A rally is a social instrument which has an appeal to all and in which all have libidinal investment. The investment may reach the intensity of cathexis and, even, overcathexis—then the encounter reaches high emotional intensity.

Rallies in analytic groups should be short-lived, or they may degenerate into quarrels or become monotonous. A rally should stimulate tangential or disparate ideas and feelings in individual members, who may, by the process of free association and through their momentary need, draw in different topics or feelings. The rally then subsides, but another may soon appear or the interview may take another turn. This variegation is in the nature of therapeutic interviews and may appear to be chaotic; but if the therapist follows the free-associative sequences, the chaos is seen to have a latent order, although not necessarily one that conforms with a syllogistic structure.

When a rally, carried on for a considerable length of time, does not generate variegated responses in some group members, it is in all probability too abstract or abstruse, or is essentially intellectual and, therefore, devoid of emotional significance and stimulus. When this is the case, it is not only of no consequence as a therapeutic encounter, but is often employed as group resistance. If it does not emanate from another patient, the intervention of the therapist may be indicated to pull the group out of this nadir.

Manifest versus Latent Themes

In a group therapy interview, the theme is not always clear, for it is at times obscured by latent content. Most often, however, the theme is apparent, coinciding with the manifest subjects of preoccupation revealed in the group conversations and interchanges. At times, however, the basic motive, or urge, reflected by the theme may be obscured by the immediacy of the material produced. The discerning psychotherapist can recognize that the subject under discussion (either as a monologue, dialogue, or a rally), flows from an underlying emotion, which, to the inexperienced or unperceptive person, may not be apparent.

For example, in a therapy group of women, one of the members initiated a discussion by narrating that her teenage daughter had accused her of not loving her. The mother defended herself by stating: "Of course I love her, but I don't have to say it to her everyday." Another member of the group expressed the opinion that it was necessary to keep telling children that they are loved, because they need reassurance. Still another said that before her group therapy experience, she used to withhold her "feelings" from her children, but now, "I let them know how I feel about them, positively or negatively. Of course, if you tell them every-day, they may become suspicious." The discussion then proceeded to a consideration of the advisability of giving presents and the possibility of "spoiling children if one overdoes it." There was again a difference of opinion that could not be resolved by the women and they turned to the therapist for her views. Instead of answering, the therapist responded by reflecting the problem to the group members and asking them how this applied to their own experiences. This provoked one of the women to relate an event that had occurred when she was eight years old. She had been subjected to an attempted sexual molestation. She never had re-ported this to her mother, because she felt that her mother would "accuse" her instead of being "sympathetic."

The first woman, mother of the young teenage girl, responded to this with the experience of her husband's brother physically touching her daughter, in a way which could be construed as hav-ing sexual intent. The mother became incensed and spoke to her husband about it. He made light of it and passed it off as mean-ingless. The woman continued by saying that she was always shy about speaking to persons in authority, because "it might create additional problems." She then spoke of her own inadequacy, her need to be passive and overconsiderate and to avoid "stepping on other people's toes." She proceeded to complain about the ill-treatment she received on the telephone from a therapist who had treated her daughter in the past, and though she wanted to complain about it, she was too shy and afraid to actually do so. Another member of the group related a similar incident of mis-treatment by a therapist. This interchange led to a discussion of tactlessness vs. frankness and honesty, and the fear of losing one's temper and becoming angry . . .

On the surface, this interview consisted of a number of sub-jects and several rallies, with no apparent theme for the total in-terview. However, examination reveals that the latent feeling underlying all these productions is sexual anxiety, and the theme

339

was the women's preoccupation with their own and their daughters' sexual impulses. This supervisory estimate proved correct, for in the next interview, the women expressed these preoccupations in more manifest forms.

SIGNALS AND CUES

As already indicated, the therapist has to draw on the manifest and latent productions of patients, in order to either stimulate, guide, or activate the interviews in a therapeutically valid direction. This activity is based on manifest verbal and nonverbal communications on the part of patients and their covert preoccupations, as well as the therapist's recognition of their therapeutic needs. The latter is derived, at least in part, from the historic background of each patient (etiology and nosology), while, in the case of the former two, he needs to recognize and follow the signals and cues that convey the patients' moods, struggles, conflicts, and transitory needs.

Cues make their appearance during verbalizations, as psychologically significant concepts or ideas which the therapist can recognize, either in terms of the patient or the group as a whole. The patient's readiness for interpretation and insight is one of the things cued to the therapist, though frequently an insignificant statement may be mistaken for a cue and picked up by the therapist despite unreadiness on the part of a patient to proceed along the lines that appear indicated. To utilize exploration and uncovering on the basis of a cue, the defenses of the patient need to be sufficiently strong so that further exploration of the particular area will not generate anxiety and resistances. The basic nature of a cue is that it is conveyed verbally.

A signal, on the other hand, is usually of a nonverbal nature. It expresses the state of being or the need of the individual through physical expressions such as posture, gestures, bodily tensions, and similar manifestations. Thus, the basic contrast between a cue and a signal is that the first manifests itself verbally while the second is conveyed nonverbally.

340

THE FACTOR OF COMMONALITY

Themes and rallies are a product of the commonality of appeal of a subject, topic, or emotion for the members of a group. A communication dealing with matters peculiar or idiosyncratic to only one member is frequently passed up by the others without response; or it may stimulate them to introduce another, unrelated subject. The value of group therapeutic interviews depends on the extent of the appeal transactions have and the number of patients they emotionally engage. The larger the numbers involved and the higher the pitch of emotion, the greater the effectiveness as a therapeutic tool. Maximal effectiveness is achieved when the group members are stirred by the *same* emotions and all have an opportunity to express and explore them, through emotional and intellectual free association, unhampered by inner inhibition or outer restraint.

The importance of *basic* group homogeneity and its relation to commonality is obvious here. The more the elements of heterogeneity (described in Chapter VII), in grouping, are introduced, the less frequently the dynamic of commonality will appear. Its absence or infrequency diminishes the appeal of group interviews and their effectiveness as reconstructive experiences to the group as a whole are reduced.

The device of "going around" (requiring patients to methodically take turns in speaking) is of dubious value and is only resorted to in the absence of adequate homogeneity and consequent lack of interstimulation.

TYPES OF THERAPY WITHIN THE GROUP

It is the presence or absence of the element of commonality that determines, to a large extent, whether therapy occurs *in* the group, *by* the group, or *through* the group. When one patient occupies the center of the group, not because of monopolistic needs or primary narcissism, but because an event in his life is so unique or an emotion so bizarre that the others cannot relate to it, the therapist is constrained to work it through with him alone.

341

Even with a limited degree of identification or empathy on the part of the group, if it is insufficient to activate them to participation, the situation still demands (individual) therapy for one patient *in* the group very similar to that received in individual treatment. When there is appeal engaging more than one patient in the interaction complex, therapy occurs either *by* or *through* the group; that is, the group takes part in helping the individual patient. Inevitably, in all group interviews, all three types of therapy are necessary at different times in the multifarious and multiphase vortex of free and dynamic interaction between disturbed and agitated adults. Here, again, we find that basic pathology homogeneity favors the *group* therapeutic process.

For some patients, the level of commonality determines the extent to which parallel individual and group treatment is necessary. Patients with a relatively high quantum of personalized or idiosyncratic problems or experiences, to which the group cannot relate, may require individual sessions to supplement the group experience or, depending on the nature and extent of the problems, the group may be used to supplement individual treatment.

Commonality should not be confused with universalization. The latter is a method planfully employed by the therapist, or automatically derived by patients (derivative insight), that helps them become aware that their own "malevolent" urges and "depraved" conduct are not peculiar to themselves, but are, in actuality, characteristics of others, too, and, potentially, of all humans. The value of this as a guilt and anxiety reducer has been detailed elsewhere in this volume, a service which commonality cannot yield. It is quite evident that commonality, in certain of its aspects, may lead to universalization, but the instrumental application of the two must be separate in the mind of the therapist.

THREAT AREAS AND INTOLERANCE FOCI

The term "interaction" designates the multifarious phenomena of mutual impact among patients of a group, both through verbal and nonverbal means. These take place on many different levels of intensity and significance. To a very large degree, the intensity stems from the patients' arousal of memories and images in one another, touching on sensitive subjects, and the hostility or (diffused) aggression that patients invariably display in general or (specific) toward each other. The emotional significance of these, to each of the participating patients or witnesses, determines the intensity of their overt or covert reactions, and forms the warp and woof of the group therapeutic interview.

The intense reactions to interpersonal stimuli result from the defensiveness, by individuals, of their "threat areas" (subjects charged with intense emotional meaning, which, when identified verbally by others or brought to the awareness of an individual, generate guilt and anxiety). There are other, less profound, reactions that touch on sensitive points but do not necessarily arouse guilt and anxiety, although they may provoke irritation, anger, rage, and other responses characteristic of an inability to readily tolerate a stimulus. Thus, an act, statement, or response may not threaten one's ego ideal, defenses, or censors, but rather recall unpleasant and anger arousing experiences or persons in one's past and tap related or accompanying feelings. The value of these for the therapeutic grist are apparent, for it is these preconscious and reflex associations that have to be dissolved by working through, by awareness, insight, and understanding. This also applies to "threat areas," but because of the narcissistic injury, threat to the ego ideal involved, and their emotional signficance, they require an incomparably more complex and prolonged procedure for narrowing or eliminating them. To a considerable extent the comparison in dealing with uncovering memories, as against exposing threat areas, is similar to that between a character disorder and psychoneuroses. That is, in the one, the patient can be confronted with his irrational and unsuitable behavior, while in the other the underlying determinants have to be eliminated, wherewith the symptom disappears automatically.

The subjects or areas which actuate responses of violent disapproval, differences of opinion, anger, and rage, we shall designate as *intolerance foci,* which, as already stated, are genetically and qualitatively different from *threat areas.*

343

Psychological Encounters

The essence of an analytic group interview is the reactions (in words, deeds, grimaces, posture, and intraorganic processes) to the stimuli in a group, which touch on each patient's intolerance foci and threat areas, for it is through these that the pathognomic elements are exposed and made available to the corrective procedures designated by the generic term of "psychotherapy." The impact of these experiences we shall designate as the *psychological encounter*. This encounter occurs on three levels: interpersonal, with therapist, with fellow patients; intragroup; and, finally, intrapersonal, which is an essential of psychotherapy.

Interpersonal Encounters

Reactions to individuals, their personalities, their mannerisms of conduct and speech, the content of their assertions and their verbalized values, precede the other encounters. As an element of the initial group-induced anxiety, each patient "takes stock" of the others—their appearance, facial expressions, weakness, submissiveness, aggressiveness, hostility, cruelty, sexuality, and even pathology. The therapist does not escape this scrutiny, and reactions to him are also registered. Each person arouses initial covert responses in everyone else, in accordance with their engrammatic memories of, and experiences with, persons of similar facial and postural expressions or stereotypes. These are stored as *attitudinal potentials* which are later transformed into overt reactions as the interviews proceed.

Observation indicates that the major and most impelling sources of attitudinal potential among patients have their determinants in sexual attraction and repulsion. The homoerotic element, repressed or disguised as the case may be, is prevalent among persons who seek psychotherapy. It may be manifested openly or it may be disguised in heterosexual acting out, in actual intercourse, or by flirtatiousness in, and outside of, the group or remain suppressed. Homoerotic and homosexual urges, or residues, are always present in patients, for, whatever the observable forms of their pathology, either its roots are in, or its consequences reflect, attitudes toward sex or sexual adequacy, as well as early condi-

344

tioned feelings toward persons of the same sex, parents and others. These states (derived from sexual sources), determine attraction and repulsion and have been found operative not only in adults and adolescents, but also in children. It should be stressed that a hostile façade may be a defensive maneuver against overcharged attraction.

When the attitudinal potentials are of a "negative" quality, that is, hostile or disapproving, conflicts arise between the patients involved which, when properly worked through, aid in the emotional maturing of the personality. When, on the other hand, the attitudinal potential is "positive," that is, nonhostile, affinities emerge which are the bases for *supportive ego* relations. These can be advantageous or disadvantageous, depending on their latent meanings to the individuals involved.[3] These phenomena are part and parcel of the network of multiple transference attitudes in groups which form the gist of the therapy.

Somewhat similar in manner, and identical in nature, are the reactions that arise toward the therapist as a part of the transference phenomena, and the therapist should be aware that hostile (negative) feelings toward him appear as projective phenomena that must be worked through for treatment to be fully effective.

Intrapersonal Encounters

Therapeutically, the most significant of the encounters are those that the patient experiences within himself and which result in his *self-confrontation,* due to the encounters he has experienced with individuals and with the group. This is the epitome of the process, without which the effort is of little productivity or even wasted. Analysis, by the patients, of the intrapersonal encounters and the defensive distortions inherent in them is the acme of the therapeutic process. The specific advantages of groups in psychotherapy (with properly selected patients) lie in this very dynamic. Other patients hold up a mirror that exposes to each, not only

[3] The terms "positive" and "negative" are here to be understood as equivalent to "friendly" and "unfriendly," rather than "favorable" or "unfavorable" to the therapeutic effort; for a "friendly" or positive attitudinal potential may prove inimical to the therapeutic effort, while negative attitudinal potential can, and usually does, advance therapy.

his acts, but also his feelings and motivations which propel him to explore their meaning in terms of his past history and his current strivings. We have already considered this dynamic in terms of resistance solvents, now it is seen in the light of inter-personal encounters; specifically, coming to grips with one's own self and one's own pathology through the activation of fellow patients.

This intimacy with the self, previously described here as com-munication between the ego and the unconscious, is the indestruc-tible part of therapeutic gains. While character residues persist and streams of the deeply unconscious surge up in adults even after the most thorough psychoanalysis, let alone after less inten-sive psychotherapy, once the capacity for self-encounter (self-examination, self-confrontation) has been established, it persists throughout life.

The ability to encounter the self and work through an emotion-ally significant situation has been referred to as "self-analysis" by some writers. Self-analysis is a real possibility, but it can be em-ployed only by those who have experienced a thorough, valid, and prolonged psychoanalysis with a competent psychoanalyst. Anyone who attempts "self-analysis" without it, is destined to sink in the mire of his defenses and descend to the nether regions of intro-spection and possible depression.

Intrapsychic encounter is particularly valuable in the treat-ment of the various character disorders (except schizophrenia), in-cluding sociogenic psychopathy. As already indicated, ego syntonic-ity is, by its very nature, inaccessible to intrapsychic encounter without external intervention, since it is devoid of inner conflict, a conflict which can be generated when the individual finds him-self at odds with his environment, especially as expressed in the disapprobation of peers which threaten his status and social sur-vival. In this, the direct and vivid encounter with fellow patients is of great importance.

Intragroup Encounters

The vortex of the diverse feelings activated in a group mani-fest responses that involve the group as a whole, as in rallies, a group phalanx, or a number of patients *vis-à-vis* an individual. These intragroup encounters have already been outlined in the discussion of transference and the other dynamics of group interaction.

INTRAPSYCHIC ENCOUNTER AND NUCLEAR PROBLEMS

In the course of his therapy, every patient has to reach his nuclear problem and resolve it. Whether the nucleus of his difficulty is a single traumatic occurrence or prolonged exposure to pathogenic stress, there is always a *core* element which has disturbed the orderly development of his psyche. This may stem from his sexuality, threats to his physical or psychological survival, prolonged hyperstimulation or other sources. These focal points in the ontogenetic development of the patient have to be reached, in sound psychotherapy, by regressive catharsis, which differentiates psychotherapy from counseling and guidance.

As a patient, in individual or group treatment, passes through a series of interpersonal and intragroup encounters that gradually and painfully force on him a view of his *real* self in all its nakedness, he slowly reaches the complex of his nuclear problem. Once this is reached, he becomes free from his emotivity, and the reactive compensations and defenses that had interfered with his adaptations and adjustments.

"PHASES" IN GROUP ANALYTIC INTERVIEWS

The sectionalization of the ongoing therapeutic continuum into "initial," "middle," and "terminal phases" is an arbitrary artifice and can cause considerable confusion and misjudgment. Anyone will find it hard to fix the boundaries of the alleged "phases." All such attempts seem to be based on the assumption that the group, as a *unit*, attains uniform levels in therapy. Another assumption is that all members have identical needs and respond at the same rate.

These assumptions are true only to a very limited extent and the exceptions are both numerous and significant. There is no gainsaying that during the initial sessions patients are all prey to group-induced anxiety. They are either wary, cautious and diffi-dent, or hyperassertive and monopolistic, either as a reaction to this anxiety or because of their basic character structure. Resistances will initially be more intense and more in evidence than later in treatment. At this stage, it is also anticipated that most patients will withhold hostilities and conceal negativism, communicate hesitantly, and discuss top realities.

This representation of early group sessions, while generally true, is conditioned by many factors. The following matter, culled from a number of the early interviews of an analytic group consisting of 15- to 16-year-old boys, in residential treatment, will illustrate some of these points.

The early sessions were replete with complaints and "gripes," against real and fantasied injustices by the institution, the teach-ers, and especially, the cottage parents. The boys bitterly com-plained of being sequestered from their homes, reiterating their wishes to be back. This outpouring was accepted and appropri-ately reacted to by the therapist. At the fifth session, the question of the bad treatment they had received at the hands of their cot-tage parents came up again and they related it to their meekness and submissiveness. Many examples of the ill-treatment were of-fered. One patient said that a boy "who was always quiet and did whatever the cottage father wanted him to do suddenly drew a knife and went after the cottage father." After a brief discus-sion (rally), all agreed that "this was not the best way of handling your feelings when you are stepped on." As the discussion pro-ceeded, with all seven group members actively participating, they arrived at the conclusion, without any comment from the thera-pist, that although life at the school was not very pleasant, in the back of their minds they were looking forward to a better life at home and in the communities where they lived; but, they add-ed, "It's not so pleasant there either." And one of the most untractable in the group added, "When I think about being home I exaggerate that things are so nice there, but when I think about it more I know that things are not so hot there either."

At the sixth session, one of the boys, who had recently returned from the "isolation cottage" as punishment for setting fire to the lawn he was put to tidying up, explained that he had done it as a result of his resentment at being put to work unjustly, as punishment by his cottage father. At the following session, when another member of the group spoke of his feelings at being rejected by his natural mother, the first boy said, "That's the way I feel and that was the reason I started the fire we were talking about." He was able to establish a connection between his act and his feelings, which otherwise seemed unrelated.)

At the same session, a boy described the feelings he had had while visiting home for Thanksgiving and Christmas. His father was away on truck delivery jobs (interstate). He had found his (alcoholic) mother "dead drunk" both times and she had remained in a semistupor the entire three days. In addition, she had chased him out of the house, screaming that he was a "no-good s. o. b." One of the other boys empathized with him and said, among other things, "I know how you feel. I worry about my mother, too, because I didn't hear from her for a long time." Three of the other boys expressed similar feelings. (Parenthetically, it may be added that the boy who was rejected by his drunken mother had behaved in a very refractory manner for three weeks, both in and out of the group. In the group he would walk around, disturb other boys, set fire to paper, and at one session verbally attacked and challenged the therapist. He had also indulged in acts that could suggest suicidal attempts.)

During the eighth session, several of the boys related dreams. One boy told of a dream in which his older brother was hurt; another had a recurring dream of two geared wheels which threatened to grind him up; a third had a recurring dream of running down the stairs "taking five steps at a time" (which he interpreted as representing his desire "to be powerful in real life"); a fourth often dreamed that a naked girl was lying next to him.

During the following session, the ninth, the boy who had discussed, at the sixth session, his feelings that led to the fire setting, reported that he had received a letter from his mother (who now lived in a far-off city and had a new set of children). She promised that she would come to see him soon. "I know inside of me," he said, "that this will never happen. She will never see me and I will never really forgive her for what she did to me." (She had abandoned him and two other siblings when he was two years old.)

During a later session, all the boys had talked about masturbation and their fears, guilts, and anxieties concerning it. They also expressed their thoughts regarding menstruation and pregnancies. (One boy's married sister had been pregnant at the time.) The boy whose mother abandoned him, remarked, during the course of the conversation, "Just because we are talking about these things here doesn't mean that we are sexy or have to *do* things. Just talking about it makes you feel comfortable inside." Another member of the group thoughtfully added, "When you understand something you are not afraid. Poking it out and understanding it makes it less frightening."

This series of communications illustrates that these matters do not emerge as isolated, single-statement revelations. It was the consistent freedom in communication and perceptive interpretation by the boys themselves (here omitted as not relevant to our topic) rather early in treatment, that accounts for the group's obvious progress. This occurred in a period which, in terms of time (sixth to ninth sessions), is still the so-called "initial phase," but the content of the productions invalidates this characterization.

The following matter, from the forty-fourth weekly session of a group of women (Chapter X), shows considerably less therapeutic advancement than the boys during their early sessions.

For about the first fifteen minutes, three of the group's six women, who had come to the session ahead of the others, talked about apartments and homes (a problem that had occupied their attention for some time in the past and which was solved by two of them satisfactorily), Open School Week and their visits to their children's classrooms, their children's adjustments to school, and similar top realities.

Mrs. W. arrived at about this time, wearing a scarlet sweater. Mrs. S. commented about it, asking her what color it was and remarking that "it was nice." Mrs. C. said that the color was "electric red" and then added archly, "It's got its points." (This was a reference to a statement, made by Mrs. C. in the preceding session, about Mrs. W.'s rather large breasts, which had embarrassed Mrs. W. very much.) Mrs. W. said laughingly that Mrs. C. is "starting again." All laughed briefly, Mrs. C. adding, "I have my points, too." Whereupon Mrs. W. retorted rather shortly, "Yes, but they're not as pronounced." Mrs. C., again with a smile playing on her face, said, "Well, let's get back to Mrs. G.," who proceeded to talk about moving to a new home.

A pause followed. The therapist (who was male) referred to Mrs. W.'s remark that Mrs. C. "is starting again," and asked Mrs. W. what she thought Mrs. C. was "starting." Mrs. W. replied that Mrs. C. "is starting again with her *pointed* remarks."[4] She then rather angrily criticized Mrs. C. for "always making disparaging or critical remarks about people." She thought that Mrs. C. had a need to always criticize. (Mrs. C. was very aggressive, had a character disorder and strong masculine protest.)

Mrs. C. defended herself against this charge and asked rather calmly (which represented a change in this rather aggressive, short-tempered woman), "What's wrong with injecting a slight sense of humor into these sessions?" Mrs. W. protested that Mrs. C. was not humorous and referred angrily to Mrs. C.'s tendency to "always tell others what to do rather than discussing her own problems," and Mrs. C.'s seeking to "be a big shot." (Mrs. W.'s permitting herself to become angry was a sign of a change in her. She had been very insecure, docile, and placating before treatment in the group.)

A pause followed. The therapist asked the group what was going on between Mrs. C. and Mrs. W.

Mrs. S. recalled that "last time" Mrs. W. had realized that she had compared Mrs. C. with her brother (whom she resented) and that Mrs. W. had, at that time, thought that she was less resent-

---

[4] This was an obvious play on words, referring to the nipples of her breasts.

ful toward Mrs. C. Mrs. W. commented, "Well, last week she (Mrs. C.) wasn't so bitchy; she had tapered off a little." Mrs. C. responded to this by saying that she was "open to criticism," and that, in the past, no one in the group had resented her (which was not the case) and only Mrs. W. resented her now. She added that Mrs. W. must be a person who resents everyone, to which the latter reacted by sarcastically stating that Mrs. C. always had to get the last word in and that she, Mrs. W., would let her have it.

Mrs. S., who appeared to agree with Mrs. W.'s attack, though unwilling to face up to Mrs. C. in open conflict, remarked that she would try to "criticize" Mrs. C. in a "a helpful manner." With obvious sincerity and with less irritation, Mrs. S. stated that, from what Mrs. C. had described in the group, she had received attention as a child only when she was "smart" but had missed out "on the other things such as love and affection." For this reason, Mrs. C. had to keep on "using smartness." During this statement, Mrs. S. pointed out several times that she thought Mrs. C. was smart but "that is not enough; something is lacking there and it alienates people." Mrs. C. seemed to accept this. (This was the first time Mrs. C. had withstood criticism without becoming hostile and vituperative.) Mrs. S. then went on to question Mrs. C. about possible envy of her siblings, but the latter denied it, saying that she was better than they in every way and that there was nothing she could be envious of in her sisters.

The discussion continued in the above vein for a short time, until Mrs. S., in an outwardly pleasant manner and with seeming casualness, remarked that Mrs. B. reminded her of a close friend during her adolescence. (The implication was that Mrs. B. was physically like that friend.) Here Mrs. C., addressing Mrs. B., said somewhat pointedly, "See, you have your *points*, too."

The therapist, sensing that Mrs. S. had wanted to convey more to Mrs. B., said that he was interested in her reasons for saying what she did about Mrs. B.'s resemblance to her friend. Mrs. S. backed down, saying that it was "just a thought," stating that, by coincidence, this friend had called her the other night. However, after a brief pause, she smiled and began talking about this friend, Sally.

With a smile, she commented to the therapist, "You got me talking," and proceeded to recall that her friend had never gotten along with her mother and then said, "There is some similarity there" (to Mrs. B.). Mrs. B. emitted a sharp, hostile laugh and exclaimed, "You're a character!" When Mrs. S. asked, "Why?" Mrs. B., with open resentment, said, "Apparently all you have to do is to go home and think about everyone else's problems." Mrs. S. commented that she must have "struck home," in her remark to Mrs. B., to set off such a strong reaction. Mrs. B. angrily denied that she was angry.

Mrs. S. stated, with conviction and emphasis, that she wondered why Mrs. B. came at all, since she apparently felt that she had no problems and denied that anything said in the group pertained to her or caused her to think.[5] In response, Mrs. B. pointedly remarked that she was too busy taking care of her home, children, and family to think about what happened in the group. She then asked Mrs. S. how her "home relations" had gone during the week. Mrs. S. quickly replied, "Yours should be as good, believe me."[6]

The therapist asked what was going on between Mrs. S. and Mrs. B. He noted that, in the past, Mrs. S. had been open in her strong resentments against her mother and had since suggested that mothers "should be forgiven," but not before Mrs. B.'s strong urging, on many occasions, that Mrs. S. forgive her mother.

Mrs. S. responded by saying that she thought she understood what the therapist was saying. During the preceding week she herself had noticed that she had been acting "quite childishly" in wanting to be "first in everything." For example, in the bakery she had pushed an old woman out of line. She at once tied this up in her mind with the very poor treatment she had received at the hands of her mother and with an incident that had happened several years ago, when her sisters had jointly given her a present of a set of dinnerware, without consulting her as to her prefer-

[5] Mrs. B., too, has a character disorder, with strong masculine identifications, and proved strongly resistive to treatment for a considerable period.
[6] This aggressiveness on Mrs. S.'s part is significant. Mrs. S. is the frightened, masochistic woman with psychogenic eczema (see Chapter X).

ence. Mrs. B. interrupted Mrs. S. and said that Mrs. S., should have taken the dinnerware set from her sisters, without criticizing them. Mrs. S., with great feeling, exclaimed, "Why should I kiss their asses?" Mrs. G. blushed at Mrs. S.'s expletive.

(At one point in this exchange, Mrs. G., who had remained quiet, giggled and said that she was going to go home, implying that she felt left out, since no one was including her in the conversation. This gave us a further clue to the underlying meaning of the argumentation going on in terms of its defense against homoerotic feelings in the group, which were started by the reference to clothes and breasts.)

Mrs. S. continued, in a more subdued manner but on the same intense feeling-level, that she was always "too humble." Close to tears, she described her constant attempts in the past to please people and to show her gratitude to them; for instance, her husband. She realized that as a reaction to all that humility and ingratiation, she had, this week, gone to the other extreme.

Mrs. C., in a supportive way, told Mrs. S. that it was permissible to go off to an extreme for a week. Mrs. C. added that she, too, would have resented the dinnerware, if it were given with no regard for her own taste or the other furnishings of her home. (This conciliatory move on Mrs. C.'s part was quite surprising in the light of her usual aggressive conduct and general hostility.) Mrs. B., however, maintained that Mrs. S. was making "too much of the whole thing."

Mrs. S. again referred to her past need to humble herself because of the way her mother had treated her. Mrs. B. continued to maintain that Mrs. S. was making too much of the situation and should have just said to her sisters, "Thank you." This prompted Mrs. W. to remark sarcastically to Mrs. B., "You're the good will ambassador, aren't you?" Mrs. B. appeared to miss the sarcasm and, instead, took this as a compliment and said, in a somewhat pleased manner, that she was generally "not bothered by such things." She went on to deny envy of her sisters, referring specifically to the fact that her younger sister sometimes received better gifts from her mother than she did. She denied feeling jealous about this and proceeded to say that perhaps, in some ways, she had more than her sisters. For instance, she had one child more than her sister had, and perhaps she was loved by her husband more than her sister was loved by hers. (This is a telling example of Mrs. B.'s resistance to treatment, which we have found to be a "character resistance." She is an inordinately hostile woman.)

The conversation lapsed and the therapist asked Mrs. S. about her current understanding of her own reactions to Mrs. B. Mrs. S. responded with the statement that she felt she understood them more clearly now. She explained that Sally (of whom Mrs. B. reminded her), was someone before whom she had always humbled herself, because she did not feel "worthwhile." In addition, Sally was small and pretty, like Mrs. B., whereas she was "tall and unattractive." (Mrs. S. is a tall, lanky, ungainly, physically unattractive woman.) Mrs. S. guessed that Mrs. B., by reminding her of Sally, had suddenly reminded her of all these feelings within herself, which had made her unhappy, and that it made her angry to remember how humble she used to feel toward people.[7]

If we take into consideration the length of treatment, the contrast is striking between the quality of the communications and interpersonal reactions in the boy's group during their sixth to ninth sessions and the women's group during their forty-fourth session. This difference clearly demonstrates the arbitrariness of dividing group treatment interviews into *distinct* initial, middle, and final phases. Unlike the women, the boys were homogeneous: they were all in the same stage of adolescence, were in similar difficulties and the same situation, lived in the same community, had seen each other frequently, had quasi-friendly relations, and, in addition, felt that their status and relationships would not suffer through their disclosures.

---

[7] It may be of interest to note that all the women in this group, except Mrs. C., were eventually either planfully discharged from treatment or moved away from the city. Mrs. C., who proved the most inaccessible of the patients in the group, was continued in another group. She remarked to the therapist, after more than four years in treatment, "Only now am I beginning to be aware of the other women in the group. Up to now they did not seem to exist for me." For her, the so-called "initial phase" continued for more than four years.

It is important for the analytic group therapist to view group interviews as a *progressively expanding,* flexible, and increasingly deepening process that occurs in fluctuating sequences, at different rates and frequencies in different groups and at different stages. Even the most convinced proponents of the phases theory describe them as "arbitrary assumptions" and "over-simplifications." Furthermore, what is expected in one "stage," as characteristic of it, may not occur in that stage, but may appear in another, because of the presence, in the group, of patients of specific types or characters.

An episode illustrating the risk of fixing definite phases in group or any other type of treatment, is supplied by the case of Dorothy (in the young adult group cited in the preceding chapter). This was a young woman who had been very promiscuous and had become pregnant when 19 years old. She had entered individual treatment at 21 years of age, after the adoption of her little daughter. She resisted by absenting herself very frequently from interviews (she had come only eight times in six months), denying the existence of any problem, and speaking only about her current boyfriends, when she did come. Two different diagnoses were obtained on this patient. One considered her promiscuity as "a need to receive mothering and to mother," which was satisfied through the sexual act. The other, suggested by the present writer, was that her sexual indulgence with numerous men was due to her basically homosexual character. The unconscious aim of her activity was to incorporate the penis of the men with whom she cohabited. This was seen as a result of identification with her father, who had died when Dorothy was 16 years old, and whom she had held in great regard. She resented her mother, a dependent and demanding woman, who gave no support to her daughter.

In the 106th group session, she became aware of her basic denial of masculinity in men and verbalized it in relation to her husband. She made him into a "neuter" and "more like a woman," but still denied that she wanted his penis for herself, when that was suggested by a fellow patient. Rather, she associated this with her physical attraction for her mother (not love) and said that the "love" of a woman was more important to her than that of a man. (It must be noted that she had slept with her mother after her father's death and before she left home to live in another state.)

Although the group was nearing termination, since it was felt that it had accomplished all it could for the six young women, Dorothy had really just entered treatment. She had arrived at the so-called "initial phase" at the group's 106th session, while the other members were in its so-called "final phase." This situation also demonstrates that a massive psychoneurosis, of a transference nature, cannot be resolved in a group. As we had suggested at the "intake conference," Dorothy would require a thoroughgoing psychoanalysis, but she was, at that time, not suffiiciently motivated for it. The group did help her to bring her problem into relief and strengthened her sufficiently so that she could bring it to awareness, readying her for individual treatment, which she then sought out.

Factors Affecting "Phases"

There is very little doubt that the "style" the therapist employs in dealing wth a group, his insight and skills, and the status and role he assumes, fundamentally affect the nature, content, and rapidity of the productions in a group, and activate those characteristics that are now attributed to "phases." Thus, an active therapist accelerates or may even skip the so-called "initial phase." Through his own enthusiasm and charismatic or catalytic effect on the group, he may, in a few sessions, bring the group to the stage which should belong to the "middle phase." On the other hand, another therapist, who, either by temperament or plan, remains passive and withdrawn or fails to respond appropriately to "signals" given by patients would extend the "initial phase." The following incident is an illustration of the latter.

At the seventh session of a group of adolescent boys, about 15 years of age, one boy asked why, when being "yelled" at, he had to impulsively stop whatever he was doing. He could not go on. This caused him much trouble with his teachers. He narrated this with much feeling, striking the table with his fist as he spoke. "What can I do about it?" he pleaded.

Because the group was engaged in speaking of superficialities, the boy's introducing a subject involving such strong affect, offered the possibility of turning the interviews into therapeutically productive channels. Instead, the therapist responded by saying, "Are you telling us that you want to get back at your teacher for yelling at you?" (The boy had related his reaction to a specific occurrence in his classroom.) The therapist then proceeded to explain that the boy may have been angry at the teacher, or at someone else of whom the teacher had reminded him. The boy immediately tied this up with his reactions to his father's dictatorial and unkind treatment of him.

However, had the therapist explained the boy's block as a resolution of his internal rage and his fear of acting on it, which resulted in immobilization, the boy and the group might have been led into uncovering, expressing, and understanding deeply repressed feelings, and into self-analysis and exploration of their intrapsychic processes. As a result, the so-called "initial phase" would have been shortened with damage to the orderly unfoldment of the treatment.

A group of homogeneous patients might shorten the period of self-consciousness, wariness, distrust, fear, and shyness, thereby entering a more advanced, so-called, "phase" much sooner than would patients who have little in common with one another. For example, prisoners in the same block of cells, patients from the same ward, or patients with similar symptomology in outpatient treatment, find it easier to communicate with one another. The characteristic diffidence which strangers feel in the presence of one another is lessened under these conditions. In the case of institutional patients, the inevitable complaints, dissatisfactions, and common negative feelings, bring them more easily into communication with one another. Through skillful direction by the therapist these "gripes" can be transmuted into therapeutic cathartic communication and into conscious and rational investigation of past and present attitudes and behavior that are of therapeutic value. Thus the "initial phase" may not appear at all and patients may begin from a point attributed to later phases.

Patients who suffer from the same type of somatic symptoms such as asthma, headaches, and gastro-intestinal disturbances, find, from the very start, subjects for conversation that set them off into therapeutic communication and interchange.

Even more serious misgivings appear in regard to the "terminal phase." Not all patients reach the identical level of improvement and are ready for discharge from therapy at the same time. Progress is achieved at different rates by different individual members of a group. Therefore, while some may be ready for "closing," others may still be far behind. Occasionally, one meets a patient, such as Mrs. C., who is still in the so-called "initial phase" after years of treatment. Therefore, to assume that there is a "terminal phase," *for a group as such,* is not in consonance with therapeutic realities. The terminal or closing phase is purely an individual matter; groups can seldom be terminated as a unit. Some patients can be closed, while others require further treatment either individually or in another group.

One must also be on guard against the onset of regressive response to therapy, at the point of its termination, when patients frequently present a façade of helplessness, dependence, and tension, similar to that displayed at the initiation of treatment. Through this, some seek to induce the therapist to continue the group, while others are informing him that he did not accomplish his task of "curing" them, just as their parents failed, in the past, to make them healthy. This resistance and negative transference has to be brought into the open and worked through. These reactions can be ignored in patients who will continue in treatment. But those who are ready for discharge may require special attention, sometimes even on an individual basis.

The "Auxiliary Therapist" Fallacy

The term "auxiliary therapist" has been introduced, to describe the patients who most frequently enter into rallies with their fellow patients, and, by their questions and explanations, assume a role analogous to that of a therapist, activating fellow patients and, quite often, helping to clarify ideas and feelings. Such patients do serve in a helpful manner, but it is both erroneous and misleading to apply the term "therapist" to them, even when qualified by the adjective "auxiliary." A therapist is one who has had specialized training and conducts himself in a calculated and thoughtful manner, in accordance with therapeutic indications based on established clinical diagnoses and valid practices. Obviously, patients who do not have the training and qualifications are acting on impulse rather than discrimination and are impelled by subjective urges rather than therapeutic judgments. As a result, they frequently conduct themselves in a manner detrimental to their fellow patients. Even if they happen to make appropriate statements and keep interviews going, they still cannot be classified as "therapists." The term "therapist" connotes a *specific* transference role (parental), which patients assign to him and which they cannot allot to a fellow patient who is a sibling substitute. Status is another element militating against patients assuming the role of therapists. This subject will be further elaborated in our discussion of the therapist (Chapter XIII).

STEREOTYPY

In the course of group interviews, the group will return to a subject over and over again, because it is of great concern and needs working through. However, when this continues for an inordinately long time and is repeated with great frequency, the phenomenon of *stereotypy* sets in, forming a plateau, which is monotonous and frustrating to both patients and therapist. Under such circumstances, it behooves the therapist to re-examine the personnel of the group, the course of past interviews, the topic around which stereotypy has arisen, the adequacy of his role, and the state of the group's resistances.

A stereotype may be repeatedly reintroduced by a compulsive-obsessional or hypochondriacal patient who is impelled to dwell on the particular point of his fixation. Patients suffering from psychic masochism, who derive vicarious satisfaction from dwelling on their suffering and mistreatment, block progress in a group interview, either through actual sympathy or because this supports the other patients' natural resistance to involving themselves in treatment. (Mrs. S., is a good illustration of this mechanism.) The patients who, due to intense oral dependence or more serious pathology, seek sympathy or need to arouse pity, also draw all discussions into channels of their own design.

When such personality determinants are not present, the therapist must attempt to trace the cause through the content and context of previous interviews: what remained unanswered that has special significance to some, or all of the patients? A therapy group, like an individual patient, can become "fixed" at a point of anxiety which has to be worked through. By some mischance, due to the vagaries of the group or oversight by the therapist, a problem of significance, charged with intense affect, may not have been resolved and the group becomes fixed at that point. Unfortunately, this may not always be easy to trace, since the problem source may be disguised or a related question may become the source of the group's block. Tracing the specific stereotype back through the sequences of former interviews gives the therapist the key to the difficulty.

Frequently, the stereotype is a subject or feeling on which insufficient light was thrown when it first arose. It is essential that the group return to the subject so as to eliminate the block to ongoing communication. Stereotypy can be considered as a form of complaint against the therapist's oversight and a demand for emotional or intellectual clarification. The significance of the topic to the members of the group has to be evaluated and its economy in the anxiety provoking situation understood by both therapist and patients, either through free association or by catharsis directed by the therapist. Therapists can induce stereotypes through their attitudes, unsuitable conduct, authoritarianism and personal preferences, all of which can prevent the flow of free association. A therapist with a "blind spot" or preoccupation with a personal problem or theoretical principle may induce stereotypes in his patients and check their communications. In many such instances, further personal psychoanalysis for the therapist may be indicated.

Most often, there are two main reasons for the appearance of stereotypes in a group. First, they serve as a signal that a topic has not been adequately clarified or a conflict adequately resolved. Second, they act as a means of resistance to treatment or to the therapist, or to both. When this is the case, an analysis of the group resistance will remedy the situation. The group's attention is called to the resistance when it is freely discussed, bringing to the surface the emotional attitudes behind it, which usually would include negative feelings toward the therapist. This will usually break the resistive wall that a group presents through stereotypy.

SILENCES

In our discussion of nodal and antinodal periodicity in groups, reasons for the phenomena were attributed to mounting anxiety, fatigue, and the need for relaxation and re-establishment of homeostasis. These elements are also discernible in the silences of therapy group interviews, but only to a slight extent. Silences in therapy groups actually have more significant meanings, in the light of the total therapeutic process.

Silences in therapy groups can be individual or of the entire group, and maybe general or selective. Both individuals and groups can resort to silence for long periods or do so only on certain occasions and briefly. Emotional, as well as intellectual, factors play a role in these phenomena.

General Individual Silences

General individual silences stem from fear, anxiety, psychoneurotic sources or have characterological determinants. Early family and peer group experiences of a repressive, inhibitive, or retro-grading nature have the effect of rendering a person cautious and nonassertive, so that he anticipates negative and rejective treatment at the hands of groupmates. Group-induced anxiety, as a result of excessive and prolonged tensions in the early home, may be ingrained (engrammatic) and automatically evoked by the compresence of a number of persons, causing one to withdraw, as a defensive and preventive measure. Another neurotic source of silence may be anality, where the child, as a measure of defiance or retaliation toward the mother, retained the feces. Later in life, this mechanism of retention is displaced "from below to above." Generalized silence in individuals can also stem from what we describe elsewhere as *catatonic defense;* that is, as a defensive weapon against assailment from, or overinvolvement with (usually) one's family or family members. Finally, generalized or frequent silences may be normal reactions in persons with schizoid character structures and specific temperaments and constitutions.

Selective Individual Silences

Among the causes of selective individual silences are topics of discussion which have no appeal or with which the individual is unconcerned; topics that, at the time, arouse excessive anxiety in one (as in the case of threat areas); fear of or unreadiness for revelation; resentment or anger against a fellow patient or the therapist; and general resistance to therapy. The last two motives fall within the category of "acting out."

General Group Silences

General group silences are most frequent in the early stages of treatment and are, with some exceptions, manifestations of resistances. In the early interviews, group induced anxiety acts as a deterrent to communication. A factor is the "psychological illiteracy" of new group members. As the sessions progress, "illiteracy" is gradually lifted. When this occurs, the flow of communication is facilitated and the incidence of silence diminished. Silences caused by "psychological illiteracy" are prevented or greatly reduced by the presence of patients who have had prior individual treatment. They communicate more freely and abundantly and act as *instigators* or catalytic agents, setting off the others in the group.

In selecting patients for placement in a specific group, the therapist who structures it should consider the potentials of some patients as instigators or seek out a few who could act in this capacity, so that the group will not flounder and ultimately disband. Group general silences that persist long into treatment can be traced to two sources: grouping and the therapist's personality and functions. There may be a lack of instigators, too great a personality and pathology diversity to attain the minimal empathic level for commonality, or individual members with an intolerable quantum of hostility that immobilizes the group. The therapist and his countertransference attitudes and acts may be of even greater damage to catharsis.

Selective Group Silences

Selective group silences are responses to specific situations that occur in groups. Some such silences are deleterious to therapeutic effort while others are salutary. As in the case of generalized silences, the selective silences may be the result of the therapist's transient countertransference reactions that set up a negative group phalanx with which the therapist can deal with relative ease. A group may also go into temporary silence as the result of a strong emotion that affects all the members, such as shock, pity, sympathy, or anxiety. It may also be caused by the group's unreadiness to deal with a particular problem or idea. Temporary silences of a salutary nature can set in when a deeply affecting event occurs in the group, such as an appropriate, well-timed interpretation of an affect-laden syndrome, or an enlightening clarification of a significant feeling or idea, to which the patients respond intensely by entering into a period of cogitation and self-confrontation (intrapsychic encounter) under the stimulation of the proceedings. Selective group silence, as all other silences, can also be a form of resistance and acting out.[8]

MONOPOLISM

Phenomenology

The term "monopolizer" is applied to a patient who consistently pre-empts to himself an incommensurate amount of the time al-

---

[8] Methods of dealing with the various types of silence are described in Chapters XII and XIII.

lotted for the group interview, depriving other members of adequate participation. This mechanism, on the part of one member, proves frustrating to all the others. The effect of monopolism is a general group "letdown," as other members are forced into spectator roles and are blocked in their therapy. Some patients, however, are relieved, as the monopolism plays into their resistance, for they are thus spared the effort and discomfort of communicating their difficulties and exposing themselves.

Monopolizing can take several forms. In one instance, the monopolizer may engage in prolonged recitals of mostly irrelevant content (possibly relating some autobiographical material) not really intended to evoke reactions from his hearers. Rather, his rapidity and the freely flowing verbosity are meant to hold the attention of the group, the orator deriving thereby the satisfactions he needs at the moment. There are monopolizers who give their hearers no opportunity to break into their monologues. Some monopolizers permit brief participation from others, but are careful to retain the group's attention, warding off all digressions or changes of subject. Usually, a true monopolizer is not aware of his role or the effect it has on his fellow group members; some may have a very vague awareness, but not enough to retreat in favor of others who may make a bid to be heard.

Another type of monopolizer is one that, though he does not hold the floor continuously, constantly and repeatedly interrupts the recitals of other patients, preventing them from a full and orderly statement of their communication. This subspecies of the monopolizer may be described as the *interrupter,* who, by this strategy, succeeds in deflecting the attention of the group from the current speaker to himself. The reaction of the group to an interrupter is one of annoyance and resentment, but for obvious reasons, his current victim suffers the most and, depending on his ego functioning, may terminate his recital or he may react with violence of varying intensity. The latter reaction, in which others may join, frequently has a corrective effect on the interrupter in certain categories (the behavior and character disorders) but are of doubtful value where the impulse to interrupt proceeds from neurotic sources.

Causation

The urge to monopolize may stem, as already suggested, from neurotic states or from character and behavior conditioning.

In neurotic monopolizers, the most common motivation is to allay anxiety. The tendency of the psycho-organism to transmute psychic tensions into motoric expression takes the form of speech in some. By occupying himself with his monologue, the speaker wards off the onset of the anxiety with which his psyche is filled. This mechanism is characteristic of compulsion neuroses, and takes the form of speech in a group monopolizer.

Another type of neurotic monopolism stems from oral dependence. Through incessant speech, the patient attaches himself to his hearers just as he once attempted, unsuccessfully and unsatisfactorily, to attach himself to mother's breast. Through this vicarious attachment, his fears about separation and being on his own are allayed. Some patients equate the stream of free-flowing, continuous speech to the free-flowing stream of urine. Here, as in the case of silence, the mechanism of "displacement from below to above" operates.

Exhibitionism and primary narcissism are other motives, while the punitive motive activates still other monopolizers, for by frustrating his fellow group members, a patient may act out his unconscious need to hurt or punish his substitute siblings, thus reliving the experiences of his first family.

The psychic masochist may use monopolism as an instrument for provoking group aggressions against himself. Somatic and emotional hypochondriacs dwell on their physical symptoms and emotional suffering.

The reason why hypochondriac patients are unsuitable for group psychotherapy, in addition to the fact that this syndrome cannot be corrected by it, is that they monopolize the group interviews. Their narcissistic preoccupations with symptoms impel them to dwell compulsively on themselves *ad nauseum*, disconcerting the others in the group. Similarly, the patient who is immersed in his own emotional suffering, despair, and depression engages in repetitive recitals of his "troubles," either as ventilation of his feelings, an appeal for pity or help, or to attain narcissistic gratifications.

The character sources of the monopolistic drive emanate from primitive orality and oral aggression. Behavioral monopolization is a continuation of earlier conditioning and results from circumstances which necessitated excessive speaking in attaining and maintaining status and in establishing relations. It can also be derived from identification with, and imitation, of loquacious parents, with oral characters.

Treatment Indications

As with all pathology, neurotic monopolism can be eliminated only through dissolution of the neurotic source in the psyche and not by directly dealing with the manifestation. The latter approach can be effective, in cases of character and behavioral monopolism through and by the group and by the therapist. Other techniques for dealing with this pattern of resistance and acting out are described in the next chapter. Most often monopolizers are found not viable in groups because of the tensions they set up in the other patients.

Basic Characteristics of Analytic Group Therapy Interviews

Group therapy interviews can be classified as transilient, dispersed, and focused.

Transilience

An interview is transilient when the subjects brought forth by members of the group are fleeting and rapidly changed, following the group members' impulsivity and resistances. Directions and interest are not sustained and do not follow a relational sequence or have organic unity. This type of conversation is inevitable in early interviews, due to group induced anxiety, and the discomfort in the participants. However, even during these early stages, it is inadvisable to allow entire interviews to pass in meaningless and desultory talk, because the patients may gain a perverse impression of the group's objective and continue unfruitful pursuits, until they lose interest and drop out.

Having initially stated the objective and *modus operandi* of the group, the therapist should feel free to call attention to the contrast between the proceedings and the stated aims (in a manner that will not label him a dictator or task master). From the very outset, patients must be convinced both of their status as free agents and the therapist's acceptance of them; but they must also become aware of their conduct. At all stages of group treatment, periods of transilience set in, even during valid and serious communication as part of resistance phenomena, mounting tensions, "emotional fatigue" and strain. These phases may be compared to "coffee breaks" for workers; they are rest periods, as it were, and are part of the nodal-antinodal phenomenon. As such, they are valuable and should be accepted by the therapist.

Dispersal

The dispersed character of interviews is manifested when communications by the group members are centered and have a common thread, but the individual contributions are variegated and disjointed, not aimed toward clarification of the question or feeling at hand. Perhaps a colloquialism would describe it best: "They spread themselves all over the lot." This, too, is usually a reaction to anxiety and resistance; the patients are either afraid or unwilling to get to the heart of a matter that would expose them or cause them narcissistic injury. In dealing with this phenomenon, the therapist may interpret it as resistance and act accordingly, or he may step in and guide the discussion toward the central focus (see also Chapter XIII).

Focusing

Focused interviews are those in which the group as a whole, or a substantial sector of it, are wrestling with a specific feeling, problem, or theme and are directing their attention and communication toward it. This type of interview is likely to cause considerable emotional drain and fatigue, but is the most therapeutically constructive. It appears more frequently as treatment progresses and the patients grow less defensive, more comfortable with each other, and more involved in therapy. The elements that constitute a focused interview are: a definite theme, frequent rallies around the theme, and meaningful interpersonal encounters among the patients.

During a given session, all three types of interview will usually manifest themselves with varying frequencies and duration. For example, during the warm-up period and at the beginning of a session some transilience or diffusion is likely to occur, until a theme is struck that engages the interest of the group. After a theme has been considered for some time, transilience and diffusion can still make their appearance, as a result of fatigue, resistance, or oversaturation with the theme. The therapeutically valuable interviews are those during which substantial time is devoted to a common theme. In a maximally operative group, themes are frequently carried over from one interview to another.

THERAPIST-INDUCED RESISTANCES

The therapist's conduct and attitudes may block a group's productivity and vitiate the therapeutic effort. Conduct and attitudes like the countertransferential manifestations of emotional "blind spots," narcissistic preoccupations, over-cathected subjects and feelings, preoccupation with a specific subject preventing free-floating attention, lack of adequate empathic personality quality, failure to perceive latent content in the patients' productions, badly timed explanations and interpretations, the invading of patients' threat areas prematurely, conveying feelings of preference for some patients, and displaying irascibility, impatience or anger.[9]

---

[9] For a fuller discussion of this topic see "Countertransference," Chapter XIII.

XII

The Analytic Group Psychotherapy Interview: Regression and Acting Out

Attitudes Toward Acting Out

Many psychotherapists have a tendency to look askance at acting out; it is considered a deterrent to psychotherapy with adults and adolescents. The term "acting out" automatically evokes, in their minds, a negative, resistive attitude in the patient, who may be, as a result, difficult to reach.

In ordinary life, the acting out of feelings is taboo, especially among the more educated and cultured; those who indulge in it are looked upon with suspicion and are frequently excluded from their social set. This stems from the anxiety aroused, in those who witness acting out, because of their fear of reacting in a similar manner and revealing their own weaknesses and inadequacy in ego controls. Anxiety is also aroused by the manifest irrational elements in the acting out behavior and fear as to its direction and result. Acting out also re-activates fears and discomfort suffered in childhood, in consequence of some acting out adults who screamed, quarreled or punished. Even the acting out of self-pity, despair, and suffering, which should arouse sympathy, causes irritability and annoyance in most spectators, since it mirrors their own weakness.

There is also an element of guilt in the spectator, because he is not in the same plight as the subject and because he feels he should help but is unable, or unwilling, to do so.

Acting out by adults is commonly considered an indication of inadequate personality integration and low ego strength, and those who indulge in it are regarded as unreliable and untrustworthy. The intolerance that our culture fosters toward character weakness and aggression is a source of much of man's mental unhealth. Society's disapproval and proscriptions cause psycho-organic disequilibrium and anxiety.

Where sublimations have not been adequately established—and it would be impossible to do this completely for all man's aggressive impulses—a health-engendering society and tolerant human relations, based on understanding and emotional flexibility, would permit a degree of acting out. Man's basic fear of anothers' ego functioning and unconscious destructive urges make such permissiveness difficult. Acceptance of aggressive acting out is conditioned by acceptance of one's own aggressions and by the security of one's own controls over them. Individuals who are uncertain as to their capacity to deal with their own aggressions (which is, in varying degrees, almost universal), fear the discharge of aggression in others. They ascribe (project) their own incapacity and weakness to them. To remain unperturbed in the presence of anger, vituperation, and destructive acts, requires a great deal of inner security and an understanding of oneself and others. These are rare attributes. A condemning attitude toward the discharge of inner stress through aggression, and the ego inadequacy it reveals, obviously cannot be acceptable in a psychotherapist.

THE PHENOMENOLOGY OF ACTING OUT

Acting out can take many forms. When a patient raises his voice in anger, grows red or pale in the face, clenches his fists, tenses his body—he is, in the strict sense of the term, acting out. More commonly recognized forms of acting out, however, are the situations in which a patient threatens to, or actually does, cause bodily harm either to a fellow patient or to the therapist; throws

371

objects; screams in anger; walks up and down the room; or smokes compulsively. Acting out also includes the patient's provoking the therapist to anger; his verbally attacking the therapist or another member of the group; his manifestations of dependence on the group, any of its members or the therapist; or when he attaches himself to the therapist or a fellow patient as a parental figure, a sexual object, a rival or a target for hostility. In addition, acting out includes any form of direct physical or sexual contact or efforts at seduction; manifest expressions of jealousy, rivalry, and monopolism; evident attempts to get pity and sympathy, protection and help; and extra-group socialization with fellow group members.

In other words, acting out by adults can be considered all acts and behavior, in a therapeutic setting, other than verbal communication.[1] Even verbalization can be acting out when employed to convey anger, spite, hostility, attack, teasing, etc. As already indicated, some types of silence, too, are a form of acting out.

To prohibit acting out would place the therapist in a position of authority and set up barriers between him and the patients. Instead of prohibition, the therapist must utilize acting out as a channel to the patient's unconscious and a link to his childhood memories, character disorder, or neurotic tensions. The patient is encouraged to reveal his feelings, thoughts, conflicts, and confusions in the present, so that the relation between them and earlier stages in his development, from which they flow, may be manifested. It is only through this connection, which the patient has to recognize and accept, that therapeutic insight and emotional maturity can be achieved.

Acting out can occur within the therapeutic setting itself or outside it,[2] where the patient indulges his narcissistic needs and

---

[1] In its wider sense, acting out can be defined as all forms of conduct in opposition to the rule, in the type of therapy in which a patient is engaged. Thus, in psychoanalytic therapy, which relies on verbalization, all physical behavior is considered acting out. Conversely, in activity or play therapy which children, refraining from motility would be acting out.

[2] This is analogous to the behavior of some child patients who conform in the home and family, but present problems and maladjustments out of the home—at school, with playmates, and with neighbors.

does not have to examine them and work them through with a therapist or a group. This acting out we describe as *ex situ,* as differentiated from acting out *in situ,* in the group.

ACTING OUT AND REGRESSION

Acting out by adults is always a sign of regression and a weak ego. Through it, the individual reverts to an earlier pattern of response to inner tensions and stressful situations or relations. It is, therefore, a mirror of the individual's ontogenetic experiences. For this reason, it takes different forms and is used under different conditions and circumstances by different people, both in therapy and everyday life. As he acts out, the individual re-enacts past responses stored in his memory, or he reverts to the use of a technique that proved effective in the past. Some of the responses are retained in organic conditioned reflexes as engrams; others in psychological memory.[3] Regression, as it relates to psychotherapy, can be *therapeutic, pathologic, parapathologic, induced, or normal.*

Therapeutic Regression

Therapeutic regression is a return to past feelings and behavior which includes a retracing of the steps in the development and organization of the individual's psyche, through a transference relation to the therapist (as a parent substitute) and to fellow patients (as replicas of siblings and other important persons in his life). Through understanding transference reactions and evolving insights, decathexis of objects, and the dissolution of defenses, the patient makes his way toward emotional maturity, personality reintegration, and toward more appropriate ways of dealing with life situations. In this type of regression, the ego of the patient remains structurally intact; only emotional elements and blockages are involved. The patient speaks about, or acts out, his feelings and works through his defenses and compulsions.

---

[3] It would probably be very difficult to establish the point at which organic reflexes end and psychological memory begins.

Pathologic Regression

In pathologic regression, the ego goes through a process of disintegration. The patient returns to earlier phases in his development not only affectively, but actually. The reality sense and reality perception (not testing) become not only *as if* but *as* that of the past. This process occurs in psychotic or organic deterioration, when the patient returns to earlier, infantile stages in his ego and libido development; the defenses and repressions are given up.

Parapathologic Regression

Parapathologic regression lies between the modalities of pathologic and therapeutic regression. This is the borderline of regressive movement, in which the ego does not become disintegrated or fragmented, but behavior and reactions do exceed the limits of either normal or therapeutic regression. Diurnal (and, to some extent, nocturnal) enuresis, encopresis, stealing, excessive masturbation, sex perversions, and other activities of this nature, indicate disorganization and dislocation, in the instinctual life of the individual, without psychoses, and can be classified as parapathologic regression.

Induced Regression

Induced regression is stimulated in one person by another, through the dynamics of induction, contagion, and identification. In therapy groups, induced regression occurs very frequently, because of the patients' weak ego development and high level of identification; and since acting out is directed, overtly and covertly, against the therapist, the latent hostile feelings toward authority are easily stirred up.

TYPES OF ACTING OUT

Being one form of regression, acting out, too, can be classified as therapeutic, pathologic, parapathologic, and induced. To these, should be added counterphobic acting out and normal acting out.

Acting out is an essential safety valve for man and has to be permitted and encouraged. The normality of acting out is determined by the strength of ego controls, the reality of the stimulus, the appropriateness and intensity of the response, the speed of recovery, and its effect on other people. The phenomenology of acting out is related to three dynamic elements: the ontogenetic experiences of the individual, the intensity of the stimulus, and the capacity of the ego to deal with stimuli.

Ideally, an individual should have ego resources adequate to deal with any demand or stress in his life setting. Of course, no one does, but the well-integrated person, though he may be unable or unwilling to expose himself to noxious external demands and pressures, is able to control his affect and impulses so as not to create undue tensions and unpleasantness. Where an individual overreacts, to the detriment of himself and others, he reveals inadequacies in the development of the ego and its inhibitive powers. Acting out, therefore, can be viewed as the id impulses overpowering the ego. Such impulsiveness is permissible in children, in whom ego development is still incomplete. In the therapy of acting-out adult patients, two aims have to be kept in mind: affect diminution (decathexis) and ego strengthening. (For my theory of ego and its correction, see Slavson, 1952a, pages 16-20, 45-53.)

Therapeutic Acting Out

In therapeutic acting out, as in therapeutic regression, the ego structure remains intact, its controls are not impaired (even though their strength is temporarily diminished), and the capacity to restore equilibrium internally, and in relation to the environment, is preserved. Given enough time, the patient would bring himself under control without outside aid. This form of acting out is made therapeutic through the skill of the therapist, and the responsiveness of other members in a group.

Acting out occurs more violently in a therapeutic situation, than under ordinary circumstances, because of transference reactions, which are always charged with intense affect, especially when feelings toward earlier important figures in one's life are stirred up. Also, in therapy, the ego defenses are threatened and the patient's established controls are undermined, which results in free-floating anxiety and hostility. Because of the transference reactions, the patient's libido is stirred up, adding to the load of his ego. Unless the ego is strong enough to deal with such added demands, it gives way to the id, and discharge of feeling takes place, much like water flooding over a dam. The therapist must be aware of the limitations of his patients' ego strengths and must prevent ego overload, which could result in withdrawal from treatment, excessive disturbance and, in extreme cases, in violence or a transient psychotic episode.

Pathologic Acting Out

In pathologic acting out, restoration of equilibrium cannot be achieved by the patient himself, without drugs, direct restraint, or some other form of therapeutic intervention. Since the ego is impaired and withdrawn from reality, external measures become necessary.

Parapathologic Acting Out

In parapathologic acting out, external measures, though less drastic, are also necessary. The narcissistic and (usually) pleasure-yielding nature of this type of indulgence, frequently makes it difficult for the ego and the rational segment of the psyche to assert themselves. The gratifications resulting from the narcissistic and biological pleasures are too strong; they silence selectivity and placate the superego; the ego is bribed, as it were. The dynamic process is similar to the dynamic process in addiction, where the ego gives way to the anticipated pleasure of diminished responsibility to control and inhibit. For example, sexual acting out, on the part of patients, needs to be prohibited in therapy and the *impulse* needs to be considered therapeutically in the treatment interviews, for the impulse is more accessible to analysis when it remains ungratified than when the tensions are eliminated through fulfillment. Similarly, addicts in psychotherapy are prohibited from indulging, even though they usually transgress the instructions. The very fact of yielding to the impulse against the therapist's or the group's wishes offers more fruitful therapeutic possibilities than does gratification without an awareness of disapproval.

On a larger scale, war and murder are parapathologic forms of acting out of primitive, animalistic drives that are often reactions to real or fantasied threat to one's biological or psychological survival. Unusual proneness to physical fights is a form of acting out of primitive emotions, where early patterning of the personality has not achieved sufficient sublimational modes of expression or adequate repression and control by the ego.

Induced Acting Out

Induced acting out appears for the same reasons as induced regression. Induced regression and acting out have minimal therapeutic value, since they are not related to nor do they stem from the intrapsychic tensions or nuclear problems of each of the group participants. Acting out, being a part of the cathartic process, has its greatest value insofar as it uncovers the source of the patient's nuclear problems.

Counterphobic Acting Out

Counterphobic feelings are another source of acting out of the preconscious and unconscious fears and anxieties with which the ego is unable to deal and which form part of the defensive system of a patient. The acting out of patients with neurotic characters ["anxiety characters" (E. Jones)] is not accessible to ordinary psychotherapy. In most instances, the phobic trends cannot be traced to their sources and a thoroughgoing psychoanalysis becomes necessary. However, it should be pointed out that counterphobic reactions and behavior exist in everyday life, in all persons, and are a normal part of human functioning; they constitute a problem only when they are of unusual quality and intensity and impede affective function and adjustment. Although aware of the presence of counterphobic states in patients, the psychotherapist need not deal with them directly in the group interviews, for they will be sloughed off or automatically corrected as a by-product of ego strengthening, improved self-image, and general reduction of the various neurotic elements in the personality.

Normal Acting Out

Acting out is the transmutation of emotional tensions into physical expression that can stem from congenital temperamental dispositions, organic imbalance, psychogenic stress, or inadequate ego controls of impulses. Transmutation of emotional tension into physical activity and motility involves the ego as well as the soma. It is a borderline phenomenon. As already stated, a degree of acting out may be essential for a given individual because his constitutional and organic structure require release through physical expression. When opportunity for such discharge is blocked, serious disturbances in the psycho-organism may occur. However, when the acting out exceeds the limits of comfort to others, is uncontrollable, or too violent, it has to be dealt with by persons other than the subject himself.

FUNCTIONS OF ACTING OUT

As a Release

Acting out serves as a release from organic tensions, pent-up emotions, and sudden upsurges of feeling, that overdrain ego strengths. As such, it is an important "regulator" of the organism, for it has, as its aim, the establishment of psycho-organic equilibrium. Its effect in ordinary life, however, may be negative in so far as it meets with social disapproval and the subject reacts with guilt and shame, because of this disapproval of his behavior. *In psychotherapy, whether individual or group, acting out, within specified limits, is accepted and even encouraged.*

As Abreaction

Closely associated to the release function of acting out, is its expression of abreactions to stressful situations in life and to the productions, behavior, and personalities in a group. The need for release stems from the internal stress with which patients come to therapeutic sessions. However, events and personalities in the group frequently set off intense feelings of anxiety, anger, and resentment. Patients whose ego strengths do not measure up to these strains discharge their feelings in some form of observable

378

behavior, such as excessive and rapid verbalization, anger, attack on other patients, leaving the room, withdrawal, silence, etc. These abreactions can be employed fruitfully in exploring the patients' feelings, their cause, and their relation to earlier or current determinants. Recognition and acceptance of the existence of motivations for an overt act and the willingness for self-confrontation strengthen the ego, in addition to other gains.

As Resistance

The most accepted view of acting out is that it is a form of resistance to treatment. This is true, and in the case of adult patients, resistance must be viewed as a salient feature of treatment. In acting out, the ego finds a shorter, easier, and more primitively direct route for discharging anxiety, guilt, and aggression, than working it through by the devious, prolonged, and arduous method of catharsis and insight. Acting out is a quick way to rid oneself of unpleasant feelings and to find rapid release from tensions.

As in other forms of resistance, acting out has to be understood in the context of the psychological syndrome. The patient is led to become aware of it and explore it in relation to himself and the situation. The therapist here needs to help the patients in the group—the person acting out and the spectators—to recognize it as resistance and relate it to specific elements in the patient or to the themes of the interview in progress. It is through uncovering such self-protective subterfuges of the unconscious and exposing them to the examination of the rational part of the ego that psychic growth and emotional maturity are achieved.[4] It is essential that any acting out resistance, whether absenteeism, silence or an attack on the therapist and others, be understood. The therapist plays an important role in this, for, though members of a group usually are alert to many of their fellow patients' stratagems, resistance is less likely to be recognized by them.

Acting out, as a form of resistance to treatment, is also employed by patients outside of the therapeutic setting. To prevent

---

[4] The therapist's maneuver in the case of Mrs. S. is an illustration of this, as is the group session narrated in Chapter X.

the painful revelations and discussions, patients take steps in their personal lives to resolve external, situational, and relational difficulties. This is done not as result of emotional maturity and intellectual clarity achieved through psychotherapy, but rather as an escape from the arduous process of treatment, as a means of pleasing or defeating the therapist, to exhibit superiority and capability, or as prevention of pain and discomfort. These acts, though, constructive in nature, and performed outside the group sessions, have to be treated as resistance to treatment. The motives and intent of seeming self-reliance and good management have to be explored. "Flight into health" is an illustration of this mechanism.

As a Reaction to Fear

Acting out through aggression, withdrawal and silence, may be reactions to fear and discomfort in group situations. This discomfort may arise from memories of pain and threats to self-esteem experienced in the original family of the patient, exhibitionistic trends, self-consciousness having a sexual source, a distorted body image, or from fear of revealing a particularly guilt and anxiety evoking thought or experience. These may be conscious, preconscious, or unconscious. In any case the patient is wary or defensive and will abreact by aggressiveness or become demure, cautious, quiet, or entirely silent.

The fear syndrome of a patient cannot be dealt with directly. Directness and efforts at exploration, too early in treatment, may cause further withdrawal, adoption of a different means of concealment, or termination of treatment altogether. Such patients require security and acceptance as a first step. The support of a group, through identification, universalization and a general atmosphere of tolerance, acceptance, and helpfulness, dissolves diffidence and fears, making the patients accessible to other, more direct, treatment procedures, as is the case in all counterphobic acting out.

The strategy of watchful waiting on the part of the therapist is not as easily applicable to patients who abreact to fear with aggression because this behavior may prove distressing to others in the group. Overacting patients not only vitiate the therapeutic atmosphere, but can actually cause the group's disruption. On the other hand, restraining such patients would only increase their panic and justify their distrust. Most patients with this syndrome are unsuitable for groups; they require individual treatment to work through the intrapsychic difficulties that necessitate this particular pattern of adaptation.

As Provocation

The aim of acting out may be to provoke aggression against oneself. The motive for this may be the need for punishment, conditioned behavior through early family relations, psychic masochism, or latent homosexuality. Provocative members are a strain on the group as a whole and can be unendurable to some neurotic and emotionally intolerant patients. However, in most instances this type of acting out is accessible to group treatment. The reaction of the group members and the mirror they provide have a salutary effect on patients who resort to it. Ordinarily, the therapist finds little need to deal with it himself, since it arouses other group members to action.

There are occasions, however, when the therapist has to step in to allay the tension and anger engendered by an especially provocative patient. He can do this by directly attacking the act, *but not the patient*, exploring and explaining it. The therapist can ask the group to explore the reasons for the behavior; he can explore, with the patient, the patient's own motives, so that he may relate his current acts to his past; or the therapist can supply the explanation himself.

Psychic masochism tends to disappear through group psychotherapy, due to ego reinforcement and an improved self-image. Unless the group reacts punitively and with rejection, patients with this character disturbance gain rapidly from group treatment. Latent homosexuality, on the other hand, is not as accessible, and this type of acting-out patient creates considerable problems in groups. By their very presence, they induce a high level of anxiety, as the unconscious of each member of the group responds to the personality of such a patient and they feel threatened. This is partly due to everyone's susceptibility to homosexuality and partly due to reactive cultural conditioning. The therapist cannot directly bring these feelings to the awareness of either the subject or the other members. This pathology requires a slow and careful unfolding in treatment, in which oral dependencies, sexual identifications, and early fixations have to be explored. This exploration can be done in groups, but it can be accomplished more easily in individual treatment.

As a Bid for Status

Acting out may be used to gain status. The forms it may take are self-assertiveness, exhibitionism, rivalry, excessive intellectualization about things related to, and, more often, unrelated to the topic under discussion.[5] Frequently, this type of patient is verbose, domineering, and critical, and attempts to choke off participation by other members, through dogmatism and authoritativeness. They attempt to displace the therapist by answering questions addressed to him and by freely giving information.

The striving for status may be a continuation of the patient's family pattern, in which rivalry and assertive conduct were fostered; a result of inferiority feelings, which he wards off through self-maximation; a reaction formation to castration anxiety; or it may be due to earlier deprivations. Often, exhibitionism reflects an erogenized intellect, which has become a substitute for genital potency. Because of early emphasis on the importance of intellectual achievement or strong physical inferiority feelings, the intellect may be invested with genital powers and significance, a clear case of displacement "from below to above." Women with masculine strivings are subject to *intellect erogenization,* but, more often, they seek status through feminine attractiveness, exaggerated charm, and emphasis on appearance. All of these are disguises for their masculine strivings, however.

Both the male and female syndromes in the striving for status can be corrected through group psychotherapy. The ease with which status is attained, negative reactions to efforts at domina-

[5] Mrs. S. recognized this mechanism in Mrs. C. and gave it the correct interpretation.

tion, new and corrected identifications, and improved self-images aided by working through and insight, counteract these and other strivings.[6] There is, therefore, no need for special measures or intervention on the part of the therapist. Patients who make a bid for status by massive exhibitionism are difficult to deal with in groups. Exhibitionism is closely related to, and is a derivative of, narcissism with strong sexual overtones. Few patients with strong exhibitionistic tendencies can be retained in groups without provoking strong hostility and consequent anxiety, the intensity of which, may, in course of time, disrupt the group or seriously undermine its effectiveness.

Patients in groups can seek status also by submissiveness, compliance, ingratiation, placation, or bribery. Their adaptive manner has to be accepted until the underlying psychological causes are overcome and the patient alters his behavior. Behind the external timidity, there always lurks latent hostility, which should be brought out into the open. The character and fear elements, and the possible sexual seduction that may be hidden, can be left untouched in the group interviews, for unless they are severe, they automatically disappear with the intrapsychic changes that result from psychotherapy. The total atmosphere, and attitudes of the patients and therapist, encourages more assertive conduct, which is later reflected in an improved personality. However, the therapist needs to be vigilant with such patients, for their manner may cover serious pathology.

As Emotional Hypochondriasis

Some patients repeatedly dwell on their tragic lives and backgrounds. Session after session, as if on a treadmill, facts and fancies are reiterated, each narration a replica of all the preceding. They recount unhappiness, mistreatment, and "insurmountable" difficulties in their past and current lives. There is little variation in this repetitive circle of events and tragedies, recounted to win pity and receive sympathy. As if entertaining a

---

[6] The exception to this rule is status strivings that stem from intense primary narcissism or secondary narcissism.

belief in the magic of words, the patient has a vague expectancy that pity and understanding will remedy his difficulties and his problems will disappear as if by magic. The pattern is analogous to hypochondria, but instead of organic complaints, emotional stress is the point of fixation. This can be termed *emotional hypochondriasis,* which contains a strong element of narcissism, in addition to affect hunger and a hidden desire to control. There may also be present a strong hysterical quality and, in some instances, a psychotic element. Reality distortion is one of the characteristics of emotional hypochondriasis, and considerable sado-masochistic elements are present.

This pattern is employed as resistance to personality change, and, therefore, to the therapeutic effort. It is magnified in groups by the fact that the pity-seeking patient frequently involves others in his emotional machinations, since the appeal is to the tender feelings of the listeners. Their superegos prevent the listeners from reacting negatively or unfeelingly; they usually offer advice that is repeated session after session, and is, consequently, impedimental to the therapeutic progress of all concerned. The behavior of one patient plays into and reinforces the natural tendency toward resistance in every member of the group. All readily fall in with the subject's needs and devote the sessions to talking about his problems, giving advice, making suggestions, and *evading* their own treatment. This is especially true of women's groups.

The patient and the group feed on each other, each encouraging the other to dwell on nonproductive recitals. Because the pity-seeking patient is so thoroughly immersed in his sadness and tragedies and strikes such a responsive note in the other members of the group, the therapist has to take a hand in breaking the vicious circle. He has to confront the group and the patient with the reality of the situation, revealing it as character resistance. The group members readily perceive this significance, though the offending patient may be slower to recognize or accept it. If the patient is too threatened, or the quantum of affect or pathology counterindicates direct interpretation, the therapist may help him explore his background and feelings and give them dimension. Periodically, he should shift the focus to other members of the group and away from the monopolizing member. These strategies repeated frequently enough, will lead the patient in question to perceive his self-preoccupation as not acceptable and he may either abandon it or withdraw from the group.

As a Defense

Acting out, especially of an aggressive nature, is employed as a defense against expectation of attack from others (counterphobic), or from a feeling of being unaccepted. While it has its roots in intrapsychic deficiencies, it is activated in interpersonal situations and is exacerbated by group tensions. As such it has valuable therapeutic possibilities, for it provides opportunities for the analysis of interpersonal transferences that may exist among the group members and toward the therapist.

Since the ability to accept human beings for what they are is an indication of emotional maturity, this opportunity to work through interpatient attitudes and feelings has valuable therapeutic possibilities. The therapist must openly and pointedly recognize the emotional tensions in the group, against which abreaction occurs, and help the patients unravel their individual feelings and the group tensions current at the time. The more sibling hostility is revealed and worked through, the better for the therapeutic activity of the group. Frequently, defensive acting out is a temporary and short-lived reaction, because the expectation of attack from the group is not confirmed. When defensive acting out takes the form of silence, the patient, in time, automatically overcomes his diffidence, as he is accepted by the group.

As a Test

Closely related to the above motive for acting out is the use of it by a patient to test the therapist and the group. This type of behavior, as well, disappears when he is assured of acceptance.

As Contagion

Acting out can become widespread in a group because of the element of contagion. Latent hostility and aggression are readily activated in a group by the hostility or aggression of one of its members who can be designated as the *instigator*. Through induction and intensification it can become a serious problem in group psychotherapy, requiring skillful handling on the part of the therapist. This problem will be dealt with later, but it is necessary to state at this juncture that it is a group phenomenon, as differentiated from acting out by an individual. The therapist has to deal here with a mass reaction, rather than with an individual, a situation fraught with difficulties and even danger. The ego reinforcement and superego sanctions that group unanimity furnishes, may cause transgression of reasonable bounds. Since the hostility is usually directed toward the therapist, the group lacks the integrative focus which he represents and it may be disrupted. The comparatively uncontrolled discharge of hostility generates anxiety and guilt, which cannot abate or be allayed without outside control. The therapist must always be on the alert against *unanimity* of any sort in therapy groups, for unanimity in groups is derived from hostility against the therapist.

Contagion in acting out, whether through overt acts or widespread silence, is derived from latent, unconscious, or preconscious hostility to any parent or authority figure; but it can also be caused by specific interpersonal dynamics in a group. Chief among these is homosexual anxiety, activated by one or more of the group members. Another libidinal source is heterosexual competition in mixed groups, and still another is widespread sibling rivalry for the attention or affection of the therapist or the group. Sexual acting out among members of heterogeneous groups is usually a displacement of libidinal strivings toward the therapist (Slavson, 1953, page 6). If the group therapist is a male, women patients gratify their sexual transference urges toward him by substituting the nearest male objects, fellow patients.

Several women patients who acted out sexually, each with a number of fellow male group members, and who had inevitably and invariably left the groups as a result, stated to their subsequent analysts that they had thought that by gratifying themselves in this manner they would be rid of their neuroses. Their behavior is analogous to acting out on the part of girls, with unresolved oedipal urges toward their natural fathers, who become promiscuous or prostitutes, or unmarried mothers.

As a Neurotic Symptom

In evaluating the phenomenology of acting out, the therapist must always be aware of its neurotic sources. Because the term "neurotic" has come into indiscriminate use, it is essential that its exact meaning be ascertained as a measure against misunderstanding.

Although the underlying causes for some of the various types of acting out may be termed "neurotic" (in so far as they are exaggerated or overintensified reactions incommensurate with the stimuli or irritants) the term is employed here in its classical sense; neurosis is the unresolved conflict between the superego and id with which the ego is unable to deal adequately. Perhaps *psychoneurotic* describes it better. Another characteristic of psychoneuroses is that the conflict originates in the sexual libido (in terms of its content) and in the oedipal conflict (in the dimension of time). The result of the unresolved conflict between the psychic forces is "the symptom," which, for reasons not always clear, manifests itself either in specific behavior reactions or in somatic disturbances.

In a comparatively small number of psychoneurotics, such symptoms may not make their appearance and instead the intrapsychic tensions propel the individual to unceasing activity, frequently of a random nature. This impulsivity serves to discharge internal tensions through action, by transmutation of emotional energy into physical energy, and it is not accessible to examination by, or the control of, the ego. The pattern becomes a part of the character organization and is structured, as it were, into the total personality. Because of this internalization and incorporation into the character structure, I have suggested the term "neurotic character" to label it. The acting out *is* the symptom.

Stemming as it does from the structure of the personality itself and being inaccessible to the ego, the behavior of patients with neurotic character disorders is difficult, if not impossible, to reach through psychotherapy. Patients with this disturbance, therefore, must be excluded from groups.[7] They are unable to contain the overwhelming anxiety and they throw it off in incessant overt acts and speech, infecting all the members of the group. They monopolize the interviews and block the free flow of group participation, thus intensifying frustration and, increasing anxiety in fellow patients.

A related type of acting out is found in "traumatophiliac" patients—patients who have a neurotic need to create difficulties for themselves and are, therefore, prone to activate rejection, attack, suffering and unhappiness. Such patients keep groups in a stir and prevent their members from participating effectively in the therapeutic process since the element of commonality is lacking. The effects such patients have is the same as those described under the section entitled "As Provocation." The difference, however, is that the basic neurotic conflict from which traumatophilia stems requires deeper analytic unraveling than groups can provide. In addition, traumatophiliac patients do not give the other group members a chance to work on their problems, and they, too, have to be eliminated from psychotherapy groups.

Compulsive talking is another neurotic acting out syndrome that affects groups adversely. Compulsive talking is generally part of a neurotic character syndrome, but may also appear apart from it. It is found in compulsive persons, in those with intense dependence needs and as a part of a character neurosis. It is doubtful whether compulsive patients, in whom the inner need for talking is intense, can be assimilated by groups, because of the inhibiting and frustrating effect they have upon fellow patients.

As Narcissism

Acting out by persons who exploit the group for narcissistic ends, presents a special difficulty. Many of the mechanisms and patterns so far described have narcissistic coloring, but there are patients whose character disturbances stem from what is clinically considered as "primary narcissism." The manifestations of narcis-

[7] "Neurotic character" has to be differentiated from "character neurosis." The latter is probably accessible to analytic group psychotherapy.

sism, its etiology and pathogenesis are too well known to require detailing here. These patients are assertive, exhibitionistic, and exploitive, and do not always fare well in therapy groups.

Groups are more helpful with narcissistic children than they are with adults, partly because of the nature of childhood narcissism as compared with adult narcissism and partly because free group life and interactions are a *growth-producing milieu,* which leads them to alter their personalities and their mode of behavior. However, where the acting out is intense and compulsive, interfering with group therapeutic activity, the patient may have to be withdrawn, after a period of trial, and again placed in a group after a term of individual treatment.

As a Character Disorder

Neurotic character compulsiveness, and narcissism syndromes are not the only categories of character disorders that produce acting out. Women with masculine, and some men with feminine, identifications are overbearing and dictatorial in manner and statements. They are hard on their fellow patients because of their interference with the therapeutic process. These women and men are not easily affected by psychotherapy, but where the character rigidities are not too intense, group psychotherapy is the treatment of choice for them, though their prognosis is never certain. The reactions of the group and the mirroring of their behavior by fellow patients do help to some extent in making inroads into their character. The models for corrective identification provided by the group support their improvement.

THE CATEGORIES OF ACTING OUT

It is clear from the preceding that the phenomenon of acting out can have many causes and its nosology, etiology and therapeutics are not uniform. Therefore, it requires diagnostic understanding and suitable therapeutic intervention, which is true also of all aspects of therapeutic activity. As already emphasized, only through such singularity can the effectiveness of the therapeutic effort be assured. While they may serve as frames of reference

389

or as conceptual orientation, blanket theories and generalizations can help but little in the actual workaday practice of the therapist. There are, however, some basic generalizations, regarding acting out, which can be helpful.

As Regression

As already suggested, acting out always connotes either regression or fixation. It is regression when an individual reverts under stress to a pattern of behavior he has outgrown and which is no longer appropriate to his chronological age or social role. The pattern that he re-enacts is one that was employed earlier in his development, especially during childhood. This genetic regression is most pronounced in the forms of acting out described under the headings of Provocation, Testing, Bid for Status, Emotional Hypochondriasis, and Abreaction.

As Fixation

Patients in psychotherapy, who have not progressed beyond infantile levels, in some aspects of their personality, remaining *fixed* at those levels, cannot be said to regress to an earlier stage or pattern, because they have never grown beyond it. They therefore behave not *as though* they are children (which is the case in regression), but *as* children. These fixated feelings, attitudes, and responses form part of the character of the person. Acting out, because of fixation, is demonstrated by Narcissism, Character Disorders, Defensiveness, Fear, and Neurotic Character.

As Ego Asthenia

Acting out is always a symptom of ego insufficiency, an attempt to deal with autogenetic (internal) stress or those external stresses that produce internal strain (exogenetic stress). Anxiety in the face of tasks too difficult for the ego powers, makes it susceptible to acting out in various (counterphobic) forms, such as excessive verbalization, heightened affect, random activity or motility (to control the environment through infantile omnipotence) or through attack (the aim of which is destruction or elimination of the offending person or situation). As the ego is threatened it defends itself against weakness and anxiety by mobilizing a primitive attack or by withdrawal. (The latter is, in some respects, similar to the death feint of some animals in danger.) Examples of this are Reaction to Fear, Striving for Status, and Contagion.

As Ontogenetic Recapitulation

The form that acting out takes is usually a replica of earlier life patterns that served effectively or were forced on the individual, in the past. Acting out has a direct relation to the individual's past and is a direct outgrowth of his adaptations and the strategies it was necessary for him to adopt in adjusting to his environment. These are stored up in the unconscious memory and when the ego and its controls are weakened by stress, they become operative, assert themselves and propel the individual to act out in earlier, forgotten or latent, ways. Abreaction, Resistance, Provocation, Emotional Hypochondriasis, Defense, Testing, Neurotic Symptom, and Character Disorder are ontogenetic acting out.

As Phylogenetic Recapitulation

The emotions of anger and hostility and the patterns of aggression and withdrawal by which regression is manifested, are not all ontogenetic; some are, rather, phylogenetic survivals of primitive stages of man's biological and social evolution; they once served as tools for survival but have become obsolete in the course of social development and remained as hidden reservoirs, as neuronic engrams, which come forth from the storehouse of the species and become operative in the life and behavior of the individual. Such primary emotions as fear, rage, love, jealousy, and hostility can only be *shaped* by experience but *not engendered* by it. Their roots are in the instinctive needs of the struggle for survival and appear in modern man in vastly modified and disguised forms that often obscure their original source. It is these phylogenetic tendencies and urges, among others, that patients act out during group sessions. The aims and results of psychotherapy are repression of some, the transmutation of others, and the sub-

391

limation of still other instinctive responses into suitable social forms. The phylogenetic recapitulation forms of acting out include Release, Fear, Bid for Status, Contagion, and Narcissism.

THE ADVANTAGES AND DISADVANTAGES OF ACTING OUT

Acting out, in group psychotherapy with adults, reveals the actual personality and ego functioning of the individual, which are otherwise frequently obscured by his masking and defensive use of language and other forms of disguise. Patients who accept their hostilities as natural and inevitable, cannot but become aware of them and the feelings that underlie them, when they contrast them with the tolerant and accepting atmosphere of the group and the therapist. The contrast between one's own behavior and the intent of the group seldom fails to impress patients. Even when this is not verbalized, the patients are half aware of it, and, in time, this grows into full recognition. The group serves as a mirror that reflects behavior, and the suitability or incongruity of that behavior is usually made apparent to the patient.

The discovery that the therapist and fellow patients accept one's acts, that were met with punishment or disapproval in the past, has a salutary effect upon the self-image and self-esteem. Acceptance by the group reduces guilt feelings and self-deprecatory attitudes toward oneself and one's conduct. The resulting relaxed feeling makes the patient more receptive to corrective experiences and re-education.

On the other hand, the friendly and critical responses of fellow patients impress one with the unsuitability of one's behavior and, unless there is uncontrollable pathology present, one gradually grows predisposed to examine the causes for acting out and to control it. Initially, examination of an individual's acting out in a group tends to activate negative and even destructive criticism and blame. This may defeat the objectives of therapy, not only for the offending patient, but also for the others, as emotional maturity is, in part, the increased capacity to accept the foibles and defects in others rather than to react punitively and critically. Mutual help, understanding, and acceptance make their appearance, as the group members work through their basic hostilities, mature emotionally, and as their egos are strengthened. They can then, calmly and more effectively, deal with the tensions and conflicts that unavoidably arise in a therapy group. In this manner, the group supplies a gauge for the therapeutic operation and for the evolving maturity of its members.

Acting out within the limits described, is a valid pattern of catharsis, communication, and self-revelation. To be of maximal benefit to patients, however, the therapist must possess high levels of ego strength, skill, and tact.

Acting out outside the therapeutic setting must be discouraged; at least, it should not be encouraged. Providing situations that favor it, such as patients having relations outside the group sessions, is to be avoided. Group psychotherapy, as a clinical tool, is effective only when practiced in a therapeutic climate. A therapy group is not a social club. It is a *partial social reality* and, at best, a structured and a conditioned one, so that reality testing is best done in the setting of the patient's everyday life away from the group associations.

On the negative side, once the adult patient has acted out his feelings, the need to explore and work them through is less impelling. The impulsion to work on an inner difficulty stems from the tensions that it engenders in the psyche. When release has been achieved, there is a lessened urge to seek resolution in the usual course of therapy. In groups, however, acting out is seldom allowed to remain unnoticed or ignored. Some react to it with sanguine intent, others with hostility and retaliation, but both force the subject into an exploration of the motives and determinants of his conduct. This leads him into a more suitable catharsis and more fruitful free-association, the foundational steps in psychotherapy. Therefore, *acting out should be allowed in analytic psychotherapy, provided it does not remain an end in itself.* Although in the initial stages of treatment, acting out may be overlooked by the therapist for the comfort of a patient and as a basis for evoking positive transference, it should not be ignored beyond this point. Induced regression cannot be avoided altogether, but it should be prevented from spreading, and patients who persist in generating it have to be withdrawn.[8] Widespread induced acting out is a manifestation of libidinal overcharge, resulting from the presence of too many acting out or susceptible patients. If permitted to run riot, they raise the quantum of anxiety beyond the group's tolerance—a limit which cannot be exceeded without jeopardizing its survival.

The nature, intensity, and extent to which acting out can be permitted is dependent on the setting in which it occurs. In private practice and in outpatient services with ambulatory patients, the intensity of acting out is likely to be lower than in residential treatment, especially in restraining institutions. Inpatients at a hospital, and prisoners, have many more reasons for resentment than do patients with the same problems in outpatient or privately conducted therapy. The patterns and intensity of acting out also bear a direct relation to the willingness to accept institutional life and its unavoidable limitations and confinement. Thus, in voluntary general hospitals, motivations for acting out are not entirely lacking but are of less urgency than in rehabilitation hospitals, prisons, or "reform" schools.

CHILD VERSUS ADULT ACTING OUT

The preceding considerations of acting out were concerned with adult nonpsychotic therapy groups, where acting out can be beneficially utilized, but it is neither essential nor a preferred method of catharsis. *Acting out by children, however, is essential, whether in groups or individual therapy.* Action, and not words, is the language of the child. His level of conceptualization, limited facility with words and ideas, still incomplete controls of mobility, and his need for manipulation and exploration, all impel the child to motility. He communicates his thoughts and feelings through action, as much as through language, which the therapist must understand and respond to appropriately. Just as the verbal communications of adults have their manifest and latent

---

[8] Mobs are actuated, in their irrational violence, through induced regression in the area of libidinal interstimulation. The sexual anxiety in all mob action should not be overlooked. Observe the rapism and debauchery that accompany mob behavior, especially in the less "civilized" populations.

counterparts, children's *action communication,* as well, consists of overt (manifest) acts and behavior which have latent meaning, discernible to a therapist trained in working with children.

Acting out is the appropriate form of catharsis in all child psychotherapy. In individual play therapy, as well as in the analytic types of groups for children (play-group and activity-interview group psychotherapy), the acting out is controlled and directed through uncovering and interpretation, as well as by direct restraint when necessary. In activity groups, it is allowed to run its course. The therapeutic results accrue from proper selection and grouping, from individual interactions, the *primary group code* as it subtly emerges, and the neutrality of, and *action interpretation* by, the therapist.[9]

Acting out and catharsis are synonymous in child psychotherapy. However, there are degrees and areas of activity catharsis that limit permissibility: the possibility of physical injury; excessive impulsivity; unpredictability of behavior, as in borderline psychotics and the brain injured (especially where other members of the group are involved); mounting destructibility; and uncontrolled physical attack on fellow group members or the therapist.

THE THERAPIST'S ROLES IN ACTING OUT

Timing and Readiness

The psychotherapist's role in acting out has been briefly indicated under the various phenomenological classifications. No blanket technique is available; the therapist's response and action have to be based on the situation, the specific patient, the effect on the other group members, the group as an entity, the therapeutic indications of the moment, and above all, the transference relations that exist between him and his patients.

All the previously discussed suggestions for dealing with acting-out patients and groups were made with the assumption that the basic transference relation is a positive one and that acting out is

[9] Because of the avoidance of interpretation and the controls that accrue from it, the selection and grouping of patients is of vital importance and essential to the survival of activity therapy groups.

a transitory negative phase of it. In the absence of positive transference, any move toward curbing or exploring behavior of patients will reinforce negative and hostile feelings in them, with deleterious, if not disastrous, results. All of the therapist's responses and acts must take into consideration the transference attitudes that prevail at a given time. The factor of timing needs to be extended to include not only the readiness of patients, but also the relation between the patient and therapist and *the therapist's own readiness*. The latter is a factor that is too often overlooked, but is especially vital in dealing with acting out.

In whatever form acting out occurs, it is always felt by the therapist as a tacit attack on himself; and in this he is right. Acting out occurs in transference, and the therapist is its sole target in individual psychotherapy and its major focus in a group. To accept attack with equanimity is no small task, even for objective and detached individuals, and therapists, being human, are not free of the need to be accepted, respected, and treated with consideration. Bearing up under direct or tacit attack is particularly difficult in a group, because of the possibility that the hostilities of other members can be mobilized, creating a phalanx against him. This does not mean that the therapist should not face this situation and, at infrequent times, even encourage it. The expression of hostility in transference is essential. What we wish to convey here is an awareness of the difficulties and strain, and the importance of the therapist's self-confrontation in this regard. He must not undertake a task that he cannot fulfill, for a display of weakness undesirably affects his role as ego ideal and object of identification. This is as true of adult patients as it is of children. A display of vulnerability intensifies and mobilizes aggression in patients and when the libidinal investment in the therapist is withdrawn, his function and value are diminished or invalidated.

An important function of the "supervisor," or one who "controls" group psychotherapists, is to prevent them, particularly those who are new to the practice, from exceeding their own tolerance. The therapist must always retain his status as ego support and object of identification for his patients and to do this he has to remain imperturbable. As he gains confidence through experience, and as his security increases, he can allow greater acting out and show of hostility. The supervisor's awareness of the therapist's limitations in this regard is of critical importance.

Evasion of Acting Out

Some group therapists shy away from acting out and employ various stratagems to prevent it. The most common of these is the assumption of a manner of extreme kindness, graciousness, and paternalism. This succeeds in holding patients' hostilities in abeyance, but the therapeutic results are greatly diminished by it. *Where there is no hostility there is no therapy.* When hostility remains unexpressed and not "worked through," one can achieve, at best, only some degree of symptom or behavioral improvement and not psychic equilibrium (that is, an efficient relationship between the id, ego, and superego), which requires the egress of hostility in a therapeutic transference relation and the insight to which it leads.

Some group therapists, who placate their patients by various means, rationalize it as playing out the "good parental role." Some even feed their adult patients during sessions! Other therapists devaluate their status by participating in the group interviews on the same level as the patients. They describe their preoccupations and reactions, even to the extent of discussing their intimate personal problems. This equalization of status of therapist and patients may be a strategy on the part of the therapist to prevent mobilization of aggression toward himself, but since he does not function *in loco parentis,* the transference reactions are not activated and, for obvious reasons, psychotherapeutic objectives cannot be attained. In a sense, this approaches the method of the "leaderless group," which is sociologically and therapeutically invalid.[10]

---

[10] By definition and phenomenological function, there is no possibility for a group to remain leaderless. It may start as such, but soon indigenous leaders appear. No group of people can function without a leader. Without leadership, groups disintegrate.

Stimulation of Acting Out

A group therapist can, consciously or unconsciously, encourage acting out in his group as some can activate resistances in their patients. Although activation of hostility is necessary at specific times, when therapeutically indicated, stirring up groups (or individual patients, for that matter) as a blanket technique is destructive.

A therapist who has retained traumatophillic needs may activate aggression in his groups either overtly or subtly, for the resulting difficulties give him unconscious satisfactions. He may gain a sense of importance and power from group turmoil or feel more effective and important when things are difficult. As a result of these and other unconscious motivations, therapists may unnecessarily encourage acting out, just as others, for equally unconscious reasons, may prevent it when it should beneficially occur.

"Alternate" and "Post" Sessions

Two of the strategies that favor acting out (especially *ex situ*) are the so-called "alternate" and "post" sessions that some group therapists employ. These are meetings where the patients meet, on different days ("alternate") or immediately following the regular sessions ("post"), without the therapist being present. Lacking a person who represents or symbolizes authority, a parental figure, and a central focus of object cathexis for the group members, their hostilities, counterhostilities, affections, and friendships are not canalized and employed therapeutically, but rather, they run riot. The libidinal cathexis, ordinarily fixed on the therapist, is diffused and is attached to various other members, which also leads, in mixed groups, to sexual acting out. The lifting of social anonymity also results in the patients becoming confused as to their roles and relationships. The conversations at sessions from which the therapist is absent have the characteristics of acting out, because they are not directed with a therapeutic intent nor are they focused, and appropriate interpretation is lacking. Usually one of the most disturbed and assertive patients takes over the direction of the group and, having no training or insight, further disturbs and confuses his fellow patients.

Though patients testify to intense discomfort during these free-for-all sessions, some may find them very pleasing, as they can give vent to the pleasure principle, feeling unhampered and uncontrolled by the presence of the therapist or by impositions inherent in the group and in society generally. But emotional re-education and intrapsychic changes are never pleasurable. Persons who seek change have to bear pain; only in suffering does change lie. "Suffering is the crucible in which the soul is purified." Whatever pleasures, peace, and "happiness" accrue are *a result* of psychotherapy. Joy is not part of its *process,* though, in its early stages, patients may feel lighthearted and even elated, resulting from the sharing of burdens, ventilation of feelings, and new-found acceptance. However, as treatment continues and deeper layers of the psyche are reached, tensions increase, causing suffering, but, more important, they serve as an impetus to further treatment.

TABLE 1

The Phenomenology of Acting Out

Forms	Types	Causes	Services	Categories	Advantages
Verbal	Normal	Organic tension	Release	Regressive	Self-revelation
Anger	Therapeutic	Psychic tension	Abreaction	Ontogenetic	Action
Spite	Parapathologic	Threats to ego	Resistance	Phylogenetic	communication
Teasing	Pathologic	defenses	Provocation		Mirror reaction
Screaming	Induced	Fear	Status striving		
Threats	*Ex situ*	Emotional	Arousal of pity		
	In situ	hypochondriasis	Defense		
Nonverbal		Contagion	Testing		
Body tension		Neurotic symptom			
Involuntary		Neurotic character			
movements		Traumatophilia			
Grimaces		Compulsiveness			
Facial color		Narcissism			
Expression		Character disorders			
of eyes		Ego asthenia			
Posture					
Throwing of					
objects					
Smoking					
Silence					
Absence					
Lateness					

XIII

The Qualifications and Functions of the Group Therapist

The qualities of the therapist involved in conducting analytic groups can be classified under the categories of (1) personal qualifications, (2) educational background, and (3) functions. In conducting group interviews, his functions are directional, stimulative, extensional, and interpretive.

PERSONAL QUALIFICATIONS

The Importance of Definition

Personal qualifications are given precedence over all the others, because in the parlance of business corporations, "The wrong person trained is still the wrong person." The term "personal qualifications" has many imponderables; yet, despite obvious semantic handicaps, it is essential that they be, as far as possible, identified and described so that they can serve as guides in selecting candidates for training. Personality qualities for other professions and trades, also intangible, have been, in many instances, successfully identified and fairly reliable objective tests for choosing suitable candidates have been devised. An effort in this direction also needs to be made for group psychotherapy.

The characteristics that are desirable in a good psychotherapist can be divided into positive and negative categories: those that favor and those that are inimical to the practice of his craft. Some of these characteristics are found in both individual and group psychotherapists, but the latter possess certain additional faculties.

The importance of personality features for effective psychotherapy, aside from knowledge and information, is best revealed in the nonverbal communications of the therapist and in his subtle reactions to his patients. Thus, what he *is* is at least as important as what he *does*.

As a Suitable Model of Identification

To varying degrees and in different ways, patients tend to imitate the therapist and to adopt his attitudes and values. As the patient's identification model in the process of ego strengthening and realigning of the superego, his character, poise, objectivity, honesty, and capacity for relatedness are of crucial importance. The manner in which he responds to, and deals with, the various transferences, especially those of a sexual nature, strongly determines the corrective process in therapy. This includes not only verbal response, but also the nonverbal reactions, such as muscular tension, posture, facial grimace, and expression of the eyes, all of which communicate to patients his state of being and his transient feelings.

Patients, by virtue of being patients, are alert to the therapist's *quality as a person* and his reactions as well as to his words. They register his frustrations, embarrassments, hesitancies, confusions, anger, anxieties, and the numberless other reactions—covert and overt—which occur during therapeutic sessions. To a great degree, this is obviated in classical psychoanalysis, where the patient does not physically face the analyst; but in the psychotherapies where therapist and patient face one another the responses cannot remain unobserved or unregistered.

Ironically, one of the requirements for a good therapist is a difficult childhood which has been adequately worked through in an analytic procedure. This gives him not only knowledge and wisdom, but aids the essential empathy with his patients. A person who has not suffered cannot emotionally "understand" the suffering of others and the outcomes of that suffering. However, the therapist must have overcome the effects of his own difficulties, resentments, hostilities and the like, without residual bitterness or cynicism, or he may reinforce such feelings in his patients on the one hand, or over-identify with them, on the other. This vitiates his therapeutic effectiveness. He must not become involved in his patients' problems; rather he needs to maintain an objective role, though with emotional resonance.

Maturity

Among the essential requirements for a good psychotherapist is the poise that comes from emotional freedom, security, a balanced judgment, and a reality sense buttressed by an appropriate philosophy of life. All of these, of course, spell maturity. One can hardly expect to achieve this state in the ordinary course of growing up in a family in our society, without the help of emotional re-education at some period; but such maturity is nonetheless an essential in the demanding role of a psychotherapist. He must, therefore, equip himself for that role not only knowledgewise but, what is more important, emotionally. It is, therefore, recommended that before attempting to practice, psychotherapists submit to a standard and extended individual psychoanalysis. So-called "group analysis" falls far short of these requirements, though a group experience may be useful as a supplement following individual analysis.

Such a psychoanalytic preparation is recommended not only for practitioners of classical psychoanalysis, but also for those who employ psychotherapeutic measures of lesser depth and intensity, including group psychotherapy. "Blind spots" in the unconscious of the therapist and his own fixated and over-cathected reactions to persons, relations, and situations (and especially to the productions and problems of his patients, whether individually or in groups), diminish his effectiveness, and in some instances may even make him unfit for the task.

Responsible group psychotherapists who, through the experience in their own proper personal analysis, have come to recognize the depth and tenacity of neuroses, find that when a therapist brings to the therapeutic relation his own unresolved problems, serious or even disastrous results may ensue.

Intuition and Perceptiveness

A therapist needs to possess the qualities that are referred to by the nebulous terms "intuition" and "perceptiveness." These are essential, since patients seldom reveal their unconscious in their verbal communications, even when resistance is minimal; nor is much that is structured or repressed in their unconscious or preconscious available to them, though this may be the core of their problems. The therapist's responsibility is to perceive these hidden elements and employ them. Such perceptiveness is characterized as "intuition," and is a major tool of a therapist. While some skills and knowledge can be acquired by training, the aptness with which they are applied is conditioned by the comprehension of unconscious (latent) significances. Such aptitude is more native than acquired, for training without inherent talent is a superstructure without an adequate foundation.

Empathy versus Sympathy

The basic capacity for empathy with the multifarious reactions and their nuances that different patients present in groups is primary. This capacity is inborn, not acquired, but it can be enhanced in persons who have come to cope with their own unconscious. No one who has not attained a degree of emotional maturity by confronting himself with his own unconscious can help another to come to grips with his irrational, archaic urges. The therapist who has not reached this level in his own development is anxious or embarrassed in the face of his patient's evasions and incapable of dealing with them therapeutically. Patients tend to activate the unconscious of the therapist, but he must be equipped not to react with countertransference feelings or acts and to maintain his own "floating" or free attention, essential in all psychotherapy.

"Free-floating" attention, rather than the therapist's pursuing his own line of thought or feelings, is imperative. Without it, he is incapable of the quick and unerring responses which will gain the confidence of his patients and cement positive transference. One of the major skills of psychotherapy is the therapist's ability to formulate thoughts of which patients are only partially aware (preconscious), and to convey his understanding of their inner struggles and problems. When a patient is misunderstood or not understood, his attitude toward the therapist may turn into hostility and resulting negative transference. To be understood is the major need of all patients.

Empathy (like-feeling with others) is made possible by having suffered and successfully worked through and overcome suffering. Sympathy is the emotion of one who is still in the throes of that suffering. In empathy there is emotional resonance because the observer has been sensitized by similar experiences; in sympathy, his own suffering is activated. Suffering, Schopenhauer wrote, is "the crucible in which the human soul is purified." This is true only when suffering results in wisdom and detachment. Suffering can also embitter: The sufferer can "go sour." Bitterness manifests itself by unhappiness, self-pity, general disturbance, a hostile and unkindly disposition, jealousy, and ill-wishes toward friends, neighbors, and relatives. Some succeed in emerging from suffering with deepened feelings, broader human understanding, increased forbearance; in other words, wisdom.

The attitude toward suffering is conditioned by a combination of the strength of native ego resources and frustration tolerance, and a philosophical (objective) outlook. The therapist's experience with depth psychology as a patient, has a salutary effect in this respect and is one of the reasons why a *real* personal psychoanalysis is recommended for prospective psychotherapists. Thus, while a therapist must respond to a patient's suffering, he must do this without becoming involved (trapped) to such a degree that his judgment (objectivity) is impaired. He should resist emotional induction. Though sympathy and the expression of it has its place in certain types of psychotherapy, and especially with certain patients needing support,[1] the therapist cannot allow him-

[1] Support can be given to a patient in the areas of reinforcement of the ego and the self-image, but his feelings of self-pity, sorrow, and the like must not be supported.

self to be drawn into their feelings and become victim of these without extricating himself as soon as it is therapeutically indicated. This type of countertransference does not help the patient, for in addition to other consequences, the therapist reveals himself as weak, vulnerable, and as confused as the patient himself.

A woman patient once brought her baby to a group session claiming that she had no one that day to entrust him to. During the session she revealed intense ambivalence toward the baby in her arms, accompanied by extreme feelings of guilt which were followed by a tearful outburst. All the members of the group, both the men and the women, were strongly moved, as was the male psychiatrist. He reacted by saying, with tears glistening in his eyes: "You know, I can cry at what you're saying." The group was disturbed by the therapist's display of sentimentality and remained subdued for the rest of the session. The therapist believed that it was the woman's recital that brought on the depressed mood in the other patients; he did not recognize the extent to which his countertransference feelings and over-identification with the baby (a result of his own personal problem), had disturbed his patients. Instead of exploring the woman's displacement of feeling, the therapist reinforced her and the other patients' infantile self-pity, bringing on their state of mild depression.

On the other hand, unresponsiveness and a cold exterior, at a time when a patient is deeply affected, may alienate him. This occurred when an elderly man was narrating with great distress how his sister had committed suicide in Hitler's Germany to avoid being sent to a concentration camp. The man burst into uncontrollable weeping and the therapist, though deeply affected by the details of the recital and the patient's emotions, studiously retained an impassive expression. The patient said nothing, but continued to weep with a handkerchief over his eyes. At a later session, after he had gained mastery over his feelings, he said that he had expected "some sympathy" from the therapist for his sister's cruel fate and for his own feelings about her. Soon after he broke off his treatment. The therapist later explained that he had behaved deliberately, just to prevent "playing into" the patient's infantile dependency mechanisms and to discourage his over-emotionality. Obviously this was not the time to employ "techniques." The situation was too realistic and too humanly tragic not to evoke an empathic and even sympathetic response. The circumstances were made even more tragic because another sister had fled to a foreign country which was about to be invaded by the Nazis. In a letter to the patient which he read during the interview mentioned, she communicated the fact that she, too, contemplated suicide if the Nazis invaded.

Detachment versus Indifference

Just as sympathy and empathy should not be confused, detachment must be differentiated from insensibility or indifference. To be a good therapist one must be sensitive; not sensitive toward himself but toward others which, in a sense, is empathy. Frequently detachment and empathy are not mutually exclusive; detachment does not mean callousness.

Motivation

Another quality essential in a good psychotherapist is a genuine motivation to help people. No matter how profound his knowledge and educational qualifications, the absence of such a desire unfits him for the job. However, this urge must be general, rather than directed toward a specific patient, for it may become an aim-directed countertransference. When such an aim is perceived by a patient or the group (and they seldom fail to do so), they may either resist improvement to defeat the therapist or present symptom improvement as an act of submission or placation.

Imagination

Few occupations draw upon the imagination of their practitioners as much as psychotherapy. Not only is the weight of responsibility very heavy, but perceptiveness and insight are totally exerted in unravelling the intricate and complex psychic processes of the disordered personality. Even greater imagination is required

407

to respond appropriately to each patient or to the group's communications and to their transient or permanent feelings. It is doubtful if this highly prized trait can be forged by educational means alone, and one cannot escape the feeling that it is a quality present in some in greater degree than in others. It is also quite likely that imagination, like the intellect, has general and specific aspects. Some individuals are to varying degrees generally imaginative; that is, they can see through their mind's eye qualities, processes, and possibilities beyond what is observable. The imagination of others is confined to a specific, or to a set of specific, phenomena.

An imagination, a sound understanding of the human psyche and its dynamism, and strong empathy are the triad of assets of a good psychotherapist, and those who possess all of them cannot but be successful in this most demanding occupation.

Narcissistic Preoccupations

A psychotherapist should be free of narcissistic preoccupations with his person and with the awareness of his abilities, excellences, and mental processes. Self-preoccupations, during treatment interviews, prevent the free-floating attention necessary to follow the productions, moods, and feelings of patients. They block the powers to observe the verbal and nonverbal cues and signals to which the therapist must be at all times on the alert. This is especially important in group psychotherapy, where a number of patients are simultaneously involved. Even when painful feelings and disturbing memories and thoughts are aroused in the therapist, he must deal with them in a controlled manner and with an undisturbed mien. Failure in this blocks the flow of the patients' free association as well as the therapist's free-floating attention.

Frustration Tolerance

To possess the stability and strength to remain passive when necessary, and to be appropriately active when participation is indicated, are essential qualities in a psychotherapist. Frustration tolerance is a major requirement. The therapist's tenseness and an uncontrollable need to discharge feelings, either verbally or motorically, engender anxiety in patients and vitiate his role as an ego ideal and identification model.

Omnipotence of Ideas

Above all, a therapist must be free of the rather common, but erroneous belief in the value of reason and ideas and of the unconscious credence in the magic and omnipotence of words. These are both extant and a source of much misunderstanding. In the words of George Fox, the founder of Quakerism, one does not talk to a person but to his *condition*. Reason is usually ineffective. Communication has to be directed to the unconscious state and needs of the patient, to the situation, and to the nuances of the relations involved. This is especially important in psychotherapy. An essential capacity is to perceive the condition and the needs of a patient *at a given moment* and react appropriately either by silence, support, explanation, agreement, exploration, or clarification—and even direction and disagreement.

It is not difficult to explain, to rationalize, and draw logical conclusions, but one cannot expect that they will be incorporated, change the personality, or eliminate conflicts. They have their place in all therapies, but when used exclusively, they at best affect transient symptom improvements in behavior and superficial adaptations due to diminished anxiety, support, and gratification of infantile dependence. Neuroses and the basic personality are impervious to rationalistic and expository procedures. Whatever observable improvements in functioning occur as a result of rationalization must only be considered temporary; the ontoarchaic patterns entrenched in the unconscious soon reappear.

Psychotherapy that relies predominantly on rationalistic, expository techniques (rather than involving feelings and the unconscious) may succeed in temporarily reinforcing defenses, in reducing anxiety, and allaying guilt; but these benefits vanish as soon as the therapeutic props are removed and the individual is again exposed to the pressures of life. One must differentiate between understanding and insight, and recognize the intention and the capacities to utilize them appropriately.

Specific Assets of a Group Psychotherapist

What has been said so far about the personality qualifications of psychotherapists applies equally to individual and to group therapy. As can be expected, groups make additional demands upon a therapist. As far as its practice is concerned, analytic group psychotherapy is in every regard the same as individual analytically-oriented psychotherapy. It does, however, demand *additional* functions and, therefore, also, qualifications. The chief of these is that the therapist, by virtue of his experience, personal background, and character, should not feel uncomfortable in a group where frank and unhibited expression and relations predominate. Some persons feel threatened and self-conscious in group situations largely because of unpleasant encounters with groups in their past—especially their families, where such difficulties usually originate. (Discomfort and unsuitable feelings in groups are caused by memories of tension, of being attacked or humiliated. They may result from hostile feelings toward groups generally, from fear of disclosure of real or fancied inadequacies, or from unresolved sexual difficulties or distortions in body image.)

Whatever the cause—and there usually is a combination of them—the discomfort may be so strong as to freeze some persons into muteness and withdrawal; others react with overassertiveness; still others with aggression that often results in disruption of the group. The fact that one chooses psychotherapy as one's profession does not cause automatic change of intrapsychic states that are unsuitable for the discharge of the duties involved. These have to be worked through in a thoroughgoing psychoanalysis before the strenuous role of conducting group psychotherapy is undertaken. In general, groups contain many potentials for engendering anxiety, but therapy groups hold many additional possibilities for anxiety responses from the therapist. Among these is his preoccupation with the pathology of each member of the group, and the effect it has on him. Since the therapist cannot exert the same control over the direction and content of interviews as he does in individual treatment, he must seek to prevent inimical effects operating on some of his group members and contaminating the others. Another source of anxiety may be the interpatient encounters: the antagonistic and deleterious affinity reactions among patients. In one case it may lead to protracted tension with possible disruption of the group; in another it may overflow into sexual acting out or overidentification with negative traits and conduct. Some types of acting out may be a threat to the group's existence, and can cause the therapist considerable concern. And there are the ever-present doubts about the suitability of some patients for a specific group and about the appropriateness of its grouping.

The possible sources of anxiety are not limited to external factors alone. The therapist's own needs, too, may threaten him. Being human, he is given to countertransference feelings not only toward patients as individuals, but also toward the group; his needs to be effective and to get results (aim-attachment countertransference). These are always lurking in the recesses of his personality. Then there is to be encountered the actual or threatened mobilization of hostility and negative transferences toward him in the entire group (or in an appreciable segment of it), with which he may decide to cope or to ignore. There are also within his personality the less definable engrams, reflex reactions, and memory traces resulting in hostility and his need to dominate, against which he must be on the alert. The content of patients' communications and hyperemotionalism may arouse in him reactive feelings, which would throw unfavorable light upon him, were he to expose them. These he must repress, or, better still, work through within himself with numerous other countertransferences that cause him internal conflict and difficulties with the group.[2]

Many other conditions and situations in groups, too numerous to recount, may cause anxiety and discomfort for therapists; such difficulties will vary with their personalities and the states of their unconscious, and may make the emotional load they carry a heavy

---

[2] This is one of the situations in psychotherapy that prove therapeutic for the therapist. The therapist is driven into the form of "self-analysis" essential for anyone engaged in this profession. This is far from a therapist's permitting his patients to analyze him; and also from the so-called "status denial" suggested by some therapists.

one. This weight can be borne only by persons who, in addition to educational and academic preparation, have attained an adequate measure of security, ego strength, and freedom from worry, excessive anxiety, projections, and defenses. Optimism and freedom from anxiety are essential to a group therapist. Psychoanalysis is helpful in attaining this condition (though there are persons who, either through temperamental disposition or favorable home and educational backgrounds, have achieved such a state without corrective procedures).

An essential requirement for adequate functioning as a psychotherapist is the ability to withstand hostility from a group without overt reactions or inner disturbance. This is particularly difficult in group treatment, since hostility and aggression are activated and intensified in, by, and among the patients, both as sibling substitutes, as displacement objects for their hostility toward the therapist (as a parent surrogate), and toward the group (as a replica of the family). That patients may discharge hostility without guilt is an essential requirement of the psychotherapy setting and, should the therapist react to it with counterhostility, irritability, resentment, disapproval, or anxiety, he would negate both the intent and the results of therapy. Anyone exposed to the acting out of hostility in therapy groups knows the emotional weight that must be borne—but borne it must be with fortitude if therapy is to succeed.

Insulation against the reactive countertransference which hostility tends to arouse is part of a temperamental disposition, but it can also be the result of reasonable freedom from personal hostilities and associated guilts achieved through adequate therapeutic procedures. The state of emotional relaxation is reinforced when a therapist accepts the fact that where there is no hostility expressed there is no therapy. A great many therapists do not accede to this therapeutic law, largely because of their own anxieties and incapacity to bear up under hostility.

EDUCATIONAL QUALIFICATIONS
The Scope of Training
Essential as they are, personal disposition and talent are not

sufficient by themselves. Talent and ability must be buttressed by appropriate training in content, functions, and related knowledge in dealing with people, for, in his daily work, the therapist has to marshal facts and insights from many sources to meet patients' diverse needs. Patients ask many questions unrelated to their problems in the course of group interviews, as peripheral and tangential ideas and challenges emerge that puzzle them.

These excursions into seemingly unrelated fields prove fruitful though they may be employed at times as resistance or evasion strategies. Nonetheless, the therapist must be competent and ready to deal with subjects that patients encounter through their free associations. Even if the therapist chooses not to be enveigled into discussions unrelated to the central intent, he should do so out of choice rather than lack of information, for transferences can be significantly affected by a show of incompetence.

The therapist who can draw upon the wisdom of the ages, cite allegories, anecdotes, and illustrations to illuminate points in interviews, finds his task of interpretation and explanation greatly lightened. These are simple but poignant roads of illumination and grasp; folk tales, folk lore, parables, aphorisms, stories, and even quips may strike at the soul of a situation and clarify it. If not overemployed, these devices are telling and time saving. The wider his culture and education, the more extensive are the potentials on which the therapist can draw to enhance his effectiveness. In dealing with humans in any field of endeavor, one cannot rely entirely upon the rigid demarcation of a specialty without the risk of becoming dull and uninspired. General cultural interests, as well as professional training, are as necessary for psychotherapists as they are for physicians, teachers, recreationists, counselors, and all others who attempt to enhance the development of people.

To deal with pathology requires knowledge and appreciation of the needs of normal people. Training should not be limited to pathology, for a pathological state is an improverished and frustrated version of normality. To reverse a pathological situation, knowledge of both normality and pathology is required.

The Content of Training

Knowledge of subjects that have direct bearing on psychotherapy is an important requirement. The basic training for group psychotherapy is essentially the same as for individual psychotherapy. In general, it is as follows: a broad and deep understanding of the human personality in its nature and development, including the organic, constitutional, biological, psychological, and social conditions and factors; an understanding of the dynamic interrelation and interaction of the human psycho-organism with the multifarious forces in the environment; a knowledge of the pathogeneses and the conditions under which they occur; skills in clinical diagnosis; knowledge of available techniques of treatment; ability to select patients for specific methods of treatment; and facility in applying these methods.

Preparation for the skills outlined above requires that the psychotherapist be versed in at least the following subjects: zoology; genetics; embryology; physiology; neurology; endocrinology; general, experimental, integrative, Gestalt, abnormal, dynamic, and depth psychologies; child development; psychopathology; clinical diagnosis; basic psychiatry; family dynamics; dynamic sociology; cultural anthropology; and economics.

Once these seemingly disparate subjects are integrated as a body of real understanding, individuals and mankind as a whole emerge as unique products of a vast number of forces and the bearing these forces have upon health and pathology becomes clear.

At first glance, some of the subjects suggested may seem to be either unrelated or remote to the central theme of psychotherapy. However, closer scrutiny will reveal their intrinsic values. A background of zoology and physiology, for example, leads to the placing of individual and species in the setting of nature and to the recognition of the basic survival devices and drives as common to all animals. Man's problems generated by the need to repress or sublimate some of the natural drives loom more significantly when viewed from the perspective of the human family structure, and from the points of view of sociology and social anthropology. When the influences, as well as the importance, of genetic factors in personality are understood, the attitude toward patients becomes more realistic. Given a set of hereditary factors or constitutional limitations, the limits of therapeutic effectiveness are appreciated. Knowledge of gestation and foetal development enriches the therapist's view of the individual as a dynamically evolving organism, and he becomes aware of its mystery and wonder. It also supplies the background, meaning, and the effect of hereditary and intrauterine, prenatal influences in the genesis of some personality deficiencies.

Neurology and endocrinology are too intimately involved in emotional responses and the conditioning of behavior to require extensive elucidation. The prevalent emphasis on psychosomatic and psychogenic disturbances has been shown by numerous independent investigators as being entirely justified. However, the connection between a specific physical symptom and its psychogenic sources remains for the most part obscure. An intimate knowledge of these in specific phenomenology would render the therapist more effective in his remedial efforts. Specificity is what is most needed in this area. But the psychotherapist needs to know also the reverse process; namely, the organic causes of psychological symptoms. This knowledge brings to awareness the unitary nature of the body-mind, but it has even more far-reaching values. It sets the limits of the applicability of psychotherapy to the correction of human maladjustments, and leads to more realistic expectation of results. A somato-psychological orientation leads to an even more pivotal conclusion; namely, the boundaries for non-medical psychotherapists.

The foregoing suggestions for training in various types of psychology are intended to evoke in students the realization for the need of a comprehensive understanding of the human psyche, its nature, aberrations, and pathology. The diversity of human responses being so great it is impossible to rely *in toto* on any system or doctrine in this most complex of all subjects. No one school of thought has the key to all manifestations in everyone. Each can explain *some* phenomena in *some* people. All that can be expected is some degree of agreement on basic frames of reference.

Boundaries for Nonmedical Psychotherapists

The question of nonmedical psychotherapists has been a bone of contention for many decades. Without entering too extensively into this contested area, it is possible to say that, basically, psychotherapy should be the responsibility of medically trained therapists. Society must have this safeguard until proper training facilities have been evolved for psychotherapists without full medical training, and their areas of service clearly defined by law and the professions involved. This need is growing. A plan was outlined as early as 1945, when the first suggestion for a "graduate school for psychotherapy" (see Slavson, 1947) was made, with details for a curriculum. Although this plan will be mentioned more fully, it is now appropriate to quote from it as follows: "It is becoming increasingly evident that medical training as such is not essential for the practice of psychotherapy, providing the therapist does not attempt to deal with psychotic and with organic patients. The lay therapist cannot be too cautious in this respect. He must be able to recognize patients who do not fall within his purview and be bound, both legally and in honor, not to undertake treatment beyond his limited competence. He should in all instances have a prospective patient examined by a general physician, a neurologist, and a psychiatrist."

Since the above was written, psychotherapy by nonmedical personnel has spread far beyond expectation, and a system of consultation, supervision, and controls has been evolved as a safeguard. Another step in this direction has been the licensing of psychologists and caseworkers in some states.

Integrating Rival Schools

No rational person would suggest that any one set of principles or dynamics is true, to the exclusion of all others. Nothing that has ever been said by rational man is either completely false or universally true. Thought and knowledge are sound only when applied to a situation to which they are suited. Equally, all knowledge is false when universally applied. Falsehood stems from the indiscriminate application of a theory or practice. Acquaintance

416

with many schools of psychological thought makes possible a broad and discriminative approach, though there is considerable risk to the neophyte in the confusion that catholicity in educational content may produce. A comprehensive view envisaged here is more sound when built upon the foundation of *one set* of convictions. It is confusing for a beginner to be exposed to fluctuating, multifarious, discrete and conflicting schools of thought. Acceptance or rejection of new ideas should arise from maturing discrimination and should relate to practice and experience. Only then are ideas assimilated. *In a sound education, a frame of reference needs to be established first and accretions and elaborations added later.* In practical training schools (as differentiated from places of academic learning), sound orientation in (and knowledge of) one specific theory and technique must form the foundation on which differentiated elaborations can later be based and applied in special circumstances. Hence, it is recommended that the basic training should be one tested and well-established system of theory and practice, but without prejudicing the student against all others.

Basic Psychiatry

The subjects offered in universities as abnormal psychology, psychopathology, diagnosis, and the body of knowledge that may be described as "basic psychiatry" are transitional from general education to specific professional equipment and are essential in the training of psychiatrists, psychologists and psychiatric caseworkers for the practice of psychotherapy. With rare exceptions even where medically trained personnel is involved, the current practice is to leave these basic subjects and learning skills of psychotherapy to post-graduation, in-service, and residency training.

Two serious difficulties are involved here. One is that hospitals and agencies are not always equipped with adequate teaching staffs, and the other is that the residency training in hospitals is geared for work with psychotics. Recent developments in chemotherapy and the convulsive therapies have occupied a central point in this training, and understandably so, especially with regard to psychotics. But, with rare exceptions, this training is done

417

at the expense of psychotherapy, which is in a subordinate position. Since the bulk of patients who seek treatment either in clinics or by private practitioners are emotionally disturbed and socially maladjusted, rather than full-blown psychotics, the need for adequate training for psychotherapy *per se* looms large in contemporary society.

The nonmedically trained psychotherapists need to know a great deal of the subjects grouped under the titles "basic psychiatry" and diagnosis to recognize the presence of serious psychopathology and somato-pathology, to determine whether patients are within their scope of competency and whether they require the attention of a medically trained therapist or psychiatrist (See Lowrey, 1946).

Child Development Studies and Their Values

The study of child development is a basic requirement. In his practice, the therapist cannot escape the need to consider children, either as patients or as offspring of the adults he is treating. He therefore needs to know the requirements of healthy childhood as well as the sources of pathology in the family, the school, and the community. Adults who become patients are those who have fixated predominantly at stages in childhood; one cannot fully understand any adult without a knowledge of the child's nature and needs, and the pathogenic deviations from them. The psychotherapist constantly deals with infantile residues which must be understood before they can be corrected. The perspective derived from the study of child development forms a continuation of the understanding of the dynamics of human personality derived from genetics and embryology.

Those who practice the healing arts are aware of the existence of basic needs rooted in the biological nature of man and the requirements of his vasomotor activity, expressed in rhythmic and other dynamic forms. The child passes through many phases in his development, each having its own place in the formation of the final product: the adult. During his orderly growth, the child passes through the manipulative-exploratory, the practical-inventive, the intellectual-epistomonic, and the social-participatory phases. (See Slavson and Speer, 1934.) All of these cycles leave their imprint upon him. Inadequate fruition of any of these destroys the harmony of the body-mind and the integrative processes of the personality. Mental health can be achieved only when growth in each phase is fulfilled, so that the subsequent stages can be achieved.

To understand development dynamically, it is necessary to consider the stages of nurture, discipline, education, and schooling, since disturbance or abnormality in these contribute to the creation of personality problems and mental unhealth, as well as do the neuromuscular, the vasomotor, and the endocrine-affect systems. The absence of adequate knowledge of these and their place in total health may lead to error in choosing and applying appropriate therapeutic procedures.

This perspective of child development is the scientific base for psychotherapy and for a fuller appreciation of the supra-complex phenomenon, the human individual, with his similarities and divergences from all others in temperamental disposition, congenital and hereditary characteristics, and differentials in potential.

It is upon these broader insights that sound psychotherapy must be based. Dealing with people is predominantly an art; but the art of psychotherapy is rooted in science which, in addition to its other values, serves to reveal its possibilities as a check upon its effectiveness, and points up its limitations.

Family Relations

This dynamic view of man's development from its primary biological sources to social atomism must of necessity include the conditions and interactions in the family and their effect in molding health and illness in the individual.[3] Whatever is human in us is given us by other humans or, as the Greeks expressed it: "Man is nothing without the work of man." Itard's (1932) *The Wild Boy of Aveyron,* and Gesell's (1944) *The Wolf Child and Human Child,* leave little doubt about this. We find dramatic confirmation of it in the contrast of personality structure, values and conduct

---

[3] I have attempted to show the effects of family upon a child and to indicate the type of parent that induces specific clinical problems in children. (See Slavson, 1952a.)

in individuals in some contemporary underdeveloped countries, as well as among the more progressive nations.

The Social Sciences

While the study of family backgrounds are more or less customary in planning patients' treatment, socio-economic and religious factors are not as frequently taken into consideration. This neglect frequently leads to serious misunderstanding of the meaning of patients' communications, delays progress, and at times causes it to bog down. The therapist must know the impact of the specific socio-economic climate on the formation of personality, the fantasies and attitudes toward the self and the value systems, first through the family, as a child, and later through direct contact with this climate.

The Methods of Training

As a result of extensive seminars, individual training, and supervision of rather large numbers of psychotherapists drawn from the various clinical disciplines, we have arrived at the following conclusion: ". . . the skills of psychotherapy are not always a part of the caseworkers' and psychiatrists' equipment.[4] There is a considerable schism between descriptive and diagnostic psychiatry and its dynamic, therapeutic counterpart. One deals with the results and symptoms of total personality breakdowns; the other with chronic or acute malintegration. . . . We have found that frequently knowledge of psychodynamics and even of psychopathology does not guarantee skill in psychotherapy. . . ." (Slavson, 1947, page 389.)

As to the training for the practice of group psychotherapy, we had the following to say: ". . . group therapy is not a specialty apart and separate from the total practice of psychotherapy. It belongs with general psychotherapy. . . . One cannot master the group techniques apart from these general understandings that are essential to all psychotherapy. . . . No one who has not had a thorough and prolonged experience in general psychotherapy ought to at-

[4] Psychologists were omitted from the list because, at the time it was written (1945), few, if any, psychologists were engaged in the practice of psychotherapy.

tempt to do group therapy in any of its forms. Dealing with groups is vastly more complicated than dealing with individuals. In the treatment of an individual, the therapist is to a considerable extent in control of the therapeutic situation. According to his understanding of the needs, at a given time, he may or may not encourage or stimulate the patient's production; he can direct the interview by means of a leading question or a remark; he can go passive and uncommunicative, or actively give interpretation.

"In groups, this autonomy, and in some respects also power, of the therapist is denied him. The catalytic effect of the group members upon one another . . . is such that the situation is taken out of the therapist's hands. . . ." (Slavson, 1947, page 388.)

It is worth re-emphasizing the fact that group psychotherapy is only a special application of general psychotherapy, and that preparation for this work is rooted in the latter; nor should practitioners limit their practice to groups exclusively, any more than they should receive training in group therapy without first mastering work with individuals. Training in group "techniques" without first being expert in individual treatment is like building an edifice without a foundation.

Therapists may or may not require a personal experience in an analytic therapy group as patients before they essay practice. This is an individual matter which depends on his security with groups and other personality considerations. Since the content and the general treatment of patients' productions are the same in analytically-oriented individual as in group treatment, a therapist with the needed personal security can make the transition without an actual group experience, provided he can obtain competent supervision until he can work on his own. Those who feel the need for a group experience should observe the work of competent therapists behind a screen or one-way mirror and microphone. Corporeal presence as "observer" or as "auxiliary therapist" is not advisable, since the character of the group and its productions change in the presence of a stranger.

The Curriculum

Training in group treatment should be available to psychiatrists, psychiatric caseworkers, and clinical psychologists who have had prolonged experience in individual psychotherapy and who have met the educational qualifications outlined above or who have taken an equivalent course of study. The curriculum dealing directly with group psychotherapy should consist of: (1) seminars in dynamic psychiatry; (2) seminars in group psychotherapy; (3) supervision in groups; (4) intensive supervision on an individual basis; (5) field work in hospitals and agencies; (6) a psychiatric consultation and guidance service for trainees, when necessary; (7) a review of the history and various theories and practices of group psychotherapy; (8) the methods of integrating group therapy into hospital and agency programs.

Training Seminars

The subjects suggested under (1), (2), (3), and (7) may be taught didactically, by discussion, or by the Socratic method. The techniques of group treatment, however, are best taught through prolonged practicum, group-case seminars, or "group supervision" (as it is sometimes referred to), under an experienced and competent leader. This method is the most effective in conveying experience and sensitizing trainees to what transpires in groups and in individual patients. Detail analysis and discussion of protocol reports of actual sessions are especially fruitful since emphasis can be laid upon the minutiae of the spontaneous process in groups. Discussion on the basis of observation of groups through screens or one-way mirrors is even more effective. Trainees should be encouraged and expected to participate in the unraveling of patients' and the therapist's actions, motives and interactions, and their latent content. Where written protocols are used as the basis for training, the conduct of the therapist whose reports are under study, or whose groups are observed, would require special attention. Appropriate or erroneous responses on his part need to be identified and reasons solicited, both from the group's therapist and the trainees. Special attention needs to be given to his responses, or lack of them, in the light of their effect upon the group and upon individual patients, with special reference to their suitability to the ongoing communication and the current

422

affect that prevails. Progress and regress need to be noted, and reasons identified in relation to the nuclear problems of the patients and their individual productions. The direction, content, and transference reactions require special attention. Following the preliminary educational and training backgrounds described, such seminars are the core and most valuable part of training.

Types of seminars can be classified as survey, didactic, exploratory, and practicum. The *survey seminars* consist of a review of the history, development, and current practices and trends in group psychotherapy. Their purpose is to widen the scope of understanding and significance of the field of group psychotherapy in the minds of the trainees, thus enriching their feeling for, and appreciation of, their chosen field. On the basis of reading and discussion, the *didactic seminars* seek to convey established and validated information and knowledge concerning individual and group psychotherapy. In these seminars the theoretical material forms the foundation, while elaborations of technique result from reading and investigation by the students themselves. Following didactic seminars, the *exploratory seminar* is used to widen the field by investigation of possible applications of group psychotherapy to clinical categories as well as to various fields and settings in which it is or can be employed. The aim here is to throw light upon specific considerations and problems with a view to deepening the students' perceptions and understanding of particular psychodynamic, nosological, and clinical entities and differentials in treatment. The *practicum seminars* concentrate upon actual practice and are based upon protocol records or tape recordings in which the total process, with special emphasis upon the function and participation of the therapist, is considered and analyzed.

In-Service and Field Training

An indispensable training area in psychotherapy is field work, or in-service practice, or internship, as it is variously called. It is essential that prospective therapists have actual experience under guidance. This form of training is offered in hospitals and clinics with other training programs, and now, it is required in the training for psychotherapy. Such control consultations are helpful also for experienced therapists, for they provide them with a "third person" assessment of the course the treatment is taking and of the therapist's part in it. The "blind spots" and unconscious countertransference feelings and resulting reactions are not always within the awareness of the person involved. The judgment, and opinion of a person who is outisde of the therapeutic complex cannot but add to effectiveness. Supervision is an essential requirement as a step toward independent practice; regardless of how conversant in theory he may be, the therapist should not undertake independent practice without prolonged guided experience.[5]

Educational Seminars versus Therapy

A word of caution is necessary against permitting the training seminars to turn into therapeutic or quasi-therapeutic sessions (which they sometimes tend to become). There is great temptation, especially on the part of neophytes, to direct interest to the feelings and motivations of the therapist whose groups are studied. Their own transference-countertransference attitudes are inevitably activated during an analytic study of a group therapy interview. Also, there is the lurking temptation to assume the role of a therapist by some of the training seminar members.

The nature of the content of the seminar discussions and the smallness of the group tend to generate a therapeutic climate to which the uncautious or the unaware may readily yield, and the leader-supervisor of the seminar has to take steps to prevent it. He has to consciously keep the interchange to its original aim; to education and not to therapy. To a large degree, he can do this by eschewing reference to the student-therapist's emotional involvement, beyond his responses and conduct or lack of them. His avoidance of exploring or calling attention to his students' feelings sets a frame of reference for the discussion and a tacit group code by which all are guided. Avoidance of therapy in the educational situation of the seminar prevents tension and anxiety which always interfere with the learning process.

---

[5] My experience leads me to the conclusion that this period should be between three to seven years, according to the innate capacities and talents of the learner.

FUNCTIONS

Four Functions

The preceding discussions of transference and countertransference, acting out, the group interviews, the nature of analytic groups, and the personal and educational qualifications of a psychotherapist, included in their context many of the therapist's functions, by implication and by direct statements. The following discussion will supplement and restate some of them in a more systematic manner.

A therapist has four generic functions: directional, stimulative, extensional, and interpretive (see Slavson, 1952).

The *directional* function is exercised when an individual or a group of patients become enmeshed in a discussion in which a number of subjects and points of view are propounded by the participants, with no objective or conclusion in sight. As one patient put it: "We are going around in circles." The therapist must perceive the frequently latent central theme with which the group is struggling and help it to concentrate on and follow the line which preoccupies their common unconscious. He thus extricates the group from its own net of confusion and gives it direction, so that the interchange can ultimately become fruitful. However, if the conflictual or confused productions are a manifestation of resistance, his interpretation of this fact falls under the category of "interpretive" function, which we shall describe presently.

The therapist may, at times, find it necessary to change the direction of the interview because of its undesirability for the group, the inimical effect it may have on some of the participants, or because, in his judgment, it will not lead to a productive end. He can accomplish this by *deflecting* the discussion to a less disturbing topic or he can directly *divert* the ongoing conversation by a question or a statement that would lead to a different channel of conversation or catharsis.

The *stimulative* role is assumed when, because of repression, resistance, emotional fatigue, anxiety, or lagging interest, a group grows impassive or indulges in a discussion of inconsequential minutiae and top realities. Under these circumstances, the therapist should employ suitable strategies to stimulate the group toward more significant productions and interactions. He may *question* a patient or the group concerning a matter or an idea that is of significance to them; *recall* a related topic, situation, or idea from a former group interview; or *retrace,* from previous interviews, the background of the content being presently produced. Such efforts eventually lead to a subject of emotional significance. In this capacity, the therapist's role can be described as that of an *instigator* or *catalyst.*

Frequently, because of a variety of emotional obstacles or blockages, a group becomes fixed on a subject, as in stereotpy, and cannot extricate itself for a period of time. When, in his judgment, a situation requires his intervention, a therapist should extend the communication beyond the arena of fixation. In so doing, he assumes an *extensional* role, he helps the group to extend their communications beyond the block through activating forward movement. He can do this by questioning, by introducing a new elaboration of the current topic or by relating it to some significant emotion or event.

The therapist can make important contributions both to the therapeutic process and to the growth of group members by increasing their "psychological literacy." There are always some patients in a group, whose comprehension of psychological processes is limited. In many instances, patients do not recognize psychogenic causes for their and others' difficulties. They ascribe the blame to physical or material causes, or insist that individuals could act "differently" if they only *willed* it. As a result, they are critical and punitive and believe in "direct action" in difficult situations. To arouse in them an appreciation of the autonomous nature of conditioned attitudes, psychoneuroses, and emotional responses is a major step in psychotherapy. Such psychological literacy is also a major ingredient in general intelligence and wisdom.

The extensional service of a therapist can serve in many instances as the foundation and even the core of (ego) treatment. There are intimate connections between the conscious and unconscious ego in individuals. This proximity varies as to areas of significance, but in many respects awareness aids in solving some behavioral and relational difficulties. Thus, extending psychological literacy can be of great value in psychotherapy, though it cannot be considered as the sole, or, even major part.

The psychotherapist can also aid in advancing an idea or understanding beyond the point that the group could on its own. He opens doors for them, without becoming academic or didactic. Though one cannot entirely rely on this procedure in a fundamental type of psychotherapy, it is possible at times to activate emotionally clarifying introspection and self-analysis, in some patients, through a pointed statement, an explanation, a remark or a question.

Interpretation, as used in sound psychotherapy, consists of the therapist's bringing to the surface meanings of a patient's communications and feelings when the patient has sufficiently unraveled repressions and resistances to the point of *readiness for insight.* In this respect, interpretation is differentiated from explanation. Explanation is directed toward intellectual understanding.

In order to be able to interpret appropriately, the therapist has to be intimately familiar with the psychodynamics and pathology of each patient, understand the significance of his production at the moment, and assess his readiness for interpretation. This involves a knowledge of the state of repressions and censors and their relation to the preconscious and unconscious of each patient at the moment. Here, the importance of free floating attention and controlled spontaneity is evident, for the therapist has to exercise selectivity in responses; he must be vigilant as to manifest productions, their latent content, and the undercurrents in transference attitudes toward himself and among the patients. Such perceptiveness of the current stream of feelings and events in the therapeutic situation needs to be buttressed by a capacity to anticipate the possible developments that may arise from his remarks, explanations, and interpretations. Such *anticipatory judgment* is essential. While seemingly dealing appropriately with a current development, psychotherapists sometimes discover that they have opened a Pandora's box. The reactions and repercussions that follow, sometimes delayed, prove inimical to the total treatment effort.

In a group, as in individual treatment, the therapist needs to differentiate between the *focal* and *peripheral areas* of an interview and, whenever indicated, guide the group to concentrate on the former. Above all, his remarks should be designed to *continue the trend* of the patients' productions if they are fruitful or promise to become so, rather than diverting them, unless the latter becomes advisable for some special consideration. By and large, free association must be permitted to flow unhampered by interruptions from the therapist and, as far as possible, by other patients.

Passivity and Creativity

This leads us to what we consider the major role of the therapist: passivity and creative listening. Regardless of his overt and covert functions and his periodic participation, his chief role is that of a passive participant who observes and registers what is going on within the psyche of each patient and the interactions in the group as a whole. In analytic group psychotherapy, passivity has different significance and meaning for different patients, as well as for the same patient at different stages.

A therapist's remarks inevitably carry symbolic authority. They are clothed in an aura of wisdom and are pregnant with meaning in the eyes of patients. This charismatic prestige status can be employed to the benefit or detriment of patients. In teaching and education, in counseling, and, to a lesser extent, also in guidance, authority status is employed directly; it is assumed that the participants are, to various degrees, in a receiving role. In psychotherapy, where internal change is sought, the individual has to *live through* and *live over,* many past experiences and freely discharge bound up feelings and anxieties. This can be done maximally only when unhampered by interferences or blockage from the outside.

The art of creative listening lies in the ability to remain receptively silent. We have all witnessed angry outbursts from persons, when we attempted to interpose a statement or ask a question while they were narrating affect-laden and deeply charged feelings. The anxiety-laden ego was unable to withhold the urge to discharge the pressures on it, even for a brief moment. What the ego desperately needed was an uninterrupted outward flow of feeling, to rid itself of its excessive load.

The therapist has to be capable of creative listening *par excellence*. If he is to encourage free association, his verbal responsiveness needs to be an exceptional phase of his functions rather than the rule, and his nonverbal reactions must be carefully controlled. The rule, though neither absolute nor exclusive, is silence and empathic listening.

Intrapsychic and behavioral passivity marks the therapist as nonjudgmental. A serious concern to patients is his possible disapproval. The therapist's emotional and behavioral passivity leaves the patient freer to reveal the content of the deepest recesses of his personality, heretofore hidden from himself and others. Unsuitable and badly timed response (verbal and nonverbal), may magnify feelings and past events or discourage revelation of them altogether, according to their symbolic meanings to the patients. Serving as a neutral screen on which thoughts and feelings can be projected, the therapist aids the flow of catharsis and self-revelation.

Restraint conveys to the patients an image of strength and power, which encourages identification transference and enhances the therapist's value as an identification model and ego ideal. Even adult patients, in their regressive states, model themselves after the therapist, as children do after their parents. Since the functioning of the ego is in great part modeled by imitation of, and identification with, parents, this process is relived in psychotherapy, though in lesser intensity and effectiveness. Nonetheless, the function of the therapist as a model of identification cannot be underestimated.

The passive role of the therapist and his capacity to maintain silence when expedient, lends weight to his remarks and interpretations when they are made. This is characteristic of all communication. The popular notion of the "strong, silent man" carries out this image. The folk unconsciously correctly perceives excessive communicativeness as stemming from weakness. Loquacity has its roots in anxiety, feelings of inferiority and dependence, as well as some psycho-organic sources. Because silence is so intimately associated with strength, the therapist has to utilize this symbol of power for the benefit of therapeutic effectiveness.

In the practice of face-to-face psychotherapy, it is more difficult to gracefully carry through the role of passivity and prevent verbal and nonverbal reactions. Should a therapist succeed in this too well, patients would feel awkward and rejected. The unaccustomed sight of someone who remains entirely untouched, while others display strong emotions, creates uneasiness and even resentment, especially in those patients who once suffered at the hands of unloving parents. To them, consistent silence spells rejection and indifference to their suffering and the therapist is perceived as an unloving, rejecting parent. Though maintaining *relative* silence and noninvolvement, the therapist must be able to *convey* nonverbally or by an occasional brief remark or monosyllable, that he is interested in the patient's communication and feels empathically with him. He must prevent blocking catharsis, either by revealing his feelings or diverting communication from the central theme, except where a longer expository statement or interpretation is indicated. Here is where the art of psychotherapy, as differentiated from its science, is of prime importance.

CHARISMA AS QUALITY AND FUNCTION

As Quality

Charisma is defined as "a spiritual gift or talent . . . power of healing, gift of tongues; or prophesying; (person) regarded as set apart from ordinary persons . . . endowed with the capacity of eliciting enthusiastic popular support in leadership and . . . direction of human affairs" (Webster's New International Dictionary, 3rd Ed.).

In the fantasy of the patient, the therapist possesses one or more of the qualities enumerated in the above definition, for without his belief in the therapist's capacity to resolve his difficulties, unburden him of his troubles and bring harmony into his life, the patient would not turn to him. This almost unconscious belief, as with many others in the life of man, is a survival of the infantile magical powers projected by the child upon his parents: the rescue fantasies of the mother and the protective powers of the father. It is also in this sense, as well as in the commonly accepted understanding of it, that the transference relation operates between therapist and patient. The therapist is endowed with suprapowers in the same manner and for the identical reasons as the physician, and the therapist has to maintain that status during the term of the treatment if he is to be effective and serve as an ego ideal and object of identification.

It is only with this attitude on the part of the patient that the therapist's statements and interpretations can carry the weight and conviction that motivate the patient to accept and integrate them into his value system and as guides in life. Thus, "status denial" by the therapist strips him of his most important source of influence in the reconstruction of personality. Some therapists establish, from the outset, a first-name conviviality with their patients in the belief that this "closeness" and informality aid the relation, and it probably does. But the relation is not a therapeutic one. The changes in personality that sound psychotherapy should effect, result from growth, just as they do from the realignment and reweighting of psychic forces. The duration and goal of this growth is set by the therapist in his *being* as well as by his *doing,* as is the case with parents in the formulation of the child's character and personality. To eliminate the charismatic component of the therapist's image is to strip him of his powers and effectiveness.

Because of their neurotic needs, many patients are happy with the elimination of the therapist's superior status, for it enhances, by comparison, that of their own. Equalitarianism in the therapeutic relation advances their image of themselves, for they do not have to assume a psychologically subordinate role which is inherent in patient-toward-therapist attitudes, and lifts them out of the stigma with which seeking psychologic help is unavoidably associated. Similarly, the rejection by the therapist of his rightful status frees him from the responsibilities that would otherwise devolve upon him. As already indicated, adults are not accessible to psychotherapy. Only children can be so treated and by the act of becoming a patient, the adult becomes (psychologically) a child in relation to the therapist. When the therapist eschews his parental (charismatic, magical) image and instead takes on the psychological guise of a sibling, his value becomes nil.

As Function

On the other hand, to the degree that a therapist overplays his charismatic role, his effectiveness is diminished. Charisma is a state of being, not of acting. The hypnotic-life effect of a dynamic display of power, if continued during the course of treatment, forces the patient to remain in the role of a submissive child. As a result, his emotional evolvement is prevented. Patients may show considerable behavioral and symptomatic improvement under these circumstances, but improvements are merely acts of submission to a powerful, directive and protective (parental) figure. The intrapsychic reconstruction necessary for permanence of change is lacking, and though patients may display improvement during, and for a brief period after, treatment, they return to their original patterns of feeling and acting when the charismatic influence of the therapist wears off.

Overplaying the parental protective, giving and guiding role by the therapist has a similar effect—the patients' emotional maturation and self-reliance are stunted, even though they may warmly respond to the manner and maneuvers of such a therapist. This relationship and the therapeutic process prove very satisfying to patients, for they are disturbed minimally, but psychic change is not attained through placidity. Real psychotherapy is not pleasant; for it is only "in suffering that the human soul is purified," and peace is attained through pain.

MACHIAVELLISM VERSUS SPONTANEITY

All psychotherapy is Machiavellian in the sense that every step taken or statement made is planned to induce the patient to respond or behave in accordance with the therapist's end. It is not an equalitarian relationship and the therapist cannot be spontane-

TABLE 1

Qualifications and Functions of Group Therapists

Personal	Educational	Functions	Countertransferences
Charisma	*Curriculum*	*Facilitative*	Positive
Maturity	Zoology	Directional	Negative
Intuition	Genetics	Stimulative	Aim-attached
Perception	Embryology	Extensional	Ambivalent
Empathy	Neurology	Interpretive	Toward group
Motivation	Physiology		
Imagination	Endocrinology		
Allotropism	Psychology		
Frustration tolerance	General		
Creative listening	Experimental		
Security with groups	Integrative		
	Gestalt		
	Abnormal		
	Dynamic		
	Depth		
	Child Development		
	Family Relations		
	Psychopathology		
	Clinical Diagnosis		
	Basic Psychiatry		
	Dynamic Sociology		
	Cultural Anthropology		
	Economics		
	Seminars in		
	Dynamic Psychiatry		
	Group Psychotherapy		
	Group Supervision		
	Individual supervision		
	History of Group psychotherapy		
	Methods of interpretation		
	Field Practice		
	In hospitals		
	In clinics		
	Psychiatric		
	Personal Guidance		
	Personal consultation		
	Types of Seminars		
	Didactic		
	Survey		
	Exploratory		
	Practicum		

ous or feel free to say or do what his impulses dictate or what, under ordinary circumstances, would be fitting. Each statement, grimace, and nuance is part of a plan to aid the therapeutic endeavor. What saves these "conspiratorial" strategies from the nefarious implications of Machiavellism is that they are intended to benefit the patient rather than the "manipulator" (the therapist). The interplay of the therapist *vis-à-vis* the patient is comparable to a chess game without the competitive element and intent to defeat. At times, a patient's strategies and pronouncements may have these aims, but never the therapist's, whose byplay and carefully chosen responses are directed toward freeing the patient rather than defeating him.

Even the group psychotherapist's very first steps are patterned. His choice and grouping of patients are done with a view toward achieving definite results, which he already envisages and toward which he will subtly push. His conduct during the therapeutic sessions and his maneuvers are dictated by his plan for each patient and for the group as a whole. The therapist may occasionally veer from his direction, but only when it fits his plans. Thus, whatever he does, whether he expresses himself freely or withholds responses, he temporizes in a thoughtful fashion. Much harm can be done by a therapist's entirely candid opinions and pronouncements, when patients are still unready for them; he may invade threat areas and threaten ego defenses with disastrous effects on the transference complex.

Thus, the therapist's sincerity lies not so much in his performance as in his intention; this is one of the very rare situations in which the end justifies the means. The therapist's directness and spontaneity increase as the patients' emotional and intellectual security is strengthened to the point where he can utilize the therapist's frankness and confrontation. This, too, is part of a design.

THE FACILITATIVE ROLE OF THE THERAPIST

In working with people, one can be authoritarian, dominant, equalitarian, didactic, or *facilitative*. In aiding children and adults toward growth and self-fulfillment, all these roles are assumed at various times, and in different relations, as well as at different

434

stages. A parent, for example, needs to be both authoritarian and facilitative in the evolvement of the child's personality. In ordinary schooling, the teacher needs to be in a dominant, didactic position and, whenever possible, facilitative as well; the more he plays the latter role, the more helpful he is in the enrichment of his pupils' personalities. Where discipline is the sole relationship pattern, as in the army, authority and domination prevail, with little possibility for other types of relations to arise between the different ranks.

In counseling and guidance, the characteristic role of the leader is predominantly didactic (though it is tempered by gentleness and understanding and is devoid of the harshness usually associated with didacticism) and facilitating. The therapist's role is predominantly one of *facilitating* the trend toward health and balance (dynamic homeostasis). His function is to set into operation the latent trends and capacities of the patient for eliminating the noxious elements and blocks to health.

The therapeutic sessions alone cannot be viewed as constituting total therapy. Rather, they are the instruments by which the intrapersonal processes are activated that lead to improvement or recovery. The therapist is both the stimulating and catalytic agent, with the corrective process internally occurring as a result of the variety of influences and stimuli he sets off for the *continuing processes between the therapeutic sessions.* This is as true of individual psychotherapy and psychoanalysis as it is of group psychotherapy. In group psychotherapy, the activating stimuli flow from the group as well as from the therapist, with the former most often predominating.

When therapists insist on freedom for patients and on "nondirective" and nonauthoritarian roles for themselves, they are emphasizing their facilitative function, a function that helps the patient's reconstruction of his psychic forces toward greater harmony through inner changes. This can be formulated somewhat differently and perhaps more clearly: The therapist, whether in individual or group treatment, creates a climate of interpersonal relations through which the patient is activated by his own effort to overcome the noxious and disturbing forces that dominate his psyche. As a corollary, authoritarian and dominating values and attitudes defeat the therapeutic intent. While didacticism may at times serve the interest of a patient, its consistent use is inappropriate in psychotherapy. An equalitarian therapist is also damaging to the group. Lacking the image of authority of the therapist (by virtue of his greater maturity and better personal and social integration), the equalitarian principle denies patients their essential feeling of security and the transferential frame of reference necessary for their own growth.

The facilitative role is the most subtle and difficult to discharge. It requires a great degree of patience, self-discipline, perceptiveness, genuine respect for the patient's personality, and above all, empathy for his herculean struggle toward self-realization. The therapist has to follow perceptively, empathically, and with patience, each patient's web of circuitous and tangential convolutions, and help him to extricate himself from the tyranny of his affects, confusions, and confabulations.

We have already indicated the autonomy and self-perpetuating nature of neuroses and their imperviousness to reason and understanding. The dissolution of the psyche's dependence on its neuroses and on the compulsion to repeat is the chief aim of psychotherapy. In this, positive transference feelings toward the therapist, are his fulcrum. Instead of relying on habitual stereotyped neurotic mechanisms, the patient can relinquish them for the security he receives from the therapist and/or the group. This transfer from the neurotic syndrome to the personality of the therapist or the group, is of singular significance in analytic therapy. The following sentence from a patient's letter illustrates this point: "It is not only what you have done for me that was so helpful through these years, but what was most important to me was that I have always felt that you had confidence in me."

It is probably in this area, more than any other, that the "values" of the therapist are of crucial importance. Whatever the therapist's social, political, ethical, and moral values may be, the values he entertains toward his patients *as human beings,* his respect for them, and his genuine interest in them, unadulterated

436

by any ulterior or vested motives, ultimately determines the success of treatment.

An Illustration of the Therapist's Functions

The following brief account of a group session rather dramatically illustrates some of the points we have made about the role of the therapist. The group consisted of mothers who had been initially involved on a guidance level in relation to their children, but were currently in treatment on their own behalf because of the seriousness of their personality problems. The following record is of the twenty-eighth treatment session.[6] The therapist was a woman.

At one point during the group interview, Mrs. C., who seemed quite disturbed, narrated an incident in her home. She began by saying that there had been a crisis in her family. Susie, her teenage daughter, had been using the phone frequently and running up a very high 'phone bill. Mrs. C. yelled at Susie, but "had done nothing else about it," and finally she told Susie that if she used the 'phone again, Mrs. C. would severly punish her. Susie used the telephone that evening and Mrs. C. told her to go to bed early. Susie refused to go, declaring that she would stay up to watch TV and "that's final." Mrs. C. "blew her top" and said everything negative about Susie that she could think of. Susie suddenly switched and agreed with everything that Mrs. C. had said: she felt that she "is terrible" and began to pull at her hair, screaming that she was afraid she was going to "lose her mind." At this point in her narrative, Mrs. C. began to cry, then checked herself and went on to say that all she could think of then was that her child needed comforting and this is what she had done. Susie then told her that the thing that she cannot stand the most is when Mrs. C. yells at her. Mrs. C. promised Susie that she would try not to yell, and even though she would punish her if she did something bad, she would try and stop yelling. Mrs. C. also told

<hr/>

[6] Though some of the patients' initials are the same as those in the group cited in Chapter X, this is a different group.

Susie that she was coming to the clinic to get help and that she was working on her problems, if only Susie would work on hers. Mrs. C. declared she "really was frightened" at what she and her husband could do to the child and she was afraid that they might actually "make her lose her mind." She turned and asked the therapist if that was possible. The therapist asked Mrs. C. what it meant to her to "lose one's mind." Mrs. G. angrily said, "Reassure her!" The therapist said again that she thought that the best way she could help Mrs. C. was to find out what this meant to her. Mrs. F. said she thought it meant "losing control."

Mrs. G. attempted to "soft pedal" the whole thing, by saying that much too much was being made of this, and that Susie was probably upset because of her poor report card from school and her outburst had had nothing to do with the home. Mrs. C. did not agree and said she was "very concerned." Mrs. S. asked if she did not have faith in Dr. C., Mrs. C.'s therapist at the clinic, and Miss E., the child's therapist. Mrs. C. said yes, but she thought that "this was something they can't do" and that she and her husband had to face it. She said that one of the things that Susie said was that she was afraid to tell Mr. C. about her poor report card, because he would yell at her, too. Mrs. C. told Susie that while they could not approve of her poor report card, she would talk to her husband about both of them trying not to yell so much. Mrs. C. admitted that it is almost impossible for her to refrain from yelling. However, she feels she must do it. Mrs. K. said she has found that if one tries to "handle something like this, the feelings come later. Even though it is not easy in the beginning, it gets easier the more you work on it."

Mrs. K. cautioned Mrs. C. that Susie will probably bait her again, and that she will yell at Susie again. This is true of her daughter, Jen, she said, but continued to encourage Mrs. C. to try to control her yelling. Mrs. F. said that Mrs. C. should ascribe less blame to herself and more to her husband. Mrs. C. replied that perhaps Mrs. F. is working on "something" of her own and projecting it on others. Actually, Mrs. C. felt she did not need so much relief of guilt. Even though the situation was very upsetting to her, at least she and Susie were now talking to each other. What concerned her at the present was whether Susie "could really lose her mind." Anxiety was mounting in the group, and the women now began to talk simultaneously and very loudly. Mrs. G. suddenly stood up and declared that it was too noisy for her and that she was leaving for about 10 minutes, and she left the room. The group was stunned and looked at the therapist, who merely said, "I wonder why Mrs. G. left?" Mrs. C. thought that this was "one of the most important things that had happened (in the group)." She expressed concern about Mrs. G., saying, "It was the talk about insanity that really bothered her and not the loudness." The whole group agreed that this must have been the reason, for they had talked this loud before and Mrs. G. had not minded it.

Mrs. C. said that Mrs. G.'s reaction was tied up with the planned placement of her (schizophrenic) son (for whom placement in an institution was planned). The women then discussed how they would react to placement of their children and to the possibility of their child "losing her mind." Mrs. C. said she felt sorry for Susie, but she also felt guilty and concerned about what other people would think of her as a mother. . . .

Mrs. G. returned and apologized in an embarrassed way. When asked why she left, she replied that "it was just too loud" for her. Mrs. C. ascribed the incident to the talk about insanity, but Mrs. G. denied this, insisting that it was "just too loud and I can't stand yelling," and she did not want to listen to "it" anymore. Mrs. S. pointed out that leaving the room was similar to what Mrs. C. did with Steven (her son) all the time, whenever the going got rough. Mrs. C. said, "That is exactly what I do." She then expressed anger at Dr. K. (the boy's therapist) for not doing more for Steven. Mrs. S. told Mrs. G. that it was she, herself, who had to decide what she was going to do.

At the end of this session, Mrs. C. said that they were all going out "with butterflies in our stomachs."

Mrs. C.'s recital of the "crisis" in her home and her fear of Susie's "losing her mind," were not adequately handled by the therapist. The "switch" from Susie's defiance to abject submissiveness and mental self-flagellation should have been explored. The change, by its suddenness and contrast, disturbed the psychologically illiterate Mrs. C. What may have come out of the exploration was that the girl had tried to placate the mother and thus evade further exacerbation of fear or guilt, or she had attempted to frighten her mother by suggesting loss of sanity. If the mother was anxious she should have been reassured on that point by the therapist. Mrs. G., in asking for reassurance for Mrs. C., actually sought it for herself, for, having a schizophrenic child, the scene that was being unfolded before her made her extremely, and unprofitably, anxious.

The therapist's hyperpassive demeanor in "exploring" what it meant to the mother "to lose one's mind," not only denoted absence of empathy for a mother in a difficult situation, but had an element of absurdity. Losing one's mind has a clear meaning, which needs no definition. When the therapist persisted on this course, Mrs. F. tried to define it as "losing control." Coming from Mrs. F., this was significant, for she was a borderline schizophrenic whose outbursts against her husband and children were extreme in their violence and loudness (which she had begun to bring slightly under control as her parallel individual and group treatment progressed).

Another subject that needed exploration was Mrs. C.'s uncontrollability with respect to yelling, but this could be initiated only after understanding its significance to her. Most often (as in Mrs. C.'s case), it is a culturally determined pattern of the uncultivated and uneducated, that can be discussed on a guidance or counseling level. It can also be a manifestation of oral aggression and, thus, a character disorder; a result of neurotic irritability with weak controls; or part of a schizophrenic syndrome with fragile defenses. If these are the bases of this pattern, the elimination of the symptom has to wait for intrapsychic changes that should accrue from treatment. Oral aggression disappears with passing from the oral to the genital phase through transference identification, insight, and awareness. When it is a neurotic symptom response, elimination of inner tensions increases frustration tolerance and results in a disappearance of the screaming. Where it is part of a schizophrenic syndrome, strengthening of the ego and defenses would have that effect. In Mrs. C.'s case it was a habit disorder.

The tension that Mrs. C.'s recital, disturbance and crying created grew intolerable to Mrs. G. She tried to "soft pedal" the tension by laying the blame on the school, saying that Susie's reaction had nothing to do with the home and Mrs. S. tried to reassure Mrs. C. by suggesting she get help from the therapist. This was done either because of their own mounting anxiety or their sympathy with Mrs. C. Mrs. C.'s guilt impelled her to return to the subject of her screaming at her daughter and she recognized the difficulty in controlling herself, again suggesting the advisability of working on this "habit" of hers. Mrs. K., having a healthier personality and better control of her impulses, had learned her lesson and held out hope for Mrs. C., suggesting a *modus operandi* for control.

This episode illustrates emotional catharsis and self-recognition of an inner problem and conflictual difficulty (by Mrs. C.); empathic response (in all the women); emotional induction (in Mrs. G.) and identification (especially in Mrs. K.); vicarious catharsis (in Mrs. F.); and efforts at interpatient therapy (by Mrs. K.). The latter and Mrs. K.'s identification, was carried further when she predicted developments in Mrs. C.'s and Susie's future interactions. Mrs. F. introduced the subject of blaming husbands. In this she associated with her own violent quarrels and constant bickering with her own husband, whom she literally drives out of the home. Mrs. C. retaliated by pointing up Mrs. F.'s projections, which was entirely correct in this case.

Mrs. C. reiterated her concern about her daughter's "losing her mind." The therapist's failure to reassure her that people do not become psychotic just because they become upset or angry, preys upon Mrs. C.'s mind. This failure unnecessarily heightened her anxiety and guilt, at the same time raising the anxiety level in the other women. The anxiety became unendurable to Mrs. G. and she left the room.

The shock caused by her departure is quite understandable. It not only brought to the remaining women's awareness the depth of Mrs. G.'s disturbance, but also served as a rebuke to them for causing it. In their guilt (by identification) and anxiety, they regressively turn to the therapist (mother figure), who instead of calming them down, thrusts them into explorations of the reasons for Mrs. G.'s flight. By identification they recognized as the motive, Mrs. G.'s feelings about her son and his impending placement in an institution, and they proceeded to empathize by verbalizing their own feelings had they been in her place.

In this episode there are two illustrations of the invasion of threat areas which occur in therapy groups but which would not be acceptable in the transactions of ordinary gatherings. One is when Mrs. C. directly identified Mrs. F.'s distortions and projections, to which the latter did not respond; the other is when the group dwells on psychoses in the presence of Mrs. G. The group's disturbance after Mrs. G. left the room would have been greatly diminished had the therapist, when the group turned to her, said in a calm voice: "I guess Mrs. G. is upset. She'll come back soon."

The fallacy of considering patients as "auxiliary therapists" is revealed in the group's response, and Mrs. C.'s and Mrs. S.'s statements, when Mrs. G. returns. The lack of sympathy with, and the rather tough treatment of Mrs. G. at their hands would seem an act of retaliation for the anxiety she had caused them.

The patients would not have left the session "with butterflies in their stomachs" had the therapist performed her function properly from the outset; namely, specifically, by reassuring Mrs. C. that her daughter cannot go insane. Failing in this, a state of anxiety had been generated, and gained momentum, which had no therapeutic value to anyone. The women responded not to their own ontogenetic anxieties, but rather to the anxiety induced by another patient, anxiety that had no justification in fact: people do not go insane simply because they are upset or angry.

Throughout the session, the therapist overacted her passive role on the one hand, and her inquisitorial, exploratory role on the other hand. The difficulty was that her explorations took the wrong directions: in one case she asked for a definition of insanity; in another, for the reasons why Mrs. G. quit the group. She failed to perceive the latent meaning and intent of what was said and what was communicated nonverbally by the patients and permitted the level of anxiety to rise too high in the group as a whole and in Mrs. G., in particular, despite her knowledge of Mrs. G.'s personality problems and family difficulties.

The malfunction of the therapist could also be understood in terms of her countertransferences.

COUNTERTRANSFERENCE

The Inevitability of Countertransference

Countertransference is one of the major concerns of the psychotherapist. Patients are always aware of, and responsive to, his attitudes, feelings, and overt and covert reactions. This awareness delimits the effectiveness of the therapeutic effort and can determine the conditions for success or failure. Patients register the psychotherapist's emotional state, his preoccupations, worries, and frustrations. His feelings of elation, pleasure, sadness, and discouragement with regard to the therapeutic events, as well as matters outside the treatment room, do not pass unnoticed by the ever-vigilant and easily affected patients. Because his thoughts, moods, and responses effect them and the treatment process, the therapist must also be aware of himself, his attitudes and feelings.

Ideally, the psychotherapist should be completely neutral and devoid of feelings both about the patients and the outcome of treatment. Of course, this is impossible. The psychotherapist, being human, cannot be entirely detached and impersonal, and patients would feel uncomfortable if he were. Patients have to feel that the therapist is interested in them and is ready to help them. Otherwise, they could not establish positive transference feelings toward him, and as a result, treatment would bog down.

The intensity of these feelings is largely determined by the nature of the therapy. In a classical psychoanalysis, where the analyst is not within the patient's visual range and communication is predominantly one-sided, detachment on the therapist's part can be much greater than in the face-to-face types of therapy. In face-to-face psychotherapy, where the transference is not as regressive, excessive detachment on the part of the therapist may antagonize and alienate the patients. They have to feel the therapist's interest in them (bilateral transference) or they become chilled into resistance, anger, and incommunicability (see Slavson, 1945, 1952a). The therapist is the object of the patients' libidinal strivings; as well as the target of their hostile and love feelings. No matter how objective a therapist is it is impossible for him to remain entirely unaffected by them. Having been born of woman, having had a father, and having passed through the usual variety of experiences in human relations in and out of the home, he cannot remain completely unaffected by what goes on in the therapy situation. Like all humans, he, too, is subject to prejudice and preference. If a male, for instance, he responds to beauty and charm in his female patients. Everyone feels uncomfortable in the face of overt hostility and aggression. The difference is in degree only. It was Freud who commented that both the patient and the analyst are neurotic; only the latter is less so.

Hence, all one can count on is that the therapist has worked through his problems, that he is aware of his condition and processes, and that his impulses are under better control. Whether he is aware of it or not, the therapist reacts differently to the personalities of his different patients and to the same patient at different times, largely because of their resemblance to people who affected him in the past, and, therefore, they arouse in him emotions associated with these memories. Such reflex emotions are not within the purview or control of the conscious. They are autonomous. The therapist is also not free of a desire to be successful in his efforts and to achieve therapeutic results. Even though he recognizes that he should not have such aims, he cannot fully divest himself of the human frailty — the desire to achieve and to succeed.

I have elsewhere described the types of countertransference as being of three categories: *positive, negative,* and *aim attachment* (Slavson, 1952, pages 35-36). A fourth type has been since suggested: *ambivalent* or *inconsistent* countertransference (Solomon, Loeffler, and Frank, 1953). Still another form of countertransference is that which involves the entire group and can be characterized as *countertransference toward the group-as-a-whole.*

Positive Countertransference

Positive countertransference manifests itself when the group therapist has a favorable and friendly attitude toward a specific patient or when he prefers some patients in a group. Such attitudes can arise from a number of sources. One of these is that the patient may represent the therapist's own ego ideal. Positive countertransference can arise from resemblance of patients to individuals in the therapist's past who have been particularly constructive, friendly, etc., to him. They can also recall members of his family, friends, or teachers, for whom he may have had feelings of a libidinal nature.

Positive countertransference can also arise from the therapist's need to be liked by his patients and he may therefore exert himself to be accepted. Though this need usually springs from an underlying negative emotional base, it is disguised by a façade of kindness or benevolence. A therapist may also have positive countertransference when a patient makes gratifying progress in treatment, either through the motives of submission or resistance, or by actual improvement. Some patients in groups help accelerate or support the therapeutic effort. Thus, by playing into the therapist's needs, they reduce his anxiety and he may become selectively well-disposed toward them, either out of gratefulness or because of feelings of success or relief. A more subtle method of activating countertransference is a patient's manner, especially when the patient is of the opposite sex.

Femininity and charm of patients may cause a male therapist to respond in a way that affects the transference relations adversely. Such a reaction is particularly deleterious in groups. One obvious difficulty is that it causes sibling rivalry and negative feelings on the part of other patients toward the "preferred child" and toward the "partial" parent figure. Such attitudes in patients toward a fellow group member and the therapist, may create serious difficulties in the therapeutic climate. The climate can become more or less permanently hostile, blocking catharsis and preventing favorable change and improvement in the patients. Hostile attitudes can be employed therapeutically only when they proceed

445

from fantasies. When they are buttressed by reality, by the therapist's real preference of some patients to others (reality saturation), working these feelings through (without involving the therapist in the therapeutic process itself) would be almost impossible. Interpretation of negative sibling transferences of this order (as repetitions of early childhood jealousies and hostilities) are of value, but the feelings must not be rooted in reality within the therapeutic setting. Their actual existence supports the latent hostile feelings toward the therapist, and the patients, as a group, may become so negative (group phalanx) as to make restoration of a relaxed atmosphere (antinodal period) difficult or impossible. The therapist's needs and the gratifications he derives from his position and status in the group can serve as pitfalls for his countertransference attitudes toward the group as a whole.

Feelings of sympathy, pity, and identification with patients, or any other emotional or physical involvement that diminishes or interferes with his objectivity and detachment, also fall in the category of countertransference.

Negative Countertransference

There are even more possibilities for negative countertransferences in groups, for the inadequately prepared therapist. The painful memories aroused in him by patients, are always likely to activate conscious or unconscious feelings of discomfort, fear, hostility, or anger in relation to one or more persons in a group. Some may resemble parents, siblings, teachers, or others who had hurt or made him unhappy as a child. Unless he has worked through these feelings and is thoroughly aware of them, he may react negatively to such patients.

Another source of negative countertransference is the patients' resistances to treatment or their antagonism to the therapist as a person. This form of countertransference is more difficult to deal with in a group than in individual treatment. In the latter, resistances can be dealt with, at times, directly through exploration and interpretation or by remaining passive until the patient exhausts his reservoir of hostility and is thus readied for a therapeutic working through of his transference neurosis. In a group, however, feelings and attitudes are contagious and intensified. Resistances and hostility on the part of one patient are usually taken on by others, damming up the therapeutic flow, with consequent frustration and threat to the therapist. Unless the therapist has a high degree of frustration tolerance and is able to remain detached and controlled, his disturbed feelings are sensed by the patients, with deleterious effects. When the therapist is aim-directed and is threatened in this by patients' hostility or resistance, counterfeelings toward them are understandably aroused. These feelings may be conveyed by subtle nonverbal means or by more obvious signs, such as change of voice, impatience, and manifest or suppressed anger.

Negative countertransference feelings can cause the group to turn against the therapist, because he appears as a punitive and rejecting parent, much as in the case of the 10-year-old boy whose 6-year-old brother was preferred by their mother and who disliked her older son and treated him punitively. Despite his preferred state, *the younger child* once told her that he was afraid, because some day she would treat him just as she was treating his older brother.[7]

Similarly, patients in therapy groups feel that once a therapist acts in an abrupt, critical, or sarcastic manner toward anyone, he is punitive and will some day treat them in a similar manner. As a result, they become suspicious, uncomfortable, and hostile. As in the case of the boy just mentioned, they feel that the time will come when the therapist will turn on them as well. Also, they discover that the therapist is weak, impatient, unkindly, has insufficient self-control and is prejudiced—in short, is just like themselves. Thus, he can no longer serve as an ego ideal and model of identification. It also justifies their latent hostility and fulfills their basic desire to see him as inadequate as they themselves are and as their parents had been.

A further reason for the group's mobilizing their resentment

[7] This supports the validity of insisting that no child be punished or rejected in activity therapy groups. Even justifiable deprivations would stigmatize the adult as a punitive person, whose punitiveness, the others would feel, could turn on them as well.

447

against the therapist lies in their sibling identifications and their solidarity against a parent figure, who is their "common enemy." This is a survival of family attitudes where children identified with one another in their suffering and united against the parents for mutual solace, protection, and support.

Countertransference toward a patient, in the therapist, may also arise from his feeling that the patient is attempting to displace him, usually as a form of acting out oedipal rivalry, by talking out of turn, impulsively interpreting statements of others, and generally attempting to take over the management of the group interview. This may affect the therapist in a number of ways: He may become resentful or threatened, particularly when the patient's influence may have an unfavorable effect on the group (for such aggressivity and monopolism eventually disintegrates it). The therapist's resulting anxiety may make him terse or impatient. This, too, can detract from his image as a positive parental figure and a strong person.

As in individual treatment, countertransferences can appear when assertions or communications by patients, set off, in the therapist, a chain of disturbing associations. As a result, he may begin losing touch with what goes on in the group interview and prevent free-floating attention. Such susceptibility indicates that the therapist is not free from his own traumata.

Negative countertransferences can be reactions to over-positive impulses toward a patient. For example, the sexual attraction that a therapist may feel toward a patient can impel him to react defensively by withdrawal, abruptness, punitiveness, or aloofness. Sometimes the defense may take the form of humor or sarcasm. A therapist needs to be constantly on guard against such subtle and indirect means of revealing himself and when such reactions are the outcome of deeply unconscious and autonomous determinants, further psychotherapy or psychoanalysis is indicated for him. The following incident clearly illustrates some of the points suggested supra.

In one of my seminars in analytic group psychotherapy, a psychiatrist reported on one of his female patients. Before treatment

448

she had had difficulties in sexual adjustment with her husband, had never achieved an orgasm, and had always remained ungratified, but as a result of treatment she was able to enjoy sexual intercourse. At this point, the therapist became aware of feelings of disappointment and resentment because of this change in his young and very attractive patient. He evidently entertained unconscious sexual urges toward her and, without realizing it, hoped to consummate them sometime. Such a reaction would also be possible if the therapist himself had some difficulties in his own sexual adjustment with his wife and had become jealous of the patient's husband, who was now being gratified. As he was narrating the situation to the seminar group, he suddenly stopped short and asked, "Well, where do I go from here?" At this, the others present burst into loud laughter, apparently perceiving his conflict and unconscious intent. It is for such subtle manifestations of countertransference that therapists must be constantly on the alert, and when they cannot be eliminated, they may have to seek help in further psychoanalysis. On occasion, patients report their disturbance at observing very subtle homoerotic trends in their therapists, which are also a form of countertransference.

Acting out by patients in groups provides an abundance of possibilities for arousing countertransference feelings. Hyperactivity, aggression, lack of consideration, active destructiveness and cruelty, tax a therapist's tolerance and controls; yet to be effective he has to deal with them with placidity and, at times, with firmness. The seeming insensitivity that some patients manifest, presents the therapist with a heavy emotional drain, but understanding of the operative psychodynamics provides him with tolerance and controls. In addition, therapists need to be supported and helped by their supervisors and consultants to accept the fact that acting out is comparable to temperature rise in medical patients. Such understanding prevents countertransference feelings, that such behavior inevitably activates. At the same time a therapist has to be on guard against demonstrating sympathy and compassion with group members who may be targets for aggression from their fellow patients.

Aim Attachment

The third type of countertransference is aim attachment. The pursuit of goals is part of the human psyche. All effort, not only in sentient beings, but in all organic life must have goals. The difference between the goals of animals and the goals of man lies in their complexity and variety. The goals of the former are directed exclusively toward physical survival as individuals and species. Although, in the last analysis the goals of man are the same, they manifest themselves in more complex forms due to his psychic potentials and his capacity for abstraction, symbolization, distortion, projection, and the multifarious patterns involved in his psychological and social survival. These occasion innumerable responses, which other animals are incapable of, though man is subject to the same basic laws as they are. One of the imperatively motivated urges is to succeed in one's objectives.

The need to be successful proceeds from a number of sources: One is the positive effect is has on the self-image; that one is adequate and potent. Another was formulated by a psychiatrist in one of my seminars as follows: "There is one aspect of success and failure in therapy that we ought to recognize. At times, a patient is about to fail, not because of anything we did or did not do, but because his problem is not accessible to treatment at a given time. This is often inevitable. However, our need to succeed is not a part of our relation to the patient; nor is it tied up with the patient himself. Rather frequently it is necessary for us, for our own personal survival, to see that our patients improve. If we are in private practice we know that patients who improve will send us other patients. If we work in hospitals or institutions we want to prove ourselves adequate to our superiors, for they have the power to pass upon our qualifications and to assure our continuance in our jobs and promotion. These external needs for success are one of the great sources of what we have been discussing here; namely, aim attachment, but they are important, nonetheless." Such external sources of aim attachment must be considered very seriously in our present-day society. It is difficult to be completely uninvolved under such circumstances, and few can ignore the imperatives of economics.

Another major element that motivates human effort is the impelling need to overcome the ever-present feelings of inferiority and inadequacy that are part of the human psyche. They are inescapable because the child, being small and living in a world of adults more capable of performing the task of everyday living, which he himself craves to do, develops an image of himself as weak and helpless. This is further increased during the oedipal period, emphasizing his sexual unacceptability and impotence, and grows even more acute during adolescence. Such feelings are always present and cannot be entirely eradicated by any known means. The therapist who fails in improving patients cannot but suspect his own inadequacy as being responsible. This is a real problem.

Another type of aim attachment arises from the therapist's need to set, in advance, an aim and a direction for a patient or a group, rather than following the needs of his patients. Some therapists aim to attain definite objectives, either in a given interview or in the total treatment process. In some instances these may be correct, but the incidence of error is increased when one directs or steers patients according to plan only. Experiences in the periods intervening between interviews and unsuspected characteristics of the patient may alter needs. Relevance and expediency are essential in the treatment of both individuals and of groups.

Another source of aim attachment is the desire to be accepted and liked by patients. One should be liked by his patients, especially in certain settings, such as social service agencies and outpatient clinics, or they would not come for treatment. Basic positive transference on the part of patients is essential in all psychotherapy, but it is valuable only when it arises spontaneously from the relation and not when the therapist makes a bid for it.

A need to be liked stems from dependency, feelings of inadequacy and insecurity, ego weakness, and similar deficits which patients seldom fail to register and take advantage of.

When the therapist has any aim in mind other than that of treating patients (such as a research study on his current patients), his judgments and conduct must of necessity be affected. Trans-

451

actions in the group assume different significance to a therapist whose interest in the patients is other than to help them. Having another aim also affects his functions and responses, and interferes with free-floating attention and therapeutically appropriate dealing with developments in the group. Divided interest prevents complete attention to patients and full-hearted concentration on the task at hand. Such divided attention would certainly affect the transference relation. Having ulterior motives, the therapist may hear selectively and misjudge or overlook developments. The attempt to study and analyze material while treatment is in progress may bias the therapist to pursue, during interviews, leads for his research, rather than follow the free association of patients. All psychotherapists (whether in individual or group treatment) should avoid collecting material for study or research while treatment is going on. The therapist should be free to do his therapeutic task without interference from secondary interests. Research should be in retrospect, after the conclusion of treatment, or carried on by persons other than the therapist.

The following episode is a dramatic illustration of the effects of divided interest and multiple roles. A group therapist in a child guidance clinic attempted to carry out, in her group, an additional task assigned to her by the administration. She was required to obtain certain personal data concerning her adolescent patients. A combination of circumstances had arisen in which the therapist's countertransference feelings were aroused when the group became disorganized and hilarious, a result of their transient hostility toward her because of her failure to understand a remark made by one of them. Instead of dealing with the group tension, the therapist, as required, proceeded to tell the girls what information the clinic wished to have about them and asked them to submit to individual interviews so that their background histories could be compiled. Not one of the patients returned to the subsequent sessions and the group had to be disbanded.

Although there were other factors operating in the dissolution of this group, a major reason was that the therapist stepped out of her role as therapist because she was constrained to do something other than understand and deal with the girls' anxiety. This changed her image and the transference was vitiated. A divided role is always a threat to the therapeutic relation. Patients perceive it as negative countertransference, seeing the therapist as being no longer interested in them alone. This is particularly harmful when it occurs too early in treatment or is otherwise improperly timed.

Ambivalent Countertransference

The concept of ambivalent or inconsistent countertransference is a useful one. It refers to successive alternations of positive and negative countertransferences toward a patient or a group and arises from the therapist's own basic ambivalent attitudes and unresolved feelings. The inability to steer a consistent course through one's reactions to situations, whether comforting or disappointing, is a problem in the therapist's ego organization rather than originating in the therapeutic situation. It is an outcome of a personal ambivalent syndrome and instability that prevents the therapist from functioning effectively.

Countertransference Toward the Group as a Whole

The preceding discussion of countertransference dealt largely with reactions to individual patients, yet attitudes toward the group may also arise. These can be considered as countertransference toward the group as a whole.

The therapist's need to exert authority over a group, as a result of his own earlier conditioning, may appear in the form of countertransference. At times it is a reaction formation against dependency or identification with an authoritarian parental figure. The therapist, then, may insist that the group pursue a definite goal or he may set problems for the group to discuss. This procedure is characteristic of a number of "repressive," didactic, and directive techniques. As a matter of fact, these techniques are preferred by some psychotherapists, because of the nature of their countertransferences. Their needs and attitudes toward patients and groups determine their choice of the "style" of treatment. When patterns and functions are determined by the unconscious needs of the therapist, rather than deliberately chosen for their therapeutic expediency, they cannot but be inappropriate.

An examination of the techniques employed by different psychotherapists may reveal that their origins stem from countertransferences peculiar to each, which in turn have their root in character structure, ego organization, or neurotic states.

A case in point is that of a therapist who was persistently challenged by his group and questioned as to the validity of his technique. His insecurity was aroused by the group's pressure and he repeatedly attempted to explain himself and impress its members with his educational background, knowledge, experience, and achievements, even listing some of his publications. One of the patients described it as follows: "I swing between loving and hating him and when I make a demand on him he 'throws the book at me.' If he could only understand what I and the others in the group are after, he would not have to impress us so much. Besides, it does not do any good, anyway."

Instead of working through the phalanx of transference of his patients and thereby advancing their emotional maturity, the therapist allowed his own feelings of inadequacy to take over. In this state of countertransference, he blindly resorted to boasting, seeking to impress his patients with his importance, in an effort to establish his status. This is an example of *countertransference toward the group as a whole*, and of its effect in blocking the therapeutic process.

DIFFERENTIAL ERROR VALENCES:
CUMULATIVE VERSUS COMPENSATING ERRORS

In every human pursuit, it is inevitable that errors will be made and psychotherapy is no exception to this. However, to prevent the breakdown of the therapeutic process, it is essential that their consistency and seriousness be minimized. Occasional mistakes can be tolerated by patients, but if their frequency and valence are too great, the therapeutic flow not only becomes misdirected, but it may come to an end altogether.

One way for the therapist to prevent committing or accumulating errors is to withhold responses in situations where there is doubt as to the meanings and intent of his patients. The adage, "When in doubt, don't" is the safest guidepost for a therapist. However, despite all precautions, one is seldom free of errors in judgment, understanding, and response, especially in a process as complex as group psychotherapy. Hence, the persistent aim should be to reduce their incidence, rather than entirely prevent their occurrence, and to be always on the alert to the most vulnerable and most significant areas of therapy.

Not all sectors of a therapeutic interview are equally weighted as to their significance and, accordingly, the effect of errors. This characteristic we designate *error valence*. There are three major sectors in which errors can be made by a therapist. These are in the realms of interpretation, defenses, and transference.

An error in interpretation (or explanation) is the least disturbing to patients, though if repeated too frequently it may affect their transference attitudes toward the therapist. To be understood is an essential need, for it symbolizes being liked or loved and indicates that an empathic relation exists between patient and therapist. An error in interpretation can be corrected at another opportunity; thus, its effect is erased at a later date. Such errors can be described as *compensating errors*.

A premature attack on or analysis of a patient's defenses, before he is ready to give them up for more benign ones, can prove very disturbing, cause intense anxiety, and result in strong resentment toward the therapist. However, this error, unless repeated too frequently can be corrected by subsequent sensitive dealing with the patient's feelings and productions. The injury is then obliterated from the mind of the patient by his conviction of the therapist's good intent and empathy. But, as already indicated, if this injury is repeated, the patient will go into a state of negative transference, from which he may never recover, and terminate treatment. Errors in interpretation, therefore, can be either "compensating" or "cumulative."

The most serious and almost always irreparable errors are those in the realm of transference. If the therapist presents a negative façade during the interviews, attacks patients, displays irritability and impatience with them, creates an image of a hostile, intolerant, rejecting parental figure, his usefulness to the group is at an end. There is no way of compensating for such errors; they are fundamentally cumulative in their nature.

XIV

Supervision

Much of the preceding chapter and some of the other chapters allude directly, or indirectly, to the teaching of psychotherapy and the supervision and "control" of practitioners at various stages in their development. This chapter is devoted to some specific aspects of the teaching/supervisory roles and of the participants.

GENERAL CONSIDERATIONS

Supervision, more than any other aspect of psychotherapy, demonstrates the genetic relation between individual and group psychotherapies (the latter being a derivative, as well as an extension and special application, of the former). Although analytic group psychotherapy has the same aims and dynamics as individual psychotherapy, the process is modified through the group. There are points of congruence in the functions of the individual therapist and the group therapist, but there are also divergences in the types of treatment which, as already indicated, have bearing on the qualifications of the therapist. Before attempting to work with groups, the therapist must have had ample preparation and extensive experience in conducting individual psychotherapy or psychoanalysis, particularly in the former. It is on this substratum in training and background that he must rely and draw in his work with groups. The supervisor of group therapists should not be called on to do basic training in psychotherapy; nor should he

457

undertake to supervise or train a therapist who is lacking the necessary foundation. Nonetheless, the practice of supervision entails two functions: direction toward the group and discussion of its various manifestations and, at the same time, aid to the therapist in understanding the mechanisms and psychodynamics of each patient.

THE SUBJECTIVE ELEMENTS IN SUPERVISION

Supervision is a highly individualized and subjective function involving conscious aims as well as unconscious values, attitudes and strivings on the part of both the supervisor and the supervisee. It also involves a subtle relationship between the two participants which, of necessity, varies depending on their characters, temperaments, levels of knowledge, and, most of all, on their unconscious reactions to each other. Both persons involved—particularly the supervisor—must be aware that the phenomena of natural attraction and antipathy, personality harmony and disharmony, and intellectual similarity and conflicts inevitably come into play. Conflict and tensions can be prevented with comparatively little difficulty if the two are professionally attuned and both have a common interest in the welfare of their patients. A supervisor may unconsciously expect a high degree of submissiveness to and conformity with his views and techniques; he may have a tendency to authoritarianism; his position may give him an exaggerated feeling of superiority, or he may feel insecure in his role. These and many other attitudes may interfere with effective infusion of knowledge and understanding to a supervisee. On the other hand, the supervisee may resist learning psychotherapy—an attitude that is not uncommon.

It is to be expected that a person who undertakes the practice of group psychotherapy has already reconciled himself with the therapist's role through work with individual patients. Yet, there may still be present personality characteristics in the supervisor, manifested in his mannerisms, overbearing use of his superior knowledge, or compulsive demands upon the supervisee, that may generate antagonism and, therefore, resistance to learning and to adopting or accepting the supervisor's suggestions and information.

As already indicated, such difficulties can be ironed out provided the persons involved are similarly motivated. However, there are definite elements in the attitudes, implied in the roles, which the two have to define and understand, taking into consideration the subtler psychic interplay of emotional forces that are involved in the relation and in their common aim.

The Factor of Sex

One of the elements that needs to be considered is the respective genders of the participants. Intersexual attitudes may be a determining factor in relationships from the very start. The rebellion of a woman to submitting to a man, which the supervisory relationship inevitably involves, is a problem which must be faced, since sometimes this impediment may doom the enterprise, regardless of conscious efforts to succeed. Similarly, the natural reluctance and even resentment of men in submitting to the supervision of a woman may in many instances generate an awkward atmosphere. Supervisory arrangements may have to be changed to obviate such a situation. By and large, it may be expected that those who have had an adequate, sound personal psychoanalysis will be much less prone to emotional attitudes that create difficulties in this relationship.

Attitudes and Values

A personal analysis helps the supervisor and therapist to understand other attitudes and feelings which may give rise to conflictual situations, making supervision either difficult or impossible. For efficiency in these roles, unconscious parapathologic and other noxious attitudes should be eliminated or brought under conscious control. This desirable inner freedom applies to the therapist's attitude toward the supervisor. He should not be resentful about accepting the role of learner or feel threatened and degraded by having his errors exposed. Nor should he as a reaction formation, be oversubmissive or overassertive toward his mentor.

Psychoanalytic therapy is also of help to the supervisor; it eliminates, or at least minimizes, egotistic, self-assertive, and sadistic trends which, while being universal traits, inevitably become more likely in the role a supervisor has to assume.

INTERRELATIONSHIP ROLES

The roles of both the supervisor and supervisee are shaped by specific elements which the two must understand. Although some of these are tacitly accepted, others must be defined, such as the type and depth of therapy necessary for a certain group or patient. This has to be clearly understood almost from the outset, either as a permanent or temporary policy which should grow out of therapeutic indications. The supervisee needs to know, for his security, that the supervisor is available for help at all times; the supervisee should have no compunction about calling the supervisor for advice during other than regularly set hours.

At times it is necessary to tell the supervisee that learning always involves a certain degree of discomfort and even suffering. The Platonic principle that learning is painful must be fully accepted by the supervisee. Learning involves disturbing intellectual and emotional equilibrium through the introduction of new facts, ideas, and values; the learning process implies an admission of inadequacy. It also involves submission on the part of the learner to the teacher. While this statement is more appropriately made as the relation takes root rather than in its early stages, it needs to be repeated in passing and, perhaps even semihumorously, more than once. The present writer has found this practice helpful in establishing and maintaining the supervisor-supervisee relation, especially when the therapist seems to manifest feelings of discouragement with his performance or anger and irritation during the supervisory interview.

The supervisor must be convinced of the prospective therapist's capacity and suitability to do group therapy, both personally and educationally. This is even more important in group therapy than in individual treatment, because tactlessness and errors on the part of the therapist may mobilize hostility and aggression of the group as a whole, resulting in a phalanx of negative transference and resistance. This is by far more formidable than in individual treatment, where the transference-countertransference relation can be worked through in a one-to-one relation without intensification through multiple reactions and mutual catalysis and induction; for, as we have seen, it is only a short step from an emotionally disturbed group to mob reaction in a miniature form. While educational deficiencies can be supplied to some extent by the supervisor in the process of supervision, it is impossible for him to fill the gaps in personal capacities and qualifications.

The supervisor is inevitably limited in his function by the level of the supervisee's knowledge of dynamics, psychopathology, and psychotherapy. His supervisory outflow needs to be conditioned by the readiness and capacity of his pupil to assimilate it. The supervisor should strive to prevent *overwhelming* the supervisee by techniques and information beyond his current perceptions, capacities, and understanding. At the same time, the supervisor must supply sufficient information and guidance as they become relevant, to render the therapeutic effort effective and advance the supervisee's knowledge and understanding. In addition to conceptualization, there needs to be at least a minimal degree of empathic suitability between the two for this fine balance to emerge and to persist.

First Steps

It is advisable that the supervisor and supervisee spend at least a part of the first session of their professional acquaintanceship in establishing a personal relationship without entering into the business at hand. This period should be devoted to sizing up and sensing the other's basic personality (not his "professional personality"). The aim is to establish an easy relationship. The responsibility for its success falls mostly upon the supervisor who, because of the image of authority which clings to him, creates the climate. However, the prospective therapist should attempt to reveal himself in his true light, at the same time preventing tension or a basis for a rift. While the supervisory relation cannot by its very nature remain consistently sanguine or harmonious, it is better that tensions should arise in the course of

461

professional interchange rather than from the initial contact. Inevitably, differences will arise and may become moderately intense. This is essential for a truly free, equalitarian relation. To completely avoid the negative aspects of another person is to eschew a meaningful human relationship. Interpersonal ease can be achieved only after the negative qualities in each have been faced, recognized, and either worked through or mutually accepted. After the inevitable and usually brief conflict passes over, feelings of mutuality and ease usually emerge. The persons involved now know each other and need not play false roles. While in the supervisor-supervisee interaction, personal relations are not as deep and strong as in some other spheres of life, they are nonetheless operative and there must be an awareness of their existence.

Also of primary importance is the supervisor's effort to put the novice at ease by explaining elements which he may or may not have learned in individual psychotherapy. Emphasis should be laid on the value of every occurrence in the group, even though at first sight it may be disturbing or destructive. Each occurrence must be considered in terms of cathartic freedom and self-revelation by patients, which lead to insight or understanding both in the patients and in the therapist. Distressing developments which occur have to be viewed as having value to the therapist for diagnosis of both the group and the individuals that are involved in it.

In the early stages, the supervisor should overlook minor errors on the part of the therapist and concentrate on serious mistakes in the therapist's deportment that may prove damaging to patients or to the therapeutic relation with the group. The supervisor may find himself in a dilemma: he cannot permit injury to patients and possible disruption of the group through repeated transgressions in the transference-countertransference complex and hazardous misjudgment of the patients' productions; yet, he has to guard against discouraging the therapist and undermining the relationship, before it is solidly established, by heaping upon him an array of faults and corrections. Such a course of action inevitably results in discouragement and anxiety which renders the therapist less effective. In some, it may even generate depressive feelings and a pessimism about their value as a potential therapist. However, as the relationship ripens and grows tolerably harmonious and the basic principles and techniques are understood and accepted, the supervisor can turn his attention to minor errors, refinements in practice, and to the subtler implications in the conduct of a therapeutic group.

LATER DEVELOPMENTS

As soon as he deems it advisable, the supervisor will do well to involve the supervisee in self-criticism. The therapist is asked to read his protocols or notes of the session to be reviewed and to reconstruct in his mind the developments and their sequences, with special consideration for individual patients according to their psychodynamics, pathology, and their participation either as instigators, neutralizers, and other interactive roles. The procedure recommended is to first ask the supervisee what questions occur to him after examination of the interview, and to encourage him to state his own reactions to them. The supervisor has to listen patiently to the supervisee's statements and ruminations without interruption, in the expectation that this intellectual ventilation will automatically provide clarification. Only after this should the supervisor offer questions and explanations to elucidate and deepen the latter's knowledge.

The Socratic method is most suitable, for it encourages the learner to exert effort in gaining understanding. Only such a procedure of self-teaching motivates true learning.

ENCOURAGING SELF-SCRUTINY

Since the ultimate aim is to prepare the supervisee for independent functioning in the future, it is advisable that the supervisor lay a foundation for it. General educational procedures do not encourage self-scrutiny or inquiry. Rather, they stress receptivity, submission, and memory. It, therefore, behooves the supervisor to alter these attitudes and thus help in the emotional as well as intellectual maturity of his charge.

463

Objectivity and self-scrutiny require a degree of intellectual and emotional security. The supervisor can aid in this by encouraging the supervisee to ask questions about the protocol or the verbal report of a session, rather than by plunging into a critical analysis of it; instead of expressing opinions or criticism, he asks for the supervisee's reactions to specific and general developments in his group and in the particular session under scrutiny. Such a procedure not only sensitizes the practitioner to his work and deepens his understanding, but it also prepares him for the self-criticism and insights necessary for independent work.

It is not suggested that the entire supervisory process can be conducted on this plan, however. Direct teaching and correction are essential, but they should come after an opportunity for self-evaluation and self-criticism has been afforded to the supervisee.

Ego Functioning of the Supervisee

The ego functiong of the supervisee and his nuclear defensive system need to be carefully considered; otherwise, his self-confidence and prospects for development may be irreparably undermined. One important fact the supervisor must always be aware of is that whatever damage he causes in his pupil, it will be passed on, in all likelihood, to his patients and group. Resentment and anger, particularly, may be acted out unconsciously against the group.

The ego functioning of different group therapists assert themselves in various ways. In some instances a supervisee's need to talk what may seem to be excessively during the supervisory session, may be his means of clarifying his thinking, while using the supervisor as a sounding board. In this case, the supervisee needs to be allowed to run his course and at a strategic point or at the end of the recital, the supervisor may either raise questions, correct errors, elaborate, explain or interpret. However, the stream of conversation may also be a form of defense against exposure of real or fancied inadequacies and errors; or a form of resistance to learning; or it may stem from hostility toward all persons in a superior position.

In the last two instances, the only recourse the supervisor has is to ignore the maneuvers and to proceed with his function as teacher and supervisor, disregarding the defensive and resistive patterns of his pupil. It is imperative that he does not fall into the trap of being drawn into a general discussion with the supervisee of these maneuvers and attitudes. An effort at analyzing or exposing the unconscious motivations would only intensify defensiveness, setting up a chain of explanations and counter-explanations that can only lead to tension and hostility. Disruption in the relation would unavoidably follow, leading to a break-up in the learning effort. Only the material at hand as reported in the protocol, and the therapeutic process involved and its meaning, should constitute the content of the supervisory discussions. As already stated, this is best achieved when the supervisee is involved in it; only very occasionally (and much later in the relationship) can the supervisor address himself to the attitudes and feelings of the therapist in a given situation in the group and toward the supervisory setting. The supervisor may ask the supervisee: "How would *you* feel in this kind of situation?" or, "Why do you think you had to do this?" Such explorations frequently involve unconscious determinants and can be employed only when the supervisor feels that they would expand the supervisee's horizon and insights, rather than cause him narcissistic injury and antagonize him.

Awareness of the Supervisee's Basic Personality

Of supreme importance is that the supervisor understand the basic personality of the supervisee, the strength of his ego, the nature of his defenses, and his threat areas. The total relationship and process needs to be based upon a consideration of these. Some therapists are less disturbed by exposure than are others; some are freer to deal with sexual material in the supervisory discussions than are others; some can bear up under direct scrutiny and even criticisms, while others feel threatened and crushed by them.

Among supervisees are to be found also persons with varying degrees of pathology and ego deficiencies and these, too, need to be carefully guarded against incursion and threat. In practice, one finds many highly skilled and resourceful therapists who crumble emotionally at the slightest suggestion of their imperfection and are paralyzed (and become hostile and intractable) by direct criticism.

The technique of encouraging the "sensitive" supervisee to examine his own conduct and reactions in his group prevents what may seem to him an inquisitorial atmosphere and excessive criticism. Therapists are not completely free of projections and distortions, particularly those with whom we are concerned here.

DEALING WITH IMPASSES

It is inevitable that from time to time an impasse should arise between supervisor and supervisee in theory and practice. In such an eventuality, the supervisor defers to the judgment of the *experienced* therapist as the best way of dealing with a situation in a group. (We repeat, the *experienced* therapist.) Imaginative as the supervisor may be, he is still corporally removed from the actual situation and, therefore, the subtle nuances and covert dynamics may escape him. The supervisee, on the other hand, having been present corporally, and involved emotionally in the event, may be closer to being correct in his judgment. Only when the supervisor has discovered, through a number of previous developments, that the judgment of the supervisee is unreliable may he insist that his judgment and suggestions prevail. Even under these circumstances it is necessary at least conditionally to enlist the supervisee's acceptance, for it is very difficult to create a therapeutic climate for a group if the therapist is compelled to act against his convictions. Functioning with full conviction is essential in creating the subtle climate required for effective psychotherapy.

A therapist who is temperamentally opinionated (rigid) and has to assert himself, defensively, in the early stages of his work, is liable to make serious errors. Here the empathic relationship and the confidence with which the supervisor had imbued his pupil come to the rescue. As a last resort, the supervisor may say, in an imploring manner: "Just have confidence in me. Do this and see how it works out. If I am wrong, tell me." Under all circumstances, the supervisor has to evade situations in which he has to be peremptorily authoritarian.

The supervisor needs to be aware that once the basic understanding of the therapeutic approach has been agreed on and acceptance established as to the nature of analytic group psychotherapy, each therapist will evolve a pattern of his own which the supervisor has to respect, both because of his regard for the integrity of the therapist and because it is the way in which the therapist can function most effectively. Such an attitude helps the learner to realize his own potentialities for the independent practice he will eventually undertake.

THE VALUES OF AFFIRMATION

Whenever it is justifiable, the supervisor may call attention to correct functioning, as he does to errors and oversights on the part of the therapist. Affirmation, however, need not take on the character of fulsome praise; rather, it should be statements of fact that point up suitable, along with unsuitable, responses.

SETTING ANTICIPATORY ATTITUDES

The supervisee can be greatly aided in the discharge of his functions if the supervisor, by virtue of wider experience and knowledge of patients and group interactions, can help him anticipate developments and prepare him for dealing with them. This may at times present difficulties and even crises, but it enriches process and content. However, the dangerous possibility exists that anticipation on the part of some therapists may, through the process described as "self-fulfilling prophecy," suggest to the group lines of action and conduct.

MULTICENTEREDNESS

The content of supervision may at various times be group-centered, patient-centered, therapist-centered, situation-centered, technique-centered, theory-centered, idea-centered, or philosophy-centered.

467

Group-Centeredness

The discussion of group-centeredness consists of the analysis of interactions in the group, the themes, rallies, and subjects that have arisen and their meanings, as well as ways of utilizing them therapeutically. Group-centered discussions would also involve the suitability of patients to the group and especially their effect upon its process.

Patient-Centeredness

The patient-centered element in a supervisory discussion would deal with the participation, responses, and reactions of individual patients; their effect upon the group, and the group's effect upon them. Changes in the personalities of patients, improvement in their specific problems, and general progress would be evaluated.

Therapist-Centeredness

The therapist-centered factor has already been discussed at various points in the preceding pages. This involves the consideration of the therapist's understanding of the relevant material, his reaction to it, failure to perceive it, as well as responses to covert communications and behavior of patients. As already indicated, on occasion this may include also an exploration of the attitude and involvements of the therapist. Not infrequently it may be necessary to call attention to over-involvement or detachment, over-function or under-function, over-confronting or evading. In other words, the therapist's total functioning, his attitudes, conduct, and behavior in the therapeutic role may have to be explored. As already cautioned, this should be kept on a nonpersonal level and viewed from functional bases; that is, in terms of action and response rather than inner motivation.

Situation-Centeredness

The situation-centered factor in supervision concerns the understanding of special situations that may arise during group interviews and interactions among its members. This factor consists

468

of an analysis of themes, subjects, rallies and their values, in terms of therapeutic needs; the rise of supportive ego relations and their value and meaning to the patients involved; affinities and antagonisms between patients; manifestations of transferences and countertransferences, with reasons for their appearance; study of antecedent communications and episodes that may have brought them on, and reasons for the involvement of the group or individuals in a particular situation, as well as their lack of involvement and apathy in other situations. (Caution should be directed here against an overabundance of themes in any one interview, that do not tend to culminate in some clarification, confrontation, or fruitful conflict; for unfocused movement in a group is nonproductive.) Special attention must be focused on the therapist's functioning, on the resistances that generate problems mentioned above, and on methods for resolving them. Preventive as well as corrective measures should be considered.

Technique-Centeredness

In the technique-centered area of a supervisory discussion, the therapist should be encouraged to evaluate his own techniques and suggest other lines of action, taking into consideration some that may have proved therapeutically ineffective. Techniques should receive the major part of the supervisor's and therapist's attention. Theory and abstract knowledge have little value unless they are transmuted into functional techniques, which have their place in a supervisory conference.

Theory-Centeredness

The question of theory in supervision is a sensitive one. Discussion of theory can become a resistive and evasive strategem on the part of the supervisee. By raising theoretical questions and involving the supervisor in discussions of theory, he can prevent his deficiencies from being exposed, and evade confronting them. The supervisor, therefore, has to be cautious not to be trapped by such maneuvers by the supervisee. And, with few exceptions (because no theoretic training in group psychotherapy is

469

available to prospective therapists), the supervisor must also be a teacher, akin to a classroom instructor, as it is essential for a therapist to have theoretic understanding as well as practice facilities. The supervisor is nearly always the person on whom devolves instruction in the dynamics of interaction and neutralization, displacement, intensification, and the many other techniques discussed in preceding pages as they appear in groups. Supervisory sessions should not be turned entirely into heuristic sessions, however. Theory needs to be subordinated to practice and flow from the analysis of actual situations and occurrences in the group and individuals under consideration. On the basis of such discussions the supervisor may recommend pertinent reading and supply the supervisee with books, pamphlets, reprints, magazines, and articles dealing with the topic in hand.

Idea-Centeredness

Idea-centered material is usually supplied by the alert and motivated supervisee who, encouraged by the supervisor, offers original ideas that suggest themselves by his work, the supervisory conferences, and his own studies and reflections. Some portion of the supervisory conferences should be given over to this adventure, even though on the surface the content may seem irrelevant or, at best, peripheral or derivative. However, the inner stimulation and the satisfaction from such original and creative mental effort enrich imagination and perceptiveness, and attune the therapist to more sensitive responsiveness to what transpires in the group and among his patients. Such creativity is regenerative, self-expressive, self-realizing, adventurous, and pioneering in the realms of thought and feeling, and renders the therapist richer as a human being, enhancing his enthusiasm for his work.

Philosophy-Centeredness

A philosophical orientation is essential in all intelligent living and functioning, and in any human occupation, no matter how humble. It is especially necessary in professions where humans are involved and where human relations are the focus. Philosophy-centered areas in supervision are essential, and the supervisor may suitably introduce them. The values a therapist entertains form an integral part of his reorienting patients emotionally and intellectually. Whether he intends it or not, his values will come through in the interpretations and explanations that he gives to his patients. Whether these values will be self-centered and promote vested interests, or socially motivated and intrinsically of common benefit, will inevitably be conveyed to the patients, regardless of the studied objectivity with which the therapist may attempt to conceal them. While discussions of philosophy are kept to a minimum in therapy sessions, the therapist needs to be prepared, nonetheless, to deal with philosophical topics when they are introduced by patients and he will unavoidably do it in the light of his own values and orientation.

In supervision, therefore, such generalized and encompassing ideas, attitudes, and values of life should be considered and discussed with a view toward helping the supervisee to clarify his thoughts and, if need be, modify them to the best therapeutic advantage. While the supervisor should encourage free expression rather than attempt to impose his values and views upon supervisees, he must help them examine their opinions in the context of the patients and their needs.

TABLE 1

Supervisory Content

Group-Centeredness
Patient-Centeredness
Therapist-Centeredness
Situation-Centeredness
Technique-Centeredness
Theory-Centeredness
Idea-Centeredness
Philosophy-Centeredness

REPETITION

The supervisor must appreciate and accept the importance of repetition; he must be inexhaustibly patient in repeating many times over to the supervisee the same ideas, responses, and sug-

471

gestions. He must do this without display of irritation, resentment, or frustration (that can only engender feelings of inadequacy and inferiority in the supervisee). Therapists in training are usually slow in absorbing and utilizing knowledge, and in assimilating the subtler implications of therapy and personality change. This low level of receptivity and retention may be due to the resistance against growing introspection (which is naturally threatening, since it exposes his inadequately repressed and carefully guarded noxious urges and characteristics); or it may be due to the difficulty inherent in the amorphous and nonheuristic nature of psychiatric materials. It is necessary for the supervisor to reconcile himself to the reality of the situation and be tolerant of it.

SENSITIZATION

The various processes briefly enumerated serve to *sensitize* the therapist to his task. Herein lies the most profound contribution of the supervisor. Important as information, knowledge, and techniques are, incomparably more important is the therapist's sensitivity and responsiveness to the nuances and subtleties that unfold before him in covert and overt intrapersonal and interpersonal reactions in his groups. Imagination cannot be taught or generated by direct means. It is a by-product of enhanced awareness, emotional resonance, and deep understanding that arises from the therapist's prolonged exposure to the imaginative, sensitive, and honest supervisory/teaching relation with a wise and sensitive supervisor. This does not result from increased knowledge of grosser facts and techniques, but from a creative, sensitive attunement that occurs within human beings through a life of ideas and ideals and in their struggle toward reconstructing their psychic organization.

XV

Analytic Group Psychotherapy With Some Character Disorders: Aggression, Hostility, and Withdrawal

ON THE NATURE OF AGGRESSION

Before we discuss the treatment of aggression through group therapy, it may be helpful to identify some of its basic characteristics. We need to come to some agreement as to its meaning, for there seems to be a variety of definitions attached to it. In the innumerable acts leading to the survival of man and of lower animals (as well as of plants), aggression against the organism's environment is the most common pattern. Life is carried on through absorption, ingestion, and direct force in lower forms of life, and by manipulation, cultivation, control, direction, and subjection of things, animals, and people in humans. Plants *force* their way through the soil, and even split rocks to expose themselves to sunshine and air, and absorb the nitrogenous substances from the earth and oxygen gases from the atmosphere to assure their life and survival. Some carnivorous plants trap insects which they *destroy* by ingestion to nourish themselves, while trees crowd each other out where sunshine is inadequate for all.

473

Aggression is more widespread and more apparent in the animal world where killing and devouring is the law of life. In humans, too, the hunter is aggressive, not only toward his prey, but also toward shrubs and bushes, as he stalks animals and the farmer as he cultivates his land. The laboratory scientist is in pursuit of knowledge, but to acquire it he is actually aggressive against the materials with which he works. Each person conducts himself aggressively as he sells and buys, makes his way socially, strives for status, and conducts the many other activities of his everyday life.

Aggression in man can be defined as the centrifugal flow of the libido toward the environment, resulting in acts which have a direction, an aim, and an object. An organism is normally aggressive only when the aggression serves its essential needs at a given time. In man this need may arise from the demands of physical, social, or economic survival as they are imposed by external realities or from impelling inner needs and strivings, cravings, and talents. Aggressive acts that serve socially and individually constructive ends, whether activated by external or internal stimuli, are considered acceptable and do not fall within the scope of psychotherapy, unless they are diffuse or accompanied by over-intense emotivity and are beyond the individual's control. By and large, aggression is considered normal when it is purposeful and adequately focused, when the individual is in control of himself, and when it is acceptable or approved by cultural mores. A behavioral pattern or act is "abnormal" when, regardless of intent, it is not within control or choice; that is, when it is compulsive and has a strong coloring of hostility or destructiveness.

One of the semantic difficulties is that the term aggression is employed indiscriminately to describe all forms of centrifugal activity in a social or group setting. This is misleading. Distinction needs to be made between playfulness, boisterousness, hilarity, provocativeness, assertiveness, outgoingness, normal aggressiveness, and hostile aggression.[1] Aggression, as differentiated from hostility, exists only as it is manifested in acts. Thus, it is correct to state

[1] For a fuller discussion of aggression, its sources, determinants, and manifestations, especially as they relate to psychotherapy, see Slavson, 1952a, pages 27-29, 52-67.

that aggression, as such, does not actually exist. Only aggressive acts are observable. What is frequently described as aggression, as a state, is actually a characteristic pattern of behavior in which there appears either insensitivity to the feelings of others or actual hostility.

Aggression in man can be atavistic, phylogenetic, ontogenetic, and instrumental.

Atavistic Aggression

This proceeds from organic (engrammatic) vestiges of the evolutionary past, in which animal survival was conditioned by direct and usually brutal attack. These vestiges are recognizable in man in his irrational and socially unproductive "instinctive" mass cruelties, and in interpersonal relations and interactions such as wars, prejudice, homicides, tortures, and genocide. Atavistic aggression, having been of great utility in biological survival, persists engrammatically in the nervous constitution of man, even though its value has disappeared. The chief aim of all education and psychotherapy is to evolve controls for the atavistic aggressions in man or to find suitable sublimations for them.

Phylogenetic Aggression

This, too, is a "savage form of survival" carried on by individuals in every society. These aggressions are passed on from generation to generation through cultural channels as folk traditions, attitudes, and values. Though their efficacy has long passed, habit, cultural lag, group induction and infection operate to perpetuate feelings and bias, and, above all, behavior patterns. As noted, these are culturally determined and are subject to alteration with changes in the societal patterns and mores. They are as engrained in the social organism through cultural determinants as are the atavistic patterns through neuro-organic imprints. In the case of phylogenetic aggression, both education and psychotherapy seek to eliminate those patterns which no longer serve the best interests of the individual and of society, and to substitute for them more appropriate means of adaptation and survival. This is also true of ontogenetic aggression, which does not serve the best interests of the individual and others in his environment.

Ontogenetic Aggression

The ontogenetic sources of aggression are the experiences and early interpersonal relations that pattern the character of everyone. The adaptations and adjustments that are imprinted on the child by the conditions under which he lives and the treatment he receives from members of his family, his models for imitation and identification, the rivalries he is subjected to, and the total social climate (especially among his peers), all combine to determine the type and intensity of aggression and assertiveness that will finally be manifested as character. The normality and abnormality of aggression should therefore be evaluated in terms of atavistic heredity, the macroculture in which an individual has been raised, and the narrower microculture of his family and neighborhood. Some circumstances may necessitate aggression more than do others; it is not considered entirely abnormal for an individual to conduct himself in ways that do not fit set norms even when some acts may not receive general social acceptance or approval. We shall presently see how these principles apply to the understanding and evaluation of patients in psychotherapy.

Instrumental Aggression

The most constructive and socially approved type of aggression is the instrumental. This term denotes aggressive acts that have a constructive and objective aim, leading to beneficial results for the individual and for his environment. In this syndrome, aggression is a means for attaining socially and personally desirable results, either immediately or in the future. It is an effective instrument of creative effort. Instrumental aggression on different levels is essential to all life and survival in the immediate setting of an organism and in man, as well as for the creation of a dynamic and expanding future. It is toward this type of aggression that the healthy human individual bends his energies and into which culture, education, and therapy transform the atavistic and other types of aggression.

Aggression versus Hostility

The object (recipient) of an aggressive act may be the aggressor himself; psychoneurotics and psychotics are their own victims. Aggression is abnormal or pathological when the factor of hostility enters either in a conscious or unconscious form, as in sadistic playfulness, humor, teasing, gossip, and derogation. In all of these the aggressor aims to provoke or injure the object. Another type of aggression is found in infantile persons: some of its undesirable features are rivalry, attention-getting devices, control of others, omnipotence and grandiosity, defenses against weakness and effeminacy, and especially masked hostility. Frustration does not invariably lead to aggression; it can also lead to withdrawal. It is more correct to state that frustration *may* lead to aggression. Frustration, rather, engenders hostility which, depending upon the conditioning of the subject and his state of ego development, may be controlled, introjected, acted out in hostile aggression, or cause withdrawal. These facts lead to another point requiring clarification.

As already indicated, strictly speaking there is no such thing as aggression; knowledge of its existence is derived from the observation of acts that correspond to a concept of aggression semantically and culturally defined. Hostility, on the other hand, is an unmistakable emotional dynamic, which may or may not manifest itself in behavior. Hostility is an attitude, an emotional quality that induces and accompanies certain acts, but may (and often does) remain unexpressed, as in passive resistance, withdrawal, passivity, and noncooperation. The aim of hostility is to injure or destroy its target, which is not the aim of aggression. Repressed or controlled hostility may be converted into a symptom, as in the psychoneuroses and the psychoses.

Hostility results from cumulative organic and psychological frustrations, affect deprivation, and cruelty. Excepting in special cases, aggression is not drawn from destructive sources alone; it is a product of necessity in the adjustment to the demands of life and circumstances. Hostility, on the other hand, is charged with strong affect whose aim is injury or destruction, while aggression can be constructive, for survival and creativity. The difference between the two is an important consideration in psychotherapy with adults, because one is accessible to psychotherapy while the other is less so (and in many instances not at all).

AGGRESSION AND CULTURE

In judging aggressiveness in a patient, it is necessary to evaluate his behavior in terms of the specific macroculture in which he has his roots, and the microculture by which his character has been shaped. What may be considered excessive aggressiveness in a person in one society or cultural group may be acceptable and even admirable in another. In our work with children, for example, we differentiate between unacceptable table manners which stem from oral anxiety and from defiance of authority, and those which stem from cultural conditioning and social and educational backgrounds. What is unacceptable in one society, group, or neighborhood is viewed as normal in another. This is equally true of manners. What may seem as excessive roughness in one social group or community is desirable and approved in another. A patient's directness, indiscretion, seeming disrespect and boisterousness may not be at all untoward if viewed from his background and cultural environment. Since everyone around him, including his parents, behaved in a similar manner, it is natural that he should adopt their pattern and mannerisms. In fact, this is not only normal but desirable, for an atypical character too different from his family and peers would be stigmatized and rejected by them. He would be considered weak and "a sissy," become the scapegoat, and generally be maladjusted in his social surroundings. Thus, the needs of social and psychologic survival in certain neighborhoods and ethnic groups require a degree of aggressiveness which may be unsuitable and undesirable elsewhere. What has been said of locality, caste, and class as determinants of aggression is equally true of broader groups such as nations and even continents. The cultures of these and the physical necessities stamp the nature, intensity, and pattern of aggressive acts. While variant behavior and mannerisms may be annoying to persons from specific local or national backgrounds, it must be recognized that such behavior is devoid of hostility, and is a conditioned automatic reflection of character organization and ego functioning. This *primary aggression* needs to be differentiated from *secondary aggression,* which is a result of pathology.

Sources of Aggression

Aggression can proceed from a number of sources and determinants. For the purpose of psychotherapeutic intervention, it can be related to character, neurotic, and psychotic sources.

Character Aggression

The sources for an aggressive adaptation stem from childhood and are determined by the conditions already described.[2] Whatever the early traumata have been, by the time the individual reaches adulthood the aggressive pattern has already become structured in character. This is inevitable, for character results from, and is conditioned by, the modes of adaptation imposed on the child for prolonged periods. When the conditions of life activate his instinctive hostility or require him to act aggressively, he will grow into maturity with a hostile or an aggressive character. Character structure in adults is resistive to change (character armor) largely because the ego is an integral part of character and its reactions, which make them ego-syntonic. Hostility, on the other hand, is by its nature ego-alien in our culture. Since it is available to the examination of the ego, hostility is accessible to individual psychotherapy.

Experience with character disorders in adults in group psychotherapy (other than neurotic characters and psychopaths) shows that this method is more effective than other forms of treatment. The advantages of groups lie in the fact that they react to and reflect the patient's aggressiveness, so that he is made aware of it in a telling and unmistakable way. He is confronted by fellow patients with the same pattern as his own, who mirror his behavior, while others, including the therapist, demonstrate nonaggressive

[2] Not all sources and determinants of aggression are enumerated here; only those that relate directly to group psychotherapy receive consideration.

ways of adaptation and response that motivate in him inhibitory trends.[3] Then there are the direct critical reactions and resistances to aggression on the part of the group. In this sense the group becomes the supplementary internalized ego which exercises a critical function as an inhibitor of behavior. Here one must rely largely upon the communication channels between the ego and the unconscious that psychotherapy aims to establish.

Neurotic Aggression

Nonhostile aggression (acting out) in adults may proceed from neurotic and counterphobic sources, such as subjective conflicts, sexual and other tensions, feelings of inadequacy and inferiority, defensiveness, and anger. Such aggression disappears when the neurotic difficulties from which they stem are eliminated. Therapy, therefore, has to be directed toward the resolution of neurotic difficulties rather than directly toward the aggressive behavior, as in character disorders.

Excessive hostility has to be considered as a neurotic manifestation, since it is derived from negatively overcathected object relations which became diffuse. Overdetermined hostility is a reaction to specific individuals and situations, but once it is internalized it becomes diffused and directed automatically toward all situations and persons with whom the subject comes in contact.

Psychotic Aggression

This stems from the overwhelming murderous hostility that underlies this type of malady, leading, in some cases, to homicide and suicide. Psychotic aggression stems from the lack of adequate ego controls and defenses, and the distorted perception of reality peculiar to the psychotic patient.

EFFECTS OF AGGRESSION ON GROUPS

In accepting and assigning patients to groups, the element of

[3] In this connection, one should keep in mind Freud's adage: "Where the id has been; the ego should be."

aggression is an important consideration. To be acceptable for analytic group psychotherapy, the patients' conduct cannot be of secondary origin; that is, it cannot stem from organic pathology, such as a brain injury, psychosis, psychopathy, glandular imbalance, autonomic imbalance, or other neurologic and organic deficiencies including constitutional ego insufficiency. Such patients require special groups, in addition to medical treatment. The potentials of the personality must be such that, after psychic balance is established through psychotherapy, the ego can deal with impulses, which it cannot in constitutional defects. Where intrapsychic resources are not sufficient, medical treatment has to be tried out before psychotherapy is initiated. In a therapy group, uncontrollably aggressive members cause panic and frustrations to other patients and set up resentments and hostilities inconsistent with therapeutic validity. Intrapsychic and intragroup tensions are fertile sources for psychotherapy only when they can be resolved. If resolutions cannot be affected because of constitutional or organic deficiencies in patients, the group climate becomes inimical.

A similar effect is produced by compulsively overaggressive patients, who are given to highly tensed reactions. As already pointed out, there are limits to a group's capacity to absorb tension or tolerate frustration; when these limits are exceeded, the intensifications characteristic of groups overstrain the ego resources of the participants. No matter how skillful and secure a therapist may be, he cannot deal with this situation, especially where the tensions are cumulative. In addition, too much aggressiveness maintains the group at a level of nodal (emotional) state so that the antinodal periods, during which therapy occurs, are not allowed to set in.

Inclusion of too many patients with aggressive characters, or even of one who is compulsively aggressive, is deleterious to both children's and adults' groups, though there are therapeutically important differences.

Because of children's maturational levels and ego development, aggression and acting out are more consistent with their personalities and group adaptation. Children can tolerate aggression more easily than adults, but both children and adult groups require "balancing," with regard to ego functioning and character, as well as with regard to clinical categories and nuclear problems of its constituents. The group should be able to recover from periods of hyperactivity and hypertension and move from nodal to anti-nodal behavior by its own forces. To achieve this, the number and quality of "instigators" must be carefully considered and balanced by "neutralizers." This is more important in children's activity therapy groups than in analytic groups. In the latter, re-straint is a by-product of interpretation, while in activity groups this source of balancing does not exist, since no verbal interpretation is employed. Where verbalization and interpretation are the rule, as in adult and adolescent groups, there can be greater lati-tude in selection and group assignment; but, for reasons already listed, too much aggressiveness in analytic groups has to be pre-vented. Several other aspects of this problem have been discussed in Chapter XII, which deals with the phenomenon of acting out.

TABLE 1

Nature and Manifestations of Aggression

Types of Aggression	Sources of Aggression
Atavistic	Character
Phylogenetic	Neurotic
Ontogenetic	Psychotic
Instrumental	

THE NATURE AND TREATMENT OF WITHDRAWAL

Definition

So far, aggression has been considered, within a defined scope, as a normal manifestation of living organisms. However, it can become undesirable or pathological when it assumes certain forms. When the intensity of aggression does not favor effective personal adaptation and group survival and exceeds the boundaries of ordi-nary controls and rationality, it can be viewed with justification as pathological. As a balance, and perhaps as an antithesis to the aggressive pattern in life and survival needs, specific conditions require avoidance and flight, and when they are so employed they, too, can be considered as normal and desirable. However, where withdrawal of energy (libido) by an individual jeopardizes his own interests and diminishes his effectiveness as a social atom, some degree of pathology is present requiring corrective measures.

For our purpose the concept of withdrawal connotes physical or psychological removal from a given situation. Withdrawal here means any block to the outflow of energy, such as mutism, stuttering, compliance, indecisiveness, lethargy, apathy, diffidence, shyness, docility, submissiveness, abstention, flight, and ingratiation — all of which can be said to be derived from two main causes, fear and hostility. In psychotherapy it is necessary to explore further their nature and forms.

A victim of psychological blocks has difficulty in relating appropriately to his environment, or in communicating with his fellows without embarrassment and suffering, or unable to mobilize energies with ease to meet ordinary responsibilities. Such difficulties are, in many respects, analogous to handicaps that limit a person's participation in the life around him and deprive him of the pleasures and satisfactions that a full, active life can offer. The desire and the channels for communication stem from healthy object relations and outward direction of libido. When assertiveness and aggression are constricted, withdrawal results, and the task of psychotherapy is to open channels of communication and mobilize the libido. To help overcome blocks to expression by correcting the conditions within the psyche that employ withdrawal as a defensive and adaptive mechanism, it is necessary first to understand the origins and causes of the blocks. As in all psychological phenomena, withdrawal is multicausal; its sources and purposes differ with individuals; but it may have multiple meanings even to the same individual. The following are some of these.

Inhibition of Spontaneity

The infant and the child are activated by energies that accompany organic and psychological growth and progressive maturation.

483

These are at first unorganized and diffuse, characterized by the absence or low level of inhibition. In orderly and healthful development, restraints and impulse organization are gradually introduced through educational controls, through identification with adults, and through the pressures and demands from individuals and groups. The manner in which primary impulses are integrated and organized in the adult personality and are employed instrumentally in the process of adjustment depends upon the treatment they have received during childhood and later formative years. Where impulses have been abruptly frustrated and harshly punished, with actual or seeming rejection, the child and later the adult may, as a result, become either violently aggressive or excessively withdrawn. In the first instance, it is rebellion against adults and is a form of counteraggression and counterrejection. This is most likely to occur when the child is very young (pre-oedipal) and has not yet established the necessary identifications with adults and the resulting willingness to give up gratifications for them. Later, during and after the oedipal period, the child is likely to inhibit his impulses to avoid punishment, prevent guilt feelings, or overcome the fear of losing his parents' love. The child senses what the adults expect from him, and he takes on patterns of behavior to please them. Usually withdrawal is accompanied by considerable anxiety and is most often laden with neurotic fears and tensions. It produces later in life a personality that is variously described as inhibited, restricted, constricted, or schizoid.

Inhibition of spontaneity is the inevitable and automatic result of association with unhappy, limited, restricted, or hostile parents or nurses. Spontaneous activation is either checked by these adults directly, or is withheld by the child, since he feels their disapproval when he becomes active. Such physical inhibition causes also emotional constriction and diminution of intellectual growth. Where the outer pressures are less great, the final personality may not be constricted, but restricted, i.e., the individual functions acceptably, but his field of operation is more limited than it might have been had he been given adequate freedom of action. Constriction results when impulses and drives for self-expression and self-realization in activity have been more inhibited than in the case of restriction. The unwise use of control and limitations imposed on the child's primitive and primary impulses by the adults important in his life may also result in inner conflict and in a character structure that resembles in its outward manifestations a neurosis. Many develop impulse neuroses and neurotic characters as they grow older, because of excessive outside inhibitive controls, especially when these have been applied very early in the child's life.

Control, restriction, and direction are essential to normal social development of the individual and to his mental health. They are pathogenic only when applied without an understanding of the dynamic needs of the human personality at its various stages of development, and when they are applied arbitrarily, with impatience, and in the absence of respect for the individuality of the child. Much of these stem from hostility, rejection, and the current philosophy of "education." When the repressive forces had been beyond the child's capacities to deal with and integrate them into his ego, the resulting withdrawal later in life may be reflected in deep emotional disturbances, the roots of which are outlined below.

With children, especially if the natural psycho-organic spontaneity has been overly inhibited, the psychotherapist's aim is to free them by supplying channels for expression. Even in the case of adolescents and adults, the permissive atmosphere, the opportunity to communicate one's feelings freely, the accepting and non-threatening parent substitute, and the example set by less frightened and less conflicted fellow members, are particularly valuable for the inhibited, the restricted, and the constricted.[4] However, in the case of adolescents and adults, the presence of neurotic difficulties from which withdrawal may proceed, necessitates individual psychotherapy. Some withdrawn patients may suffer from obsessional fears or other pathology that require treatment other than group therapy. In most instances, however, the opportunity to act out (activity catharsis) counteracts the barriers to

[4] In children's groups there is also a very valuable outlet: work with various types of manipulative materials and games.

centrifugal flow of the libido in action and creativity. New perceptions, coupled with the euphoric feelings that naturally flow from self-fulfillment and the exercise of power—physical, aesthetic, intellectual, and emotional—balance the patient's psyche so that withdrawal is less needed.

In most adults, those withdrawal stems from early impulse inhibition, diffidence and nonassertiveness become the stamp of his character that mark his relations throughout life. Such adults have few friends and are in contact with few persons outside their immediate families. Even with the latter they remain uncommunicative and withdrawn. They avoid group associations, and when they find themselves in groups they remain isolated.

Therapy groups for such individuals are eminently valuable. Their passive participation turns in time (often a very long time) into active communication and sharing with other members in the groups. The security of full mutual acceptance, the noncritical and permissive relations, and the role of the therapist, activate such adults to take part with others in matters that concern them all. These are the patients who should be encouraged to participate in such ancillary activities as plastic and graphic art, dramatics, and various types of manual and social activities, in addition to the group interviews. Group art therapy is especially valuable. However, the therapist should always keep in mind the limitations put on psychotherapy by the rigidities of the adult character.

Failure in Sibling Rivalry

When a child has consistently failed in competition and rivalry with siblings, either because of age, personality differences, preference of parents for the contending sibling, or because of naturally more limited talents, he may withdraw from the competitive arena, and later may refuse to take part in activities, learning, and occupations in which the rival sibling is successful. He may also become either too assertive and demanding, and generally present a series of behavior and habit disorders of an aggressive nature; or he may renounce all effort and aggression and in extreme instances behave as though his energies are paralyzed. He will eschew activities and participation in which differences and

486

conflict are involved, and avoid all competitive situations. Fear and indecisiveness become dominant characteristics, and his self-image becomes one of weakness, inadequacy and inability to succeed in any effort. In addition, he may refuse to recognize any value in achievement, preferring to immerse himself in self-absorption, emotional and intellectual inactivity, and sometimes even physical immobility.

Frequently this condition is accompanied by a satirical attitude and a nihilistic philosophy of life: achievement is considered unworthy and the values placed on things by the world is regarded as exaggerated. Thus, the child dawdles, becomes a school problem, is lackadaisical and slow. As an adult, he is satisfied with a station in life and in professions and occupations far short of his talents, and is seemingly indifferent to the opinions of his fellows. Bohemians, beatniks, and other unconventionals are predominantly people with this adjustment pattern. While most such people are passively resistant there are also among them overt aggressives who are more likely to join the ranks of economic and political organizations with defined and active revisionistic or radical objectives.

Extreme cases of withdrawal due to sibling rivalry may appear as schizoid characters, but structurally they are widely different from the schizoid. In the latter, the character defect is constitutional and, so far, has not yielded to psychotherapy (though considerable improvement in adaptive functions had been affected), while withdrawal, being an adaptive pattern, responds to corrective evocative stimuli of psychotherapy.

Nonparticipation, dawdling, and general isolative demeanor on the part of the rejected, and the failures, have additional secondary gains. Through them, the child, particularly, sets himself off as different from the more successful sibling. This difference gives him a special mark or brand that is exclusively his own. Being the extreme opposite makes him in his own eyes a person with a definite individuality, different from his rival. Thus, his self-identity is in a rather ironical way bolstered, through his insufficient adaptations.

Another secondary gain that accrues from withdrawal and its accompanying behavior reactions is that it draws attention from parents and teachers. Thus it serves at once as an attention-getting device and as a counter-hostility measure. Because of annoyance, adults turn their efforts to correcting the child's demeanor, and he feels gratified at being able to disturb them and cause them concern, as retaliation for the real or fancied rejection he feels he had suffered at their hands. Thus, what seems on the surface to be withdrawal, is actually a form of passive aggression, shielding strong feelings of resentment, hostility, and rebelliousness, which may even be covered up by exaggerated affection, submissiveness to, and protectiveness of, the more successful sibling. In the course of treatment of persons who had suffered deeply by failure in relation to siblings, it is not unusual to uncover repressed death wishes against them and the parents, as well as guilt, and fear of being killed by them.

To a patient who, as a child, was the victim of sibling rivalry, satisfying constructive and substitute (restitutional) relations and ego gratifications are of the utmost value in corrective psychotherapy. In a therapy group, these relations are supplied in the persons of the other members, who are substitute siblings, but in an atmosphere that favors the positive aspects of such a relation. Acceptance and recognition counteract passive aggression, controlled jealousy and masked resentment, which at first are felt toward fellow members (siblings) and toward the therapist (parent).

The changed self-image, the feelings of power and success, and the reconditioned attitudes toward others combine in the emergence of channels for centrifugal libidinal flow toward the environment and the persons in it. In children's, adolescents', and adults' analytic groups the intrapsychic problems are not worked out in relationships alone; they also yield to interactions. The habitual attitudes and withdrawal patterns are reacted to, discussed, and traced to their origins, and distortions and displacements are revealed.

In many adult patients, failure in sibling rivalry and intense hostility toward siblings, form the center of neurotic difficulties that require working through in a thoroughgoing transference psychotherapy. The intrapsychic anxiety stemming from the con-

488

flict between felt hostility and the disapproval of it by the superego (which is conditioned by social mores and family ritual), results in great tension and anxiety which is discharged either by
aggression or by defensive withdrawal. One of the serious consequences of this is that the hostility is usually displaced on mates
and offspring.

The problem of hostility in adults toward siblings and the feeling of failure in relation to them cannot be resolved by situational therapy alone, as with children. Adults have to unearth the
past events buried in their own unconscious or preconscious, and
the accompanying feelings that caused protective diffidence and
shyness. Only when these become available to the ego can the desired character change occur. This can be accomplished in individual as well as in group psychotherapy, with some advantages
on the side of the latter. In any case, a group should be an integral part of the treatment of such patients, either as concomitant,
tapering off, or subsequent experience as reality testing.

Withdrawal as a Reaction to Guilt

The fear of revealing unconscious guilt-provoking content and
evoking the disapproval of others may cause withdrawal and the
blocking of freedom in communication. Hostile and homicidal
urges toward members of one's family, incestuous strivings and
fantasies, past or current, masturbation, and numerous socially
forbidden acts and thoughts, often lead to self-incapsulation as a
conscious and unconscious preventative against inadvertent self-
revelation. Withdrawal and diffidence diminish the risk of being
found out, but result in a constricted personality. Unless these
superego-alien and socially censored thoughts, memories, and fantasies are dislodged from the unconscious or preconscious, the
neurotic tensions and the resultant behavioral patterns become imprinted as the permanent character of an individual.

In a treatment group for adults, an unmarried young woman
aged 32, greatly inhibited and withdrawn, participated little in the
interviews; instead she did many paintings, red being the predominating color. They were usually abstract and of a distinct
character which revealed, to a discerning eye, considerable re-

pressed sexuality. A special feature of her artistic efforts was that when she finished a painting, she invariably blotted it out with black paint. She continued this practice for some months when her need to blot out her work disappeared. She was no longer embarrassed to have her paintings exposed to view. Simultaneously, her participation in the group discussions increased. She now spoke more freely and her general appearance also improved. Her friends remarked on this and on the marked increase in her communicativeness and friendliness. The blotting out of the drawings was a physical counterpart of her need to blot out memories; it was a form of preventing the rise to the surface of guilt-evoking thoughts and sexual fantasies. While this type of withdrawal, laden with a neurotic content, requires deep uncovering psychotherapy, the behavioral (character) components had been alleviated through activity catharsis and vicarious therapy in the group.

Universalization assuages guilt and reduces the resulting anxiety, and helps patients grow less fearful and less ashamed of their impulses. Members of groups may speak of untoward acts and fantasies, which helps others gain courage to face their own hitherto warded off feelings; thus they, too, are freed to communicate.

At a group interview of adolescent girls, one of their number said: "From this group I learned how to talk properly. I feel that I have gotten a kind of 'lady poise.' " She attributed her gains to the fact that the girls did not "make fun of me, even though they called attention to my many mistakes. From listening to the girls," she said, "I now understand people better than I used to because I understand myself better. I used to think that I had a strange character, but I found out here that other girls did the same things I did. Mrs. K. (group therapist) used to tell me things (in individual interviews) and often gave me examples of how other people act and behave, but I never believed it. I thought she was leading me on. In this group I saw and heard the kind of things Mrs. K. used to talk about." When asked what she meant by a "strange character," Pearl responded by saying: "I was a little bit like R. (another member of the group). I used to stay at home and indulge in daydreams. Now I know that other girls, too, did the same things. I belonged to another club once, but there I used to talk nonsense, because down deep I was afraid I was different. Here I became serious. I didn't act nonsensically after the first meeting, when I felt more accepted by the girls." The girls also helped her to a better vocabulary and she improved it by "thinking before I speak." Laura recalled that Pearl used to laugh "about nothing at all, just giggle." Pearl explained that it was because she did not feel secure; she did not know how she would be accepted because she thought herself "strange."

Considering patients from the behavioral aspect only, we have found in our work both with children and older patients that the withdrawn and diffident improve much more quickly than do the assertive and the aggressive. This does not mean that the basic problems of the withdrawn are more accessible than those of the aggressive. Rather, their conduct (ego functioning) is more readily affected by group treatment: they grow more assertive, release an impressive quantum of hostility, and become strikingly less isolative and diffident. This improvement can be explained by the fact that psychotherapy allies itself with, and buttresses, the natural and inherent tendency of all living organisms for centrifugal flow of the libido or *élan vital*, which is a prime requirement for biological survival.

Narcissism and Withdrawal

The inversion of libido because of primary narcissism is one of the causes of object relations insufficiency incompatible with the accepted standard of normality. When relationships perpetuate the basic narcissism of a child and allow it to persist beyond the appropriate age levels, a narcissistic character is the result. Among the conditions that determine this development are denial of love which necessitates the subject's investment of love upon himself rather than upon outer objects, the encouraging of exhibitionism by parents and others, excessive attention, overgratification, and conditions that favor autoeroticism rather than investment of sexual libido in external objects.

These and similar conditions lead to psychological isolation, and the subject becomes what Dr. Adolph Meyer has described as egotropic (in contrast to being allotropic, which is the normal

491

state for an individual living in a social setting). Extreme narcissism, especially that of a secondary nature, is characteristic of the psychoses; but we are concerned here with nonpsychotic states in which these extremes are not present. The ego in the latter is neither libidinized nor erogenized but, rather, the self-image is defective, the ego is preoccupied with the self, and its boundaries are not adequately defined. As a result, the independence/dependence balance is faulty.

Narcissistic character disorders in adults are almost inaccessible to individual psychotherapy and psychoanalysis because of their inability to establish a positive transference. They are also difficult in group psychotherapy, since the basic requirement for motivating treatment is social hunger; that is, the desire to be with people and belong with others. Social hunger has the same relation to group psychotherapy as transference does to individual psychotherapy. Both are motivations for continuing treatment and both have an identical relation to the treatment medium.

Although the foundations for object relations are weak, there are patients in this category that may gain from a group more than they would in individual treatment. In a group there is less demand for "relatedness" and the reactions of other members may make an inroad into a patient's psyche, penetrating the wall of his incapsulation, provided, of course, that he continues in treatment despite the threat to his ego. Thus, though the narcissistic character disorders in adult patients present a poor treatment prognosis, some individuals can gain from the experience. They have to be carefully screened, however, because narcissistic patients tend to antagonize and disturb groups and are, therefore, attacked and rejected. Nonetheless, some areas of personality and behavior can be modified to a certain extent, but that the basic character can be changed is questionable.

Reactions to Stigmata

Physically or socially stigmatized persons tend to withdraw from social situations and remain more or less isolated and uncommunicative. Any feature or characteristic that distinguishes a person from those around him generates "self-consciousness" and, therefore, diffidence. Cripples, persons of unusual build or stature, members of racial, ethnical, and cultural minority groups feel themselves different from their surroundings and grow timorous (though some individuals may also react by overassertiveness), and hence, cluster in ghettos.

It has been observed that unusually tall persons are quiet and withdrawn, as the diminutive, contrariwise, are aggressive and loud. The tall person who stood out as a child (and especially as an adolescent) felt different from his peers and grew apprehensive of attack or scapegoating. Tall youngsters are also aware that they represent physical threat to their playmates and, in order not to be attacked or ostracized, assume a recessive, nonthreatening mien, which in time becomes set into a character pattern. Similarly, redheaded persons are by and large less assertive and more sensitive than others who are of a more usual coloring. It is quite possible that the reputed quick temper of the redhead is a reaction to the discrimination they were exposed to and to the self-imposed frustration in earlier years. Adults who have been brilliant youngsters also tend toward a withdrawal pattern, due to the discomfort they once felt in being the center of attraction and the victims of derision from peers.

Physical stigmata, such as lameness, clubfeet, facial disfigurements, hunchbacks, blindness in one eye, stuttering, and similar handicaps, all contribute toward the impairment of freedom in relations, communication, and comfortable social adjustment. We have found that children with visible physical stigmata, except for stuttering, cannot be placed in therapy groups because they are liable to be traumatized even further by name-calling and possible rejection by other group members.

In therapy groups, adults can explore their feelings concerning the stigmata and handicaps; the reactions and support of others who are not so handicapped is of inestimable help to them. The objectivity, acceptance, and support of the group, the ease and simplicity with which this threat area is treated cannot but help them to accept themselves and to live more comfortably with their handicaps. In the group, the physically stigmatized discovers that, though physically intact, his fellow members, too, are handicapped by emotional and social difficulties as much as he is by his physical deviation.

Defective Self-Image

Low self-esteem (from causes other than actual stigma or defects) can proceed from many sources: from failure in sibling rivalry, affect deprivation, and excessive punishment and rejection by parents, as well as from feelings of unworthiness emanating from a severe superego or a weak ego.

A child unloved by his parents is dominated by a feeling that he is unworthy of love, inferior and worthless, for self-esteem is only an incorporation or introjection of the esteem of the parents for the child. A mother's praise makes a child feel praiseworthy; her respect engenders self-respect; and her faith makes him capable and responsible. But when parents view the child negatively and are persistently critical, discouraging, and denying of tenderness and love, the self-perception of the victim will be at a low ebb and weigh him down until the end of his days.

Much of the psychic masochism, self-denigrating acts, attitudes, and relations manifested in incompatible marriages and unutilized talents, as well as general maladjustment, are traceable to lack of faith and respect. Persons who have been subjected to such treatment in childhood may grow submissive, unassertive, placating, and generally withdrawn. Boys may doubt their sexual potency and girls may feel unattractive. Both boys and girls either become shy or aggressive and may commit antisocial acts, leading to delinquency and criminality.

The heightening of the self-image is among the five major aims of sound psychotherapy; but as we have attempted to show, the effects of three of the other aims of psychotherapy—corrected libido distribution, ego strengthening, and a regulated superego—also enhance the self-image. Group psychotherapy *per se* has a direct bearing upon overcoming the damage to self-esteem. In groups, this occurs in consequence, firstly, of the fact that patients are unconditionally accepted for what they are and, therefore, come to feel worthy. Secondly, success in reality testing is a constant process and further adds to an improved self-image.

Thirdly, healthful identifications with fellow group members and the positive, poised, understanding, and tolerant therapist further help the process and fourthly, a feeling of greater adequacy in discharging biological destiny is achieved.

Group interviews of adults are replete with complaints of feelings of weakness, inadequacy, and unworthiness. These feelings are most often all-pervasive, diffuse, and directed toward all relations and situations, especially the marital relation. Men and women reveal themselves as feeling inferior to their mates and sexually inadequate. This can be expected, since in the marital relation, more than in any other, all facets of the personality are engaged. Here men and women are faced with biologically most vital and culturally most cathected functions. Success in sexual responsiveness and consummation is highly prized in the value system of society as well as by the individual, and one who fails, considers himself as lacking. Group members help one another greatly in this as in other areas. Not only is there consolation in the fact that others, too, have similar difficulties, but the free discussions of the subject remove fears and repressions which are in many instances at the root of the difficulty. This results in improvements in sexual adjustment in some less serious cases.

Similarly, patients help each other to re-evaluate feelings in other areas and relations originated in childhood. This leads them to understand emotionally the relics of their infantile feelings and childhood cravings and fantasies, all of which arouse new and more appropriate attitudes concerning the self and its worth and powers.

Submission to Parents

Among the most usual material that appears in therapeutic interviews is the child's relationship with his parents and, especially, his domination by them. While children's submission to parents is not unnatural and, within certain limits, desirable, the memory of it, however, is a serious problem when they become adults.

The roots of this pattern are inherent in the nature of the child-mother relation. The demands for obedience and submission are made upon the child at a very early age, during the nurturing and discipline phases in his development. Because of the mother's part in his survival and her role in gratifying the child's primary needs, he submits to her discipline. But, as the child grows older, he should be progressively freed of his dependence and submission.

When, in an adult, dependence and submissiveness persists to a point where he finds it difficult to discharge his functions as a mate and parent without consultation with his parents, or when he feels compelled to placate them at a cost to his own family and children, the relationship is deleterious and can be of a parasitic, symbiotic, or of a domination-submission nature. (See Slavson, 1944a.) These relations can be charged with intense affect and anxiety; they can bear a strong incestuous or homosexual tinge, have a psychotic base, or result in psychic masochism. It is therefore necessary for the therapist to ascertain the nosology with every degree of certainty possible before going too deeply into treatment.

In an impressive number of cases, groups have been very effective in supporting patients so that they could throw off the yoke of dominating and demanding parents. Groups have diminished or dissolved the psychic masochism, and supported latent schizophrenics to a point where their relations with parents have changed. The criticism, advice, and direct suggestions as to ways of dealing with the interfering parent, coupled with the interpretive analyses of the dynamics and etiology of the relations, buttress the patient's weak ego and reduce the fear of asserting himself. After a number of such discussions, patients came to the group sessions glowing with joy, to announce triumphantly that they had put their parents "in their place" or that they had talked matters over with them frankly and directly as "advised" by the group.

Here, as in other situations, the group as a whole serves *in loco matris*. In many essential respects, the group assumes the role in the psychic economy of the patient of a good mother. Because the group accepts him unconditionally, is interested in him, protects, supports, advises, and guides him, and is in every way a positive source of strength and courage, its psychic image becomes that of a loving mother.

Schizoid Withdrawal

One type of apathy encountered in psychotherapy is intrinsic to the schizoid personality. The accepted view of the nature of this condition is that it is an inherent predisposition of a constitutional origin, and is unalterable by any known educational or therapeutic means. The basic structure of the schizoid personality is marked narcissism, while the observable manifestation is quietude, withdrawal, and isolationism, though at times periods of hypermotility may appear. At the present state of our knowledge of this condition, this is normal to certain persons and, being rooted in the individual's constitution, is not alterable, though the patient can be helped by skillful and cautious psychotherapy. Schizoid persons can be helped to fit into the economic structure of society, but they are more useful in occupations that require minimal interaction with people, where the reality demands are low and the content and duties of the job deal predominantly or entirely with objects or accounts that are not too variable.

Both the nature and degree of withdrawal in the schizoid varies. While the difference can be accounted for on constitutional grounds, there is also every likelihood that the manner in which the patient was treated by parents and teachers as a child (especially in relation to his narcissism), may be a determining factor. Efforts by parents to activate the child with schizoid tendencies by drawing him into conversations and helping him share in activities in the home and the school, thus extending his field of reality contact and communication, may hold the schizoid trend within boundaries. When parents protect the schizoid child against rejection and narcissistic injuries, the narcissistic regression (autism) does not reach as high levels as in children whose experiences served to strengthen them. Similarly, schools have to accord these children special treatment to prevent fear, anxiety, and failure, which further increase their flight tendencies.

Schizoid adults are intensely sensitive and harbor intense hostility, which remains for the most part either unexpressed or indirectly expressed. It is probably of the schizoid that it was said: "Still waters run deep." Their lives are rich in feeling and thought, but they remain comparatively removed from the maelstrom and bustle and activity of the world around them. They remain immured in the deep caverns of their own psyche. Because of their sensitivity, schizoid personalities have to be treated offhandedly, though with respect and consideration, but no effort at a close relation should be made. Every step toward closeness or intimacy constitutes an invasion into the closely guarded precincts of their privacy, threatening their insufficient and loosely held together ego forces.

Many persons with schizoid characters function at their highest capacities and, as such, require no treatment. However, some present problems of adjustment and overintense anxieties with which they cannot deal, and require psychotherapy. Treatment of these patients always presents a serious risk, since their hold on reality is a tenuous one and their ego defenses are fragile. Direct psychotherapy may, therefore, set in a psychological break. As in schizophrenia, here, too, treatment needs to be in the direction of ego support and reality testing.

The schizoid patients, especially in certain moods, communicate little, and groups in which they can participate in vicarious catharsis and identification therapy are suitable to selected patients in this category. The fact that they are able to remain quiet at will rather than be expected or forced to speak as in other therapies, is both a source of comfort to them and an easier approach to their problems. Because of their defective object cathexis and low capacity to relate, the diluted relations in a group are well suited to this type of patient.

At best, reality to the schizoid is hazy, and while he is capable of reality testing he does it with less enthusiasm and thoroughness than does the average person. As already mentioned, the schizoid functions best and can retain his hold on himself and on reality where the demands on him are minimal. These principles also govern his therapy. The emotional strain and self-confrontation in a group may be much less a drain on schizoid persons than in a one-to-one relationship. The group, however, is not free of presenting them with stresses and the therapist with risks. Insensitive and aggressive members may, by their manner and directness, cause much anxiety to the schizoid and force him into further narcissistic regression and withdrawal. The selection and assignments of such patients must, therefore, be done with great caution and on a test basis. Experience with adult schizoid patients in analytic groups shows that in time they become activated sufficiently to participate in a limited way in the group discussions, but that they usually address themselves to the problems of other patients rather than their own. Although their sensitivity prohibits self-exposure, they show improvement, but at a less rapid rate than other patients. They grow more related, somewhat more spontaneous and, as it seems to the observer, happier persons.

In activity groups, children who present either schizoid or, what is more likely, schizoid-like behavior, display impressive improvement in social adjustment in comparatively short periods. They become activated quickly by the manual occupations, by the interactions with other children, and by the dynamic atmosphere. However, schizoid children have to be placed in mild groups, for excessive and violent acting out frightens them into quitting the group.

Catatonic Defense

Environmental pressures and demands may become so threatening to a person with ego deficiency that he may defend himself against it by a detachment so complete as to give the impression that the situation leaves him entirely unaffected. In extreme instances, persons given to this reaction behave as though they do not register what goes on around them. While in the course of daily events they may discharge major responsibilities, such as holding a job, with a tolerable adequacy, they remain emotionally unresponsive to other events and communicate little or nothing. They leave the management of most affairs to others, usually to a mate. Such persons have been characterized as "living corpses," but the term *catatonic defense* describes them more correctly.

This defense is usually adopted not as a general pattern of life, but in particularly stressful areas. An individual may function effectively on a job but adopt this withdrawal mechanism at home. Contrariwise, difficulties with a partner in business or a demanding, authoritarian, and abusive boss may cause a person to assume this defense at work, and yet be activated and comparatively lively at home, where he feels accepted and secure.

In a distressing situation the individual with catatonic defenses maintains what appears as a studied quiet. He removes himself psychologically (and sometimes also physically) from the unpleasant situation, as a defense against being hurt and probably also as a means of expressing resentment and hostility. A case in point was that of a father of a boy in treatment. Whenever a home visit was made to follow up on the boy's adjustment, the mother, a power-driven, aggressive, authoritarian woman, managed the interviews. The husband sat by quietly, either averting his eyes or reading a newspaper. On some occasions he walked toward the window and stood looking out, with his back toward the interviewer and his wife. This was his defense against an overpowering wife as well as a gesture of his hostility toward her.

A classical illustration of catatonic defense is Henry in the film, *Activity Group Therapy*. Henry was about eleven years old, completely isolated and in his daily life spoke no more than a few words to his mother and a boy cousin. He had never played with children and, when encountering a group at play on a sidewalk, he would cross the street to avoid passing them. When placed in an activity therapy group on a trial basis, he remained completely immobile for weeks, making no contact and speaking to no one, children or therapist. In his anxiety he would stay rooted to one spot far away from the others and with downcast eyes and with lips ceaselessly moving in a sucking action, would move some objects with his hand back and forth in monotonous repetition for hours on end; or he would crawl into a box and sit in it for more than an hour in a tightly cramped position; or later, he would bounce a Ping-Pong ball up and down with a paddle with monotonous regularity for interminable periods.

As is usual in these groups, no one paid attention to him and he slowly began making contact with the other boys. By sidelong furtive glances (which lengthened in point of time as he grew more secure) he observed the children's activities and, after many weeks, he played table tennis with the therapist and later with one more boy participating. Gradually, as he overcame his paralyzing fear and discomfort, he joined with the others in their simple games and to a limited extent also in their conversations, though he has never become normally communicative or assertive. He remained on its periphery throughout his three years in the group. Henry's mother reported that he had carried over this change to his daily associations. He played ball with boys in his neighborhood, for which he seemed to have a special talent.

We have had no experience in group treatment of adults with catatonic defense. It can be assumed, however, that interpersonal and group activation should be of some value, either exclusively or supplementary to individual therapy, depending upon the nosology of the particular case. In some instances, patients might give up their defenses more easily in a group than in individual contacts. However, since psychotherapy directs its efforts at the cause rather than the symptom, what is required here is the resolution of the intrapsychic and interpersonal conditions that necessitated the adoption of such a defense.

Withdrawal as Retaliation

One way in which children retaliate against parents, and adults against each other, is by silence and by withdrawal from participation in a relationship and responsibilities. This action is intended to annoy its object, and the more the latter reacts with annoyance, anger, anxiety, or worry, the more likely is withdrawal to be used as retaliatory passive aggression.

Occasionally this pattern appears as an act of hostility and spite in children who are strongly attached to a parent when he withholds his attention from the child. Anger and spiteful withdrawal are activated when a child is forced to take charge of younger siblings. In such a situation strong hostility arises, not only against the siblings but also against all children, who become the targets of displacement of his negative feelings. He may then either attack them or withdraw from associating with them.

A boy of ten once vividly described his feelings of paralyzing fear as he sat alone at home watching over his sleeping younger brothers and sisters, while his parents were occupied with their

501

social and political interests out of the home. This boy was inordinately withdrawn at home, failed in his studies at school, had no friends, and was unable to play children's games or participate in any other children's interests. In addition, he was intensely effeminate, performing house chores in his home and in the homes of neighbors for a scheduled fee. He made flowers for sale, but could not play ball, fight, run, or take part in any boyish activities. Through the combination of activity group therapy with a man and an individual relation with a woman, he was helped to overcome his basic dislike for children and to acquire facilities for working and playing with them, thus making a satisfactory social recovery. The group helped him in overcoming his defective identification and self-image, and gave him a field for testing himself against reality, for which he was encouraged by the others in the group. In the individual relation, he was able to ventilate his complaints against his parents and siblings and thus bring his hostilities under the control of his strengthened ego.

The use of withdrawal as an act of spite and hostility is not limited to children. It is also found among adults, such as an adult offspring and his parents and, more frequently, between married couples. All are aware how bitter is the silence of one's friend and partner, and few can tolerate it. Silence can represent scorn, rejection, hostility, which the object seldom fails to perceive and react to.

By its very nature, group psychotherapy can be effective with such patients, though the nature and intensity of each case of negative object cathexis must be considered and its accessibility determined.

Withdrawal as Psychoneurotic Symptom

In addition to the neurotic elements inherent in the various types of withdrawal already described, there are patients who manifest this characteristic as a result of neurotic intrapsychic conflicts that constitute a true psychoneurosis. As such, the withdrawal is a symptom that serves to protect the ego from tension and anxiety by flight or retreat. Nonpsychotic withdrawal emanates from the neurotic discomfort a patient feels in the presence of other persons, from the dread of being exposed, disapproved of, or criticized, or from a fear of responsibilities that, consciously or unconsciously, he feels unable to assume.

To some patients in this category, successful, aggressive effort represents culmination of unconscious or preconscious incestuous coitus and to prevent the onset of anxiety that accompanies success, the patient recoils from it. Patients suffering from this syndrome tend to leave their works unfinished or poorly performed, thus defeating themselves. One of the means for self-defeat and for evading the full consummation of effort is frequent change of jobs and residence, and general evasion of permanence and success. Adult patients with this deep disturbance require intensive transference and insight psychotherapy, and individual treatment is recommended for them.

THE TRANSMUTATIONS OF WITHDRAWAL INTO AGGRESSION

The reader will readily recognize that many of the causes described which give rise to withdrawal (as the concept is used here), may also lead to aggression through the dynamic of "reaction formation." The reaction of an individual to frustration and rejection, fear and insecurity, is determined by many factors. Chief among these are constitutional and temperamental predispositions, identification, supportive relations or lack of them, the degree of real pathology of authoritarian and repressive parents.

An important observation should be made here pertinent to general psychology, and especially to the phenomenology of character formation and the theory of psychotherapy. It is commonly accepted that aggression can be counterphobic (a compensatory mechanism against intense fear), that it can be a mechanism for concealing feelings of weakness to prevent deflation of self-esteem and to uphold a "social image." But withdrawal, too, is employed for the same ends, and to disguise underlying feelings of hostility and aggression. It is, therefore, necessary in psychotherapy to ascertain the causes of withdrawal and its latent or concealed meanings and determinants before proceeding to deal with it.

503

GENERAL VALUES OF GROUPS TO WITHDRAWN PATIENTS

General Release

Analytic group psychotherapy helps inhibited patients to overcome their trends through activation. They overcome fears and anxieties through the support of fellow group members, and find outlets for expression of their reactivated libido, which in the past, they were forced to withdraw through fear and anxiety engendered by unfavorable conditions and relations. The groups supply a friendly, accepting and, therefore, releasing atmosphere; opportunities for patients to act out or verbalize tensions, fears, and conflicts; models of identification and imitation; supportive relations with fellow members and the therapist; ego strengthening opportunities; discharge of hostility without fear of punishment or retaliation; and insight into adaptive mechanism.

The child mobilizes power more easily and more rapidly than do adolescents and adults, because his inhibitions are not as deeply rooted, and rigidities of character and defenses have not been as yet fully formed. As the individual grows older, defensive and reactive withdrawal are structured into character, which makes him less easily (if at all) accessible to treatment. The group demonstrates to patients that, to get what they want, they need not wheedle, placate, or bribe; neither is it necessary to repress impulses to be accepted or to escape tension and anxiety. Anxiety can be acted out with impunity, and as the ego is strengthened and self-esteem improved, the individual functions better in his family and social community. The newly-gained strength and the discovery that one need not fear one's impulses and aggressions lift the bars that blocked self-expression, communication, and creative effort.

The Consistency Element

An important element in group psychotherapy is its consistent environment. The factor of consistency is a major source of security. Patients derive security from consistency in the room in which they gather, its furnishings, and their arrangement, the relationships they may encounter, and the general content of the interviews; unexpected changes in these and similar factors make patients insecure. In this unvarying *environment* they need not make new adjustments or meet new challenges until they are ready to do so.

Supportive Ego

Another major factor that helps patients overcome their diffidence is that of supportive ego. Because of fear of facing the realities of the situation, a member of the group may choose one of the others as support to help him overcome fears and misgivings. Usually, a series of supportive egos are chosen, in accordance with the evolving personalities of patients, before they become a part of the total setting.

It has been observed by all who employ the group as a treatment tool that patients overcome their withdrawn traits much more rapidly than do the hyperactive their characteristic. Groups may at first restrain newcomers, but ultimately they have a releasing effect. The first effect in developing attitudes in a group, beyond the acclimatization period, is activation. The setting encourages acting out of repressed impulses, fantasies, and infantile strivings, and each member of a group has a catalytic effect upon every other. Thus, by and large, a group is indicated for the shy and withdrawn, unless the neurotic syndrome is such that association with others in an intimate relation is undesirable when the patient requires individual treatment.

TABLE 2
Sources and Treatment of Withdrawal

Sources of Withdrawal	Groups in Treatment of Withdrawal
Inhibition of spontaneity	Release
Failure in sibling rivalry	Consistency
Reaction to guilt	Supportive ego
Narcissism	
Reaction to stigmata	
Defective self-image	
Submission to parents	
Schizoid character	
Catatonic defense	
Retaliation	
Psychoneurosis	

505

GENERAL PRINCIPLES OF THERAPY

It may be helpful to re-emphasize two points relative to the treatment of aggression and withdrawal, which apply to all therapies. One is that it is necessary to ascertain as early in the treatment as possible the etiology of these manifestations in the light of each patient's biographical development. This knowledge facilitates the therapist's understanding of the patient's conduct and verbal communications, and helps him utilize them in therapy appropriately.

The therapist needs to determine especially the *core* of the character, conflict, or stress in the light of early traumata that propel the patient toward the behavior or symptoms he manifests. This central difficulty we designate as the *nuclear problem,* that is, the nucleus from which the observable difficulties emanate and around which they are built and from which the derivative or *peripheral problems* flow.

Once the nuclear problem has been established, a choice of treatment directed toward that problem can be made. In the light of this observation, it is evident that aggression and withdrawal, as such, are not the targets of therapy; they have to be viewed as symptom manifestations. Therefore, psychotherapy needs to be directed toward the neurotic syndrome or the character formations (as the case may be) from which they stem. The treatment of aggression and withdrawal involves the totality of the psychological syndromes of the patient and cannot be viewed apart from the total personality.

XVI

Group Psychotherapy and the Nature of Schizophrenia

Specificity in Treatment

The primary requirement for effective psychotherapy is that the nature and dynamics of the patients' syndromes be thoroughly understood in the light of available knowledge. The therapist must be, at all times, willing to re-evaluate, amend, and change his orientation and techniques in the light of newly acquired knowledge and the changing, or newly recognized, needs of patients. Because of the vast differences between patients, *conditional tentativeness* and flexibility are essential in dealing with the emotionally and mentally disturbed. No one technique can be applied to all patients in a blanket fashion, not even to those in the same clinical category, for character idiosyncracies, and the changing states and conditions of each patient during the course of treatment, require modifications in approach. Variations in technique are even more important with patients in different diagnostic categories.

In the treatment of a psychoneurosis, the task of psychotherapy is to resolve or diminish the intrapsychic conflict between the id and superego; in the instance of character disorders, the therapeutic procedure is essentially to expose the patient to "mirror reactions" and interpersonal experiences, through which he may be-

507

come aware of the quality of his attitudes and behavior. What has been ego-syntonic has to be rendered ego-dystonic,[1] largely through the transference attitudes of the patient and, especially, his identification with the therapist, fellow group members, and the group as a whole. A compulsive symptom, for example, may be approached directly in many instances, even though the compulsion neurosis itself is not accessible to such treatment.[2] We have described, in some detail, the therapeutic processes in various clinical categories, except that of schizophrenia. This chapter is devoted specifically to that subject.

THE NATURE OF SCHIZOPHRENIA

Quantitative and Qualitative Aspects

Without fully defining this malady, it is possible to state that its basic characteristic is a massive deficiency in the ego reserves necessary to deal with the stresses of living. This is the *quantitative* aspect of the schizophrenic's personality structure. Since there are many individuals with ego deficiencies who do not react with psychotic defenses against the stresses of life (e.g., conversion and compulsive symptoms and hypochondriasis), it is postulated that, in the schizophrenic's psyche, *qualitative* elements produce his characteristic reaction of withdrawing from reality into a world of delusion.

We have seen that the maximal quantum of ego reserves available to an individual varies in accordance with his organic-constitutional state, which is determined to a very large extent by hereditary and other biological conditions. The utilization and distribution of these energies or reserves are determined, however, by conditioning, using this term in its broadest sense.

Although much of the research on the nosology and etiology of

---

[1] This process is often formulated as "making the patient neurotic, and then treating the neurosis," on the assumption that the difference in clinical categories is only quantitative. We cannot agree with this hypothesis. Psychopathy, psychoneuroses, and psychoses, for example, differ from each other in essential nature and structure and, therefore, are not transmutable.

[2] Prohibition is used when the neurotic content has been made manifest and is understood by the patient. The direct approach serves mostly to "break the habit," the conditioned reflex or engram that has been established through long usage.

schizophrenia is still inconclusive, in recent years considerable light has been thrown on its nature and manifestations. It seems quite certain, at the present time, that schizophrenia is a syndrome; that *true* schizophrenia is a process that, unless checked, leads to progressive deterioration; and that basic constitutional and organic factors are involved, such as the functioning of the hypothalamus and the adrenals. In all likelihood, other organs are also involved, though the evidence for this is less conclusive; the brain enzymes and protein content are definitely altered and some enzymes are absent; chemical analyses of urine, blood, and liver show definite differences between schizophrenic patients and the general population; and intestinal function, circulation, autonomic control, average weight, and other anatomical and physiological details, differ between the "normal" and schizophrenic populations.

Numerous genetic studies, carried on independently in various parts of the world, seem to leave little doubt as to the constitutional nature of schizophrenia and the linkage of the DNA plasma and the genes as a determining factor in the predisposition to, if not the passing on of, the actual malady, though there is strong evidence for the latter as well. Very impressive experiments in the chemical induction of hallucinations and delusions, as well as the remissions that have been obtained in many patients by the use of chemotherapy, are further evidence for the hypothesis that schizophrenia involves biochemical processes, constitutional deficiencies, and toxicity.

A study of the fingerprints of a hundred male patients in a mental hospital showed that they have a high incidence of unusual fingerprints, as classified according to the Federal Bureau of Investigation system and that of Scotland Yard. The striking difference from the general population was found to be in the high incidence of whorles (lines that make almost complete circles) and arches (lines that rise to a peak) and the presence of fewer lunar loops (lines forming ovals). There was also a striking difference from the norm in the presence of short broken lines in the center of whorls instead of the normal orderly concentric circles (T. Raphael and L. G. Raphael, 1962). In view of the fact that fingerprints develop during the third and fourth months of pregnancy, this variant is of significance in support of genetic foundations for schizophrenia.[3]

The results of another recent study, by Dr. Harry VanderKamp of the V.A. Administration in Battle Creek, Michigan, further support the theory of the biological basis of schizophrenia. Dr. Vander Kamp found an "abnormal" substance in the white blood cells of sixty schizophrenic patients which was not present in forty normal persons tested. Dr. VanderKamp concludes that the tendency to develop the illness is inherited, but believes that environmental conditions contribute to its development.

The Three Basic Characteristics

The three observable characteristics of the schizophrenic personality are overwhelming fear and anxiety, hostility (homicide), and incestuous urges, far beyond those in the average person or in nonpsychotic patients. The intense fear probably stems from two sources: the inadequacy of the ego to meet even simple demands and stresses and the cruel treatment the schizophrenic actually received in the past, at the hands of parents, relatives and others, because of his deviant reactions from childhood on. The anxiety may also stem, in part, from the feelings of inadequacy in relation to outer conditions and events, but it stems even more from the devastating, murderous hostility which is an integral part of the schizophrenic syndrome and which the patient attempts to hold in check. It has been suggested that "if he (the schizophrenic) is ever forced to make a choice between fragmenting his own ego or damaging an emotionally significant external object, his involuntary choice will be the former. He is willing [sic] to sacrifice his own ego, to destroy his precious self, to prevent himself from harming such an object." (Spotnitz, 1957.) Dr. Lewis B. Hill (1955) expressed the same thought, when he said that the schizophrenic "does not have any belief in the possibility of self-realization, except in terms of sacrifice to preserve the mother."

[3] Abnormal fingerprints have been linked also to such congenital conditions as epi lepsy and mongolism.

The overwhelming destructive drive of the schizophrenic was well demonstrated by a 14-year-old girl who had attempted suicide on four occasions, without success. She explained to her psychiatrist that, "I really want to kill my father and mother and my sisters and brothers, but I can't kill them, so I want to kill myself."[4] We see in this the third characteristic of the schizophrenic personality—hostility—which in some cases emerges as either murder or suicide. Since the homicidal schizophrenic is ever on the threshold of breaking through the insufficient controls at his disposal, he lives under constant anxiety.

Quantitatively, the schizophrenic suffers from ego deficiency, with the additional lack of adequate, normal ego defenses, which require, for their development, energy and suitable objects for identification. We have described the latter in some detail elsewhere, with special emphasis on the function of parental images in the genesis and pathogenesis of the ego and its defenses. But what is of special concern to the psychotherapist is the qualitative aspect of the ego phenomena. The schizophrenic's ego is strongly cathected, both because of its fragility and because of the noxious treatment he has received from others. The libido energies that are employed by the average person in object relations are invested by the schizophrenic in himself. This is a result of his primary autism, on the one hand, and his noxious interpersonal relations, on the other. Because of this and many modifying constitutional and interpersonal conditions, the schizophrenic is, in his development, arrested on the oral level. The intensity of orality in this condition is widely recognized in psychiatry and psychotherapy.

While it may, or may not, be necessary to feed regressed adult patients via a baby bottle as they recline on the lap of the therapist (as suggested by some psychiatrists), certainly the efficacy of an appeal to orality is seldom disputed. Two very striking, as well as convincing, examples are contained in two papers that appeared in the *International Journal of Group Psychotherapy* (Beard, 1958, and Hinckley, 1957). In one instance, a catatonic patient was drawn into a work project without a preliminary relation hav-

---

[4] Related to me by Dr. Simone Blajan of Paris, France.

ing been established between him and the therapist. While the patient showed impressive improvement in the months of the project's duration, he returned to his former state as soon as the project was terminated. In the second instance, the therapist had taken weeks to arouse response in a patient who had remained in bed and was incontinent and completely unresponsive. The therapist paid regular daily visits to the patient's room, and never failed to leave food for him. When the patient became somewhat activated, the therapist wooed him and waited on him "hand and foot," as it were. As a result, the patient became ready to be involved in a special type of group where he received particular attention from the therapist and from another patient who took him under his wing. The patient recovered, left the hospital, has held a job for some years now, and even owns and drives a car.

There, the appeal was made to the oral incorporative needs of the patient. This was accomplished not only by means of giving food, which was an important element, but—even more significant —by becoming the giving person without reservation, so that the therapist (mother) was (symbolically) orally incorporated by the patient.

Freud speaks of the three types of identification (Freud, 1940), one of which is oral incorporation. In the schizophrenic, this occurs symbolically, which means denying the object all autonomy and right and making him an integral part of the subject, which is characteristic of infantile narcissism. As we shall presently see, symbolic incorporation is one of the services the therapist offers to the patient in the early stages of treatment until his ego has been strengthened sufficiently to differentiate between object and subject (himself). The therapist serves as the good, all-giving mother whom the patient, like the baby, ingests with the nipple (incorporates). As the patient does so, he also incorporates the ego strengths of the object, in this case the therapist, as does the baby who feeds on (or through) his mother.

The oral incorporative urge of the schizophrenic is a vestige of an instinctive primitivism, which, in some extreme instances, takes the form of an acted-out cannibalism. Wertham has reported on such cases; for example, a man who killed a small girl and ate parts of her body (Wertham, 1949). In one case we suspected schizophrenia in a boy who ate raw chicken meat. The suspicion was later confirmed by clinical tests. In another case, a teenage boy shot birds and ate their raw flesh. A woman stated that whenever she went into the bathroom of her home she thought of her husband's penis and had an uncontrollable urge to tear the condoms he used with her teeth (Anthony, 1959).

The difficulties that confront schizophrenics in social adaptation arise from the unconscious counterreactions of persons around them to their oral incorporation (hostile) urges. The psychotherapist, therefore, must not become involved in the psychotic's emotional vortex to the degree that he reacts negatively. He needs to possess sufficient skill to lead the patient from his deep self-involvement to a more realistic perception of his ego boundaries.

A frequent "complaint" of borderline schizophrenics and patients in remission is reflected in the phrase, "I feel so empty." Significantly, this remark is made by many patients in diverse circumstances and from different social strata. This universality suggests that the "feeling of emptiness" is a characteristic feature of the schizophrenic syndrome and reveals both the schizophrenic's incorporative needs and the affect deprivations to which he has been subjected. The deprivations often have taken place on the oral level and are "felt" and carried through life. It is this feeling of emptiness and the gnawing craving "to be filled" that lead us to conclude that cannibalistic urges are present in the schizophrenic and that therapy needs to play into his oral incorporative needs.

Only when the therapeutic approach is made via this primitive avenue, both actually (by giving the patient food) and symbolically (through acceptance), can the schizophrenic be "filled" sufficiently to reciprocate and enter into a relationship instead of fearing it or continuing in an emotionally and physically parasitic state.

Real versus Induced Schizophrenia

Our present knowledge leads us to believe that schizophrenia does not have a single cause, but rather, multiple and varied ones. Recent researches seem to confirm the fact that, fundamentally, *true* schizophrenia is a disorder in biochemical and metabolic processes. Delusions and hallucinations have been induced in normal persons through chemical means, by blood transfusions, and through ingestion of the species of mushrooms known as Amanita Muscaris, A. Pantherina, and A. Mappa, all of which contain Buforenine (also by drinking the mushroom eater's urine). It has been further established that as the organism throws off these noxious substances, the individual is restored to normality.[5] It would seem that in the schizophrenic, some noxious compounds (some of which have been identified) are produced in the body chemically and are introduced into the blood stream. There is evidence that the ductless glands are involved.

Evidence pertaining to the physical basis of schizophrenia was advanced in a paper read before the American Psychiatric Association's Annual Convention in 1960. The paper, entitled "Steps Toward the Isolation of a Serum Factor in Schizophrenia," was prepared by a team of workers at the Lafayette Clinic in Detroit, Michigan, consisting of Drs. Charles E. Froman, Elliot D. Luby, Garfield Towney, Peter G. S. Becket, and Jacques S. Gottlieb. The implication of their report is that a substance in the blood may be at least a partial cause of the illness and if its presence is discovered early enough it may be possible to prevent the development of schizophrenia.

Observations of families with schizophrenic children indicate that the parents and other relatives are contributing factors in the illness. Studies of mothers of schizophrenic offspring show that the majority of them are themselves schizophrenic. It can be assumed that the children have come by the disease through heredity or, when constitutionally intact, by identification. As the baby and child internalizes the mother's image, the latter's defects are also absorbed. Thus, *schizophrenia can be acquired as a result of induction,* which we describe as *induced schizophrenia,* as differ-

[5] No evidence has been advanced to show that these substances produce schizophrenia *per se;* rather, they induce hallucinations only (which are also part of full-blown schizophrenia).

SCHIZOPHRENIA

entiated from *actual schizophrenia,* which is constitutionally determined.

By induced schizophrenia, we mean schizophrenic-like reactions or behavior displayed by a person who is organically and constitutionally healthy, but whose ego has been exposed to continuous and massive stress at an early age (probably beginning with the preverbal and preconceptual stages), is depleted, or has been prevented from flowering into full bloom. An interesting theory on the psychogenesis of schizophrenia was suggested to the writer in a personal communication by Dr. David Mendell of Houston, Texas. He suggested that schizophrenia can be induced when too great demands for emotional "giving" are made on a young child, by a weak or deficient mother, which demands the child cannot meet. This suggestion deserves further elaboration and may apply to at least some cases in the category of induced schizophrenia. This concept may also serve as a basis for understanding the component of orality and the intense hostility of the schizophrenic. They are a result of the profound and basic maternal deprivation in a parasitic mother-child relationship which inevitably gives rise to the conflicting feelings of oral dependence and rage.

Schizophrenic-like reactions, however, are not caused by deprivation alone. Maternal overgratification and overprotection, too, can result in depletion of ego energies and ego integration. Ego growth, ego strength, and the ability to mobilize resources dealing with inner and outer demands are blocked and prevented, to varying degrees, by overgratification by the mother. Individuation is prevented and the child, with underlying intense resentment and rage, becomes orally tied to the mother, a state from which he is unable to escape for the rest of his life. Having no resources of his own to deal with life adequately, and being afraid and anxious, he responds to the normal stresses of living in characteristic schizophrenic-like or schizoid manner.

There are two additional aspects of this familial interpersonal situation to be considered. One is that the patient has derived his superego from his mother rather than his father (he lives by a "maternal superego"), and, second, he has failed to establish

515

effective ego defenses, both of which conditions are fertile soil for anxiety. When the mother is either overrejecting or overprotective, she becomes the central focus of cathexis and her superego is internalized by the child, becoming confused (and even fused) with feelings of love and security. Love, dread, and hate become a conglomerate in the psyche, each struggling for ascendency, with love usually being the loser.

The following delusional monologues of a 29-year-old male hospitalized patient in a therapy group, illustrates the fact that there is a strong identification with the mother and that she is perceived as a threatening (punitive superego) figure: "Everywhere you look you have a feeling there's a woman there. Maybe she tells you how to handle yourself or how to eat . . . I get sort of panicky and frighten myself into believing I am a woman . . . I guess it would be all right (to be a woman) if the public would allow it . . . I change around the opposite way, then a woman won't come at you. *It's their conscience that argues with you* [italics mine] . . . Well, naturally these must be my mother's upper lip and lower."[6] (Alikakos, Starer and Winch, 1956.) The authors correctly comment: "He [the patient] appears here to be talking about introjecting the aggressive, dominating mother and becoming like her in order to get along with her and manage her and be liked by her." It should be noted that the mother in this case had been committed to a mental hospital ten years previously and that the patient had been, at different times, homosexual and heterosexual.

At different times, the patient had made the following statements in relation to his confused identification and love and dread feelings: "They [women] break up your thoughts. . . . Somehow your lips are her [mother's] lips and your nose is her nose." "I'm left-handed. I'm built more like a mother . . . I more or less have the woman feeling all the time. It scares me through and through." These statements reveal the dread under which the

[6] This and the other quotations in this chapter can be examined from the aspect of symbolic logic, which in hallucinations takes the form of paralogia, etc. However, since we are interested here in psychotherapy, it is more advantageous for us to interpret them in terms of their latent content.

schizophrenic lives, a dread that emanates from a superego derived from a person who should have been the source of love, protection and security.

One of the chief characteristics of the schizophrenic is the absence of ego defenses in full-blown schizophrenics and their fragility in the borderline and latent states. Civilized man lives by and through the ego defenses he has established against the impact of the many forces operative both within and from without. These defenses are called into action when stress and/or strain grow in intensity beyond the ego's normal capacity to bear them. When this limit, which is different for each individual, is reached, anxiety sets in and the ego defenses come to the fore, very much as military reserves are drawn up in defense of a wavering front line in a war. The effect of the ego defenses is to prevent overstrain of the ego and its fragmentation, manifested by psychotics in hallucinations and delusions and in others as a "nervous breakdown."

It is the absence of adequate defenses, coupled with insufficient constitutional reserves of ego energies, that results in the schizophrenic pattern. The strengths of the ego and its defenses derive from and are determined by the earliest interactions of the child with the significant persons in his life, particularly the mother; they are achieved through the processes of imitation, identification and internalization. Thus, the weaknesses or strengths of the ego structure and the conduct of the parents are absorbed into the structure of the offspring's ego, setting the pattern of his life.[7] In this situation lies the genesis of both real and induced schizophrenia. When the hereditary constitutional predisposition is present, it is reinforced by parents with schizophrenic personalities. When the offspring is constitutionally healthy, he may still fail to develop effective defenses or he may internalize the weak defenses of his parents, resulting in induced schizophrenia.

Schizophrenia as a Defense

Just as *distortion of reality* is inherent in psychoneuroses, *re-*

[7] For a fuller discussion and elaboration of this point see Slavson, 1952a, pages 16-19, 45-52, 162-163.

treat from reality is inherent in schizophrenia. Because of ego deficiencies and lack of adequate defenses, the only recourse the schizophrenic has, in his efforts in life, is to deny the distressing and frightening actuality and substitute for it ideas and feelings that are devoid of threat. These are the delusional and hallucinatory images, which are consistent with the psychotic's powers to comprehend, recognize, and cope. They, too, have their roots in experience and actuality, but in so distorted a fashion as to render them unrecognizable. Delusions and hallucinations are present in full-blown episodes and may become permanent in chronic patients. Full retreat from actuality (reality) may also occur in less regressed cases, such as borderline and latent schizophrenics, brought on by situations of excessive strain or shock, as the weak defenses give way. Psychotic breaks are less likely to occur in induced than in real schizophrenia.

The above considerations point to the utilitarian value of *schizophrenia as a defense*. The schizophrenic's destruction of his own ego, rather than carrying out destructive drives toward emotionally significant persons, is a defense against homicide. It also serves as a defense against incest. For example, the male patient previously quoted repeatedly referred to his mother at every group session. At one of these he said: "I'd kiss a woman on the cheek and that's as far as I'd go . . . Some people get murdered trying to talk to girls. My dad is a killer somehow." Here incest and its punishment, death, and the father as a prohibitive destructive force in preventing incest are revealed as they appear in the patient's thoughts, though there is also strong homosexual coloring present.

Borderline Schizophrenia

Where the process is only partial or mild, as in borderline or latent schizophrenia, both the ego reserves and the ego defenses are not as weak and can hold up under moderate stress, although with great effort, anxiety and hostility. In borderline cases, as the name implies, the patient is on the verge of a break, but his ego and its defenses can withstand the stresses, provided they do not exceed the limits of his powers, which, as we have seen, differ for each individual. In latent schizophrenia, there exists a "fault," such as one finds in geological formations, and as in the case of rocks, the structure remains intact as long as the forces are in "equilibrium under tension." (See Slavson, 1952a, pages 68-70.) However, when this equilibrium is disturbed, both in rocks and the human personality, a break occurs—a "slide" in the former and a retreat from reality in the latter.

In varying degrees and in accordance with inherent or evolved strengths, the borderline and latent schizophrenic also tends to re· treat from actuality. But this retreat is not as complete as it is in hallucinatory and delusional psychotics. Rather, the borderline schizophrenic operates through unconscious (instinctive) selective maneuvers, evading overinvolvement and remaining passive, though extremely anxious, under emotional stimuli or in overly difficult tasks. His panic is made manifest by bodily responses, facial grimace, darting expression of the eyes, and other somatic manifestations. In repose, on the other hand, the borderline schizophrenic presents a mien of flat affect and bland facial expression. This might be, to some extent, the result of an actual failure to register stimuli, but it is more likely a reflection of the defenses that prevent strain and fragmentation by avoidance of response and involvement.

CATEGORIES OF SCHIZOPHRENIA

As a guide to the planning and carrying out of treatment, schizophrenia can be divided into the functional classifications of *constitutional, traumatic,* and *defensive* schizophrenia. Understanding a patient in these terms aids in planning and directing the course of treatment, and, even more important, establishes the limits on which the therapist can set his sights.

Until biochemical antidotes are developed, in cases of constitutional (real) schizophrenia, chemotherapy and convulsive therapies would seem to be primary, with psychotherapy as an ancillary technique. Psychotherapy serves to integrate the effects of chemotherapy and convulsive therapies, and to establish new patterns of response and new engrams or reflex reactions. When organo-traumatic factors, such as in the "cerebro-organic pseudo schizophrenias" (Rumké), are involved, the therapist needs to set limited objectives for himself and even rely, in some instances, on surgery. Perhaps the most fertile field for psychotherapy is the defensive schizophrenias, among which are included many of the borderline, latent, and induced types, discussed at some detail in other parts of this chapter.

SYMBOLIC REALIZATION

When asked by a harassed young pyschotherapist, who found himself with a few borderline schizophrenics among his clientele for the first time, what the chief characteristic of the treatment of such patients is, the present writer replied: "To understand the symbolism of the patient's productions." Delusional and even hallucinatory content has meaning. The meaning is peculiar to each patient and is obscure to the average mind, but there is logic and "reality" in the psychotic's confabulations, which reflect his preoccupations and concerns, but the "logic" is often incomprehensible to the "orderly" thinking of the nonpsychotic. Word symbolisms of a schizophrenic, even when he is not delusional, have different meanings than they have for the average person. Even when stripped of the bizarre quality of the hallucinatory monologue, the meanings which a borderline person attaches to ordinary words and common thoughts are vastly different than intended by a nonpsychotic communicant. Perhaps it is because of dread and paranoia that the schizophrenic reflexly reinterprets ordinary statements into distorted meanings. Anyone who has attempted to communicate with persons in this category, especially in a dispute or difference of opinion (when feelings rise), has found himself frustrated by failure to "get through." The inability to receive meanings from others is undoubtedly the result of the narcissistic encapsulation of the schizophrenic, his rigid defenses, and the absence of empathic capacity, which are characteristic of the schizophrenic, whether latent, borderline or real.

Putting language to idiosyncratic use that results in a symbolic communication is probably the result of confabulation, condensation and distortion of ideas and meanings, analogous to dreams. In a case cited previously (p. 516), the male psychotic patient speaks of introjecting the female superego symbolically, in a manner that borders on ordinary language ("It's their conscience that argues with you."), but then he jumps to a quite bizarre statement (". . . these must be my mother's upper lip and lower"). In another session he said, "I have roots in my mouth. Maybe that makes a tree grow." As he continued his monologue, he produced the following statement (which probably throws light on his preoccupation): "F. [another patient] had a feeling I was a queer [homosexual]. I'm not a queer I have teeth."

One may have a clue to the meaning of these productions only when one knows the background and developmental history of a patient, his relationships in his home, and other forces that were exerted upon him, against which he defends himself by his delusional system. But despite the lack of this information, it is possible to speculate on the meaning of this patient's communications, especially when we also consider the following verbal perambulations. At various sessions he dropped remarks like, "I kissed a lot of things. I kissed balls and all that . . . ." and his father was "forcing me to be a homosexual." From juxtaposing the various statements, it would appear that they form a "logical" system of the patient's preoccupation with sex and incest. The mother's upper and lower lip may refer to her vagina which does not have teeth and he is a man because his mouth has teeth. A tree growing from his mouth may represent the act of fellatio ("I kissed balls and all that"). This seems plausible because of his bisexual practices in the past and the tree growing from his mouth may represent reproduction, thus carrying out his fantasies of being a woman as well as a man.

The symbolisms of nonhallucinating patients are neither as involved nor as obscure and can be understood by the therapist who has been trained for this work and who knows the background of the specific patient and the strongly cathected experiences and feelings against which he defends himself. It was Dr. Marguerite Sechehaye (1951) who introduced the concept of "Symbolic Realization." More recently, Dr. Beulah Parker describes (1962) the treatment of a latent schizophrenic boy, in which his symbolic language was the sole medium of the therapeutic process. The extent to which symbolic realization can be employed in groups, especially in the presence of nonschizophrenic patients, is a moot question, and the process should be attempted only with great caution. However, since patients in this category should be in parallel individual treatment, *reality bombardment* can be carried out in the individual interviews.

BASIC PRINCIPLES OF PSYCHOTHERAPY OF SCHIZOPHRENIA

The Four Tasks of Treatment

From the preceding brief discussion of the nature of schizophrenia, four elements emerge to which psychotherapy has to address itself: orality, hostility, ego deficiency, and retreat from reality.

Orality

In his interpersonal orientation, the schizophrenic *substitutes* the therapist (and other persons *in loco parentis*) for his parents and maintains toward him the same hostile, homicidal urges and infantile, cannibalistic, oral incorporation drives as he did toward his parents. In order to lay a basis for emotional growth, these urges must first be satisfied, before the patient can establish ego strengths and boundaries and move on toward progressive development and integration of his personality. The latter are at all times subject to the limitations of his constitutional resources. Thus, the patient has to "ingest" the therapist, symbolically, as a baby does its mother. This very complex process is at least partially achieved by the therapist's unconditional acceptance of the patient's aggression (within the boundaries of the latter's inner controls) and his permission to be used by the patient at will (e.g., unrestricted accessibility, either in person or by telephone). The therapist also has to display affection to the patient in tangible ways, including feeding. A patient in private individual treatment once bitterly complained that she was not "loved" by the therapist. Among the accusations she listed against him was: "You even never give me anything to eat!" There is also the example of the frozen catatonic incontinent patient (described supra) who achieved protracted improvement and who probably would not have been reached without weeks of feeding him.

522

Patients constantly seek to involve the therapist in their psychotic network of feeling and hallucination, which he must allow them to do, while remaining fully aware of their maneuvers as well as his own behavior and response, a task that few can achieve with real success. It is through his own awareness and his skill to pull the patient back to reality that the therapist helps him become more reality oriented.

Hostility

The second task of the therapist with a schizophrenic patient is to deal with the latter's overt hostilities, without any trace of counterhostility, of which the patient has been a victim nearly all of his life. It is this task, more than any other, that creates strain and difficulties in treatment. In this respect, therapists can be divided into two categories: those who respond to the schizophrenic's hostility and those who respond to his utter helplessness; only the latter will be successful in treating a schizophrenic. A psychotherapist who experiences counterfeelings of hostility, which can be very easily aroused by the patient's aggressions, should not attempt to treat schizophrenics. This in no way disqualifies him from doing therapy with other types of patients, but therapy of schizophrenics requires *special* attributes in the therapist that make it possible for him to empathize with them sufficiently to absorb their murderous drives and yet withstand the drain.

Ego Deficiency

As important as these two services—gratifying his orality and accepting his hostilities—are to the patient, the actual therapeutic dynamics in the cure or improvement of the schizophrenic are the resultant ego strengthening and defense building, on the one hand, and the evoking of a sense of reality and the testing of reality, on the other. As already indicated, major dynamics are conditional upon each patient's inherent limits and capacities.

The first of these processes—the structuring of the ego—occurs automatically. As the patient internalizes the therapist, he also internalizes his ego strengths, just as the baby internalizes the parental ego with the food he receives from the parent. This ego reinforcement is the pivot of the treatment here. But it can take place only after the patient *accepts* the therapist as the good parent, and this he does only after a prolonged period during which the therapist accepts the patient's orality and hostility. It is this *good* parent that the patient incorporates, together with his ego. At the same time, the therapist needs to build a bridge between the patient's ego and reality by subtly holding him down to reality, by introducing realistic values, and, above all, by experiences and activities that involve actual situations.

As the patient's ego is strengthened by these various techniques of reinforcement, it abandons its former defenses of violence and retreat and substitutes the more normal defenses. At this point, the patient is introduced to more strenuous conditions and demands. He must be helped to succeed in these by the therapist and other persons whose help the therapist enlists, and, in this fashion, the patient can eventually be led to function on his own. One must remember, however, that the newly acquired or reinforced defenses can never be as strong in a "cured" or improved schizophrenic as in a nonschizophrenic. The *foundations* of his personality structure will always be weaker and its maximal capacities for withstanding stress will always be lower than in the ordinary person. One should keep in mind the dictum: "Once a schizophrenic, always a schizophrenic."

Retreat from Reality

The objective evaluation of health and illness is always made, rightly or wrongly, on the basis of manifest behavior, and behavior is judged by the manner in which an individual deals with actuality (reality). The aspect of the psychotic's behavior that concerns persons close to him, and the community generally, are not his internal strains, his anxiety, and his delusional state; rather, it is the way he deals with reality. Society is not interested in the individual; it is interested in his works. There are and have been numerous borderline and actual psychotics among geniuses and among many outstanding persons of lesser excellence. Nor is the community concerned with those borderline cases who sufficiently discharge their responsibilities. The effectiveness with which an individual deals with actuality is the current measure of health and illness and is also the frame of reference for improvement and recovery.

Like the young child, the psychotic operates on his *perception* rather than through testing reality and the validity of his perceptions through *experience*. The psychotic's perceptions are determined by his development (which is arrested at levels of primitivism), by the *phantoms* which populate his psyche, and by the perception of his own identity, or lack of it.

The levels of his development are orality, hostility, homicide, and incest. The psychotic, therefore, perceives the world as hostile, threatening, and destructive. This feeling has to be overcome through the discovery that, in actuality, the world is not as he perceives it, a change that can be achieved only by his testing that world and by testing himself against it, which he can at first accomplish only with the support of the therapist's (borrowed) ego. He can venture on this exploration only in a setting that is commensurate with his current (though growing) strengths, that is, in an environment *that does not overload his ego*. This environment is best achieved in institutional treatment, either in a day or residential hospital, according to need. The patient involuntarily adjusts to it. Its chief, favorable characteristic is that of *graded reality*—an environment which is graded in complexity and demands as the patient's ego is strengthened and his inner resources increase.

The Principle of Graded Reality

The principle of graded reality is borrowed from the field of education where it is applied when the learner is presented with information, materials, and situations of gradually increased difficulty and complexity as readiness is achieved through organic maturation and acquired skills and learning. In modern hospital treatment, this principle is followed as patients are transferred from the "maximum security" wards to "minimum security" and later to "open" wards, followed by "temporary paroles" and, finally, discharge.

In direct therapy, whether individual or group, the therapist consistently and persistently faces the patient with reality and brings into focus, and sometimes even exposes, the patient's confusions and irrational ideas and perceptions. An important dynamic of treatment is the therapist's holding up to the patient the mirror of actuality against which the patient can measure his own perceptions. This *bombarding of the patient with reality* is the surest means of dissolving delusional ideas and images. Throughout all this, the patient must feel he is loved and accepted. Without such feeling, all therapeutic endeavors are perceived as hostile and destructive and the patient will turn away from treatment, in rage and disappointment, to increased pathology.

Confrontation versus Exploration

In a group of psychotics in a mental hospital, a male patient repeatedly boasted of his "pushing women off" subway stations into the path of oncoming trains. After this boast was repeated a number of times, the psychiatrist correctly asked the patient: "Did you really push these people under trains, or do you only imagine it?" This was an appropriate question, for it *confronted* the patient with the need to examine the reality of his claim. The patient stopped short, cogitated a minute or two, then responded in a hesitant voice: "I am not sure. I think I did. But I am not sure." The next question, however, was a grievous error. The therapist asked: "Did you ever want to kill your mother?" The patient became visibly disturbed, cast his eyes down, remained silent throughout the remainder of the session and had difficulty in resuming conversation in the following session.

This episode illustrates one important rule in the treatment of all schizophrenics, whether full-blown, borderline, latent, real or induced. The rule is that *in the treatment of the schizophrenic patient we employ confrontation, not exploration*. Exploration is essential in the treatment of psychoneuroses. Confrontation is the most effective tool in the therapy of all character disorders, and is the basic tool in the treatment of psychoses. In the above episode, the patient's recurring delusional idea might have been treated more effectively through confrontation. The therapist should have asked the patient in considerable detail where and when the acts occurred, what the women looked like, where they had been standing, where he was standing, how far the train was from the locale of the act committed, etc., thus stripping the idea of its delusional elements. It is not impossible that after being confronted with requests for details the patient would say: "I guess this is all in my imagination." Such an eventuality would truly have been a therapeutic achievement. The patient's psychotic (delusional) content would have been *slowly* dissolved through a *conceptual process* and in its place reality recognition would have appeared. It is possible that the patient might have balked at answering the series of questions or would not have come to the desired conclusion. However, it is only by enlisting the patient's thinking process again and again that a degree of sanity is attained.[8]

The inadvisability of exploration is illustrated by an experience of a young psychologist, who found that many of his hospitalized patients became very disturbed during and after interviews with him. When asked about the content of the interviews and how he approached them, he disclosed that he always opened by asking the patients, "How do you feel today?" or "How are you?" He wondered why these friendly questions should be so distressing to the patients. The distress increased, he said, as he continued to inquire about their backgrounds, the members of their families, and similar "pertinent" matters. Schizophrenics (borderline or full-blown) should not be asked how they are or feel, because the question activates great anxiety and hostility toward the inquirer. It brings to their awareness their condition and inadequacy. Interviews should be initiated by talking about nonpersonal matters and personal (threat) areas should only be touched on later, if at all.

The following episode shows how remarks from a therapist could have helped dissipate the phantoms in a patient's psyche and his fear of his own aggressions. In ball catching games in a mental hospital, in which the therapist participated, one of the patients, instead of throwing the ball to the therapist persisted in walking

[8] More recently the *paradigmatic* technique was introduced in dealing with such situations by re-emphasizing and maximating a delusional claim to a point where the patient himself recognizes its absurdity.

over and handing it to him. This was correctly understood as the patient's fear of hurting the therapist (parent) as a reaction formation to his desire to do so. The practice was allowed to go on, on the assumption that the patient would eventually overcome his diffidence through "kinesthenic adaptation," to use the therapist's phrase. After many sessions and numerous tries, the patient did throw the ball, but still not directly to the therapist; he bounced it instead. Apparently, the "kinesthenic adaptation" or, perhaps, more correctly, the growing security through imitation, did take place, but the fear of injuring his partner continued. It would have been far more efficacious for the therapist to encourage the patient to throw the ball *at* him early in the game by recognizing the fear. The therapist could have said: "Throw the ball to me, John. Don't be afraid. It won't hurt me." And if the patient did so and the ball was caught, the statement could have been, "See, it did not hurt." This is a procedure analogous in every regard to the education of a child. It is by such steps that the patient tests both external and internal reality.

With patients in remission, with good "contact" and ego strengths, para-analytic and even analytic group therapy can be tried, but it should be attempted cautiously. Psychotherapy in which there is uncovering of unconscious urges, motivations, and affect-laden traumatic memories and experiences, especially those relating to parents and siblings, is usually not suitable for schizophrenic patients. This general rule depends on the defensive resources of the particular patient. Thus, some ambulatory patients can participate in discussions in a group of nonpsychotic patients in private practice or an outpatient clinic. The ego of such patients being weak and fragile in its defenses, makes intensive psychotherapy a possible risk. The strain on the defenses that occurs in uncovering and insight therapy may prove deleterious and even dangerous, as the defenses may give way and the patients retreat from reality into delusions.

In one case, a schizophrenic woman, though not diagnosed as such initially, refused to use the couch after several psychoanalytic sessions. When asked why, she explained that she was "afraid" of her analyst. An adolescent girl broke off her analysis after a few sessions because, as she explained, "I felt uncomfortable . . . that shadow (of the analyst) on the wall bothered and frightened me." This patient, too, was not initially recognized as being a latent schizophrenic.

Exposure may not be as dangerous in a group as it is in individual treatment, since, as we have seen, a group provides one with many escapes. Chief among these are silence and withdrawal, which are not available in a one-to-one psychotherapeutic situation. Despite such escapes, however, the schizophrenic may become disturbed, beyond permissible limits, by the communications of other patients, through identification and "spectator therapy". The suggestibility of psychotics and their proneness to emotional contagion (as witnessed by occasional disturbances and hospital riots, basically due to their weak ego defenses) may activate pathology. Still another factor that operates here is the possibility of the schizophrenic becoming the scapegoat in the group. Such treatment, which may be a re-enactment and reliving of hostilities experienced in families and in the home community, causes only further regression and ego fragmentation.

Phantoms, Hallucinations, Delusions

Every one carries, in his unconscious, symbols, phantoms or images. While man feels lonely, he is never alone; while he can isolate himself physically, his conscious, and, particularly, his unconscious, are ever populated by introjected phantoms and memory traces of persons and images. These are an integral part of himself and determine to a large extent his reactions and relations. One of the outcomes of good psychotherapy, and especially sound psychoanalysis, is to rid the psyche of those phantoms that interfere with full adjustment and prevent realistic dealings with life situations.

The phantoms that infest the mind of the psychotic are horribly disturbing and threatening. The male patient previously referred to, hallucinated along these lines: "A woman is trying to drown me. How can I be saved. . . . Some woman causes all the trouble around here. This problem won't be solved until the woman is away." Again, "She [the woman within himself] talks like a woman and forces me to talk like one. She tries to pull off my hair. She is a throat-cutter." Or, "I am built more like a mother . . . It scares me through and through." On a number of occasions he stated that his father had forced him to be a homosexual. Then again, "My dad is a killer somehow." Such delusions have to be dealt with directly and an attempt must be made to help the patients recognize their unreality.

My own experience, with a post-lobotomy patient, during a visit to one of the large mental hospitals in the United States, may illustrate the limitations of our efforts in this direction and the persistence of delusional thinking. This encounter was with a very attractive, sensitive, and intellectual looking young man, who was the only patient with the freedom of the hallways on the floor on which his ward was located. His fellow patients could be seen through the locked glass doors, languishing in various postures, consumed by boredom and ennui, while a rough-looking guard sat on a somewhat elevated platform reading a newspaper.

The young man stopped the visitors abruptly and said: "They cut out the snake from my brain. You know, I had a snake in my brain; they cut it out, but they forgot a piece and now it wriggles in my brain. The snake talks to me. It's in that closet and it talks to me." In an effort to dissolve his hallucination we asked the guard on the floor to unlock the closet and we asked the young man: "Well, where is the snake?" He stopped short, in momentary surprise and said, somewhat disappointed: "It ran away." Apparently, he needed to hold on to the delusion that a part of a snake was wriggling in his brain.

The dissipation of delusional content and the substitution of reality is the main task of the therapeutic effort. Various means suggest themselves that are suitable for different patients and different stages in treatment. One effective means is not to talk about the patient, his feelings, attitudes, problems, and not attempt to explore his background. Rather, the interviews can be ordinary everyday conversations about social, scientific, literary, or other cultural developments and events, or current sports and news items that may be of interest and on the level of the patient. These *tête-à-tête* conversations, as between two friends on an even base, can have many salutary effects and meanings. The patient feels he is accepted as an equal; his self-image is improved as a result; he is made aware of his intellectual powers and capacities and, above all, his mind is preoccupied with reality. Thus, his ego is strengthened through participation in an equalitarian relationship with a parent-surrogate and he introjects the ego strengths and defenses of the therapist, thereby displacing his earlier introjected, threatening phantoms by a new and helpful image (the therapist). The effect of being reality-oriented during these conversations, must be viewed as of great value in evoking the sense and power for reality testing.

A psychiatrist complainingly said to the present writer: "I have a borderline schizophrenic young man as a patient who comes to me a few times a week. We do nothing but just talk. We talk about anything that happens to interest us. I don't think I do anything for him, but his family bless me for the improvement the boy seems to show at home. I feel sort of guilty for I know I do nothing for him." The therapist, in this instance, was not aware of the process of ego reinforcement and the importance of identification and introjection in all psychotherapy, especially with borderline patients. It was explained to him that the patient was actually *borrowing the therapist's ego* which he later used in his daily living. As far as our present knowledge of such patients goes and the treatment tools now available, he may need such support, although probably at a reduced frequency, all his life.

The therapist's understanding of the schizophrenic process, especially as related to a specific patient, the needs of the patient at a given time, and, above all, the therapist's own temperamental disposition and ease, will determine the procedures he will adopt. The equalitarian conversational approach obviously cannot be used with regressed patients. It is suitable for borderline or latent schizophrenics. Procedures are determined by the degree of contact with reality, ego strengths, intellectual and educational levels, and other such factors. To make accurate judgments requires considerable training and prolonged experience, in residence in a hospital, under proper tutelage.

A psychotherapist once consulted the present writer on the treatment problem presented by a very disturbed ambulatory schizo-phrenic girl. When the plan of ordinary conversation, described above, was suggested, the therapist replied with an admixture of depression and irritation: "She is the kind of person with whom I cannot find anything to talk about." When asked if she felt irri-tated by her, the emphatic reply was, "Yes, she makes me mad, and I can't control it."[9] The therapist seemingly reacted to the patient's hostility rather than her helplessness, and was angry be-cause she was frustrated and had a feeling of failure. Just as a physician cannot feel failure in the unsuccessful treatment of in-curable cancer, the psychotherapist cannot feel frustrated in the treatment of schizophrenia.

Self-Identity and Schizophrenia

The problem of personal identity is another consideration in the treatment of this malady. In full-blown, regressed cases, the awareness of the self is sometimes nonexistent or is so shifting as to approach nonexistence. Again, we quote from the rumina-tions of the patient on whose statements we have often drawn. He said, at the first group session, "Well, maybe it isn't your [his own] body after all, but naturally a man [himself] has a right to see who he is supposed to be . . . I'm more or less on the girls' side. I don't know whether to be a girl or to be a man. Yet I am a man. I can't stand it that way." In the twelfth session, he said, "When you're talking to a woman, you ain't talking to me . . . I'm just a baby doctor . . ." At the one-hundredth session, he said that he was pregnant and later declared that his name was Charmaine and that he had long, blond hair.

Full-blown schizophrenics, in their retreat from reality, may lose their identity and assume (as do little children) the identity of animals or inanimate objects. In one group of hospitalized schizophrenics, one patient insisted that he was God and when the other members of the group refused to accept him as such he turned his back on them, saying that unless they acknowledged his sacred identity, he would have nothing to do with them. The

---

[9] This episode took place in one of the Scandinavian countries.

other patients continued to discuss his reaction and one of them said: "Tom was never loved by anybody in his life, so he has to love himself. He loves himself so much that he must think he is the only one in the world. He is God." This penetrative remark helped Tom to "come to his senses."

Though very much less damaged than in the fully regressed psychotic, the self-identity in the borderline schizophrenic is also inadequate and unstable. Before we discuss this aspect of reality testing in the mentally ill, it may be of some value to consider the genesis and function of self-identity in the "healthy" psyche.

Self-identity has its roots in inner kinesthetic sensations, urges, and drives, but it is established with outer reality as a frame of reference. The awareness of self probably originates during the "eight-month anxiety" when the baby's senses seem to mature sufficiently to perceive (and perhaps recognize) objects and persons outside of himself. Weaning, spoon feeding, toilet training, and the sensations of hunger and pain, arouse awareness of "self" which, in later stages of development, is extended to wider areas in the surrounding world, especially people. The development of a full measure of self-identity is either aided or hampered by the type and healthfulness of the various identifications, introjections, and ego ideals that take place in the course of life. Both overidentification and unstable and inadequate identification interfere with the normal and orderly development of self-identity, self-esteem, and the self-image.

In the psychoneurotic, and even more so in the borderline psychotic, identifications are faulty; in the latter they tend to remain unstable and shifting. Borderline patients, largely because of their weakness and infantile dependence, become readily attached to warm and friendly persons and identify with them. An example is the borderline, oral-dependent young woman, to whom we have referred, who identified with a sexually promiscuous member of her therapy group and duplicated the other's life by becoming sexually promiscuous. When her model left the group, she chose another as an object of identification and entirely altered her life pattern. The possibility of establishing a sound and permanent self-identity in the schizophrenic patient, through the process of identification, is questionable; but when a supportive identification with the therapist is achieved, it can become a permanent crutch for him. This, together with ego reinforcement, may be the reasons why a prolonged relation is necessary in such cases, even if it is carried on, in later years, by no more than correspondence or telephone.

HOSPITAL COMMUNITY PSYCHOTHERAPY

Values of a Hospital Community

Full-blown, regressed schizophrenia requires hospital treatment, at least initially, so that the schizophrenic may receive chemotherapy and/or convulsive therapy when indicated, as well as supervision by trained and experienced personnel. Commitment to a special hospital also serves as protection for both the patient and the community. The need for segregation, and its length, are determined by the severity of the illness, the degree of contact with reality, and the suitability of the patient's environment and living conditions in the general community.

The chief value of a good hospital community is that through understanding guidance, it can supply re-educational opportunities in reality testing and in ego-strengthening, through group living, status, and identifications that would be impossible to supply *in situ*. Another value of a properly conducted mental hospital is that reality can be *graded* commensurate with the ego strength, clarity of thought, and comprehension of the patients. It is only when these conditions are met, that a hospital can serve the ends of therapy. If they are not met, then only custodial services are supplied, without any results beyond the limited number of cases who improve or recover spontaneously.[10] Aside from the important medical services that it offers, a hospital conducted on the plan of a therapeutic community is a growth-inducing and re-educa-

---

[10] "Spontaneous recovery" can be explained by the fact that under the custodial care, the patient's ego is freed of the burdens and tensions to which it had been subject prior to hospitalization, where the ego had been "overloaded." Another explanation is that the organism has been cleared, through the passage of time, of noxious poisons that blocked cerebral associative functions and controls.

tional instrumentality. It utilizes the native centrifugal flow of the libido which, because of unfavorable inner states and external conditions, had been blocked.

By creating a dynamic community, in which all patients are actively engaged in productive and creative pursuits, the dream worlds in which the patients have been immured are dissipated and they emerge into a new tangible world of reality, which they can influence and mold through their own efforts and newly-found powers. What this means to the individual would be difficult to estimate, but wherever a dynamic community has been created, immeasurable improvement was obtained. However, the basic characteristics of such a hospital must be emphasized, lest they be misunderstood to be mere activity and freedom of locomotion, just "open wards," or what was more recently added to the psychiatric terminology, "the open door."

Occupations and work-jobs must be made *significant* to the patient, both because they are of interest to him and because they are of value to the group and the community of which he is a part. The resultant feeling of belonging and being accepted engenders new awareness of self and a more sound self-identity. Through the influence of the milieu and the group and individuals in it, the patient is activated toward reality and motivated to mobilize his powers. This brings him closer to rational conceptualization and reality testing and supplies a frame of reference in reality to replace illusory ideas and phantoms.

A patient who had been successfully carried in treatment by a very competent psychiatrist for some twenty years, making it possible for him to adequately fill his role as head of the family and attain enviable success in business, had had periodic "breakdowns." The severity of one of these necessitated placement in a private hospital, from which he emerged, recovered, after a few weeks. When this very bright man was asked by this therapist what he considered to be the most important factor in his recovery, he unhesitatingly exclaimed: "The group! It's being with the others and talking and doing things with them that brought me back."

Staff

Such salutary results cannot be achieved solely by a group or a community. They may be the effective instrumentalities for improvement or recovery, but the transition into the group must be supplied by a member, or members of the hospital staff with whom the patient can establish a warm relation. This is dramatically illustrated by the two cases of catatonia previously cited, both of whom had been involved in group activities. One recovered, and stayed recovered, because he was helped to introject the therapist's ego and was supported throughout by the latter, while the other, lacking these, regressed as soon as the construction project was ended. It has been observed that the psychological effect of the very act of being given tranquilizers (real or placebo) in a mental hospital has, in itself, a beneficial effect on patients. The fact that they *receive* (i.e., that they are loved), whereas they had previously been ignored, temporarily quiets them down and renders them more amenable to controls.

The staff, therefore, and their constructive attitudes and functioning are the pivotal factor in the therapeutic hospital community. The feeling of acceptance or rejection that they convey are the soul and substance of such a community. The open ward and useful activities, though important, are secondary to the social and emotional climate. Except in cases of frozen catatonia, this is not to be construed to mean that the patients have to be pampered or overgratified. Rather, they have to be treated firmly but gently and realistically, as small children are treated by intelligent loving parents. Firmness is essential, for it conveys ego strengths, which the patients incorporate. But the firmness must proceed from empathy and genuine kindness. "For only he who loves may chastise," said the poet, Rabindranath Tagore. Deprivations, as well, are a part of love and reality, but they have to be administered only when the particular patient is ready to bear up under them and then only according to the principle of graded reality.

The following is a case in point that demonstrates the importance of understanding the patients. A psychiatrist in training in

Switzerland, involved one of his psychotic male patients in gardening, in which both were participating. At a group supervisory
case conference, in which the present writer took part, the therapist characterized the patient as "an awful liar" who constantly
prevaricated, and he described his own "impatience and rage" at
this. The therapist was unable to "get anywhere with him" because the patient "never told the truth." It was evident that
this was not a case of *pseudologia fantastica,* but rather a defensive fencing against the manner in which the interviews were being conducted, that apparently threatened the patient, and a
reflection of the defective relationship that existed between the
two of them.

A few days before, during the gardening project, the patient
had insisted on planting the vegetables in a certain order, of which
the therapist disapproved, and was ordered to do it as he, the therapist, thought proper, which the patient failed to do. When the
therapist asked him about it, the patient again "lied" to him. "I
got so mad," said the therapist, "that I grabbed him by the
shoulder and shook him. I gave him quite a shaking, too!" After
this the patient refused to participate in gardening altogether.

Obviously, the therapist did not understand the patient's assertiveness for what it was, an attempt to throw off the yoke of the
authoritative parent figure and, by destroying his authority, to
destroy him. We explained to the therapist that had he played
into this need of his patient by adopting his plan, his own standing would have been improved so that the patient would not have
had to use lying as a defense, and treatment would have progressed.

In the creation of a therapeutic emotional climate in residential treatment, *all* members of the hospital staff are involved, medical and lay, ranging from menial workers to the superintendent
or director. Rejection and frustration, from any source, is injurious to the patients. Matters unacceptable to patients need to
be taken up during group discussions, so that other patients, in
better contact, can help in controlling the disgruntled members of
the hospital community. In fact, the more the various groups are

involved in planning, the more the improvement in patients is likely to be accelerated.

Application of the Group Process

Small group discussions, as well as large meetings and therapy groups, should form the core of the program in a therapeutic community. It is desirable that all, or almost all, matters pertaining to the life and conduct of the hospital shall be subject to discussion, planning and participation by patients, in small and large groups. Matters pertaining to a ward or a residence cottage become the problems to be solved by those who live in them. Decisions are made by the group as a whole. Even the menu needs to be planned by the patients, let alone the program of activities and social affairs. The hospital should supply classes for the teaching of academic, trade, and general cultural subjects, in which interest is displayed or where patients can be induced to participate. Participation in the planning discussions, and trade school classes on and off the campus, provide situations and responses that extend reality testing possibilities and ego strengthening experiences. Whenever opportunities are offered in the nearby communities, patients, according to their readiness, should be allowed off-grounds participation. "Paroling" patients for home visits has been found valuable as reality testing experiences, and courses of study and work outside the hospital can be employed to the same end.

Recreational activities and classroom instruction can be held with great benefit for improved and nonregressed patients, on an extramural basis (as a transition to the larger community and for their therapeutic possibilities). It is more profitable for such patients to visit a cinema or watch an athletic game away from the hospital, than to see the same thing on the hospital grounds. Similarly, contact with mentally healthy persons, in a learning and protected job situation, offers great advantages to some patients.

Classroom instruction for very small groups of four and five, where individual attention by the therapist-instructor can be provided and intimate interactions and mutual helpfulness can emerge, is an essential step in rehabilitation. Frequently, there is a need to instruct some emerging regressed patients in the basics of the three R's. Geography, especially raised map making so that neuromuscular activity is involved, is a fertile subject for activating and widening interest in the world. Visual aids such as photographs, maps, and movies are valuable in this connection.

Occupational therapy is of immensely greater value if the manual activites are carried on in groups of two or three, or sometimes even larger numbers, rather than individually, for the latter encourages self-absorption and isolation. Situations that require sharing, co-operation, and mutual helpfulness are far more conducive to personality development and ego integration than are isolating occupations. Such activities are easily introduced when the occupational therapist is oriented toward co-operative effort and is skilled in stimulating it. However, care must be taken not to force the issue. There is much value in the satisfaction of personal achievement and the recognition and praise that it brings. The value of various stimulating and evocative activities is epitomized in a statement by the German psychiatrist, Dr. Richter.[11] "Catatonic schizophrenics," says Dr. Richter, "were seen more frequently in the days when patients were allowed to deteriorate in the wards, and they appear to be becoming less common now in hospitals where occupational therapy is stressed." This observation is of no small significance, not only because of its advocacy of meaningful occupations for schizophrenic patients, but for its suggestion that the schizophrenic process *can* be halted before maximal damage has taken place.

The groups that can be employed in this broad therapeutic and re-educative effort in a hospital can be classified as follows:

Living groups (in wards or cottages)

Planning groups (for activities, parties, social affairs, menus, management and discipline, etc.)

Mass discussion groups (of matters that concern the hospital as a whole, current events, and topics of general interest)

Recreational groups (games, hikes, picnics, parties, social clubs, dramatics, etc.)

[11] At the Second International Congress for Psychiatry, Zurich, 1957.

539

Classroom instruction (in academic, trade, and cultural subjects)

Socialized occupational therapy groups

Music and dancing groups

Remotivation groups (see Project Method).

This list can be augmented or reduced as needs and interests indicate and as personnel is available to conduct the groups.

Effects of Small Groups

Perhaps the most salutary result of participation in small group discussions by patients in good contact or remission, is their growing relatedness resulting from the comfort, intimacy, and sharing that occur in such a setting. At the fourth session of a group of five hospitalized, open ward patients with considerable autistic trends, one of their number appeared very depressed and withdrawn. After about fifteen minutes of desultory talk due to the atmosphere generated by the depressed patient, one of the group suggested that they go down to the cafeteria for coffee. The therapist consented and the patients left by themselves. At the next session, two days later, the group spent some time talking about how they "pulled out" their fellow group member from his state and expressed much gratification that they were able to help each other. "We are now friends," they concluded.

One can assume that, with some exceptions (such as homicidal and suicidal patients or pyromaniacs), patients able to participate in an analytically oriented therapy group can be discharged from hospital care for private or outpatient treatment. The selection of patients for analytically oriented groups must be made with utmost care. In a study of the effects of activity group therapy on children, differential results were found in the cases of four borderline schizophrenics. The pre- and the post-treatment Rorschach, and other projective tests, showed "of the four borderline cases, three gained from the group experience. This highlights an area for further study as to the differentiation between success and failure in various types of borderline cases. The following is offered as a tentative finding: If a child in the borderline category presents pathology which does not cause him to be markedly or too obviously different from his peers, and thus too threatening to them, inclusion in an activity therapy group may be indicated." (Nagelberg and Rosenthal, 1955.) While this deduction may be valid, one can assume that original ego strengths and defenses, and general mental health, also play important roles.

Whether the findings with children in a special type of therapy group hold for adult patients cannot be ascertained at this stage. Some of the factors that should be considered, however, in addition to ego strengths and frustration tolerance, are the degree of reality contact, level of intelligence, education and social background and verbal facility that favor comprehension of ideas and controls of behavior, and supportive relations in the environment.

Reality-Oriented Groups

Even for patients in good contact, *reality-oriented* discussions are of much more therapeutic effectiveness for a long period in the treatment than are psychoanalytic, uncovering sessions. Some individuals may be suitable for the latter, in which case, they should be reassigned to groups of nonpsychotic patients, where they would be a small numerical minority. This would prevent the reinforcing of latent psychotic trends and buttress their reality-oriented movement.

Planning, didactic, and discussion groups have one common element of special value; they are reality-oriented. Group activities supply continuous, effective, and meaningful experiences in this direction. The value of groups is greatly enhanced if they culminate in action. Since they contain the elements of social and interpersonal relations, activities that flow from group discussions and group planning have greater meaning than those that originate with and are carried out by individuals alone or at the direction of staff.

The Project Method

What is known in education as the *project method* is very suitable for inpatient activities for small groups in a hospital. This is a method of teaching in which a class of pupils undertake a study or an investigation *as a group*. Individuals or small subgroups undertake specific areas or tasks that contribute to the total project.

Some school subjects and activity projects may be suitable for some adult psychotic patients. Though there are many common elements in the psyche of normal young children and psychotic adults, their interests and capacities vary in many and important respects. Considerable imagination and resourcefulness is needed in applying re-educational group techniques in mental hospitals and the readiness and capacities of each of the participants must receive attention if traumatization and regression are to be prevented. As far as possible, projects should flow from the realistic needs of the hospital community as well as from the creativity of the participants.

Among suitable projects are decorating rooms or wards; making curtains, shelves, and simple furniture; upholstering; sewing pillow cases; arranging a bazaar, social affair or party; giving a play or concert; planting gardens that belong to the group; publishing a magazine or a newspaper, and so on.[12] In one instance, excellent results in activating a group of catatonic patients were obtained through the teaching of reading, writing, and simple arithmetic. If these, and similar elementary school subjects, are employed, learning and achievement must not be sought as ends in themselves, but rather considered in the light of their therapeutic value. They can also be employed as a starting point in treatment and lead to more realistic projects and discussions.

The educational plan suggested here requires personnel with special training in orthopedagogy. Such skills are, at present, not readily available, but can be acquired by persons drawn from peripheral or related fields, such as nursery school teachers, progressive educators, social group workers, occupational therapists, and group therapists. The recent trend, in the United States, toward training "psychiatric group workers" is a step in this direction.

---

[12] See Slavson, 1954, for a description of activities introduced in a community of delinquent patients.

However, all work in a mental hospital, whether educational or recreational, must be under continuous supervision and in consultation with a properly qualified and imaginative psychiatrist.

GROUP PSYCHOTHERAPY IN OUTPATIENT TREATMENT

In patients treated *in situ,* the schizophrenic syndrome differs less qualitatively than quantitatively from those we have considered thus far. The factors of orality, hostility, and anxiety are all present, but are either less intense or are under control of the healthy portion of the patient's ego (though still tenuously). Under favorable circumstances, an equilibrium may be maintained, in many instances, throughout life. In others, the equilibrium can be secured through support when external conditions grow difficult. In some instances, an individual may be constantly on the brink of a break, have brief or fleeting episodes of auditory or ideational hallucinations and commit bizarre acts.

The defenses of patients suitable for outpatient treatment are, in important repects, different from those of the full-blown schizophrenics. Instead of retreating into hallucinations and delusions, they fall back on either a "schizoid defense" or an obsessional-compulsive life pattern. In a full-blown schizophrenic, the protection against overloading the ego is achieved by noninvolvement and withdrawal; in the outpatient, this protection is obtained from reducing the need for choice and decision to a minimum. Someone once said that it requires less effort to run a trolley (which is on tracks) than to drive an automobile. This simile characterizes the value of the compulsive pattern that some schizophrenics adopt. In psychotherapy, it is of the utmost importance to recognize the nosology of this complex and leave it untouched —whether it be a character (anal) trait, a psychoneurotic (anxiety) symptom, or some other pseudo-neurotic manifestation—if it serves as a defense against a schizophrenic breakdown.

Among the many difficulties one encounters in dealing with patients in this clinical category is their awareness of their condition, though not always of their acts and motives; they are inordinately perceptive and penetrating and, therefore, readily see through the therapist's maneuvers; they are extraordinarily intuitive and can "read the mind" of the therapist, as it were.[13]

There is also the question of whether psychoanalytically oriented therapy groups are suitable for ambulatory patients in the borderline and latent categories. As already indicated, the uncovering procedure may threaten their already unstable and fragile ego defenses to a nonpermissible extent. Nonetheless, such patients have been observed to gain considerable ego strength and insight when placed in small numbers, in groups of nonpsychotics. These salutary results depend on a number of factors. First and foremost is a proper assessment of the current strength of the patient's ego and his defenses. It is also necessary to consider the supportive agencies in his life, such as his family, his job, and the therapist; the possibility of his becoming a scapegoat or the target of other members' attacks; the degree of active support that he may require from the therapist in difficult situations in the group; and, finally, his capacity to share the therapist with other patients.

No more than one or two borderline patients can be included in an analytic group. A larger number creates what may be called a "psychotic climate," with deleterious results both to them and to the nonpsychotic patients, who may be frightened and either drop out of the group or become aggressive and punitive toward the psychotic member. There are advantages to the borderline patients in being a part of a "healthy" (nonpsychotic) group environment and identifying with the healthier patients. The introjection of nonpsychotic egos and defenses has a desirable effect. Nagelberg and Rosenthal found that "the collective group atmosphere created by the more normal individuals composing it, would appear to exert a strengthening effect upon the weakened ego structure of the borderline case. In turn, the borderline . . . himself may contribute to the group by acting as an instigator in expressing primitive fears for the others." (Nagelberg and Rosenthal, 1955, page 390.) These findings apply to adults as well as

---

[13] A psychiatrist, exceptionally gifted with psychotic patients, told the present writer that during interviews, he consciously thinks of matters that do not relate to the patients. He found by experience that when his thoughts concerned them, they often perceived the content of those thoughts.

children. But it is essential that the prepsychotic patient should not be bizarre or so markedly different from the other patients as to make them uncomfortable.

Because of the patient's fear of all relationships, especially multiple relationships, a prolonged period (sometimes years) of individual therapy may have to precede assignment to a group, which should be timed with the patient's psychological readiness. Individual therapy should be continued parallel with the group treatment for a long period. Only when the patient is ready, and willingly accepts exclusive group treatment, should this arrangement be made available to him. The individual and group therapist have to be the same person, a fact that presents the borderline patient with a specific difficulty, since the patient's tie to the therapist is threatened when he must share him with others.

Reactions stemming from the patient's anxiety, fear, and feelings of worthlessness must be counteracted, if increase in pathology is to be prevented, and this can be accomplished in two different ways. One is through parallel group and individual treatment and the other is through the use of strategies to prevent the onset of excessive anxiety during the group sessions.[14] Even in the advanced stages of his group treatment, and regardless of the high degree of improvement, the schizophrenic cannot be exposed to the full impact of the negative blasts of a therapy group without some form of support from the therapist. Sometimes this support comes from another patient (supportive ego), but in the case of schizophrenics, it is usually less effective than that offered by the therapist.

PSYCHONURSING

Experience has shown that true schizophrenia, whether in its most extreme form or in the borderline state, requires prolonged treatment, most often throughout life, by support and ego reinforcement. Until such time as curative treatment is evolved through biochemical means, patients in this category will require what may be termed *psychonursing*. The term psychonursing is equivalent to medical nursing during physical convalescence or

[14] For an excellent treatise on this subject, with detailed illustrations as to strategy. see Spotnitz, 1957.

permanent debility, in which the nurse responds to, and meets, the needs of the patient so that he may manage everyday life.

The psychotherapist in private practice (who should be medically trained and have experience in a mental hospital) should be available to patients for support and guidance, either through visits of varying frequency, by telephone or correspondence, or by attendance in a paratherapeutic group. We include the totality of these contacts, in their various forms, in the concept of psychonursing.

DEFENSE AGAINST THERAPY

Differentiation must be made between resistance and *defense against therapy*. Some patients, who remain uninvolved in treatment for prolonged periods or break it off altogether, do not always do so because of the usual resistances to self-revelation, narcissistic injury, damage to the ego ideal, superego prohibitions or censors, or fears of self-confrontation; but rather as a defensive measure against ego fragmentation and psychic break. Where the ego defenses are weak, as in latent or borderline schizophrenia and some hysterias, exposure to the stress involved in analytic psychotherapy, if continued, may cause the ego to retreat from the overbearing strain and bring on a temporary, or permanent, psychosis.

Making an exhaustive study of the personality structure of a prospective patient is one way to prevent damage. Another, is by cautious dealing with the patient during the early observation period in treatment, until the limits of his endurance and the maximal load his ego can carry without sustaining fragmentation is ascertained. At times, it is not possible to do this in advance by any known means (such as etiology and projective tests). It is, therefore, incumbent on the therapist to cautiously watch the behavior and reactions of each patient before pressure is applied toward therapeutic involvement. The therapist must, at all times, be on the alert for signs of serious pathology and stress limits. It is particularly necessary to be vigilant against activating some deeply hidden weaknesses in the patient's psyche, exposing him to excessive strains, or employing a procedure inappropriate to his problem or personality structure. A case in point is the teenage girl who could not proceed with the psychoanalysis, but who might have been able to accept and benefit from ego-supportive psychotherapy. Another illustration is the couple in classical psychoanalysis, during which the husband, himself a psychiatrist, began to hallucinate and his wife insisted on sitting up because she was "afraid" of her analyst. In each of these instances, the patients did not *resist* treatment (in fact, the couple returned to psychotherapy, not psychoanalysis), but rather, all three *defended* themselves against an unsuitable (for them) approach. Should they have continued, the results may have been disastrous.

The reaction of the group patient who went into silence when asked by the therapist if he had ever wanted to kill his mother, was also not resistance, but rather, a defense against the threat to his psychic integration and a means of escape from further hallucinations and delusions. Schizoid defenses also serve a similar purpose —to prevent overloading of the ego.

An even more transparent example of this type of defense against therapy in a borderline schizophrenic, is the case of the woman who, though presenting many bizarre features and extreme anxiety and hostility, was treated for two years in individual, analytically oriented psychotherapy by two skillful therapists, without any results. She was characterized as "a most resistive" patient. When placed in a "guidance" group, in which discussions were reality oriented and where she received ego support and guidance from the group members and the therapist, her progress was so marked that her husband, an obsessional-compulsive cleric, voluntarily applied for treatment for himself. She, herself, had become so aware of her relief that when she met one of her former therapists she said, "This [the group] is what I always needed. I couldn't talk to you about myself." Her former therapist described the patient as so improved in appearance that at first she did not recognize her. (Slavson, 1958, Chapt. 4).

It is essential that therapists do not conclude that all noncommitments, blockage, and uninvolvement in treatment are resistances. Seeming "resistances" often serve the ends of maintaining psychic wholeness and conserving the limited and tenuous resources of the patient.

References

Ackerman, N. W. (1958), *The Psychodynamics of Family Life.* New York: Basic Books.

Alikakos, L. C., Starer, E. and Winch, W. (1956), Observations of the Meaning of Behavior in Groups of Chronic Schizophrenics. *Internat. J. Group Psychother., 6*:184.

Allee, W. C. (1938), *The Social Life of Animals.* New York: Norton.

Anthony, E. J. (1959), A Group of Murderous Mothers. Proceedings, *Second International Congress on Group Psychotherapy* (Zurich). Basel: S. Karger, pp. 137-142.

Beard, J. H., et al. (1958), The Effectiveness of Activity Group Therapy with Chronically Regressed Adult Schizophrenics. *Internat. J. Group Psychother., 8*:123-136.

Einstein, V. W., ed. (1956), *Neurotic Interaction in Marriage.* New York: Basic Books.

Freud, A. (1945), Indications for Child Analysis, *The Psychoanalytic Study of the Child,* I. New York: International Universities Press, p. 145.

Freud, S. (1927), *The Ego and the Id.* London: Hogarth Press.

—— (1940), *Group Psychotherapy and the Analysis of the Ego.* New York: Boni and Liveright.

Gesell, A. (1944), *The Wolf Child and Human Child.* New York: Harper.

Graham, F. W. (1960), Group Treatment of Married Couples. *Internat. J. Group Psychother., 10*:161-165.

Hill, L. B. (1955), *Psychotherapeutic Intervention in Schizophrenia.* Chicago: University of Chicago Press.

Hinckley, W. W. (1957), The Chestnut Lodge Kiosk: Observations on a Psychiatric Hospital's Work Project—Parts I and II. *Internat. J. Group Psychother., 7*:327-336, 437-449.

Itard, J. (1932), *The Wild Boy of Aveyron.* New York: The Century Co.

Kropotkin, P. (1955), *Mutual Aid as a Factor of Evolution.* Boston: Sargent.

LeBon, G. (1897), *The Crowd: A Study of the Popular Mind.* New York: Viking, 1960.

Lowrey, L. G. (1946), *Psychiatry for Social Workers.* New York: Columbia University Press.

Metchinkoff, E. (1903), *The Nature of Man.* New York: G. P. Putnam & Sons.

Nagelberg, L. and Rosenthal, L. (1955), Validation of Selection of Patients for Activity Group Therapy Through Rorschach and Other Tests. *Internat. J. Group Psychother.*, 5:380-391.

Parker, B. (1962), *My Language is Me*. New York: Basic Books.

Powdermaker, F. and Frank, G. A. (1953), *Group Psychotherapy*. Cambridge, Mass.: Harvard University Press, p. 25.

Raphael, T. and Raphael, L. G. (1962), Fingerprints in Schizophrenia. *Journal of the American Medical Association*, 180-215.

Sechehaye, M. (1951), *Symbolic Realization*. New York: International Universities Press.

Shaw, G. (1932), The Effects of Biologically Conditioned Water upon Rate of Growth in Fishes and Amphibia. *Ecology, 13*:263-278.

Slavson, S. R. (1937), *Creative Group Education*. New York: New York Association Press.

—— (1938), The Group in Development and Therapy. Proceedings, *National Conference of Social Work*, pp. 339-343.

—— (1939), *Character Education in a Democracy*. New York: New York Association Press.

—— (1943), *An Introduction to Group Therapy*. New York: International Universities Press.

—— (1944), Current Practices in Group Psychotherapy. *Ment. Hyg., 28* (no. 3).

—— (1945), Types of Relations and Their Applications to Psychotherapy. *Amer. J. Orthopsychiat.*, April.

—— (1951), Current Trends of Group Psychotherapy. *Internat. J. Group Psychother., 1*:7-15.

—— (1952), *Analytic Group Psychotherapy*. New York: Columbia University Press.

—— (1952a), *Child Psychotherapy*. New York: Columbia University Press.

—— (1953), Common Sources of Error and Confusion in Group Psychotherapy. *Internat. J. Group Psychother., 3*:1-28.

—— (1954), *Re-Educating the Delinquent*. New York: Harper.

——, ed. (1956), *Fields of Group Psychotherapy*. New York: International Universities Press, pp. 273-289.

—— (1957), The "Adolescent Crisis" in Mental and Community Health. Growing Up in a Changing World. Proceedings, *Conference of the World Federation for Mental Health*, (Copenhagen), London, England.

549

—— (1958), *Child-Centered Group Guidance of Parents*. New York: International Universities Press.

—— (1962), A Critique of the Group Therapy Literature. *Acta Psychother.* (Basel), *10*:62-73.

—— and Speer, A. (1934), *Science in the New Education*. New York: Prentice-Hall, pp. 290-299.

Solomon, A., Loeffler, F. J. and Frank, G. A. (1953), An Analysis of Co-Therapist Interaction in Group Psychotherapy. *Internat. J. Group Psychother.*, *3*:171-180.

Spanjaard, J. (1959), Transference Neuroses and Psychoanalytic Group Therapy. *Internat. J. Group Psychother.*, *9*:31-42.

Spotnitz, H. (1952), A Psychoanalytic View of Resistance in Groups. *Internat. J. Group Psychother.*, *2*:3-9.

—— (1957), The Borderline Schizophrenic in Group Psychotherapy. *Internat. J. Group Psychother.*, *7*:158-174.

Symposium (1954), Applications of Group Psychotherapy Techniques in Nonclinical Settings. *Internat. J. Group Psychother.*, *4*:131-217.

Ward, L. (1911), *Pure Sociology*. New York: Macmillan, p. 3.

Wertham, F. (1949), *The Show of Violence*. New York: Doubleday.

Wolf, A., et al. (1954), Sexual Acting Out in the Psychoanalysis of Groups. *Internat. J. Group Psychother.*, *4*:369-380.

Index

Abreaction, acting out as, 378-379, 390, 391
Abruptness, as resistance, 160, 161, 163
Absenteeism, as resistance, 159, 197, 379
Acceptance
  acting out as, 370-371, 392-393
  fear syndrome and, 380
  importance of, 173-174
  need for, 34, 451
  self-image and, 494
  withdrawal reactions to stigmata and, 493
Ackerman, N. W., 224n
Acting out, 78, 363, 364, 370
  advantages and disadvantages, 162, 171, 392-394
  "alternate" and "post" sessions and, 398-399
  as abreaction, see Abreaction
  as bid for status, 382-383, 390-392
  as character disorder, see Character disorder (s)
  as communication, 261, 393
  as contagion, 385-387, 390-391, 392
  as defense, 385, 390, 391
  as emotional hypochondriasis, 383-385, 390, 391
  as fixation, 390
  as narcissism, 388-389, 390, 392
  as neurotic symptom, 387-388, 390, 391
  as provocation, 381-382, 390, 391
  as reaction to fear, 377, 380-381, 390-391, 392
  as recapitulation, 391-392
  as release, 378, 392
  as resistance to therapy, 379-380, 391
  as symptom of ego insufficiency, 390-391
  as test, 385, 390, 391
  attitudes toward, 370-371
  categories of, 389-392
  child vs. adult, 394-395
  counterphobic, 377, 380

countertransference and, 449
group psychotherapy and, 185-186
id and ego impulses in, 375
induced, 377
nonverbal, 370-372, 400
normal, 375, 378
pathologic and parapathologic, 376-377
phenomenology, 371-373, 375, 400
pleasure drive and, 376-377
regression and, 220-221, 373-374, 390
sexual, 66-67, 386-387
sources of, 480
therapeutic, 375-376
therapist's role in, 379, 380, 393-394, 395-399, 425-426
transference and, 375-376, 395, 396, 397
traumatophilia and, see Traumatophilia
types of, 374-378
verbal, 372, 400
Action (s)
  groups, 73, 74
  intensification of in therapy and nontherapy groups, 48-49, 55, 73
  in therapy, 90-91
  see also Interpretation, Insight
Activity catharsis, see Catharsis
Activity group psychotherapy, 31, 75, 79
  acceptance of new members, 52
  acting out in, 395
  catharsis in, 145, 146-147, 176 (tab)
  derivative insight in, 165, 166
  dynamics in, 175-176
  for schizophrenia, 540-541
  group types in, 128
  nodal behavior in, 55
  permissiveness in, 69
  requirements for therapist in, 81
  schizoid personalities in, 499
  supportive ego in, 212-213
Activity-interview group psychotherapy, 145, 176, 395

551

Activity-verbal catharsis, 146
Actuality, *see* Reality
Adaptation, 19-20
Adler, Alfred, 31
Adolescence, Adolescents, 266
  age grouping of, 227
  catharsis in, 145-153, 177
  coordinated family group therapy for, 225-226
  dynamics in group therapy for, 177
  group relations of, 14
  identifications of, 132, 134
  para-analytic group psychotherapy for, 117-118
  supportive ego choice by, 213, 214
  therapy for inhibited, withdrawn, 485-486
  therapy with, 370
Adults
  acting out by, 370, 392-395
  age and grouping of, 227
  aggression tolerance of, 481-482
  catharsis, 145-153
  ego and superego derivation and, 10
  ego energy distribution in, 250-251
  nodal behavior of, 56
  reality perception by, 167-168
  struggle between child and, 10
  supportive ego choice by, 213, 214
  see also Parents
Affirmation, in supervision, 467
Age, grouping and, 226-227
Aged, para-analytic group psychotherapy for, 118
Aggression, 33, 156, 371, 380, 386, 473-475, 477-479, 484, 503
  abnormal, 474, 476, 478, 482-483
  and sibling rivalry, 486, 488
  character, 479-480
  childhood training and, 9-10
  culture and, 478-479
  effects, in therapy groups, 480-482
  ego energy and, 250-251
  hostility and, 474-475, 477-478
  normal, 474, 476, 478, 482-483
  ontogenetic, phylogenetic, 475-476
  security in group and, 290-291
  therapy for, 491, 506
  see also Hostility
Alikakos, L. C., 516
Allee, W. C., 19
"Alternate" Sessions, 398-399; *see also* "Post" Sessions

Ambivalence, 249; *see also* Countertransference
American Group Psychotherapy Association, training program for group therapists, 79-83
Anality, 9, 239, 243-245
Analytic group psychotherapy, 90-94, 128-129, 182, 193-196
  catharsis in, 137, 148, 151, 177
  communication in, 259-282
  dynamics of, 90-94, 129, 175, 177, 330-369
  for character disorders, 473-506
  in withdrawal, 504-506
  passivity in, 428
  phases in, interviews, 347-359
  process, 255-258
  symptom improvement in, 29
  transference in, 118, 137, 177
  treatment levels in, 85-89
  with schizophrenics, 528
  see also Group psychotherapy and *sub* specific topics
Analytic interview group psychotherapy, 75
Animals
  ego manifestations in lower, 236-238
  group anxieties in, 32
  group relationships of, 18-19
Anonymity in therapy and nontherapy groups, 65-67
Antagonism, between sexes, 221-222; *see also* Aggression, Sibling rivalry
Anthony, E. J., 334, 513
Antinodal behavior, 53-57, 147, 362, 481, 482
Attention-getting, 276, 488
Anxiety
  acting out and, 370-371
  and catharsis, 146
  ego and, 235, 250-251
  endogenous vs. induced, 333-335
  essential vs. neurotic, 40-42
  group-induced, 31-33, 34
  group relations and, 14
  homoerotism and, 216-217
  hostility and, 289
  in psychopathy and psychoneuroses, 206
  in schizophrenia, 510
  monopolizing and, 366
  of therapist, 410-412
  reduction of in psychotherapy, 39-42, 240
  silence and, 363

Anxiety (cont.)
  treatment of, 182, 190, 191, 193
  withdrawal and, 484
Anxiety neurosis, 185, 190
Assimilation, in therapy and nontherapy
    groups, 49, 52, 73
Associative thinking, 149-150
  as resistance, 160
Attitude (s)
  age and, 226-227
  anticipatory, in supervision, 467
  improvement of, 91, 157
  potential, origin of, 344-345
  supervision and, 459-460
  therapist, in reality saturation, 139
Authority in therapy, 428, 434-437, 453
Autism, 8
Auxilliary therapist fallacy, 151n, 165n,
    269n, 359-360
Awareness, origin of in childhood, 8-9

Beard, J. H., 511
Becket, Peter G. S., 514
Behavior
  acting out, see Acting out
  animal, 236-238
  ego and, 235
  group modification of, 33-34, 184
  improvement in, 91, 157
  nodal and antinodal in groups, 53-57,
    147; see also nodal behavior
  periodicity of, 362, 481, 482
Behavior disorders, 9, 13, 78, 194, 208, 234
Betlheim, S., 70
Bipolarity, 28
Blajan, 511n
Briehl, W., 200n
Burrows, T., 251

Case histories, 2, 109-116, 119-126, 500-501
Caste system, grouping and, 228-229
Catalysis, 69-70, 155, 163-164, 257, 290,
    336
Catatonic defense, 499-501
Catharsis, 1, 38, 48, 62-63, 88, 91-93, 116,
    118, 129, 137, 142-158, 171, 176-177,
    223, 256, 260, 278, 280-281, 364, 393,
    395, 485-486
Cathexis, 11, 53, 70, 337
  libidinal, 26-27, 39
  of three primary orifices, 239, 243-245
Character, 164, 204-205
Character disorders, 13, 174, 208-209, 343,
    346, 492

acting out as, 389, 390, 391
  aggression in, 479-480
  ego in, 234, 252
  grouping and, 208, 211
  treatment of, 78, 183-186, 193-194, 221n,
    387-388, 507-508
Character resistance, 186
Charisma of therapist, 430-432
Children, Childhood, 56, 167, 174, 227,
    266
  acting out, 372n, 375, 394-395
  aggression tolerance, 481-482
  catharsis, 145-153, 176
  development, 7-18, 418-419
  disciplining of, 9-11
  ego in, 241-250
  identification, 132
  nurture, training and schooling, 8-10,
    244-245
  spontaneity inhibition in, 483-486
  submission to parents, 495-496
  supportive ego choice, 212-213, 214
  treatment of, 38, 45, 165-166, 224-225,
    331-332, 389, 485, 499, 540-541
  withdrawal as retaliation, 501-502
  see also Adolescence, Infancy, Sibling
    rivalry
Classroom instruction in hospital com-
    munity, 538-539, 540
Clinical categories for grouping, 208-211
"Closed system," therapy group as, 69-71
Cognition, conation and, in psychothera-
    py, 38-39
Cohesion, group, 50-52, 60-61, 73, 258,
    277-279
Collaboration, in therapy and nonthera-
    py groups, 60-61, 65, 73
Commonality, 58, 60, 341-342
Communication, therapeutic, 259-282
  acting out as, 261, 393
  as resistance, 160-161, 269
  cues and signals in, 340
  therapeutic validity of, 142-143
  see also Nonverbal communication
Community, 15-16, 229
Comprehension levels, communication
    feedback and, 276-277
Compromise, in groups, 45-46, 73
Compulsive symptom (s)
  talking as, 230-231, 388
  see also Obsessive-compulsive states,
    Neurosis, obsessive-compulsive
Conation, cognition and, 38-39
Conceptualization, 38, 332

"Confessionals," 142-143
Confrontation, 526-529
Congruence, 273-274
Consistency, 504-505
Contagion, acting out as, 385-387, 390-391, 392
Counseling
  aims and dynamics of, 37, 101-102, 104, 105, 107, 115-116, 126, 129, 231
  associative thinking in, 150
  group, 102, 128
  leader's role in, 101-102, 435
  marriage, 222
Countertransference, 443-456
  in group and individual psychotherapy, 141-142
Creativity, of therapist, 428-430
Crowd, 25-26
Culture
  aggression and, 478-479
  ego and superego derivation and, 10
  group psychotherapy and, 4-5
  levels, grouping and, 227-228
Cybernetics, 262
Cyclothymic personalities, 190
Group therapist, 76, 410-412, 460-461
  training of, 5-6, 77-83, 420-421
  see also Therapist

Death instinct, 238
Defenses, 12, 164, 257, 543
  acting out as, 385, 390, 391
  against therapy, 281-282, 546-547
  analysis of, 455
  catatonic, 499-501
  ego, 200-201, 267, see also Ego and sub specific defense mechanisms
  schizophrenia as, 517-518, 520
Defensiveness, 267-268, 343
Definitions, importance of, 2, 95-96
Deflection, 159-160, 163, 275-276
Deliberating groups, see Groups, deliberating
Delusions
  chemically induced, 514
  in schizophrenia, 518, 520-522, 529-532
  treatment of, 190
Depressed states, 190, 209-210
Depth of therapy, see Therapy
Derivative insight, 1, 63, 75, 163, 164-165, 166
Destruction, drive for, in schizophrenia, 510-511

Detachment, of therapist, 407, 443-444
Development
  childhood, see Children
  ego in, 30, 233-234
  evolutionary, 21-23
  group in individual, 7-18
  identification in, 132
Diagnosis, 76, 199
Didactic seminars, 423
Directed catharsis, 150-151; see also Catharsis
Direct insight, see Insight
Directional function of therapist, 425
Directive therapy, 128, 175
Discipline, 9-11, 242, 496
Displacement, 159, 163
Distraction, 160-161, 163
Dreams, 118

Education, 3n, 8n, 174
  of therapists, 412-424, 433
Ego, 79, 103-104, 146, 180, 234-236, 492
  defenses, 164, 200-201, 204, 206-207, 251, 267, 518-519; see also defenses and sub specific defense mechanisms
  deficiencies, 240, 390-391, 508, 510, 511, 516-518, 523-524, 528
  educability of, 238-239
  energies, distribution of, 245, 250-251
  functioning, 9-10, 12-14, 25-26, 30, 33-35, 68-69, 156, 204, 233-234, 240-245, 256-258, 392, 464-465
  "group," 67-69
  id and, 239, 240, 246, 375
  importance of, in psychic illness, 30-31
  in schizoids, 189, 190
  libido and, 246-247, 249
  manifestations in lower animals and man, 236-238
  overloading, 144-145, 253, 255
  relationships, 37-39, 107-108, 129
  strength, 56, 87-88, 90, 115, 371, 373
  structure, 9-10
  supportive, 211-214, 345, 505
  therapy, 231-235, 251-258
Egotropism, 13-14
Einstein, V. W., 224n
Emotional
  hypochondriasis in acting out, 383-385, 390, 391
  maturity, 169
  re-education, 156-157

Emotional *(cont.)*
see also Emotions
Emotions, 38, 51, 276, 378
in therapy and nontherapy groups, 48-49, 55, 73, 288
manifestations of, 259-260
mutual support and, 156-157
of therapist, 403-404
see also Emotional
Empathy, 151-152, 240, 277, 404-407
Encounters, interpersonal, intrapersonal and intragroup, 344-347
Environment, consistent, in therapy groups, 504-505
Errors, of therapist, 454-456
Evasion, 269, 397
Evolution, 21-23
Exhibitionism, 276, 366, 382, 383
Exploration, in therapy, 526-529
Exploratory seminars, 423

Father, see Family, Parents
Father figure, group leader as, 27
attitudes, 447-448
coordinated group psychotherapy of, 224-226
ego formation and, 241-242
group as substitute for, 26-27
group relationships of, 20-21
of patient, 53n
of schizophrenics, 514-517
personality development and, 4, 14
relations, 32-33
see also Parents, Sibling rivalry
Family, 11-12, 49, 203-204, 382, 419-420
Fantasy, 220
Fear (s) , 40, 289, 487, 510
acting out as reaction to, 377, 380-381, 390-392
ego energy and, 250-251
group effects on, 33-34
neurotic, 247-248
Feedback, 275-277
Feeding patterns, 8-9
Feelings, see Emotions
Field training of therapists, 423-424
Fingerprints, in schizophrenia, 509
Fixation, acting out as, 390
Fixity, group polarity and, 53, 54
Flexibility, in therapy, 507-508
Forced groups, 72, 74
Frank, G. A., 336, 444
Free association, 35, 71, 74, 91-93, 107, 146-149

Freedom, in psychotherapy, 91-92 253-254, 289
Freud, A., 251
Freud, S., 1, 24-25, 28, 29, 64-65, 236, 238, 246; see also Freudian concepts
Freudian concepts
on group psychotherapy, 1, 4, 23-30
on identification, 27-28, 131, 133, 512
on libido, 31
see also, Freud, S.
Fries, M., 279
Froman, C. E., 514
Frustration, 408, 447, 477

Genetic factors, in schizophrenia, 509-510, 514, 517
Gestalt, 50, 52
Gottlieb, J. S., 514
Graham, F. W., 200
Group (s) , 2-4, 41, 171, 182
anxiety induction by, 31-34
associations, 11-13, 26, 33-35
basic, 13-14
crowd and, 25-26
dynamics, 45-62
genesis differentials, 71-74
individual development and, 7-18
induction in, 69-70, 73; see also Induction
in nature and society, 18-19
interaction in, 2, 45-46, 48, 53, 55, 58, 61, 66, 69-70, 73, 342-343
leader's importance in, 26-27, 397n
psychology, 24-28
restraints and, 33-34, 48-49
therapy vs. nontherapy, 45-71, 73, 74
see also Group psychotherapy; Themes, group; Relationships, group; Therapy group (s)
Group counseling, 102, 128
Group guidance, 104-105, 106, 128; see also Guidance group
Groupplay therapy, 75, 395
Group psychology, individual psychology and, 24-27, 28
Group psychotherapy, 208, 258, 345-346, 538-545
aims of, 30, 52, 90-94, 116-119, 129
analytic, see Analytic group psychotherapy
and individual psychotherapy, 4, 75-76, 81-82, 87, 194-196, 457-458
as ego therapy, 231-235, 251-255
catharsis in, 142-158, 176-177

Group Psychotherapy *(cont.)*
  coordinated family, 225-226
  culture and ethos in, 4-5
  diagnosis in, 76, 77
  dynamics of, 109, 130-177, 211-214
  ego basis of, 30-31
  family consultation in, 224-225
  focus on individual patient in, 77-78, 90, 96
  for character disorders, 479-480
  for homosexuals, 190-191, 215-216, 381-382
  for psychic masochism, 189-190, 496
  for schizophrenics, 528-529
  for withdrawn patients, 486, 491, 493-494, 502
  Freudian concepts and, 1, 4, 23-30
  group dynamics and, 57-62
  historical background of, 3-4, 79-85
  insight in, 164-167, 176-177
  integration of with other therapy methods, 96-97
  libido and, 140-142
  outpatient, 543-545
  para-analytic, 116-129, 177, 528
  psychiatry and, 78-79
  reality testing in, 167-171, 176-177
  resistance and, 159-164, 176-177
  results of, 330-331, 332
  self-image and, 494-495
  settings for, 1-2, 38-39
  sibling rivalry and, 488-489
  somatic factors and, 205-206, 359
  sublimation in, 172-174, 176-177
  transference in, 131, 135-137
  unconscious in, 86, 88-89, 166
  see also Grouping of patients; Psychotherapy; Selection of patients; Therapy group(s) ; and *sub* specific condition and/or dynamic
Grouping of patients, 1-2, 92, 96, 189-190, 198-232, 358-359, 492
  aggression and, 480-482
  commonality and, 341-342
  homosexuality and, 190-191, 215-216, 381-382
  intellectual parity in, 227-228, 276-277
  neuroses and, 28-30, 208, 209, 211
  reality saturation and, 139-140
  schizoid personality in, 498-499
  schizophrenics in, 207-208, 544
  sex as criterion for, 199-200, 218-222, 386
  silences and, 363-364

  see also Selection of patients
Groupism, 21-23
Guidance group, 37, 101-107, 115-116, 126, 129, 231-232, 435; *see also* Group guidance
Guilt, 40-41, 247-248, 251, 289, 489-491

Hallucinations, 190, 514, 518, 520-522, 529-532
"Here-and-now" method, 170, 219
Heterosexual groups in therapy, 199-200, 218-219, 221, 222, 386
Hill, L. B., 510
Hinckley, W. W., 511
Homeostasis, 40-41, 56
Homoerotism, 216-218, 344-345
Homogeneity, in grouping, 199, 201-206, 341-342, 358-359
Homosexuality, 190-191n, 215-216, 381-382, 386
Hospital community psychotherapy, 534-545
Hostility, 224, 444-446, 477-479
  countertransference and, 446-447
  essential to therapy, 148-149, 397, 412
  free discharge of in therapy, 40, 289-291
  in schizoid personality, 497-498
  in schizophrenia, 510, 511, 513, 523
  in therapy groups, 278-279
  toward mate, 223-224
  withdrawal as, 501-502
  see also Aggression
Hypochondriasis, 191, 366-367; *see also* Emotional hypochondriasis in acting out
Hysteria, 191-192

Id, 87
  psychotherapy and, 68-69, 107-108, 129
  ego and, 235, 239, 240, 246, 375
Identification, 131-135, 156, 182-183, 194, 367, 495
  catharsis and, 151-153, 157-158, 247
  correction of defective, 88, 211-214, 257-258
  countertransference and, 446
  ego functioning and, 240-242
  Freudian concept of, 27-28
  in therapy and nontherapy groups, 47-48
  model for, 170-171, 402-403, 429, 447, 448
  as resistance and, 163-164

Identification (*cont.*)
   self-identity and, 533-534
   see also Incorporation
"Identification transference," 27-28, 88, 131-133, 254-255
Images, internalized, 330-333
Impulses, inhibition of childhood, 483-486
Incestuous strivings, 66-67, 510
Incorporation, 512-513
Individualism, 15-18
Individuality, 49-50; *see also* Individualism
Individual psychology, 24-28
Induction, 47, 73, 152, 163-164, 514-515; *see also* Group (s) , induction in
Infancy, 8-9, 533
Inhibition, 199-200, 278, 483-486
Injury, psychic, 197, 200-201, 266, 288-289, 546-547
Inservice training, 423-424
Insight, 75, 156, 256
   derivative, *see* Derivative insight
   in therapy, 63, 108, 116, 118, 129, 163-167, 176-177
   understanding vs., 38, 409
Instincts, 240
Integration into groups, 49-52, 56-57, 73
Interaction, *see* Group interaction, Relationships
Internalization, 132-133, 241
Interpretation, 75, 165, 285-287, 291, 427-428, 455
Interstimulation, in groups, 46-48, 55, 73
Intervention, *see* Therapist, intervention by
Interviews
   dynamics of, 330-369
   hostility discharge in, 289-291
   phenomenology of, 283-329
Intrapersonal communication, 261-264, 270
Intrapersonal psychologic encounters, 345-346, 347
Intuition, 404
Irrelevance, as resistance, 160
Isolation, 34

Jones, E., 377

Kinesthesis, 40-41
Kropotkin, P., 18
Lateness, as resistance, 159

Leader (s)
   group, 26-27, 45, 51-52, 58-61, 64, 67, 397n
   in counseling, 101-102, 435
   in guidance, 105-106, 435
   see also Group therapist, Therapist
Learning process, 460
Levine, L., 222
Libido, 131, 140-142, 179
   acting out and, 394
   aggression and, 474
   cathexis, 26-27, 37, 39
   disturbances, 31, 35
   ego and, 246-247, 249
   in schizophrenia, 511
   redistribution, 37-39, 90, 115, 129, 164, 233, 246-247, 252-253
Literacy, psychological, grouping and, 231-232
Loeffler, F. J., 444
Low, A. A., 143
Lowrey, L. G., 418
Loyalty, effects of excessive, 50, 52
Luby, E. D., 514

Maladjustment, group associations and, 12-13
Married couples, in therapy group, 200, 222-224, 225
Masochism, psychic, 189-190, 366, 381-382, 496
Men, in therapy groups, 216-217, 221
Menninger, K., 245
Metchnikoff, E., 237-238
Meyer, A., 491
Mobility in therapy and nontherapy groups, 52-54
Mobs, actuation of, 394n
"Monopolizers," 230-231, 364-367, 388
Mother (s)
   -child relations, 8, 495-496
   of schizophrenics, 514-517
   see also Parents
Motivation
   for therapy, 492
   of "monopolizers," 366-367
   of therapist, 407
Murder, by schizophrenics, 511
Mutual induction, 47, 69-70, 152, 240
Mutual support, 103, 240, 380, 493
   as resistance solvent, 163-164
   catharsis and, 155-157
Mysticism, psychotherapy and, 171-172

Nagelberg, L., 541, 544
Narcissism, 34, 383, 492, 497
  acting out and, 376-377, 388-389, 390, 392
  monopolizing and, 366-367
  of therapist, 408
  treatment of, 190, 191
  withdrawal and, 491-492
Nature
  aggression in, 473-474
  ego manifestations in, 236-238
  groups in, 7, 18-19, 32
Need (s)
  aggression and, 474
  aim attachment and, 450-451
  childhood, 8
  determination of, 101
  group and acceptance, 34
  individual, 86-87, 92
  of therapist, 445-446, 453-454
  psychotherapeutic process in meeting, 42-45, 77-78
  self-protective, 66
Neurosis, 13, 31, 43, 78, 247-248, 387, 485
  anxiety, 185, 190
  grouping and, 28-30, 208, 209, 211
  obsessive-compulsive, 190, 508
  perversions and, 216
  situational, 143n, 194, 255
  therapy of, 31, 35, 84, 185-186, 193
  transference, 31, 35, 84, 142, 166, 190, 221n, 252
Neurotic character, 217-218, 387-388, 390, 391, 480, 485
Neutralization in groups, 45-46, 73
Nodal behavior, 53-57, 147, 362, 481, 482
Nonverbal communication, 265, 340

Obsessive-compulsive states, 190; see also Compulsive symptoms
Occupational group, 14
Occupational therapy, 539, 540
Orality
  ego and, 239, 243-245
  identification and, 132-133
  monopolizing and, 366, 367
  in schizophrenia, 511-513, 522-523
Outpatient treatment, 543-545

Para-analytic group psychotherapy, see Group psychotherapy, para-analytic
Parent, 494, 497
  ego functioning in children and, 241-242

group leader as substitute, 26-27
  spontaneity inhibition by, 484-485
  submission to, 495-496
  see also, Family, Father, Mother
Parker, B., 521
Participation, importance of free, 91-92
Passivity
  as resistance, 161
  of therapist, 428-430
Pathology, grouping and, 199, 202, 204-206, 342
Patient ('s) , 35, 155, 188, 468
  acceptance of new, into group, 52, 70-71
  anonymity, 65-67
  as "co-therapist," 151n, 165n, 269n, 359-360
  ego tolerance, 87
  group variables applied to, 192-196
  individual needs, 34, 42-45, 77-78, 86-87, 90, 92, 94
  in psychologic encounters, 344-347
  psychic injury to, 197, 200-201, 266, 288-289, 546-547
  stereotypy and, 360-361
  therapeutic communication, 271-272
  treatability, 37-39, 84-85, 96
  see also Grouping of patients, Selection of patients, Therapy group (s) , and sub specific concept and/or dynamic
Permissiveness, 68-69
Personality, 37, 190, 371
  development, 4, 8-9, 14, 131-132, 330-332
  group associations and, 11-14, 20-21
  growth in therapy and nontherapy groups, 58, 61-62
  integration, 56-57
  of supervisor, 458-459
  of therapist, 2, 401-412, 430-433, 465-466
  psychopathic, 13
  structure, in schizophrenia, 508, 510-513
  supportive ego and, 212-213
Perversion, 190, 216; see also sub specific perversion
Pity, seeking of, 383-385
Play group psychotherapy, 38, 75, 395
  catharsis in, 145, 147, 176
Pleasure drives, 235, 376-377,
Polarity
  in ego, 239-240

Polarity (*cont.*)
  in therapy and nontherapy groups, 52-53
  "Post" sessions, 398-399; *see also* "Alternate" sessions
Powdermaker, F., 336
Pratt, J. K., 143
Problems, therapeutic, 115, 129, 203-205, 210, 221, 335, 347, 379-380, 506; *see also sub* specific categories
Project method, 541-543
Projection, 182, 267, 343
Psychiatry, 78-79, 417-418
Psychoanalysis, 31, 35, 38, 75, 99, 113-114, 131, 166, 179-180, 186, 233-234, 403, 405, 410, 412, 443
Psychodrama, 92, 282, 332
Psychology, individual vs. group, 24-28
Psychoneuroses, 174, 206-209, 252, 257, 266, 343, 387, 477, 502-503, 517, 533
  therapy for, 57, 84, 231-232, 253, 507, 526
  see also Neurosis
Psychonursing, 126, 128, 545-546
Psychopathy, 13, 206-208, 234
Psychosis, 13, 145, 207-208, 492
  aggression in, 477, 480
  ego in, 234, 252
  identification in, 132, 533
  therapy of, 190, 526
Psychotherapist, *see* Therapist
Psychotherapy, 36-42, 53n, 99, 101, 391-392
  associative thinking in, 149-150
  case history need of, 111-112
  confrontation vs. exploration in, 526-529
  defense against, 546-547
  dynamics of, 36-40, 88, 101, 107-109, 115-116, 129
  ego and superego functioning in, 68-69, 79
  ego therapy in, 251-255
  for sexual disturbances, 179-180
  freedom in, 253-254, 289
  hospital community, 534-543; *see also* Hospital community psychotherapy
  identification transference in, 27-28
  importance of hostility in, 148-149, 397, 412
  individual combined with group, 75-76, 87, 194-196
  individual needs in, 42-45

individual vs. group, 4, 81-82, 131, 135-137, 139, 141-142, 182, 258, 457-458
integrating rival schools of, 416-418
multiplicity of approaches, 89-90
mysticism and, 171-172
reality and, 168-169
reality testing in, 138-139
specificity of, 507-508
status-seeking, correction for, 382-383
superego relationships and, 107-108, 129
with schizophrenics, 126-127, 511-512, 519-520, 522-525, 543-545
see also Group psychotherapy, Therapy, and *sub* specific condition and/or dynamic
Punishment, need for acting out and, 381

Rallies, 336-338, 341
Raphael, L. G., 509
Raphael, T., 509
Rationalization, 257, 268, 269, 333
Reality
  basis in therapy, 220-221
  concept, in schizoid personality, 498-499
  distortion, 517
  figures vs. internalized images, 330-332
  fragmentation, 190
  in hospital community, 541
  in psychotherapy, 139, 149-150
  principle of graded, 525-526
  retreat from, in schizophrenia, 518, 519, 524-525, 532
  saturation, 138-140
  sense of, 167-168
  therapy and, 168-169, 223-224
  see also Reality testing
Reality testing, 63, 167-171, 176-177, 256, 494
  group as arena for, 196
  in psychotherapy, 75-76, 88, 108, 116, 118, 129
  in schizophrenia, 528
  paroling patients and, 538
  role of, in psychotherapy, 138-139
Recapitulation, acting out as, 391-392
Recreation, in hospital community, 538, 539
Regression, 35, 37, 146, 207, 374
  acting out and, *see* Acting out
  in therapy, 108-109, 142, 144, 359, 373
Reidentification, as psychotherapeutic dynamic, 88, 211-214, 257-258

Relationship (s)
  importance of group, 20-23
  in supervision, 460-463, 465
  interpersonal, 3, 168-169
  minimal, for group therapy participa-
    tion, 178-179, 190
  patient, anonymity and, 65-67
  supportive ego, 211-214
  see also Interaction Transference
Release
  acting out as, 378, 392
  in therapy groups, 504
Relevance, 275, 291
Repression, 11
Resistance, 29, 142, 144, 269, 282, 338, 362,
    369, 384, 547
  acting out as, 379-380, 391
  communication as, 160-161
  countertransference and, 446-447
  deflection as, 159-160, 163, 275-276
  interpretation and, 285, 287
  overcoming of, 163-164, 231-232
  patterns of group-induced, 159-164, 176-
    177
  signs of, in therapy groups, 278-279
  silences as, 161, 163, 363, 364
  transference, 186-187
Restraints
  group effects on, 33-34, 48-49
  in group psychotherapy, 169-170
Retaliation, withdrawal as, 501-502
Rigidity, 42-45, 53
Richter, A., 539
Rivalry, sibling, see Sibling rivalry
Roback, A. A., 239
Role playing, 92, 282, 332
Rosenthal, L., 541, 544
Rümke, H. C., 520

Schizoid personality, 188-189, 487, 497-
    499
Schizophrenia, 145, 197, 206-207, 266, 282
  delusions and hallucinations in, 518,
    520-522, 529-532
  ego in, 508, 510, 511, 516-519, 528
  role of family in, 514-517
  genetic factors in, see Genetic factors
  graded reality principle for, 525-526
  group assignments in, 207-208
  hospital community psychotherapy for,
    534-543; see also Hospital community
    psychotherapy
  orality in, 511-513, 522-523

psychonursing for, 545-546
pseudo, 134
real vs. induced, 513-517
self-identity and, 532-534
somatic factors in, 509, 510, 514, 517,
  519-520
symbol interpretation in, 520-522, 530
therapy for, 117, 126-127, 190, 208, 496,
  511-512, 519-520, 522-529, 543-547
Schooling of children, 8-10
Sechehaye, M., 521
Security
  ego functioning and, 242
  fear syndrome and, 380
  hostility and, 290-291
  transference and, 332
Selection of patients, 1-2, 92, 96, 101, 178-
  179, 192-197
  ego strength and, 180, 190
  for analytic groups, 181-193
  for group guidance, 105
  for group psychotherapy, 76, 77, 84-85,
    86-87
  for para-analytic group psychotherapy,
    117-119
  for psychonursing, 127
  see also Grouping of patients
Self, 34
  confrontation, 345-347
  determination, 49-50
  image, 8, 37-39, 66, 90, 115, 158, 248-
    249, 251, 253-254, 267-268, 450, 487-
    488, 492, 494-495, 532-534
  polarity of ego and, 239-240
Sex (ual)
  acting out, 66-67, 386-387
  adjustment, 495
  antagonisms, 221-222
  as factor in therapy groups, 199-200,
    218-219, 221, 222, 386
  attitudes, 459
  attraction, countertransference and,
    444, 445, 448-449
  competition, acting out and, 386
  disturbances, group therapy participa-
    tion and, 179-180, 183, 190
  problems, universality of, 203-204
  urges, ego and, 239, 243-245
Shaw, G., 19
Sibling rivalry, 187-188, 386, 486-489, 494
Silence, 197, 362-363, 379-380, 529
  as resistance, 161, 163
  as retaliation, 501, 502

Silence *(cont.)*
of therapist, 428-430
Situational neurosis, 143*n*, 194, 255
Social adaptation, group and, 13-14
Social hunger, 48-49, 173-174, 492
Society, survival and, 19-21
Solomon, A., 444
Somatic factors
ego and, 243, 249-250
group therapy and, 205-206, 359
in schizophrenia, 509, 510, 514, 517, 519-520
withdrawal and, 492-494
Spanjaard, J., 35
Specificity, in therapy, 2, 94, 252, 268, 507-508
"Spectator therapy," 48, 88, 153
Speer, A., 418
Spontaneity
inhibition of childhood, 483-486
in therapy, 432, 434
Spotnitz, H., 510
Starer, E., 516
Status
acting out as bid for, 382-383, 390-392
of patient, 275, 360
of therapist, 430-432
Stereotypy
as resistance, 161-162
in analytic group interviews, 360-362
Stigmata, withdrawal as reaction to, 492-494
Strategy, therapy and, 434
Sublimation, 256, 371
groups and, 13-14, 63
in therapy, 38, 116, 118, 129, 172-177
Submission to parents, 495-496
Suicide, 511
Superego, 41, 87, 206, 247, 289, 494
derivation, 10, 241, 515-516
development, 180-181, 190
group, 67-69
group and, 12, 26, 33-35, 67-69
in therapy, 37, 38, 39, 90, 107-108, 115, 129
Supervision, 457-472
Survival
aggression and, 473-476
ego and, 238, 239
natural groupings and, 18-19
society and, *see* Society
struggle for, 391
Symbolic realization, 520-522

Symbolism, 520-522, 530
Symptoms
aggression and withdrawal as, 506
homogeneous, 358-359
of need for psychotherapy, 37-39
origin of, 262
see also sub specific symptoms
Syndromes, grouping and, 199, 202, 204, 205-206
Synergy, 60-61, 63-65, 73

Tagore, R., 536
Target multiplicity, 333
catharsis and, 154-155
transference resistances and, 187
Tension
catharsis and release, 146
group, 33-34, 188, 333-335, 481
in supervision, 461-462
Terminology, 2, 95-96
Themes, group, 336-341
Theories of psychotherapy, 36-37, 42-45
Therapist, 59-61, 64, 108, 144, 165, 214, 284, 336, 340, 383, 425-443, 446
aim attachment of, 450-453
as model for identification, 212-213; *see also* Identification, model for
attitudes of, 139, 218
countertransference of, *see* Countertransference
creativity of, *see* Creativity
errors of, 454-456, 462-464
frame of reference of, 42-45
frustration tolerance of, 408-409, 447
group cohesion control by, 278-279
hostility and, 159, 290-291, 386
in acting out, 379, 380, 393-399
in behavior control, 55-56
incestuous strivings toward, 66-67
in communication, 261, 264-265, 268, 269, 271-274, 287
in ego-centered therapy, 254-255
in schizophrenia, 522-525
interpersonal encounters with, 344-345
intervention by, 285-287, 291, 395-397
nonmedical, 416, 418
personality of, 401-412, 430-433, 465-466
phases in analytic group interviews and, 357-358
protection of patient by, 197, 266, 288-289, 546-547
qualifications of, 2, 82-83, 401-412, 430-433
role of in psychoanalysis, 233-234

Therapist (*cont.*)
  silences and, 363-364
  supervision of, 457-472; *see also* Supervision
  stereotypy and, 361, 362
  training of, 5-6, 77-83, 412-415, 420-422
  transference toward, *see* Transference
  see also Group therapists
Therapy
  acting out and, 370-371, 372*n*, 375-376
  aims of, 98-129, 391-392
  authority in, 428, 434-437, 453
  defense against, 281-282, 546-547
  educational seminars and, 424
  ego function in, 233-234
  general principles of, 98-129, 506
  hostility and, 40, 148-149, 289-291, 397, 412
  self-image and, 115, 129
  setting, 1
  spontaneity in, 432, 434
  "spectator," 529
  sublimation in, 38, 116, 118, 129, 172-174, 176-177
  terminal, 359
  types of, within a group, 341
  see also Group psychotherapy; Psychotherapy; Communication, therapeutic; and *sub* specific concept, condition and/or dynamic
Therapy group (s)
  acceptance of new members in, 52, 70-71
  acting out in, 385-387, 390-392
  aggression in, 480-482
  anxiety induction and, 333-335
  anxiety of therapist and, 410-412
  as "closed system," 69-71
  behavior modification and, 184
  catalysis in, 69-70, 155, 257, 290, 336
  characteristics of, 90-94
  cohesiveness in, 50-52, 60-61, 258, 277-279
  common tensions in, 333, 334-335
  communication in, 264-273
  congruence and misunderstanding in, 273-274
  countertransference toward, 453-454
  ego therapy and, 255-258
  feedback sources of, 274-277
  freedom in, 91-92, 253-254, 289
  homoerotic stimuli in, 217
  homogeneity and commonality in, 341

  homosexuals in, 216, 381-382
  identification with, 157-158, 171
  identification transference in, 131
  importance of balanced, 481-482
  inductions in, 47, 69-70, 152
  interactions in, 45-46, 48, 53, 55, 58, 61, 66, 69-70, 73, 342-343
  in therapist's presence and absence, 265*n*, 269*n*, 398-399
  intragroup encounters in, 346-347
  leadership, 58-61, 64; *see also* Therapist (s)
  mutual support in, 155-157, 380
  nodal and antinodal behavior in, 53-57, 147, 362, 481, 482
  nontherapy groups compared with, 57-69, 73, 74
  patients as "co-therapists" in, 151*n*, 165*n*, 269*n*, 359-360
  rallies in, 336-338, 341
  reality-oriented, in hospital community, 541
  reality setting and, 220-221
  reality testing and, 167-169
  reidentification and, 211-214, 257-258
  relationships in, 212-214
  resistance induced by, 159-164
  sex as factor in, 66-67, 199-200, 218-219, 221, 222, 386
  size of, 25-26, 92-94, 540-541
  social hunger and, 173-174, 492
  supervision centered around, 468
  target multiplicity in, 154-155
  tension activators, 188
  themes in, 336, 337, 338-340, 341
  therapists as patients in, 421
  therapist's communication with, 272-273
  transference modification and, 135-138
  types of, 128
  unanimity in, 278-279, 386
  values, in withdrawal, 504-505
Threat areas, 266
  communication feedback and, 276-278
  defensive projection and, 182, 267, 343
  in schizophrenia, 527
  intolerance foci and, 342-343
  therapeutic communication and, 265-268
Timing by therapist, 285-287, 291, 395-397
Togetherness, 14-16
Tolerance

Tolerance (*cont.*)
  aggression, 481-482
  frustration, 408-409, 447
Towney, G., 514
Training
  basic psychiatry in, 417-418
  child development study in, 418-419
  content of, 414-415
  curriculum, 421-422
  methods, 420-421
  of group therapists, 5-6, 77-83
  of infants and children, 8-10, 244-245
  scope of, 412-413
  seminars, 422-424
Transference, 115-116, 129, 176-177, 256, 492
  acting out and, 375-376, 395-397
  bilateral, 137, 444
  catharsis and, 144, 151-152
  constants and variables in, 135-137, 176-177
  in analytic group psychotherapy, 118, 129, 137, 177
  in group psychotherapy, 131-142, 176-177, 186-187
  in homoerotism, 217-218
  in guidance, 104, 129
  in para-analytic group psychotherapy, 118, 129
  in psychoanalysis, 131, 443
  in psychotherapy, 38, 108, 129
  insight and, 165
  in therapy and nontherapy groups, 62, 70
  negative, 147
  positive, 332
  reality saturation and, 138-140
  role of therapist in, 360, 455-456
  sex distribution of group and, 199-200
  symptom improvement and, 29
  target multiplicity and, 154-155
  therapeutic regression and, 373
  see also, Transference identification, Transference neurosis
Transference identification, 27-28, 88, 131, 133, 254-255

Transference neurosis, 31, 35, 84, 142, 166, 190, 221*n; see also* Transference
Traumatization, 197, 200-201, 228-229, 266, 546-547
Traumatophilia, 41, 388

Unanimity, in therapy groups, 278-279, 386
Unconscious
  ego and, 239-240, 263, 346
  group psychotherapy and, 86, 88-89, 166
Understanding, *see* Insight
Unisexual groups in therapy, 199-200, 219
Universalization, 156, 158, 163-164, 240, 342, 490-491

Value systems, 4, 226-227
Vander Kamp, H., 510
van Ophuijsen, J. H. W., 85
Vectors, in group communication, 270-273

Ward, L., 21
Wells, H. G., 22
Wertham, F., 512
Winch, W., 516
Withdrawal, 380, 482-483, 529
  as catatonic defense, 499-501
  as guilt reaction, 489-491
  as psychoneurotic symptom, 502-503
  defective self-image and, 494-495
  frustration and, 477
  gains from, 487-488
  group values in, 504-506
  narcissism and, 491-492
  schizoid, 497-499
  sibling rivalry and, 486-489, 494
  spontaneity inhibition and, 483-486
  therapeutic principles, 491, 506
Wolf, A., 67
Women
  homoerotism in, 216, 217
  in therapy groups, 221
Word symbolism, in therapy groups, 273-274
Working through, 91, 108, 260